Seventh Edition

GROUPS

A COUNSELING SPECIALTY

Samuel T. Gladding
Wake Forest University

PEARSON

Boston Columbus Indianapolis New York San Francisco Hoboken Amsterdam Cape Town
Dubai London Madrid Milan Munich Paris Montréal Toronto Delhi Mexico City
São Paulo Sydney Hong Kong Seoul Singapore Taipei Tokyo

Vice President and Editorial Director: Jeffery W. Johnston
Vice President and Publisher: Kevin M. Davis
Editorial Assistant: Marisia Styles
Executive Field Marketing Manager: Krista Clark
Senior Product Marketing Manager: Christopher Barry
Project Manager: Lauren Carlson
Procurement Specialist: Deidra Skahill
Senior Art Director: Diane Ernsberger
Cover Art: Xuanhuongho/Shutterstock
Full-Service Project Management: Kelly Ricci, iEnergizer Aptara®, Ltd.
Composition: iEnergizer Aptara®, Ltd.
Printer/Binder: Edwards Brothers—Malloy
Cover Printer: Phoenix Color—Hagerstown
Text Font: Times LT Std

Credits and acknowledgments for material borrowed from other sources and reproduced, with permission, in this textbook appear on the appropriate page within the text.

Every effort has been made to provide accurate and current Internet information in this book. However, the Internet and information posted on it are constantly changing, so it is inevitable that some of the Internet addresses listed in this textbook will change.

Library of Congress Cataloging-in-Publication Data

Gladding, Samuel T.
    Groups : a counseling specialty / Samuel T. Gladding, Wake Forest University. —Seventh Edition.
        pages cm
    Includes bibliographical references and index.
    ISBN 978-0-13-390520-5—ISBN 0-13-390520-9
    1. Group counseling.   I. Title.
    BF636.7.G76G55 2015
    158.3'5—dc23

                                                                                            2015000800

10 9 8 7 6 5 4 3 2 1

PEARSON

ISBN 10:   0-13-390520-9
ISBN 13: 978-0-13-390520-5

To my wife
Claire
and my children
Ben, Nate, and Tim
Who have all taught me anew that
sensitivity is a strength,
listening is a skill,
love is an action, and
life is a gift to be shared.

ABOUT THE AUTHOR

 Samuel T. Gladding is a professor in the Department of Counseling at Wake Forest University in Winston-Salem, North Carolina. He has been a practicing counselor in both public and private agencies since 1971. His leadership in the field of counseling includes service as president of the American Counseling Association (ACA), the Association for Counselor Education and Supervision (ACES), the Association for Specialists in Group Work (ASGW), the American Association of State Counseling Boards (AASCB), and Chi Sigma Iota (international academic and professional counseling honor society). He has also been the chair of the American Counseling Association Foundation (ACAF).

Dr. Gladding is the former editor of the *Journal for Specialists in Group Work* and the author of more than seven dozen refereed articles in counseling journals, 41 books (including revisions), and five counseling videos. In 1999, he was cited as being in the top 1% of contributors to the flagship journal of the American Counseling Association—*Journal of Counseling and Development*—for the 15-year period from 1978 to 1993. Some of Dr. Gladding's most recent books are *Family Therapy: History, Theory, and Process* (6th ed., 2015), *Counseling: A Comprehensive Profession* (7th ed., 2014), *The Counseling Dictionary* (3rd ed., 2011), *The Creative Arts in Counseling* (4th ed., 2011), *Becoming a Counselor: The Light, the Bright, and the Serious* (2nd ed., 2009), and this seventh edition of *Groups: A Counseling Specialty*.

Dr. Gladding's previous academic appointments have been at the University of Alabama at Birmingham (UAB), Fairfield University (Connecticut), and Rockingham Community College (North Carolina). He was also Director of Children's Services at the Rockingham County (North Carolina) Mental Health Center. Gladding served as a Fulbright Specialist in counseling to Turkey (2010) and China (2013). His books have been translated into several languages including Turkish, Chinese, Korean, Russian, Polish, and Indonesian.

Gladding received his degrees from Wake Forest (B.A., M.A.Ed.), Yale (M.A.R.), and the University of North Carolina–Greensboro (Ph.D.). He is a National Certified Counselor (NCC), a Certified Clinical Mental Health Counselor (CCMHC), and a Licensed Professional Counselor (North Carolina). Dr. Gladding is a former member of the North Carolina Board of Licensed Professional Counselors (NCBLPC) and the Alabama Board of Examiners in Counseling.

Dr. Gladding is the recipient of numerous honors, including the Lifetime Achievement Award from the Association for Creativity in Counseling; the Eminent Career Award from the Association for Specialists in Group Work; the Thomas J. Sweeney Professional Leadership Award from Chi Sigma Iota; the Gilbert and Kathleen Wrenn Award for a Humanitarian and Caring Person from the American Counseling Association; the Professional Leadership Award and Outstanding Publication Award from the Association for Counselor Education and Supervision; the Research Award from the International Association of Marriage and Family Counselors; and the Ella Stephens Barrett Award for Leadership and Service to the Counseling Profession from the North Carolina Counseling Association. He is also a Fellow in the Association for Specialists in Group Work and in the American Counseling Association.

Gladding is married to the former Claire Tillson and is the father of three children—Ben, Nate, and Tim. Outside of counseling, he enjoys tennis, swimming, writing poetry, and humor.

PREFACE

Groups are a part of everyday life. We are born into a family group, and many of the most important events of our lives take place in the educational, recreational, and work groups of which we are a part. Almost everyone is influenced daily by some type of group, and it can be justifiably argued that we truly become human through our interactions in groups. Sometimes just the memory of a group experience or the attractions of an upcoming group event can have a powerful impact on us. The groups with which we directly and indirectly associate affect us all.

The helping professions have worked with people in groups since the end of the 19th century. Professionals realize that, if used properly, groups have the power to help, heal, direct, and support. Working with persons in groups has become an increasingly popular, diverse, and viable means of promoting change and the accomplishment of tasks. Because each group is different, group workers must be equipped with a variety of skills.

NEW TO THIS EDITION

My purpose in writing this new edition of *Groups* was not only to update the text with the latest research but to make the seventh edition more user friendly, interesting, scholarly, and relevant. To improve the book, I initially looked at how it was organized and how the flow of the chapters could be enhanced to help readers more readily learn the essentials of working with groups. With this goal in mind, I focused particularly on incorporating into the text examples and exercises that could give the reader more practical techniques for conducting a group. I also wanted to give the reader more examples of different types of groups and to provide creative methods for working with groups.

I was able to accomplish all of these goals, and thus there are a number of substantial differences in this seventh edition when compared to the previous edition of this book. Major and important new features to this seventh edition are as follows:

- More than 120 new references have been added and incorporated into the body of the text. These references are all new from the last edition. Numerous older references have been deleted as well, making the book more current than ever and more evidence based.
- Chapter overviews have been added, giving the reader an idea of the important points covered in the chapter.
- Brief introductory stories have been added to the beginning of each chapter.
- The number of chapters has been reduced from 17 to 16.
- The chapter in previous editions on the history of groups has been shortened, simplified, and made into Appendix A with an accompanying chart (Appendix B) to make it more readable.
- New material and updates on previous material covered in the book have been added to each chapter. Some of the most notable additions include those that focus on social justice, creativity (particularly the work of Keith Sawyer), different specialty groups throughout the life span, technology and group work, brief groups, and groups for older adults.
- A new appendix, Appendix C, has been added, entitled "Some Prominent Self-Help Group Organizations." It lists prominent mental health associations that deal with troublesome behaviors, such as addiction and eating disorders, and do so largely in self-help/mutual help formats.

ORGANIZATION

This book, like previous editions, examines essential skills required to be an effective worker with groups in multiple settings.

Part 1 of this text (Chapters 1–7) concentrates on types of groups (task/work, psychoeducation, counseling, psychotherapy, and mixed) and how they develop, including their stages and dynamics. Skilled group workers must be aware of and comfortable in dealing with the dynamics and the development of groups over time, from their forming to their adjourning.

Part 2 (Chapters 8–10) focuses on ethics, legal issues, diversity, social justice, creativity, and special kinds of groups. Ethical and legal aspects of working in groups are discussed, along with specialty groups and the influence of culture, social justice, and creativity on groups.

Part 3 (Chapters 11–14) examines the role of groups throughout the life span. These chapters cover issues and procedures for working with groups that focus on children, adolescents, adults, and older adults. Each of these age-and-stage groups has special needs that can be addressed positively in a group setting. Different types of groups appropriate for various life-span periods and circumstances are highlighted and discussed.

The final part of this book (Chapters 15 and 16) concentrates on theoretical approaches to leading groups, describing eight of the most prominent approaches. Each theory is examined in regard to its premises, practices, leadership, emphases, outcomes, strengths, and limitations. The specific theories explored here are transactional analysis, reality therapy, Adlerian, person-centered, existential, Gestalt, rational-emotive behavior therapy, and psychodrama.

A PERSONAL NOTE

I decided to write this book after reflecting on my own experiences in groups. In the late 1960s and early 1970s, I was exposed to a variety of groups, including what were then known as T-groups. I participated in group marathons, psychoeducational groups, self-help groups, task groups, and counseling groups. I took formal courses in conducting groups at Yale, Wake Forest, and the University of North Carolina at Greensboro. Later, I joined such organizations as the Association for Specialists in Group Work (ASGW) and the North Carolina Group Behavior Society. In my initial employment at a mental health center, I was required to lead psychotherapy, counseling, and psychoeducational groups. In private practice and in my duties as a college professor and administrator, I have added task/work groups as a part of my experience.

Fortunately, I have had some excellent instructors and colleagues over the years. They include Wesley Hood, Larry Osborne, Peg Carroll, Diana Hulse-Killacky, Jerry Donigian, Bob Conyne, Chuck Kormanski, Rosie Morgannet, Beverly Brown, Janice DeLucia-Waack, Marianne Schubert, Johnne Armentrout, and John Anderson. I have also been enriched as a practitioner and a writer from my experience as president of the ASGW and editor of the *Journal for Specialists in Group Work*.

ACKNOWLEDGMENTS

I am grateful for the input of professional group workers who reviewed various editions of this text since its original publication in 1991. They include Adrian Blow, St. Louis University; Roberto Clemente, University of Northern Iowa; Robert Conyne, University of Cincinnati; Dana Edwards, Georgia State University; Thomas Elmore, Wake Forest University; Stephen Feit, Idaho State University; Richard Hawk, Tuskegee University; Diana Hulse-Killacky, University of New Orleans; Dennis Kivlighan, University of Missouri, Columbia; Brent Mallinckrodt, University of Oregon; Diana McDermott, University of Kansas; Bernard Nisenholz, private practice, California; Susan Orr, California State University, Sacramento; John G. Pappas, Eastern Michigan University; Sally E. Thigpen, Northeast Louisiana University; Charles Weiner, Henderson State University; Fred Bemak, George Mason University; Brian J. Den, Georgia State University; Jean E. Griffin, University of Nevada–Las Vegas; Susanna A. Hayes, Western Washington University; Barbara Couden Hernandez, Indiana State University; Kathleen M. May, University of Virginia; J. J. McWhirter, Arizona State University; Steven Pfeiffer, Florida State University; Daniel Eckstein, Sam Houston State University; Kathy Evans, University of South Carolina; Walter Frazier, Mississippi College; and Elizabeth Sites, Liberty University.

I want to especially thank the following reviewers for their helpful comments and suggestions for the seventh edition: Joel F. Diambra, University of Tennessee; Mary E. Dillon, University of Central Florida; Diane M. Waryold, Appalachian State University; Jonathan Ohrt, University of North Texas; and Brian Wortham, Texas A&M University–Central Texas.

Others who have been of great assistance to me with this project are former graduate students Jo Spradling (University of Alabama, Birmingham), Paul Myers (University of Alabama, Birmingham), Regan Reding (Wake Forest), Beverly Huffstetler (Wake Forest), Erin Binkley (Wake Forest), and Katie-Anne Burt (Wake Forest). All have been exemplary in helping me ferret out original sources, in proofing pages, and in making changes at times in my sentence structure to improve the clarity of this text. My youngest son, Tim, now in his early 20s, has also been very helpful in making constructive suggestions, and my most recent graduate student, Derek Rutter (Wake Forest), has been of assistance as well, in locating recent articles on groups. Then, of course, the professionals at Merrill Education/Pearson—including my former editors, Vicki Knight, Linda Sullivan, Meredith Fossel, and present editor, Kevin Davis—gave me much to think about as well as encouragement.

My family group, to whom all editions of this book have been dedicated, has been patient and supportive during my writing and rewritings. My wife, Claire, has given me encouragement, support, and a healthy helping of humor throughout this process. My children—Ben, Nate, and Tim—were 4, 2, and just born, respectively, when I began this project. They are now 28, 26, and 24. Time goes by quickly, and writing a revision of the book every four years has helped me keep track of their lives and mine individually and collectively.

CONCLUSION

In concluding the seventh edition of *Groups,* I am more aware than ever of the importance of collaboration in accomplishing goals and fulfilling dreams. The poet John Donne was correct in reminding us that we are not isolated islands sufficient unto ourselves. We are connected to humanity and have the power to help or hinder one another's growth and development. It is in the mixing of personalities and processes that the heart of group work lies, through which our past gains meaning, and from which our present and future are created.

Samuel T. Gladding

BRIEF CONTENTS

CONTENTS

CHAPTER 1

Types of Groups and Group Work

I live in a group
that contains many groups
all spinning in different cycles
like planets around the sun.
In each I am me,
differently,
distinctively,
collectively,
and freely.*

*From "Planets" © 2010 by Samuel T.
Gladding. Reprinted by permission from
Samuel T. Gladding.*

Monkey Business/Fotolia

CHAPTER OVERVIEW

From reading this chapter, you will learn about

- Different classifications of groups and examples of each:
  - task/work,
  - psychoeducational,
  - counseling,
  - psychotherapy,
  - mixed

AS YOU READ, CONSIDER

- The need for each type of group
- The intended outcomes of each type of group
- What types of groups you have been in or seen demonstrated and their effectiveness

On April 11, 1970, Apollo 13, the third Apollo mission intended to land men on the moon, was launched from Cape Canaveral, Florida. As portrayed in the movie *Apollo 13*, a mid-mission oxygen tank explosion not only aborted the goal of the mission but put the lives of the astronauts aboard in jeopardy. To survive, the crew of the mission shut down the command module and used the lunar module as a "lifeboat" during the return trip to Earth. Despite great hardship caused by limited power, loss of cabin heat, and a shortage of potable water, the crew returned safely to Earth on April 17, but only because a group of engineers devised a method to help them meet their needs. The engineers took materials available within the spacecraft that had been designed for one function and found ways to connect them to serve other functions so that the astronauts could survive. If there ever was a time when the wisdom and power of a group prevailed in the face of overwhelming odds, it was this mission, and the creativity that went on within the engineering group behind the scenes after the astronauts sent back word to Mission Control: "Houston, we've had a problem."

Groups, whether on rescue or routine missions, are a part of everyday life and are defined in many ways. Not every gathering or collection of people qualifies as a group, because they may lack an awareness and purpose of seeing themselves as such (Meneses, Ortega, & Navarro, 2008). The following definition, adapted and modified from Johnson and Johnson (2013), encompasses the main qualities of groups. A **group** is a collection of two or more individuals who meet face to face or virtually in an interactive, interdependent way, with the awareness that each belongs to the group and for the purpose of achieving mutually agreed-on goals. From family councils to town meetings, groups are an important component of everyday life. Healthy groups are contextually unique, are complex in regard to their multiple transactions, and are open systems as well (Conyne & Bemak, 2004).

Groups vary according to type and purpose. There are four distinct group specializations: task/work, psychoeducational, counseling, and psychotherapy. The Association for Specialists in Group Work (ASGW) (1991, 2000) has defined and developed standards for each. Within these types of groups are multiple purposes—for example, remediation, development, prevention, skill training, and problem solving. There may be several types of groups that meet the purpose of individuals joining them. For example, a psychoeducational group may be preventive and skill focused, whereas a task/work group may be remedial, preventive, and problem solving. Thus, it is prudent to focus on types of groups initially, because a number of types of groups can be beneficial to individuals seeking help.

That group work is effective has been established through multiple research-based studies (Ward & Ward, 2014). Developing standards and competencies for group workers was a major breakthrough complementing the evolution of the group work literature. Explicitly defining specific group types and establishing skills that need to be acquired and developed in each has fostered evidence-based interventions (Ward, 2006). Furthermore, exemplary training models set up in educational institutions for each type of group have promoted the growth of competent group leaders. Having such models allows programs that prepare group specialists from a variety of disciplines to point to examples of what should be done in the preparation process of forming a group as well as in the implementation of groups (Conyne, Wilson, & Ward, 1997).

Groups, if run well, are dynamic. They include numerous **activities**, which are verbal and nonverbal undertakings a group and its members participate in, such as expressing themselves in different ways and interacting with others. Activities rarely produce meaningful learning in and of themselves. "Rather, it is the carefully selected and planned use of an activity, targeted for a specific purpose with a specific group," that when processed effectively is likely to lead to or promote change and understanding (Nitza, 2014, p. 95). For example, Jill may be asked to describe herself in five words to other group members as the group begins. If Jill is not asked or allowed to explain why she picked the words she did, the activity will soon be forgotten and useless. However, if Jill is given an opportunity to explore the words she picked and why, she and other group members are likely to understand her better.

In human service occupations, groups have usually been thought of as dedicated to mental health issues, but they may focus on task and education agendas as well. Today, the concept of group work is broad. That is why the Association for Specialists in Group Work (2000) defines **group work** as

> a broad professional practice involving the application of knowledge and skill in group facilitation to assist an interdependent collection of people to reach their mutual goals, which may be intrapersonal, interpersonal, or work related. The goals of the group may include the accomplishment of tasks related to work, education, personal development, personal and interpersonal problem solving, or remediation of mental and emotional disorders. (pp. 329–330)

This chapter explores each type of group that has been well defined and that has educational standards to match (task/work, psychoeducational, counseling, and psychotherapy groups). Group work in the context of its purpose, structure, and intended outcome is also covered. In addition, other models, past and present, for classifying groups are discussed, especially the goals and process (GAP) model. The ways in which group purposes and skills can be combined are also illustrated through an examination of the ways in which self-help groups operate. By being aware of different types of groups and their purposes and group work as an entity, you should gain immediate knowledge and insight into a growing and essential field of working with people.

CLASSIFYING GROUPS

Before exploring the four different types of groups, it is important to briefly examine how they came into being. In truth, there is no systematic way these groups came to be recognized. Rather, the process was one that has developed over time and has come in spurts. In fact, the classification system for categorizing group work is still being debated, as is discussed later in this chapter.

Need was part of the reason for the development of different types of groups. Group workers needed a way to describe what they were doing and what could be expected. For example, **contact-focused group theory** was an early forerunner of the group type model. The focus of this theory was on the purpose of groups. Three primary contact groups described in this theory were group guidance, group counseling, and group psychotherapy. Mahler (1971) differentiated among these groups as follows: (a) the group's initially defined purpose, (b) the group's size, (c) the management of the content, (d) the length of the group's life, (e) the leader's responsibility, (f) the severity of the problem, and (g) the competency of the leader. To further distinguish among these three groups, Gazda (1989) emphasized that guidance, counseling, and psychotherapy groups could be viewed along a continuum with overlapping goals, professional competencies, and unique distinctions.

A model that was even more comprehensive and useful in conceptualizing groups was the **specialty/standards model** pioneered by Saltmarsh, Jenkins, and Fisher (1986). This model evolved out of the realization that groups differ in their purpose and functioning. Not all groups are created equal, and to try to conduct them in similar ways is neither prudent nor possible. Thus, Saltmarsh et al. set up a model of group work known by the acronym TRAC, with each letter representing an area in the total picture of group work: tasking, relating, acquiring, and contacting (see Figure 1.1).

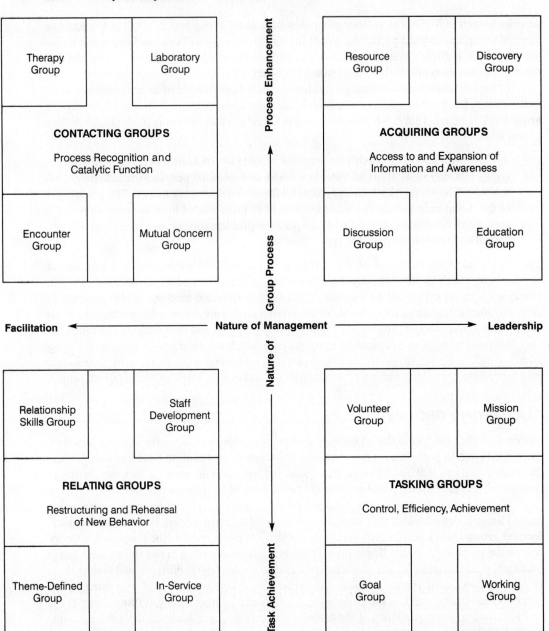

FIGURE 1.1   The TRAC map of group processes and management.   *Source:* Robert E. Saltmarsh, Stephen J. Jenkins, Gary L. Fisher, Figure 1.1: The TRAC map of group processes and management, "The TRAC Model: A Practical Map for Group Processes and Management" *Journal for Specialists in Group Work, 11,* p. 32, Taylor & Francis—US Journals, 1986, 32.

The main characteristic that distinguishes one type of group from another in this model is the focus. *Tasking groups* are focused on task achievement. *Relating groups* emphasize the options for movement within the life of each person. *Acquiring groups* are directed toward learning outcomes that members can apply to others. In contrast, *contacting groups* are focused on the individual growth of members. (Saltmarsh et al., 1986, p. 34)

It is possible by using this model to explain how groups that start out in one major area (e.g., tasking) may move into other areas (e.g., relating). For example, a group set up for a special event, such as staging a race for a charity, may evolve into one where members simply enjoy getting together and hold frequent "reunions." The **TRAC model of groups** clearly delineates group process and management and the types of specific groups found in each of four areas. It was the forerunner of the ASGW (1991, 2000) *Professional Standards for the Training of Group Workers,* which delineated the four types of groups that we now discuss: task/work, psychoeducational, counseling, and psychotherapy.

TASK/WORK GROUPS

Task/work groups "promote efficient and effective accomplishment of group tasks among people who are gathered to accomplish group task goals" (ASGW, 2000, p. 330). They are the "only group type not inherently formed with personal psychological learning as a primary objective" (Ward & Ward, 2014, p. 45). There are as many types of task/work groups as there are kinds of everyday jobs and assignments. The major types of tasking groups, according to Saltmarsh et al. (1986), are volunteer groups, mission groups, goal groups, and working groups. Task/work groups also take the form of "task forces, committees, planning groups, community organizations, discussion groups, and learning groups" (ASGW, 1991, p. 14).

Regardless of type or form, all task/work groups emphasize accomplishment and efficiency in successfully completing identified external work goals (a performance, an assignment, or a finished product) through collaboration (Falco & Bauman, 2014; Stanley, 2006). Skillfully led work groups engage workers in a process where problems are identified and explored and collaborative solutions are developed and implemented (Letendre, Gaillard, & Spath, 2008). Unlike other groups, task/work groups do not focus on changing individuals. Whether the group is successful depends on **group dynamics**—the interactions fostered through the relationships of members and leaders in connection with the complexity of the task involved.

Because task/work groups run the gamut from informal subcommittee meetings to major Hollywood productions or corporate transactions, the number of members within a task/work group may be large, but this type of group usually works best with fewer as opposed to more people. In an analysis of group size, development, and productivity, Wheelan (2009) examined 329 for-profit and nonprofit work groups in organizations across the United States. She found that groups

> containing 3 to 8 members were significantly more productive and more developmentally advanced than groups with 9 members or more. Groups containing 3 to 6 members were significantly more productive and more developmentally advanced than groups with 7 to 10 members or 11 members or more. The groups with 7 to 10 members or 11 members were not different from each other. Finally, groups containing 3 to 4 members were significantly more productive and more developmentally advanced on a number of measures than groups with 5 to 6 members. (p. 247)

From her study Wheelan concluded that work-group size is a crucial factor in increasing or decreasing both group development and productivity. In small groups, unintended subgrouping does not occur and members may focus more on the tasks at hand.

The length of a task/work group varies, but most are similar to other groups in that they have a beginning, a working period, and an ending. Total quality groups found in business settings are a good example of task/work groups. These groups apply group methods "to solve problems related to consumer satisfaction and quality" (Smaby, Peterson, & Hovland, 1994, p. 217). Juries are another good example of task/work groups. The movie *12 Angry Men* not only illustrates how some task/work groups operate but shows the many facets of group process as well (Armstrong & Berg, 2005).

Like other types of groups, task/work groups run best if the following assumptions are met:

- If the purpose of the group is clear to all participants,
- If process and content issues are balanced,
- If the systems of the group as a whole, leader, member, and subsets of members are recognized and acknowledged,
- If time is taken for culture building and learning about each other,
- If the ethic of collaboration, cooperation, and mutual respect is developed and nurtured,
- If conflict is addressed,
- If feedback is exchanged,
- If leaders pay attention to the here-and-now,
- If members are active resources,
- If members learn to be effective and influential participants,
- If leaders exhibit a range of skills for helping members address task and human relations issues,
- If members and leaders take time to reflect on what is happening. (Hulse-Killacky, Killacky, & Donigian, 2001, pp. 21–22)

There are, however, at least two major differences between task/work groups and other types of groups. First, these groups may disband abruptly after accomplishing their goal. In this way they have the most similarity to psychoeducational groups that may end hurriedly because of time constraints, especially in a school setting. If members or leaders pay little attention to the termination stage in a task/work group, then members may feel incomplete when the group is finished. A second difference between task/work groups and other types of groups is that task/work group members and leaders may have considerable contact with others in an organization in which the group is housed. The reason is that task/work groups need input and feedback from people who are not group members.

Reflection

Task and work groups can either be rewarding or disappointing. What is the most satisfying task/work group you were ever in? What made it so? What was the worst? What factors contributed to your being disappointed in the group?

An Example of Task/Work Groups: Teams

Task/work groups "have great importance for our everyday lives, our jobs, our government, and our world" (Stanley, 2006, p. 27). A special type of a task/work group is a team. A **team** is a group of "two or more people who interact dynamically, interdependently, and adaptively and who share at least one common goal or purpose" (Azar, 1997, p. 14). In this respect, a team is more than the sum of its parts. Just think of athletics teams, for instance, such as those in the Olympics or at the college or professional level. There may be some players who are more skilled than others, but if the team as a whole does not cooperate and work together to maximize strengths and abilities, the team will fail to reach its potential.

Teams differ from other types of groups in four main ways (Kormanski, 1999; Reilly & Jones, 1974): (a) They have shared goals, as opposed to individual goals, as in most groups; (b) they stress interdependency more; (c) they require more of a commitment by members to a team effort; and (d) they are by design accountable to a higher level within the organization. "A lack of commitment to the team effort creates tension and reduces overall effectiveness" (Kormanski, 1999, p. 7).

Teams differ from task/work groups in at least a couple of ways. For one thing, more interdependence and accountability are evident in a team than in a task/work group. In addition, in a team effort, there is more sharing of information and work toward a common goal than in a task/work group. The result is usually a greater bonding of members to one another and more cooperation and unity in achieving a common objective (Katzenbach & Smith, 1993). Table 1.1 describes other differences between teams and task/work groups.

Although teams can be classified in many ways, one of the more common is by setting. From this perspective, teams are primarily found within work, sports, and learning situations (Johnson & Johnson, 2013). Examples of teams can be found in environments in surgery (such as the 4077th M*A*S*H medical unit of film and television notoriety), exploratory excision

Table 1.1 Task/work groups versus teams.

Working Groups	Teams
A strong, clearly focused leader is appointed.	Shared leadership responsibilities exist among members.
The general organizational mission is the group's purpose.	A specific, well-defined purpose is unique to the team.
Individual work provides the only products.	Team and individual work develop products.
Effectiveness is measured indirectly by group's influence on others (e.g., financial performance of business, student scores on standardized examination).	Effectiveness is measured directly by assessing team work products.
Individual accountability only is evident.	Both team and individual accountability are evident.
Individual accomplishments are recognized and rewarded.	Team celebration. Individual efforts that contribute to the team's success are also recognized and celebrated.
Meetings are efficiently run and last for short periods of time.	Meetings with open-ended discussion and include active problem solving.
In meetings members discuss, decide, and delegate.	In meetings members discuss, decide, and do real work together.

Source: From Johnson, David W.; Johnson, Frank P.; *Joining Together: Group Therapy and Group Skills,* 5th ed. © 1994. Reprinted and Electronically produced by permission of Pearson Education, Inc., Upper Saddle River, New Jersey.

(such as Lewis and Clark's mapping of the Louisiana Territory), and flying (such as the miracle landing on the Hudson River of a USAirways plane by its pilot, Captain Chesley "Sully" Sullenberger). In a work team, the emphasis is on interpersonal interaction in which members' proficiency and success in doing their jobs are maximized and their efforts are coordinated and integrated with those of the other team members.

A second way to classify a team is by how it is used. Common uses include problem solving (e.g., ways to improve quality, efficiency, and the work environment), special purpose (e.g., facilitating collaboration between unions and management), and self-management (e.g., a small group of employees who produce an entire product or service).

A final way teams can be classified is in regard to what they recommend, do, or run. Teams that recommend include task forces that study and help find solutions for problems, whereas teams that do focus on performance (Katzenbach & Smith, 1993). It is rare for a team to run something, such as an organization, especially a large and complex one such as Microsoft or AT&T.

A number of guidelines should be considered in establishing teams. First, it is important that teams be kept small, half a dozen members or so at most, because large numbers of people generally have difficulty interacting constructively in a group. Second, team members should be selected for their already-established expertise and skills as well as those they have the ability to master. Therefore, effective teams are heterogeneous, and their members possess a variety of abilities. In such groups, team members will often serve as "external memory aids" for one another and "divvy up what needs to be remembered about a task, with individual members remembering different aspects of the task and everyone knowing who knows what" (Azar, 1997, p. 14). A final necessity for forming a team is to bring together the resources necessary to function, including both tangibles and intangibles, such as materials, support personnel, space, and time.

Once a team has been established, it must be structured and nurtured. A crucial ingredient in this process is giving the team a mission and the independence to operationalize the goals that go with the mission. Teams function best when they have a meaningful and worthwhile purpose, such as winning an athletic competition or finding a cure for a disease. A further necessity in structuring and nurturing a team is to provide opportunities for team members to interact face to face or virtually and promote one another's success (Johnson & Johnson, 2013). Frequent and regular meetings are one way this may be done in a face-to-face way, but electronic communication, such as e-mail, Skype, and phone time, can also be counted as time spent together.

Other matters that must be attended to in structuring and nurturing a team, according to Johnson and Johnson (2013), include the following:

- Paying particular attention to first meetings, especially what those in authority do in such meetings because they are the role models for the members
- Establishing clear rules of conduct, especially pertaining to attendance, discussion, confidentiality, productivity of members, and constructive confrontation
- Ensuring accountability of the team as a whole and its members individually
- Showing progress, especially obtaining easy goals early in the life of the group
- Exposing the team to new information and facts that help them redefine and enrich their understanding of their mission, purpose, and goals
- Providing training to enhance both task/work and teamwork skills
- Having frequent team celebrations and opportunities to recognize members' contributions to the team success
- Ensuring frequent team-processing sessions so the team can examine how effectively it is working and discuss ways to improve

Overall, teams that function best emphasize continuous improvement of themselves on an interpersonal, process, and product basis. They work as a group to create a culture that is supportive for members—one that gives them a sense of identity. At the same time, team members focus on specific goals and missions they wish to accomplish and make sure their energy is constantly focused on outcomes that are directly related to their purpose. Effective teams also train together, with the result being better performance over time, increased productivity, and fewer mistakes (Azar, 1997). Teamwork is a set of skills that must be developed through practice and feedback (Levi, 2014).

Case Example

Bradley at the Bat

Bradley has always loved baseball. He was never a great player, but he has now joined the city recreation league and is a member of his company's team. He plays second base, and his colleagues applaud him for both his effort and, at times, his efficiency.

Bradley is the lead-off batter. His job is to get a hit and get on base. He finds that whenever he comes to the plate his teammates cheer for him whether he gets a hit or not. That makes him feel good, and as a result he tries harder.

Bradley has noticed recently that he is becoming closer to his fellow workers at his company. There seems to be a spillover effect, and whether he is at the ballpark or at his computer, Bradley is trying hard to do a good job. He notices that he and others now, regardless of where they are, use phrases such as "Let's have a winning attitude here" and "Let's do this—for the team!"

Questions

When have you seen a team positively affecting one of its members? What do you think this says about the power of teams and teamwork?

PSYCHOEDUCATIONAL GROUPS

Psychoeducational groups were originally developed for use in educational settings, specifically public schools. "The developmental nature of psychoeducational groups [proved] very useful when working with children's self-concepts and attitudes toward school" (Villalba, 2003, p. 264). One of the first types of groups to evolve in the development of group work, psychoeducational groups were premised on the idea that education is treatment not only because of the knowledge acquired in the process but also because of the perceptions that may be changed as a result (M. Young, 2013). Basically, psychoeducational groups, with well-organized and structured activities and exercises, help increase the self-worth of participants (Villalba, 2003). Because of their structure, psychoeducational groups, in many instances, lend themselves to work with cultural diverse populations (Champe & Rubel, 2012). Furthermore, drawing on Yalom's research on therapeutic factors, these groups provide information, socializing techniques, hope, and modeling (Waldo, Kerne, & Kerne, 2007). Sometimes psychoeducational groups are simply referred to as **educational groups** or **guidance groups**.

Regardless of the name, "psychoeducation group work emphasizes using education methods to acquire information and develop related meaning and skills" (Brown, 1997, p. 1). Thus, psychoeducational groups are able to function on multiple levels and with a wide variety of clients. They can be preventive, growth oriented, or remedial in their purpose and focus. Because of their versatility, psychoeducational groups are increasingly being used in various settings outside of schools, including hospitals, mental health agencies, correctional institutions, social service agencies, spiritual settings, and universities (Champe & Rubel, 2012; Christmas & Van Horn, 2012; Morgan, 2004). They include "discussion groups, guided group interactions, recovery groups, support groups, orientation groups, educational groups, or student-centered learning groups" (Rivera, Wilbur, Roberts-Wilbur, Phan, Garrett, & Betz, 2004, p. 391). Lefley (2009) has found that psychoeducational groups help members who have serious mental illnesses "combat social isolation, redeem self esteem and hope, and improve their life situation" (p. 369). Emotional support and education rather than psychotherapy in many cases is what is needed and valued.

"The overarching goal in psychoeducational group work is to prevent future development of debilitating dysfunctions while strengthening coping skills and self-esteem" (Conyne, 1996, p. 157). For instance, Hage and Nosanow (2000) reported that an 8-week, 90-minute psychoeducational group for young adults from divorced families helped participants "reduce isolation, establish connectedness, and build a stronger sense of their own identity and empowerment" (p. 64). In addition, Morgan (2004) states that cognitive-behavioral or behavioral approaches for offenders and mandated clients work well, especially if the psychoeducational group is structured on a topic such as stress management, problem solving, or life skills. Because of their flexibility and efficiency, psychoeducational groups may even be preferred in counseling and psychotherapy environments "when managed care policies demand brief and less expensive treatment" (Brown, 1997, p. 1). They may also be preferred when the leader has less clinical experience and wants the group members to realize immediately why they are in a group.

The size of psychoeducational groups will vary across settings (e.g., whether the activity is in a self-contained classroom or in a public lecture hall), but a range from 20 to 40 individuals is not unusual. In such large groups, discussion and skill practice can take place in subgroups. However, if subgroups are set up, they must be small enough to ensure that each member of the subgroup is not seriously limited in the available **airtime** ("the amount of time available for participation in the group"; Brown, 1997, p. 4). Therefore, subgroups should be limited to 10 to 12 adult members at most, and fewer if the members are children.

The leader of psychoeducational groups is in charge of managing the group as a whole, disseminating information, and breaking groups into subgroups when necessary. "Effective leaders are those who are skillful at managing time, are able to redirect the focus of the session when appropriate, provide considerable structure for the group, and are competent at helping members set clear, specific, and concrete goals" (Riva, 2014, p. 150). A leader who is not an expert in the group's focus area must bring in someone who is. The leader's responsibilities then include managing the expert's presentation as well as the group's activities. The juggling of data, along with processes ensuring that group members benefit from the group experience, is demanding. Timing is crucial, and the group leader must be cognizant of group members' readiness to approach certain activities (Jones & Robinson, 2000). To do the job well, a psychoeducational group leader should take preventive steps before the group's first session. These include planning for session length, session frequency, number of sessions, and what will occur within sessions (the curriculum). Follow-up planning for subsequent sessions is crucial.

In the planning process, it is vital that the leader focus specifically on the design of the group. Such attention to detail is a highly involved endeavor but has a tremendous payoff in keeping the group focused and on course (Furr, 2000). In designing a group, Furr advocates a six-step process: (1) stating the purpose, (2) establishing goals, (3) setting objectives, (4) selecting content, (5) designing experiential activities, and (6) evaluating. Such a procedure leads to purposeful and meaningful outcomes.

Although the length, frequency, and number of sessions of psychoeducational groups will differ according to the ages of the people involved and the stage of the group, these groups usually last from 50 minutes to 2 hours. In general, psychoeducational groups work best when they have a regular meeting time, such as once a week. The number of sessions offered will depend on the purpose, but the range varies from 4 to 20 or more sessions. The average number of sessions is 8 to 10. Regardless of the number of sessions, psychoeducational groups should have opening and termination sessions and at least one session dedicated to each of the goals of the group (DeLucia-Waack & Nitza, 2014). However, all of these parameters are subject to change as "emerging policies on parity for insurance coverage of mental health services . . . influence the length and focus of many psychoeducation groups, as part of the mental health care system" (Brown, 1997, p. 13).

In general, psychoeducational groups stress growth through knowledge (ASGW, 1991, 2000). Summing up previous comments about such groups, Rivera et al. (2004) state that the focus of psychoeducational groups is on transmitting, discussing, and integrating factual knowledge. Because of this focus, psychoeducational groups are "amenable to certain technological applications," such as computer-assisted programs, video and audio transmissions, and computer simulations (Bowman & Bowman, 1998, p. 434). Content includes, but is not limited to, personal, social, vocational, and educational information. Activities in these groups can take many forms but usually are presented in the form of nonthreatening exercises or group discussions (Bates, Johnson, & Blaker, 1982). For instance, in working with individuals who have undergone cardiac transplantation and their families in a psychoeducational short-term group, Konstam (1995) found that framing anger in a positive way helped the group to discuss this normally "taboo" emotion for heart patients. Furthermore, the group process helped members realize they were not unique in their experiences of anger. By the end of the group, anger had significantly decreased.

One way to improve psychoeducational groups is to give members *out-of-group homework exercises* (Morgan, 2004). For instance, instead of just talking about the positive aspects of anger, group members might be assigned a photo opportunity of taking pictures of anger at work in a positive way. They might find that mild forms of anger or frustration can lead to people planting gardens, paving roads, or clipping hedges, all of which have a positive outcome.

Reflection

When have you been a member of a psychoeducational group? What did you learn from the experience? How did it help you or give you fresh insight or knowledge?

An Example of Psychoeducational Group Work: Life-Skills Development Groups

A special form of the psychoeducational group is the life-skills development group. The concept of the **life-skills group** began to emerge in the 1970s when theorists such as Ivey (1973) and Hopson and Hough (1976) started using terms such as *psychoeducation* and *personal and social education*. In the 1980s, the momentum for this approach gained further impetus through the social skills and life-skills training methods advocated by Gazda (1989). The emphasis on life-skills training and its importance in society continues.

Life-skills training focuses on helping people identify and correct deficits in their life-coping responses and learn new, appropriate behaviors. Sometimes these corrective measures are achieved in individual counseling, but often they are carried out in a group setting. One example is helping parents relate effectively to their children with disabilities (Seligman, 1993). The focus of life-skills training is on immediate remediation and future prevention. The training itself is primarily developmental, with the group emphasis being on "how to." Activities within the group may include the use of films, plays, demonstrations, role-plays, and guest speakers.

A life-skills emphasis is appropriate for individuals in schools, colleges, families, work settings, clubs, and other natural group environments. Because many troubling situations arise in groups, the group setting provides an excellent place in which to work on resolutions. Because of the focus on life skills, such as increasing appropriate interpersonal communications or assertiveness abilities, "the growth process proceeds more comfortably, more observably, and with more precise attention given to the specific ingredients that induce change" (Zimpfer, 1984, p. 204).

Through life-skills training, people can be taught on an intrapersonal level how to prevent potential problems, such as depression, from occurring (Sommers-Flanagan, Barrett-Hakanson, Clarke, & Sommers-Flanagan, 2000). They can also be reinforced for taking corrective measures on behavioral and cognitive levels if difficulties arise. For example, Waldo and Harman (1999) found that the communication and interpersonal relationships between state hospital patients and staff improved and became more enjoyable when Bernard Guerney's (1977) Relationship Enhancement (RE) therapy approach was used in a group with both.

A number of steps are involved in learning life skills, many of which are the same as those that Johnson and Johnson (2013) describe in learning group skills:

1. Understand why the skill is important and how it will be of value to you.
2. Understand what the skill is, what the component behaviors are that you have to engage in to perform the skill, and when it should be used.
3. Find situations in which you can practice the skill over and over again while a "coach" watches and evaluates how you are performing the skill.
4. Assess how well the . . . skill is being implemented.
5. Keep practicing until the skill feels real and it becomes an automatic habit pattern.
6. Load your practice toward success [set up practice units that can easily be mastered].
7. Get friends to encourage you to use the skill.
8. Help others learn the . . . skill. (pp. 53–54)

Through implementing these procedures, group members enable both themselves and others. The result is a kind of snowball effect wherein skills continue to build on skills in an effective and complementary way.

Life-skills development groups ideally offer both the opportunity to learn new ways of behaving and the support necessary to continue to exercise them. Leaders and members can learn through each other's feedback and evaluations whether the strategies they employed have been useful and thereby improve their mastery or delivery of skills for future situations. Participants who profit most from these types of groups are those who have enough time and practice to fully integrate what they have learned in the group into their real-life situations.

Case Example

Patrick Practices His Psychoeducational Group Skills

As a group leader, Patrick wanted to experiment in finding out what methods worked best in leading a psychoeducational group for preteens. Therefore, when he made his lesson plans for his four fifth-grade classes, he used different ways of presenting the material: role-play, lecture, PowerPoint, and a combination of these methods. He gave each class a pre- and posttest to see what they knew and what they learned. He also measured how much they enjoyed the class.

Patrick was not surprised to find that the more active role-play format received the highest rating. He was also not shocked to find that the lecture method was least well received. Interestingly, the classes learned about the same amount of information regardless of the method used, and in a follow-up test a few weeks later, Patrick found that the class that used a combination of methods had the highest knowledge retention.

Questions

Patrick's results might be different from others because of his circumstances. Therefore, think of your own life experience and how you have learned best and with the most enjoyment when in a psychoeducational group. Were there methods used, other than those just mentioned, that helped you grasp or retain the material that was presented? What were they?

COUNSELING GROUPS

Counseling groups are preventive, growth oriented, and remedial. These groups are "generally considered to be a treatment mode that is equal in effectiveness to individual counseling" (Stockton, Morran, & Chang, 2014, p. 133). The focus of counseling groups, which are also referred to as **counseling/interpersonal problem-solving groups**, is on the improvement of interpersonal relationships and the intrapersonal growth of members through the help of the group. Members are not in need of psychotherapy or remediation (Ward, 2010). Although goals are personal, the group as a whole may share them. For instance, some counseling groups may concentrate on ways for each individual in the group to deal with disabling emotions, such as anger, whereas others may focus on disagreeable and crippling feelings, such as anxiety. Regardless, the interaction among people is highlighted, especially in problem solving. These groups emphasize group dynamics and interpersonal relationships and tend to promote cohesion (Waldo et al., 2007). Although psychoeducational groups are recommended for everyone on a continuous basis, counseling groups are more selective. They "are generally for people who may be experiencing transitory maladjustment, who are at risk for the development of personal or interpersonal problems, or who seek enhancement of personal qualities and abilities" (Merchant & Yozamp, 2014, p. 20). In other words, these groups are ideal for individuals experiencing usual, but often difficult, problems of living that information alone will not solve.

The size of counseling groups varies with the ages of the individuals involved, ranging from 3 or 4 in a children's group to 8 to 12 in an adult group. The number of group meetings also fluctuates but will generally be anywhere from 6 to 16 sessions. The leader is in charge of facilitating the group interaction but becomes less directly involved as the group develops.

Usually, the topics covered in counseling groups are developmental or situational, such as educational, social, career, and personal. They also tend to be of short-term duration. Counseling groups are a more direct approach to dealing with troublesome behaviors than are psychoeducational groups because they target specific behaviors and are focused on problem solving, instead of being aimed at general difficulties that may or may not be pertinent to every member's life. For instance, Finn (2003) described a nine-session counseling group to help students cope with loss in which members used artistic means, such as drawing, music, and drama, to access the underlying feelings and thoughts common to grief and process what they were going through. The focus in this counseling group was on a common experience, loss, that had taken many forms but that was disruptive in these adolescents' lives until dealt with openly.

A major advantage of counseling groups is the interpersonal interaction, feedback, and contributions group members experience from one another over time. Certainly that was true in the grief group just described.

One form a counseling group may take is **adventure groups**. This type of group was originated by educator Kurt Hahn to enhance emotional and physical abilities in clients by having them deal with safe but risk-taking events in the wilderness (Gillen & Balkin, 2006). Like other groups, these groups go through a number of stages. They focus on the promotion of long-term change and the opportunity to learn new coping skills. They may be used as adjuncts in hospital and clinical settings. Fletcher and Hinkle (2002) found that integrating an adventure component into an institutional setting produced positive results in participants, such as enhanced self-confidence, self-concept, and well-being. Other findings support enhanced benefits, such as more immediate insight and quicker movement through developmental stages within the group.

Reflection

If you started a counseling group, do you think you would incorporate physical activities, such as the arts or movement, into it, or do you think you would concentrate mainly on having members talk about their concerns? Why would you do what you do, and how would it help the group develop?

An Example of a Counseling Group: A Counseling Group for Counselors

Often counseling groups are conducted in schools or agencies with clients who want or need to focus on a developmental or situational problematic aspect of their lives, such as making a career decision or resolving negative feelings toward specific people or experiences. The purpose of the group and its members is clear.

The counseling group chosen as an example here, a counseling group for counselors, can be enhancing for several reasons. For example, it promotes a dialogue among members of a profession who may otherwise not meet together at any other regular time. One of the most important dimensions of this type of group, however, is to help counselors deal with what Kottler (2010) describes as the "toxic effect" that comes from working with people in pain. The **toxic effect** includes physical and psychic isolation, repeated feelings of loss in regard to client termination, and interpersonal distancing from family and friends who may perceive counselors as interpreting their words and actions. Thus, as Guy (1987) recommends, counselors need periodic, regular counseling to keep themselves well and functioning in an adequate and effective manner.

A counseling group for counselors can be conducted in a number of ways, but Emerson (1995) has set up an open-ended group model that appears to be most appropriate for practitioners in local communities. Her model is premised on Coche's (1984) suggestion that experienced group counselors reexperience participation in a counseling group. Specifically, Coche states that this reexperience can help group workers go beyond blasé and stereotypical responses, make them more aware of group participants' feelings, and resensitize them professionally to their power as group leaders.

In a counseling group for counselors, just as in other group counseling, self-disclosure and exploration of one's strengths and weaknesses are important for the development of the group members and the group as a whole. **Yearbook feedback**—that is, saying nice but insignificant things about a person, as high school students do when they write in annuals—is a tempting but nonproductive strategy. Instead, group members must deal with anxieties about their concerns as the group develops in an atmosphere of mutual trust where calculated risks are taken. When this type of behavior occurs, people who risk making themselves known and attempt to engage in new or different behaviors gain the most from the group experience.

Like other participants in counseling groups, counselors in counseling groups may experience some negative as well as positive outcomes. For instance, Gene may have suppressed anger and may erupt over what seems like an innocent remark directed at him. In such a case, the group needs to help Gene recognize both from where his anger is coming and toward whom or what it is really directed. Likewise, secrets may keep Bogusia from sharing significantly with the group and may inhibit the group's development if they are not acknowledged and shared. On the positive side, the awareness of personal growth that comes in problem solving and sharing may lead to members developing greater confidence in themselves as counselors, friends, family members, or parents. For example, Cassandra may discover from feedback in the group that she is perceived in a positive way congruent with her own self-concept. Thus, she may become even more open and available to those around her.

Case Example

Cassie Tries a Counseling Group

Cassie was in a natural disaster and was having trouble coping afterwards. A friend suggested that she sign up for a counseling group offered by the local mental health authority. Cassie was reluctant at first, but after a few more sleepless nights, she relented and joined a group.

The group leader, Martin, made it clear that members were free to work on issues that were of most concern to them. Cassie chose her experience in the natural disaster. She was not the only person struggling with reliving such a bad memory. In the group Cassie was able to verbalize her anger, angst, and anguish. She was able to come to terms with what she did and did not do to help others and herself. As the group ended, Cassie, who kept a journal, told the other group members: "I was wrung out when I came to the group, now I'm right on."

Questions

When have you felt it would be helpful to be in a counseling group to deal with a life issue? Is that still an issue you could use some help with?

PSYCHOTHERAPY GROUPS

A psychotherapy group is sometimes simply called **group psychotherapy** or group therapy. It is a group that addresses "personal and interpersonal problems of living . . . among people who may be experiencing severe and/or chronic maladjustment" (ASGW, 2000, p. 331). Such a group is remedial in nature and emphasizes helping people with serious psychological problems of long duration by confronting them with "their unconscious conflicts so that they may be resolved" (Lev-Wiesel, 2003, p. 240). As such, this type of group is found most often in mental health facilities, such as clinics and hospitals. The emphasis in psychotherapy groups is on therapy *by* the group rather than therapy *in* the group (Grossmark, 2007). As an entity, a psychotherapy group may be either **open-ended** (admitting new members at any time) or **closed-ended** (not admitting new members after the first session).

One of the primary aims of the group psychotherapy process is to reconstruct, sometimes through depth analysis, or to rectify through various treatment modalities the personalities or intrapersonal functioning of those involved in the group (Brammer, Abrego, & Shostrom, 1993; Gazda, Ginter, & Horne, 2001). The literature rather clearly documents group psychotherapy as an effective intervention for a wide variety of disorders, with client improvement supported in a vast number of studies (Hoffmann, Gleave, Burlingame, & Jackson, 2009). For instance, Semmelhack, Hazell, and Hoffman (2008) used a group-as-a-whole method with 11 severely mentally ill adult clients residing in a long-term care facility over 30 weeks. The **group-as-a-whole approach** is one where the therapist makes comments directed to the whole group that "reflect processes operating in the group in the here and now that seem to be out of the group's current awareness" (p. 44). Through this approach they were able to bring about "a significant decrease in anxiety and a reduction in depression" when this population was compared to a control group (p. 58).

The size of psychotherapy groups vary from 2 or 3 to 12 members. The duration of the group is measured in months, or even years. The leader of the group is always an expert in one of the mental health disciplines (psychiatry, psychology, counseling, social work, or psychiatric nursing) and has training and expertise in dealing with people who have major emotional problems. The leader's responsibility is to confront as well as to facilitate.

It should be noted that, although group psychotherapy is focused on severe problems, it is not wise or effective to include only individuals with personality disorders or diagnosable mental disorders, according to the latest edition of the American Psychiatric Association's *Diagnostic and Statistical Manual of Mental Disorders* (Yalom & Leszcz, 2005). Instead, a variety of individuals (a heterogeneous group) works best. To select such a group, leaders must prescreen carefully, preferably using prescreening instruments, such as the Group Therapy Questionnaire (GTQ) (MacNair-Semands, 1997). Leaders of psychotherapy groups most often operate from a theoretical position (e.g., psychoanalysis, Gestalt, existential). Three primary forces are operating at all times in a psychotherapy group: individual dynamics, interpersonal dynamics, and group-as-a-whole dynamics (Bernard et al., 2008).

Reflection

How do you think group counseling and group psychotherapy differ? How are they the same? What concerns, besides those already mentioned in the text, do you think would be appropriate for a psychotherapy group?

An Example of Group Psychotherapy: Group Work with Abusers and the Abused

Working with abusers or the abused requires a different approach from that used in other forms of group work. Individuals who are abusers, or who have been abused by others, have great difficulty in establishing healthy intrapersonal and interpersonal relationships (Vinson, 1992). They suffer from a variety of symptoms ranging from poor impulse control in the case of abusers to poor self-concept in the case of the abused. Many people in either category have trouble working through their problems on an individual level. Abusers "usually have long histories of abuse, extremely strong defenses against change, and relatively little ability to follow through on commitments" (Fuhrmann & Washington, 1984, p. 63). The abused, especially those who have been sexually molested as children, tend to shut down, suppress, or distract themselves to the point of not dealing with what happened to them (Emerson, 1988; McBride & Emerson, 1989). In both types of cases, denial is a major means of dealing with present and past situations.

Group psychotherapy is often effective with such individuals for at least two reasons. First, many perpetrators of abuse and their victims are socially isolated and, therefore, welcome a structured experience in which they can "tell their story" and become more connected with others. Second, groups composed of members with similar backgrounds, such as abusers, are more resistant to manipulation by their members.

Almost all psychotherapy groups for abusers and the abused make use of basic group techniques, such as role playing, modeling, feedback, and confrontation (Fuhrmann & Washington, 1984; Vinson, 1992). The degree and type of change that occurs in group therapy is related to both the emphasis in the group and the group's developmental stage (Wheeler, O'Malley, Waldo, Murphey, & Blank, 1992). Psychotherapy groups that work best are composed of volunteers who are prescreened before being selected. However, because of the seriousness of abusive disorders, some groups are mandated as a part of court-ordered treatment and are filled with openly resistant clients. In such situations, group leaders must know how to work with resistance, such as not opposing it, but talking it through. Because of the volatility present in abuse groups, co-leaders are often recommended.

Probably the abusive disorder in which group psychotherapy strategies are most prevalent is with addiction, ranging from "foodaholism" (Stoltz, 1984) to chemical dependency (Clark, Blanchard, & Hawes, 1992; Kominars & Dornheim, 2004). In such groups, it is helpful but not always necessary to have leaders with experience in working through the abuse involved. A group leader does not have to have been abused or have been an abuser to be effective with group participants in this personality reconstruction process, but a thorough understanding of the individual, group, family, and community dynamics that contribute to abusive disorders is essential. For example, if Zelda undertakes conducting such a group, not only does she need to have established expertise in dealing with the dynamics underlying the abused or abusers, but she also must have established a network of community resources she can utilize in helping her group members reconstruct their lives. See Figure 1.2 for a summary of the four main types of groups.

Case Example

Garrett and the Psychotherapy Group

Garrett has been in and out of the state mental hospital three times. Having read the book *A Mind That Found Itself,* he realizes that he is much like the author, Clifford Beers, who had moments of clear thinking amid times of despair. In one of his clearest moments, Garrett decides to enroll in a psychotherapy group to help himself.

The group is open-ended, with new members coming in all the time and old members leaving. Yet, Garrett finds that the constant leadership of the group worker keeps him focused on not getting too upset when his day is interrupted or when he makes

mistakes. He takes his medicine every day and talks about the time when he may no longer need medication. Overall, he is better adjusted than before because he is becoming more aware of himself and what he can do to help himself.

Questions

What people do you know, either from a distance or up close, who you think could benefit from a psychotherapy group? Do you think most people who need psychotherapy groups are or should be on medications? Why or why not?

Type of Group	Emphasis	Setting	Size	Duration Number of Sessions
Task/Work	Promote efficiency and effective accomplishment of group goals	Almost any environment—work, school, religious settings, community organizations, civic groups	Work best with 12 or fewer members because otherwise subgroups may form	Time depends on task, but most task/work groups last from a half hour to 2 hours. Meetings may be regular or spontaneous depending on objective and whether setting is formal or informal
Psychoedu-cational	Acquire information and develop related meaning and skills	Hospitals, mental health and social service agencies, educational and religious settings, work environments	20 to 40 is average	50 minutes to 2 hours. Regular meetings usually weekly— average number of sessions 8 to 10, although many may be just for one session
Counseling	Prevention, growth, remediation, interpersonal and group dynamics	Schools, universities, mental health agencies, employee assistance programs, etc.	8 to 12 adults, smaller size for children, may vary depending on whether open or closed ended	20 to 90 minutes on average with longer lengths for adults. Regular meetings usually weekly
Psychotherapy	Personal and interpersonal problems of living—some severe; remedial, reconstructive	Hospitals, clinics, mental health and social services agencies	Depends on whether open or closed ended	60 to 120 minutes. Regular meetings often last over a number of months or years

FIGURE 1.2   Comparison of four basic types of groups.

MIXED GROUPS AND A PROPOSED REGROUPING OF CATEGORIES

Some groups simply do not fit into any of the four major categories of groups just described; that is, it is hard to classify them as mainly task/work, psychoeducational, counseling, or psycho-therapy groups. "Overlapping and blending of group types in the same group experience often best represents the reality of the evolving practice of group work" (Ward, 2006, p. 95). Further-more, as Waldo and Bauman (1998) assert, the four main categories of groups are problematic "in that the goal and process dimensions of group work are combined within each category" (p. 164). Groups that defy classification are sometimes described as **mixed groups** because they encom-pass multiple ways of working with their members and may change their emphasis at different times in the development of the group. For instance, the Doctor Interactive Group Medical Appointment (DIGMA) is a "group intervention that combines the services of behavioral health and primary care" while combining elements of psychoeducational and support groups (Westheimer, Capello, McCarthy, & Denny, 2009, p. 151). It has been found effective in help-ing hypertensive male veterans reduce their blood pressure and promote healthy behaviors. Yet, it is a mixture of different types of groups.

Waldo and Bauman (1998) have proposed using multiple dimensions to describe groups. They point out that, although there are at least five dimensions that could be used in categorizing groups—goals, process, members, setting, and leader—"it is possible to arrive at a meaningful and practical categorization of groups through the use of the first two dimensions, goals and process" (p. 169). Their nomenclature for goal category includes the terms

- *development,* that is, forward motion and expansion;
- *remediation,* that is, overcoming or correcting manifest problems; and
- *adjustment,* that is, assisting members in coping with problems or circumstances that cannot be remediated.

The process dimension of their proposal retains three of the titles and process descriptions currently employed by the ASGW: psychoeducational, counseling, and psychotherapy. Therefore, when goals and process are placed as two dimensions of a matrix, they form nine categories of group work.

Waldo and Bauman (1998) have validated their goals and process, or **GAP matrix for groups**, by having independent raters categorize randomly selected articles on group work under this system as well as the ASGW's four types of groups. They found much more agreement (100% vs. 33%) for raters using the GAP model and point to the utility, specificity, and research implications of their system as opposed to the four-group specialty system.

In response to the GAP matrix for groups, Conyne and Wilson (1998) point out that, although the system has many merits, if it were to be adopted as proposed it could undermine the ASGW training standards, which are a firm foundation for training, research, and practice and "whose positive effects are only now just beginning to emerge" (p. 183). Another drawback to the GAP model is that it does not consider task/work groups (Keel, 1998). Furthermore, the model is not as applicable as it would seem to such areas as psychoeducational groups for college students and, in fact, may complicate training for professionals entering student development and related fields (Taub, 1998b). Another drawback is that the model itself may need further refinement. For instance, the GAP model might be more useful if three dimensions (members, settings, and leaders) initially discussed by Waldo and Bauman were included as well as the dimensions of goals and process (Gerrity, 1998).

In response to the criticisms of their GAP model, Bauman and Waldo (1998) have revised their system to incorporate the four ASGW group classifications. Regardless, there are many examples of how groups may overlap in purpose, process, and content. For instance, a group might begin with multiple purposes (psychoeducational, psychotherapeutic, and task oriented). Such groups can be found among a number of self-help or mutual help groups.

Self-help groups and **mutual help groups** (i.e., **support groups**) are synonymous (Klaw & Humphreys, 2004, p. 630). They take two forms: those that are organized by an established, professional helping organization or individual and those that originate spontaneously and stress their autonomy and internal group resources—self-help groups in the truest sense (Riordan & Beggs, 1988). Although distinctions in support groups and self-help organizations can be made regarding leadership and control (Silverman, 1986), these groups share numerous common denominators, including the fact that they are composed of individuals who have a common, or single-life, focus and purpose. They are psychoeducational, psychotherapeutic, and usually task driven. In addition, members of these groups frequently employ basic counseling techniques, such as reflection, active listening, and confrontation.

The civil rights movement of the 1950s and 1960s laid the foundation for the self-help and mutual help/support group movement. Minorities, especially African Americans, realized during this time that they would have to band together and rely on their own resources if they were to make substantial gains and obtain major changes in American society. Other factors, such as the success of earlier self-help and support groups (e.g., Alcoholics Anonymous, Weight Watchers) and the failure of federal programs to take care of needs they were intended to address, also contributed to the momentum behind this movement.

Many support and self-help groups seem to be successful in assisting their members to take more control over their lives and function well. The narrow focus of these groups is an asset in achieving specific goals. For instance, support groups for survivors of natural disasters, such as Hurricane Katrina, Superstorm Sandy, typhoons in the Philippines, or tsunamis, had an immediate positive impact on problem solving. Furthermore, they may have had a preventive effect in decreasing posttraumatic stress disorders by normalizing stress reactions and stress symptoms, providing a means for members helping others physically and psychologically, and being a source of understanding where individuals really felt listened to (Fernando, 2009).

There are hundreds of self-help organizations in the United States alone and "more than a 1,000 national, international, model, and online self-help support groups for a variety of stressful life situations—including mental health, addiction, bereavement, parenting, abuse, and more" (Merchant & Yozant, 2014, pp. 34–35). "Indeed, mutual help organizations exist for almost every major chronic condition and leading cause of mortality" (Klaw & Humphreys, 2004, p. 631). Furthermore, these groups are used: "approximately 7% of American adults (about 11 million people)" participate in them every year, and approximately 18% have done so in their lifetimes (p. 632).

A national survey revealed important facts about the characteristics of self-help group participants. First, with the exception of groups for eating problems (whose membership is composed almost entirely of White women), African Americans and Whites are equally likely to attend all types of self-help groups. Furthermore, individuals with low incomes (from $0 to $20,000 per year) are more likely to participate than are middle-class and affluent individuals. Finally, individuals who are divorced or separated and have less social support are more likely to attend groups than are married individuals and individuals with extensive social support. Given these data, we may conclude that self-help groups have significant potential to benefit diverse racial groups and individuals with low financial and social resources (Klaw & Humphreys, 2004).

In addition to the foregoing, within a self-help group context, a group member is empowered because he or she provides as well as receives services, and the positive self-identity of these individuals grows. Furthermore, "self-help groups can be successfully incorporated into professional programs in a fashion that enhances outcomes with little additional cost" (Klaw & Humphreys, 2004, p. 635). Thus, mental and physical health can be improved through the use of self-care groups. They can lower health care costs if used by health care and health promotion programs.

Some of the most common self-help groups are those for chronic conditions such as arthritis (Young at Heart) and psychiatric disabilities (Recovery, Inc.), as well as those established to combat leading causes of mortality such as tobacco (Nicotine Anonymous) and illicit drugs

(Narcotics Anonymous). A list of names and addresses of some of the most prominent self-help group can be found in Appendix C of this text.

Reflection

What surprises you about self-help groups? What facts about these groups did you already know or assume?

An Example of a Mixed Group: A Consumer-Oriented Group

A support group that encompasses self-help and functions from a psychoeducational and task/work perspective is a consumer-oriented group. Consumer-oriented groups, which are often groups that advocate for change and social justice, are formed on the basis of need and may be either short term or long term, depending on the problem or concern. For instance, consumer-oriented groups may revolve around long-term themes, such as protection and promotion of the environment around low-income neighborhoods. In such cases, these groups tend to be ongoing, with individuals joining or dropping out of the group depending on the sociopolitical climate and the impact of specific events on their lives. Short-term consumer groups focus on immediate issues, such as safety in particular locales, taxation, property values, or zoning permits in a community. These groups are usually spontaneously organized and less hierarchical than long-term consumer groups. After their issue is settled (e.g., new stop lights are installed, school zones are redrawn), the short-term groups usually disband. They work in such cases much like task/work groups.

Consumer groups are sometimes impaired, at least initially, because there is no immediately recognized leader. When this occurs, the group must wait for one to emerge. Considerable chaos may ensue while members jockey for positions and direction. Consumer groups that are successful have both *rigor* (structure and a plan of action) and *vigor* (constant communication and contact with officials), whereas those that fail primarily have only one or neither of these qualities.

Consumer groups that meet in public and wish to elicit community support need to identify responsible people who will arrange for a variety of tasks that must be carefully and efficiently carried out if the group is to be successful. Many of these tasks are rather mundane and mechanical, but they are crucial in promoting the outcome of the group—for instance, arranging for audiovisual equipment and food, if necessary.

One of the more important dimensions to planning consumer group meetings is the seating arrangement of the room. At least three arrangements will enhance or detract from the task of the group, depending on how they are used (Wilson & Hanna, 1986) (see Figure 1.3). Consumer group leaders should be aware of these designs when setting up their meetings to enhance the use of their time and the resources of the people involved. For instance, if Benjamin, the leader of a consumer group, mainly wants the group to hear new information, he may arrange the room and program as a symposium or a panel discussion. However, if he wants group members to become active and discuss strategies for dealing with a particular matter, he may use a round-table format and arrange as many tables as needed to accommodate the size of the group. After discussing issues for a specified length of time, each table leader can then report back to the group as whole.

Roundtable

Symposium

Panel Discussion

FIGURE 1.3   Three ways of helping groups gather information and make decisions.

Case Example

Charlie and the Moving Chairs

Charlie loved working as the leader of an advocacy group of young professionals. He noted how smart and aware they were and how they were driven to achieve tangible goals. However, Charlie noted that of late, the group had become more lethargic, and not as much was being done inside or outside the group by the members. Therefore, he decided to shake things up, starting with the way the chairs were arranged in the room. Each week Charlie haphazardly arranged the chairs in different formations. In some of the formations, members could see each other directly. In others, members' views were partially blocked or they actually saw the back of other members' heads. Charlie noticed there was more physical motion in the group after he started moving the chairs around, but he could not tell that it made a difference in any other way.

Questions

What do you think of Charlie's experiment? What else do you think he might have done to have helped the group refocus itself and be more successful?

Summary and Conclusion

This chapter has covered past and present proposed categories for classifying groups. Past models include those that were contact-focused or specialized, yet flexible, as in the TRAC model. In 1991, the four major types of groups (psychoeducational, counseling, psychotherapy, task/work) as proposed by the ASGW became a standard for categorizing groups. This system was revised in 2000 when it was realized that some groups, such as many self-help groups, are mixed and incorporate multiple dimensions of the four ASGW group emphases in their functioning. The GAP group model is the most recent innovation in the group classification system. Its usefulness is now being openly discussed among group experts.

Group workers who narrow their skills to working with only one type of specialty group will limit their flexibility in working with people in groups. Although specifics can increase expertise in a particular area, human service professionals, such as counselors, psychologists, social workers, and psychiatric nurses, are called on to deal with a variety of clients in multiple ways. Sometimes conducting a psychoeducational group will be more productive than running a psychotherapy group, and sometimes psychoeducational group skills are necessary to facilitate a psychotherapy group (MacNair-Semands, 1998). Working in task/work groups will be required regardless of what else the clinician does.

From case conferences to task force teams, everyone who works as a professional helper needs to know how to facilitate a group that is focused on achieving a product other than individual change. Therefore, it is essential to adhere to and master the standards and competencies that professional associations have laid out. Group work involves different types of groups. It is a complex and demanding process in its actual application.

Classroom Exercises

1. In a group of three, identify two life skills, such as applying for a job or making conversation in a social situation, that you think could be taught in a psychoeducational group. Outline the ways you would teach these skills. Confer with another threesome about the skills they have selected and the approach they have decided to use. Select one skill and approach from your combined group of six, and as a group present it to the class.

2. Read recent periodicals in your library to gain a sense of how task/work groups and teams are used in business and nonbusiness environments. In a group of three, discuss the articles that each of you has selected. Share your ideas about ways to use task/work groups and teams in the helping professions.

3. In dyads, read and critique a recent research report or journal article on the effectiveness of a counseling or psychotherapy group. Report your findings to the class as a whole.

4. You have been asked to train a group of novice group workers and teach them about the four major types of groups. From what you have read in this chapter, how would you go about accomplishing this task? Would you incorporate the GAP model into your training? If so, how? Share your outline for presenting your material with your class.

CHAPTER 2

Group Dynamics

Emotions ricochet around the room
fired by an act of self-disclosure
in an atmosphere of trust.
I, struck by the process,
watch as feelings penetrate the minds of members
and touch off new reactions.
Change comes from many directions
triggered by simple words.*

*From "Group Dynamics" © 1989 by Samuel
T. Gladding. Reprinted by permission from
Samuel T. Gladding.*

Monkey Business/Fotolia

CHAPTER OVERVIEW

From reading this chapter, you will learn about

- Group content and process and the importance of balancing them
- Group dynamics
- The differences and similarities between working with groups, individuals, and families

AS YOU READ, CONSIDER

- How much group structure is related to the success of a group
- How positive and negative internal and external variables can affect a group
- The importance of preplanning a group

In William Golding's book *Lord of the Flies*, the reader is taken through a process of events that depicts how young English boys gradually decline from proper to savage behavior. The boys are marooned on an island in the middle of the ocean after a plane crash, without any link to the world. They initially start to help each other out just as adults would do. But the group deteriorates, and violence and bloodshed result. In contrast, B. F. Skinner's *Walden Two* starts and ends differently. A thousand inhabitants of a planned utopian community live happy and healthy lives thanks to adhering to the principles of behaviorism. Both novels represent different aspects of group dynamics and how such dynamics affect a group.

Regardless of what groups people may be a part of, they need to be aware that groups are dynamic entities that have a direct and indirect impact on their members (Bion, 1959; Yalom & Leszcz, 2005). "In any group, it is a mistake to ever conclude that nothing is happening within or between its members" (Conyne, Wilson, & Ward, 1997, p. 32). The presence of others may improve or impair the performance and development of persons, depending on their background and preparation (Zajonc, 1965). When individuals are accustomed to working with others and well prepared for a group experience, the group enhances their performances, and they add to the group. In contrast, when individuals are used to working alone and are not well prepared for a group experience, their behavior may be detrimentally affected by being in the group, and they may detract from the group as a whole. Thus, a **social influence** emerges in a group that manifests itself by altering actions, attitudes, and feelings (Asch, 1951; Festinger, 1954; Sherif, 1937).

Research taken from three separate disciplines—individual psychology, social psychology, and sociology—focuses on explaining these and other interactions that occur in groups and how groups influence their members (Munich & Astrachan, 1983). Basically, people act differently in groups than they do by themselves. As a general rule, **primary affiliation groups** (those with which people most identify, such as a family or peers) exert greater pressure on individuals than **secondary affiliation groups** (those with which people least identify, such as a city or a confederation).

Case Example

Alberto Wreaks Havoc

When he is with his family, 13-year-old Alberto is polite and well behaved. So it was a shock when Mrs. Hernando received a call from the director of the camp Alberto was attending during the summer asking that she and her husband come and get him. When the Hernandos arrived at the camp, the director informed them that Alberto had broken into the kitchen with several other boys and dumped flour all over the tables and chairs. When questioned, Alberto could not give a rational explanation. He said he simply thought it was funny and that the camp staff would not care. He was having a good time with his new friends. His behavior at camp was far from what he displayed at home with his family and peers.

Questions

What do you think happened to Alberto? Based on what you have read, why might it have occurred?

The influence of groups on members, and what has grown to be known as group dynamics, was first studied as a phenomenon in work environments. Indeed, "the origins of group dynamics are largely in social and industrial psychology and stem from the efforts of experts in these fields to understand group influence on individual behavior and on productivity in the workplace and in other human groups" (Friedman, 1989, p. 46). Elton Mayo and associates at the Hawthorne Plant of the Western Electric Company conducted the initial landmark study on the influence of groups (Mayo, 1945). This research group investigated the effects of manipulating physical features in the work setting. It was discovered that physical aspects of the work environment were not as important as social factors within the work group. Changes in behavior as a result of observation and manipulation of conditions in an environment became known as the **Hawthorne effect**.

Although Mayo's work involved group dynamics, he did not describe it in that way. Rather, the term came from Kurt Lewin (1948), who was the first to use it. For Lewin, group dynamics includes everything that goes on in a small group. He was especially interested in how the climate of a group and its processes influenced the interactions of group members and ultimately outcomes. He thought many factors contributed to the overall concept of group dynamics, including the group's purpose, communication patterns, power, control issues, and member roles. For instance, a psychotherapy group for survivors of natural disasters, such as a forest fire or earthquake, has a purpose and intensity quite different from those of a research group formed to study the Internet's effects on community values. Member roles and interactions are not the same, either. The intensity or temperature of these types of groups differs dramatically. By understanding forces operating within a group and their interplay, group specialists are able to discern the nature of groups and how interactions among participants affect a group's development.

Reflection

What role(s) do you play in your primary groups, such as in your family or on your athletic or artistic team? How does your behavior differ in these circumstances compared to that when you are in a secondary group setting, such as riding on a train or plane?

GROUP CONTENT AND GROUP PROCESS

Included in the term *group dynamics* (forces within a group) are two powerful elements that have a major bearing on a group's development and productivity: **group content** (information within and purpose of the group) and **group process** (interactions and relationships among members within the group). The amount and mixture of group content and group process ultimately determine the dynamics within a group.

Group Content

Group content involves the actual words, ideas, and information exchanged within a group as well as the purpose of the group. For example, in a psychoeducational group, participants may talk about the facts surrounding the purpose of the group, such as how to prevent the spread of acquired immunodeficiency syndrome (AIDS) or ebola. However, groups do not run well on facts and information alone. After some time in most groups, members have enough basic knowledge to accomplish their goals. This point does not mean that new and pertinent information should not be added to the group over time—quite the contrary, because groups absorb and deal with information developmentally. Rather, it means that more information is not necessarily better. Large quantities of information in short periods are not useful because it cannot be adequately digested. For instance, in a group for victims of a disaster, information on recovery is given in pieces over time because otherwise group members become overwhelmed, confused, or discouraged.

People in groups, just like people individually, do not make most of the important decisions of their lives based on cognitive knowledge. Instead, good decision making involves interaction with others in pursuit of a purpose. It is based on members having pertinent information, an opportunity to understand their options, and a chance to assess what they are thinking and feeling with other people they trust and value. That is where group process comes in.

Case Example

Professor Drone Goes On and On

Despite his sincerity and sense of caring, Professor Drone gets terrible student evaluations. He complains to his colleagues and tries harder each semester without making any substantial progress. He is knowledgeable and amicable, but his students do not like being in his class and do not learn a lot. The reason:

He drones on with lecture notes from the minute he starts class until the bell rings. Students do not interact except to occasionally squirm and roll their eyes.

Questions

What would you advise Professor Drone to do besides "try harder"? Be specific.

Group Process

Group process is the interaction of group members with one another, often in some meaningful way. For example, Joe may feel he cannot speak up in a group because another group member criticized one of the first things he said in the group. His lack of trust and inhibition detracts from the group because he remains silent. If Joe is an especially astute observer of people or has insight that would really help the group, his nonparticipation in the group hurts that much more. Regardless, other members will eventually notice Joe's withdrawal. Then either the group will spend time attending to Joe—trying to coax him into contributing when they could be focusing on other goals—or they will criticize him even more, thereby alienating him significantly from the group. Thus, attending to process within the group is vital to the group's well-being.

As groups develop, less time generally is spent on content material, and more is focused on process functions. There is often a relational paradox. Individuals, especially those who have been in nonmutual relationships, want to become connected with others. Out of a sense of fear or hurt, however, as with Joe in the preceding illustration, they simultaneously employ strategies that restrict or limit their ability to become close to others (Comstock, Duffey, & St. George, 2002). Therefore, they disconnect. They may reconnect (when trust is built) and enhance their connection (when they feel safer yet).

Seven types of group processes that most frequently occur in groups related to this paradox and the dynamics surrounding it have been outlined by Donigian and Malnati (1997):

- *Contagion*—In this process, member behavior elicits group interaction. For instance, if Bette talks to others in a group about her emptiness and loneliness, then she may elicit an emotional and physical reaction from other group members as some cry and some lean forward to listen more intensely.
- *Conflict*—Matters involving conflict usually revolve around significant issues in people's lives, such as authority, intimacy, growth, change, autonomy, power, and loss. All group members and leaders experience conflict during the life of a group. How a group leader

handles conflict makes a difference. For example, if in a group counseling session Rex, the group leader, pushes Stu to have a fight with Keith, Rex may be vicariously meeting needs he never satisfied in adolescence, but he may not be helping Stu or Keith to resolve their differences.

- *Anxiety*—The tension involved in anxiety and the uneasy feelings that go with it are universal. To cope with the discomfort of some emotions in a group, members typically employ one of two strategies. The first is a *restrictive solution*, such as changing the subject, attacking a group member, intellectualizing, detaching from the group, or ignoring a group member. Thus, if Karen feels uncomfortable discussing her personal life, she may flippantly say, "But my situation is just like everyone else's."

    A second, healthier strategy for dealing with anxiety is to employ *enabling solutions* (Whitaker & Lieberman, 1964). These types of solutions revolve around open listening and discussion about the anxiety that is present. In such a situation, Roosevelt might say to Regina, "Tell me more about how you felt when your mother criticized you." Overall, "anxiety is a mobilizer of group process," especially if it is faced openly and honestly (Donigian & Malnati, 1997, p. 62).

- *Consensual validation*—The process of consensual validation involves checking one's behaviors with a group of others. In this interaction, people are questioned, confronted, or affirmed either individually or within the group. Thus, in a group for overeaters, members might question one another about their interactions involving food to find out how unusual or common their behaviors are.

- *Universality*—It is comforting to know that others within a group have similar experiences and feelings. Such insight helps people feel they are in the same ballpark as the rest of the group members. In the universality process, this discovery enables group participants to identify and unify with one another. For instance, in a psychoeducational group involving families with adolescents, families in the group may be relieved to know they are not the only ones having difficulties with parent–teen communications. If a group is going to be productive, it is essential for universality to occur early in its development.

- *Family reenactment*—Families of origin continue to influence people throughout their lives (Kerr & Bowen, 1988). Because groups resemble families in many ways, it is natural that some behaviors by group members are connected to issues they never resolved in childhood. The group is either helped or hindered by such actions, depending on whether group members are assisted in focusing on the present or allowed to lapse into the past. In the first case, the group member and the group work through issues. Thus, Pedro may say to Veronica, "I need you to help me hear what you are saying. Your actions are a lot like those of my mother, with whom I was constantly arguing." In the second scenario, group interactions become distorted or toxic. An example of this type of behavior is when Sally repeatedly tells David, "I'm not listening to you. You sound just like my father, and he never had anything worthwhile to say."

- *Instillation of hope*—In some groups, especially those involving counseling and therapy, many members may feel hopeless. They believe their environment controls them and they will never be different or change. It is, therefore, vital that these group members be helped to come to terms with their own issues. Through such a process, all group members can come to realize that their issues are resolvable. In such a situation, Kathy may begin to believe she can be different because William has gotten better and his problems were similar to hers when the group began.

Focus Questions:

FIGURE 2.1   Balanced process and content.   *Source:* From "Leadership in Groups: Balancing Process and Content," presentation at the annual convention of the American Counseling Association, April 1994. Reprinted with permission of Diana Hulse-Killacky, Becky Schmacher, and Kurt Kraus.

Balance Between Content and Process

Process must be balanced with content regardless of the type of group being conducted (Kraus & Hulse-Killacky, 1996). Process, along with content, is at the heart of decision making. Leaders can use two sets of questions to guide the interplay between content and process (Hulse-Killacky, Killacky, & Donigian, 2001).

Content questions include:

> What do we have to do?
> What do we need to do to accomplish our goals?

Process questions center on:

> Who am I? [intrapersonal]
> Who am I with you? [interpersonal]
> Who are we together? [the whole group] (p. 9)

One way to think about process is to liken it to a river, whereas content is like a boat on the river (Geroski & Kraus, 2002). Regardless, interpersonal dimensions of a group take on increased importance as the group moves toward its objectives (Armstrong & Berg, 2005; Luke, 2014). The ideal balance between content and process can be seen in a bell-shaped curve (see Figure 2.1) in which content and process look like a single thread even though they are two separate fibers (Hulse-Killacky, Schumacher, & Kraus, 1999). However, achieving such a balance is not easy (Champe & Rubel, 2012).

When process and content are out of balance, there may be too much of one, or the two may not be intertwined. For example, a group can begin with an overfocus on process (see Figure 2.2). In such a group, an experiential activity that does not tie in with the rest of the group session is used to get members emotionally involved. For example, a leader may take one of the energizer

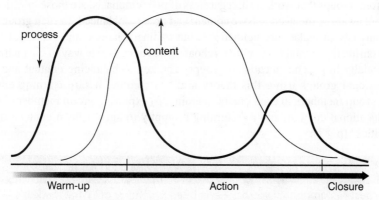

FIGURE 2.2   Process first, content after.   *Source:* From "Leadership in Groups: Balancing Process and Content," presentation at the annual convention of the American Counseling Association, April 1994. Reprinted with permission of Diana Hulse-Killacky, Becky Schmacher, and Kurt Kraus.

exercises from Keene and Erford (2007), such as "It's Snowing" (p. 26), where everyone represents himself or herself as a snowflake in the introduction segment of the group and highlights unique personal qualities. However, in this unbalanced scenario, the activity is then never connected to the work of the group. Another such scenario may occur if Peggy, the group leader, has group members talk to one another initially about the most important event that shaped their lives and then moves onto having the group solve a problem concerning the selling of tickets to an upcoming play, without connecting the group experience to the work activity.

The opposite of such a scenario is for a group to stay focused on content (Figure 2.3). This type of arrangement occurs frequently in task/work groups in which members may not even be introduced to one another before the group leader states what the group will do for the day. In a

FIGURE 2.3   Content-inhibiting process.   *Source:* From "Leadership in Groups: Balancing Process and Content," presentation at the annual convention of the American Counseling Association, April 1994. Reprinted with permission of Diana Hulse-Killacky, Becky Schmacher, and Kurt Kraus.

content-dominated group, process is inhibited, and members often withdraw from the group mentally or physically because they never felt a part of it to begin with.

Therefore, groups that work well, regardless of their emphasis, are those in which members and leaders are aware of the need to have content and process balanced. In such groups, everyone works continuously to make sure neither gets out of line. Champe and Rubel (2012) suggest using focal conflict theory, a theory with psychoanalytic roots, as one way of balancing these two entities, especially in psychoeducational groups. The key to balancing content and process in psychoeducational groups using this theory are: "1) creating a safe learning environment, 2) engaging group members in each others' learning, 3) exploring group members' relationship to psychoeducational content, and 4) returning promptly to agreed upon content and content-related activities" (p. 87).

Reflection

What is the best-run group that you have ever been a member of? What made it so? What was the worst? What made that a bad experience? In your evaluation of these groups, think how content and process were handled.

THE GROUP AS A SYSTEM: A WAY OF EXPLAINING GROUP DYNAMICS

Because content and process must be balanced to have productive group dynamics, a question that arises is "How?" One answer is to think of the group as a **system**, a set of elements standing in interaction with one another (Agazarian, 1997; Connors & Caple, 2005). Each element in the system is affected by whatever happens to any other element. Thus, the system is only as strong as its weakest part. Likewise, the system is greater than the sum of its parts (Gladding, 2015). An example of a system is a living organism, such as a plant or an animal. However, a group can be conceptualized as a system, too. As such it is made up of three crucial parts: the group leader, the group members, and the group as a whole (Donigian & Malnati, 1997).

For the system to be healthy and productive, each of these parts must function in an interactive and harmonious way as a unit and with the other two parts of the system. Thus, if group members are constantly in conflict with one another, then the group will not work well as a whole regardless of how talented the leader might be. Likewise, if group members work well together but are led by a leader who is unable to use this strength, then the group as a whole will underfunction. Finally, if group members and the group leader are both healthy, but no one in the group knows anything about how a group functions over its life span or the group has no goals, then the group as a whole will suffer.

Systems theory goes a long way in explaining how groups work and group dynamics (O'Connor, 1980). In a systems context, group members are always deciding between their needs for *differentiating themselves* (taking care of their needs to do things by themselves) and *integrating with others* (doing things with others) (Matthews, 1992). From a systems perspective, group leaders must orchestrate their efforts in helping members and the group as a whole to achieve a balance of individual and collective needs as the group develops. Multiple factors—such as interpersonal relationships, the mental health of the individuals involved, and the skill of the group leader—affect the group. The dynamics within the group are complex and connected. Although some factors influence others directly (in a **linear** or cause-and-effect way), most factors influence each other **systemically** (in a circular manner) (Bertalanffy, 1968; Donigian & Malnati, 1997; Matthews, 1992).

From a systems perspective, even small or seemingly insignificant events make a difference in the group. For instance, the presence or absence of a group member affects how a group operates. Similarly, the withholding or divulging of feelings has an impact. Even inevitable events, such as the passage of time, influence both the lives of group members and the life of the group as a whole. Consider, for example, the Beatles. During the 1960s, each member of this band—Paul McCartney, John Lennon, George Harrison, and Ringo Starr—changed not only himself but also the outward appearance, musical style, and performance of the others and the group as a whole. The Beatles of 1969 were not the same group in the way they operated (or even looked) as the Beatles of 1964 (Forsyth, 2013). The point is that groups as systems with many parts are constantly in a state of flux. In a more mundane illustration, if Bill feels uncomfortable in the presence of Norm and Nancy, then their absences from the group will most likely result in Bill being more active, which in turn will lead to new information being added to the group and a new interactive group process.

The complexity of working with groups as distinct types of entities must be properly understood to promote healthy atmospheres within them (Korda & Pancrazio, 1989). People who are uninformed or ignore how groups function usually become frustrated and bewildered. They do not help the group grow and may even behave inappropriately by encouraging behavior that group members are not ready to handle yet.

Case Example

Retro Rick

Rick is 50, married, and the father of three children. He works in information technology. Because he wants to expand his circle of male friends, he joins a local "growth group" of men who are at various life stages. Instead of talking about his own situation, Rick tries to be "cool." He talks about himself in singular terms and as if he were single and still in his 20s. He seeks out the younger men in the group to "hang with." Everyone is confused as to what Rick is doing. As one of the men his age says to him: "You are not 'youthing,' you are aging. 'Time passages' is more than a song by Al Stewart."

Questions

What do you think is happening with Rick? What is happening in the group? What aspects of health and dysfunction are present? How is the group working as a system?

One method of assessing which types of factors most influence certain group situations is by studying the research on groups as systems in such journals as *Small Group Behavior,* the *Journal for Specialists in Group Work, Group Dynamics,* and the *International Journal of Group Psychotherapy.* Good research that is clearly and concisely written can convey a considerable amount of information. Direct group observation or participation is a second means of comprehending the evolving nature of groups and how members are influenced by one another and external forces (e.g., cultural surroundings). This method gives firsthand knowledge about how a group is operating. A third way of assessing group influences is feedback from outside objective observers or a critique of group videotapes. This last means of obtaining data, especially if outside observers use video, allows a thorough examination of the group as a system and enables viewers to both see and hear what is occurring within.

INFLUENCING GROUP DYNAMICS

Given that group dynamics can be explained from a systems perspective, it behooves group workers to take advantage of this knowledge. They can do so by setting up conditions and structures that will help the group potentially run better and more smoothly in both the long and the short run. Although veteran group leaders "develop skills to assess the dynamics of group members and use their skills to anticipate and react to group movement" (Gerrity, 1998, p. 202), most group workers are wise to spend time and energy attending to the preplanning part of a group, the group structure, group exercises, group interaction, and members' roles.

Preplanning

The dynamics of a group begin before the group convenes. In the pregroup stage, the leaders plan what type of group to conduct, in what setting it should be held, how long it will last, who should be included, and how it will be evaluated. All of these considerations are an essential part of facilitating a successful group (Glaser, Webster, & Horne, 1992). If leaders are not sure of the type of experiences they wish to set up and for whom, then the group will most likely fail.

The first factor that must be considered in preplanning is **clarity of purpose**—what the group is to accomplish. For a group to be successful, it must be relevant and meaningful for all of its members. Otherwise, they are likely to withdraw or disengage. For instance, a psychoeducational group focusing on careers may have an appeal to senior high school students but not be relevant to primary school children unless it is modified to their level and presented so that they see a connection between themselves and future careers.

In addition to clarity of purpose, a **group setting** (its environment) will influence how well it runs. Settings should be rooms that are quiet, comfortable, and off the beaten track. This type of environment, one that promotes positive group dynamics, is not found by accident. It must be carefully selected because the group's functioning ultimately depends on it. Members who feel secure in an environment are more willing to take risks and use themselves and the group to the fullest.

A third factor that must be considered in preplanning a group is time. A group session should not be too long or too short. Sessions running more than 2 hours may cause members to become tired and lose interest. Likewise, with the exception of some children's groups, most groups need about 15 minutes to "warm up" before they start working. Therefore, groups that meet for less than half an hour, except for children's groups, do not have time to accomplish much. The ideal time frame for most groups is between an hour and an hour and a half. A few groups, such as marathons, use extended periods to help lower defenses through the effects of fatigue. In this way, they promote identity and change. Most groups, however, meet weekly within the period just described. Such a schedule allows group members and the group as a whole to obtain a comfortable pace or rhythm.

Even in a small group, size makes a difference in group dynamics. Research indicates that increasing the size of a group (beyond 6 to 14 members) decreases its cohesiveness and member satisfaction (Munich & Astrachan, 1983). One study indicated a significant reduction in interaction among group members when the group size reached 9, and another marked reduction when the group size reached 17 or more (Castore, 1962). In such cases, **subgrouping** (in which two or more members develop a group within the group) tends to occur. The result of subgrouping is that some members become silent while others dominate. Competition for airtime, focus, and inclusion becomes intense (Shepherd, 1964), and the atmosphere of the group changes. Groups with fewer than 5 members (except those composed of elementary school children) tend not to function well, either. In such groups, too much pressure is placed on each group member to perform or contribute. There is virtually no opportunity in a group of 5 or fewer to choose not to participate.

Another component of a group that affects its dynamics is membership, in regard to both the mixture and the number of people in it. **Heterogeneous groups** (those composed of people with dissimilar backgrounds) can broaden members' horizons and enliven interpersonal interactions. Such groups may be helpful in problem solving, such as in psychotherapy and counseling groups. Yet, **homogeneous groups** (those centered on a presenting problem or similarity in gender, ethnicity, sexual orientation, or sociocultural background) are extremely beneficial in working through specific issues. They normalize "one's experience and the sense of shared struggle in a common area" (Perrone & Sedlacek, 2000, p. 244). Task/work groups, as well as some counseling and therapy groups, are often homogeneous for this reason. A potential drawback to homogeneous groups, however, is "when group members gain the belief that only others who are similar (adult children of alcoholics, abuse survivors) can fully understand or help" them (MacNair-Semands, 1998, p. 209). That aside, it is the nature and purpose of the group that usually determines what its member composition will be.

Other factors affecting group dynamics that must be preplanned are the fit between members' goals and group goals (expected or planned outcomes), the level of membership commitment (whether members are joining the group voluntarily or because of external pressures), the openness of members to self and others, a commitment to take or support risks, members' attitudes toward leadership and authority, and the leader's attitude toward certain member characteristics. The point is that group dynamics are a result of interaction patterns that develop because of careful or careless preplanning (see Table 2.1).

Group Structure

Group structure refers both to the physical setup of a group and to the interaction of each group member in relation to the group as a whole. Both types of structure influence how successful or harmonious the group will be and whether individual or group objectives will be met. Leaders and members have the ability to structure a group for better or worse. In this section, the physical structure of a group is examined; the essence of group interaction will follow in a later section.

The **physical structure** (the arrangement of group members) is one of the first factors to consider in setting up a group. Physical structure has a strong influence on how a group operates.

Table 2.1	Factors involved in preplanning a group.
Clarity of purpose	What the group is to accomplish
Setting	The environment
Time	The length of the group meeting
Size	How many people will be involved
Membership	Heterogeneous or homogeneous
Goals	Expected or planned outcomes
Commitment	Voluntary or mandated attendance
Openness	Consideration of novel ideas and actions
Risk taking	Engaging in new thoughts and behaviors
Attitudes	How members and leaders perceive tasks and others

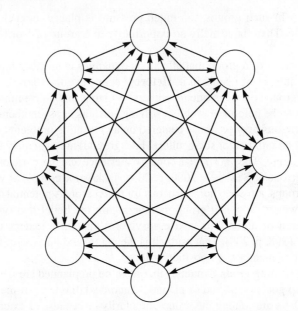

FIGURE 2.4   Optimal group structure/interaction.   *Source:* Adapted from "Some Effects of Certain Communication Problems on Group Performance" by H. J. Leavitt, 1951, *Journal of Abnormal and Social Psychology, 46,* pp. 38–50.

If members feel they are physically removed from the group or are the center of it, then they will act accordingly.

The seating arrangement in a group is, therefore, important. Many groups, regardless of purpose, use a **circle** format. In this configuration, all members have direct access to one another (Yalom & Leszcz, 2005). Equality in status and power is implied as in the famous Knights of the Round Table stories from the legends of King Arthur. The disadvantage of a circle arrangement is the lack of a perceived leader in the structure unless the identified leader is active and direct. Overall, the circle lends itself to being a democratic structure for conducting group work and is probably the best structure for ensuring equal airtime for all group members (see Figure 2.4).

However, the circle is not the only way to set up a group. Other formats yield different types of interactions. In an experiment to determine the effects of various structures on group performance, Leavitt (1951) devised three communication networks in addition to the circle (see Figure 2.5): the "chain," the "Y," and the "wheel."

In the **chain** arrangement, people are positioned or seated along a line, often according to their rank in the group. Communication is passed through others from a person at one end of the configuration to a person at the other end. The chain is a popular way to run some group organizations. For example, the military conceptualizes its command structure as "the chain of command." However, a chain is seldom used outside a hierarchical association because of the indirectness of communication, the lack of direct contact with others, and the frustration of relaying messages through others. In a group, for instance, Janet will probably become exasperated if she has to communicate her wishes and thoughts through Georgia, who in turn has to relay them to Penny, who then conveys them to the leader.

In contrast, the **wheel** arrangement has a "center spoke," the leader, through whom all messages go. Although members have the advantage of face-to-face interaction with the leader in this

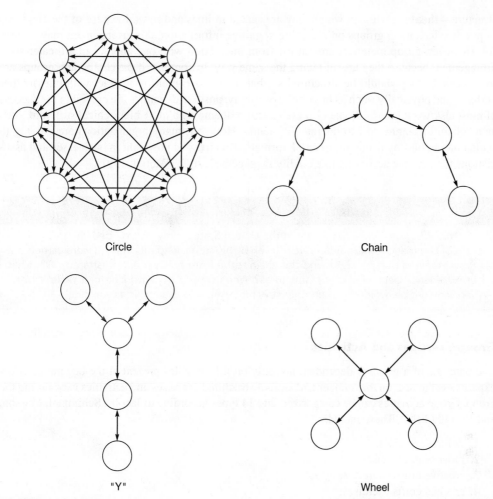

Circle

Chain

"Y"

Wheel

FIGURE 2.5   Effects of group structure on group performance.   *Source:* Adapted from "Some Effects of Certain Communication Problems on Group Performance" by H. J. Leavitt, 1951, *Journal of Abnormal and Social Psychology, 46,* pp. 38–50.

structure, they may become frustrated by the inability to communicate with another group member directly. In the wheel configuration, some members are not informed about what their colleagues are doing. For example, supervisors in a factory may work as the center spokes in a wheel formation and have different personnel report to them. If they do not give as well as receive information, then their workers will not know how the plant is operating or which issues need to be addressed.

The final type of group structure Leavitt (1951) experimented with was the **Y,** which combines the structural elements of the wheel and the chain. In this arrangement, there is a perceived leader. The efficiency of the unit is second only to that of the wheel in performance. Like a chain, however, the Y may frustrate group members who wish to have direct contact and communication with one another. Information is not equally shared or distributed.

In most cases, the importance of structure will vary according to the type of group being led. For instance, in a psychoeducational group, members may be arranged in yet another structure—**theater style**—in which they are seated in lines and rows. Because of the emphasis in psychoeducational groups on obtaining cognitive information, this arrangement may be useful. However, group members are cut off from interaction with one another in a theater-style arrangement because they are all facing the same way. In contrast, if psychotherapy groups are to work well, they should be structured so that members can easily interact with one another verbally and physically, such as in a circle. Similarly, positive dynamics are crucial to the success of most task/work groups. Some of these groups will employ a more hierarchical structure, such as a "chain of command," to operate efficiently. However, many organizations are moving to flatten hierarchies by using group circle formats. This trend is prevalent in businesses and associations that operate according to a quality management style (Walton, 1991).

Reflection

In my mid-20s, I was a first lieutenant in the United States Army. There I became used to the "chain of command" where orders were given by higher-ranking officers and were carried out by lower-ranking personnel. I found the chain to be both efficient and frustrating. What has your experience been with group structures? When do you think working in a circle is best? When should it be avoided and another structure used? Be as specific as you can.

Group Exercises and Activities

The outcome of a group is dependent not only on the variables present at the beginning of the experience, but also on the number and kind of structured exercises and activities used during the group. Group activities can be categorized into 14 types according to Jacobs, Schimmel, Masson, and Harvill (2016). These include:

1. written exercises,
2. movement exercises,
3. creative props exercises,
4. arts and crafts exercises,
5. fantasy exercises,
6. common reading exercises,
7. feedback exercises,
8. trust exercises,
9. experiential exercises,
10. moral dilemma exercises,
11. group-decision exercises,
12. touching exercises,
13. rounds, and
14. dyads and triads.

The question of whether prepackaged activities have a place in groups is one that group leaders and members must deal with constantly. There are certain advantages and disadvantages to employing exercises in a group setting (Carroll, Bates, & Johnson, 2004; Jacobs, 1992). For example, if the leader knows that a particular game or exercise is likely to result in a positive outcome, then it may be used as a catalyst, especially early in the group's life, to bring people together. In such a capacity, games and exercises can play a vital part in promoting group dynamics. However, group leaders should always ask themselves why they are doing a particular activity at a specific time and what they hope to achieve as a result.

An example of a purposeful activity a leader might use to begin a group is the exercise "Adverbs" (Gladding, 2011b). In this activity, group members pass around a pencil to one another in a circle saying and demonstrating any word that ends in "-ly" in the process. Thus, Juanita might say to Charlene who is seated on her right, "I am passing this pencil to you quickly" and in the process give the pencil to her quite fast. Charlene, in turn, would then turn to the person on her right and use another "adverb" and motion such as "slowly," "clumsily," or "hesitantly." The process is repeated until the pencil has gone around the group several times. At that point, the leader and members talk about ways of doing things and behaving in the group that the exercise demonstrated.

Overall, **group exercises** can be beneficial if they promote a positive atmosphere in a group. Jacobs et al. (2016) state that exercises have the following benefits:

1. They may generate discussion and participation, thus stimulating members' energy levels and interaction.
2. Exercises may help the group focus on a particular topic or issue. This is especially true in task groups.
3. Group games help shift the focus from one area to another. Although effective group leaders should be able to redirect the focus without employing games, some exercises provide a natural bridge to important group topics.
4. Games and exercises promote experiential learning, which means that members will probably go beyond their thoughts in self-exploration. Furthermore, exercises such as rounds provide the group leader with useful information about the group and what needs to be done to move forward.
5. They increase the comfort level of participants and help them to relax and have fun. Learning is best when it is enjoyable.

Group exercises and activities "are commonly used in groups to activate the group, encourage members to take risks, and provide a learning experience that moves the group members" (Riva, 2004, p. 63). Basically, these ways of working with a group are "either intrapersonal or interpersonal, and the type of communication is either verbal or nonverbal" (Trotzer, 2004, p. 77). "Interpersonal activities involve interacting with other group members in dialogue—for example, introducing oneself to the group and answering questions. If the activity is nonverbal, words are not used, such as the exercise 'changing seats'" (asking select members or an entire group to change seats). "Intrapersonal activities are those in which an exercise is done alone at first" (such as drawing a line that represents a present feeling) "and then shared and explored with others at a later time. . . . Nonverbal activities include private, personal experiences" (Carroll et al., 2004, pp. 116–117). Overall, when combined, four possible categories emerge that are of low, medium, or high intensity in the four following types:

1. *Verbal intrapersonal*—A low-intensity verbal intrapersonal exercise would be having group members draw pictures of how they perceive the world and using these pictures to introduce themselves verbally to the group.
2. *Verbal interpersonal*—An example of a low-intensity verbal interpersonal activity would be having group members divide into small groups and discuss their sibling positions. Then the group as a whole would reassemble and members would talk about how they view the world based on past perceptions.

3. *Nonverbal intrapersonal*—A low-intensity nonverbal intrapersonal exercise would be what is known as "body relaxation," where the leader would talk members through relaxing parts of their body starting with the feet and ending with the head. Members' eyes would be closed the whole time.

4. *Nonverbal interpersonal*—In a nonverbal interpersonal activity, members might line up from most to least about any concern that is relevant for the group at the moment such as anxiety. Members would then get a chance to compare where they stand in regard to others in the group.

In summary, exercises and activities take multiple forms and can be used almost anytime in the group process, as long as they do not become gimmicks and are processed afterward so that members:

gain insight into themselves personally,

become more aware of themselves as members of the group, and

understand group dynamics more fully.

Processing usually lasts twice as long as activities themselves. The important point to remember in using exercises and techniques in groups is that timing and instructions are crucial. A poorly timed event with unclear instructions may damage the group instead of promoting cohesion, insight, and movement. If employed too frequently, group activities can negatively influence the group by taking the focus off its purpose. There are also some ethically questionable exercises that promote anxiety and do harm; thus, group leaders who use them should do so cautiously.

Group Interaction

Group interaction can be described as the way members relate to one another. It consists of nonverbal and verbal behaviors and the attitudes that go with them. Group interaction exists on a continuum, from extremely nondirective to highly directive. For example, in some psychotherapy groups, members may be quite reserved and nondirect in their interactions with others, at least initially. In many task groups, however, members may be direct and verbal. The type of group interaction (e.g., nonverbal, verbal communication) as well as its frequency makes a difference in how or whether the group develops. Each factor is examined separately here, even though none of these components operates in isolation from the others.

Nonverbal behaviors make up "more than 50 percent of the messages communicated in social relationships" and are usually perceived as more honest and less subject to manipulation than verbal behaviors (Vander Kolk, 1985, p. 171). The four main categories of nonverbal behavior, according to Vander Kolk, are *body behaviors, interaction with the environment, speech,* and *physical appearance*. Group leaders and members have many nonverbals to watch. For example, when Sue wraps her arms around herself, does it mean that (a) she is physically cold, (b) she is imitating Heather, or (c) she is psychologically withdrawing from the group? The meaning of nonverbal behaviors cannot be assumed. In addition, the same nonverbal behavior from two different people may not convey the same message. Walters (1989) has charted behaviors frequently associated with various group members' emotions. Nonverbal behavioral expressions should always be noted (see Table 2.2).

Verbal behavior is also crucial in group dynamics. One of the most important variables in group work to track is who speaks to whom and how often each member speaks. On a formal basis, there are ways to chart such interactions, such as **sociometry**, a phenomenological

	Table 2.2	Behaviors frequently associated with various group member states.					
	Head	Face	Mouth	Eye Contact	Hands	Posture
Despair/ Depression	Down	Sad frown (eyebrows down at outer ends)	Tightness	Little or none; may cover eyes with hand	Autistic behaviors; body-focused self-stimulating movements	Approaches fetal position
Excitement/ Euphoria	Mobile movement	Mobility of expression	Smiling; laughing	Tries to capture and to hold eye contact of all other persons ("Look at me.")	Sweeping, expansive movements	Frequent change; seductive
Fear/Anxiety	Stiff movement; chin down	Flushing	Tightness; clenching teeth	Darting glances to others; wants to keep watch on others by not meeting their gazes ("I'll watch you.")	Tightness; gripping; sweaty palms ("clenched and drenched")	Frequent movement; crouching; hunching shoulders
Hostility/ Rejection of another person Active/Overt	Head, and often chin, thrust forward and/or tilted upward	Angry frown (eyebrows down at center)	Lips tensed and pushed forward slightly	Defiant	Clenching; fist; thumping (symbolic hitting)	Poised on edge of chair
Passive/Covert	Down; turned away slightly	Squinting of eyes	Closed; normal	Aversion; blank staring	Body-focused movements; self-inflicting behaviors	Infrequent change
Dependency/ Attraction toward another	Head slightly down while making eye contact ("Poor me.")	Mirrors expression of other	Frequent smiling	Frequent	Reaching motions	Quasi-courtship
Resistance to Learning	Turned; rolled back	Rigidity of expression	Tightness	Avoidance	Clenched; looking at watch; body-focused movements	Held in; stiffness of limbs

Source: Gazda, George M.; Walters, Richard P.; *Group Counselling: A Developmental Approach*, 4th ed. © 1989. Reprinted and Electronically produced by permission of Pearson Education, Inc., Upper Saddle River, New Jersey.

FIGURE 2.6 Sociogram depicting choices and rejections of classmates.

methodology for investigating interpersonal relationships (Treadwell, Kumar, Stein, & Prosnick, 1997). For example, by using a **sociogram** (a tool of sociometry that plots out group interactions), a group leader might learn that Melissa addresses most of her comments in the group to one of three people. Such data might be helpful to the leader and the group in examining or modifying their interactions (see Figure 2.6).

However, most leaders operate informally and map in their minds awareness of how group members speak and to whom. They also pay attention to silence and how it is observed and respected. It is difficult for some groups to deal with silence but less likely to be bothersome in certain psychoeducational and task groups in which members are not especially attuned to it.

Group discussion is usually important to the functioning of a group. In task, psychoeducational, counseling, and psychotherapy groups, discussion allows members to process information relevant to making decisions (Forsyth, 2013). Alternative courses of action can be considered more thoughtfully when the group as a whole discusses them. The amount of time spent in an active discussion of issues influences the quality of the group's decision (Laughlin, 1988).

Sometimes groups will use their time unwisely and collectively engage in what is known as the **Law of Triviality** (Parkinson, 1957). According to this law, the time a group spends discussing any issue is in inverse proportion to its consequences. For example, in an hour-long task group, 50 minutes might be spent talking about whether a group celebration should be held on a Thursday or a Friday and 10 minutes might be spent in planning the activities and considering a budget for the event.

Case Example

Debra the Diligent

Debra decided to form a work group for student leaders at her university. She wanted the group to go well and was determined to give group members all of the help she could. Therefore, when the group met, Debra had an outside observer make notes on how often people spoke, who spoke, what was discussed and for how long, and what decisions were made. At the end of the semester, Debra had the outside observer give this information to the group as a whole in the way of feedback. The response was mixed. Most of the group members who had been most active liked it. However, when Debra tried to reform the group at the beginning of the next semester, she found several members were not interested in being a part of it.

Questions

What do you think of Debra's method for helping the group? What could she have done better? What might you have done from the start if you had been Debra?

Members' Roles

A **role** is "a dynamic structure within an individual (based on needs, cognitions, and values), which usually comes to life under the influence of social stimuli or defined positions" (Munich & Astrachan, 1983, p. 20). The manifestation of a role is based on the individual's expectation of self and others and the interaction one has in particular groups and situations. For example, Mabel, a reflective and introverted person, might take the role of a "group observer" in an active counseling group. By so doing, she could give feedback to the group as a whole without exposing personal feelings. Every person has multiple roles he or she can fulfill. When groups change or when people change groups, roles are frequently altered.

Roles are usually different from the overall identity of individuals. For example, people may play certain roles in their vocational lives, such as being a sales clerk or a computer operator, but not envision themselves exclusively as their occupations. Therefore, although Terri sells shoes, she does not consider herself as a shoe salesperson. Nevertheless, roles strongly influence how individuals act in a group (Shepherd, 1964). For instance, entrepreneurs may want to push their point of view regardless of how it affects their acceptance into the group. Sometimes roles become so strong that people have a difficult time separating themselves from the roles they play. Such a situation may be enacted if people mainly see themselves in terms of a role they played in childhood. For example, adult children of alcoholics (ACoAs) often play one of four roles to adapt to their environments: hero, scapegoat, lost child, or mascot (Harris & MacQuiddy, 1991; Wegscheider, 1981). In such circumstances, the individuals may become trapped in dysfunctional ways of relating that will detrimentally affect them in all but psychotherapeutic groups.

When group leaders become aware of roles and behaviors that are detrimental to the group as a whole, they have an obligation to act. Their behavior can take a number of forms, such as having a one-on-one conversation with the person about their behavior, asking the person to assess his or her behavior in the group and note how it affects the group, or, in extreme cases, removing the person from the group (Goodrich & Luke, 2012). These basic forms of addressing a problematic group member hold true regardless of the type of group being run.

TYPES OF ROLES

One way to conceptualize most roles in groups is to view them as primarily functioning in one of three ways: facilitative/building, maintenance, and blocking (Capuzzi, 2010).

A **facilitative/building role** is one that adds to the functioning of a group in a positive and constructive way. Members who take on such a role may serve as initiators of actions and ideas, information seekers, opinion seekers, coordinators, orienters, evaluators, or recorders. Group facilitating and building focuses on helping everyone feel like a part of the group. Members who function in this way help the group develop while keeping conflict to a minimum. Group facilitators and builders do their best work during the initial formation of a group. For instance, in a task group, Dot may take the role of being an opinion seeker. Before the group moves on its decisions, she makes sure all views are heard by asking more quiet members for their input.

A **maintenance role** is one that contributes to the social-emotional bonding of members and the group's overall well-being. When interpersonal communication in the group is strained, there is a need to focus on relationships (Wilson & Hanna, 1986). People who take on such roles are social and emotionally oriented. They express themselves by being encouragers, harmonizers, compromisers, commentators, and followers. For example, in a counseling group, Ned may help by serving in the role of a harmonizer as he assists members in seeing the differences they have and pointing out how these differences can give each group member a new perspective on the world. In group maintenance, group members are encouraged to openly express "both positive and negative feelings, supportive responses to member concerns and contributions, and acceptance of differences" (Shaffer & Galinsky, 1989, p. 25).

A **blocking role** is essentially an antigroup role. Individuals who take this role act as aggressors, blockers, dominators, recognition seekers, and self-righteous moralists. For instance, those who perceive themselves as outsiders—such as Lucy, who has been placed in a psychoeducational group for punishment—may actively attempt to keep the group from discussing a proposed topic. Such a member may also seek to divert attention away from the group's goal by being negative and preventing the group from accomplishing anything.

Fortunately, few members act out a pure role.

PROBLEMS IN CARRYING OUT ROLES

Sometimes problems arise in the fulfillment of roles (Hare, Blumberg, Davies, & Kent, 1994). Both internal and external factors contribute to these problems, and there is seldom a simple cause. Four major forms of role difficulties are role collision, role incompatibility, role confusion, and role transition. In **role collision**, a conflict exists between the role an individual plays in the outside world (e.g., being a passive observer) and the role expected within the group (e.g., being an active participant). In **role incompatibility**, a person is given a role within the group (e.g., being the leader) that he or she neither wants nor is comfortable exercising. **Role confusion**, sometimes known as *role ambiguity*, occurs when a group member simply does not know what role to perform. This may happen at the beginning of groups or in leaderless groups where members do not know whether they are to be assertive in helping establish an agenda or passive and just let the leadership emerge. Finally, in **role transition**, a person is expected to assume a different role as the group progresses but does not feel comfortable doing so. For example, in self-help groups, experienced members are expected to take on leadership, rather than "follower," roles. Yet, some group members do not feel comfortable doing so.

In most groups, maintenance and task roles need to be balanced. "Too much attention to socioemotional functioning can cause the group to wander and lose sight of its goals; in similar fashion, overemphasis on task can result in disruption and dissatisfaction if members have no outlet for their grievances and no way to resolve their conflicts" (Shaffer & Galinsky, 1989, pp. 25–26).

> ## Reflection
>
> When have you ever been placed in a role where you felt uncomfortable? What did you do? Looking back at the time and circumstance, what else could you have done or wished you had done?

THE EFFECT OF POSITIVE AND NEGATIVE VARIABLES ON GROUP DYNAMICS

Many group specialists (e.g., Corey, 2012; Jacobs et al., 2016) have listed a number of variables within groups essential to group life and functioning. Psychotherapeutic and counseling groups seem to have been especially targeted by experts in this regard. Yet, the factors generally noted are applicable to most psychoeducational and task/work groups. These variables include member commitment; readiness of members for the group experience; the attractiveness of the group for its members; a feeling of belonging, acceptance, and security; and clear communication. These factors are collectively conceptualized as **positive group variables**. For example, if group members speak from an "I" position, everyone in the group becomes clear about what they are saying and can respond appropriately. Positive forces within the group, when expressed to the fullest extent possible, can lead to a group that is both cooperative and altruistic (McClure, 1990).

Yalom (Yalom & Leszcz, 2005) was among the first to delineate positive primary group variables based on research he conducted with others on therapy groups. He has called these positive forces **curative (therapeutic) factors within groups**. These variables are expressed in successful groups through a variety of means. They often affect the interactions of members and the group as a whole in complex ways. For counseling and psychotherapy groups, these therapeutic factors are as follows:

- *Instillation of hope*—Assurance that treatment will work. For example, the leader might say at the beginning of a group: "I think we will be able to accomplish most of your goals through our work in this group."
- *Universality*—What seems unique is often a similar or identical experience of another group member. For example, the leader might say: "Isaiah, it seems that you and Austin share a similar concern about how you can find balance in your lives."
- *Imparting of information*—Instruction about mental health, mental illness, and how to deal with life problems through group discussion. For example, a member might share that she has read that to stay mentally healthy, a person needs 8 hours of sleep at night.
- *Altruism*—Sharing experiences and thoughts with others, helping them by giving of one's self, working for the common good. For example, Jessica might inform the group that she is going to work a night at the homeless shelter and invite them to work there, too.

- *Corrective recapitulation of the primary family group*—Reliving early familial conflicts correctly and resolving them. For example, Louise may find that through her interactions with Roscoe she is able to find ways of disagreeing with a male who is slightly older, like her brother Taylor, without becoming emotionally upset.
- *Development of socializing techniques*—Learning basic social skills. For example, Aiden may come to realize through the group experience that people like to be invited to do activities rather than carped at to do them.
- *Imitative behavior*—Modeling positive actions of other group members. For example, Jayden may learn ways of requesting what he wants by imitating the behavior of Colin.
- *Interpersonal learning*—Gaining insight and correctively working through past experiences. For example, Virginia may see through talking with members of the group that her bossy behavior in the past has gotten her nowhere.
- *Cohesiveness*—The proper therapeutic relationship among group members, group members and the group leader, and the group as a whole. For example, after everyone in the group shares their thoughts about racism, they may feel closer together.
- *Catharsis*—Experiencing and expressing feelings. For example, Julia may cry softly when she realizes how much hurt she has been carrying around for so long.
- *Existential factors*—Accepting responsibility for one's life in basic isolation from others, recognizing one's own mortality and the capriciousness of existence. For example, Sebastian may come to the realization through talking with older members of the group that his life is half over and that he needs to work hard on improving himself if he is ever going to live his dreams.

Yalom (Yalom & Leszcz, 2005) contends that these variables constitute both the actual mechanisms of change and conditions for change. The interplay of the factors varies widely from group to group. However, these factors help members gain insight into themselves and their relationships with others. "For instance, altruism, catharsis, and group cohesiveness enable . . . members to feel supported, emotionally connected, and as though they belong" (Marmarosh, Dunton, & Amendola, 2014, p. 8).

To this list, Bemak and Epp (1996) have added what they consider to be a 12th factor—love. They believe that although love may contain aspects of some of Yalom's other factors, it stands alone as a contributor to the healing process in group psychotherapy. "Love's nature and dynamics in groups . . . can have many variations"—for instance, transference as well as genuineness (p. 119). According to Bemak and Epp, "the unmasking of transference and the fostering of open expressions of giving and receiving love are essential healing factors in the group therapy process and in the development of healthier human beings" (p. 125).

Yalom's (Yalom & Leszcz, 2005) conceptualization of group dynamics, with the addition of Bemak and Epps's (1996) contribution, is extremely useful for conducting group counseling and psychotherapeutic sessions. It gives group leaders and members ideas and experience-based realities on which they need to focus. Such variables are like a map that can guide the group process. For instance, if a group member, Sarah, refuses to work through past family impasses and treats another group member, Charles, as if he were a rejecting parent, then the leader and other members can take steps to correct this behavior. In this case, the group might confront Sarah with how she is acting and role-play situations to help her recognize and resolve previous dysfunctional patterns that are interfering with her present functioning.

In addition to positive variables and therapeutic forces, **negative group variables** operate. These variables include, but are not limited to, avoiding conflict, abdicating group responsibilities, anesthetizing to contradictions within the group, and becoming narcissistic. If most or all of these variables are present, then a group will become regressive and possibly destructive (McClure, 1990, 1994). In such cases, the whole group and the individuals within it lose.

Avoiding conflict involves the silencing of members who expose the group's shortcomings or disagree with the majority's opinions. Silencing is often done through coercion or acts of domination. For example, whenever Dee tries to tell the group she does not feel understood by the other members, she is belittled through comments such as "That's touchy/feely stuff, Dee, get real" or "You are being oversensitive." As time passes, Dee learns not to speak. A destructive dynamic is set in motion by avoiding conflict and silencing dissent. If it remains unchallenged and unchanged, then the group becomes unhealthy.

One of the most destructive behaviors for groups to take is to become narcissistic. "**Narcissistic groups** develop cohesiveness by encouraging hatred of an out-group or by creating an enemy . . . . As a result, regressive group members are able to overlook their own deficiencies by focusing on the deficiencies of the out-group" (McClure, 1994, p. 81). The leaders of North Korea are sometimes cited as a national group that is narcissistic, as in their reaction to the motion picture *The Interview*. In the process of projecting their feelings onto others, group members create an illusion of harmony that binds them together. In a more mundane example, a student newspaper is launched with the intent of attacking the president of a university. Within the group, members focus on "digging up dirt" and disregard any positives they find. A bunker mentality develops in which the president becomes the enemy and the student newspaper, the source of all truth. Member disagreement is handled by dismissing anyone from the paper who does not agree with the party line. Cohesiveness is developed through rewarding member writers who can find the most damaging material to print.

Occurring in regressive groups, along with the avoidance of conflict and the development of group narcissism, is **psychic numbing**, in which members anesthetize themselves to contradictions in the group. In the student newspaper example, writers may break into an office to get information they want and not feel guilty about breaking an ethical or legal code. Overall, a regressive group expresses an abdication of responsibility for the group and a dependency on its leader. Members do not take on the role of being leaders or facilitators of the group but rather become obedient followers. They do not take risks and, in effect, give their power away to influence the group. In such cases, the group is left without means to correct itself and will continue to be destructive unless a crisis occurs that influences its members to behave differently (Peck, 1983).

Case Example

Philip Puts the Positives Before the Group

Philip has had mixed results with the groups he has run. After reading about Yalom's positive factors, Philip decided he would make a copy for all group members of a task group he was running. He asked each member to study the factors carefully. He also told the group about negative factors that could affect the group. To his delight, Philip's group ran well. He thought it must be because of the materials he distributed and the way he asked members to pay attention to them. However, the next time Philip tried the same procedure, the group did not run as well.

Questions

Why do you think Philip's method worked the first time but failed on his second try? How important is it for group members to have the kind of information Philip provided?

LEARNING GROUP DYNAMICS

Knowledge of group dynamics that is both experiential and cognitive can help a group worker either lead or be in a group. Such learning may take place in multiple ways. One model is based on interdisciplinary education and involves five activities that help participants gain greater insight into the ways their group is functioning (Marrotta, Peters, & Paliokas, 2000).

1. *Videotaping*—Through observing their personal and collective interactions in a group, participants may note verbal and nonverbal behaviors of members and how these actions affected the group and its development. They may also note group roles, if any, that stand out.
2. *Journaling*—A journal is a weekly log of the content and process that occurred in a group and one's reactions to particular activities, exchanges, or the group as a whole. By writing immediately after a group is completed, participants capture present thoughts and feelings related to what happened in the group. By reading their logs later, they may gain insight into patterns occurring within the group.
3. *Outdoor experiences*—Participating in an outdoor exercise can help individuals explore their cooperative and competitive styles and how these mesh with the group as a whole. The group can be seen more fully as a dynamic entity in events such as rope courses, where if the group is to be successful, everyone must participate and negotiate in regard to overcoming an obstacle or completing a task.
4. *Simulation games for team building*—"Problem-based learning situations in the classroom are isomorphic to issues that professionals will encounter in the workplace" (Marrotta et al., 2000, p. 21). A task such as having a group, along with the teacher, design a logo for a class can bring out or highlight behaviors that either help or hurt the group in reaching a goal. By having the group analyze what happened in the process, members can see more clearly the dynamics involved in what happened and how they contributed.
5. *Sociometrics and learning integration*—A final way to help facilitate the learning of group dynamics is to employ sociometric techniques. These activities can provide perspective on each member's learning style and on various aspects of group dynamics, such as leadership, boundaries, and subgroups. All of these can be depicted through visual models. For example, individual students might be given Tinkertoys to create a visual model of their understanding of the development of cohesion. The crucial component in this activity, as with the others, is debriefing, discussion, reflection, and the fostering of insight.

GROUP, INDIVIDUAL, AND FAMILY DYNAMICS

Working with groups is both similar to and different from working with individuals or families. Individual, group, and family approaches to helping have some parallels in history, theory, technique, and process. However, because of the unique composition of each, the dynamics of these ways of working are distinct (Gladding, 2015). The numbers of variables and interactions differ, as does the focus. A skilled group worker who has knowledge of individual and family helping dynamics is able to compare and contrast what is occurring in the group with what might be happening in another setting and, more importantly, to assess what may be needed. **Awareness** of individual and family helping dynamics assists a group worker in realizing whether referral of a member is in order. The complexity of working with others is a process that involves knowing what to do, when to do it, and what the probable outcomes may be. In this section, the dynamics of individual, group, and family work are discussed in regard to persons, processing, and consequences.

Persons

In examining the entities of groups, individuals, and families, one immediate common denominator is apparent. All are bodies, singularly or collectively, with defined boundaries and interrelated parts. An intervention cannot be made at any level without affecting other aspects of the body. For example, even on the individual counseling level, a counselor cannot work from a strictly behavioral perspective without influencing the cognitive and affective aspects of the client. However, in working with individuals, only one person is the focus of attention. The influence of others may be discussed, but they are not a part of any direct form of helping. In addition, single individuals may or may not be behaviorally or emotionally connected with others. Therefore, attention is almost always centered on intrapersonal issues.

With groups and families, the focus is on more than one person. It is often simultaneously intrapersonal and interpersonal. Trotzer (1988) and Vinson (1995) point out that groups share many similarities with families. For instance, both have hierarchies (power structures), roles, rules, and norms. In addition, groups and families move through phases and stages during the counseling process, with group leaders being more active in the initial sessions of any therapeutic interventions. In groups and families, a tension also is manifest overtly and covertly that must be resolved or managed if members are going to work well together. A final similarity between groups and families is that all members in their units affect both. Thus, if a member of a group or family is dysfunctional, then the entire group or family will work in a dysfunctional way.

Groups are distinct from families in that the members come together initially as strangers for a common purpose (Becvar, 1982; Hines, 1988). They have no experience of working together. Families, in contrast, have members with a shared history of interactions. This history may hinder or facilitate any actions taken in trying to offer assistance, but interventions made in family work usually occur faster and with more impact because of the family's common background. Another difference in working with groups and families is the purpose for the treatment. In groups, intrapersonal change may be just as important as interpersonal change, whereas in families the focus is usually on changing the family system. Although groups may resemble families at times in how they work, groups dissolve after a set time, whereas families continue. Overall, as Becvar (1982) states, the group is not a family, and the family is not a group.

Processing

In group work, **processing** refers to an activity that helps group members and the group identify, examine, and reflect on their behaviors and what occurred in a group in order to increase understanding, extract meaning, integrate knowledge, and improve their functioning and outcomes. Processing activities and events in the group helps group members better understand their experiences in the group and relate these to their personal lives (Ward, 2014).

Processing with individuals, groups, and families is similar in several ways. One important similarity involves an examination of what is involved. In essence, all effective processing can be thought of as following the **PARS model (Processing: Activity, Relationship, Self)**, even though this model was originated for group work (Glass & Benshoff, 1999). Processing following this model includes three stages: reflecting, understanding, and applying (see Figure 2.7).

In *reflecting,* individuals retrace the steps of a particular activity and essentially ask, "What did we do?" An individual may reflect with a counselor, group members may reflect with one

| Reflecting |
| Understanding |
| Applying |

FIGURE 2.7 The PARS Model.

another and the leader, and family members may reflect with one another and the therapist. "Reflection allows participants the opportunity to recreate the experience by describing actions the group [or the individual] went through to complete the exercise" (Glass & Benshoff, 1999, p. 18).

In the *understanding* stage, the focus is on participants discussing specific interactions as well as offering explanations and interpretations of what occurred, especially in relationship to others. On the group and family level, this stage is more complete because of the others immediately involved. Finally, in the third stage of PARS, the emphasis is on *applying* what has been learned through experience and interaction in the session to one's own life. Without this last stage, which involves a transfer of insight and learning, processing is not complete.

In addition to the PARS processing model, some common counseling and psychotherapy theories are used as guides in individual, group, and family work (Horne, 2001; Patterson, 1986). For instance, Bowen and Adlerian theory may be employed in helping adolescents differentiate themselves from their families in a counseling group format and thereby become less anxious personally and within their family context (Nims, 1998). Likewise, person-centered and behavioral theories have been translated to working with people in individual, group, and family environments. However, an individual theory of helping may not be appropriate for use in some group and family situations, just as some approaches created by group workers and family therapists are not geared for individually oriented helpers.

Consequences

In addition to both subtle and obvious differences in processing and employing theories, a major difference in working with individuals, groups, and families is what happens after helping ends. Success and failure have different consequences. If the individual or the group work does not go well, then those involved may be disappointed. However, with few exceptions, they leave the experience and those involved with it behind them. Families, however, live together through any attempts at helping, and change may promote tension both during and after the process.

Overall, individual, group, and family approaches overlap and yet are distinct from one another. The participants, how they are involved, and how they relate to the professional clinician and the others outside of treatment sessions must be taken into consideration in any comparison. Likewise, a crucial aspect of the process of working with these populations in different phases and stages of their development is which theories of helping are used and how. The leader's role in each differs in regard to what is highlighted in inducing change.

Reflection

How do you think your family-of-origin background has influenced you in your interpersonal relationships with others? What strengths and liabilities do you carry from your family of origin that could help or hurt you as you work with groups?

Summary and Conclusion

This chapter has focused on group dynamics. In most groups, it is crucial that group leaders and members be aware of these dynamics because such forces help influence group development. Several key areas of group dynamics have been discussed. For instance, the content and process in a group must be recognized for what they are and what they contribute. It is also crucial that content and process be balanced. Furthermore, in fostering change, it helps to perceive the group as a living system with interacting parts that affect one another.

In influencing the dynamics of groups, leaders must preplan and clarify the purpose of their groups. This type of action before the group begins can be instrumental in positively affecting the way the group functions. In addition to a clear purpose, leaders should plan for a quiet, conducive environment for their groups. Planning groups with regard to time, size, mixture of people, and goals is also crucial. Group structure in terms of member positioning and group interactions, especially verbal and nonverbal behaviors, must be taken into account. If groups are to prosper, they must spend their time wisely and be as inclusive of all their members as possible.

Members' roles must also be considered. In healthy groups, members may switch roles and be facilitative or supportive. Antigroup roles, such as being aggressive, must be dealt with to prevent groups from being regressive and destructive. At the same time, positive group variables, such as clear communication and acceptance, must be promoted. Ways of helping groups include the limited use of group exercises and employing basic helping skills. Learning activities that promote insight into how groups operate are helpful, as are teaching devices that highlight group dynamics. In working with groups, leaders are best able to understand and make appropriate interventions if they are aware of the differences and similarities in group dynamics compared with those of individuals and families in helping situations.

In summary, groups are a unique way to work with individuals in resolving past problems, accomplishing present tasks, and undertaking future goals. Those who wish to participate or specialize in them are wise to realize that groups are dynamic entities with lives of their own that differ from those of their members. Those who are knowledgeable about how groups operate know what to expect and can help facilitate positive action in themselves and others.

Classroom Exercises

1. In groups of three or four, discuss what you consider to be the most important positive group variables mentioned in this chapter. Are some variables more important for some types of groups than for others? Which ones does your group think would be most crucial in the following types of groups: (a) a group for troubled adolescents, (b) a social skills learning group for mentally challenged adults, (c) a grief group for those who have lost loved ones, and (d) a task/work group planning for a lecture series? Compare your discussion with those generated by other class members.

2. Pick a role mentioned in this chapter with which you feel comfortable. Why do you find this role attractive? Think about whether you have played this role in groups before. Also describe what role in the group you consider least desirable and why. Discuss your findings with another class member.

3. This chapter mentioned ways of influencing a group. Discuss in subgroups three ways you might pragmatically exert a positive presence in a group. Especially concentrate on the importance of factors that affect group dynamics, and identify whether these factors are primarily those related to content or process.

4. Observe or recall a group that you are or have been involved in, and note which factors mentioned in this chapter are or were prevalent in the life of the group. How do you think the group could be improved? What is your feeling after this observation about the influence of groups on people and people on groups?

CHAPTER 3

Photographee.eu/Fotolia

Effective Group Leadership

Before me is an opening in time
behind lies a lifetime of training,
Strategically located around a circle,
are those who depend on my skills
as they wait in anticipation.
Within me there is measured anxiety
outside I show a calm facade;
The group begins
with the soft sound of words,
quiet nervous laughter, and a few faint smiles,
all deft attempts to join with others
and create an environment of trust.*

From "In Anticipation" © 1989 by Samuel T. Gladding. Reprinted by permission from Samuel T. Gladding.

CHAPTER OVERVIEW

From reading this chapter, you will learn about

- Group leadership and how it affects the functioning of a group
- Skills needed to run an effective group
- Group leadership training and group supervision

AS YOU READ, CONSIDER

- What your preferred style of leadership is
- How the personal and professional skills needed to run a successful group match with the skills you already have
- How comfortable or uncomfortable you would feel co-leading a group

George Washington lost more battles than he won. Yet, he kept the American Revolution alive at the end of 1776 by crossing the Delaware River with his army and capturing the Hessian garrison at Trenton, New Jersey. Washington's victory has been idealized in paintings, films, and verse. However, because of bad weather, illnesses, scarce supplies, and unexpected delays, it was anything but glamorous. Yet, the victory was possible because of the general's careful planning, encouragement, and coordination of troops. Washington had his men work together with a specific goal, and his success probably energized all in the colonies who supported independence from England at the time.

Washington's example shows how leadership and groups are eminently connected. "Leadership is necessarily concerned with group activity" (Gardner, 1990, p. 80). Hundreds of research studies have been conducted to identify personal or professional attributes of leaders (Johnson & Johnson, 2013). Some characteristics associated with group leadership (e.g., caring, openness, strength, awareness, warmth, flexibility, sensitivity, creativity) have been pinpointed (M. Young, 2013). However, many unknown dimensions exist. In fact, leadership is probably "one of the most observed and least understood phenomena on earth" (Burns, 1978, p. 2). Nevertheless, the role of the leader is crucial to the overall functioning of groups (Rubel & Kline, 2008). "The leader plays a vital role in both the dynamics of the group and the outcome of its members" (Riva, Wachtel, & Lasky, 2004, p. 37). In addition, "a group is a mirror of its leader. A group draws definition from its leader. It will be only as good as the leader, as good as his or her skills, and as good as the leader's own being" (Bates, Johnson, & Blaker, 1982, p. 73).

Many issues surround group leaders and leadership. Some of them deal with substance, such as the mastery of skills; others, with style and personality. There are different types of leaders, just as there are distinct types of groups, and the appropriateness of an individual for a particular group depends on many complex and interrelated factors. The way a leader functions in one group may be totally inappropriate in another (Forsyth, 2013; Kottler & Englar-Carlson, 2014). For example, a **transformational leader** (a person who empowers group members and shares power with them in working toward the renewal of a group) may be needed when a group is floundering. However, a **traditional leader** (a person who is controlling and exercises power from the top down as an expert) may be appropriate in running a hierarchical group that is diverse and whose members are physically separated.

In this chapter, multiple aspects of leadership are examined—for example, styles, personalities, and core and specific skills. Which behaviors and competencies work best in particular circumstances is also considered, along with other group leadership functions, co-leadership, training, and supervision. However, first we turn our attention to defining *leadership*.

LEADERSHIP: A CONCEPT IN SEARCH OF A DEFINITION

The word *leader* first appeared in the English language in the early 1300s, and the word *leadership* in the early 1800s (Johnson & Johnson, 2013). Yet, despite the long history associated with defining leaders and leadership, much disagreement persists among social and political scientists about exactly what a leader is. There is no one definition of either word. Indeed, the concepts *leader* and *leadership* have been defined in more different ways than almost any other concept associated with group structure. For example, Bass (1995) states that

> leadership has been conceived as the focus of group processes, as a matter of personality, as a matter of inducing compliance, as the exercise of influence, as particular behaviors, as a form of persuasion, as a power relation, as an instrument to achieve goals, as an effect of interaction, as a differentiated role, as initiation of structure, and as many combinations of these definitions. (p. 38)

Clearly, disagreement prevails about what a leader and leadership are in both the theory and the practice of group work (Barker, 1997; Milsom, 2011; Stockton, Morran, & Velkoff, 1987).

Despite definition disagreements, some common factors in leadership can be distinguished. Forsyth (2013), for instance, defines leadership as "a special form of social interaction: a reciprocal, transactional, and transformational process in which individuals are permitted to influence and motivate others to promote the attaining of group and individual goals" (p. 343). This definition encompasses many of the most important factors of leadership (social, reciprocity, legitimate influence, motivation, and cooperation for the achievement of common goals) and distinguishes leadership from control (Parsons & Shils, 1951) and power (French & Raven, 1960). Forsyth's definition is the basis on which leadership is conceptualized in this chapter. It is assumed that a leader is one who implements a number of facilitative qualities in a group, such as envisioning goals, motivating people, and achieving a workable unity in an appropriate and timely way.

GROUP LEADERSHIP STYLES

Leaders help groups get organized and develop. Therefore, the style that a group leader displays has a direct effect on the behavior of group members and group dynamics (Sampson & Marthas, 1981). Leaders who operate exclusively from one point of view are more likely than others to influence members' behaviors in a specific way. For example, leaders who are always telling group members what to do may get immediate tasks accomplished but at the price of membership flexibility and innovation. Most effective group leaders show versatility (Kottler, 1994) and modify their leadership pattern to coincide with the purpose of the group and its membership.

Choosing a style of leadership depends on a multitude of factors, such as the leader's personality and the purpose of the group. Lewin (1944) identified three basic styles of group leadership: authoritarian, democratic, and laissez-faire. Lieberman, Yalom, and Miles (1973) describe six basic styles: energizers, providers, social engineers, impersonals, laissez-faires, and managers. Hansen, Warner, and Smith (1980) contend that most models are either refinements or elaborations of Lewin's concepts; therefore, the focus of this section is on Lewin's three styles, what the choice of each yields, and so-called leaderless groups.

Authoritarian group leaders envision themselves as experts and tend to be rigid and conventional in their beliefs (Cheng, Chae, & Gunn, 1998). They believe they understand group dynamics and, therefore, are best able to explain group and individual behavior. These leaders interpret, give advice, and generally direct the movement of the group much as parents control the actions of a child. They demand obedience and expect conformity from their followers. Authoritarian leaders are often charismatic and manipulative (McClure, 1994). Frequently, they structure their groups using the wheel model (explained in Chapter 2), which results in an autocratic **leader-centered group**. All information is filtered through them, and they decide which information to share with the group (see Figure 3.1). Such leaders may coerce group members under their charge because they basically believe people are not ambitious and are somewhat lazy. This style of leadership is sometimes referred to as *guru oriented* (Starak, 1988). McGregor (1960) characterizes this type of leader as a so-called **Theory X leader**. Adolf Hitler, Fidel Castro, and Mao Zedong exemplified this type of leadership, although some charismatic political and corporate leaders may display characteristics of this style in a more healthy way. Most leader-centered groups place a strong emphasis on the personality of one individual, giving that person a great deal of power and trust. In these groups, chaos erupts when the recognized leader is absent.

Authoritarian Leader

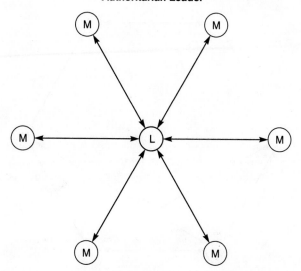

FIGURE 3.1 Authoritarian leadership. *Source:* From Hansen, James C., Richard Warner, and Elsie Smith. *Group Counseling*, 2e. © 1980 Wadsworth, a part of Cengage Learning, Inc. Reproduced by permission.

Some group workers prefer an authoritarian leadership style. They equate group leadership with instructing or controlling. Authoritarian leaders may achieve much during periods of crisis because of their commanding style and the needs of followers. Authoritarian leaders are powerful and usually safe from exposure of any personal vulnerability. They direct action and yet are protected by structure and function from self-disclosing.

Democratic group leaders are more group centered and less directive than authoritarian leaders. Those operating from this perspective, such as Carl Rogers (1970), trust group participants to develop their own potential and that of other group members. These leaders serve as facilitators of the group process and not as directors of it. They cooperate, collaborate, and share responsibilities with the group. Those who embrace this perspective are more humanistically and phenomenologically oriented (see Figure 3.2). McGregor (1960) refers to group-centered leaders as **Theory Y leaders**. They think that people are self-starters and will work hard if given freedom. Leaders who have exemplified this approach to a group facilitate conditions to "promote self-awareness and options to develop the guru within" (Starak, 1988, p. 104). Mohandas Gandhi and Martin Luther King, Jr., led using this style.

Leaders who are inwardly comfortable and trust group members to take care of themselves and others use this approach. The advantage is a sharing of power and responsibility. Group members can interact openly. Trust, once established, is fostered under this type of leadership, as is calculated risk taking.

Laissez-faire leaders are leaders in name only. They do not provide any structure or direction for their groups, so members are left with the responsibility of leading. As a result, the group operates from a **group-centered perspective**, focusing on members and interpersonal processes. The disadvantage of this type of leadership is that the group as a whole may be slow to establish agendas and achieve goals. Some inexperienced group leaders choose this style in an attempt to be nonthreatening; others pick this style to avoid making any hard decisions, thereby increasing

Democratic Leader

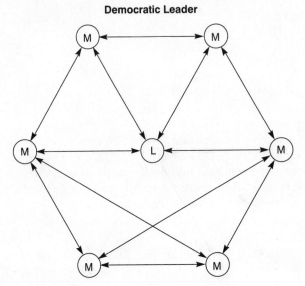

FIGURE 3.2 Democratic leader.   *Source:* From Hansen, James C., Richard Warner, and Elsie Smith. *Group Counseling*, 2e. © 1980 Wadsworth, a part of Cengage Learning, Inc. Reproduced by permission. www.cengage.com/permissions.

their popularity. (Being liked or popular is not a key characteristic of being an effective leader, by the way.) Still others believe that this group style works best and that the group must take care of itself from the beginning. Unfortunately, many laissez-faire group leaders and their groups do not accomplish anything because no clear purpose and goals emerge. Interactions within a laissez-faire group are represented in Figure 3.3.

Laissez-Faire Leader

FIGURE 3.3 Laissez-faire leader.   *Source:* From Hansen, James C., Richard Warner, and Elsie Smith. *Group Counseling*, 2e. © 1980 Wadsworth, a part of Cengage Learning, Inc. Reproduced by permission. www.cengage.com/permissions.

At the extreme of a group-centered approach is what Ouchi (1981) describes as Theory Z, which stresses that a group will manage itself through the participation of its members. A **Theory Z leader** is a facilitator who helps encourage group members to participate in the group and to trust that individual and collective goals will be accomplished through interaction.

Whether a group is leader or group centered depends on who set it up, under what circumstances, and for what purpose (Gardner, 1990).

So-called **leaderless groups** rotate the leadership role among their members, and there is no designated leader/facilitator (Brown, 2014). In these groups, leaders emerge as the group develops. One type of leaderless group is the self-help group (e.g., Alcoholics Anonymous, Parents Anonymous). Another form is the mutual support group, exemplified by some women's groups that form around such concrete and specific purposes as the accomplishment of goals, babysitting cooperatives, or a hobby or interest such as hiking or quilting (Kees, 1999). In many forms of these groups, peer leadership works well. In such cases, nonprofessional leaders develop as their group progresses. They usually end up creating a leadership style that feels comfortable for them, such as being confrontational or collaborative. Occasionally, they undergo brief leadership training by reading manuals or taking courses. Although some leaders of leaderless groups are effective, this approach is basically developed through trial and error. It has the potential to be destructive as well as constructive.

Case Example

Omar's Emergence

When Jared joined the Gamblers Anonymous group, two aspects of the group struck him. First, he was one of the younger members. Second, the group was led by a rather old, grizzly man by the name of Omar. Jared was not sure if he could relate to anyone in the group that well, but Omar immediately made him feel welcomed and a part of the group by relating part of his life story. It seems that Omar had come into this group several decades ago at about the same age as Jared. An older member, who was then the leader of the group, had helped him understand both the nature of his problem and himself. Omar had been grateful and had vowed that he would do the same if given the chance. Now he was the leader and he was fulfilling his pledge.

Questions

When have you received the guidance and attention of someone who was older and wiser than you? How do you think it helped you?

Another type of leaderless group meets alternately with and without a leader. Such groups may increase the creativity and participation of individuals and the group as a whole. However, notable group specialists (Gazda, 1989; Yalom & Leszcz, 2005) warn about the dangers of these groups, especially when they are composed of moderately or severely disturbed individuals. In such cases, if a leader is not present, the group may get out of hand and do considerable damage to its members. As a result, the group regresses, and everyone suffers (McClure, 1990).

LEADERSHIP STYLES FOR DIFFERENT GROUPS

"Expert leaders describe their effectiveness as perceiving, understanding, and formulating observed group experience into action" (Ward & Ward, 2014, p. 18). However, different types of groups demand specific styles of leadership. For example, in psychoeducational and task/work groups, leaders do best when they are direct and keep the group focused on the topic or job at hand. Psychotherapy and counseling groups, though, require that leaders provide support, caring, and sometimes confrontation and structure. They are more intrapersonal in nature. Regardless, the ASGW Professional Standards for the Training of Group Workers (2000) "specifies a minimum level of 1 hour a week of planning time for group leaders (either individually or with a co-leader). According to these standards, leading effective groups demands constant assessment of leader skills and interventions, group development, and individual progress of group members" (DeLucia-Waack & Fauth, 2004, p. 137).

Luke (2014) states that according to **Group Systems Theory** (Connors & Caple, 2005), group leaders have the option to focus on one of three levels of the group as a system: the intrapersonal, the interpersonal, or the group as a whole. The **intrapersonal style of group leadership** stresses the inward reactions of individual group members and the **interpersonal style of group leadership** focuses on transactions among individuals in the group, whereas the **group as a whole** hones in on the development, the dynamics, and experiences of the entire group. These distinct styles of leadership have their place in a group, and effective group leaders use all of them at times. For instance, as a group leader of a counseling group, Don may ask Phyllis to reflect on her last outburst directed toward Mary Ann. Later, Don may solicit opinions from the group as whole about how Phyllis could relate more positively with Mary Ann. Ideally, counseling group leaders begin by concentrating on the group as a whole and then move to interpersonal dimensions. Later, when members are more comfortable with one another, leaders integrate intrapersonal material into the group. Other types of group leaders, such as those who lead psychoeducational groups, may engage in the process in an entirely different way.

Leadership may also focus on the accomplishment of tasks versus the development of personal relationships as well. Whether a leader exercises task or relationship leadership depends on who he or she is, what is happening, and when (or whether) goals must be accomplished. For example, if the group leader is heading a work group whose members know one another well, then he or she may focus on the task to be accomplished because members already have a sense of "we-ness." If, however, a leader is conducting a psychotherapeutic group, then he or she is most likely to focus on the cohesiveness of personal relationships before attempting to work on individual or group goals. Hersey and Blanchard (1969) have elaborated on different styles of leadership dealing with people and tasks over a group's life cycle. In their model, leaders choose an emphasis depending on whether they are people or task oriented. In reality, most group leaders will consider both aspects of a group.

Regardless of emphasis, leaders need to be attuned to and use "core mechanisms of group process and change" (Polcin, 1991, p. 10). These **core mechanisms of group leadership** are emotional stimulation, caring, meaning attribution, and executive function. Lieberman et al. (1973) first described these universal central factors and distinguished them from a group leader's orientation (theoretical approach).

In all types of groups, leaders must promote sharing on an effective as well as an intellectual level (**emotional stimulation**). Feelings, as well as thoughts, need to be expressed. For example, instead of asking Stephanie what she thought about Wanda's remarks, the group leader could ask her how she felt about them. Furthermore, group leaders must show **caring** (a genuine concern for others), through their openness and honesty with group members. Thus, Logan needs to let Dominic know that he honestly wants to know what he is thinking and that he values their relationship whether they have the same ideas or not. **Meaning attribution** refers to the leader's ability to explain to group members in a cognitive way what is occurring in the group. For instance, the leader might say, "Members of the group seem reticent to talk today about themselves. It appears we are having a hard time trusting one another." To function optimally, group leaders need "to learn how to attribute meaning to the events and experiences occurring during the life of a group" both for others and for themselves (Conyne, 1998, p. 255). Finally, in the **executive function** role, leaders manage the group as a social system that allows the group and its members to achieve specific goals (Polcin, 1991). In this role, leaders remind the group periodically what it has done and what it is doing in regard to agreed-on goals formulated earlier. For instance, the leader may say: "We have formulated a plan. Our challenge now is to implement it."

Reflection

Which of the core mechanisms of group leadership do you see yourself best at implementing? What experience(s) in your life give you insight into that strength(s)?

PERSONAL QUALITIES OF EFFECTIVE GROUP LEADERS

Every group leader brings his or her personal qualities to a group, including preferred ways of perceiving the world and experiences in relating to oneself and others. Group leaders must ask themselves such questions as "Who am I?" "Who am I with you?" and "Who are we together?" (Hulse-Killacky, Schumacher, & Kraus, 1994).

The way the questions are asked, as well as the answers that are derived, plays a strong part in determining how one's personal qualities translate into leadership. For example, if a person does not have a strong sense of self, then it is doubtful he or she will be effective as a group leader. Similarly, if an individual cannot keep his or her identity while appreciating others, then it is unlikely that this leader will exert a strong influence in the group. Personal qualities of effective leaders have traditionally been explained through examining their personality traits or learned skills. Effective group leaders probably use the strongest aspects of their personalities and knowledge and combine these with experiences in their leading of groups (Johnson & Johnson, 2013).

The Trait Approach

A traditional school of thought in human history is that some persons emerge as leaders because of their personal qualities. This point of view was advocated by Aristotle, Thomas Carlyle, and Henry Ford (Forsyth, 2013) and remains popular today in some circles. Some group specialists have compiled long lists of ideal qualities they believe are essential to the personality of an effective group leader, a so-called **trait approach** to group leadership. Proponents of this viewpoint believe that specific personality characteristics are essential for successful leadership.

Two examples of this approach are those given by Slavson (1962) and Corey, Corey, and Corey (2014). Slavson posits that the personal qualities of group leaders include poise, judgment, empathy, ego strength, freedom from excessive anxiety, a desire to help people, tolerance of frustration, imagination, intuition, perceptiveness, and an ability to avoid self-preoccupation. Corey et al. include such qualities as courage, willingness to model, presence, goodwill and caring, belief in group process, openness, nondefensiveness in coping with attacks, personal power, stamina, willingness to seek new experiences, self-awareness, humor, and inventiveness. The number of ideal qualities appears to be almost infinite, and it is unlikely that many potential group leaders will possess them all.

The trait view of leadership, although popular and appealing, has little support in research. No single personality type is best suited to be a group leader. Rather, effective group leaders possess a combination of certain personal qualities—a "personality profile" that facilitates their communication with group members. These qualities promote the successful integration of the leader and the group and help the group work more efficiently toward common goals (Stogdill, 1969, 1974). Although research indicates that some personality qualities correlate with leadership, it is the combination of factors (e.g., emotional stability and independence) working in interaction that makes a difference (Brandstatter & Farthofer, 1997).

PERSONALITY AND SPECIFIC GROUPS

As indicated previously, studies point out that people who are effective in some groups, such as those that are relationship oriented, may not be skilled in other groups, such as those that are task oriented (Forsyth, 2013). For example, Stockton and Morran (1982) and Yalom and Leszcz (2005) found that those who conduct counseling and therapy groups are most effective when they are (a) moderate in the amount of emotional stimulation they give the group (e.g., challenging, confronting, emphasizing the disclosing of feelings), (b) moderate in the expression of executive function (e.g., setting rules, limits, norms), (c) high in caring (e.g., offering support, encouragement, and protection), and (d) high in the use of meaning-attribution skills (e.g., clarifying, interpreting).

Research also indicates that ineffective group leaders are characterized as aggressive, authoritarian, pressure oriented, disrespectful of members, confrontational, egocentric, inappropriately self-disclosing, and poorly timed interveners (Lieberman et al., 1973). Experienced leaders act more like one another than inexperienced leaders do (Kottler, 1994).

Leaders who have been well trained in personal counseling are often assumed to be able to transfer their relationship skills to conducting groups. However, such is not the case. The dynamics associated with working with individuals, as opposed to groups, differ considerably. Just wanting to be a good group leader is not enough; one must have experience. Indeed, "group leaders must experience the power of group dynamics both as a member and a leader to truly understand them" (DeLucia-Waack, 2000c, p. 325).

Consequently, would-be group leaders need to explore through both experience and reflection whether they are suited by temperament and skills to operate as the leader of a group. Bates et al. (1982) recommend that potential group leaders examine their own personalities by using Jungian-based instruments, such as the Myers-Briggs Type Indicator, to understand how they might function in a group. Other group experts recommend different ways of assessing oneself.

THEORY AND EFFECTIVE GROUP LEADERS

The principles that guide group leaders are known as **theory**. The word *theory* receives mixed reactions in the field of group work because it is overused and often misunderstood. Basically, a theory is "a way of organizing what is known about some phenomenon in order to generate a set of inter-related, plausible, and, above all, refutable propositions about what is unknown" (Blocher, 1987, p. 67). A theory guides empirical inquiry and is useful in testing hypotheses. It is different from a *philosophical assumption* (which is largely untestable and focused on values) and a *process model* (which is a "cognitive map" that provides a "direct and immediate guide for counselor action" [p. 68]).

On one hand, some individuals believe that theory is of minor importance and has little effect on practice. This position was especially prevalent in the 1960s, when many new types of groups sprang up without solid theoretical foundations. In contrast, some think knowledge of well-developed theory is essential to becoming a competent practitioner (Lewin, 1951). The place of theory in group work depends on the type of group being conducted.

Most major theoretical positions consider the use of groups as a preferred mode of treatment. Operating from a theoretical base has definite advantages. However, choosing a theory or theories can be problematic, especially in group work. Among the advantages of theories is that they are practical. A good theory helps a practitioner understand and find meaning in experiences by providing a conceptual framework. "Like the scientist, a counselor [or a group worker] uses scientific theory to organize his or her knowledge of behavior" (Claiborn, 1987, p. 288). The lack of a theoretical framework can result in confusion.

A second advantage of theory is that it serves as a guide to expected behavior. In group counseling, for instance, a **settling-down period** usually occurs in which members test one another and the group before the group unifies. Group leaders guided by such theoretical knowledge are better prepared to respond appropriately to settling-down times than those who are unaware.

A third advantage of a theory is its **heuristic** (research) dimension. Theory is the foundation on which research is built. Research, in turn, strengthens the quality of theory. It is difficult, if not impossible, to have a theory without a research component. Another advantage of knowing and operating from a theoretical perspective is that the practitioner and group may make more progress than they would otherwise. Group leaders without any theory behind their interventions will probably find that their groups never reach a productive stage.

A further argument for the employment of theory in groups is that it helps practitioners formulate their own personalized approach to the groups in which they work. Patterson (1985, 1986) has made the point that some practitioners continue to repeat mistakes of the past or rediscover events of past decades because they are ignorant about how theories developed. Leaders who are most aware of what has been will most likely be skilled innovators of new methods and more highly developed in their ability to integrate and personalize information and process.

Finally, knowledge of theory generally helps group leaders formulate a specific approach for each group member. It is the leader-as-scientist's task to enhance the fit between the hypothetical group member and the actual one. Theory allows for the making and testing of predictions about how the group member will behave in response to particular environmental conditions, including selected interventions (Claiborn, 1987).

Case Example

Manuel Makes a Change

Manuel never had formal training in conducting groups. Instead he was asked one day to lead an inpatient group at the hospital where he worked, and for several years he had done so. He was therefore surprised when a new employee, Mattie, was assigned to conduct the group with him. He was even more taken aback when Mattie asked him what theory he employed in leading the group.

After realizing he lacked theoretical skills, Manuel got training. He became a reality therapist and in the process cringed as he remembered how he used to be obsessed with getting his group members to delve into their pasts. He now realized that focusing on the present is more practical.

Questions

What have you seen group leaders do that works? Has there been a theory behind their actions?

Group leaders may have difficulty choosing a theory because some theories tend to be "either too specific or too general to account for all the elements involved in the complexity of human behavior" (Ohlsen, Horne, & Lawe, 1988, pp. 48–49). Theories are also incomplete, and practitioners who stick with one theory may be hard pressed to explain certain actions in their groups.

A second problem in selecting a theory is that theories may become political. Practitioners of specific approaches tend to reinforce one another and exclude others. This practice may produce theoretical enrichment, but it sets up a **we/they mentality** in which practitioners of other points of view are seen as "uninformed," "naive," or "heretical." In such cases, potential contributions to a theory from outside sources are never made, and questionable assumptions are not examined.

A third drawback of theories is that they have many overlapping dimensions. For example, terms originated by Alfred Adler and Carl Rogers, such as *empathy, acceptance,* and *inferiority complex,* have essentially been incorporated into major leadership theories. As a result, the meanings of these concepts can be quite different from their origins. Such imprecise usage can be confusing to novice practitioners and the general public.

Another troublesome aspect about theories involves research. Some research (e.g., Korchin, 1976) supports the premise that theoretical orientation and outcome are unrelated. Basically, this research states that experienced therapists tend to be more effective and similar in what they do than inexperienced therapists. If research continues to uphold this finding, then group leaders, especially those with a counseling background, may pay less attention to theoretical orientations.

A further limitation of theories, and a potentially dangerous one, is that group leaders who use theory may notice only select details about their group members (Kottler, 1994). In such cases, both members and leaders are placed in potential jeopardy. For example, if Kathy ignores the more angry side of Brandon and other group members because her theory is based on emphasizing positives, then she may find that she is unable to deal with the group's collective anger.

Related to this limitation are group leaders who become locked into a theory so tightly that they become rigid, inflexible, and mechanical in practice. These leaders have poor interpersonal relationship skills because they are focused on what the theory directs rather than what their group members need. For instance, if a theory directs leaders to simply reinforce and not confront, then group members will find select behaviors influenced positively and other actions and considerations stunted.

KNOWLEDGE AND SKILLS OF EFFECTIVE GROUP LEADERS

Group leader knowledge and skills are displayed in different ways at various stages during the life of a group. Therefore, to make appropriate leadership decisions, group leaders must be well educated and know what to do and how to do it. In addition, the leader must be timely and appropriate. A variety of group techniques are possible, but effective group leaders use themselves, other group members, and the group process in helping facilitate change. No "cookbook" is available detailing exactly when to use specific interventions. Responsibility ultimately falls on group leaders to determine what to do, when to do it, and how.

Core Group Knowledge and Skills

Regardless of the type of group, some critical knowledge and core skills must be exercised if the group is to be successful. The ASGW's (2000) "Professional Standards for the Training of Group Workers" lists knowledge and skills needed for groups that include:

- Course work (at least one course in group work) and experiential requirements (at least 10 clock hours of direct observation and participation in a group experience as a member or leader)

- Knowledge of specializations, theories, and research as well as skills such as preparing a professional disclosure statement, applying theoretical concepts, and using scientific findings. Assessment of group members and social systems in which group members live and work is also expected
- Planning and implementing group interventions
- Leadership and co-leadership
- Evaluation
- Ethical practice, best practice, and diversity-competent practice

Overall, group leaders need to realize they must have a knowledge of group members and group skills if they are going to run a group constructively. For example, if Patricia, the leader, gives feedback to her group about their overall behaviors but claims negative feedback she receives from group members she does not know is the result of projection, the group will not work well. The reason is that Patricia is disconnected from the group personally and has not acquired a skill to help her handle group feedback.

Reflection

Think of groups you have been in that were productive. Then go back to the list of basic group skills just covered and note which ones you think were in the group in which you participated. In your opinion, are some core knowledge and skill sets more important than others?

Specific Group Skills

In considering which competencies to use, group leaders should recognize that a number of group skills are the same as those displayed in working with individuals. For example, group leaders must be empathetic, caring, and reflective. At the same time, a number of special skills are unique to group leaders and to the groups they are leading. Group work is an interactive system in which attention to one group member or topic will have an impact on all group members and the group process. Thus, group leaders must be engaged in

- opening and closing group meetings in ways that keep the group moving, focused, and on task and respectful of individual members,
- ensuring that all members have the opportunity to express themselves.

Corey (2012) has formulated a chart based on Nolan's (1978) ideas about group leadership. It points out essential skills that group leaders must have at their command (see Table 3.1).

Among the specific skills that differ significantly between group and individual work are:

- *Facilitating*—In groups, the leader facilitates by helping open up communication among group members (e.g., "Ryan, how do you want to respond to Kyle?"). In individual counseling, facilitation involves a more personal focus (opening people up to themselves, such as "Melissa, how did that feel to you?").
- *Protecting*—The skill of protecting is two dimensional in group settings. On one hand, it involves the leader safeguarding members from unnecessary attacks by others in the group. On the other hand, protecting "refers to a broad category of leader interventions aimed at preventing members from taking unnecessary psychological risks in the group"

Table 3.1	Overview of group leadership skills.	
Skills	Description	Aims and Desired Outcomes
Active Listening	Attending to verbal and nonverbal aspects of communication without judging or evaluating.	To encourage trust and client self-disclosure and exploration.
Restating	Saying in slightly different words what a participant has said to clarify its meaning.	To determine whether the leader has understood correctly the client's statement; to provide support and clarification.
Clarifying	Grasping the essence of a message at both the feeling and the thinking levels; simplifying client statements by focusing on the core of the message.	To help clients sort out conflicting and confused feelings and thoughts; to arrive at a meaningful understanding of what is being communicated.
Summarizing	Pulling together the important elements of an interaction or session.	To avoid fragmentation and give direction to a session; to provide for continuity and meaning.
Questioning	Asking open-ended questions that lead to self-exploration of the "what" and "how" of behavior.	To elicit further discussion; to get information; to stimulate thinking; to increase clarity and focus; to provide for further self-exploration.
Interpreting	Offering possible explanations for certain behaviors, feelings, and thoughts.	To encourage deeper self-exploration; to provide a new perspective for considering and understanding one's behavior.
Confronting	Challenging participants to look at discrepancies between their words and actions or body messages and verbal communication; pointing to conflicting information or messages.	To encourage honest self-investigation; to promote full use of potentials; to bring about awareness of self-contradictions.
Reflecting Feelings	Communicating understanding of the content of feelings.	To let members know that they are heard and understood beyond the level of words.
Supporting	Providing encouragement and reinforcement.	To create an atmosphere that encourages members to continue desired behaviors; to provide help when clients are facing difficult struggles; to create trust.
Empathizing	Identifying with clients by assuming their frames of references.	To foster trust in the therapeutic relationship; to communicate understanding; to encourage deeper levels of self-exploration.
Facilitating	Opening up clear and direct communication within the group; helping members assume increasing responsibility for the group's direction.	To promote effective communication among members; to help members reach their own goals in the group.
Initiating	Taking action to bring about group participation and to introduce new directions in the group.	To prevent needless group floundering; to increase the pace of group process.
Goal Setting	Planning specific goals for the group process and helping participants define concrete and meaningful goals.	To give direction to the group's activities; to help members select and clarify their goals.

Table 3.1	*(continued)*	
Skills	**Description**	**Aims and Desired Outcomes**
Evaluating	Appraising the ongoing group process and the individual and group dynamics.	To promote deeper self-awareness and better understanding of group movement and direction.
Giving Feedback	Expressing concrete and honest reactions based on observation of members' behaviors.	To offer an external view of how the person appears to others; to increase the client's self-awareness.
Suggesting	Offering advice and information, direction, and ideas for new behavior.	To help members develop alternative courses of thinking and action.
Protecting	Safeguarding members from unnecessary psychological risks in the group.	To warn members of possible risks in group participation; to reduce these risks.
Disclosing Oneself	Revealing one's reactions to here-and-now events in the group.	To facilitate deeper levels of interaction in the group; to create trust; to model ways of making oneself known to others.
Modeling	Demonstrating desired behavior through actions.	To provide examples of desirable behavior; to inspire members to fully develop their potential.
Dealing with Silence	Refraining from verbal and nonverbal communication.	To allow for reflection and assimilation; to sharpen focus; to integrate emotionally intense material; to help the group use its own resources.
Blocking	Intervening to stop counterproductive behavior in the group.	To protect members; to enhance the flow of group process.
Terminating	Preparing the group to end a session or finalize its history.	To prepare members to assimilate, integrate, and apply in-group learning to everyday life.

Note: The format of this chart is based on Edwin J. Nolan's article "Leadership Interventions for Promoting Personal Mastery," *Journal for Specialists in Group Work*, 1978, 3(3), 132–138.

Source: From Corey, G. *Theory and Practice of Group Counseling*, 5e. © 2000 South-Western, a part of Cengage Learning, Inc. Reproduced by permission.

(Morran, Stockton, & Whittingham, 2004, p. 93). It is not a skill usually used in individual counseling. For example, as Emma struggles in controlling her anger, the leader wants to make sure she does not receive hostile and unsympathetic responses from others and that she does not go too far, too soon, in disclosing reasons for her anger.

- *Blocking*—Blocking is related to protecting. In blocking, the leader intervenes in the group activity to stop counterproductive behavior. This intervention can be done on a verbal or nonverbal level. In individual and counseling sessions, the leader will block a person from counterproductive behavior, such as rambling or storytelling, by confronting, intervening, or cutting off (Morran et al., 2004). Therefore, if Darlene dominates the group for 10 minutes with a story that seems to have no point, the leader may give her both a hand signal and a verbal message that she needs to conclude what she is saying.

Seven other skills not included in Corey's chart are also vital in some group work settings: linking, diagnosing, reality testing, modification, delegating, creativity, and emotion regulation.

- *Linking*—Linking is "an intervention often used to connect what one group member is saying or doing with the concerns of one or more other members" (Morran et al., 2004, p. 96). For instance, in a psychoeducational group, the leader might link Matthew and Cheri together by stating, "I hear that both of you are concerned about what to say to other people after you have said 'hello.'" Through linking, interaction among members is encouraged within the group. Linking also promotes the development of facilitative relationships that have been found to be essential for effective group functioning (p. 96).

- *Diagnosing*—In this activity, the leader identifies certain behaviors and categories into which a person or group fits. Diagnosing in groups does not usually include psychological instruments but is based more on leader observations. For instance, in a task/work group, a leader may notice that the group has a tendency to blame rather than to develop constructive ideas for different ways to do things. To help the group grow, the leader must be a good observer who knows how to overcome distractive or disruptive behavior.

- *Reality testing*—This skill is used when a group member makes an important decision, such as changing jobs or taking a risk. At such moments, the leader will have other group members give feedback to the one who is contemplating a change on how realistic they consider the decision to be. For instance, members might tell Jack that they think he has the skills to be successful in sales as well as in public relations. Through this process, the person is able to evaluate more thoroughly his or her decision.

- *Modification*—Modification is a skill "designed to elicit potentially productive feedback from a group member" (Clark, 1995, p. 14). It is primarily employed when one group member gives another group member negative feedback that the second group member either cannot accept or becomes defensive about. Its purpose is to safeguard members and create a constructive atmosphere in the group. For instance, if Jayne tells Dylan, "You are selfish and never share your thoughts with the group," she could be asked to restate her thoughts and end up saying, "I think you have something to offer the group, and I'd like to hear more from you." In modification, the group leader must use a logical sequence by first "acknowledging the emotional reaction of a member" receiving negative feedback and then affirming the "potentially constructive intent" of the sender (Clark, 1995, p. 16). Finally, by using a convincing tone of voice, the leader needs to persuade the sender to restate the feedback message so it can be properly heard and received.

- *Delegating*—In delegating, the group leader assigns a task to the group or one or more of its members. The task can be as simple as observing and sharing impressions of what is happening in the group. For example, "Yvonne, I would like for you to let the group know when you think there is a lot of energy in it." Delegating can be complex, too, such as asking a member or members to lead the group. The idea behind delegating is to share the responsibility for the development of the group with the group.

- *Creativity*—The act of creativity is one where a person takes elements within the environment and arranges or rearranges them in such a way that something new and useful is formed. Often insight, meaning, and synergy occur in the process. By its very nature, group work is creative; therefore, group leaders need to be skilled in divergent ways of thinking and behaving (Bowman & Boone, 1998). Group leaders with a heightened capacity for creativity can help themselves and the group be more productive in times of crisis and form a sense of community. When creativity is employed, problems can also be viewed differently, and lives and interaction patterns transformed.

- *Emotion regulation*—Effective emotion regulation is crucial to group leadership (Champe, Okech, & Rubel, 2013). Strategies connected with emotion regulation include "behavioral and cognitive methods by which individuals influence the type, timing, intensity, and expression of emotion" (p. 353). For instance, by making a cognitive change of a statement, an emotional reaction may be altered. Thus, when Ruth Ann says, "I don't like what we are doing in this group," Brandon, the group leader, may change his thinking—instead of taking the statement personally that he is doing something wrong and getting angry, he can modify his thoughts to wondering what Ruth Ann was expecting and what she sees happening. In that way, he can logically ask Ruth Ann to help him understand what is upsetting her.

Overall, more than two dozen leadership skills can be used in various types of groups. Initial research by Toth and Stockton (1996) suggests that general group skills, such as here-and-now interventions (immediacy) as well as specific skills (e.g., blocking), can be taught using a systematic, microskills format as first devised by Ivey (1971). The implementation of this research is yet to come, but the identification and mastery of leadership skills are important. By being familiar with the skills and how they are employed, group leaders increase the range of alternative actions (Ivey, Ivey, & Zalaquett, 2014) that they can use at appropriate times in the life of the group.

GROUP LEADERSHIP ROLES AND FUNCTIONS

In addition to displaying a wide variety of skills, group leadership requires that leaders function in specific roles at various times during the life of a group (DeLucia-Waack, 1999c). A group leader must be versatile and focused in various ways at different times. Experience, coupled with training, permits leaders to operate in such a manner. There are six essential roles and functions that leaders must carry out over the life of the group: "(a) group member selection, (b) pregroup preparation, (c) positive leader-member relationship, (d) leader's use of structure, (e) group cohesion, and (f) leader communication and feedback" (Riva et al., 2004, p. 38). The specifics of these roles are discussed in later chapters. However, it is crucial to remember that there are skills and behaviors associated with each distinct role and function. For instance, at the beginning of the group, a leader is much more likely to function in an active and direct way than during the middle phase of the group process, when group members are busy with their own activities.

It is also important to realize that group leaders operate in certain ways whether the groups are counseling, therapy, psychoeducational, or task/work oriented. Leaders must recognize which strategies will work best and when. Bates et al. (1982) characterize four main roles and functions that group leaders need to display at various times: traffic director, modeler of appropriate behavior, interactional catalyst, and communication facilitator.

Each of these roles takes specific skills. In the **traffic director** role, for instance, leaders "help members become aware of behaviors that open communication channels and those that inhibit communication" (Bates et al., 1982, p. 96). The role is both proactive and reactive in the prevention of certain behaviors (e.g., blocking "why" questions, focusing on the past, gossiping) and the promotion of others (e.g., actively listening, responding in a nonjudgmental way). In a similar manner, in the role of **modeler of appropriate behavior**, leaders must consciously pick actions they think group members need to learn through passive and active demonstrations. These ways of modeling can include deliberate use of self-disclosure, role-plays, speech patterns, and acts of creativity. For example, when group leaders employ voice tones that signify happiness or sadness, they are directly and indirectly helping their group members learn ways to express their feelings.

The **interactional catalyst** role requires that leaders promote interaction between group members without calling attention to themselves. One way to do this is to look at various members when it might be appropriate for them to respond. Being an interactional catalyst is a functional process that continues throughout the group and can take various forms, such as questioning whether two or more group members have something to say to each other and then being silent to see what happens.

Case Example

Nolan Gets a Nod

Nolan characterized himself as a "shy guy" who was "willing to try almost anything once." So when he joined a singles group, he thought he would have plenty of opportunities to try many things. Instead, the group was dominated by a few individuals, and Nolan had a hard time getting a word in edgewise, until one day when the group leader looked around the group during a moment of silence and gave a nod to him as if saying: "Please feel free to speak and share your opinions." That is what Nolan did, and almost immediately afterward, he became more involved.

Questions

Have you ever been brought out in a group by someone using either verbal or nonverbal means? What happened? Do you recommend that others use such means? Why?

Finally, in the **communication facilitator** role, group leaders reflect the content and feeling of members and teach them how to do likewise. For instance, leaders may note that when someone is conveying that they are depressed, they do not smile or have a lilt in their words. Therefore, this process focuses on both the expression of words and the emotion behind the communications. In addition, the importance of speaking congruently is stressed—that is, using "I" messages to state what one wants or what one thinks.

Leaders and Group Conflict

In addition to the four tasks just described, a primary function of group leaders is dealing constructively with conflict. The display of conflict is normal within a group and is especially prevalent in certain group stages, such as "storming" (Tuckman, 1965). Conflict and challenges in groups, if managed properly, offer opportunities for growth within the group. However, "one of the most difficult aspects of group leadership is the ability of the group leader to respond to conflict or challenging incidents in the group" (Kraus, DeEsch, & Geroski, 2001, p. 31).

Five specific techniques for managing conflict in groups have been proposed by Simpson (1977) and elaborated on by Kormanski (1982): withdrawal from the conflict, suppressing the conflict, integrating conflicting ideas to form new solutions, working out a compromise, and using power to resolve the conflict.

- *Withdrawal from the conflict*—This strategy involves leaders distancing themselves from conflict and postponing interventions. It has the advantage of letting leaders gather more data and observe longer without becoming excessively involved. It also allows leaders to consult and use resolution strategies later if issues are not settled. The disadvantages of this approach are that conflict may escalate, and withdrawal is completely ineffective in dealing with a crisis.

- *Suppressing conflict*—As a strategy, suppression consists of playing down conflict. It is often used when issues are minor. It keeps emotions under control and helps group leaders build a supportive climate. Suppression is most effective when conflict issues are unimportant or when focusing on a relationship is more important than concentrating on an issue. The disadvantages of suppression are that it fails to resolve conflict and allows feelings to smolder and possibly erupt later. In addition, leaders may be perceived as weak or insensitive when they use this strategy.

- *Integrating conflicting ideas to form new solutions*—Consensus is the idea behind integration. In using this strategy, group leaders try to get all parties to reexamine a situation and identify points of agreement. The goals are to develop new alternatives, learn how to open up lines of communication better, and build cohesive unity and commitment. One example of integration is **mediation**: having a third party hear arguments about a situation and then render a decision. The disadvantages of the integrative approach include the large amount of time it takes to implement and the unwillingness of some individuals to set aside their own goals and work for the good of the group.

- *Working out a compromise*—In this method, each party involved gives up a little to obtain a part of what they wanted and avoid conflict. The result is a win–win situation in which cooperative behavior and collaborative efforts are encouraged. This approach is effective when resources are limited and group members are flexible—for example, in a work group in which little money is available to spend on research and salaries. Compromising is a good strategy to use in avoiding win–lose situations. Negotiation is a good example of compromise. The disadvantages of compromise are that some parties may inflate their wants, and the eventual action taken may be ineffective or less than desirable.

- *Using power to resolve the conflict*—The power strategy involves "the imposition of someone's will on someone else" (Kormanski, 1982, p. 116). The source of power may be derived from either a person's status or from his or her personality. **Position power** is most often used when immature relationships between individuals exist (Hersey, Blanchard, & Natemeyer, 1979). It is derived from the status of people's titles, such as "group leader" or "group facilitator." **Personal power** is employed more frequently in mature relationship situations. The source of power in such a situation is from the individual and his or her ability to persuade others to follow a selected course of action.

By using power, a leader is able to resolve a crisis quickly. However, the use of power creates a win–lose atmosphere in which the losers may harbor feelings of resentment or powerlessness and may seek revenge on those who have won. Arbitration is an example of a typical use of power.

Reflection

Which of the leadership strategies for managing conflict do you prefer? When have you used that strategy?

Overall, a prerequisite to becoming an effective leader is learning which strategies and roles to employ in conflict situations and when. Kraus et al. (2001) encourage leaders to approach such situations first by attending to and valuing them. Leaders must "internally process challenges in part by asking themselves supervision-like questions before effective interventions can follow" (p. 32). Kraus et al. suggest a "menu" of six nonexhaustive and nonexclusive questions that cover such important topics as member selection, systems theory, group dynamics and stages, individual members' group issues, emerging themes, and leader introspection. "By leaders carefully considering which perspective—which cuisine—may offer the best opportunity to harness the positive energy present in the group at that moment, an appropriate approach will follow" (p. 44). Other experiences, such as observing or co-leading groups, can also be enlightening in learning how to handle conflict and not become defensive when challenges occur.

CO-LEADERS IN GROUPS

A **co-leader** is a professional or a professional-in-training who undertakes the responsibility of sharing the leadership of a group with another leader in a mutually determined manner in order to facilitate counseling, therapy, or group member interaction. The use of co-leaders in groups occurs often, especially in groups with a membership of 12 or more. The efficacy of using co-leaders depends on many factors, including economic considerations, advantages to the group, agreement on confrontation styles, and the personal compatibility of the leaders (Bridbord & DeLucia-Waack, 2011). It is usually thought that co-leaders will be most effective when they share cognitions about the group they are involved in but are dissimilar in terms of their skill sets and behavior within the group. However, the process is more complicated than that (Miles & Kivlighan, 2010). "Group co-leaders' concerns about their competence . . . [are] among the most significant factors influencing the development and enactment of their co-leader relationship" (Okech & Kline, 2006, p. 166). In order to promote co-leader relationships, Huffman and Fernando (2012) recommend using the interpersonal process of intimacy where at each stage within the group, a supervisor facilitates intimacy between leaders "by inviting self-disclosure and partner responsiveness around the issues most relevant in their relationship and their group" (p. 161).

Advantages

The advantages associated with co-leading a group, according to Carroll, Bates, and Johnson (2004), Corey, Corey, and Corey (2014), and Jacobs, Schimmel, Masson, and Harvill (2016), include the following:

- *Ease of handling the group in difficult situations*—When two leaders are present, they may help each other facilitate the movement of the group. For example, one leader can shift the topic or the focus of the group if the other leader gets bogged down. Before and after group sessions, co-leaders can plan strategies and discuss problems that they, members, or the group as a whole are experiencing.
- *Uses of modeling*—With co-leaders, group members are exposed to two models of human interaction. They see how individuals can relate to each other in positive ways and how they can disagree and still cooperate. When co-leaders are of the opposite gender, members may grow by more fully realizing and reliving earlier family dynamics and working on any unresolved issues that are brought up.
- *Feedback*—Regardless of the issues members discuss, they usually receive twice the leader feedback when the group is co-led. This input helps members realize more fully how others perceive them and gives them a different perspective than they would receive otherwise. For example, one co-leader may comment on intrapersonal aspects of a group member's behavior, whereas the other focuses on interpersonal relationships. In such situations, leaders may also stimulate each other more and take corrective measures to avoid **burnout** (becoming physically and emotionally exhausted). Leaders, like members of the group, may grow more than they would if they were leading the group alone.

- *Shared specialized knowledge*—In groups with co-leaders, there is a primary advantage for all concerned when the leaders share specialized training with each other and the group. This type of sharing can come in response to a situation in the group, such as dealing with anger, and can be done privately or publicly. In these cases, everyone benefits because information is presented and discussed in a more dynamic and expanded manner than is possible in a one-leader group.
- *Pragmatic considerations*—In a co-led group, it is possible for one leader to cover for the other if a group session must be missed because of illness or professional considerations. Coverage allows the group to continue and evolve.

Limitations

The limitations of co-leading a group are also important to consider. The disadvantages this effort entails have the potential to be very destructive. "Unless partners can work as a complementary team, much group time can be wasted in power plays, bickering, and mutual sabotage" (Kottler, 1983, p. 178). Among the potential liabilities of co-leading are the following:

- *Lack of coordinated efforts (Okech, 2008; Okech & Kline, 2006)*—The degree to which a group grows depends on the coordination of its leaders. When leaders do not meet to process what has occurred in the group or to agree on where they want to lead the group, destructive conflict within the group may occur, and the outcome of the group may be less than desirable. In such situations, the leaders may work, knowingly or not, at cross purposes.
- *Two leader focused*—The old saying that "too many cooks spoil the broth" may apply to some groups with two leaders. In these cases, the presence of two leaders, especially if both are strong personalities and leader centered, will work against the good of group members because too much attention is concentrated on the leaders. One leader may also dominate another and call attention to the leadership role instead of the goals of members. In such cases, the impact of both group leaders is eventually diminished.
- *Competition (Okech, 2008; Trotzer, 2007)*—Competition between group leaders is often the result of a lack of *reflect practice,* where leaders do not reflect individually and together on their experiences about helping people. This lack of insight and awareness may be manifest in several ways—for example, through trying to gain the attention of the group or through using opposing theories. The point is that competition between group leaders will cost the group part of its efficiency and productivity. Leaders may lose respect for each other in such an atmosphere.
- *Collusion*—In the collusion process, a co-leader forms an informal alliance with a group member to address disliked qualities of the other co-leader. The result is an unloading of unexpected emotion onto the nonaligned leader and a splitting of the group into factions.

Overall, when leaders decide to lead a group jointly, they must work as a team. Such an approach takes considerable preparation. The process develops over time and goes through stages (Fall & Wejnert, 2005; Okech & Kline, 2006). For example, in the initial forming stage of a group, co-leaders "are uncertain about the expectations of the group and of one another" (Fall & Wejnert, 2005, p. 315). Likewise, co-leader relationships develop over time and co-leaders experience storming, norming, performing, and adjourning in a parallel manner to that of group members. Okech and Kline (2005) found that co-leaders believe that their effectiveness as co-leaders depends on the quality of their relationships. Thus, co-leading is a double-edged sword in that it can both relieve and promote stress depending on how well the leaders relate to one another.

Gazda (1989) states that "supportive feedback, mutual trust and respect, and a liking for each other appear to be at least minimal requirements" for co-leaders to work well together and be of benefit to the group (p. 64).

In addition to developing a strong relationship, co-leading requires that both leaders be competent to begin with and that they be able to express a wide range of facilitative skills (e.g., self-disclosure, timing) in an appropriate manner. Co-leaders must also be consistent and non-competitive. The three main models of co-led groups are those in which the lead is (a) **alternated** (one leader takes responsibility for a specific period or a session, and the other leader provides support); (b) **shared** (each leader takes charge momentarily as he or she sees fit); or (c) **apprenticed** (a more experienced leader takes charge of the group to show a novice how to work with groups).

Overall, co-leading can be either a bonus or a bust to group members and to group leaders. When co-leaders develop a positive relationship in their group approach, they have a greater capacity for helping individuals and the group than does a single leader (Trotzer, 2007). It is the development of the right conditions that either makes or breaks co-led groups.

Case Example

Casey Strikes Out

Casey wanted more experience in leading a group, so she asked her best friend, Jenny, to co-lead a grief group with her. Jenny had been a group worker for about 4 more years than Casey, and Casey was sure the two of them would do well together because they had been friends since college. However, from the first group session on, there was friction between the two leaders—not enough to throw the group off balance, but enough that the two co-leaders noticed it. After the group was over, Casey asked Jenny to sit down with her and process what had happened

and why. Both women were honest in their observations—and then it dawned on Casey. Jenny was an existentialist, and Casey was a reality therapist (choice theory). They were operating from two different theoretical viewpoints.

Questions

How do you think Casey could have avoided the difficulty she experienced as a co-leader of the grief group? What could Jenny have done to help? Do you think it is essential for co-leaders to have the same philosophical viewpoints? Why or why not?

GROUP LEADERSHIP TRAINING

"Training in group counseling typically includes four essential components: academic, observation, experiential, and supervision" (Riva & Korinek, 2004, p. 55). Yet, one of "the weakest areas of the group work movement throughout the decades has been the lack of attention paid to the training of group leaders" (Shapiro & Bernadett-Shapiro, 1985, p. 86). Until recently, little was published about training group leaders (Dye, 1997). Indeed, in the early days of group work (the 1950s and 1960s) before training standards were established, almost anyone could claim to be a group leader and start a group. Many such individuals were well intentioned but used predominantly individual counseling techniques with groups. The results were less than desirable and many times harmful. The self-anointed approach is no longer recognized or considered ethical by major group associations. Such an approach does not ensure quality or uniformity in treatment.

Most people are not natural leaders of groups. It takes time and training to perfect group leadership skills. Yalom (Yalom & Leszcz, 2005) strongly advocates that potential group psychotherapy leaders participate in groups as a part of their training. This is a group process model of training (Stockton, Morran, & Krieger, 2004). Yalom notes that the accreditation committee of the American Group Psychotherapy Association has recommended a minimum requirement of 60 hours of participation in groups for those in training to become leaders. Yalom also believes leadership training should provide an opportunity for a beginner to serve an apprenticeship with a more experienced clinician. Jacobs et al. (2016) also point out the importance of being in groups to fine-tune skills. The idea behind this approach when used as a model for training group leaders is that people must experience the power of the group as followers before they can become group leaders. Indeed, many self-help group leaders hone their skills in this way. However, just being in a group is inadequate for becoming a group leader. Likewise, a sole emphasis on simple didactic instruction or observation of a group at work is deficient as the major way to train group leaders.

In addition to an experiential base, group leaders must have specialized knowledge in the theories, dynamics, and interpersonal, ethical, research, and stage components of group work (Association for Specialists in Group Work, 2000). Leadership skills for conducting groups require input and cultivation of many sources. Effective group leaders must be able to perceive what is occurring in the group, select appropriate interventions, and risk implementing the interventions they have chosen (Stockton, McDonnell, & Aldarondo, 1997). Only the well-trained professional can make therapeutic moves in a group on a consistent basis (Vriend, 1985).

Among the methods that have been established to train group leaders are (a) group-based training (Pearson, 1985), (b) the group generalist model (Anderson, 1982), (c) the educational and developmental procedure (Tollerud, Holling, & Dustin, 1992), (d) systematic group leadership training (Harvill, Masson, & Jacobs, 1983; Harvill, West, Jacobs, & Masson, 1985), (e) the critical-incident model and intervention cube concept (Childers, 1986), and (f) skills-based training models (e.g., DeLucia-Waack, 2001a).

The first way of obtaining the specialized training necessary for working with groups that is examined here is **group-based training** (Pearson, 1985). In this model, trainers first identify and define specific skills used in groups, providing examples in which each skill might be used. The flexibility of using various skills is stressed. Next, both videos and role-plays are used to show trainees how a particular skill is employed. The third step in this procedure is structured practice, in which each trainee demonstrates how he or she would use the skill that has been demonstrated. This enactment is then critiqued. Finally, group leader trainees, after learning all the group skills, are asked to demonstrate their group facilitation skills in 20-minute, unstructured practice sessions. They are observed leading a group and are given feedback on the use of skills they implemented during this time as well as those that they did not use.

A second way of preparing group facilitators is the **group generalist model**. The model includes a five-step process outlined by Anderson (1982). The first step is having a group leader model behaviors for a group followed by having the group break down into subgroups with each subgroup member becoming a leader of the subgroup in a small group discussion. The third step is to have subgroup members process their behavior in the discussions followed by a critique of the subgroup leaders' behavior. Finally, the whole group shares observations and insights they gained from the experience.

A third model for training group leaders is the **educational and developmental procedure**. It consists of four components: (a) content, (b) decision making, (c) eventual leadership style, and (d) dual process (Tollerud et al., 1992). All of these components are connected to a supervisor, "whose role is to make timely decisions as to how and when these components are implemented into the training" (p. 97). The focus of content is on factual information. Decision making involves choosing what to do and how to do it based on an understanding of group dynamics and self-knowledge. Leadership style deals with the complex set of expectations and tasks that face new group leaders. Finally, dual process is the idea that group leaders-in-training are members of two groups at once. The first group is composed of those trainees are leading; the second is composed of peers. The experiences from each group can be used in the other.

Systematic group leadership training is a fourth way of teaching basic skills to beginning group leaders. It is a six-step method that includes the video recording of trainees as they lead a group before they are introduced to the skill to be learned (steps 1 and 2). Then trainees read about and see a new skill demonstrated (steps 3 and 4). Finally, trainees critique their original videos and then make new videos demonstrating the skill they have just been taught (steps 5 and 6) (Harvill et al., 1983). As first proposed, systematic group leadership training focused on six group leadership skills:

- *Cutting off*—This skill is used to stop group members who continue to speak in an unfocused way and help them concentrate on a point. For example, the leader might say, "Sharon, you seem to be repeating yourself. See if you can make your point in a sentence. Then let's hear from someone else."
- *Drawing out*—Drawing out occurs when the leader "directly invites comments or involvement from one of more group members. It is often used to encourage participation from members who find it hard to share with others or with those who share on a surface level but avoid deeper issues" (Morran et al., 2004, p. 95). For example, as the leader, Rudy might ask Fred and Alma if they have thoughts about the matter before the group because they have been quiet during the group's discussion.
- *Holding the focus*—This skill helps members concentrate on a specific topic or person for a set length of time. For example, if the group has been talking about risk taking and Wanda changes the subject, then the leader may simply say, "Wanda, let's conclude our discussion on risk taking before we deal with anything else."
- *Shifting the focus*—Sometimes leaders need to move group members to a different topic or person. For instance, the group leader may say to the group as a whole, "It appears we have exhausted our ideas about how to take risks. I would like to see us talk about the drawbacks, as well as the advantages, of risk taking."
- *Using eyes*—Scanning the group and noticing nonverbal reactions is a helpful skill for group leaders. For instance, the leader may notice that Kathryn's eyes are focused on the floor instead of on Jean, to whom she is talking.
- *Tying things together*—When leaders tie things together, they connect members with one another in regard to their similarities just as in linking. Therefore, Inez and Pablo are connected or "tied together" by a leader who realizes they both have a passion for computers and software and who points this commonality out in the group.

Research findings support that four of these skills—cutting off, drawing out, holding the focus, and shifting the focus—are significantly improved following systematic group leadership training.

Reflection

Why do you suppose there is no consistent empirical evidence to support the improvement of skills such as "using eyes" and "tying things together" following systematic group leadership training? Do you think the lack of supportive research for these two skills means they are of lesser value than the skills that do have empirical support: cutting off, drawing out, holding the focus, and shifting the focus?

The **critical-incident model** and **intervention cube** concept make up a fifth way of training group leaders. This approach, as first set forth by Cohen and Smith (1976) and later expanded on by Donigian and Hulse-Killacky (1999), focuses on a number of critical incidents in the life of a group. The trainee, after studying group dynamics, watches a video of his or her instructor handling a number of different situations in a group. Then the trainee co-leads a group under the instructor's supervision, during which he or she makes strategic interventions geared to the incidents in the particular group (Childers, 1986). Trainees are taught self-management skills and ways to deal with specific group situations. They learn on both a personal and a professional level. This type of training, when combined in an integrative way with the type of nonperfectionistic thinking pattern proposed by Miller (1986), can help beginning group leaders be less rigid and more sensitive, caring, and helpful to others.

Skills-based training models for group workers have also become more prevalent and popular, and a number of instruments have been developed to assess group leadership skills (DeLucia-Waack, 2001a). A particularly strong model, the **Skilled Group Counseling Training Model**, has been proven to be effective through research (Smaby, Maddux, Torres-Rivera, & Zimmick, 1999). It is especially helpful in assisting beginning group workers to "learn and transfer group counseling skills to actual group counseling sessions" (Downing, Smaby, & Maddux, 2001, p. 158). This model, which can be tested through use of the **Skilled Group Counseling Scale**, "includes 18 skills organized into three stages of counseling: exploration, understanding, and acting" (p. 158). An equally important instrument for measuring skills is the **Group Leader Self-Efficacy Instrument (GLSI)**, a 36-item scale that measures group leader self-efficacy (Page, Pietrzak, & Lewis, 2001). **Self-efficacy**, according to Bandura (1986), is a person's judgment of his or her capability to organize and execute a course of action required to attain a designated type of performance. The GLSI appears to have sufficient validity and reliability to measure the self-efficacy of individuals learning to perform group leader skills and, therefore, can be employed to ensure that new leaders are competent in their purported abilities.

Overall, the concepts and methods used in most of these approaches to training include the basic prerequisites for an effective group leader as articulated by Trotzer (2007). They also incorporate, for the most part, the literature on the training needs of preservice group leaders as summarized by Stockton and Toth (1996), which states that group leaders need to be grounded in theories, have an opportunity to observe and personally participate in groups, as well as practice leading groups under careful supervision.

Yalom (Yalom & Leszcz, 2005) concurs with this holistic, research-based, balanced, and multidimensional emphasis in training. He stresses that group leadership training goes beyond techniques in emphasizing the importance of helping students to evaluate their own work in a critical fashion and to maintain sufficient flexibility (both technically and attitudinally). According to Yalom, becoming a mature clinician requires evolving. Every group is a learning experience.

An open attitude toward learning is especially important for effective and mature group leaders, regardless of their specialty area in working with groups.

GROUP SUPERVISION

"Supervised experiential training is a key component of group leader instruction" (Stockton & Toth, 1996, p. 280). Supervision increases supervisees' independence and self-confidence (Linton, 2003). It helps supervisees broaden their understanding from a focus on individual issues to interpersonal and group-as-a-system issues (Rubel & Okech, 2006). Therefore, group supervision is an essential and complementary activity for becoming competent at group leadership (DeLucia-Waack, 2002). It may be done in conjunction with the other three components of group leadership training.

Supervision for group workers is also essential after formal training. Without ongoing supervision and evaluation, original errors made by a group leader may be reinforced by simple repetition (Yalom & Leszcz, 2005). For example, Isabel may continue to gloss over feelings in group members unless she is confronted about both what she is doing and why. Furthermore, supervision enables group leaders repeatedly to address problematic thoughts and issues they may have, such as those involved in eating disorders (e.g., perfection, independence), so that they do not become troublesome and intrusive (DeLucia-Waack, 1999b). Group workers who do not have supervision "get stuck in patterns of dysfunctional behavior and do not know how to get out" (DeLucia-Waack, 1999c, p. 132).

One way to minimize problems and processes in group supervision is to make them developmental, comprehensive, and diverse. "At any particular moment, the supervisor must consider the level of cognitive complexity of the supervisee, the developmental level of the group, the level of training of group members, and the interactive effects of these variables with one another" (Hayes, 1990, p. 235). The anxiety of the group leader must also be assessed and dealt with in supervision because "anxiety may impact cognitive development" and the functioning of the leader in the group (Duncan & Brown, 1996, p. 252).

The American Group Psychotherapy Association recommends a minimum of 180 hours of supervision for group leaders-in-training. According to Trotzer (2007), one good way of being supervised is to have two potential group leaders co-lead a group under the supervision of a more experienced leader. This type of supervision is less threatening to a novice group leader than trying to co-lead with an experienced group leader. It requires less time on the supervisor's part and allows him or her to be more objective in critiquing the new group leaders. This technique may also include video recording and observations by a group team behind a one-way mirror that in turn can result in further supervision by a supervisor working with the observation group.

Case Example

Sally Skips Supervision

Sally was an excellent individual counselor who was learning how to become a solid group counselor. As a part of her training, she led a psychotherapy group of women who had been hospitalized for mental disorders. Because she was sensitive and well trained as an individual clinician, Sally did well with the group. Members seemed to like her, and she felt good about her abilities, as did her clinical supervisor. One day, however, after a grueling week, Sally decided to skip supervision, stating to a friend, "I am sure both my supervisor and I can find better things to do this week."

Questions

What was wrong with what Sally did? What was right about it? What do you think would have been the best course of action for Sally to take in this situation?

Peer group supervision is another way of providing group leaders with supervision. "The support for peer group supervision is based on the belief that it offers opportunities for vicarious learning in a supportive group environment. It is argued that once established, this environment contributes to decreased supervisee anxiety, increased self-efficacy and confidence, and enhanced learning opportunities" (Christensen & Kline, 2001, pp. 81–82). This type of supervision may reduce hierarchy and dependency needs found within individual supervision. Furthermore, it may make the most of supervisory time and expertise, although in the beginning it requires an investment in structuring the group. Research by Christensen and Kline (2001) using a process-sensitive peer group found peer group supervision to be an effective way of helping supervisees learn essential skills "that enable them to supervise each other in a peer supervision environment" (p. 97). There are essentially five aspects of peer group supervision as the illustration below shows.

A less effective way of supervising is through listening to an audio recording of a group. In this type of supervision, voice tones and member input are readily picked up, but other nonverbal dimensions of the group are missed. The least effective way of conducting group supervision is having a supervisee report either orally or in writing what occurred in the group. Such self-reports are usually selective and miss subtleties (Freeman & McHenry, 1996).

Another way supervision may occur is to have group leaders in a group that is supervised. This type of group supervision saves time and resources (Gillam, Hayes, & Paisley, 1997). It is usually reserved for novice counselors who are learning generic counseling skills, but it can be employed with group leaders either during formal education classes or as continuing education (Werstlein & Borders, 1997). In such a process, group leaders bring in videos or role-play problematic situations in the group and receive supervision from the supervisor in charge of running the group and from their peers. In academic and practice settings, a group of this kind may function primarily as a task group, and "highly task-oriented behaviors may predominate across all stages" of its development (Werstlein & Borders, 1997, p. 132).

The supervision of group work (SGW) model developed by Okech and Rubel (2007) is a final way of providing supervision. The SGW model is adapted from the discrimination model of supervision (Bernard & Goodyear, 2013). "The model highlights conceptualization, personalization, and intervention skills, which parallel the domains of awareness, knowledge, and skills necessary for diversity competence. In addition, the model brings focus to the group interaction levels (individual, interpersonal/subgroup, and group-as-a-system)." Overall, it illustrates "the need for supervisor and supervisee diversity competence and group work-relevant awareness, knowledge, and skills at each level" (Okech & Rubel, 2007, p. 264).

Reflection

Which of the ways of acquiring group supervision appeals most to you? Why do you think you prefer it over other models? What does this tell you about yourself?

If supervision is successful, then group leader trainees will grow in four areas (Bernard, 1979; Freeman & McHenry, 1996; Lanning, 1986). First, they will improve their **process skills**—that is, observable behaviors used to run groups, such as summarization, immediacy, and confrontation. DeLucia-Waack (2002) recommends that a Group Processing Sheet be used in the process skills area. This sheet is made up of two parts: Group Process Notes to record "the events of the group session as part of the official notes for the group and/or individual client files" and a Processing of the Group Session section "to help group leaders analyze what happened in the group in terms of therapeutic factors, critical incidents, effective interventions, and counter-transference" (p. 346). By improving process skills, group leaders become more versatile in their interactions with group members and the group as a whole.

A second area in which group leader supervisees will become better through supervision is in using **conceptual skills**—that is, thinking skills that enable them to delineate dominant themes and the concerns of clients while simultaneously choosing a particular helpful response. Conceptual skills deal with the whole picture of what is occurring within the group and are crucial to the development of a group. Conceptualizing is helped through filling out the Group Processing Sheet, as is the third area in the domain of **personalization skills**. These skills are associated with using one's own personal attributes, such as openness or humor, to full advantage in a group setting. Finally, in supervision, supervisees are assisted in improving their **professional skills**, such as behaving appropriately in a crisis, safeguarding confidentiality, and turning in reports connected with the group on time. Overall, supervision contributes to both specific and general learning experiences of group leaders in training.

Summary and Conclusion

This chapter has focused on the complex nature of group leadership. The concept of leadership is often misunderstood, but some of its common factors include multiple relationships in which there are reciprocity, legitimate influence, motivation, and cooperation for the achievement of beneficial goals. To be an effective group leader, a person must show some versatility and realize that different styles of leadership are appropriate in certain situations. Leaders who are too rigid and use one style (e.g., authoritarian, democratic, laissez-faire) may be less helpful than those who are flexible and developmental.

The personal qualities of group leaders are also important. No one trait is essential for leaders to possess. However, the display of some personal qualities (e.g., support, warmth) in certain quantities will facilitate the movement of the group and the growth of members. Which qualities and quantities are vital depends on the dynamics of a particular group. The way theories and theoretical skills are employed is also linked to the nature of the group being led. Some theories are helpful and advantageous to the leader and members; others are not.

Some skills are unique to certain groups, whereas others are universal to all areas of human relations. As group work has grown, it has become increasingly important for group workers to become skilled in core competencies appropriate for running any type of group as well as for them to master specific group competencies targeted for specialty groups. General core group skills come first. From these skills, group workers can hone and refine their abilities when working in specialty areas. No one skill is crucial for a group leader to possess, but knowing what to do and when to do it is essential. Leadership in skill deployment is developed through experience, course work, and supervision. Skills, if properly applied, can help members and groups achieve individual and overall goals. Knowing when and how to use a particular skill separates successful and unsuccessful group leaders.

Group leaders function in a variety of ways—for example, as traffic directors, catalysts, and managers of conflict. Therefore, leaders must be sensitive to themselves and their constituents. Sometimes working with a co-leader can be helpful in learning how to integrate personal and professional skills, especially if the experience is under supervision.

Group leadership training is a must for those who expect to work on more than a one-to-one basis. Such training will often be composed of three elements: telling, doing, and showing. It is important that group leaders get a feel for what working with a group is like before they actually direct one. The process of updating leadership skills is continuous, as is supervision. Models for learning skills and receiving supervision have proliferated and improved in recent years.

In summary, groups are a unique way to work with individuals in resolving problems or accomplishing tasks. Group leadership involves being not only knowledgeable about group operations, but also skilled through an integrative experience in how to help members and the group as a whole move in productive directions.

Classroom Exercises

1. Why do you think the terms *leader* and *leadership* are so misunderstood? What qualities do you consider essential for a group leader? If possible, tell about a leader who has personally influenced you and how you were affected. What did that person do with the group you were in that you admired most?

2. List personal and professional qualities and skills you possess that would help you lead a group of your choosing. Which qualities and skills do you think you need to cultivate more? Discuss your self-assessment with two other class members. Notice how your ideas and theirs change or remain the same in this process.

3. Find an article on the supervision or training of group leaders (consult the *Journal for Specialists in Group Work, Small Group Behavior,* or *Counselor Education and Supervision*). Share the content with the class and your instructor; other class members will do the same. From the ideas presented, discuss what the process of supervision entails in group work.

4. Discuss how you feel about conflict in a group with another class member. After you have identified your feelings, look at the five ways of managing conflict suggested in this chapter. Which ones are you most uncomfortable with? Why? Describe a specific way you can work to improve your management of group conflict.

CHAPTER 4

Forming a Group

WavebreakMediaMicro/Fotolia

Knowing that most beginnings are awkward
we wait anxiously for words or actions
to break the silence of this gathering
and give our group its genesis.
Strangers to each other,
and to ourselves at times,
we slowly move into awareness
of our own uniqueness
coupled with impressions
of the specialness of others.*

*From "Beginnings" © 1993 by Samuel T.
Gladding. Reprinted by permission from
Samuel T. Gladding.*

CHAPTER OVERVIEW

From reading this chapter, you will learn about

- Steps in the forming stage of a group
- Tasks and problems at the beginning stage of a group
- Useful procedures for the beginning stage of a group

AS YOU READ, CONSIDER

- How you usually feel when you are beginning something new
- How you feel about following rules in a group setting and how you react to those who do not
- What behaviors of someone else make you feel welcome and what actions put you off

Twyla Tharp, as a dance choreographer, is famous for interviewing many more dancers than she needs for any of her productions. However, her list of awards, including a Mac-Arthur Fellowship, a Tony, and numerous honorary degrees, far surpasses her peers. She has the tenacity and ability to selectively choose individuals who will perform at extremely high levels individually and within a group to make her productions most memorable. It is Tharp's contention that effort spent in forming a dance assembly is crucial if the group is going to function at the highest level.

Tharp's ideas about the importance of being careful in forming a dance assemblage is applicable to the beginning and ultimate outcome of any group. The reason is that groups either develop in healthy ways or end up in disarray. Understanding how to begin and nurture a group significantly improves the chances that the goals of the group and its members will be achieved and chaos will be avoided.

Almost all functional groups go through developmental stages. More than 100 models of group development exist, but the generally agreed-on number of stages in their evolution is between four and five, with Tuckman and Jensen's (1977) five-stage model—*forming, storming, norming, performing,* and *adjourning*—being the most widely recognized (M. Young, 2013). Similar to the Tuckman and Jensen models are those by Kormanski and Mozenter (1987), who state that groups develop out of **awareness** and then move on to *conflict, cooperation, productivity,* and finally *separation,* and Trotzer (2007), who conceptualizes groups as moving through the stages of *security, acceptance, responsibility, work,* and *closing.* Ward (1982) characterizes group stages in a four-part sequence as *power, cohesiveness, working,* and *termination,* and Gazda (1989) does the same in including the stages of *exploration, transition, action,* and *termination.* I describe a four-stage process as well—*formation/orientation, transitioning* (storming and norming), *performing/working,* and *mourning/closing.* On the outskirts of this stage norm is Yalom (Yalom & Leszcz, 2005) with three stages—*orientation, conflict,* and *cohesiveness*—and Corey (2012) with six stages: *formation, orientation, transition, working, consolidation,* and *follow-up/evaluation.*

Not all theorists agree that stages do or must exist in groups, at least in a progressive fashion (Yalom & Leszcz, 2005). However, developmental stages have been identified in learning groups (e.g., Lacoursiere, 1974, 1980), therapy groups (e.g., Brabender, 1985), and training groups (e.g., Dunphy, 1968). More recently, Yoon and Johnson (2008) have identified seven stages in virtual learning teams: orientation, scheduling, exploration, work and decision, progress check and evaluation, refinement and formatting, and termination.

Regardless of how many stages there are in group development, the beginning stage is an important and usually a multidimensional event. The most obvious beginning of a group is when group members and leaders assemble for the first session. However, before the initial meeting, many processes have already been completed—for example, formulating the idea for the group, screening members, and selecting preliminary individual and group goals. Even after the group meets initially, it continues to evolve and can be conceptualized as forever forming, with certain issues returning from time to time to be explored in greater depth—the so-called **cyclotherapy process**. Some of the issues with which groups continually struggle are anxiety, power, norms, inclusion, identity, interpersonal relationships, and personal growth (Cohen & Smith, 1976; Ivers & Newsome, 2011; Kormanski, 1999).

The focus of this chapter is on what is considered to be the **forming, or orientation, stage of the group**, which is a time of initial caution associated with any new experience. Personal relations are characterized by dependence, and group members attempt to be accepted and safe by trying to keep things simple and free of controversy so they can avoid being rejected by others, the leader, or even themselves. This feature of the group is particularly strong in counseling or psychotherapy groups in which individuals do not know each other well, but it can also be part of task/work and even psychoeducational groups where members have a common shared history. Regardless, discussions are usually superficial during forming, centering around historic or future events that do not have a direct impact on the group or its members.

Stages/Transitions of Group Development according to Eight Group Experts

Group experts	Stage/Transitions
Tuckman & Jenson	1) Forming 2) Storming 3) Norming 4) Performing 5) Adjourning
Kormanski & Mozenter	1) Awareness 2) Conflict 3) Cooperation 4) Productivity 5) Separation
Trotzer	1) Security 2) Acceptance 3) Responsibility 4) Work 5) Closing
Ward	1) Power 2) Cohesiveness 3) Working 4) Termination
Gazda	1) Exploration 2) Transition 3) Action 4) Termination
Gladding	1) Formation 2) Transition 3) Performing 4) Closing
Yalom	1) Orientation 2) Conflict 3) Cohesiveness
Corey	1) Formation 2) Orientation 3) Transition 4) Working 5) Consolidation 6) Evaluation

Reflection

What is your typical behavior when meeting someone new? Is the behavior different when you are with friends in a group or by yourself? Would you like your initial behaviors on meeting someone new to change? If so, how would they change? If not, why not?

STEPS IN THE FORMING STAGE

Forming is a process that involves several steps. Although some of these steps may be completed concurrently, none may be skipped if the group is going to form properly and prosper. Group workers are wise to consult such documents as the Association for Specialists in Group Work's (ASGW) *Best Practice Guidelines* (Thomas & Pender, 2008) if they want to have successful groups and work within appropriate ethical and professional standards.

Step 1: Developing a Rationale for the Group

A group begins conceptually with the generation of ideas. Behind every successful group is a *rationale* for its existence. The more carefully the reasons for conducting a group are considered, the more likely it is that there will be positive responses and outcomes. Therefore, a clear rationale and focus are of uppermost importance in planning. Group leaders who are unclear about their purpose will end up being nonproductive at best and possibly harmful.

For example, school counselors may wish to make sure that all members of a sixth-grade class learn appropriate ways of interacting with the opposite sex. One counselor decides to run a series of psychoeducational groups with the sixth-grade students based on the rationale that students first need knowledge before they can act properly. This counselor plans a sequential series of interactive presentations. Another counselor at the same school does not think through the process and impulsively decides to conduct counseling groups with the sixth graders to deal with this same topic. There is no rationale for such groups. They are ill suited for children who have not expressed a concern about this subject, and they take considerable time to conduct. The outcome of the two groups would vary greatly because of the initial thought processes in the planning of each.

Step 2: Deciding on a Theoretical Format

In addition to developing a rationale for which type of group to conduct, group workers must consider the theoretical format from which they will work. Some group leaders pretend not to work from a theoretical basis, claiming they will let their groups decide how to develop. Yet even this type of purported atheoretical stance is really a theoretical statement about how the leader thinks and conducts a group.

Ward (1982, 1985) notes that each major theory of group work has limitations and strengths. Leaders who are most aware of these areas before groups begin can choose a format appropriate for their group even if it is **eclectic** (a composite of theoretical approaches). All groups deal with individual, interpersonal, and group foci. Thus, a theoretical format should function on intrapersonal, interpersonal, and extrapersonal matters, but in varying degrees. The theoretical base of the group should match the needs of participants and the group as a whole.

Waldo (1985) has conceptually described levels of functioning in a group as **I/We/It**. His thoughts parallel Hulse-Killacky's ideas concerning process and content. "I" is the individual, intrapersonal focus on beliefs, attitudes, and feelings; "We" is the interpersonal dimension, or the relationship among group members; and "It" is the extrapersonal emphasis on issues, tasks, or group concerns. Leaders who wish to facilitate interpersonal ("We") development of members might choose a theoretical format that promotes this process, such as a person-centered counseling group, whereas those emphasizing individual ("I") development might plan to employ an active psychoeducational group. Regardless of the approach chosen, planning for a group must consider that groups contain many variables, among them people, processes, and products. "Group work is challenging and complex because groups are complex" (Ward, 1985, p. 59).

Case Example

Joan and the Sound of Silence

Joan has seen a need in her school to address bullying. She wants to run an interpersonal group based on person-centered theory. She also wants to have the group focus on prevention and be developmental. Joan thinks it would be best to start her group with the younger children first. She assembles first graders, whom she screened to select those who are most passive and the least likely to complain about being picked on. However, during the first session of the group she is frustrated because no one talks about themselves or their feelings. Although Joan has good intentions, she has overlooked the fact that a homogeneous group of shy kids is not one that is likely to be verbal, especially using a person-centered approach.

Questions

What would you suggest she do? When? How? Why?

Step 3: Weighing Practical Considerations

After a clear, convincing rationale and theoretical format have been determined, group proposals should stress specific, concrete, and practical objectives and procedures. Considerations such as meeting time, place, and frequency cannot be overlooked if the group is to be successful (Jacobs, Schimmel, Masson, & Harvill, 2016). Group leaders must be sensitive to political and practical realities as well. Some good group ideas never get implemented because colleagues fear, misunderstand, or disapprove of the group leader's plans. For example, a high school guidance group focusing on understanding human immunodeficiency virus/acquired immunodeficiency syndrome (HIV/AIDS) might be prohibited or canceled if the principal of the school thinks sexuality is the group's main agenda item. In a case like this, the group leader should first thoroughly brief the principal and then the parents of the teens on the emphasis of the group in order to prevent a negative reaction.

Case Example

Careful Candace

At the beginning of the school year, Candace sent out a needs survey to her 10th-grade students. She found that one area a majority of them wanted more information on was on the impact of over-the-counter drugs on health. Rather than start a group on "Drugs 101," Candace talked to her principal about the survey results and then sent an e-mail to her students and their parents. She followed this communication up by gaining permission from her administration to conduct a psychoeducational group on over-the-counter drugs and then explain-

ing to the PTA what she had in mind. Before recruiting group members, she sent out another e-mail to the 10th-grade class and their parents informing them about what she planned to do and how and inviting their questions and comments. When she did recruit and conduct the group, no one seemed upset, and the group went well.

Questions

What did Candace do to make sure her group would not be controversial? What else do you think Candace could or should have done?

Overall, the setting in which the leader works will influence the formulation of a group proposal. For instance, an employee assistant professional might propose an adjustment group for recent retirees in a community center, whereas a college counselor might focus on offering a series of guidance presentations on careers in the student university center. Counselors and therapists in private practice will generally have more flexibility and fewer administrative procedures than those who work in the public domain. However, institutions do not protect private practitioners who conduct groups. Therefore, private practitioners must be as careful and meticulous as other group practitioners in their proposals. A partial secret of success in all cases is detailed preparation. A good model that reflects adequate preparation is a proposal that includes the broad range of information presented in Figure 4.1. This model can be adapted to meet the needs of group leaders interested in serving other populations.

Step 4: Publicizing the Group

Corey, Corey, and Corey (2014) note that how a group is announced influences both the ways it will be received by potential members and the kind of people who will join. Some of the best ways of announcing the formation of a group are through word of mouth with professional

Proposal for a group

I. Type of Group

This will be a (task/work, psychoeducational, counseling, psychotherapy) group for people between the ages of (_____ and _____) or with the following interests or aspirations: (_____). The group will specifically focus on _____. It will not concentrate on _____. The group will meet for a (limited, unlimited) time starting with a meeting on (fill in specific date, length of meeting, and place).

During the initial session, the leader will give specific suggestions to participants in getting the most from their group experience.

The fee (if any) for this group will be _____.

II. Rationale, Goals, and Objectives

The rationale for conducting this type of group is as follows:

1.
2.
3.

Goals and objectives for the group are as follows:

1.
2.
3.

III. Rights and Expectations of Group Members

Group members have rights as well as responsibilities. It is expected that group members will be active participants. However, members will decide at what level they participate, how much they reveal about themselves, and when they wish to share information. Ethical guidelines of _____ will be followed.

IV. Group Leader

Name(s) of the group leader(s), degrees, professional and personal backgrounds and experiences, qualifications for leading groups, and other pertinent information.

V. Basic Ground Rules

To obtain the most from the group, members will be asked to suggest ways of conducting it. However, these generic rules will be followed:

1.
2.
3.

VI. Topics for the Group

Certain topics will be given emphasis, but group members will have the opportunity to discuss the aspects of those topics that are most meaningful to them. Following is a sample of some possible topics for the group to explore. Other topics of concern to group participants can be developed.

1.
2.
3.

FIGURE 4.1 Checklist of specific issues on content.

colleagues, personal contact with potential members, and written announcements to a targeted audience. There are advantages and disadvantages to each of these ways of **publicizing a group**. For example, announcing the formation of a group through word of mouth to professional colleagues may personalize the information but fail to reach a large number of individuals who might wish to participate. The same is true if a group leader simply contacts those he or she thinks might benefit from the experience. Written announcements to selected audiences are likely to reach the most people, but they may not be clear enough to specify who should be a member of the group. Therefore, some persons who are not suited for the group may apply, or too many persons may apply, requiring the group leader to spend a large amount of time screening them.

The *Best Practice Guidelines* published by the ASGW (Thomas & Pender, 2008) is a definitive and comprehensive document that provides guidance on the proper conduct expected of those who lead groups, including preparation procedures. Professional group workers have also focused on specific issues regarding content that should be addressed. Among the best of these checklists is one by Tollerud, Holling, and Dustin (1992). Another checklist on specific issues regarding content is found in Figure 4.1.

Step 5: Screening and Pretraining

The maturity, readiness, and composition of membership play a major role in determining the success of a group (Riva, Lippert, & Tackett, 2000). Therefore, potential group members should be **screened** (interviewed either individually or in a group before the group's first meeting in regard to their suitability for the group) and carefully chosen whenever possible (Riva & Lange, 2014). Exceptions to selecting members are likely to occur in some psychoeducational and task/work groups. In the pregroup screening process, the leader must address potential group members' readiness to be in a group and their goals (MacNair-Semands, 1998).

Most experts in the group field endorse either an **individually conducted pregroup screening procedure** or a **group-conducted pregroup screening process** (Conyne & Diederich, 2014; Rapin & Crowell, 2014). Both formats are essentially intake interviews—ways of determining who should join a particular group and who should not. In pregroup screening sessions, the group leader and potential members can interview each other about different aspects of the group process and themselves. The group leader may ask a number of questions of potential group members during the screening, but queries that are open ended and elicit personal responses and interpersonal styles seem to work best (Gladding, 1994a; Riva et al., 2000). For example, a prospective member of a group might be asked: (a) "What has been your past experience with groups?" (b) "What has led you to want to be a part of this group?" (c) "What can you contribute to this group?" and (d) "How do you express your emotions, especially your negative ones?"

In the pregroup screening process, the group leader must determine the level of interpersonal behavior or comfort with others that potential group members have. Such a determination is "essential to groups that focus primarily on group interaction and group process" (Riva et al., 2000, p. 167). The goal is to determine whether a particular group is right for a particular person at a specific time. Through screening members, premature termination is avoided, while goals and processes involved with the group are clarified, and members are empowered to take an active part in the group.

According to Couch (1995), there are a number of interdependent steps necessary for conducting an effective pregroup screening interview:

1. *Identify needs, expectations, and commitment*—Of these factors, commitment is considered the most crucial. Thus, the group leader might ask: "Since there are a number of group

experiences from which you could choose, why do you particularly want to be in this group? What do you want to get out of it?"

2. ***Challenge myths and misconceptions***—It is crucial that potential members have accurate information and not misinformation like that sometimes given on television or in the movies (Childers & Couch, 1989). Some of the common misunderstandings about groups, especially counseling and psychotherapy groups, include "groups are for sick people," "groups are artificial," and "groups force people to lose their identity." The group leader might help in clarifying this matter by asking a potential member: "How do you perceive this group developing? What are your concerns in being a member of it?"

3. ***Convey information***—The nature and limits of confidentiality are particularly helpful to communicate, but group stages, roles, and the importance of balancing content and process may be quite useful to explain as well. To address this matter, the group leader might simply talk about the length of the group, what might occur, and the importance of a member paying attention to nonverbal as well as verbal interactions.

The uniqueness of school environments may make the pregroup screening process distinct for school counselors who lead groups. These group workers may concentrate on developmental issues when interviewing potential members. They may also form groups based on program goals and student standards (Hines & Fields, 2002). Written parental consent for children under 18 to participate in a group is needed as well.

One way, other than screening, to ensure that members are ready for the group is through **pretraining** (orienting group members on what to expect of the group before it ever meets). "Such an investment should enhance the functioning of the group, speed its work, reduce dropouts, and increase the positive outcomes" (Zimpfer, 1991, p. 264). Pretraining has been positively associated with cohesion, member satisfaction, and comfort with the group (Burlingame, Fuhriman, & Johnson, 2004). Pretraining can be done on an individual or a group basis. When it is conducted individually, the possibility always exists that a leader will accidentally leave out some vital details about the group. The advantage of an individual process, however, is that the rapport between the member and the leader may increase. A group session, in contrast, is a more uniform, although less personalized, way of pretraining. Such a session focuses on topics that might be explored in the group and gives members an opportunity to assess whether they wish to invest themselves in this particular group. It also gives the leader an opportunity to see how potential members of the group interact in a group setting. Group pretraining is not required; however, the more thoroughly prepared potential members and the group leader are, the more likely it is that the dropout rate will be low, the communication clear, and the cohesion of the group as a whole great (DeRoma, Root, & Battle, 2003; Yalom & Leszcz, 2005).

An example of pretraining illustrates its essence. In a group that is voluntary and therapeutic, potential members should be informed of which techniques and procedures will be used, the qualifications of the leader, fees (if any), types of records kept, member responsibility, personal risks involved, and the types of services that can realistically be provided (ASGW, 2007). They may be shown clips of selected group videos, such as those created by Irvin Yalom, Rex Stockton, Gerald Corey, or Peg Carroll. Their questions about the group should be answered as well.

When the group leader is unsure about how specific to be, it is better to err on the side of caution and give group members a thorough explanation of group and administrative procedures. In no case should the leader make promises or guarantees. Facts concerning the formation and procedure of a group are preferably put in writing.

Step 6: Selecting Group Members

The selection of group members is usually a two-way process. Exceptions occur in some psycho-educational groups, in which material is presented to a captive audience, such as in schools or the armed forces, and in task/work groups, such as in businesses, where individuals are grouped with one another because they work in the same office. When potential group members and the leader are mutually involved in the selection process, both have input into deciding who will be included or excluded.

People who are invited to join the group should be individuals who are likely to benefit from the experience. Essentially, they should be those who have specific goals in mind, who have allayed their fears of what a group might do, and who feel comfortable in their roles and sensitive to their surroundings.

Individuals who do not appear likely to contribute to the growth of the group or who lack personal maturity are prime candidates for exclusion from it. Such persons include those who are extremely hostile, self-centered, unmotivated, crisis oriented, or mentally unbalanced, as well as those who are unable or unwilling to self-disclose, express feelings, or tolerate anxiety (Corey, 2012; Riva et al., 2000). Other individuals who may be excluded from a particular group are those who are either too different or too similar to other potential group members. Many of these individuals may benefit from personal one-to-one counseling.

Members of extremely heterogeneous groups may not relate well to each other and may experience a good deal of interpersonal conflict (Melnick & Wood, 1976); members of extremely homogeneous groups, in contrast, may relate too well, may not work hard on individual or group tasks, and may stay on a superficial level. Over time, heterogeneous groups may be most effective for intensive group therapy procedures in which the emphasis is on personality change (Kellerman, 1979), whereas homogeneous groups may be most appropriate for individuals who need support or have more focused problems, such as solving a dilemma on a job-related task. Clearly, both advantages and disadvantages are inherent in heterogeneous and homogeneous groups.

A potential group member should never be coerced to join a group. Likewise, if a potential group member and the group leader determine that group work "does not show promise as a source of help," then the group leader should work with the interviewee in looking for other sources of assistance (Ohlsen, Horne, & Lawe, 1988, p. 37).

Case Example

Savage Sue

Henry had one spot open in a counseling group he was forming at his agency for adults in midlife. The group was heterogeneous, and Henry thought that Sue, a mid-40s White woman, would be a good fit for the group. When he broached the subject of the group with her, Sue declined. Undeterred, Henry persisted and finally got Sue to join by telling her that if she did not, the group would fail and that the other group members really needed the experience.

The group turned out to be a bad experience for everyone involved. Sue did not show up half the time, and when she did come, she was passive-aggressive. Henry really got mad toward the end of the group and blasted Sue for her behavior. Her response was: "Well, I told you I did not want to be a part of the group in the first place."

Questions

Put yourself in Henry's shoes. What would you do now? What would you do the next time you start to form a group?

Step 7: Selecting a Group Leader

Certain qualities distinguish an effective group leader. Some of these have been discussed previously and will not be reiterated here. The selection of a leader by a potential group member is emphasized because the selection process hinges partly on professional qualities and partly on personal qualities. It is easier to deal with professional issues because, in the pregroup screening procedure, the potential group member can and should ask about the group leader's qualifications. The group leader can voluntarily offer information about his or her educational preparation and experience in conducting groups. Such professional disclosure is considered a must at this point in group formation.

Personal information about the group leader's style in sessions is also important (Trotzer, 2007). The leader's style may incorporate humor, self-disclosure, confrontation, or other helping modalities. The leader's style and personality are important aspects of the group for the potential member to consider. If the potential group member does not think that the group leader is one with whom he or she can comfortably work, then it is best to find another group to join.

TASKS OF THE BEGINNING GROUP

Group leaders and members have varied tasks to accomplish during the first sessions of a group, including these: (a) dealing with apprehension, (b) reviewing members' goals and contracts, (c) specifying more clearly or reiterating group rules, (d) setting limits, and (e) promoting a positive interchange among members so they will want to continue (Weiner, 1984). Failure to accomplish any of these tasks may result in the group not functioning properly. Each of these tasks is examined individually.

Dealing with Apprehension

Apprehension is synonymous with anxiety. Too much or too little anxiety inhibits the performance of the group and its members (Yalom & Leszcz, 2005). Therefore, it is appropriate that group members and leaders have a moderate amount of apprehension when they begin a group. It helps them key in on what they are experiencing and what they want to do. Apprehension differs in psychotherapeutic and psychoeducational groups, in which there is an individual focus to the apprehension, and task/work groups, in which there is a group focus to the apprehension. For example, in a therapy group, Ellen may be anxious about whether others will see her as capable, whereas in a task group, she may be anxious about whether the group can perform its assignment.

It is helpful, and sometimes necessary, after each group session for group leaders to deal with any misunderstandings that may have arisen because of anxiety. For example, if James is berating himself in front of his counseling group for being defensive when asked a question about his attitudes toward race, then the leader may say, "James, I hear you are concerned about two aspects related to the question Jan asked you about race. One is your verbal answer; the other, your failure to live up to your own expectations. I wonder what feelings got in the way of your handling of Jan's question." Such an observation and invitation give James a chance to deal with his emotions, especially his apprehension about saying the right words and being perfect. By clarifying what has happened, James and the group as a whole are able to move on.

Reviewing Goals and Contracts

Goals are specific objectives that an individual or the group wishes to accomplish. Group goals are announced at the time a group proposal is formulated and again during the pregroup interview.

As a member of this group, I, John Smith, make this contract to achieve the following goals.			
What (i.e., goal)	*How*	*When*	*Where*
(1) share my thoughts	verbal	each session	in group
	verbal	each day	home
	verbal	each class	school
(2) eat healthy	choice	each meal	everywhere
(3) exercise	discipline	each day	home
(4) control anger	choice	each time	home
	choice	each time	in group

John Smith
signature

January 31, 2001
date

FIGURE 4.2 Sample contract on goals for an individual group member.

Group members should keep these objectives in mind throughout the group process. Likewise, individual goals are worked out in the pregroup screening session and are consistent with the group's overall goals. In counseling, psychoeducation, and task/work groups, such goals may have a universal quality about them—for example, understanding careers. In psychotherapy groups, especially with individuals in severe distress, the goals and contracts may vary widely. For example, such groups may contain members who are trying to resolve grief as well as those who are attempting to overcome depression.

A thorough way of clarifying group and individual goals is to have the group leader restate the purpose of the group during the first session and have each member elaborate on his or her goals. In some cases and with some theories (e.g., Gestalt, transactional analysis), members are asked to formulate a **contract** (an agreement of what will be done and when) (Corey, 2012; Donigian & Hulse-Killacky, 1999). A written contract helps members specify what, how, when, and where they will work to make changes related to their goals (see Figure 4.2).

However, as important as it is to formulate and verbalize goals, "simply asking members to write about their group or asking members to write specific goals prior to the beginning group are not sufficient to influence group process, perceptions of involvement, or ability to give feedback significantly" (Bridbord, DeLucia-Waack, Jones, & Gerrity, 2004, p. 301). It is in the verbalization and feedback interaction that goals tend to be clarified and strengthened.

Reflection

When have you had a goal that you did not openly discuss with someone? What happened to that goal? Was it clear? Did you achieve it? How important do you think it is to write goals down and keep them in a place where you can see them?

Specifying Group Rules

Rules are the guidelines by which groups are run. They are established both before and during the group process. In pregroup screening sessions, leaders take the initiative in setting up rules. For example, most groups have rules set by the leader, such as no physical violence, no drugs, and attendance at all meetings. Rules should be stated in a positive rather than a negative way; thus,

"No physical violence" is better expressed as "Members will respect the physical and psychological space of others at all times."

During the first session of the group and afterward, members make contributions to rules by which the group will abide, for example, "Smoking will be permitted outside the group room but not during the group session." It is important to formulate a rationale behind every group rule rather than to set rules in an arbitrary and "thou shalt not" manner that invites violations and game playing (Yalom & Leszcz, 2005).

One rule that is usually agreed to, but difficult to enforce, is **confidentiality**—the explicit agreement that what is said in the group will stay in the group. It should be noted here that confidentiality is the "ethical cornerstone" of group counseling and psychotherapy (Plotkin, 1978). It is also a valued component of many task/work and psychoeducational groups, for it is "a prerequisite for the development of group trust, cohesion, and productive work" (Gazda, 1989, p. 303). However, confidentiality is sometimes violated, either intentionally or unintentionally. At the beginning of the group, members and leaders should review possible ways that confidentiality might be violated, including revealing identification information about group members or talking about group interactions outside of the group.

Leaders need to be sure of their responsibilities regarding confidentiality—for example, protecting group members' files or computer records and erasing or destroying audio and video recordings after they have been used to critique group progress. Leaders often take responsibility for keeping confidences by reviewing group codes of ethics and legal precedents. They usually do so outside the presence of the group. However, the extent to which leaders go to maintain confidence may be productively discussed in the group, especially if members raise issues pertaining to it.

When breaches of confidentiality occur, they disrupt the functioning of the group and promote distrust among members. Therefore, it is crucial that group rules or procedures be in place to deal with such possibilities. The group that can agree in the initial session on the nature of rules and the consequences for breaking them is ahead of the group that bypasses this procedure.

Setting Limits

Limits are the outer boundaries of a group in regard to behaviors that will be accepted within the group. Limits are set both explicitly and implicitly in group settings. Explicitly, they take the form of rules regarding acceptable behaviors and procedures related to time (Napier & Gershenfeld, 2004). When members violate an explicit limit, the group corrects them. For example, if Kathy tells Connie what Louise said in confidence in a group counseling session, then Kathy may be dismissed from the group, asked to apologize to Louise, or taken to task by members about the seriousness of what she did.

Implicit limits are more subtle and involve such actions as the attention of the leader to a particular member or the verbal reinforcement or discouragement of certain content topics. For example, the leader may instruct group members who ramble on about their families: "Keep your comments about past family matters brief and to the point so the group can help you." The leader may also use eye contact to encourage or suppress dialogue. Skilled group leaders use their power of facilitating and setting limits in both direct and indirect ways.

Promoting a Positive Interchange Among Members

Promoting a positive interchange among members of a group is initially the task of the group leader. If positive interchanges among group members can be facilitated, then group members will begin to share openly with one another, and the group atmosphere will be enhanced.

The leader can establish a positive tone by (a) being enthusiastic, (b) drawing out members, (c) holding the focus on interesting topics, (d) shifting the focus when the topics are irrelevant or interesting to only a couple of members, and (e) cutting off any hostile or negative interactions (Jacobs et al., 2016). The leader can also set a positive tone by emphasizing similarities among members so that everyone feels included and a part of the group (Ward & Ward, 2014). If such a productive tone is not created, then group members may drop out, close up, or attack each other.

Another way to promote a positive interchange within the group is to use **interactive journal writing**. In this process, members keep logs of their thoughts, feelings, impressions, and behaviors within a group and exchange them in all directions—members to leaders, members to members, and leader to members (Parr, Haberstroh, & Kottler, 2000). When conducted so that members are well prepared for it, this type of process may promote group cohesiveness, trust, altruism, catharsis, hope, and self-understanding. It can be used in all stages of a group.

Reflection

What is your reaction to someone responding to you positively as opposed to responding to you negatively? How similar or different do you think your reactions are to those of most people you know? How do you think a negative tone would influence the work of a group?

RESOLVING POTENTIAL GROUP PROBLEMS IN FORMING

A number of problems can occur during the formation of a group and afterward. Some of these difficulties involve people; others are related to procedures. One of the best ways to handle potential group problems is to prevent them. Prevention involves following the steps for forming the group already mentioned in this chapter. When prevention is not possible, the leader and group can work to bring about resolution. Member interaction patterns that are particularly troublesome are addressed first in this section, then initial group procedures.

People Problems

Despite careful screening, some group members display difficult behaviors early in the group process. Those who cause the most concern, especially in counseling groups, are individuals in the group who monopolize, withdraw, intimidate, verbally ventilate, focus on others, seduce, or show intolerance (Edelwich & Brodsky, 1992). **Subgroups** (cliques of members who band together) may also be troublesome. Sometimes, group leaders will become too involved in the content of what is being expressed in the group and not notice interactional patterns. By concentrating on the styles of different group members, however, leaders are better able to plan and lead future sessions. Seven common membership roles often displayed during the first session are covered here, along with the problem of subgroups. In dealing with people problems, group leaders are advised to avoid labeling individuals. The tendency that goes with labels is to stereotype individuals and to perceive situations as falling within a certain behavioral range (Kline, 1990).

MANIPULATORS

Members who are **manipulators** are characterized by their subtle and not-so-subtle use of feelings and behaviors to get what they want. Often they are angry and bring into the group unresolved life problems centering on control. For example, Jose, in his manipulator role, may say to the group, "If you're not going to give me what I want, then I'm leaving this group."

Reframing, conceptualizing potentially destructive acts in a positive way, may help manipulative individuals. For example, the leader may say to Leonardo after he has falsely and vigorously accused the group of breaking confidentiality, "Sounds like what you want from this group is specific help in learning how to trust them." The group leader or members may also intervene by blocking manipulating actions, such as threatening or pleading. At the beginning of a group, manipulators will often struggle with group leaders for control. They should not be allowed to usurp the leader's function, or the group will fail.

RESISTERS

Resisters are often angry or frustrated and bring these feelings with them to the group. They do not participate in group exercises or tasks and act as barriers to helping the group form. For example, Brandy may say to the group, "I don't see any sense in telling you how I feel. That won't really help me."

Leaders can help resistant group members build trust in the group by inviting them to participate but not insisting that they do. This is an affirmation approach and allows resisters and leaders a chance to explore this behavior later (Larrabee, 1982). A second way of working with these individuals is to confront and interpret in a reflective manner what is happening with them (Vriend & Dyer, 1973). For instance, in the previous example, a group leader may say to Brandy, "I hear you have been disappointed with the groups in which you have previously participated. They have not been very productive for you." Often the feelings of resistant members are dealt with best in the working stage of the group.

MONOPOLIZERS

People who are **monopolizers** dominate the conversation in a group and do not allow other members a chance to verbally participate. Monopolizers initially offer group members relief because they focus attention on themselves and away from everyone else. These individuals are dealing with underlying anxiety but often become sources of irritation for other group members. One soliloquy does not a monopolizer make, so anxious members should not be characterized as exhibitors of this behavior too early. At the same time, members who display this pattern from the beginning need the help of the leader and other members to realize how certain behaviors hurt their interpersonal relationships and which other actions they could take to improve them. The sooner the nonproductive talk of the monopolist is addressed, the more productive an outcome can be reached. The technique of cutting off, highlighted later in this chapter, is an excellent way to deal with monopolists.

SILENT MEMBERS

Silent members may or may not become involved with the group. Sometimes, silence is used to cover hostility (Ormont, 1984) . . . and sometimes not. Members who are silent are often nonassertive, reflective, shy, or just slow in assessing their thoughts and feelings. The best way to determine the meaning of silence is to give a person a chance to respond to a question and to notice what happens. A simple question such as "What do you think about what other group members have been saying?" is often enough to draw a silent member out.

Acceptance of silence by the group leader and the creation of opportunities by the leader for silent members to become more involved usually rectify any negative impact that may be associated with these individuals or this behavior. If a group member remains silent throughout the group experience, then he or she will probably not get as much from the process as more active members (Conyne & Silver, 1980).

USERS OF SARCASM

Persons who express themselves through **sarcasm** differ from those who are outwardly angry. **Users of sarcasm** mask their feelings through the use of clever language that has a biting humor. For instance, the sarcastic member may say, "Oh, joy, now I get to tell you about how I feel. Isn't that just thrilling!"

The group leader can help the sarcastic member work on expressing anger directly. This skill is accomplished by identifying what is happening in the group member's life and by having the group member explore what the behavior means for him or her both now and where it was learned. The leader may also invite other group members to give the sarcastic member feedback on how they respond to sarcastic ways of relating.

Case Example

Irksome Erika

Erika entered the psychotherapy group because she was unhappy with her life. She thought it would be easy to change, but after 4 weeks she became skeptical. She expressed her feelings through belittling others. For example, she would say: "Oh, my god, has Cora gotten cold feet?" or "Oscar, aren't you filled with confidence today! I can just see it oozing out of your skin."

When Erika did not stop these kinds of remarks, the group jumped in to confront her. For instance, Blanche told Erika: "I don't think your comments are helpful to you, the group, or the person you are addressing them to. They just have a bitter flavor about them."

Although Erika did not change quickly, she did begin to soften her tone.

Questions

What might you have said to help Erika? What else might have been helpful to her besides words?

DIAGNOSTIC ANALYZERS

Individuals who have a passing knowledge of psychology or mental illness may attempt to diagnose or explain other group members' problems in clinical terms. These people get caught up in thinking that everyone in the group has a deep-seated problem that can and should be explained by using the *Diagnostic and Statistical Manual* (DSM). Their belief is that once an explanation of a behavior is given, group members will act differently. Thus, diagnostic analyzers are quick to provide cures and an abundance of answers and explanations to others. They focus on solving other people's problems.

The group leader can help counter this tendency and assist the diagnostic analyzer by pointing out that everyone has difficulties and that only those with extreme troubles are diagnosed by DSM standards. More importantly, the leader can assist the analyzer by having this group member focus on what he or she would like to get out of or take away from the group. This type of personal gain and centering can aid the analyzer in realizing that he or she has more to get from the group than is possible by concentrating on others.

FOCUSERS ON OTHERS

This final category of behavior involves **focusers on others**—those who become self-appointed group "assistant leaders" by questioning others, offering advice, and acting as if they did not have any problems. These individuals are often challenged by group members and can be helped to overcome this other-focused behavior by being taught that self-disclosure is more helpful to most people than a style devoid of personal involvement. They may also be given permission during this stage of the group to make wishes for themselves. For instance, the leader may ask, "Latoya, if you could have some new traits for yourself, what would they be?" In essence, other-focused group members must be helped to realize the value of becoming personally committed to the group.

Overall, it is important that group members be given time to express themselves and not be labeled or stereotyped early in the group process. Leaders must trust their feelings and reactions in regard to difficult group members. In some instances, a difficult group member may have to be removed from the group, but this measure is a last-resort strategy (Kline, 1990). Such a process creates anxiety in other members about whether they might also be removed. Before ever taking such a step, the leader needs to try to help the group help itself by working through thoughts and feelings about certain behaviors. Allowing group members to give and receive feedback enables them to obtain insight and change the troublesome and disruptive behavior. In short, "the presence of 'problem members' is a golden opportunity to facilitate group development and move the group to greater levels of intimacy and heightened functioning" (Kline, 1997, p. 95).

SUBGROUPS

Group leaders may help prevent the formation of subgroups by focusing on the uniqueness of each individual and his or her connectedness with the group as a whole. Leaders may discourage the formation of subgroups by making their expectations known in regard to such groups in the screening interview, pregroup training, and the initial group session. When subgroups do develop, however, they must be dealt with directly, or they may have a deleterious effect on group member interaction. Trotzer (2007) describes three ways of handling subgroup behavior (in addition to prevention):

1. "Bring all coalescing, colluding, and subgrouping behavior that occurs in the group to the group's attention." For example, point out that John, Jim, and Mary seem to be acting as a team on their own and not with the other members of the group.
2. "Establish a guideline and expectation that the group be informed about extra group activities among members." In such a case, one of the group rules can be that all meetings of group members outside the regular schedule of the group be reported to the group at large before sessions begin.
3. "As a group leader, do not collude with subgroups overtly or covertly by not disclosing what you perceive and/or know about the subgroup." If a group leader remains silent on realizing that a subgroup has formed, he or she is hurting the group as a whole. Speaking out may risk alienating members of the subgroup for a while, but not doing so poses an even greater risk of losing the group as a whole.

Group Procedural Problems

Both the group leader and members often feel anxiety, awkwardness, and anticipation at the beginning of an initial group session. Because every group is different, even veterans of group experiences may feel some apprehension. Most group members will try to put on their best behavior and be friendly and positive, but potential problems may arise at certain points. The best way to deal with these areas is to prevent them from developing. However, corrective measures may need to be taken.

OPENING THE GROUP

Beginning the first group session is often a difficult experience, especially for the novice leader. It is what Donigian and Hulse-Killacky (1999) describe as a **critical incident in the life of the group** (an event that has the power to shape or influence the group positively or negatively). How it is handled can make a major difference in what happens later in the group. Some practitioners, such as Coulson (1972, 1974), choose to begin a group in silence, but most group leaders are more structured. Sufficient structure at the beginning of a group helps members become less anxious and not be overwhelmed by the group process (Marmarosh, Dunton, & Amendola, 2014). Group leaders have general openings, or leads, at their command, such as "Let's get started" or "It is time to begin" (Carroll, Bates, & Johnson, 2004). These openings signal to the members that the group is beginning and focus attention on what is about to occur.

Along with these general leads, several other options are available for beginning the first group session. Jacobs et al. (2016) suggest eight different ways. Each is dependent on the style of the leader and the purpose of the group.

1. "Start with an opening statement about the group; then conduct an introduction exercise." This type of procedure is usually employed with psychoeducational or task/work groups, although it may be used in therapeutic groups. It involves the leader taking about 5 minutes to describe the format and purpose of the group and introduce himself or herself, followed by a brief exercise, such as members introducing themselves.
2. "Start with a long opening statement; then get right into the content of the group." In this style, which is often used in educational and task groups, the leader begins by giving members an explanation of the group's content or purpose. He or she then quickly gets group members involved in the group without introducing them to each other because either the group is too large or members already know one another.
3. "Start with a long opening statement about the group and its purpose; then conduct an introduction exercise." This procedure is used when the group's focus is educational or task based. In the long opening statement, the leader reminds group members of their purpose and then helps the group get down to business by describing what the group is going to do. This option works best when the information given is interesting and informative. A mistake that may be made is for the leader to talk too long—for example, over 15 minutes.
4. "Start with a brief statement about the group; then get into the content." This opening is ideal for task/work groups in which members know one another and the group's purpose is clear. In this opening, members freely exchange ideas and suggestions at the initial group meeting.
5. "Start with a brief statement about the group; then have the members form dyads." In this type of opening, the purpose of coming to the group is clear, and members have some comfort in being in the group. Breaking into dyads helps group members focus more on content or the purpose of the group experience.
6. "Start with a brief statement about the group; then have members complete a short sentence-completion form." The sentence-completion format is useful in helping members focus on the purpose of the group. It is employed in task/work, psychoeducational, and therapy/counseling groups when no introductions are needed.
7. "Start with an introduction exercise." This type of introduction is employed when group members have a strong idea of the group's purpose. This process helps members introduce themselves and immediately focus on the content of the group. A number of creative exercises can be used. For example, Lessner (1974) suggests that group leaders use nondidactic

poetry, such as that written by Lawrence Ferlinghetti or A. R. Ammons, when they begin a new group. The selection is read aloud, and then all group members describe how they are like an image in the poem, such as a leaf, a rock, or a tree. Then they introduce themselves to the group by stating not only their name but also an image with which they identify. Texts such as Jacobs's (1992) *Creative Counseling Techniques* are excellent resources for picking or modifying a procedure with which to begin. For example, Jacobs points out that props, such as cups and chairs, can often illustrate to group members what words alone cannot convey.

8. "Start with an unusual opening—one that grabs the members." The idea behind this type of beginning is to get group members' attention in ways that would otherwise not be possible. For example, a leader might stage a verbal argument with a co-leader on ways to effectively communicate. Group members would then be asked to offer feedback on what they saw. A discussion would ensue about communication and ways to do it effectively.

Overall, there is no single type of introduction that will work consistently for every group or every group leader. The style of introduction is largely determined by the interpersonal skill of the leader and the nature of the group.

Other aspects of the group at its beginning that will be problematic if not addressed are structure, involvement, cohesion, hope and risk taking, and the termination of the session. Therefore, these processes are examined more thoroughly here.

Reflection

Think of the groups you have been in during your lifetime. How did the groups that were most productive start? How did those you least enjoyed and profited from begin?

STRUCTURE

Group leaders in the initial stage of a group must make decisions on **structuring the group** (running the group according to a prescribed plan or agenda). Those conducting task/work and psychoeducational groups will be much more direct than leaders of counseling and psychotherapy groups. The advantages of structuring a group are that it promotes group cooperation, lessens anxiety, highlights individual performance, and facilitates the inclusion of everyone in the group (Bach, 1954). Structuring may also give leaders confidence and help them concentrate on group goals. The disadvantages of structuring are that it may discourage personal responsibility and restrict freedom of expression. Unstructured groups, though promoting more initial anxiety and discontent, also ultimately create high group cohesiveness and morale (Trotzer, 2007).

Regardless of who promotes involvement, the structuring of a group is inevitable. As Corey, Corey, and Corey (2014) remind group workers, the proper question is not whether a group leader should provide structure but rather what degree of structure should be provided. A major guideline for the amount of structure will be the leader's theoretical stance. Overtly and covertly, members look to the leader for structure and answers, as well as for approval and acceptance (Yalom & Leszcz, 2005). It is important that the leader not overstructure or understructure the group experience during the beginning sessions.

Dies (1983) has given some guidelines for proper structuring in the initial stage of group development. These ideas include awareness by leaders that directly structuring the group in its early stages facilitates the group's development and may promote the establishment of trust and the accomplishment of goals. However, structuring depends on the type of group. It can include indirect modeling of behaviors by the leader as well as confrontation of actions. Once the group begins to work well, leaders who use a lot of structure ease up on this process.

INVOLVEMENT

Involvement of group members, in which they actively participate with one another and invest themselves in the group, is necessary for first sessions to work best. Structured exercises, such as those proposed by Johnson and Johnson (2013), are excellent in bringing people together in a creative and enjoyable way. However, there is no instant intimacy or involvement of group members with one another.

During the first sessions, group leaders must facilitate member interaction. The use of structured activities is one way to accomplish this goal. By discussing specific concerns related to the exercises, group members are able to stop concentrating on group acceptance issues and start focusing on individual goals. Therefore, there is a place in some groups for these activities on a limited basis. In deciding how to get members involved, leaders should focus on the primary purpose of the group before they decide on a strategy for achieving this goal. The most productive groups are composed of members who deal realistically with themselves, others, and issues.

GROUP COHESION

"The effective development of any group requires that members share an image of the group" (Hansen, Warner, & Smith, 1980, p. 492). Unfortunately, in the initial stage of group work, "members bring individual images of the group" (p. 492). Not only is a common identity lacking, but often group members are unsure of themselves, resist any directions from the group leader, or "play it safe" by showing a reluctance to join with others.

One way to break down this difficulty and build **group cohesion**—that is, a sense of "We-ness"—is to allow individuals to voice their concerns freely and fully. By participating in this way, members gain a sense of ownership in the group because they have invested in it. Another way to enhance group cohesiveness is through the use of the arts (e.g., drawing, photography, literature) in helping group members express their feelings and thoughts more clearly (Gladding, 2011b; Shechtman & Perl-Dekel, 2000). Art techniques in groups are usually fun and nonthreatening and involve self-disclosure. The participatory process promotes a sense of openness, trust, and security in the group as a whole as well as in its members. These perceptions lead to positive group member interactions, such as cooperation on tasks, resolution of differences, and agreement on group goals.

Although group cohesion usually does not manifest fully until the norming (or identity) stage of the group, the seeds for its development are planted early. They are rooted in attachment, as members learn to trust and interpersonally relate (Pistole, 1997).

Case Example

Colleen's Cohesive Experience

Colleen was skeptical about being involved in a women's group. She was drawn to it because of her social isolation, but she was wary of it because she thought it would be too "touchy feely" and that all she would get from it would be an emotional purge.

When she expressed her skepticism about the group during its initial session, she was surprised to hear other women voice the same concern. That made her feel closer to these strangers.

Colleen was drawn into the group even more when the leader asked members to draw a line with markers showing the emotions they were experiencing as they began the experience. Colleen used a bright orange marker. Her line was jagged up and down the page. When processing it, she was not sure if it represented anger, frustration, or nervousness. She laughed as she told the group, and in a good-natured way they laughed, too.

Questions

What do you think Colleen thought about the group after these two experiences? What else might you have done as the leader to have helped Colleen find her place in the group?

HOPE AND RISK TAKING

Promoting hope is one of the basic "therapeutic" factors described by Yalom (Yalom & Leszcz, 2005). If members are hopeful that their situations can be different and better, then they are likely to work hard within the group. Leaders can instill hope during the initial sessions of the group in several ways. For instance, they can convey information to members about group process, validate commonalties among members, and accentuate the positive (Couch & Childers, 1987). They can also use humor or give general examples of how hope has been conveyed in other groups.

If members are able to experience a sense of **universality** (commonness with others) within the group, then the group will feel more cohesive (MacKenzie & Livesley, 1983). They are then more likely to take risks that, when successfully completed, will add to their sense of accomplishment and attractiveness to the group. "The degree of risk should not be excessive at this point, or the disclosure too threatening to other members" (MacDevitt, 1987, p. 79). Therefore, leaders must strive for balance in the area of self-disclosure. Leaders who can facilitate the disclosure by members of limited and nonthreatening information in the early stages of the group are appropriate in what they are doing and on their way to conducting a successful group.

CLOSING (TERMINATING) OF THE SESSION

The closing or terminating of a group session is filled with many feelings—anxiety, relief, sadness, and joy. It is just as important to end a group session appropriately as it is to begin it correctly. Too often, not enough attention is focused on closing a session; a group leader may simply announce, "Time is up." Corey, Corey, and Corey (2014) recommend that at least 10 minutes be set aside at the end of a group for reflection and summarization. Otherwise, group members may become frustrated and fail to gain insight into themselves and others. The Coreys also suggest that, at the end of regular sessions, group members leave with some unanswered questions, some reflection about their involvement in the group, some self-report about what they are learning, some concentration on what they would like to explore during the next session, and some feedback from others about positive changes in their behaviors.

The initial sessions of a group are crucial in establishing such a pattern. Even if a group does not make it through more than a few sessions, many group members may experience "considerable relief" because they are able to release repressed feelings (catharsis), see themselves as possessing commonalties with others (universality), find themselves caring about the fate of others (altruism), and experience hope about their personal futures (Zimpfer, personal communication, December 1989).

USEFUL PROCEDURES FOR THE BEGINNING STAGE OF A GROUP

No one method or technique is appropriate for all aspects of a group as it begins. The reason is simple: each group is unique. Yet, there are some universal group procedures that seem to work well in most groups, especially at the beginning of the group. The following are a few of these.

Joining

Joining is the process by which members connect with one another psychologically and physically. Joining requires that leaders and members exert some effort to meet and find out more about each other. Joining can occur in several ways. Probably the most common is for members to introduce themselves, stating their names and some brief background information. A more exciting way of joining is through an **icebreaker**—that is, an activity designed to promote communication between two or more people. Such an activity can take many forms, but its purpose is to energize, reduce anxiety, provide structure, facilitate members' introductions to each other, and promote universality among members by eliciting some personal information from each (Brown, 2014). An example of an icebreaker is where members simply take turns stating their name and a favorite food or activity. A more energizing, but demanding, icebreaker would be for each person to have to introduce a person seated nearby. Whether superficial or more complex, icebreakers are appropriate in most task/work and psychoeducation groups.

Counseling and psychotherapy groups, however, are better served when members go into more depth about themselves and explain their reasons for becoming a part of the group. They can do this in a straightforward verbal way. They can also do it more creatively by engaging in activities, such as "making bags" that are decorated on the outside with symbols of their life, for example pictures, and that contain within more symbolic information about concerns they have and that they will disclose when ready (Gladding, 2011b).

Linking

Linking is the process of connecting persons with one another by pointing out to them what they share in common. It strengthens the bonds between individuals and the group as a whole. For example, the leader may point out how two participants are dealing with issues involving loss or transition. The leader may also help the group realize through linking sentences that one of the issues during the session has been the establishment of trust. In such a case, the leader might say, "I have observed today that some of you are struggling with a common problem. Henry, Alice, Alicia, and Ernie, you all have talked about being unsure of whether you can say what you really feel in the group. The issue of trust seems important and one that is shared."

Linking is employed throughout the life of a group, but it is especially powerful at the beginning stage. Through linking, group cohesion is developed. Some group workers consider linking to be development because, as the group progresses, more themes, interpersonal relationships, and issues tie the group together and facilitate a sense of interrelatedness (Trotzer, 2007). This developmental quality of linking is more likely to occur if the process is used from the start of the group.

Reflection

Think of when someone helped you become aware of an interest or hobby that you shared with another person. What was it like for you to gain this awareness? What did you want to do with this knowledge?

Cutting Off

Cutting off is defined in two ways. First, it is making sure that new material is not introduced into the group too late in the session for the group to deal with it adequately. For instance, if

Janice, a group member, relates that she would like to share an important secret with the group and only 5 minutes remain in the session, then the leader may cut her off. The cutoff will most likely focus on the limited amount of time left in the session. In such a procedure, the member is invited to bring up the secret information next time, and the group can begin the session with it.

The leader might phrase a cutoff statement this way: "Janice, I think the group is receptive to hearing from you but is unable to because of the time. I regret that what you wished to share has surfaced so late in the session. I need you to save this material until next session so we can deal with it properly and give it, and you, the consideration you are due."

Cutting off is also preventing group members from rambling. For instance, if Mark begins to relate his life history to the group, when all he has been asked to do is briefly introduce himself, then the group leader may cut him off by saying something such as, "Mark, we will go into more depth about our backgrounds as the group goes on. Now we need to move on to the next person to make sure everyone has an opportunity to be introduced." By cutting Mark off, the leader keeps the group on task and teaches proper conduct to Mark and others in the group.

Drawing Out

The opposite of cutting off is **drawing out**, in which the leader purposefully asks more silent members to speak to anyone in the group, or to the group as a whole, about anything. For example, the leader might say, "Andy, we haven't heard from you about this matter." By using the drawing-out technique, the leader helps members feel more connected with one another. Drawing out helps members invest more in the group as well as recognize their thoughts. At the same time, other group members receive valuable information about the person who is being drawn out. This technique is particularly appropriate for group members who tend to be introverted or reflective.

Clarifying the Purpose

Sometimes members unintentionally bring up material that is not appropriate for a beginning session or the overall purpose of the group. In such situations, the leader should **clarify the purpose** of the group with the individuals and the group as a whole, the stage the session has reached, or which behavioral interactions are appropriate. For example, the group leader may say, "Frank, your comments are quite interesting, but I am not sure where you are going with them in regard to the topic we have been dealing with. Remember, in this group we are focusing on improving our interpersonal communication skills."

Summary and Conclusion

Beginning a group is a major undertaking filled with complex tasks. Group leaders who are not prepared properly can be overwhelmed by all the demands associated with this responsibility. Therefore, carefully prepared proposals and selection of group members are musts if the group is to be successful. These processes take time and effort but are likely to pay off for the leader in such ways as receiving approval from colleagues, obtaining appropriate group members, gaining clarity on group and individual goals,

and ensuring as much as possible confidentiality and proper procedure. Groups that begin well are more likely ultimately to do well.

Group leaders need to be prepared for developmental and unexpected events within the group, such as members who play certain roles and processes that contribute positively or negatively to group and individual growth. Structuring the group and confronting problems when they occur are important for an overall successful outcome. There is no way to know exactly what will happen when, but group leaders who have knowledge about how to open and close first group sessions, as well as how to help group members get what they both want and need, are valuable resources whose importance cannot be underestimated.

Classroom Exercises

1. Draw up a proposal for a group you would like to lead following the model presented in this chapter. Present it to three other people in a small group of four and elicit their feedback about ways to improve your ideas. Take turns listening to others in the group and making positive suggestions to them on ways to refine what they are proposing.

2. Using seven volunteer class members, assign one to play the role of the group leader who will screen the others as potential group members for a personal growth group. Have the leader interview members individually and in subgroups of two or three. Notice which questions are asked and how the interview process differs on an individual and small-group basis. Then have the leader screen members for a task-oriented group. How do the questions differ? Discuss as a class what you observed.

3. Invite a group leader to speak to your class about how he or she conducts the initial sessions of groups and gets them off to good beginnings. Specifically focus on how the leader deals with the matter of confidentiality and troublesome group procedures such as those discussed in this chapter.

4. What ground rules do you consider essential for conducting an initial group session? How would these rules differ if the group were therapy oriented as opposed to task oriented?

CHAPTER 5

The Transition Period in a Group: Storming and Norming

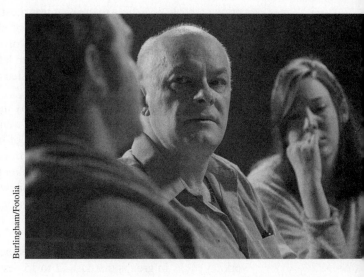

In the midst of struggles, stagnation, and stress
we gather as pilgrims on a journey
to explore the territories of our minds
and the spaces that separate us from others.
The air is tense with anxiety
as we venture into the unknown.
Like the settlers of yesterday's time
we strive to take in all we encounter.
Enlivened by a new awareness
we are moved to consider change.*

*From "A Restless Presence: Group Process
as a Pilgrimage," in School Counselor, 27,
pp. 126–127, © 1979 by Samuel T. Gladding.
Reprinted by permission from Samuel T.
Gladding.

Burlingham/Fotolia

CHAPTER OVERVIEW

From reading this chapter, you will learn about

- The group stage of storming and how it may be worked through
- The group stage of norming and how it may be promoted
- Techniques for overcoming resistance and resolving conflict

AS YOU READ, CONSIDER

- When you have felt competitive with someone in a group and what you did as a result
- When you identified with a group and how you acted as a result
- What you have done in the past to make others feel like they were part of a group

In 1620, a band of Pilgrims landed at Plymouth in what is now the state of Massachusetts. There they sought religious freedom and a new beginning in the American wilderness. The spirit under which they began helped sustain them through many hardships. However, the adversities they endured, especially sickness and the death of half the colony, changed them from a primary idealistic society to one that was most practical and focused on surviving and thriving in a new and hostile world. In the process of change, the colony expanded its worldview and adapted to its environment. The transition involved disagreements at times, or a type of storming, but eventually the group of settlers who were left and joined by other settlers established a way of life and a way of working together that lasted as an entity until 1691 when Plymouth ended its history as a separate colony.

Groups and their members seldom stay the same. The enthusiasm that is prevalent in the initial group meeting, for instance, usually wanes by the second or third meeting, and participants may experience a letdown. This type of behavior is to be expected. Another predictable development is the movement of members from talking about past history to concentrating on the here and now. The shift to an emphasis on the present may not occur without the leader's guidance, but in most groups it takes place on two levels—the personal and the group as a whole (Sklare, Keener, & Mas, 1990; Yalom & Leszcz, 2005). This event, in which members are willing to risk more and move past the superficial, signals the end of the forming stage and the beginning of transition.

The **transition period** in the group is the time after the forming process and before the working stage. In groups that last 12 to 15 sessions, this period begins in the second or third group session and usually extends for one to three meetings. In other words, the transition period in a group takes an average of 5% to 20% of the group's time. This period, which is a two-part process, is characterized by the expression of a number of member emotions and interactions.

Transition begins with a **storming** stage in which members start to compete with others to find their place in the group. This unsettling aspect of the group involves struggles over power and control that may be both overt and covert (Carroll, 1986). Anxiety, resistance, defensiveness, conflict, confrontation, and transference are frequent feelings that surface at this time (Corey, Corey, & Corey, 2014; Gladding, 1994a). If the group successfully weathers this turbulence, then it moves on to a **norming** stage in which there are resolutions, the building of cohesiveness, and the opportunity to move forward in growth (Greason, 2011; Ward, 1982). The purpose of the group and the skill of its leader influence the general ebb and flow of these processes, but the personalities and needs of members and their levels of trust, interest, and commitment also play a major part (Jacobs, Schimmel, Masson, & Harvill, 2016; Zimpfer, 1986). Because every group is unique, leaders and members have to pay special attention to group dynamics and personal feelings to maximize the benefits from these two experiences.

In this chapter, attention is concentrated on how the qualities displayed in the storming and norming stages of a group (the transition period) are influenced (Tuckman, 1965; Tuckman & Jensen, 1977). Each group and group experience is different, but the development of the group involves the interdependence of task goals and interpersonal relationships (Napier & Gershenfeld, 2004). Characteristics associated with transitions in the group follow some general universal patterns, whether they are stage (development) or theme (issue) oriented. The overall patterns must be considered if the group is to effectively negotiate through this period and eventually be productive. The two predictable processes in the group's transition—storming and norming—have characteristics uniquely their own.

STORMING

Storming is a time of conflict and anxiety, when the group moves from **primary tension** (awkwardness about being in a strange situation) to **secondary tension** (intragroup conflict) (Bormann, 1975). During this period, if the group is functioning well, it works out its "threshold for tension" and reaches a balance between too little and too much tension. Group members and leaders struggle with issues related to structure, direction, control, catharsis, and interpersonal relationships (Hershenson, Power, & Waldo, 2003; Maples, 1988). Although frustration and noise sometimes increase during this stage, **quiet storming** in the form of avoidance may also take place. It is important that "the group and its members express and explore differences between and among members" if the group is to be productive (Donigian & Malnati, 1997, p. 64). Members need to work through past nonproductive ways of relating, create new repertoires, and establish their place in the group.

Case Example

Olivia Gets Stuck in Storming

Olivia is a new group leader. She has never read a book on leading groups or received supervision. Yet she thought it would be fun to form a group within her service club. For the first few sessions, all went well as members bantered about as they did at their weekly meetings. Then when the discussions got more serious in regard to what the group would do to better the club, tension arose. Put quite simply, there are three competing ideas out on the floor and there is a lot of competition to see which one emerges as the strongest. The group now has three subgroups and a few independent thinkers. Tempers are beginning to flare just a bit, and Olivia is worried that someone may get either mentally or physically hurt.

Questions

What would you recommend Olivia do? When? How?

Each group experiences the storming process differently. Some may encounter all the problems associated with this period, whereas others may have few difficulties. A group's development may be arrested here by either dwelling on conflict or ignoring it, and the group may never move on to the working stage (Forsyth, 2013). When this happens, conflict becomes destructive, and disagreements spiral upward, "characterized by power, manipulation, coercion, threats, and deception" (McRoy & Brown, 1996, p. 12). Therefore, it is essential that the group leader help members recognize and deal with their conflict and any anxiety and resistance associated with it (Gladding, 1994a; Mahler, 1969). They may do so through either conflict resolution or conflict management.

Conflict resolution "is based on the underlying notion that conflict is essentially negative and destructive" (Rybak & Brown, 1997, p. 31). Therefore, the primary focus is on ending a specific conflict. For instance, the leader may ask Kevin and Opal to stop calling each other names or making absolute, general statements about each other. **Conflict management** is premised on the "basis that conflict can be positive" (Rybak & Brown, 1997, p. 31); thus, the focus is on directing conflict toward a constructive dialogue (McRoy & Brown, 1996). For instance, if Peter and Heather accuse each other of being insensitive, then they may be asked to show each other which actions they would like to see in the other.

When group leaders employ either a conflict resolution or a conflict management approach, the potential benefits of conflict in a group are numerous. For instance, conflict can open up relationship development in the group by highlighting interpersonal boundaries between members. It can also help the group as a whole overcome resistance to change from receiving more information. Other positive functions of conflict that come from resolving or managing it include releasing tension, strengthening relationships, and reevaluating and clarifying goals (McRoy & Brown, 1996). Satisfactorily dealing with conflict results eventually in a "degree of interdependence versus independence that is acceptable in the relationship between members and within the group as a whole" (Rybak & Brown, 1997, p. 31).

Storming has some central characteristics that determine which way conflict will be handled and how the group will progress: peer relationships, resistance, and task processing.

Peer Relationships in Storming

During the storming stage, group members are initially more anxious in their interactions with one another because they are afraid of losing control, being misunderstood, looking foolish, or being rejected. Some avoid taking a risk by remaining silent at this time; others who want to establish their place in the group deal with their anxiety by being more open and assertive (Yalom & Leszcz, 2005). For instance, Cheryl may remain quiet during storming and simply observe the group members' interactions. However, Tony may be verbally aggressive and express his thoughts about every idea raised in the group.

The concern for power is also prevalent during storming. **Power** is "the capacity to bring about certain intended consequences in the behavior of others" (Gardner, 1990, p. 55). The struggle for power occurs soon after group members have oriented themselves to the group formation. Attitudes toward power become important because the ways in which group members deal with this issue influence how conflictual or cooperative a group will become (Johnson & Johnson, 2013).

Power within a group can take many forms. **Informational power** is premised on the idea that people who know more are able to exert control over situations, including those involving people. **Influential power** is based on the idea of persuasion and manipulation of others through convincing them that a certain course of action is correct. **Authoritative power** is predicated on social position or responsibility in an organization. Authoritative means, such as "pulling rank," may be employed to try to influence members of groups that include individuals of unequal status, such as those in task/work groups.

Reflection

When have you seen any of the three types of power just explained displayed? When have you exercised power of any type, especially in a group? How do you feel about exerting power? How do you feel when power is exerted on you?

The principles that operate in dealing with power are similar regardless of the type of power being expressed. At first, members will attempt to resolve power concerns in ways that resemble those they have used outside the group—for example, by fighting or fleeing. If these strategies work, then members will continue to employ them. If not, members will formulate new ways of handling potentially conflictual situations. For example, when Tracy finds that yelling at other group members does not influence them and make them respect her, she may try having one-to-one conversations or persuading the group that she should be respected by telling members stories about what she has done in the past.

Members' attitudes about trusting the group and its leader are also an issue during storming. There is usually a good deal of mistrust in others during the storming stage, based partly on lacking experience in dealing with the group and partly on resolving anxiety and power issues while moving from a superficial group toward becoming a unified one. Too much mistrust will hinder people in the group from becoming cohesive. However, blind trust uninformed by experience (e.g., telling group members your intimate thoughts before getting to know them fully) is also inappropriate.

Connected to the issues of anxiety, power, and trust among peers is the question of the quality of verbal interaction. Negative comments, judgments, and criticisms are frequent during storming as members deal with issues of control, conflict, and dominance in the establishment of a hierarchy (Maples, 1988; Schutz, 1971; Yalom & Leszcz, 2005). For instance, members may focus on the content of the message. In such situations, their responses would most likely be statements such as "I cannot understand why you allowed that to happen to you," "I don't think you were very smart in letting that occur," or "If I were you, I would have. . . ."

Case Example

Critical Carl

He swore he was only being truthful, but every time a group member brought up a situation in which he or she had been wronged, Carl pounced on the event like a lion on a gazelle. He was relentless in his criticism and judgment. Members either fought with him or stopped talking to him. Finally, several members of the group pointed out to Carl what he was doing. He protested but to no avail. It took considerable time, but finally Carl realized what he was doing and modified his behavior.

Questions

Why do you think Carl was resistant to changing his critical demeanor? What strategies outside of verbal confrontation do you think would help an overly critical person modify a behavior?

If all goes well during the storming stage, then group members come to understand themselves and one another better. They begin to develop empathy for one another, too. However, to make progress, the group must work collectively through its resistance to change.

Resistance During Storming

Resistance is best defined as any behavior that moves the group away from areas of discomfort, conflict, or potential growth. It appears to increase especially during the early part of the storming stage (Higgs, 1992). Forms of resistance are multidirected and aimed at discussion material (e.g., "I don't want to talk about that"), the leader (e.g., "You're the leader; you show me how to change"), other members (e.g., "I think Jim doesn't like me. I'm leaving"), questions of control (e.g., "I don't feel safe in here and I'm not going to say anything until I do"), or the group in general (e.g., "You guys are a bunch of losers. I don't have anything in common with you").

Group leaders who are unprepared for such experiences may become defensive when this kind of behavior happens. In such situations, the group is thrown into chaos, and the leader may feel personally attacked or insulted. When this behavior occurs, responses by members and the leader are usually angry and unproductive. For example, Helen may say, "June, if you don't like this group and what is being discussed here, you can quit and find another group." June may reply by yelling, "You aren't in charge and have no right to tell me what to do!"

Some forms of resistance are more subtle than others. For example, group member behaviors may appear to be accepting on the surface but are really resisting underneath. The most prevalent forms of subtle *indirect resistance* are described in the following subsections.

INTELLECTUALIZATION

Intellectualization is a behavior characterized by an emphasis on abstraction with a minimal amount of affect or emotion (Clark, 1992). The person uses thoughts and a sophisticated vocabulary to avoid dealing with personal feelings. Such a process helps the member become detached from the group. For example, a psychotherapy group member might say to the group, "Many people think they are being threatened when others disagree with them." Unless this comment contains some personal feelings, such as "I feel that this group is rejecting me when members disagree with me," it is difficult to make a meaningful response.

QUESTIONING

In interpersonal relationships, a question is often a disguise for a statement. If members are constantly **questioning** one another, then they are safe from exposing their true selves. Questions keep the group focused on why something occurred in the past and thereby prevent members from concentrating on what is happening now. In a resistant counseling group, members may use questions such as, "Do we really have to talk about how we feel?" or "How come John is not saying as much as Susan about his past group experience?"

To counter questions, group leaders need to take corrective actions. One of the best strategies is for leaders to ask members to use the word "I" before beginning a sentence, such as "I feel nervous." A complementary strategy is for leaders to simply say, "Since most questions are really statements, I want each of you to rephrase your query as such." Thus, in the examples just given, statements would be "I do not want to talk about my feelings" and "I wish John would say as much as Susan about his past group experience." Through such approaches, members and the group as a whole are invited to examine their thoughts and feelings in a productive way.

ADVICE GIVING

Advice giving involves instructing someone on what to do in a particular situation. Advice is seldom appropriate or needed in most groups (Sack, 1985). It prevents members from struggling with their own feelings (Greason, 2011) and keeps the advice giver from having to recognize shortcomings in his or her life. In a resistant group member, advice may be general or specific, but it is usually not helpful. For example, Jan may say to Wanda, "I think what you need to do is to exercise more. Until you feel better about your body, you will never feel good about yourself." This advice may have merit but, because the members do not know one another well at this time, it will probably be seen as criticism and separate Jan and Wanda even more.

Reflection

When have you ever been offered advice? How did you feel as the recipient? Is there a danger to giving advice to someone in the midst of the struggle he or she is having about a decision? What is the downside to such action? What is the upside?

BAND-AIDING

The cleverly named concept known as **band-aiding** involves the misuse of support. It is the process of preventing others from fully expressing their emotional pain through ventilating their feelings (catharsis). Band-aiders soothe wounds and alleviate feelings when just the opposite would be more appropriate. For example, in a psychotherapy group, Rad may try to calm Jason physically and psychologically when Jason is shouting about the way he was treated by his parents. If Rad succeeds in his effort, then he prevents Jason from releasing his feelings and thereby dealing with them. Jason may then continue to be angry and, at times, project his emotions onto others. This may result in extending the storming stage of the group.

Case Example

Band-Aid Bob

He had been hurt badly in the breakup of an intimate relationship, and Bob still carried the wounds. He thought he had joined a grief support group, but he soon found out he had become a member of a denial troupe. The members simply did not want to listen to or hear about pain. Therefore, Bob became more and more frustrated. He wanted to get his feelings out. Instead, he was being blocked from moving on in his life.

Questions

What are some ways Bob could have handled this situation besides becoming frustrated and mad about it? When have you seen people or groups band-aid someone? What was the result?

DEPENDENCY

Group members who display **dependency** behaviors encourage advice givers and band-aiders. They present themselves as helpless and incapable but refuse to listen to feedback. They are "help-rejecting complainers" (Yalom & Leszcz, 2005). For example, Joyce may say to Tom, "What would you do in my situation? You are more experienced than I am. I need your help." If Tom responds by taking charge of Joyce's life, then neither he nor Joyce is helped because Joyce becomes more dependent on Tom, and the two begin to relate as unequals in a one-up/one-down position.

Other forms of resistance, discussed next, are more direct and potentially more destructive.

MONOPOLIZING

Monopolizing occurs when a person or persons in the group dominate the group's time through excessive talking or activity that is often irrelevant to the group's task. At other times, their points are pertinent but so full of unimportant details or movement that group members are unable to process what they have heard. In either case, this form of resistance keeps the group from working on either individual or group projects.

Monopolizers may be helped by (a) confronting them, (b) teaching them new skills to deal with anxiety (e.g., progressive relaxation), or (c) giving them feedback on how their old or new behaviors affect interpersonal communications (Krieg, 1988; Yalom & Leszcz, 2005). In some cases, the group leader may display a hand signal to remind the monopolizer that he or she needs to change behaviors.

ATTACK ON THE GROUP LEADER

An **attack on the group leader** is probably the most direct form of resistance that causes groups difficulty. Such attacks are somewhat common in involuntary groups where members are mandated or assigned to come. Many theories view an attack on the leader as an opportunity to shape new norms and enhance group movement (Donigian & Hulse-Killacky, 1999). Regardless, it is vital that the group leader not ignore an attack. Sometimes attacks are justified, especially if the group leader has been insensitive to members' needs. However, such is not always the case.

Processes that contribute to leader attacks in almost all groups, if they are voluntary, are subgrouping, fear of intimacy, and extragroup socializing. For example, if subgroups develop in the group, then isolated thoughts and ideas may germinate in regard to the leader's competence. It does not take long for such negative thoughts to surface and be expressed. These difficulties and attacks can be prevented if members are thoroughly screened, pregroup training takes place, and rules for the group are clearly defined in the beginning. For example, in a psychotherapy group, Zack may be asked to wait to participate in the next group being offered because he appears unable to think through situations by himself. When the leader has doubts about whether someone is ready for a group, it is probably better to err on the side of caution and deny the person a particular group experience.

When an attack on the leader comes, however, it must be addressed and dealt with immediately. Otherwise, the group will become unsafe for any risk-taking behavior and will disintegrate into a series of attack sessions in which members feel threatened and drop out (Yalom & Leszcz, 2005). In other words, *perpetual storming* will prevail. One of the best strategies for group leaders to use in dealing with attacks is to face them directly and attempt to determine the underlying variables that have led to them, such as unresolved feelings. It is best that the leader do this in a nondefensive and open manner. For example, if Ben, as the leader, is being attacked for not creating a safe and trusting atmosphere, then he may state, "As I listen to what you are saying, I'm aware that you would like me to do more. I'd like to know what you have specifically in mind. I'd also like to know how you would like others in the group to act so that you would feel safer and more trusting."

Task Processing in Storming

Task processing (ways of accomplishing specific goals) appears to regress during storming. No longer do members or leaders concentrate as directly on objectives as they did at the beginning of the group. Rather, there is a great deal of attention on personal matters, such as group safety, leader competence, trust, and ways of interacting. It is healthy that this "pause" in the group takes place, for it allows everyone the opportunity of reevaluating goals and directions. More important, it provides a chance for group participants to "look" before they "leap" toward the process of change.

A potential problem in this suspension of effort to accomplish a task is that someone in the group may be blamed, or scapegoated, for the group's lack of achievement (Rugel, 1991). To **scapegoat** is to project the group's problems onto a single individual instead of the group taking responsibility for creating and resolving its difficulties. If such an event occurs, then the group spends additional time and energy working on interpersonal issues that must be resolved before the group as a whole can get back on task. It is crucial that members and leaders take responsibility for their own actions at this point in the life of the group. For example, in response to Marc being blamed by several group members for present problems, Jean may say, "I think the situation we are currently in is the result of more than one person's actions. We have all contributed in our own unique ways to this situation. If we are going to help one another, then we need to explore what we have done up to this point and try to do some things differently."

If members can be helped by the leader and one another to express their feelings in relation to individual or collective goals, then scapegoating is less likely to happen, and greater awareness will most likely evolve (Saidla, 1990). This process is helpful in the eventual achievement of selective tasks and the healthy growth of the group and its members.

Working Through Storming

Several methods have already been mentioned for working through particular forms of problematic intrapersonal and interpersonal group issues during storming. However, there are global and uniform means of helping the group as a body during this time as well. One way to help group members work through their feelings in storming is to use a **process observer** (a neutral third-party professional who observes the group and gives it feedback on its interpersonal and interactive processes). As Trotzer (1997) states, "The foundation for effective problem-solving and conflict resolution is effective group process. . . . Impasse and polarization arise with conflict when group process is defective or ignored" (p. 6).

By giving the group feedback as to what he or she sees occurring, a process observer can help the group become more open in acknowledging and constructively responding to tensions and anxieties that may be present in group member relationships. For example, the process observer may say to the group, "I have noticed that Rick and Darla seem to be struggling with each other regarding what the group will focus on today while the rest of the group is silent. This pattern has been going on about 10 minutes now. I wonder what is happening with the group?" Framing an observation in such a factual way allows all members of a group to hear it and allows members besides Rick and Darla to deal with what appears to be a covert conflict. By starting early to observe what is going on among group members, the members and the group as a whole can attempt to change behaviors or modify ways of interacting.

A second way to work through the storming stage is to use the process of **leveling**, in which members are encouraged to interact freely and evenly (Kline, 1990; Kottler, 1994). In leveling, the leader draws out group members who are underparticipating, and those who are excessively active are helped to understand the impact of their actions through group feedback. For instance, if Tonya is always making a comment after each group member voices a concern or makes a statement, then the leader may intervene by saying, "Tonya, do you realize how your active participation in the group affects other members' abilities to get involved?" If Tonya does not acknowledge any awareness, then the leader may ask the group to help Tonya become more sensitive to how her actions are preventing others from becoming involved in the group. A slightly different strategy would work for Al, who is not speaking up in the group. An open invitation by the group leader might be, "Al, we haven't heard from you today. What's on your mind?" If leveling works well, then the verbal behavior within the group is modified so that members participate evenly. When everyone in the group interacts, issues that have the potential to cause conflict may surface and be resolved sooner.

Another method for working through storming is for group members to acknowledge what is occurring in the group independent of a process observer. If group leaders or members deny that the group is in unrest or even conflict, then confusion will arise. In addition, members will not trust themselves, take risks, or believe the leader. In most groups, members can handle honesty better than denial or deception. They may agree with Walter, who says to Michelle and Megan, "I wish you guys would resolve your personal disagreement so we can move on toward working on our goals." By facing the fact that storming is happening, members and leaders know what they are up against and can thereby give themselves permission to be less frustrated and display greater tolerance of what is happening. Acknowledgment also enables members to make plans and develop a greater sensitivity to the situation so that it can be improved.

A fourth global way of dealing with the storming part of transition is to get **feedback** from members about how they are doing and what they think needs to be done (Greason, 2011; Ponzo, 1991). Feedback either encourages change or supports the current status quo. The feedback process can take place in a formal or an informal way. Using **informal feedback**, the leader may ask members to give their reactions to a group session in an unstructured way at any time they wish. Such an invitation is likely to increase spontaneity and sensitivity. For instance, Bettie may say, "Oh, I just realized something I'm doing. Every time Patricia talks, I tune her out. She reminds me of my mother with whom I had real trouble. Yet, just now, Patricia, I heard your comments about your own pain, and I suddenly became aware that you are your own person."

Formal feedback is structured. It may be set up, for example, through the use of what is known as **rounds** (having each person in the group make a comment). In rounds, each individual has the same amount of time, usually 1 or 2 minutes, to say whatever he or she wishes. Through using rounds, especially those that are time specific, everyone gets equal "airtime" to give input and make suggestions. In formal feedback rounds, the views of the group as a whole are heard. Formal feedback may also include the use of **logs** or **journals** (members' written comments made after a group). Ideally, logs are written and read between group sessions by the group leader, who gives feedback to group members and even the group as a whole regarding specific and general comments. "Collected logs can be a robust diary of the entire group experience, documenting ups and downs, the progress or lack of it, and can sometimes serve as a map showing members' growth" (Riordan & White, 1996, p. 98).

A final way of working through storming is the use of **motivational interviewing** (MI), a client-centered, directive method for resolving ambivalence that impedes change (T. Young, 2013b). The spirit of MI is founded on the client-centered principles of autonomy (that the group member has a right and ability to make choices), collaboration (the opposite of confrontation), and evocation (as opposed to education). By using MI techniques such as keeping questions open-ended, intentionally using reflections, recognizing readiness, and guiding members in setting personal goals, the leader may help a group member and the group itself move on.

Reflection

Which of the strategies just described do you think you would employ in a group that was storming? Which would you not employ? Why?

Results of Working Through Storming

When the group works through storming, especially in regard to resistance, the group will take on a new dimension characterized by members making emotional space for one another and being accommodating. Additional changes will include "more plain talk, open risk taking, overt agendas, increased intimacy, greater appreciation for one another, more intense emotions, and an emphasis on the present" (Ormont, 1988, p. 44). Members may decide to revise their goals or alter their style of interpersonal relationships as a result of working through storming.

Altering interpersonal relationship style is especially important to the group's future development. Often members enter a group with a limited response range. For example, in the area of conflict management, members may only know or feel comfortable using one or two of five dominant **conflict management orientations**: competing, accommodating, avoiding, collaborating, or compromising (Thomas & Kilmann, 1974). These conflict management styles can be characterized as follows:

- *Competing* occurs when individuals pursue their own concerns at other people's expense—for example, Heather insists that she be picked up from school at 5 p.m. even if it means others have to rearrange their schedules to do so.

- *Accommodating* happens when individuals neglect their own concerns to satisfy the concerns of others—for example, Anna gives up an hour of sleep each night so that she can fix breakfast for her suite mates.
- *Collaborating* occurs when individuals work with others to find solutions that fully satisfy the concerns of both—for example, the Brown family searches until they can find a movie that they all want to see.
- *Avoiding* is seen when individuals do not immediately pursue their concerns or those of other persons—for example, Sam lets his wish to be a pilot take a backseat while he checks out the reactions of others to his tentative choice of a job.
- *Compromising* is in effect when individuals attempt to find an expedient, mutually acceptable solution that partially satisfies both parties—for example, in peace negotiations, representatives from countries may have to give up some of the things they want in order to get a final agreement.

Although each of these responses has advantages (e.g., in regard to time limits, competing may work best), group members who are limited in their responses may restrict their ability to relate to all members of the group. Such a case would occur if Kenneth constantly challenged other members of his work group to "put up or shut up." By altering their style of conflict management, members increase their flexibility and the probability that the conflicts they have with other members will have a more positive than negative outcome (e.g., provide vivid feedback, motivate individuals to search for creative alternatives) (Mitchell & Mitchell, 1984).

Different types of groups will vary in the length and depth of their experience in storming and amount of conflict (Jacobs et al., 2016). For psychotherapy groups, the impact of the storming period on the group itself will be greater and last longer than for psychoeducational groups. In fact, psychoeducational groups are usually low in interpersonal conflict, and the duration of such conflict is relatively brief if it occurs at all. Psychotherapy groups, in contrast, are generally intense, and the storming period can be quite long. Regardless of the time and intensity, storming provides a time for group members to become realistic and active in examining their goals and working out relationships in their interactions with others. For most groups, the interdependency among group members and the stability of the group as a whole cannot deepen until intragroup hostility has surfaced, been acknowledged, and been dealt with (Greason, 2011). Therefore, the work done during storming is the foundation on which most groups will be built (Mahler, 1969).

NORMS AND NORMING

There is both a distinction and a relationship between the concept of norms and the group experience of norming. **Norms** are expectations about group members' behaviors that should or should not take place (Forsyth, 2013). "Group norms regulate the performance of the group as an organized unit" (Napier & Gershenfeld, 2004, p. 101). Words commonly associated with norms are "ought, should, must, or better" (Shepherd, 1964, p. 123). In some groups, especially those that are open ended, group norms may be unclear, confusing, ambiguous, arbitrary, and restrictive. In most groups, however, norms are clear and are constructed both from expectations of the members for their group and from the explicit and implicit directions of the leader and more influential members (Yalom & Leszcz, 2005). Therefore, most norms are based on input from everyone involved in the group and ensure group predictability and survival.

At the beginning of a group, norms may not be as clear or as well defined as they will be later. As the group develops, group members and leaders become more aware of the verbal and nonverbal rules they wish to follow to achieve their goals. They also become better acquainted with one another.

Group norming is the feeling of "We-ness," identity, groupness, or cohesiveness that comes when individuals feel they belong to an association or organization larger than themselves. The process of norming is often characterized as one of the major aspects of groups (Tuckman, 1965; Tuckman & Jensen, 1977). Like storming, norming is a crucial part of the group process because it sets the pattern for the next stage: performing (working). In the norming stage, enthusiasm and cooperation are expressed (Hershenson et al., 2003). In many ways, it parallels the forming stage in its emphasis on positive emotions. However, because group members are more informed and experienced with one another, they can concentrate on themselves and one another better in the group. Although some groups experience norming as a distinct stage in their development, others find the process to be continuously evolving. Two main aspects of norming are peer relations and task processing.

Peer Relationships During Norming

During the norming stage, several important changes occur in peer relationships. Among these are outlook and attitude. Group members usually have a positive attitude toward others in the group and the experience itself during norming. They feel a newfound sense of "belongingness" and "groupness" (Saidla, 1990). This positive mindset is likely to result in learning, insight, and feelings of support and acceptance. Members are willing to give of themselves and committed to taking needed actions. They expect to be successful. Peer interactions are manifest through identification, here-and-now experiences, hope, cooperation, collaboration, and cohesion.

IDENTIFICATION

A sense of **identification** is a "normal" developmental process in which individuals see themselves as being similar to one another (Freud, 1949). For example, in a counseling group, Allison and Lynn may come to realize they have many similar tastes, from food to clothes to reading materials. Identification explains why group members often become emotionally attached to their leaders and give them power. It also explains why some strong friendships begin in groups. Identification must be taken into account when considering the behavior of groups of all sizes. Those groups in which there is more identification with the leader or other members will be more cohesive and less resistant to change than those that are not. In norming, identification with others grows.

Case Example

Buford Becomes Mobile, Agile, and Hostile

When Buford was 20, he went through basic training in the U.S. Army. The training molded him into a person who thought of himself as a part of a greater whole. Although individually he was "mobile, agile, and hostile" (who crawled on his belly like a reptile), he also identified himself as part of a larger group that was the same. His identity went beyond his dog tags. He was a part of the armed forces and realized that when he was instructed to "take a hill," "take a hike," or "take a 5-minute rest period," he needed to do as instructed for the good of the group.

Questions

Buford's experience is not that different from what you may have experienced in being a member of a club, art group, or athletic team. What words, slogans, logos, and mascots have you identified with in the past and why? Gauge the strength of your relationship to these entities with which you have identified. How important has it been for you to do as instructed in the groups to which you have belonged? Why?

HERE-AND-NOW EXPERIENCES

Although group growth can be charted on a session-by-session basis, the best way to help individuals and the group make progress is to deal with immediate feelings and interactions (**existential variables**). Conflict, withdrawal, support, dominance, and change all need to be acknowledged as they occur. Feelings from ecstasy to depression must be addressed as they surface. Group leaders and members can link the present with past trends, but it is crucial that behaviors and emotions be recognized and worked on when they arise. Some individual and group experiences will focus on what Yalom and Leszcz (2005) describes as personal issues about one's own life and death. Others will be directed toward obtaining specific goals, such as learning to accept others who differ or finding new, appropriate ways to interact with members of the opposite sex (Carkhuff, 1971; Rose, 1982; Watson & Tharp, 1981).

HOPE

The experience of **hope** occurs on both a cognitive and an emotional level in groups. Cognitively, hope is the belief that what is desired is possible and that events will turn out for the best. Emotionally, hope is the feeling that what one wishes for will occur. The importance of hope is that it energizes group members and the group as a whole. Furthermore, hope helps groups envision meaningful, but not yet realized, possibilities.

In norming, groups and their members need to hope and usually do so. Psychotherapeutic group members may hope, for instance, that they have the courage to overcome past tragedies, whereas counseling group members may hope they can purposefully plan a future different from their past. Task/work group members may express hope in combining their talents so that new products can be marketed. Likewise, psychoeducational group members may hope they can learn to integrate new life skills into their daily lives.

COOPERATION

Cooperation occurs when group members work together for a common purpose or good. During norming, group participants become relaxed and work better together. Vying for position, which is so prevalent in storming, diminishes. In some task/work groups, cooperation increases because there is increased awareness of a group goal and members realize more fully what each can do for the other (Johnson & Johnson, 2013). In psychotherapeutic groups, cooperation is often the result of better understanding and communication worked out in the storming stage. In such cases, it is based on a hope for change (Weiner, 1984).

COLLABORATION

Collaboration goes hand in glove with cooperation. Members who think they can work in a harmonious, cooperative manner are likely to share facts and feelings about themselves and other matters with the group; that is, they collaborate. Furthermore, they are prone to work with other group members in sharing a vision and making that goal a reality.

Collaboration is probably seen most clearly in task/work groups in which members work on a tangible product. However, in counseling groups, collaboration is expressed when members assist one member in obtaining a personal goal even when there is no observable reward for the rest of the group.

Reflection

When have you seen a group work hard for the benefit of one of its members? Even when it appears that only the member benefits, what else might be happening?

COHESION

The last factor in the interpersonal process of norming, **cohesion**, has received a great deal of attention. It is widely recognized as central to the success of groups, and, although not sufficient in itself to make a group effective, it is necessary (Forsyth & Diederich, 2014). In fact, cohesiveness is often cited as the most important factor in shaping the outcome of groups because without it, groups would not stay together (Nitza, 2005; Pender & Prichard, 2009). Cohesion can be thought of as a sense of "groupness" or "We-ness." Groups that establish such a spirit (and keep it) run harmoniously as a unit. Morale, trust, attendance, commitment, and solidarity increase, as do actions involving self-disclosure, whereas premature termination decreases (Marmarosh & Van Horn, 2011). The chief concern of the group during this time is intimacy and closeness (Yalom & Leszcz, 2005). In a cohesive atmosphere, emotional closeness becomes acceptable and valued.

There is a difference between "total group cohesiveness and individual member cohesiveness (or, more strictly, the individual's attraction to the group)" (Yalom, 1985, p. 49). Yet, a positive correlation often exists between the two, with members of groups attracted to a particular group contributing to it. Group and individual cohesion can be measured by behaviors, such as attendance, punctuality, risk taking, self-disclosure, and dropout rates. Cohesive groups are more effective in their communication patterns, and members communicate with one another frequently. Cohesive groups also appear to have considerable fun together and yet are achievement oriented, especially on difficult tasks (Johnson & Johnson, 2013). They are able to express their hostilities and conflicts openly and come to some resolutions. Well-functioning athletic teams are cohesive.

The advantages and limitations of group cohesion are notable. On the positive side, it has generally been demonstrated that members of cohesive groups "(1) are more productive; (2) are more open to influence by other group members; (3) experience more security; (4) are more able to express hostility and adhere more closely to group norms; (5) attempt to influence others more frequently; and (6) continue membership in the group longer" (Bednar & Lawlis, 1971, pp. 822–823). There is even an afterglow benefit to group cohesion, because members in more cohesive groups continue to improve after treatment has ended more than those in less cohesive groups (Conye, 2010), and those who feel valued and accepted in a group can actually increase in self-esteem and self-acceptance (Waldo, Schwartz, Horne, & Cote, 2011).

However, cohesion can be problematic. Among the potential difficulties with cohesion is that group participants may decide they like the positive atmosphere so much that they are unwilling to talk about anything that might be upsetting. In such groups, harmony is stressed over everything, and a type of **pseudo-acceptance** (false acceptance) prevails. This type of atmosphere prevents anxiety, but it keeps the group from progressing. Groups that finally settle down into the performing or working stage are those that can discuss negative, as well as positive, material.

Case Example

Anxious Alan

Alan grew up in an environment where he had to be tough to survive and get what he needed, let alone get what he wanted. Therefore, he vowed that he would make life easier for others whenever he could. That vow included those in the groups Alan was asked to run for an agency where he got his first job. At his 3-month review, Alan's supervisor noted that feedback from the groups Alan ran was consistently negative. He was described as a passive leader and one who insisted that everyone be upbeat. One feedback statement even portrayed Alan as "on a mission to have everyone like everyone" and "in the end hold hands and sing 'Kumbaya.'" Alan told his supervisor that he just did not have it in him to be negative. He wanted to be sure there was minimum to no tension in his groups so he purposely smoothed things out in a glib way whenever he saw tension developing in the context of the group.

Questions

If you were Alan's supervisor, what would you do first? Second? Third? If you were Alan, how would you take this feedback? What do you think Alan should do from here on out?

Task Processing During Norming

One main task objective in the norming stage is for members to reach an agreement on the establishment of norms, or rules and standards from which to operate the group. Some norming is done on a nonverbal, mostly unconscious, level, but other aspects of norming are conducted verbally. Through norms, group members learn to regulate, evaluate, and coordinate their actions (Gibbs, 1965). Groups typically accept both *prescriptive norms,* which describe the kinds of behaviors that should be performed, and *proscriptive norms,* which describe the kinds of behaviors that are to be avoided (Forsyth, 2013).

Norms are value laden and give a degree of predictability to the group that would not be there otherwise (Luft, 1984). Often, they evolve so gradually that they are never questioned until they are violated. Basically, norms allow the group to begin to work, although not all norms are productive (Wilson & Hanna, 1986).

Another main, task-related goal of the norming stage is **commitment**. The commitment is to the group as a whole and its rules as well as to individual goals. The group and its members begin to operate on a higher level when commitment is a central part of the group. Eventually, participants come to "evaluate their performances and the performances of others in terms of accomplishment of the group's goals" (Napier & Gershenfeld, 2004, p. 194). This sense of commitment carries over and intertwines with the group at work (Schutz, 1958). It is at this point that the group and its members can begin to see the tangible results from their dreams and efforts. Groups in which members are most committed to one another are more likely than not to be productive in achieving tasks as well as successful in feeling good about the group experience.

Examining Aspects of Norming

Norming is generally characterized in terms of behaviors and feelings expressed by group members toward one another. Although it is difficult to measure the impact of emotion on the group, there are ways of examining behaviors during this stage that are both concrete and scientific. One way involves peer relationships. This method uses a research-based theory of personality and group dynamics that is referred to by the acronym **SYMLOG** (System for the Multiple Level Observation of Groups) (Bales, 1980; Bales, Cohen, & Williamson, 1979).

The SYMLOG model yields a field diagram that pictures how members of a group are rated on three dimensions: dominance versus submissiveness, friendliness versus unfriendliness, and instrumentally versus emotionally expressive. In addition, it yields a total of 26 roles found in groups. One way to use this instrument is to rate each group member's tendency to engage in any of the 26 roles on the instrument and then to summarize the scores along the three dimensions. For instance, an industrialist such as Henry Ford might be classified as UF (assertive and businesslike), whereas a talk-show host such as Jimmy Fallon might be UPB (entertaining, sociable, smiling, and warm). By using SYMLOG, the interactional dynamics and personality of the group can be better understood because the homogeneous or heterogeneous nature of the group is clearer.

Promoting Norming

Norming can be promoted through actions by either the group leader or group members. Several human relations and specific group skills can be used in this process. Chief among these skills are supporting, empathizing, facilitating, and self-disclosure.

SUPPORTING

Supporting is the act of encouraging and reinforcing others. Its aim is to convey to persons that they are perceived as adequate, capable, and trustworthy. Through the act of supporting, group members feel affirmed and are able to risk new behaviors because they sense a backing from the group, a secure base (Harel, Shechtman, & Cutrona, 2012). The result is often creative, surprising actions that are novel and positive because self-defensiveness is reduced and self-confidence is increased. An example of what supporting in a counseling group can do is when Trip (speaking for the group) says to Burgess, "I, and we as a group, really think you can be more assertive in letting your spouse know what you want." The results are that Burgess comes into the group the following week and presents a one-person play called "How to Be Assertive" in which she humorously, yet sensitively, shows how she used the group's support to ask her husband for what she wanted.

EMPATHIZING

Empathizing means putting oneself in another's place in regard to subjective perception and emotion while keeping one's objectivity (Brammer & MacDonald, 2003). It demands a suspension of judgment and a response to another person that conveys sensitivity and understanding. Again, during the norming stage, expressing empathy takes on special significance. Members need to listen to both the verbal and nonverbal messages of others in the group and be responsive. For instance, in a psychotherapy group, Nancy may say to Fred, "It seems to me you are sad. Your voice is low, and your eyes are focused on the floor." Such a message reflects an understanding of another person's voice and body signals and opens up potential dialogue and problem-solving avenues.

FACILITATING

The act of **facilitating** involves using clear and direct communication channels among individuals. It is an activity usually assumed by a group leader, although members of the group may engage in this process at times. Part of facilitation is to make sure messages are sent and received accurately. The leader may say, "Tammy, when Mark said he was glad you had resolved your differences, you looked a bit perplexed. I wonder what you were thinking?" In this case, Tammy may shrug off the suggestion that anything was bothering her, or she may confess that it feels unusual for her not to be at odds with Mark. In either case, Mark, Tammy, and the group as a whole get the benefit of making sure these two group members are feeling connected so that underlying problems do not arise later to the detriment of the group as a whole.

SELF-DISCLOSURE

One of the strongest signs of trust in a group is **self-disclosure** (revealing to group members information about oneself of which they were previously unaware) (Jourard, 1971). Self-disclosure is enhanced when members feel safe. Through self-disclosure, barriers that inhibit communication among individuals are torn down. A sense of community and camaraderie is established. Leaders may model disclosure behaviors to show which materials should be revealed and how. It is best to first disclose materials related to individuals and experiences in the group. Through such a process, members' bonds become stronger.

Reflection

When have you felt closer to someone because of self-disclosure? When have you felt farther from someone because they did not self-disclose? When have you felt someone went too far in self-disclosing? What do these experiences tell you about self-disclosing in a group?

Results of Norming

If the process of norming goes well, then the group will be ready for the next step in its developmental process—working. Members will feel connected with the group and will be able to concentrate on being productive, rather than protecting themselves. Just as Maslow's (1962) hierarchy of personal needs builds from the basics up, such is also the case in groups. When members feel secure and linked with others, they are free to begin cooperating and coordinating their efforts to achieve specific goals.

Norming gives group members guidelines under which to operate. They are, therefore, able to gauge how well they are doing individually and as a group. If discomfort is evident in the group, then members may realize that they or the group as a whole is regressing instead of progressing. It is from the baseline of norming that the group is measured or referenced.

Overall, norming has the effect of helping members in the group feel good about themselves and the group as a whole. Norming is like a breath of fresh air after the turmoil of successfully resolving the difficulties of the storming stage. Norming allows members to clear their minds, reassess their goals from a realistic perspective, feel good about themselves and the group's progress, and make new plans for the working stage of the group. Such processes help group members and groups as a whole renew their efforts toward achievement.

Summary and Conclusion

The transition period of groups is multifaceted and complex. If it is successful, then this time will be a takeoff point for the group's work. Ideally, transition is a two-part process. Group members resolve conflict in the storming stage of the transition period. Then they are able to set up and follow rules (norms) as well as form a cohesive bond with one another (norming). In such cases, the group ends the transition period ready to get down to work collectively and personally and to be productive.

In practice, groups are unique and differ in the way they develop because of their members, leaders, climates, and goals. A number of procedures can be enacted to facilitate the group's development and that of its members during this time. Some of these activities are as simple as recognizing what is happening (promoting awareness). Others are more complicated and require that the leader learn appropriate skills or enlist members' help and participation (e.g., empathy, support).

In this chapter, common aspects and problems of the transition period of group work have been discussed, particularly in regard to personal and task-related consequences. In the processes of storming and norming, group leaders and members must be cognizant of and emotionally attuned at all times to each other's intrapersonal and interactional patterns. If the overall outcome of groups is to be productive, then individuals and the group as a whole must make a transition from the more superficial stage of forming to the more demanding stage of working. To do so, they must learn to relate to one another as well as to plans and purposes.

Classroom Exercises

1. Under your instructor's direction, have group members enact resistant roles: withdrawing, monopolizing, attacking the group leader, and so on. After about 15 minutes of role playing, ask group members what they think would be helpful to them in overcoming resistance to specific situations. Discuss their ideas and classmates' ideas in regard to dealing with resistance.

2. Discuss with a classmate and then the class how you, as a group leader, would promote cohesion. Refer to different techniques mentioned in this chapter as well as to other ideas or procedures you think would be beneficial.

3. Which types of self-disclosure have you seen in groups to which you have belonged? What impact did these revelations have on you? Talk with classmates about how the act of self-disclosure differs for individuals in task/work groups as opposed to counseling, psychotherapy, and psychoeducational groups.

4. What part do you think hope and commitment play in the storming stage of group work? What other factors have you seen successfully employed in helping individuals reach a settlement of conflict or differences? Discuss your ideas and experiences with your class.

CHAPTER 6

The Working Stage in a Group: Performing

Monkey Business/Fotolia

In the calmness of reflection
we examine the depths of our lives
and the purposes for which we have come together.
I am amazed that out of silence
and through sharing
a whole new group has evolved.
In the process of working
we have welded an identity
from where we shall stand
and likewise be moved.*

*From "In Reflection" © 1993 by Samuel T.
Gladding. Reprinted by permission from Samuel T.
Gladding.*

CHAPTER OVERVIEW

From reading this chapter, you will learn about

- Peer relationships, task processes, and team building during the working stage of a group
- Problems that may arise in the working stage of the group
- Strategies for assisting groups in the working stage and achieving positive outcomes

AS YOU READ, CONSIDER

- What part(s) you have played in being a part of a team
- Difficulties you may have had as a member of a team or a group
- Ways you have helped others in a group or the group itself reach a goal

Henry Ford is credited with converting the automobile from an expensive curiosity into a practical and affordable reality. He did so by making use of specialized groups. He changed the ways automobiles were made from one at a time to a moving assembly line where workers would add a crucial part to the car at every station. In a 20-year period (starting in 1908), more than 15 million Model T cars were sold. Ford had proven that small groups of skilled workers can cooperate to make a finished product one step at a time. The adjustment and innovation Ford implemented paid off, and its modern equivalent is found today in total quality groups where camaraderie and expertise are blended together.

Although their groups are broader and more complex than the groups Ford set up, members of successful, ongoing groups in all walks of life usually experience a number of adjustments and changes before they begin to work. However, after a group makes the transition from forming to resolving conflicts and norming, the **working stage** begins. This stage focuses on the achievement of individual and group goals and the movement of the group itself into a more unified and productive system.

The working stage is described as the group's "performing stage" (Tuckman & Jensen, 1977) and its "action stage" (George & Dustin, 1988). It is a time of problem solving that usually lasts longer than any of the other group stages. In groups of all types, somewhere between 40% and 60% of the total group time will be spent in this stage. Task/work groups will generally spend a higher percentage of their time here than will counseling, psychotherapy, or psychoeducational groups because of their purposes and the ways they are run. The working stage is often regarded as the most productive stage in group development and is characterized by its constructive nature and the achievement of results.

During the working stage—as compared to the other stages—group leaders and members feel more freedom and comfort in trying out new behaviors and strategies because the group is settled and issues, such as power and control, have been worked through enough for members to trust one another. At this stage in the group's development, "therapeutic forces," such as openness to self, others, and new ideas, "are well-established" (Ohlsen, Horne, & Lawe, 1988, p. 88). A healthy group, regardless of its purpose, displays a great amount of intimacy, self-disclosure, feedback, teamwork, confrontation, and humor. These positive behaviors are expressed in interpersonal relationships among members (in peer relations). Other behaviors of the group during this stage are primarily focused on task-related endeavors, such as achieving specific goals. Both peer- and task-related dimensions of a group in the working stage are considered in this chapter, along with generic core skills.

PEER RELATIONSHIPS

In the working stage of most groups, members appear to show genuine concern for one another on a deep, personal level. Participants are more *intimate* after control problems have been resolved. Feelings of empathy, compassion, and care abound, and groups gradually grow closer emotionally. This interpersonal bonding, or **cohesiveness**, usually increases, even in task/work groups, as group members interact and understand one another better. This process has positive repercussions in terms of member satisfaction as well as individuals' feelings about themselves and the group as a whole (Perrone & Sedlacek, 2000).

Emotional closeness is especially likely to grow if group members can identify socially with one another and if they have been successful in working through their struggles together. An appreciation of cultural differences is helpful in this process. Whereas the previous stages of the group were characterized by concerns of being *"in and out"* (becoming a member of the group, as opposed to being an outsider) and *"top to bottom"* (establishing one's place in the group structure), the working stage of the group focuses on *"near and far"* (Schutz, 1966). Participants establish how physically and psychologically close they wish to be to others and behave accordingly.

Along with positive feelings about the group and the constructive behaviors of its members comes a greater willingness to self-disclose (reveal information about oneself to the group). Society generally discourages self-disclosure (Jourard, 1971), and in some groups, such as task/work groups or psychoeducational groups, it may be inappropriate for members to be too open. For example, if members talk extensively about family secrets in psychoeducational groups, they most likely have overstepped appropriate limits. However, self-disclosure has a place in most groups.

Self-disclosure involves more than simply talking about oneself. It is a multidimensional activity. It involves listening and receiving feedback as well as speaking. It is related to many other factors, such as the type of group that one is in, the level of others' disclosures, group norms, and timing (Morran, 1982; Stockton & Morran, 1980; Wilson & Hanna, 1986).

Case Example

Self-Disclosing Sally

The group Sally has been in for the past 5 weeks is a counseling group composed of women who have all been abused. Sally has had little to say, although she has been very involved mentally. However, in the middle of the session after Tameka has shared, Sally speaks up. She discloses to the group not only the abuse of the past but the reasons why she did not leave her situation earlier. It is something that is hard for her to do and yet something she feels "comfortable"

in doing. At the end of her self-disclosure, Sally admits she was scared to bring up her situation. Yet, she says that the disclosures of others and the fact that she is feeling comfortable with others made her want to let them know about her situation.

Questions

What do you think is healthy about Sally's actions? What are some potential dangers or drawbacks?

The **Johari Awareness Model**, sometimes called the *Johari Window,* is a good representation of what happens in the arena of self-disclosure when a group is in the working stage (Luft, 1984). This model also illustrates how appropriate disclosure develops during the life of the group (see Figure 6.1).

The first quadrant (the **open quadrant**) contains information that is generally known to self and others. For example, Flo knows that the group is aware that she chews her nails. In the working stage, this quadrant expands. Members learn one another's names, stories, and likes and dislikes. With an expansion of knowledge, participants are able to interact more fully and freely with one another. Exchanges of thoughts and feelings move to a deeper and more personal level. What was previously hidden from others and even from oneself is now exposed and dealt with openly.

The second quadrant (the **hidden quadrant**) contains undisclosed information known only to oneself. This quadrant shrinks during the working stage, through self-disclosure. For example, group members become aware of the experiences others have had, such as the fact that Larry has traveled extensively or that Jackson studied abroad. This information would not be apparent unless it was willingly revealed. Members become increasingly comfortable with one another as a result of finding out more about one another. This comfort leads them to take further risks in revealing hidden secrets to the group as a whole, as Sally did in the example given earlier. When

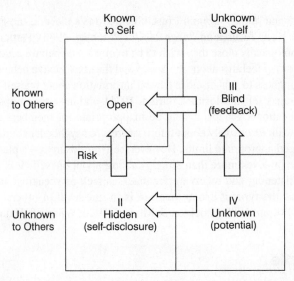

FIGURE 6.1   Johari Window.   *Source:* From J. Luft (1963). *Group Processes: An Introduction to Group Dynamics.* Copyright © 1963 by The McGraw-Hill Companies. Reprinted by permission.

this process happens, members who have opened up, and the group as a whole, are freer to explore other personal and interpersonal dimensions of relationships that were previously limited to them.

The third quadrant (the **blind quadrant**) is originally unknown to oneself but known to others when the group began. For instance, Tom may be unaware that his face twitches slightly before he speaks in the group, but everyone else sees it. In the working stage, the personal unknown area diminishes. Feedback is a key ingredient in this process, as members share their impressions of one another. There is a risk in giving and receiving feedback of this nature, for not all comments may be positive. Therefore, group leaders need to monitor and, if necessary, intervene to be sure effective feedback takes place at this time and throughout the group. Through sharing on a number of levels, members come to know about how they are seen and are able to interact on a deeper and more authentic level in the group.

The fourth quadrant (the **unknown quadrant**) is full of potential. It contains material hidden from self and others because of a lack of opportunity. As the group progresses, this quadrant shrinks. It may be developed in the group because of crises or opportunities. Basically, the possibilities and potentials that individuals possess lie dormant until opportunities arise to express them. In the working stage of the group, some situations develop in which, unknown to the group or the person, an untapped talent emerges. For example, Brenda, a shy group member, may suddenly take the lead when the group is in the midst of a dilemma, such as searching for ways to deal with a rival group in a positive way. Although unexpected, this type of emergent behavior is usually welcomed by all within the group because it represents growth.

Overall, in the working stage of the group, members become increasingly aware of individual participants and the world of each person. More sharing of past and present experiences and perceptions ensues, and risk taking increases. The group and its members achieve growth and freedom. New discoveries open the group and its members to other insights and actions as well. A long-term, closed group membership is especially prone to display these behaviors.

Reflection

When have you seen someone and the group they were in be surprised by that person's actions? What do you think happened to trigger such new behavior? How was it similar or different to the process that has been described in the fourth quadrant (IV) of the Johari Window?

TASK PROCESSES DURING THE WORKING STAGE

The major emphasis in the working stage is productivity, whether the results are tangibly visible or not. Group members focus on improving themselves or achieving specific individual and group goals. One way productivity may be increased is by encouraging equal member airtime through making **rounds** (Yalom & Leszcz, 2005). This procedure has been elaborated on previously, but its importance as a process in a group that is working cannot be overestimated. Members who are given time during the group to discuss issues of concern to them will invest more deeply in the group with each session and will do the type of work that can benefit themselves and the group as a whole. For example, if in a counseling group Timothy realizes the group will help him in finding new ways to overcome his shyness with women, then he is likely to attend all group meetings faithfully and participate actively. The only problem with the technique of rounds is having enough time for all members to articulate and work on situations to the extent they wish.

A second way tasks are accomplished in the working stage is through **role playing**. In role-plays, members are given a chance to assume an identity that differs widely from their present behavior. Role playing is a tool for bringing patterns of behavior and their consequences into focus "by allowing participants to experience the situations concretely . . . gain insight into their behavior, and practice the skills required to manage the situation constructively" (Johnson & Johnson, 2013, p. 55). This psychodramatic technique can be powerful in helping group members see and feel how certain actions will be experienced before they actually occur outside the group (Shaffer, 1997).

Trust and caring are vital in the role-playing process, and specific ideas about what the group member wants to accomplish are helpful. In a role-play, the participants set up an imaginary life situation and ask others in the group to play certain parts while they respond in a prescribed way, such as remaining calm. After the action is completed, the member and the group discuss benefits, consequences, and alternative ways of behaving in the given situation.

Case Example

Name-Calling Nanette

Nanette is an overweight, unkempt, and lethargic sixth grader. She is teased a lot in school. The counseling group she is in is working with her on controlling her temper. She is asked to play the role of being nonchalant when others poke fun at her. She pretends the words are like raindrops bouncing off a finely waxed car. She is in the driver's seat and can remain cool instead of revving up. Nanette finds her role refreshing and she is surprised that she can control her temper.

Questions

How do you think the car metaphor helps Nanette? What other roles might Nanette play that would help her? How might she transfer what she does in a role-play to real life?

A group member can have a frustrating experience in a role-play and still benefit from it. For instance, Helen asked her psychoeducational group members to role-play a situation with her in which she confronted her boss about his rude and demeaning behavior to her. Although group members tried to assist Helen in their enactment of roles, Helen was not sure after the role-play ended whether she had found a way to address her boss or not. However, as she continued talking, Helen began to realize that, although she had not achieved all that she wished, she did feel some relief and confidence about the situation and had a base from which to continue.

Another task process that is prevalent in the working stage is **homework**, or working outside the group itself. Group members often find that they need to carry behaviors they practice within the group to situations outside the group. Although the group or its leader may not give members a specific assignment, they will often try out new skills and bring their experiences back to the group to process. In this way, participants receive twice the benefits they would otherwise: they get to practice skills in a real-life situation, and they get to interact with the group about the experience.

An example of homework is a member practicing being calm when his colleagues in a work setting make demands on him. In returning to the group, he can not only relate how his homework went but receive support and suggestions from other group members on future homework assignments. Homework generally varies in its intensity and importance. Sometimes, simple and less noticeable acts, such as calling friends, going to a meeting, or inviting someone over for refreshments, are vital homework tasks.

Reflection

Outside of an educational setting, when have you had homework or given yourself homework? How did that work for you? How have you seen homework benefit others?

A final dimension that must be considered in the working stage of the group is **incorporation** (a personal awareness and appreciation of what the group has accomplished on both an individual and a collective level). When the working stage of a group ends, members should have a feeling and knowledge of what was achieved and how. Through incorporation, members realize the value of the group in their lives and remember critical times in the group regarding what they or other members of the group said or did. Incorporation prepares members to move on to the termination stage. For example, in thinking about the group as it progressed, Eileen was able to realize that she took risks in the group by disclosing information she had never revealed before. Instead of being devastating, this experience gave her a sense of relief and direction. She was able to take satisfaction in what she had done and began to see that she could accomplish goals outside the group. Her gratitude for the group and for what she learned as a result of being in the group increased.

TEAMWORK AND TEAM BUILDING DURING THE WORKING STAGE

Teamwork and team building are vital in the working stage of groups (Klein et al., 2009; Kline, 2001; Ward, 1997). A **team** is "a number of persons associated together in work or activity" (*Merriam-Webster's Collegiate Dictionary,* 2003). The outcome of a team effort is seen most graphically in athletic or artistic competition in which members of a group act and perform in a coordinated way to achieve a goal in a unified and coordinated manner, such as scoring points in a basketball game or a dance contest (as in the television show *So You Think You Can Dance?*).

Groups sometimes function as teams, whether planned or not. However, selecting members of a group who have excellent emotional intelligence will function best in a team environment because they will add to the group's expressive astuteness and ensure the best possible results (Peterson, 2012). Two ways of selecting members are by using the **Team Player Inventory (TPI)** or the **Group Emotional Intelligence Individual Regulation (GEI-IR)**. The TPI is a 10-item assessment instrument that denotes the degree to which individuals are predisposed toward organizational team-working environments (Kline, 1999). It is practical in determining whether "there are team members who view team work environments as primarily negative" as well as identifying individuals who "are positively predisposed to working in a team environment" (p. 110). The GEI-IR is a three-pronged instrument with a group efficacy scale, a group trust scale, and a group cohesiveness scale. It has practical applications in that it can be used both during a group's life and at its conclusion.

After team members are selected, the next major step in team building is promoting a team spirit. Increasing team spirit increases the likelihood that a group will work together constructively. It is done through encouraging **teamwork** (all members of a group working together cooperatively) through team building. The process of **team building** takes time and may assume different patterns over time (Klein et al., 2009; Kormanski, 1999). For example, some teams may build through completing tasks together, whereas others may do so through extended group discussions. Groups that work to achieve consensus, promote interpersonal relationships, and minimize conflict perform best.

In psychoeducational groups, teamwork and learning are promoted by emphasizing how groups can achieve tasks that cannot be accomplished by an individual alone (Gough, 1987). For instance, if an academic class is given a long reading assignment that could not be covered by one class member in the time allotted, a study group team could come together and distribute the readings. Then each member could become an expert on an area that he or she would later teach the group when they reassembled (Light, 1994).

Teamwork is considered so important to many organizations that teachers from graduate business schools to elementary schools often break their classes into teams at the beginning of a term to help them to master material and to learn how to work cooperatively with others. A team can be a socializing as well as a productive experience. The founder of reality therapy, William Glasser (1986a), considers teams to be an essential part of his theory, especially as it relates to control within self and others. Teamwork and the team building that goes with it can also be applied to counseling and psychotherapy groups in stressing the importance of the interpersonal dimension in one's own growth and development.

Effective development of a team (team building) can take other forms as well. Maples (1992) has proposed one model of developing a group into a team. She premises her model on the assumption that group members trust one another and are motivated for success. Basic components of this model involve choice and ownership. Groups that make positive choices that lead to success do so from a stance of openness, honesty, compassion, enthusiasm, integrity, and a commitment to communication. The ownership of the group is achieved in such cases through patience, objectivity, personal responsibility, and investing energy in the group. Keeping focused in the present, being sincere, and at times being introspective or humorous are other factors that help the group achieve a sense of unity as a team. Maples suggests that groups also need **ice-breaking exercises** (introductory activities that link people together). Such exercises increase the group's awareness of one another or remind members of what they did in previous sessions.

Case Example

Bulldozing Barney

Barney believes that it is always best to get down to business as soon as possible. Therefore, when his task group comes into a room, he gives them an agenda and tells them what they are going to do. He then begins the meeting by going item by item through the handout. Barney's group appears to be unmotivated, and they are behind other groups at the same company who have had a similar assignment.

Questions

What do you think is going on inside Barney's group? How do you think Barney is feeling? Thinking? What do you think the group members are feeling and thinking?

Ward (1997, pp. 115–116) has listed six other factors that either contribute to or distract from the development of teams:

1. *"Leadership style"*—A democratic style works best in building teams because of its cooperative emphasis.
2. *"Member maturity and motivation"*—The more of each, the better.
3. *"Group task or purpose characteristics"*—Some tasks lend themselves to cooperative work more than others.
4. *"Membership stability and group size"*—Irregular attendance is distracting, and having either too many or too few members prohibits the development of a team effort.
5. *"Time availability"*—It is crucial that group goals match time availability.
6. *"Organizational, institutional, cultural, and societal expectations"*—The setting in which a group is conducted will influence whether teamwork is valued, as will the backgrounds of those involved.

PROBLEMS IN THE WORKING STAGE OF GROUPS

Despite good intentions, some groups are more productive than others for a variety of reasons, including pregroup preparation, the composition of group members, the group's focus, and group leadership/followership interactions. Among specific problems that arise during the working stage are fear and resistance, challenges to leaders, and a lack of focus on achieving individual and group goals. These problems are expressed in numerous ways, such as intense emotionality in members, projection or scapegoating of a member, and lack of constructive participation. Focusing on issues outside the group, such as gender or race, or turning inward as a group to be protective (collusion) are also problematic and are considered here.

Racial and Gender Issues

Matters pertaining to race and gender are manifest in some groups more than others, but they occur in most types of groups in both subtle and blatant ways. The thoughts and feelings surrounding these descriptors of persons reflect societal attitudes in general. In regard to race, Rokeach, Smith, and Evans (1960) propose that racial prejudice is based on assumptions about the beliefs and attitudes of persons of a given race. Some groups may struggle or engage in high conflict because of racial prejudices among members. Other groups deal with racial issues through denial (Lanier & Robertiello, 1977). Individuals who hold stereotyped views and act accordingly are **culturally encapsulated** (Wrenn, 1985) and behave in a rigid and stereotyped manner (Ivey, Pedersen, & Ivey, 2001). Contact with others from different cultures in a group context often helps members become more aware of their racial feelings. It can have "the healthy effect" of making them realize their ethnocentric assumptions and limiting beliefs, "thus leading to a broader view of human nature" (Walsh, 1989, p. 547).

The same dysfunctional/functional and nonproductive/productive dynamic of prejudice and stereotypes may occur in regard to gender, too (Sullivan, 1983b). In such cases, the words *male* and *female* are highlighted at the expense of the concept *person.* The result is that males and females must learn new roles within the group that give them greater freedom to be flexible and competent. Sometimes others hamper this new learning, but it has a good chance of success if it is begun early in the group's development. Leaders must work with the group to prevent or limit negative outcomes among members by increasing sensitivity and decreasing the escalation of conflict (Korda & Pancrazio, 1989). Generally, the issue of gender is highly visible and dealt with constructively by group leaders and members as part of larger issues in the working stage.

Group Collusion

Group collusion involves cooperating with others unconsciously or consciously "to reinforce prevailing attitudes, values, behaviors, or norms" (Butler, 1987, p. 1). The purpose of such behavior is self-protection. Its effect is to maintain the status quo in the group. For example, in work groups, when subordinates agree with their boss to keep from being fired, they are engaging in a collusion process. The same is true in psychoeducational groups when students concur with their professors to receive a good grade.

Most groups experience some degree of collusion but, in extremes, group collusion prevents open discussion, critical thinking, and problem solving. Such closedness, and the conformity promoted by it, may lead to a destructive process that is regressive in nature. Janis (1982) has called this phenomenon **groupthink**. In a groupthink situation, there is a "deterioration of mental efficiency, reality testing, and moral judgment that results from in-group pressures" (Janis, 1972, p. 9). Forms of groupthink may become destructive and even deadly. Evidence of the lethal nature of groupthink can be found in the Bay of Pigs invasion of the Kennedy administration; the mass suicide that occurred in Jonestown, Guyana, under the leadership of the Reverend Jim Jones; and the Branch Davidian tragedy in Waco, Texas. In less severe cases, groupthink inhibits growth and represses individual and group development. For example, in some work groups, criticism of a new or existing product may be suppressed because of groupthink. Ignoring the groupthink attitude and expressing criticism may cause talented individuals to lose their jobs and influence in a company. The cartoon "Dilbert" regularly illustrates examples of groupthink.

To prevent group collusion from occurring to any great extent, group membership should be diversified. In addition, open discussion should be promoted, and goals and purposes should be continuously clarified. As a precautionary measure, some type of **devil's advocate procedure** should be actively implemented. This procedure entails asking one or more members in the group to question group decisions with a firm skepticism before the group reaches a conclusion. Such an approach is especially helpful "when the decision scenario involves high uncertainty (little predictability) but plenty of available information" (Chen, Lawson, Gordon, & McIntosh, 1996, p. 589). Interpersonal relationship skills should be strengthened as well. "Groups who wish to structure themselves to avoid faulty decision making are well advised to have impartial leadership and methodical procedures where they avoid overestimation of the group, closed-mindedness, and pressures toward conformity" (Schafer & Crichlow, 1996, p. 429).

Case Example

Danielle as the Devil's Advocate

Danielle is not very popular in her work group. She is always questioning. She wants to know what the expected outcome of an action might be, and if she does not get a specific answer, she will not cooperate with the group. Everyone in the group is tired of her "attitude" and they are now signing a petition to get her transferred.

Questions

Why do you think the group's action is a good or bad idea? What else might they do? What else might Danielle do to help make the group more productive?

THE WORKING STAGE OF THE GROUP AND GROUPS THAT WORK

Just as there is a difference in the dynamics that underlie the working stage of a group's development, there is also a difference in working and nonworking groups. For instance, members of working groups have a sense of cohesion and trust with one another. They work in the present and are willing to take risks in self-disclosing or sharing ideas. When disagreement exists in the group, members acknowledge it and deal with it in an open manner. Communication is clear and direct, and members use one another as resources. In addition, working groups are aware of the group progress and process. They accept responsibility for doing their part within the group in relation to either their own or group goals. They give honest feedback to one another without fear of reprisal. They are hopeful and secure within the group and are, therefore, able to maximize their thinking, feeling, and behaving capabilities. Corey, Corey, and Corey (2014) have identified about 20 characteristics that compare working and nonworking groups. These characteristics include such factors as trust, clear goals, functional leadership, cohesion, acceptance, feedback, clear communication, diversity, and cooperation.

Corey et al. believe that leaders and members both play a vital, interactive part in the success or failure of the group. Research confirms such a view. Leaders who have prepared themselves and their members adequately beforehand are more likely than not to be successful. However, despite preparation, incidents may happen within the working stage of a group that cause problems. For example, the death of a loved one may influence a group member to focus on his or her internal agendas rather than the group's task. Likewise, an unresolved conflict between group members may break down the harmony and constructive nature of the group.

STRATEGIES FOR ASSISTING GROUPS IN THE WORKING STAGE

When groups are not doing well in the working stage, several approaches can rectify the situation: modeling by the leader (Borgers & Koenig, 1983), exercises (Corey, Corey, Callanan, & Russell, 2014), group observing group (Cohen & Smith, 1976), brainstorming (Osborn, 1957), nominal-group technique (NGT) (Delbecq & Van de Ven, 1971), synectics (Gordon, 1961), written projections (Hoskins, 1984), group processing (J. Donigian, personal communication, July 8, 1994), and teaching of skills (Toth & Erwin, 1998).

Modeling by the Leader

The **modeling** method is used to teach group members complex behaviors in a relatively short time by copying or imitating. Modeling depends on timing, reinforcement, the amount of positive feedback received, the view of the group leader, the degree of trust, and the amount of motivation for imitation. Borgers and Koenig (1983) stress that group members borrow from leaders and other members what they need to function better and become more their own persons. Leaders can promote working in the group by displaying behaviors congruent with this stage, such as self-disclosure, or by having a core of group members with whom others can readily identify display such actions. The latter strategy of having peers help peers is especially effective if the members who are modeling behaviors are similar to those they are helping in regard to age, gender, and background (Cox, 1999).

Exercises

Exercises involve less direct showing and more an experiential integration. "The term *exercise* is used among group leaders to refer to activities that the group does for a specific purpose" (Jacobs, Schimmel, Masson, & Harvill, 2016, p. 219). There are different views about whether preplanned exercises should be used in groups and when. On one end of the spectrum is a view represented by Rogers (1970), who advocates the avoidance of "any procedure that is planned" (p. 56). On the other end of this continuum are leaders who simply employ a series of exercises in their groups from group exercise books (e.g., Pfeiffer & Jones, 1972–1980).

A more moderate approach is using exercises in groups at specific times for particular reasons (Carroll, Bates, & Johnson, 2004). As Jacobs et al. (2016) point out, a leader may employ group exercises for at least seven reasons:

1. To increase the comfort level
2. To provide the leader with useful information
3. To generate discussion and focus the group
4. To shift the focus
5. To deepen the focus
6. To provide the opportunity for experiential learning
7. To provide fun and relaxation (p. 205)

All of these reasons make it likely that sometimes group leaders will employ a prestructured exercise during the working stage of the group. Preplanned exercise experiences should not be used indiscriminately or even frequently in the working stage of most groups. However, interventions such as these, when well planned and tailored to a particular situation, can increase member awareness and responsiveness to self and others. Whether exercises are used in group work depends on the need for these devices, the comfort of the group and its leader with them, and the potential benefits and liabilities of using such procedures (Wenz & McWhirter, 1990).

As previously discussed, an icebreaker at the beginning of a group can be a potent stimulant, as can a well-timed intervention at a critical moment in the group's development. For instance, if a counseling group appears to be anxious and overly concerned about one of its members, Michelle, and is talking *about* her instead of *with* her, then the leader might simply ask the group to gather in a tight circle with arms interlocked. Michelle would then be invited to try to break through the circle, which, even if she is successful, would be frustrating and aggravating. From this brief exercise, the leader could help the group focus on its dynamics and the group processes that keep the group from discussing their anxiety about Michelle with her.

Regardless of the types of exercises used, "it is the processing of those activities that translates what happens in group into interpersonal and intrapersonal learning for group members" (DeLucia-Waack, 1997b, p. 82). Through processing of an experiential exercise, group members may "develop a plan of action for transferring . . . learning to their lives outside of the group" (Kees & Jacobs, 1990, p. 23). This benefit may be especially powerful because it offers group members new possibilities for influencing the course of their lives positively.

Despite benefits, group exercises have disadvantages, too (Gladding, 2011b). If they are used too often, group members may become overly dependent on the leader. Exercises may make some group members angry or resentful because members may feel a lack of control over what will happen next. Finally, if employed too frequently, exercises can disrupt the natural development of a group. Therefore, prudence is called for when exercises are used in groups.

Reflection

When have you been in a group where the leader used exercises? How did you like the experiential nature of what you did? What drawbacks or doubts did you have in following the leader's directions? If you were running a group, when might you use exercises? Why?

Group Observing Group

Group observing group requires that the group break up into two smaller groups in any way the leader directs and that each watch the other function (as outsiders). This process is sometimes called a **fishbowl procedure** (see Figure 6.2).

After the group observations are completed, the group reunites, and members give one another and the group as a whole feedback on what was observed. The intent of this activity is to

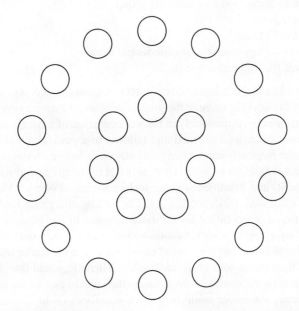

FIGURE 6.2 Group observing group.

help members focus on common concerns that outweigh differences and to begin working harder on shared agendas.

For example, Carolyn might notice that the group she is observing struggles with the problem of making sure everyone who wants to contribute gets heard. This awareness helps her realize that her own group is not unique in its quest to be fair to all members and make sure they have a say. She also realizes some things she could do differently in her own group, such as being an encourager of those who are most reflective and less likely to participate overtly.

A variation on the fishbowl is the two-way fishbowl, that is, the 2-FB model (Hensley, 2002). This model is primarily a group training approach that can be used in academic classes. Participants learn about group theory, process, and leadership by taking on and integrating four different roles: class participant, group member, observation team member, and group leader. Each role provides students with a different lens through which to view and then reflect on the evolution of working groups as they move in and out of these various roles.

Brainstorming

Brainstorming, a way to stimulate divergent thinking, requires an initial generating of ideas in a nonjudgmental manner (Osborn, 1957). The premise of this approach is that critical evaluation of ideas and actions often holds back creativity and member participation. Therefore, in this procedure, the ideas of every person are recorded first before any comments are made. Quantity is emphasized in this process—the more ideas, the better. Only after a large number of ideas have been written down do members go back and evaluate the feasibility of what they have contributed. This results in an increase in group activity and responsibility as well as an emphasis on reality. However, by the time ideas are judged along qualitative lines, many thoughts have been contributed that would not have been voiced otherwise.

Nominal-Group Technique

Another helpful procedure for getting the group to work is the **nominal-group technique (NGT)**. This process has up to six steps (Delbecq, Van de Ven, & Gustafson, 1975). In the first step, the group leader introduces the problem or issue briefly and then asks members to silently, and individually, generate a number of ideas or solutions connected with the statement. Members are given 10 to 15 minutes to complete this exercise and are asked to do it in writing. The second step involves members' sharing of ideas, with each person stating an idea in a round-robin fashion and the group leader writing that idea and an identification code on a blackboard or flip chart before the next person speaks.

The third step requires a discussion of ideas for clarification, with "What did you mean when you said . . . ?" dialogue. The fourth step has members write their top five ideas or solutions on an index card. The leader then collects the cards, a vote is tallied, and the information is fed back to the group as a whole. In the fifth step, a short discussion of the vote follows. At this time, members can again raise points, seek clarification, or solicit comments. The final step is a possible revote, which usually takes place if the discussion on the original vote has brought out new information that members want to consider in light of their earlier decision.

NGT does not require the open exposure of members as much as brainstorming. However, it is quite useful in getting group members to think and to work on problematic situations, especially in task/work groups. Overall, NGT places more objectivity in the group decision-making process than almost any other method.

Synectics

A novel way of helping groups in the working stage become more productive is **synectics**. The word *synectics,* from the Greek, means the joining together of different and apparently irrelevant elements. Synectics theory applies to the integration of diverse individuals into "a problem-stating, problem-solving group" (Gordon, 1961, p. 1). Synectics follows the general pattern of group discussions—problem statement, discussion, solution generation, and decision. There are several important differences, however.

First, throughout the discussion, members are asked to analyze all sides of an issue by adopting a spectrum policy. This policy is the recognition that few ideas are totally good or bad. Next, members are encouraged to express their wishes and hopes throughout this process. Although they may not receive what they wish for, members are able to clarify what they want more clearly through this process and to relieve some pent-up frustrations.

A very refreshing and stimulating part of synectics is called **excursions**. In these activities, members actually take a break—a vacation—from problem solving and engage in exercises involving fantasy, metaphor, and analogy. For example, members might play with how many career paths they could take to get elected president of their country. The idea is that the material generated in these processes can be reintegrated into the group later, specifically to issues that are of individual and group importance.

Written Projections

Written projections are yet another means to help a group during the working stages. Members are asked to see themselves or their groups in the future having been successful and to describe what the experience was like. Group members are able to play with their fantasies at times as well as be realistic. An example of projection that captures the spirit of this approach is the writing of a **therapeutic fairy tale** (Hoskins, 1984). Within 6 to 10 minutes, members are to write their story beginning with "Once upon a time" and including (a) a problem or predicament; (b) a solution, even if it appears outlandish; and (c) a positive, pleasing ending. The time limit helps members focus on the task and prevents resistance.

A group member in a therapeutic group once wrote this fairy tale:

> *Once upon a time, there was an old woman who had managed, like the woman in the shoe, to raise a number of children. The only problem was that the children now knew what they wanted to do with their lives and the old woman did not. At first, she got depressed and thought if she got sad enough the children would come back to her. They did, but they were angry and put her in a mental health facility. She tried getting even more down, but her strategy just didn't seem to help. The children abandoned her.*
>
> *One day the old woman woke up and said to herself, 'Today, I'll wear purple, a healing color, and I will go out in the wards and say hello to everyone I meet.' She did and, to her amazement, most of those she encountered responded back in a positive way. She felt better, they felt better, and as a result she realized all the world could now be her surrogate children. So, she left the hospital with a good feeling and a great plan and lived happily both with her children and her neighbors.*

Group Processing

Another strategy for helping groups maximize their resources in the working stage is through group processing. "Processing can be defined as capitalizing on significant happenings in the here-and-now interactions of the group to help members reflect on the meaning of their experience; better understand their own thoughts, feelings, and actions; and generalize what is learned to their life outside the group" (Stockton, Morran, & Nitza, 2000, p. 345). **Group processing** "refers to the dynamics that naturally occur in the group" (p. 345) or, as Yalom and Leszcz (2005) have characterized it, "the nature of the relationship between interacting individuals" (p. 143). To enhance processing for group workers and group members, the strategy of note-taking is recommended (Falco & Bauman, 2004; Hall & Hawley, 2004). Such a procedure prevents **memory decay** (where more frequent life events of members overshadow previous group experiences). In addition, making process notes provides group members with an opportunity for self-reflection and growth by motivating group leaders and members to "recall each session in detail in order to provide meaningful insights" (Falco & Bauman, 2004, p. 186).

Reflection

When have you made notes about an event in your life, that is, a journal, log, or diary? Were you surprised when you reread this material and remembered events you had forgotten? How do you think making notes in a group would help you in the group? What might be some drawbacks?

As previously discussed, another way to make the most of processing is to bring a process observer into the group. This person is a professional human services worker (e.g., counselor, psychologist, social worker) who is neutral in regard to the group agenda and personalities in the group but who helps the group understand the dynamics within their setting by observing and feeding back to them what is occurring between members and in the group itself. The job of the process observer is not to judge but to inform the group objectively about what is occurring (Benson, 2010; Trotzer, 2007). For instance, in a task group, the observer might say something like the following: "I noticed during this portion of the group that Beverly was trying to make sure the group was aware of the ramifications of investing money in the foundation. She did this through providing the group with a lot of facts. Bree, you were most supportive of Beverly and encouraged her. Chuck, you were also supportive but you seemed to grow impatient as Beverly's presentation continued. Michael, on the other hand, I observed you wanted to end the discussion and kept asking the group if there were other agenda items to cover. I'm not sure exactly what that was about."

Hearing such feedback, group members are then free to discuss and process what the observer has presented. They may do so through talking with one another, owning their feelings, or asking the observer for more detailed or clearer information. In any case, through process observation, the work of the group is enhanced because members begin to see patterns in themselves and others and to address issues related to who they are with one another as well as the content on which they are focusing (Kormanski & Eschbach, 1997). It is prudent for most groups, regardless of their emphases, to have the process observer "report" either right before or after they take a break or when they seem to be getting bogged down. Process observing energizes the group as well as gives it useful information.

Teaching of Skills

A final strategy for improving performance in the working stage of a group is teaching skills. Sometimes group members are not successful because they do not know how to relate well to others, such as giving and receiving interpersonal feedback (Toth & Erwin, 1998). Novice group participants may be especially lacking in feedback skills.

Through teaching members skills, group functioning improves. The reason is that members feel more confident in their abilities and indeed improve them. Basic counseling responses in groups can be learned in a systematic and interesting way (Haney & Leibsohn, 2001).

OUTCOMES OF THE WORKING STAGE

The end result of the working stage of a group is usually tangible. Goals have been worked on and achieved. Some of these goals take the form of personal objectives. For example, in counseling and psychotherapy groups, members are usually involved in improving particular areas in their lives. Other goals evolve as the result of a combined group vision and effort. Group members often gain a clearer idea of what they have accomplished in the working stage when they put their group session goals down on paper before each session.

One of the most productive aspects of the group in the working stage is the learning and sharing of ideas and information among members. As a result, the entire group membership is enriched. Some groups achieve the ability to generate new thoughts spontaneously. "Group stuckness" cannot remain if the group is really working.

An important aspect to realize about any group is its cyclical nature between task and social/emotional vectors (Bales, 1951). Certain roles are primarily task oriented, such as presenting material in a psychoeducational group. Others are either positive or negative in regard to the creating of social/emotional atmospheres, such as welcoming people to the group or ignoring them. Leaders and members must be vitally aware of roles, because by being so, they can best promote strategies and resolutions.

Other procedures used in the working stage of a group overlap with techniques previously described in prior group stages. For instance, in counseling and psychotherapy groups, as participants make discoveries about themselves, they often experience a **catharsis**—a release of pent-up feelings. In such cases, they may cry, laugh, become angry, or tap into any other emotional state that has been released. For example, in a psychotherapy group, Irene found herself still mad at her childhood peers for teasing her about matters over which she had no control, such as where she lived and what her parents did for a living. Her awareness and release of bottled-up feelings were therapeutic, as was the discussion she had later with her group members. However, catharsis by itself does not create lasting change. As Yalom has stated: "No-one ever obtains enduring benefits from ventilating feelings in an empty closet" (Yalom & Leszcz, 2005, p. 90).

Thus, group members need to add actions to the emotions they are experiencing during the working stage. Such a process allows participants to gain insight and become more cognitively aware of themselves and their options. If this developmental process occurs, members **cognitively restructure** their lives (they begin to think of and perceive themselves differently). They see that, although change is difficult, they are not helpless and the situation is not necessarily hopeless (Ellis, 1977, 1986; Watzlawick, 1983). Expressing negative emotions without cognitive restructuring only reinforces such feelings and in the end leads nowhere.

However, with heightened awareness come increased intermember exchanges and a giving and receiving of honest, direct, and useful information. Group members seem to genuinely care how others perceive their behaviors in the working stage. The impact of their actions in promoting or inhibiting relationships becomes valued. The focus is on the present, and it may include **confrontation**. The idea behind confrontation is for members to challenge one another to examine the discrepancies between their words and actions. For example, in a counseling group, Paul may say to Allison, "I hear that you really want to make your own decisions, but I see that you are constantly asking your mother for advice. Help me understand how these two behaviors relate." Confrontation does not usually lead to conflict or withdrawal. Instead, members become more thoughtful about what they are doing and why.

Feedback, which is known as "immediacy," "here-and-now interventions," and "impact disclosure," is the pantheoretical intervention in group work (Claiborn, Goodyear, & Horner, 2001). It refers to the response of one individual to the words and actions of another and is used in the working stage of a group and indeed throughout the group. Feedback usually involves sharing relevant information with other people, such as how they are perceived or how they behave, so they can decide whether to change. Information should be given in a clear, concrete, succinct, and appropriate manner. Feedback is not usually unidimensional (about one thing) (Bednar & Kaul, 1985; Morran, Robison, & Stockton, 1985) but rather often encompasses a variety of information, both conscious and unconscious. Timing and the type of feedback given are important variables on its impact. Positive feedback is generally received more willingly and has a greater impact than negative feedback (Dies, 1983; Morran et al., 1985). However, research shows that the positive–negative sequencing of feedback increases the acceptance of negative feedback (Kivlighan & Luiza, 2005). Likewise, group members rate specific feedback about behaviors as being more effective than general or nonspecific feedback (Rothke, 1986; Stockton & Morran, 1980).

In giving feedback, it is important to "carefully assess" a person's readiness to receive a corrective message (Stockton, Morran, & Harris, 1991, p. 253). It is also essential to allow enough time for processing feedback messages. If adequate time is not allowed, then group members may rationalize or forget the messages they receive. Overall, the quality of feedback is higher during the latter stages of the group, and feedback is likely to be more accepted, especially if it is given by other group members (Ward & Ward, 2014). This may be due to a number of factors including less projection or transference (Lev-Wiesel, 2003). Regardless, it is important that feedback be given within the group throughout the entire group experience. The group leader can do much to facilitate feedback exchanges in a group. Activities that may be employed include

- structured feedback exchange exercises (where the leader sets up ways for members to give exchanges to one another, such as in writing),
- modeling (where the leader regularly gives feedback to members in a direct and caring manner),
- connecting (where the leader helps a group member relate feedback to a goal or behavior),
- consensual validation (where the leader uses other group members to give their reactions to feedback directed at a particular group member), and
- feedback paraphrasing (where the leader has the recipient of feedback repeat what he or she heard in his or her own words) (Morran, Stockton, Cline, & Teed, 1998).

Using a variety of feedback methods may be most helpful in getting messages across.

Case Example

Unaware Olga

Olga joined the psychotherapy group because she felt that she had a way of alienating people from her. Sure enough, she did. When QuiQue stated that he was thinking of taking a social skills class, Olga said: "That's stupid! Be a man!" Zack, the leader, and the rest of the group wrote Olga notes of concern about her action, but Olga did not slow down in her blatant criticism of others. She thought Julie was "a tramp" for flirting with men and told her so.

At this juncture, Zack asked if someone in the group might model other ways for Olga to express her disdain for what Julie was doing. Katie did, using milder language. Others followed. Still, Olga was outspoken and usually hurtful when she responded to others. The next time Olga exploded, it was at Zack, who this time responded by paraphrasing, saying: "Olga, it sounds like you hate me."

Olga finally got it. "Oh," was all she could add. "I didn't realize my words were so powerful."

After that, Olga watched her words and actually asked others to help her frame her thoughts in a gentler style.

Questions

What do you think about the way Olga received feedback? Would other ways of giving feedback have been more effective? For instance?

The **corrective emotional experience** is another benefit that can come in the working stage of the group. Yalom and Leszcz (2005) describe this experience as the hallmark of the working phase of therapy groups. A group supportive enough to permit the risk taking that goes with this experience must have been developed beforehand. If it has, then the corrective emotional experience has several components. The first is that the group member must risk making "a strong expression of emotion, which is interpersonally directed." "Reality testing," which allows the group member "to examine the incident with the aid of consensual validation from the other members," is also necessary. Then the group member must recognize "the inappropriateness of certain interpersonal feelings and behavior or the inappropriateness of certain avoided interpersonal behavior." Finally, the group and its leader must help the member going through this experience in every way possible "to interact with others more deeply and honestly" (p. 26).

In addition to increased intimacy, openness, and feedback, another quality that is useful, important, and likely to be helpful during the working stage is **humor**—the ability to smile or laugh at oneself or a situation in a therapeutic and nondefensive manner. Groups that last make more frequent and longer use of humor than those that are short lived (Scogin & Pollio, 1980). In a successful working stage, seriousness may be interspersed with laughter as members gain better insight into themselves, others, and the dynamics of life inside and outside the group. Humor may have a potential benefit for a group by easing tension, distilling hostility, promoting positive communication bonds, and fostering creativity (Baron, 1974; Fine, 1977; LaGaipa, 1977; Murstein & Brust, 1985).

The exact role humor plays in a group is not always easy to determine. Certainly, it may distract members from their work or be used to make put-downs. Therefore, it is important for groups to notice when and how humor is used to determine its impact. There are always opportunities to cultivate humor by taking advantage of paradoxes within the group, discrepancies, the unpredictable, the unanticipated, universal truths, the absurd, and the familiar. For example, in a round, the group leader asks members to remember a funny experience in their lives that made them more aware of their humanness. Sam relates that because of his cultural background, he had not understood that a "Danish" was a sweet pastry as well as a person from Denmark. When he was invited by his group to "go get a Danish," he just looked at them in amazement and questioned why they would want to do something like that. It was only when his peers escorted him to a bakery that he fully understood what they were talking about and laughed with them at the misinterpretation (Gladding, 2010a).

Well-conducted counseling, psychotherapeutic, task/work, and psychoeducational groups often make use of humor. Sharing a lighter moment from one's personal experience or enjoying an illustration that makes a point while being amusing helps people remember and enjoy a laugh together at no one's expense. Humor also helps individuals and group members as a whole bond and gain insight by smoothing group interaction, forming a collective identity, separating the group from others, and securing appropriate behavior (Fry & Salameh, 1993; Rothwell, Siharath, Bell, Nguyen, & Baker, 2011). It influences them positively about working together. In fact, several major companies, such as Southwest Airlines, General Electric, IBM, and AT&T, have found that successful organizational humor can have a positive impact on a variety of group processes (e.g., effective communication, development of group goals, and management of emotion) and outcomes (e.g., group productivity, group viability, and development of group members), which contribute to overall group effectiveness (Romero & Pescosolido, 2008).

Reflection

What type of humor have you seen in the groups in which you have been a member? When have you seen humor be therapeutic in a group? When have you seen humor be detrimental to a group? If you were to use humor in a group setting, what kind of humor would you employ—for example, paradox, jokes, exaggeration?

Summary and Conclusion

The working stage is when the group should be most productive in resolving or solving personal, task, or educational issues. If for some reason this stage of the group does not go well, then group members may leave the group frustrated and disheartened. In addition, attempts at termination will be impeded. Members who have had a bad experience in the group during this stage are less likely to want to participate in collective efforts again. In contrast, when the group functions well in the working stage, members are positively influenced.

Some of the factors of which group leaders and members must be aware and execute to help groups help themselves have been highlighted. Among these important elements in assisting the group to be productive are modeling, structured exercises, groups observing groups, brainstorming, the nominal-group technique, synectics, written projects, group processing, and teaching skills. When groups are successful in the working stage, they achieve goals and move toward termination. Members of such groups increase their insight and use of basic therapeutic devices through such devices as feedback, confrontation, corrective emotional experience, and humor. In successful groups, the working stage is one that is remembered fondly and proudly by its members.

Classroom Exercises

1. Divide into groups of four. Discuss the use of humor in groups for facilitating the group process. What are the advantages and limitations of using humor in task, guidance, and therapy groups?
2. Write a "therapeutic fairy tale" about some aspect of your life. In groups of two, discuss how you reacted to this exercise and for which populations you think it would be appropriate. Share your story and ideas with others in the class.
3. How does a representation such as the Johari Window help you understand the similarities and differences between working and nonworking groups? Be specific.
4. Discuss the nominal-group technique. Use the technique to generate ideas about how, when, and with whom NGT would be most effective.

CHAPTER 7

Wavebreak Media Micro/Fotolia

Closing a Group

I travel back to the land of my genesis
as a different man in a changing world,
like Joseph, after his stay in Egypt.
At the end of night, I will begin,
by exploring the light and hope of dawn,
recalling the length of just past days,
and feeling the warmth of lasting friendships.
Amid the abundance of still fresh memories
I will journey on a path of transition
into the unknown and ever evolving
as I experience the fullness of time
that leads to closure and permanent growth.*

*From "Transitions" by Samuel T. Gladding,
© 1994, Samuel T. Gladding. Reprinted by
permission from Samuel T. Gladding.*

CHAPTER OVERVIEW

From reading this chapter, you will learn about

- How to prepare for and close a group
- The effects on individuals of ending a group
- Specific ways of closing a group, problems in the procedure, and the importance of follow-up sessions after a group has ended

AS YOU READ, CONSIDER

- Your usual reaction to ending or closing an event or experience
- Your thoughts and feelings about giving other members of a group feedback when a group ends
- Strategies you consider effective or have used to help you end one experience and start another

few years ago, I conducted a retreat for a small liberal arts college. On the last day, I woke up to a serenade. The words the young women were singing, were these:

"I want to linger, a little longer. I want to linger here with you.
And as the days go by, I'll think of you and sigh.
This is good day and not good-bye."

The sentiment was wonderful but alas the retreat ended and the students went back to campus and to classes with mixed feelings, of course, but with a song in their hearts. That scenario of a defined completion is one that happens with functional and productive groups. It is crucial to the health and well-being of those involved that groups conclude properly.

Closing a group, whether for a group session or for an entire group experience, received little attention in professional group publications until the 1970s. For example, it was not until 1977 that Tuckman and Jensen added the stage "adjourning" to the developmental model of groups devised by Tuckman in 1965. Part of the reason for the neglect of endings in group work was the assumption that closing a group experience on any level is a natural phenomenon that most leaders and participants know how to do.

Yet, ending a group is never simple. Group leaders, members, and the group as whole may handle it awkwardly or ineptly, and the results in such cases may be harmful or hurtful (Mangione, Forti, & Iacuzzi, 2007). Through design or neglect, proper preparations are sometimes not made in the adjourning process. Ending a group is filled with thoughts and feelings that tend to influence individuals long after the group experience is just a memory (Stein, 1993). According to Corey (2012), the closing stage is equal in importance to the beginning stage of a group. During the forming stage of a group, members get to know one another better; during the closing stage, they come to know themselves on a deeper level. If adjourning is properly understood and managed, it can be an important force in promoting change in individuals. "A successful completion of the group has a strong impact on group members' self-esteem, sense of accomplishment, and self-confidence" (Shechtman, 2014, p. 591).

Primary activities of group members in closing are to (a) reflect on their past experiences, (b) process memories, (c) evaluate what was learned, (d) acknowledge ambivalent feelings, and (e) engage in cognitive decision making (Brabender, 2010; Wagenheim & Gemmill, 1994). Through members' participation in these activities, they are helped to integrate and use information gleaned from the group experience in outside situations (Lieberman, Yalom, & Miles, 1973). They are able to generalize learning from one situation to another (Shulman, 2012). For instance, if Maria realizes in the group that she has the ability to confront individuals and does not have to placate them, then she can use this skill in her work situation when individuals constantly make demands on her.

Overall, closing is a transition event that ends one set of conditions so that another experience can begin (Hackney & Cormier, 2012). It is considered the last stage of the group process, but in reality it marks a new beginning. Closing provides group members an opportunity to clarify the meaning of their experiences, consolidate the gains they have made, express their joys as well as their regrets, measure their growth, and make decisions about the new behaviors they want to carry away from the group and apply to their everyday lives. It is influenced in a positive or negative way by the leader's action and direction (Benson, 2010). It differs for members in closed-ended versus open-ended groups because members of closed-ended groups prepare for and experience the closing collectively, whereas members of open-ended groups prepare for and experience closing individually.

There are many issues and processes in ending a group. One concern is **emotional ambivalence**. Often there are feelings of loss, sadness, pain, and separation (Mangione et al., 2007; Shulman, 2011). Frequently, these feelings are mixed with those of hope, joy, anticipation, and accomplishment. Almost always, there are issues involving "unfinished business," transference, and countertransference (Tudor, 1995). How to solidify and translate learning accomplished within the group to outside experiences is still another aspect of ending a group. Therefore, it is crucial to the health and well-being of everyone in a group that ending the group be handled correctly. If the change, loss, and grief that are a part of closing a group are not acknowledged and overtly handled, then gains made within the group by its members will be minimal.

In this chapter, several different aspects of closing a group are covered. First, proper preparation for closing is examined. Second, the effect of ending on the individual is explored. Next, ways of handling premature endings are discussed, especially when the ending is involuntary. Fourth, proper methods of ending single group sessions are noted, along with appropriate ways of ending the group as a whole. Finally, the issues of problems in terminating a group experience and of group member follow-up are addressed. In each of these situations, the responsibilities of leaders and members are highlighted.

PREPARING FOR CLOSING A GROUP

Proper preparation for ending a group begins in the planning stage. Leaders should have in mind not only what type of group they wish to conduct but also how long it will meet and how it will end. They are guided in these decisions by theoretical and pragmatic considerations, such as which approach has shown positive results with certain populations and problems as well as which facilities are available and when.

To ensure proper group procedures from start to end, leaders must establish appropriate boundaries. **Boundaries** are physical and psychological parameters under which a group operates, such as beginning and ending on time or sitting in a certain configuration, such as a circle (Carroll, Bates, & Johnson, 2004). Leaders who do not keep these dimensions of a group in mind basically "are abdicating their responsibility and reinforcing a perception many group members may already have—that people often don't mean what they say, that they cannot be trusted" (Bates, Johnson, & Blaker, 1982, p. 88). Therefore, planning for closing should go hand in glove with other theoretically based group procedures and be a coordinated process. The impact of ending on the growth of individuals and the group as a whole is both direct and subtle.

Case Example

Ernie Tries to End a Group

The last thing Ernie thought he needed was instruction on how to end a group. He had been in groups before that just seemed to end, and he thought he would know both the time and the way to finish the counseling group he was leading. The trouble was that he did not have the foggiest idea how he would know what to do and when. Therefore, week after week group members attended, and Ernie pretended that that was what was supposed to happen.

About 6 months into the group, members began to attend irregularly. There was a lack of energy in those who did attend, and everyone looked to Ernie to make the situation better.

Finally, Ernie announced to the 7 of 12 members still coming that after the day's meeting that the group would not meet again. Many of the members were upset or mad. They shared their anger with him. He was visibly shaken by the time everyone left. It was not as he had hoped.

Questions

What could Ernie have done to have made the transition smooth? Do you think group members were justified in being angry at him? How would you have felt had you been one of the members?

Closing occurs on two levels in groups: at the end of each session, and at the end of a certain number of group sessions. Both types of closing have step processes within them that are predictable. In considering closing, group leaders should make plans accordingly. One of the best guidelines for making plans to terminate is based on a model for ending family therapy sessions, whose main idea is that, regardless of theory, closing entails four steps: (a) orientation, (b) summarization, (c) discussion of goals, and (d) follow-up (Epstein & Bishop, 1981).

During orientation, the subject of closing is raised. At times during the process, group members are reminded when a session or a group will end. During summarization, material that has been covered and processes that have occurred in the group are reviewed. Ideally, both the group leader and group members participate in this summary. During the discussion of goals, the group focuses on what members will do after the session or the group ends. In the final step, follow-up, group members inform one another of the progress they have made in obtaining their objectives. Through reminding themselves of these steps and procedures, group leaders help themselves, group members, and the group as a whole come to a successful ending.

In open-ended therapy groups, such as those for psychiatric patients, endings are highly individualized, but even these situations contain some predictability. For example, Yalom (Yalom & Leszcz, 2005) states that most psychiatric patients in outpatient groups require approximately 12 to 24 months to undergo substantial and durable change. Working though issues in these types of groups takes time. Therefore, trying to end a group before its members are ready for closure is ill advised and can be detrimental.

In closing a group session, a leader should inform members that the group is ending about 5 to 30 minutes before its conclusion. Such an announcement (orientation) does not have to be elaborate. Rather, the leader can simply say during a pause or a brief interruption, "I see we have about 15 minutes left. What do we need to do collectively or individually to end on time?" In a therapy group, the amount of time needed to bring about closure is almost always greater than in a task/work or psychoeducational group. Regardless, this orientation to the end makes it possible for the group members to summarize, set goals, and plan for follow-up if they wish.

In ending a total group experience, the orientation to closing involves a planned number of sessions that are devoted to the topic of termination. In closed-ended counseling and psychotherapy groups, at least two to four sessions should be focused on the ending (Gazda, 1989; Maples, 1988). Task/work groups may decide to disband more rapidly, but they also need time to get used to the idea of no longer being a group. The time is needed because, in some task/work groups, members hinge part of their identity on the group (Stein, 1993). Ideally, group members review what was completed, assess output versus objectives, assess the group's ability to meet the evaluation of those who use or view group output, and prepare group output for final disposition (Keyton, 1993). In psychoeducational groups, members are usually aware in advance that the group will be time limited. However, a reminder is often appreciated and keeps the group on task and mentally prepared for the final ending. A straightforward orientation to closing followed by the other steps in the termination process helps members accomplish their pregroup goals and clarify any questions they have of themselves or others. Members who gain the most from a group experience are informed in advance what will happen during the time they are together and what is expected of them.

Reflection

With what groups have you most identified in your life? How did it feel to leave these groups? What was the best experience you had when the group ended? What was the worst? How can this knowledge inform you about terminating a group?

EFFECTS ON INDIVIDUALS OF ENDING A GROUP

Ending a group has an impact on individuals. How much depends on many factors, including whether the group was open-ended or closed-ended; whether members were, in fact, prepared in advance for its ending; and whether the speed and intensity of work within sessions was at an appropriate level to allow participants to properly identify and resolve concerns or problems. If handled inappropriately, ending a group may adversely affect persons and inhibit their growth. "If handled adequately, the process of termination in itself can be an important role in helping individuals develop new behaviors" (Hansen, Warner, & Smith, 1980, p. 539). Often from the death of relationships, whether physical or psychological, comes a new understanding of who one was with others and who one is now as a result (Hulse-Killacky, 1993). However, for such benefits to occur, group members must work through their feelings just as people who experience death and grief do (Kübler-Ross, 1973).

The behavior of group members at the end of the group indicates how they think and feel as well as what they have experienced. Members who are anxious at or during the closing may feel they cannot function without the group's support. Participants who are sad may be afraid they will not see others in the group again. Those who are angry may think they have not accomplished what they should have done (Ellis, 1988). For example, if Jane says to the group that she is "upset" about its ending and wishes to continue longer, she may be indirectly stating that she wants reassurance from group members that she is competent to deal with situations by herself.

Usually the range of feelings among individual group members is wide. In some cases, group members emphasize only the positive aspects of what has occurred in the group instead of what they have learned. This type of focus is known as **farewell-party syndrome** and tends to avoid the pain of closure (Shulman, 2012). However, the most likely overriding emotion at the end of a group is one that can best be described as mixed or bittersweet (Goodyear, 1981).

The best way for individuals to end a group is to reflect on what they have experienced and make way for new beginnings outside the group. However, the achievement of this ideal is not always possible. Therefore, group leaders may have to focus special attention on the issue of separation with some people more than others. For example, the leader may have to spend more time with Jason at the end of a psychotherapy or counseling group because of his unstable background. In contrast, the leader may spend less time with Jacob because of his emotionally secure past. For Jason, the fear that he will be unable to find supportive relationships in other settings can be countered by a leader who helps him remember the risks he took in the present group and ways he achieved his group goal in a personal and satisfactory way.

Regardless of how careful and thorough the leader is during the closing stage, a few group members may occasionally need more help. For these people, three options are productive:

1. individual counseling, in which unique concerns can be given greater attention;
2. referral to another group or organization, in which more specific or specialized assistance can be rendered; or
3. **recycling**, in which the individual can go through a similar group experience again and learn lessons missed the first time.

In all of these cases, the focus is on helping group members maximize their capabilities and obtain their goals. Through these procedures, group members discover more about themselves, try to better understand others, and take steps toward creating the types of communities or organizations they need.

PREMATURE CLOSING OF A GROUP

Sometimes, individuals quit a group abruptly or the group experience ends suddenly because of actions by the leader. Both cases are examples of **premature termination** and may result in difficulties for the participants (Donigian & Hulse-Killacky, 1999). Various theoretical perspectives and practitioners handle such situations differently. For example, a person-centered group and leader may trust a group member's judgment that leaving before the group is scheduled to end is the best action, whereas a group and leader with a reality-therapy orientation may concentrate on trying to persuade a member not to leave.

There are guidelines (e.g., Association for Specialists in Group Work, 2007) to follow in premature ending cases regardless of the reason for the action or the group leader's theoretical persuasion. Most of these guidelines apply to psychoeducational, counseling, and psychotherapy groups because the impact of premature endings is greatest on these types of groups. Task/work group members and leaders, however, may also make use of these guidelines.

Generally, three types of premature endings must be dealt with: the termination of the group as a whole, the successful ending of a group for an individual member, and the unsuccessful ending of a group for a member (Yalom & Leszcz, 2005).

Premature Closing of the Group as a Whole

The premature closing of the whole group may occur because of a group leader or group member action. Group leaders may appropriately terminate the group prematurely if they become sick, move, or are reassigned to other duties. In all of these situations, group members may feel incomplete and try to reestablish contact with the leader (Mangione et al., 2007; Pistole, 1991).

To handle these types of premature closings properly, leaders need to have at least one group session to say good-bye to the group as a whole, or they need to be able to contact group members directly. The logistics of making such arrangements is sometimes difficult. Inappropriate premature endings, however, are even more stressful. Group leaders who prematurely terminate groups because they feel personal discomfort, fail to recognize and conceptualize problems, or feel overwhelmed by members' problems do themselves and the group a disservice by leaving the group and its members with unresolved issues.

Premature Closing Initiated by Group Members

For individuals, premature termination may be due to appropriate or inappropriate reasons, and the experience may be successful or unsuccessful. Yalom (Yalom & Leszcz, 2005, p. 233) lists a number of reasons that are often given by individuals who leave psychotherapy and counseling groups prematurely: (a) "external factors" (e.g., scheduling conflicts, external stress), (b) "group deviancy" (members who do not "fit in" with others), (c) "problems of intimacy," (d) "fear of emotional contagion" (a negative personal reaction to hearing the problems of other group members), (e) "inability to share the doctor" (wanting individual attention from the group leader), (f) "complications of concurrent individual and group therapy," (g) "early provocateurs" (overt, strong rebellion against the group), (h) "inadequate orientation to therapy," and (i) "complications arising from subgrouping." Of these reasons, those involving external factors, not fitting in, and complications of concurrent individual and group therapy are most likely to be appropriate factors in deciding to end a group experience early. It should be cautioned, however, that group members may rationalize reasons for premature endings.

The other reasons given by Yalom, with the exception of inadequate orientation, are associated most often with the immaturity of group participants. Immature individuals, who are usually unsuccessful in the group process, avoid dealing with loss by physically removing themselves from the group. They deny their need for self-exploration and understanding. They often prevent themselves from experiencing deep personal growth by making a few changes in behavior and then leaving. At other times, if such group members do not remove themselves but consistently and disruptively act out, then the leader may have to ask them to leave. This type of behavior is in marked contrast to successful group members who terminate prematurely for legitimate reasons and take the time to say good-bye to others in the group before they go.

Case Example

Edith's Exit

Edith felt more uncomfortable with her counseling group every week. She thought others were talking more, gaining greater insights, and growing healthier than she was. That bothered her a great deal. She thought of leaving but decided her parents would not approve. Therefore, she struggled in the group. One day she simply arrived early, left a note on the leader's chair, and went home.

When she received phone calls later that night after the group, she did not answer. Instead, she binged on ice cream from her freezer and turned up the volume of the television.

Questions

What do you think Edith could have done that would have been more constructive and productive? How? When?

Preventing Premature Closing

If a group appears to have a high potential for a premature ending, steps can be taken to prevent it. For instance

- groups should start and end on time,
- members should commit to attend a number of sessions,
- members should be treated in a personal and professional way,
- clarity and conciseness should be used in talking about individual and group issues, and
- reminders should be sent to members if there are long intervals between group sessions (Young, 2013).

Other steps can be taken to soften or alleviate a premature ending and its potential negative impact. The first action is for the leader or members to inform the group as soon as possible about their departure from the group. Individuals need time to prepare for transitions and loss. The more time available, the better, especially if the departure is unexpected. For example, a leader who must move because his or her spouse is relocating may telephone group members to prepare them for this event before the next session, especially if the move is unforeseen or sudden.

A second procedure group leaders can follow when faced with a member wanting to leave prematurely is to discuss thoroughly the ramifications of such a move with the member and the group in a safe, protected atmosphere (Corey, Corey, & Corey, 2014). Members might not leave a group prematurely if they are given a chance to talk things out and explore their feelings more thoroughly. For instance, Peter may think he has been slighted but may feel differently once he has had a chance to face the issue in the group. Through this type of contact, he may recognize his tendency to flee situations when he is uncomfortable and acknowledge that he may have to change his lifestyle if he stays in the group.

Finally, in the case of premature closure, members should be helped to realize what they have gained from the group and what positive steps they can take in the future to build on these achievements. Giving members feedback is one valuable way to help them adjust to an abrupt ending (Wagenheim & Gemmill, 1994).

Case Example

Penny's Project

Penny joined a task group to help her gain skills in decision making and follow-through. After several sessions with the group, she decided she wanted to work on the project on her own without input from the group. Because the task group had completed only about half of its sessions, Penny was unsure how to leave. She did not want to be passive aggressive and just not show up. Therefore, she told the group at its seventh session about her plans.

To her surprise and delight, members were understanding. Directed by the group leader, they each told her what she has meant to them and the group as a whole. For instance, Dick said: "Penny, I have really benefited from the energy you have generated in this group," and Robin responded, "Penny, I find what you want to do to be refreshing and inspiring." When the feedback was finished, Penny felt good about her experience, as did members of the group. She left on a positive note and was able to consolidate the benefits she had derived from the group.

Questions

When have you seen people depart from a group or a project early and receive positive feedback? How do you think you can apply this example to your present or future life as a group member or a group leader?

Occasionally, a member will drop out of the group with no warning and without saying good-bye. In such cases, the group leader should follow up and ask the absent member why he or she left the group prematurely. The member should be invited back to discuss his or her thoughts and feelings with the group as a whole and to say good-bye and achieve closure when appropriate. Best practices guidelines for groups (Thomas & Pender, 2008) and ethical codes state that no undue pressure should be used to force a person to remain in or to return to a group. However, the benefits and liabilities of staying in the group can and should be explored openly.

CLOSING OF GROUP SESSIONS

There are numerous ways to end individual group sessions. For each group session, the appropriate format for closing will depend on the type of group that was conducted, the purpose of the particular session, and the content of the session. The leader should vary the ending of the group whenever possible so members do not get bored with the same routine (Conyne, Crowell, & Newmeyer, 2008). Among the most effective formats for closing a session are having the members summarize, having the leader summarize, using a round, using dyads, scaling activities, and getting written reactions, such as journaling or logs (Jacobs, Schimmel, Masson, & Harvill, 2016). Rating sheets and homework are also recommended (Wagenheim & Gemmill, 1994).

Member Summarization

In member summarization, one or more members of the group summarize what has occurred during the session, describing what has happened to them individually and how they have gained from the particular session. If done regularly, summarization challenges members each week to think about what they are both giving and getting from the group. At least 10 minutes should be allotted to this exercise, but it is important that group members not become bored. Thus, each member who speaks must keep his or her summary brief. For example, member comments at the end of a session might go as follows:

DANIEL: I've learned a lot just by listening today. I've found out I share many of the same feelings about taking risks that Russell does.

MARY GRACE: I was surprised that the focus of the group today centered on risks. I expected we would talk about past events, not present challenges. This session has got me thinking about what I will do in regard to my work situation.

RUSSELL: It was a risk for me to speak up today and talk about my feelings in regard to taking risks, such as moving to a new city. Although I still have mixed emotions about what I am going to do in the future, I'm glad I spoke up.

CHIP: I'm glad you initiated our focus on risk taking, Russell. There are some situations in my own life that involve risks that I want to talk about next time.

Leader Summarization

When leaders summarize, they give a personal reaction to what they perceive to have occurred in the group. Leaders may comment on the cohesion of the group, the degree to which members freely brought up topics for work, the willingness of members to take risks and talk about unsafe topics, the degree to which members interacted with one another, and the willingness of members to discuss negative concerns or feelings (Corey, Corey, Callanan, & Russell, 2014).

Case Example

Samatha Summary

Samatha realized that a lot had happened in the session of the counseling group that she was leading. As it was coming to a close, she decided to try to capture the most important interactions, so she gave the following summary.

"As we close today, I'd like to tell you what I observed. It may be helpful to you as you leave and as you think about what you will do in the group next week. I noticed Julie confronted Joe on the issue of anger during the session. I don't know that the two of you resolved how anger should be handled, but at least you started a dialogue. I was also pleased to see Sheree assert herself. Sheree, I have

wondered about your silence, so it was good to see you come out. Markus, I was impressed with your comments, too, about trying new behaviors when in a different environment. I'll be interested in what you do this week in that regard. Thom, it seemed to me that you were avoiding confrontation with Diana today. It might be productive for you and Diana to talk about that next session. Well, that's it. See you next week."

Questions

What do you think of Samatha's summary? Would you have said less or more? Why? How might your style differ from that of Samatha?

The advantage for leaders in summary situations is the emphasis they can place on certain points and comments. The disadvantage is that leaders may neglect some important developments during the session or fail to mention the contributions of one or two members. Also, leaders may misinterpret behaviors or interchanges.

Rounds

The exercise of rounds (sometimes called **go-rounds**) is a variation on member summarization, except in this procedure every group member comments briefly (usually in a sentence or two) about highlights of the group session. Rounds are a way of completing loose thoughts, ending on a positive note, and ensuring that each member feels involved in the group (Trotzer, 2007). Every group member gets equal airtime and leaves with a feeling of having participated in the group.

Case Example

Robin Makes the Rounds

At the ending of a group, Robin wanted to make sure everyone had a say about the way the psychoeducational group had gone. Although it was unusual, she decided to let each person present say a sentence or two about what they had learned in the group. To her surprise, the process went well, and as one member put it toward the end of the round, "Everyone has reminded me of important points I do not want to forget."

Questions

When have you ever been reminded of ideas by someone? How often has it been in a group setting? How frequently has it been at the close of a unit of study or an interpersonal experience? How might you use what you know from these experiences in your work at the end of a group?

Dyads

By having members form into groups of two, or **dyads**, at the end of a session, group leaders make sure all members are involved in the closing, and at the same time, the group is energized. Often, group leaders may decide to pair participants up at the end of a session if they are working on similar concerns or problems. For example, if Tom and Jeanne are both striving to be better listeners and more empathetic, then they may be put together to talk and practice skills connected with their concerns. If there are no obvious pairings, then members are free to choose their partners or work with those assigned to them.

Scaling Activities

Scaling activities are a way of finding out the level of satisfaction group members have in a quick and efficient fashion. Scaling can be done one of two ways. At the end of a group session or at the end of a group itself, the leader can ask members to rate their satisfaction of the group experience from 1 to 10, with 10 being the highest. This numerical exercise can be followed up by members either talking about their rating or elaborating about it in writing. If writing is chosen, the information gleaned is more tangible and useful for the group leader. For instance, if Diana rates the group as a 6, she might write, "I liked the group but I felt if you (the leader) had cut some of the more verbal members of the group off, and had drawn out the more introverted members, we would have had more ideas and better discussions."

Written Reactions

Writing is frequently used at the end of group sessions. It is an aid to promoting reflection because of the time and structure group members have to devote to it. Furthermore, writing can demystify the group process, encourage deeper participation, validate members' feelings about group experiences, and increase cohesiveness among members of the group (Cummings, 2001).

Several forms of written reactions can be used at the end of group sessions besides elaborating on scaling. One such activity is an exercise in which members are asked to take a few minutes during the closing of a session and write their reactions to what has happened. This procedure is conducted infrequently, and members may or may not share their writing, depending on the time left in the session and the leader's instructions.

A second form of this procedure is for group members to write regularly at the end of each session in journals, or logs (Gladding, 2011b). In this process, group members are required to write their reactions to the events of each session. This process enables them to spot inconsistencies in their reactions more quickly than if they simply talked about them. In effect, a paper trail is established that group members and the group leader may later consult in charting the personality of the group. "Indeed, the collected logs can be a robust diary of the entire group experience, documenting the ups and downs, the progress or lack of it, and can sometimes serve as a map showing members' growth" (Riordan & White, 1996, p. 98). There is no one agreed-on time at which logs should be written after the end of a session. "Logs written immediately following the session will tend to reflect more accurately the emotions experienced within the session, while those written following a reasonable time lapse will present observations digested and organized in a fashion compatible with the self-concept" (Riordan & Matheny, 1972, p. 381). Either way, some information and insight will usually surface.

Writing and exchanging **journal letters** is a third way of ending group sessions (Cummings, 2001). In this practice, group members and the leader write about their experiences in an ongoing group and give their letters (usually one or two pages) to each other (members to leader and leader to members). In the case of students learning about groups, such an exchange helps "correct misperceptions, encourage risk taking in self-disclosure and in challenging of other group members, reinforce helpful leadership behaviors that members had used in the sessions, and answer questions posed by group members" (p. 11).

A fourth form of writing is to combine the written word with either music or drawings (Wenz & McWhirter, 1990). For example, in summing up a session or a group, members may be invited to draw logos that represent their lives or to bring in music that symbolizes through lyrics or a melody what they are. In the case of Elaine, she drew a tree that was green and full as her logo, with words underneath it:

I have grown to be me,
All that I hoped in the gr oup I could be .
Now I am moving on .

Logos can be created by first asking members of groups to doodle. After a few minutes, they are invited to find part of the doodle to expand in making their logo. They are also encouraged to think of words and phrases that come to mind as they embellish their drawings and to jot these descriptors down for when they write about what they have drawn.

Finally, the group leader can make written notes about or to members at the end of each session, which may or may not be shared with the group or individuals. When the leader chooses to write notes about members, this usually takes the form of a private, clinical record. When the leader writes notes to group members on their logs, the response is aimed at promoting insight and communication with individuals. In some group exercises, the leader or other members give written responses to the group as a whole.

> ### Reflection
>
> When have you received a letter or a written statement that you valued? What is the advantage of writing out reactions or suggestions as opposed to verbally saying them to a person? What care must be taken when writing? Give examples.

Rating Sheets

Another way of closing a group and obtaining an accurate picture of how the group assessed the session is by having the leader distribute a **rating sheet** to members that they fill out and return before they leave. Members can rate themselves, other members, and the leader on a number of dimensions, including involvement, risk taking, goals, emotional involvement, feedback, and productivity (Corey, Corey, Callanan, & Russell, 2014). They can give their opinions on how satisfactory the group was for them and how they think it could be improved. To be effective, a group session rating sheet should be brief. Sometimes it can be set up in the form of incomplete sentences, as follows:

1. The thing I liked most about today's group was _____.
2. My best and most productive time in today's group was _____.
3. The thing I will remember most about today's group is _____.
4. I think that today's group could have been improved if _____.
5. My suggestions for making the group even better are _____.

Homework

The closing of a group may often occur with the assignment of **homework** (work done after the group session is over). Such "real-world," nongroup experiences can include thinking, feeling, or behavior experiences. Homework may be especially important in task/work groups in which members need to complete assignments so the group can finish a project. Homework is also important in counseling and psychotherapy groups because it helps members find ways of transferring learning in the group to everyday events in their lives. Getting homework assignments at the close of the session allows group members to be more concrete in determining their between-group goals.

> ### Reflection
>
> When have you found homework assignments helpful to you? What made them that way?

FINAL CLOSING OF A GROUP

The final closing of a group is filled with a mixture of emotions and tasks. It is a time when members' behavior undergoes noticeable changes (Davies & Kuypers, 1985). In successful groups, there is an increase in positive feedback and a certain amount of distancing as members anticipate change. In unsuccessful groups, anger and frustration may emerge along with distancing as members realize they will not attain individual or group goals. "Embedded in the process of closing are issues of the individual's separateness, autonomy, and independence from the group" (Ohlsen, Horne, & Lawe, 1988, p. 93). Leaders and members who successfully complete this stage of the group have and employ certain interpersonal and process skills. These interpersonal and process skills are concentrated on here because they serve as a model to emulate.

Movement into the stage of finally ending a group rests squarely on the shoulders of group leaders. Although members of all groups realize the group will end, it is leaders who provide the type of guidance that will make the process positive and productive. One way leaders do this, as previously noted, is through setting a **time limit for the group** (a set number of meeting times that is announced in advance). A second way they help the group terminate is through **capping**— easing out of emotional interaction and into cognitive reflection (Bates et al., 1982). Skilled group leaders realize that if members leave groups too stirred up emotionally, then they may not remember much, if any, of what they learned within the group. Therefore, leaders make a purposeful attempt to promote more cognitive interpersonal and intrapersonal interactions as the group moves into disbanding.

A third way group leaders can bring a group to its final ending is to use appropriate closing skills and call the group's attention to what needs to be done to terminate. For example, to properly establish final closure of a group, members may be asked to reflect on the group experience:

What was most helpful?

What did they learn from the group?

What are they taking with them from the group that will be helpful in other experiences?

Even more specific than reflections may be when members are asked to identify aspects of the group that were most useful and to identify individual members who were most caring (DeLucia-Waack, 1998). In this process, group leaders approach the group in a matter-of-fact and reflective manner and help focus group members' memories and thoughts.

A number of capping (closure) skills enable the group to close appropriately. In their interactions with the group as a whole, leaders must use these skills to the maximum. Because time and modeling processes have been covered previously, capping skills, especially as they relate to effective aspects of the group, are focused on here.

Capping Skills in Closings

Some groups need less time to close than others do. For instance, task and psychoeducational groups usually end when they have completed their mission. The group members may make **summarizing** reflections that recall significant events or learning experiences in the group at its end. However, other procedures are not always used. In contrast, psychotherapy and counseling groups may struggle with multiple issues during closure because of the more personal and intense nature of material covered. In actuality, all types of groups can benefit from capping skills in closure. When these skills are employed properly, group members gain a sense of completeness that the group has ended and a new time in their lives has begun. Some of the most important capping skills for groups to employ at the final closing of the group as a whole are as follows:

1. Reviewing and summarizing the group experience
2. Assessing members' growth, change (or achievement)
3. Finishing business

4. Applying change to everyday life (implementing decisions)
5. Providing feedback
6. Handling good-byes
7. Planning for continued problem resolution (Jacobs et al., 2012, p. 382)

Reviewing and summarizing the group experience is the first way to ask members to cap the group. This procedure involves having members recall and share special moments they remember from the group. One way to implement this review is by asking members to recollect their most salient memories from each of the group sessions. Giving the members copies of their feedback sheets on individual sessions may enhance this experience, but it is not absolutely necessary. At review and summary times, group leaders or other group members may guide participants through the process in ferreting out important points they wish to remember or contribute to the group.

For example, in her review of the group, Carolyn became stuck in remembering exactly when she made her first major contribution to the group.

CAROLYN: I think it was during the fifth session that I noticed how we all shared a common concern about not being recognized for the work we do and pointed it out to the group as a whole. I was pleased that I did that, and I think you, as members of the group, were, too. I just wish I could remember when I did that.

GROUP LEADER: Carolyn, although you cannot remember the exact session, what would you like for us as a group to remember?

CAROLYN: Two things. First, I made a contribution, and second, I helped us all realize more clearly a common bond—concern over not being recognized. I think the second contribution was important to the group as a whole in what eventually happened here.

Assessing is a technique similar to reviewing, but in **assessing members' growth and change**, the emphasis is on individuals' memories of themselves at the beginning of the group and now. The idea of such a capping exercise is to have members see and share significant gains with themselves and others. If group logs have been used, then members may consult them before sharing with one another. The important point of this exercise is for members to recognize their own growth. For instance:

MARGE: When I came here, I was scared. I felt I was the only one who was self-conscious about how she looked physically. Through this group, I have grown to understand that everyone, including really attractive people like you, Betsy, worry about how you present yourself. I am more confident than I was when we began this group that I can overcome my feelings. I have also learned, through my conversations with you, some things that I can do to enhance my appearance.

Finishing business is a crucial task at the end of a group. **Unfinished business** is basically "when someone hurts another, or is hurt by someone, and fails to resolve [the] problems with the relevant person" (Ohlsen et al., 1988, p. 128). Unfinished business may develop in groups because of their fast pace and lack of time to process all of the material that arose. Unresolved, unfinished business festers like an untreated wound and can hamper personal functioning. The "hurt" may distract a person from concentrating on what he or she needs to do and has a negative impact on the group itself. In either case, clear communication, congruence, and direct confrontation of the event with the significant person are needed for resolution and to start the healing process. During closing, group members are encouraged to complete this process, feel relief, and start mending and growing. Different theoretical approaches will direct exactly how this may be done, but sometimes the learning of a new behavior is required. In completing this task, it is crucial not to bring up new business.

For example, if Tamara thinks Wendy has put her down in the group, she needs to voice her concern during the closing stage, if not before. Then, if she is shy, she may need to assert herself and ask for what she wants or thinks she needs, such as an apology or an explanation. From that point, there is clarification, negotiation, and, if successful, resolution. When the process is over, Tamara and Wendy should be able to move on with their lives, each other, and the group.

The process of *applying change to everyday life* involves rehearsal, role-play, and homework. **Rehearsal** can be done in the group setting with members showing others how they plan to act in particular situations. This type of demonstration can be made more concrete and meaningful when others in the group play the roles of significant people in such environments. Some common mistakes that members make in rehearsals and role-plays are focusing on the change in others instead of self, becoming impatient with the slowness of others' change, and relying too much on the group's jargon (Corey, Corey, Callanan, & Russell, 2014; Shulman, 2012). Usually, rehearsals and role-plays will occur in the working part of the group and only be reviewed at closing.

Sharing homework is a transitional exercise that often follows rehearsal and role playing in which group members actually practice in public what they have done experientially in the group. Homework is usually specific and allows group members to report their results to the group, decide more clearly what they wish to change, and make a transition from group to personal norms. Homework has been covered before, but the important points to remember are that it (a) is a continuous technique that may be employed in many different types of group sessions and (b) should always be processed.

Providing feedback is crucial to the closure of a group and is an integrating experience. It provides an opportunity for leaders and members to reinforce each other for the progress they have made as well as to deal with their thoughts and feelings about making meaningful changes. Feedback should be honest, specific, sincere, and as positive as possible, although leaders and members occasionally can use it "to confront members who are still denying problems or who have not taken responsibility for their behavior" (Jacobs et al., 2012, p. 385). It is helpful for members to write down specific feedback. Otherwise, they tend to forget what was said. After the group has ended, members can use written records of feedback to see whether they are continuing to make progress toward being the type of person they were becoming when the group ended.

Expressing farewells allows the group to wrap up, at least on an effective/cognitive level. By **saying good-bye**, members are encouraged to own their feelings and express their thoughts at this time, especially in regard to what others in the group have meant to them. Members may reminisce about significant group events at this time, remind each other of the way they were, and give personal testimonials about how much they have been helped. The group leader may also deal with feelings about separation if they come up.

Sometimes there is a resistance to saying good-bye, for this is the final capping experience. In such cases, group leaders can set the tone for the closing moments by sharing their feelings of satisfaction with the work the group has done and by inviting members to express themselves in a farewell. For some members, there is a need for touching, shaking hands, or hugging. Depending on the type of group, one or more of these demonstrative ways of saying good-bye may be appropriate, but it is best for leaders and members to err on the side of caution if they are ever in doubt as to how to say good-bye. This means using a verbal approach. The important thing in good-byes is that thoughts and feelings be expressed in a constructive manner.

Reflection

What feelings do you have about loss? How do those feelings relate to closing a group? What does capping do to help alleviate feelings that might be a part of a closing experience? Can you see yourself cognitively capping the closing of a group? How would you do it?

Often, especially in closed-ended groups, structured exercises can be used in this farewell process (Conyne et al., 2008; Pfeiffer & Jones, 1969–1975; Schutz, 1967; Trotzer, 2007). These exercises can help bring a ceremonial close to the group and reach a climactic and conclusive ending. One such structured exercise is the awarding of certificates for attending the group. Another is a **pat on the back**, in which members draw the outline of their hand on a piece of white paper that is then taped on their back. Other group members then write closing comments on the hand outline or the paper itself that are positive and constructive about the person (see Figure 7.1).

The final step in closing a group is *developing a specific plan for continuing each member's progress* after the group ends. This *planning for continued problem resolution* may be completed

FIGURE 7.1   A pat on the back.

before or after individual good-byes are said. It should include when and how certain activities will be carried out, but others' expectations should not be part of the plan. In essence, this activity is a variation on what Corey (2012) describes as **projecting the future**, in which group members are asked to imagine the changes they would like to make in the short and long term. However, this planning process is more concrete and may involve the use of a written contract between the group member and the group that spells out in a realistic way how the member will implement the plan. Such a procedure can be quite productive in a task/work group as well as a therapeutic group. For example, Bob may state to the group and to himself that within the next 3 months he will complete his survey to find out how customers in his department like the services they are being offered. He will then send group members the data he collects.

PROBLEMS IN CLOSINGS OF GROUPS

Sometimes group members (and occasionally group leaders) have difficulty with the ending of a group. In such cases, they attempt to deny that they are close to ending and do not work on closure and transition. At other times, they will encounter difficulties in transference issues with the leader or other members. Another scenario may be the group leader's countertransference in relationship to one or more members. Finally, the issues of closure and transition may or may not be handled correctly. Each of these four possible problem areas is examined here.

Denial

Denial is acting as if an experience, such as a group, will never end. It can be expressed in a group on a limited or mass level. Usually the denial of termination is an individual matter, although some groups at times act as if the group experience will continue indefinitely. In cases of denial, the group leader must remind participants, especially in closed-ended groups, when the last session will be and encourage them to prepare accordingly (Carroll et al., 2004). In cases in which the group or individuals refuse to deal with closing issues, the leader needs to focus specifically on these areas. This focus may involve consultation with another professional, as well as individual sessions with denying members, or a special session or two with the group as a whole.

For example, when John led a six-part psychoeducational group on home repairs, members of the group told him after the fourth session that they would not let him end the group. Collectively, they insisted they wanted more and would not stop learning. To John's credit, he thanked the group for its confidence in him and compliments to him, but at the beginning of the fifth session, he stated firmly and matter-of-fact way that the group would end in one more session. He gave group members additional information about other courses they might find of interest and referred them to the community college's director of continuing education for further information.

Transference

Transference is the displacement of effect from one person to another. It has many sources but basically operates on an unconscious level and is manifest most directly when individuals attempt to relate to other persons in ways inappropriate for the situation.

Within a group, a variety of transference processes may emerge. For instance, "transference may occur among the group members themselves, between each member and leader, and between each member and the group as a whole" (Lev-Wiesel, 2003, p. 227). Group leaders and members in counseling and psychotherapy groups are often the objects of multiple transferences—that is, distorted perceptions. However, transference can occur in task/work and psychoeducational groups, too. For example, at various times in the group, leaders and members may be perceived by other participants as experts, authority figures, superheroes, friends, or lovers. There is a tendency for many group participants, especially adult children of alcoholics (ACoAs), to interact in the group as they did in their family of origin (Brown & Beletsis, 1986).

One way of dealing with transference perceptions is to become aware of them and recognize them for what they are initially in the group. Group members can then be encouraged to give both positive and negative feedback to each other throughout the group process regarding transference issues. This is a tricky process to keep in balance, and group leaders may be wise to seek consultation or supervision in such situations. The curative factor for multiple transference characteristics in groups, according to Yalom (Yalom & Leszcz, 2005), is the primary recapitulation of the primary family group. It represents a second way to deal with transference. Yet a third way of dealing with this difficulty is called the group stories fabric technique (GSFT) (Lev-Wiesel, 2003). In this last method, group members recount personal stories and give as well as receive feedback to these stories by other group members. The stories within the stories told by members, that is, the *metastories*, reflect individuals' transference issues. Implementing the GSFT is complex and takes time. It involves the group leader weaving the stories of group members into a "single, unified story that reflects the issues and concerns of all the group members" (p. 233).

Regardless of which method is used, if transference is still present at the end of the group, the group itself may be used as a whole even more to help individuals deal with their unresolved issues, including revealing feelings and realistically exploring them. Individual counseling for persons with transference problems, after the group terminates, may be appropriate.

Case Example

The Group That Would Not Die

Shelby had done all he could to inform the counseling group he was leading that it would end. However, he agreed to extend it for four more sessions. Yet when the time came, members insisted that the group be extended again. Shelby did not think that was wise and tried to wrap the group up in the last of the sessions.

Nevertheless, the group kept going even without its leader, and members kept calling Shelby and asking him to return. Because he feared that the group members would eventually become tired of one another and that the group might deteriorate, Shelby came to the third meeting of what he called "the group that wouldn't die." At that meeting he explained once again the benefits of a time-limited group and the fact that once an experience ended, participants could begin a new group and learn even more. His words finally had an impact, and the members of the group, after doing rounds, decided to quit.

Questions

What do you think you might have done had you been in Shelby's shoes? Why?

Countertransference

Countertransference is usually thought of as the leader's emotional responses to members that are a result of the leader's own needs or unresolved issues with significant others. However, in addition to leader–member interactions, countertransference can occur between members of unequal status. "Countertransference origins likely to be evoked in group therapy include reactions to authority, conflict, and anger; narcissistic needs; cultural values; excessive need for control; family issues, and separation-individuation issues. . . . Countertransference *triggers* are the therapy events and/or client characteristics that evoke therapists' unresolved conflicts" (DeLucia-Waack & Fauth, 2004, p. 139). Group leadership may also trigger a group worker's unresolved conflict because of its complex and interactive nature.

The first step in dealing with countertransference is to recognize how it is being manifest. Watkins (1985) states that countertransference is being exhibited when leaders are overly solicitous, distant, protective, nonconfrontational, competitive, resistant, overly identified with, or romantically or socially attracted to group members. There are a number of ways to manage countertransference, including denial and repression. However, the best way to combat these feelings and actions is direct supervision and individual therapy. It is crucial in ending a group that countertransference issues be resolved.

Handling the Closing of a Group Correctly

As evidenced in the literature on the termination of groups, there is no one way to handle such a process correctly. However, some specific signs indicate that the closing of a group is being conducted incorrectly. For example, if a group is closed abruptly and issues about ending are not processed, then the group is being closed improperly. "More often than not, this problem is observed when the group is of the short-term, weekend encounter variety where there is no follow-up period built into the process" or when the group leader is "from out-of-town and conducts a combination training-therapy workshop" (Gazda, 1989, p. 307).

Another sign that the group is being terminated incorrectly is when members are left with a number of unresolved issues. In open-ended groups, this problem may be handled by extending the number of sessions in the group (Yalom & Leszcz, 2005). In closed-ended and time-limited groups, leaders must try to resolve as many of these issues in the time left in the group and make appropriate referrals or offer individual counseling to those who still have difficulties when the group ends.

Overall, closing a group is a gradual process, and group leaders who handle it properly let it evolve over time. "Embedded in the process of termination are issues of the individual's separateness, autonomy, and independence from the group" (Ohlsen et al., 1988, p. 93). The pain and anxiety of separating from the group (if they occur) are best dealt with at this time by using capping techniques. As stated previously, capping involves a cognitive sharing of events that are removed from immediate here-and-now situations. Examples of capping include reflecting on past experiences, remembering meaningful group events, reminiscing about the way one entered the group, and talking about present and future plans. The sharing of this information can be done on an individual basis through a brief leader–member exit interview before the group's final session or within the confines of the last few sessions of the group itself.

FOLLOW-UP SESSIONS

Follow-up is the procedure of reconnecting with group members after they have had enough time to process what they experienced in the group and work on their goals or objectives. It is beneficial to members and to leaders in evaluating the experience they had in the group and reflecting on what was learned. Usually follow-up is planned for anywhere from a few weeks to 6 months after a group ends, either with the group as a whole or with the leader and a group member. There are several ways to follow up with group members once a group has ended. The first is to arrange for a private interview with each group member. These interviews focus on the achievement of individual goals of group members. They give leaders and members a way of assessing what has happened to members since the group terminated. At these times, the impact of the group on members can be examined, and any unresolved business can be discussed. Leaders also have an opportunity at such sessions to suggest other resources or opportunities for group members.

A second variation on the follow-up of group members is to hold a reunion of the group as a whole. These sessions may take the form of parties or may be conducted in a business-style manner. Regardless, it is important that leaders and members be given the opportunity to reconnect with one another and share their unique experiences. The best way to plan for reunions is to announce them before the group officially ends. In this way, group members are more motivated to follow through on changes to which they have committed during the group.

Another way to conduct a follow-up is with an **evaluation questionnaire**. This type of follow-up serves the purpose of helping group members be concrete in assessing the group in which they have participated. These questionnaires can take many forms but are best if kept brief. An evaluation questionnaire should cover at least (a) the leadership of the group, (b) the facilities in which the group was held, and (c) the group's effectiveness in achieving its objectives.

Leadership can be assessed through asking such questions as whether the leaders (or co-leaders) were personally and professionally responsible and whether they were effective in helping the group and its members. Questions related to whether the group began and ended on time are appropriate, too.

Queries related to facilities should focus on the location, comfort, and usefulness of the room in conducting a group. If a room is too noisy or cold, or even if it is the wrong shape, the group will be affected.

Final inquiries on a follow-up questionnaire should deal with the effectiveness of the group. If the individuals involved had their personal and collective needs met through the group, then the group was successful. It may take months before such an assessment can accurately be made.

The last frequently used method to evaluate a group is through writing a journal. A journal, or log, may be a valuable document for later examining what actually happened and when within the group. Individuals who keep journals may discover through reading their writings how they progressed during the group. Leaders may especially benefit by sharing their journals with other professionals as a means of supervision and feedback. In such a process, they may gain insight into their own strengths and weaknesses in handling particular group stages, difficult group members, and forms of group behavior. For example, Tyro may note his initial concern about Alicia in his journal. Later, he may look back to his writing and recognize how she has grown, regressed, or stayed the same. The key to this insight would become clear because of his writing.

Among the benefits of keeping a journal are its immediacy and availability for the group member or the leader. A journal is a paper trail that can be kept in a special place so that it is always accessible. Journals also allow group members to release their emotions and check the reality around them. By recognizing themes within one's journal, a person can examine predominant ways of reacting toward a person or a situation. If such expression is irrational or irresponsible, then the group member can work within or after the group to become more skilled in making another response. Finally, journals help group members clarify their thoughts. For example, by journal writing, Jill may discover she is mad at herself for not taking risks rather than angry with Amy for talking too much.

Summary and Conclusion

Closing is an important stage in groups, both on an individual session basis and as an overall process. The impact of ending on group participants and the group as a whole can be either positive or negative. Thus, it is crucial that group leaders and members have an awareness of when the group will end and its importance even before the group starts.

Until the late 1970s, the termination of a group was not given much attention because it was assumed that group leaders would know how to close off groups. Since that time, however, ending a group has increasingly been recognized as a distinct process in group work and has been the subject of numerous research studies. On an individual level, group members may either resist or gradually move toward termination. Some members, who have not been properly screened or who are immature, may leave the group early. Leaders and members must deal with these situations as well as with unavoidable premature exits due to circumstances beyond a leader's or a member's control. Ways of handling these situations vary, but general guidelines exist. One of these guidelines is to recognize that major theoretical positions deal differently with prematurely ending a group.

Another guideline is to be aware that terminating a group is a gradual and stepwise process.

Appropriate ways of ending individual sessions and the group as a whole also exist. Group leaders must take precautions and necessary steps to see that groups run on time and members realize the importance of participating in the group while there is time. Ways of encouraging members to do so include offering structured exercises, such as making the rounds, as well as setting up parameters and focus. It is the leader's responsibility to make sure the group stays on track in closing and to help members who have unfinished business or other problems at the time of termination. Follow-up on either an individual or group basis is a way of helping members concentrate on what they have achieved within the group as well as what they wish to accomplish. Structured exercises used throughout the closing process, such as journal keeping or feedback questionnaires, will help leaders and group members to end a group positively and productively.

Major characteristics of the five group stages covered in the last four chapters (chapters 4-7) are summarized in Table 7.1 as this section of the book is concluded.

Classroom Exercises

1. As a class studying groups, bring in song lyrics, poems, or short stories that deal with the theme of ending. Examine how writers treat the subject, and discuss those who the class feels personify these themes.
2. In a group of three, think of an exercise you could use to help a group terminate—for example, the making of a group collage. As a triad, formulate directions to do your exercise and demonstrate it before the class as a whole.
3. Discuss in a group of three what you would do as a group leader in the following situations:
   a. A group member at the last session angrily attacks you as the leader and says his experience in the group has been worthless.
   b. Five of eight group members ask you during the last session to extend the group for at least four more sessions.
   c. After the close of an individual group session, a member lingers and tells you she must talk about something she did not reveal in the group today.
   Share your strategies for dealing with these situations with the class as a whole.
4. Role-play a group session in which one member gets up and leaves the group (during the fourth session). Have group members and the leader react in ways they feel at the moment. Then have other class members who have been on the outside of this demonstration give the inside group feedback about what they observed and what they might do.

Table 7.1	Characteristics of the five group stages.			
Forming	Storming	Norming	Performing/Working	Mourning/Termination
Characterized by initial caution associated with any new experience; attempt to avoid being rejected by others.	**Characterized** by a time of conflict and anxiety; group moves from primary to secondary tension; attempt to balance between too much and too little tension.	**Characterized** by a feeling of "We-ness" that comes when individuals feel that they belong to the group; often enthusiasm and cooperation at this time.	**Characterized** by a focus on the achievement of individual and group goals and the movement of the group into a more unified and productive system.	**Characterized** by participants coming to know themselves on a deeper level; primary activities in termination—reflect on past experiences, process memories, evaluate what was learned, acknowledge ambivalent feelings, engage in cognitive decision making.
Peer relationships: group members tend to be superficial and center conversation around historical or future events that do not have a direct impact on the group.	**Peer relationships:** group members tend to be more anxious in their interactions with one another; concern for power is prevalent.	**Peer relationships:** identification with others in the group; hope, cooperation, collaboration, cohesion.	**Peer relationships:** genuine concern on a deep, personal level by members for one another; greater willingness to self-disclose on the part of members; increased awareness in the group about individual participants and the world of each person.	**Peer relationships:** feelings of empathy, compassion, and care abound; participants relate to one another on a deep and sometimes emotional level; feelings of warmth and sorrow often occur simultaneously.
Task processing: dealing with apprehension; reviewing members' goals and contracts; specifying more clearly or reiterating group rules; setting limits; promoting positive interchange among members so they will want to continue.	**Task processing:** concentration on direct objectives diminishes; a healthy "pause" takes place; scapegoating might take place.	**Task processing:** members must agree on the establishment of norms from which to operate the group; groups accept both prescriptive and proscriptive norms; importance of commitment is stressed during this time.	**Task processing:** major emphasis on productivity whether the results are tangibly visible or not; maintenance of interpersonal relationships must be attended to and balanced with productivity.	**Task processing:** major emphasis on promoting a successful end to the group and relationships in the group; consolidation of gains, finding of meaning in group, making decisions for new ways of behaving; prepare for a new beginning after group ends.
Useful procedures: joining, linking, cutting off, drawing out and clarifying purpose.	**Useful procedures:** leveling, feedback, informal and formal feedback.	**Useful procedures:** supporting, empathizing, facilitating, self-disclosure.	**Useful procedures:** modeling, exercises, group observing group, brainstorming, nominal-group technique, synectics, written projections, group processing, teaching skills.	**Useful procedures:** summarization, rounds, dyads, written reactions, rating sheets, homework, time limits, capping skills, and modeling.

CHAPTER 8

Diversity and Social Justice in Group Work

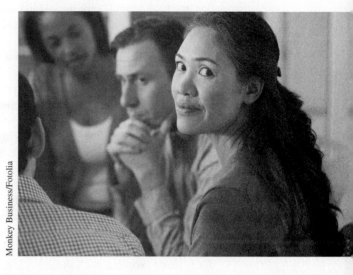

Monkey Business/Fotolia

With age she has learned
to forgive the groups
that mistreated her
because of her color.
Each Saturday she now bakes bread
and takes it to the local mission
where she stays to cut and serve it
with love and a main dish.
Her grace has overcome years of hatred
angry words and hours of sadness
her brightness exudes a subtle warmth
everyone calls her "Rainbow."*

*From "Rainbow" © 1997 by Samuel T.
Gladding. Reprinted by permission from
Samuel T. Gladding.*

CHAPTER OVERVIEW

From reading this chapter, you will learn about

- The history, challenges, myths, and goals of culturally diverse groups, leadership of these groups, and social justice issues connected with them
- Major characteristics and concerns of six diverse cultural groups: African Americans, Native American Indians, Asian Americans, Hispanics/Latinos/as, European Americans, and Arab Americans
- Groups for gays, lesbians, bisexuals, transgenders, queers, and questioners

AS YOU READ, CONSIDER

- The myths, challenges and goals you have when working with groups composed of individuals who differ from you and social justice matters related to them
- What you know about the six different cultures covered and how knowledge of cultures affects group work
- How you perceive and work with individuals who have the same or a different sexual orientation from you, and social justice issues connected with sexuality

Charles Darwin is the naturalist we most often think of in regard to diversity. Darwin came up with his theory on the evolution of species by doing one simple thing: observing. He recorded his findings, and the proof of his surveillance overwhelmingly backed up his reflective ideas. Until fairly recently, diversity was not a major concept in counseling or in group work. Yet, the background, appearance, and environments of individuals are important and influence their behaviors in groups. The presence or absence of social justice makes a difference, too, in the way society operates.

Diversity and social justice exist separately and together in a variety of ways. **Diversity** is associated with terms such as race, ethnicity, language, culture, gender, socioeconomic class, sexual orientation, religion, ableism, and disability (Diller, 2014). Diversity is a fact of life in complex, pluralistic societies like those in North America and Europe, which are composed of people who differ widely in regard to their lifestyles and worldviews and where differences in communication styles, messages, and behaviors affect the ways in which groups are set up and conducted (Conyne, Wilson, & Tang, 2000; Shechtman & Perl-Dekel, 2000). **Social justice**, although a relatively new term, is like diversity in examining differences among people and striving for "the fair and equitable distribution of power, resources, and obligations in society of all people" regardless of their backgrounds (Hage, Mason, & Kim, 2010, p. 103). In group work, social justice emphasizes "empowerment, self-determination, advocacy, and change" (Singh & Salazar, 2010, p. 97) in order to confront injustice and inequality in society (Kiselica & Robinson, 2001).

Early group workers, such as Jane Addams, Joseph Pratt, and Jesse Davis, laid the foundation for how to define the integration of group work and social justice today. "Each committed to a career involving advocacy with historically marginalized individuals and communities" (p. 97). Each also viewed a form of group work as a powerful intervention for promoting empowerment and healing of individuals who were often at society's forgotten edges.

Overall, diversity, multiculturalism, and social justice are closely interwoven constructs and activities. Group leaders can engage in diversity-competent practice without embracing social justice principles, but their work can be enriched by developing awareness of systems of power, privilege and oppression that impact group members. On the other hand, group leaders attempting to engage in social justice group work "without concomitant diversity competence are in danger of doing harm due to lack of awareness of culturally based perceptions, needs, and experiences of group members and their communities" (p. 101).

In this chapter, diversity and social justice are examined separately, with the realization that they are closely related in many ways. If group workers strive for social justice, they must do so with a knowledge and appreciation of diversity. Major aspects of social justice are discussed first, followed by a focus on cultural diversity, specifically six culturally diverse population groups. By cooperating collaboratively with persons who are not like themselves, individuals in groups can achieve common goals and in the process can also (a) bridge the gap of differences, (b) become more creative in their problem solving, (c) grow in their cognitive and moral reasoning, and (d) learn to view matters from a new perspective (Johnson, 2013).

A BRIEF HISTORICAL OVERVIEW OF DIVERSITY AND SOCIAL JUSTICE IN GROUPS

The emphasis on cultural diversity and social justice in group work is a rather new frontier. It is only recently that group professionals or associations have dealt with these two concepts in depth. For instance, it was not until 1996 that the Association for Specialists in Group Work (ASGW) set up a task force to incorporate multicultural competencies into its standards. Still later, in 1997, the ASGW endorsed the *Multicultural Counseling Competencies and Standards* of the Association for Multicultural Counseling and Development (Sue, Arredondo, & McDavis, 1992). In 1999, the ASGW adopted its own *Principles for Diversity-Competent Group Workers*. However, it was not until 2012 that ASGW provided a larger framework for working with culturally diverse groups when it adopted its own document, *Multicultural and Social Justice Competence Principles for Group Workers* (Singh, Merchant, Skudrzyk, & Ingene, 2012).

Three reasons account for this delay in dealing with diversity and social justice in groups. First, despite early work in the late 1940s by Kurt Lewin and his associates "to train community leaders to work more effectively in reducing tensions among interracial groups and to facilitate changes in racial/ethnic attitudes," this emphasis of the group movement was forgotten and discarded soon after Lewin's death in 1947 (Merta, 1995, p. 567). Second, during the development of the group movement of the 1960s and 1970s, culturally diverse group members were not considered to be significantly different from dominant group members in regard to concerns and issues. Finally, traditionally cultural minority members were not thought to have a great deal more influence on group dynamics than those from the dominant cultural group.

However, recent thinking has returned to Lewin's emphasis on the use of groups both to promote racial and ethnic harmony and to help people from different backgrounds understand themselves and others better. Over a 25-year period (1982–2007), group treatment among minorities in the United States has found that group work can reduce depression and promote positive psychosocial health among African American women, decrease rearrest rates for Latino and African American young men on probation, and increase problem-focused coping and social problem-solving skills with pregnant and parenting Latina teens (Stark-Rose, Livingston-Sacin, Merchant, & Finley, 2012).

In addition, reports from group leaders working with older populations indicate that the cultural backgrounds of group members often have a powerful impact on interpersonal relationships and the work that the group does (Conyne et al., 2000; Rose, 2001). In such groups, "culture becomes the foreground rather than the background for the group process" (Baca & Koss-Chioino, 1997, p. 130). Therefore, an effective group worker must consider the cultural background and influences of group members in all types of groups (Anderson, 2007). "Culturally sensitive practice plays a critical role in the delivery of group counseling services" and in group work in general (Johnson, Torres, Coleman, & Smith, 1995, p. 144).

Case Example

Deidra Diverges from Diversity

In setting up an advertising task group at work, Deidra decided to form a homogeneous group of her peers. She was single, young, attractive, and well educated, and she had a quick wit. She thought having a group with characteristics similar to her would be fun and productive. At first it was. The group came up with a number of new ideas for promoting the company's product.

Then, the group began to falter. They were good at targeting a population like themselves, but as Lawrence, a member of the group, said: "We really don't know what it's like to be Hispanic or disabled." Thus, after a heady start, the group disbanded in disgrace. They simply ran out of ideas.

Questions

What do you think might have happened had Deidra formed a heterogeneous group? Why?

STAGES OF SOCIAL JUSTICE

In the twenty-first century, thanks to the diversity and multicultural movement and its conscious-ness-raising impact on counseling, social justice is a term and a movement that is alive and well. There is even a division within the American Counseling Association entitled Counselors for Social Justice. The concept of social justice has been refined by Ratts, Anthony, and Santos (2010) into a description that is both a process and a goal. They break down the dimensions of social justice into five stages, starting with an intrapsychic and ethnocentric-based perspective and ending with an advocacy position where "group members and leaders . . . step outside the traditional group setting to advocate with and on behalf of a cause or issue" (p. 165).

Stage 1 is *naivety*, "a lack of awareness of how issues of diversity impact the intra and interpersonal interactions within the group" (Berg, Landreth, & Falls, 2013, p. 16). In these types of groups, the group leader assumes that all interactions are universal and equal. Multicultural variables are not examined or brought up. It is as if they were not there. Thus, some members of the group feel misunderstood, undervalued, and even oppressed.

Stage 2 is one of *multicultural integration*. In this stage, the "group leader moves out of an ethnocentric lens and fully recognizes the richness of the cultural elements of each member" (p. 16). Although cultural identities are interwoven into the flow of the group and the potency of the group is improved, there is not a lot of depth to discussions, and awareness levels regarding culture and diversity stay on a surface level.

Stage 3 is known as *liberatory critical consciousness*. In this stage, each member of the group "gains a more expansive understanding of self and the conditions that help form their beliefs" (p. 16). They are exposed to other's learning as well and thus are able to place their own and others' learning into the context of something bigger.

Stage 4 is *empowerment*. Ratts et al. (2010) note that in this stage, group members find their voice as the atmosphere within the group promotes self-advocacy. Social justice issues are integrated into a wide range of group work applications. Members role-play different ways of acting and receive feedback as they use their knowledge of diversity and multiculturalism to become more aware of how they wish to address issues such as racism and oppression.

The final stage, 5, is described as *social justice advocacy*. Group members expand their advocacy skills into the larger community and society as a whole. Not every group reaches stage 5, and there is anxiety associated with the stage because it may bring group members into conflict with other professionals. Basically, step 5 is social justice in action.

Going even further than Ratts et al. (2010), Burnes and Ross (2010) offer strategies to assist in group discussions on social justice issues such as marginalization, privilege, and oppression. For instance, they advise: "Be intentional about having diversity of group member-ship and avoid representation/token members of a marginalized community," "Use structured activities to talk about issues of privilege and oppression," and "Facilitate consciousness rais-ing and create awareness of social justice in group members by processing issues of oppression in the moment" (pp. 171–174). They state that their strategies are applicable to "all types of group work, including brief groups, psychoeducation, psychotherapy groups, and counseling groups" (p. 175).

Although there is still much discussion and debate over social justice and group work, it is clear that the concept and practices that go with it will continue (Hays, Arredondo, Gladding, & Toporek, 2010). Topics both now and for the future surrounding social justice and group work will include "consciousness raising, group empowerment, community organizing, definition of social justice, attribution theory, and sociopolitical identity development" (p. 177).

CHALLENGES OF CULTURALLY DIVERSE GROUPS

As has been implied indirectly and stated explicitly, groups vary in multiple ways. This fact is true for culturally diverse groups, of course. Groups that are culturally diverse are found in a number of settings. However, the contexts in which they are most likely to be conducted are:

- **(a)** racial-cultural sensitivity groups, increasingly being held on college and university campuses,
- **(b)** alcohol and other drug abuse recovery programs,
- **(c)** groups conducted inside correctional facilities, and
- **(d)** career development and job training programs (Johnson et al., 1995).

To work effectively with diverse populations in a group context, group leaders must understand the subjective, as well as the objective, experience of group members (Tate, Rivera, Conwill, Miller, & Puig, 2013). To do this, they must make three modifications in the traditional ways of working in a group. First, they must understand what a culture is. A number of definitions of **culture** exist, but Sternberg (2004) gives one of the best in stating that culture is "the set of attitudes, values, beliefs, and behaviors shared by a group of people, communicated from one generation to the next via language or some other means of communication" (p. 325). Because many different groups of people live in the United States, Canada, the United Kingdom, and other pluralistic nations, *most group work is multicultural in nature.* Indeed, the term *multicultural,* which stresses this diversity among people, has become quite common in the professional helping literature as well as society at large.

Second, group theory and technique must be modified and applied to different cultures in ways that are congruent with the beliefs and behaviors of those cultures (DeLucia-Waack, 1996b, p. 218). This type of behavior is beginning to occur. A notable example is the application of cognitive appraisal theory to psychoeducational multicultural groups (McCarthy, Mejia, & Liu, 2000). In this model, based on the work of Roseman, Antonion, and Jose (1996), group members are taught to identify linkages between appraisals of events and people and their emotions. They learn, for instance, that individuals can make various interpretations about events and people, including negative, positive, and surprise. A four-stage model is useful in presenting this information and includes a didactic introduction, discovery, deeper insight, and a final integration and appraisal flexibility phase. In the process, participants might learn that changing their appraisal of an event by attributing the cause to themselves, instead of to other persons, leads to a different emotion and may consequently result in a greater understanding of cultures outside of their own.

Reflection

When have you been in a group, or even just with another person, and found that your interpretation of an event was different? What do you think was behind this difference in perception? How did it make you feel? How did you see similar events from then on?

Finally, for group work to be multicultural and diverse, group theory and techniques must be developed that "acknowledge, explore, and use group member differences to facilitate change and growth" (DeLucia-Waack, 1996b, p. 218). This last change, which stresses the use of differences to enhance group effectiveness, has been slow to emerge. Greeley, Garcia, Kessler, and Gilchrest (1992) and Johnson et al. (1995) were early leading authors in this particular area. More recently, Merchant (2009) has spearheaded efforts to help group workers be aware that diversity-related groups are of three types:

- **culture-specific groups**, which focus on a specific cultural population where members are of the same or a similar background
- **interpersonal learning groups**, which are designed to promote greater understanding across cultural groups and contain members from different cultural backgrounds
- **other-content-focused groups**, which mainly focus on other topics, such as substance abuse, but at the same time pay attention to the diversity of their members as an important group issue

Salazar (2009) has edited a book on favorite multicultural activities from leading group experts in order to guide novice and experienced group workers in choosing, planning, conducting, and processing their work in diversity. Still, almost all formalized group approaches, especially in the Western world, are based on European American models (Bemak & Chung, 2004).

Further complicating the issue of conducting multicultural groups are the various definitions of multiculturalism that have been advocated. Multiculturalism as a movement has been defined traditionally in terms of cultural, ethnic, and racial differences. In this somewhat narrow definition, an emphasis is placed specifically on the collective history of a people as an identified group as well as individual differences among members (Atkinson, 2004; Harper, 1984; Vacc & Wittmer, 1980). However, culture may be defined broadly, too, and may include such factors as demographic variables (e.g., age, gender, residence), status variables (e.g., social, educational, economic), and affiliations (both formal and informal) (Pedersen, 2000). Thus, there is a fine line between too narrow and too broad a definition of culture.

A broader definition of culture is probably preferred because of its inclusive rather than exclusive focus. Under such a definition, the almost 20% of Americans who have some type of disability as defined by the Americans with Disabilities Act of 1990 are included. So are persons with varied sexual orientations (Brown, 1996). Unquestionably, most groups are multicultural in this broadest sense of the word, in that they are heterogeneous and incorporate within them people with a number of differences (Yalom & Leszcz, 2005). For purposes here, the word *multicultural* is used in the broadest way. However, because of space limitations, the focus in this chapter is on a narrow number of distinctly recognizable cultural groups: African Americans, Hispanics/Latinos/as, Asian Americans, Native Americans, Arab Americans, European Americans, and gays/lesbians.

MYTHS ABOUT MULTICULTURAL GROUPS

A number of myths surround multicultural groups, some perpetuated by professionals with the best of intentions. Yet, the fact is that myths are only partially true and, therefore, must be resolved if people from different cultures are to work well together. DeLucia-Waack (1996b) and Locke and Kiselica (1999), among others, have articulated myths that need to be dispelled if diverse groups are going to be productive. Four of them are as follows.

Myth 1: Discussion of racial or cultural differences is offensive to group members and is best never mentioned. The reason some group workers do not address cultural issues is that they fear that a discussion of these matters will offend group members or make them uncomfortable. Yet, as DeLucia-Waack points out, "in reality, the acknowledgement of cultural differences may increase group cohesion" (p. 219). The reason is that, once acknowledged, the subject area is no longer taboo, and what was in effect known by everyone on a covert level is now overt. This knowledge can be especially useful if it is addressed in a sensitive manner. Thus, within a group, the leader might say to Lilly, "As an African American housewife, how does what Jane, as a European American housewife, is advocating resonate with you?" In such a situation, Jane and Lilly may find both similarities and differences in what they think based on culture and status. By discussing cultural differences openly, they will not misunderstand or misperceive each other based on silence or presumptions. They may also discuss social justice issues.

Myth 2: ***Groups can be homogeneous so focusing on diversity is not needed.*** Even when groups seem homogeneous, they are not. People are unique in many ways (e.g., gender, age, marital status, family of origin, occupation, beliefs/values). Therefore, a surface resemblance may be exactly that—veneer. Once group workers can break through the myth of homogeneity, true progress can be made in highlighting differences and similarities among people. The group is then freed to use the unique as well as the universal potential within itself as a whole (Pedersen, 1997b). Thus, after the leader acknowledges that Raphael and Jorge differ in their thoughts and objectives, even though they are brothers, the two group members and the group as a whole will begin to make progress in achieving individual goals.

Myth 3: ***Group member differences do not matter and seldom, if ever, affect the process and outcome of task and psychoeducational groups.*** The basis of this myth is that task and psychoeducational groups are not affected by processes inherent in them as much as counseling and psychotherapy groups are. These groups are believed to be primarily content oriented. Yet, in getting to content, task and psychoeducational group members are influenced by the beliefs, experiences, and cultural interactions that are a part of their background. Therefore, culture plays a major part in how and when members in task and psychoeducational groups interact. For instance, DeLucia-Waack (1996a) relates the story of trying to lead a stress management workshop for a group of eight male Italian students who were new to the United States. Although well intentioned and well prepared, she found that these men did not think a woman should be teaching a class of men and that their cultural norms did not permit the disclosure of weaknesses to other men, let alone a woman!

Myth 4: ***Group work theories are appropriate for all clients all the time.*** Theories on groups and how they work, at least in most of North America, are, as pointed out previously, "based on Eurocentric notions of mental health and functional relationships" (DeLucia-Waack, 1996b, p. 221). These tenets of health include a focus on the individual, verbalization as the primary means of communication, unstructured interactions among group members, an emphasis on risk taking, and the importance of the group leader or facilitator. In reality, these emphases are not shared worldwide. Group members are unique, and what may be the norm for one may not be the norm for another. Thus, if groups are going to work, members must discuss norms and work out a framework that will be helpful to all.

If group leaders and members notice and address myths before the group begins, such as in the screening stage of the process, then greater understanding and a better outcome will most likely result. Along with a focus on myths, group workers must help the group to formulate and reach appropriate goals, which may include advocacy as well as understanding and appreciation. The fact is that "multicultural group work represents a powerful tool for helping and healing in the context of human diversity" (Anderson, 2007, p. 224).

Case Example

Myra's Myths and Mindsets

Myra had been told all of her life that Whites were all pretty much alike. Her family had told her not to trust them, because they would take advantage of her whenever they could. Thus, when a White woman befriended Myra in her counseling group, Myra was suspicious. She knew the woman must want something and that she would pay a price for friendship. Therefore, Myra avoided the woman and seldom spoke to her.

Later, when the group had a reunion, Myra was surprised to find out that the woman she had avoided was good friends with many of her friends.

She was shocked. She could not believe it. Not only that, the woman had some situations similar to Myra's. By avoiding her White group member, Myra had missed a number of opportunities for companionship, support, and insight.

Questions

How do you think myths and mindsets can be overcome? What historical examples can you think of where the thinking of one or more persons was changed? What insights can you glean from such examples?

GOALS OF DIVERSE AND MULTICULTURAL GROUPS

Like all successful forms of group work, diverse and multicultural groups are goal directed. Although goals will differ from group to group, these objectives may be described as falling into categories that are primarily remedial, preventive, or task oriented. Goals also focus on intra- and interpersonal processes. In addition, goals are geared toward both general and specific topics that are of concern to those within their ranks (Corey, 2012). Thus, a primary challenge of conducting diverse and multicultural groups relates to the different views, values, and interpersonal styles that members display, as well as how these forces are managed and highlighted in productive ways. If the group is conducted properly, then members who differ from one another will begin to trust and help one another in learning new, different, and productive ways of acting and inter-relating (Pedersen, 1997b). Through such a process, individuals, subgroups, and the group as a whole will benefit. For instance, if Maria assists Jon in verbalizing his frustrations with school policies, then the two may become emotionally closer to each other and work more closely with their fellow group members in proposing new and better school policies as part of an agenda that promotes fairness, equality, and social justice.

According to DeLucia-Waack (1996a), diverse and multicultural groups, regardless of their emphasis, have three common goals: (a) to understand the situation that brought the person to the group from a cultural perspective; (b) "to approach all events and behavior in the group from a functional perspective" (p. 171); and (c) to help members make sense of "new behaviors, beliefs, and skills within a cultural context" (p. 171). These goals hold up across group types, including task/work, psychoeducational, counseling, and psychotherapy (Anderson, 2007). If participants do not comprehend why they are in a group, what they can learn from the group, and what implications their new behaviors, beliefs, or skills have for them within the context of where they live, then the group experience will be of minimal use to them.

Reflection

When have you ever been in a group where it was obvious that one or more members did not want to be a part of the group? How did their actions affect the group? How do you think their actions could have been muted, modified, or clarified so that the group would have functioned better?

ASSESSING CULTURAL DIVERSITY IN A GROUP

It is imperative that group workers understand the cultural backgrounds of their clients before attempting to work with them and that they have a broad and culture-centered perspective. As previously noted, groups composed of people from culturally different backgrounds will have diverse values and worldviews (DeLucia, Coleman, & Jensen-Scott, 1992). By recognizing these differences and the cultures from which they spring, group leaders can design appropriate interventions (Leach & Aten, 2010; Pedersen, 1997a). However, the extent of diversity is dependent on a number of factors, including time, acculturation processes, people's socioeconomic environment, and even the number of group members from a particular background. (By the way, including just one member of a distinct group in a larger group is usually not productive. That person may have difficulty identifying with others in the group and may be stereotyped by the group.)

Therefore, group workers need to assess multiple factors that will either benefit or hinder the group's development. This type of assessment is complex. For instance, some people may be deeply affected by their collective history, whereas the influence is minimal for others. In making an assessment, the pregroup screening stage of forming the group is the place to begin. In screening, group leaders may keep in mind that some cultural groups do better in certain types of group environments. For instance, many Asian Americans do not respond well to traditional group psychotherapy processes because their culture teaches them not to share personal problems or confront others in public (Chung & Bemak, 2014; Singh & Hays, 2008). In contrast, other cultural groups, such as African Americans and Hispanic/Latino/a Americans, often do extremely well in a variety of group settings (McWhirter, McWhirter, & McWhirter, 1988).

For most cultural groups, core group skills and principles will work on some level. However, for other groups, depending on their specific composition, there is a need to develop culture-specific strategies. Thus, in planning and implementing a culturally diverse group, the leader must conceptualize and work broadly, in terms of what is generally known, and specifically, in terms of the persons who actually make up the group. Outcomes in groups "are dependent, in part, on the match between the group leader's and the client's respective stages of racial consciousness" (Johnson et al., 1995, p. 145). Therefore, before Dwight, a European American, decides to lead a multicultural counseling group, he must ask himself questions about his own awareness of his heritage and the heritage of others in the group and how it will affect the final results.

LEADERSHIP IN CULTURALLY DIVERSE GROUPS

As implied previously, before beginning a group, it is important for leaders to examine their own thoughts and feelings about people who are culturally or otherwise distinct from themselves. Self-awareness regarding cross-cultural interactions is a "must" for those who would lead (Bieschke, Gehlert, Wilson, Matthews, & Wade, 2003). Such an examination allows leaders to deal constructively with prejudices, biases, and racist elements in their lives that have either been passed on from a previous generation or learned through isolated incidents and generalized. For example, a group leader of Asian American descent who grew up in an affluent but isolated neighborhood might have negative feelings about working with Mexican Americans if he or she has never encountered persons from such a background before and has heard disparaging remarks about them as a group. The point is that when thoughts and emotions about culturally different groups of people are not dealt with before a group begins, they may well play themselves out detrimentally within the group itself. For example, the leader in the illustration just given might hold stereotypes of Mexican Americans, such as that they are all illegal immigrants and not well educated. Such stereotypes might psychologically impede the leader's ability to hear and communicate accurately with Mexican American members of this group.

In conducting groups that include members who are culturally distinct, leaders must sensitize themselves continually to cultural variables and individual differences so that they become more conscious of the issues of culture that influence their own backgrounds and those of group members (DeLucia-Waack, 2004). Anderson (2007) has developed a "diversity wheel of salient human differences" that encompasses five factors that every group leader needs to be conscious of: culture, worldview, identities, statuses, and demographics. "A culturally responsive group leader is aware of his or her own cultural values, assumptions, and biases and how these might impact upon the group process" (Brinson & Lee, 1997, p. 47). He or she also is "autonomous"—that is, the group leader is comfortable with his or her identity and able to empathize with culturally different group members' feelings.

Skilled diverse and multicultural group leaders realize that among group members, multicultural differences tend to occur early in the life of a group "and discomfort associated with multicultural issues tends to occur towards the end of groups" (Bieschke et al., 2003, p. 325). This process of examination and "becoming" inevitably lasts a lifetime. However, parts of it are achieved in stages, with the group leader becoming more skilled with each culturally diverse group conducted (Marbley, 2004). Such groups give life and possibility to those involved with them because differences in group members become assets, not liabilities, in the group's development. In addition, there is an understanding of how values and beliefs are shaped and influenced by social environments.

The awareness and abilities of group leaders in culturally diverse groups may be increased in multiple ways. Strategies most often employed are

    (a) consultation with minority counselors about working with groups they may already be serving;

(b) having group leaders become immersed in culturally enriching and sensitive traditions such as the observation of significant holidays or festivals;

(c) proactively taking note of the needs and issues of minority groups; and

(d) taking language lessons and pronunciation training so as to be comfortable and correct when speaking a culturally specific circumstances (Johnson et al., 1995).

A fifth strategy is for group leaders to examine their family as the place where they learned about their culture and relationships with others (Ivey, Ivey, & Zalaquett, 2014). Constructing a genogram and interviewing family members about their cultural experiences and expectations can often give insight into the sources of particular beliefs and outlooks.

A final strategy is the employment of both didactic and experiential education. On the didactic side, there is the study of cultures and the heritages of people. This type of knowledge can be obtained through reading books and articles that relate to global and specific traditions and customs in the lives of various people (Chiu, 1997). On the experiential side, course work can be set up to sensitize group workers to themselves and group members who differ from them. Integrating this cultural knowledge into real groups is the challenge.

Group leaders-in-training may need to work through the strong emotional reactions and paralyzing feelings they experience when dealing with multicultural issues on any level. One way to handle the intense emotions, such as guilt or shame, that come with such a process is through the use of small, supportive, and accepting groups (Parker, Freytes, Kaufman, Woodruff, & Hord, 2004). This type of group, which is nonjudgmental in nature, may help neophyte group workers share thoughts, feelings, and actions that they would not do otherwise. Through such a process, multicultural counseling competencies are enhanced.

In summary, to be a leader of a diverse and multicultural group with skills and competencies, an individual must

- have "an awareness of different cultural worldviews and the subsequent impact on group work interventions,"
- have a self-awareness, in particular of racial identity and personal and cultural worldviews, and
- have a focus "on the development of a repertoire of culturally relevant group work interventions" (DeLucia-Waack, 2004, p. 167).

Case Example

Edward Enters a Multicultural Group as a Leader

Edward is a native of Africa and the son of immigrant parents. He is bilingual. Until age 4, he lived in Kenya. Since then, he has lived in Canada. As a mental health worker, he has decided to start a group for recent immigrants from Africa. He is aware of his heritage as well as his values, but he is not as familiar with the lives of recent immigrants.

Because he is married and the father of young children, Edward does not have time to participate in a lot of new cultural experiences. However, he approaches his group with new knowledge he has attained through attending a recent course on the lives of African immigrants. He has also conducted personal interviews with some recent immigrants. Therefore, he believes he is prepared to address situations affecting his group members when the group begins.

Questions

What else might Edward do to make himself more competent? What do you consider to be your greatest strength in addressing diversity and multicultural issues?

WORKING WITH DIFFERENT CULTURAL POPULATIONS IN GROUPS

The 2014 U.S. census data indicated increasing diversity in the population of the United States. The following percentages reveal how many of the 318 million respondents reported themselves to be of a particular race: African American, 12%; Native American, 1%; Asian American, 5.6%; Hispanic, 14%; European American (White Non-Hispanic), 65%; two or more races, 2% (U.S. Census Bureau, 2014).

Accompanying this growing diversity is the increasing need for professional and personal sensitivity to others in groups, especially multicultural groups (DeLucia et al., 1992). "Implicit in multicultural group work is the fostering of acceptance, respect, and tolerance for diversity within and between members" (Bemak & Chung, 2004, p. 36). Therefore, group workers from all cultures in the United States will need to expand their knowledge about cultural variables. People from various cultures do not think or act alike, nor do they come to groups for the same reasons. Among the most important pieces of knowledge group workers need regarding diversity in groups is information about group process in naturally occurring groups—for example, the African American church, Latino/a clubs, Native American Indian tribal councils, and Asian American family groups. "In many cases, group process in these kinship units often significantly predates what we know as group work" (Lee, 1995, p. 4).

One dynamic that occurs in multicultural group counseling is the use of defense mechanisms, particularly splitting and projection identification, which are used "in groups to protect against feelings of inadequacy and vulnerability, which underlie racial and cultural prejudice" (Cheng, Chae, & Gunn, 1998, p. 373). Excessive splitting and projection identification lead to scapegoating that in turn leads to fragmentation and a failure to build a sense of community within the group.

While acquiring process knowledge, group workers should attune themselves as well to the nonverbal behaviors of group members. Nonverbal behavior can have various meanings among different cultures. For instance, cultural differences in eye contact abound (Ivey et al., 2014). European Americans usually value direct eye contact when listening and less while talking, whereas African Americans often have the reverse pattern. Likewise, direct eye contact may be avoided entirely by some groups of Native Americans when talking about something serious. Distance is another nonverbal behavior that should be understood. Conversational distance of an arm's length is comfortable for many North Americans, but many Hispanics/Latinos/as prefer half that distance. The point is that, in conducting any group, cultural heritage will influence levels of comfort and patterns of interaction for better or for worse, depending on the knowledge of group leaders and other group members.

"Although extensive literature testifies to great interest in multicultural work, little is known about group counseling outcomes with specific U.S. racial minorities" (Stark-Rose et al., 2012). Some of the qualities that affect particular minority and majority cultural groups that we are aware of follow. It should be noted that although these characteristics may generally apply, they "warrant ongoing scrutiny because they are based more on anecdotal reports than on systematic research and because they often fail to consider within group differences (e.g., socioeconomic status, acculturation level) and between group differences (e.g., between Japanese Americans and Vietnamese Americans)" (Merta, 1995, pp. 573–574). Individuals within a group and even groups in different regions of a country will vary in their customs and traditions. Therefore, group workers can never assume that persons from certain backgrounds will behave in a set way. In fact, to make such an assumption is to stereotype and act with prejudice.

African Americans

Group work with African Americans has been written about more extensively. However, more than 50% of articles have focused on women and youth, with a noticeable shortage of articles on groups for men (Stark-Rose et al., 2012). As a group, African Americans are quite diverse, and within-group differences are great. Yet, collectively, most African Americans share a common bond that is the result of the legacy of slavery and bondage that prevailed in the United States from 1619 to 1865. During those almost 250 years, African Americans were bought and sold as chattel. The history of discrimination that followed their freedom from slavery, such as Jim Crow legislation, segregation, and other forms of racism, has influenced most members of this group in significant ways. For example, skepticism or suspicion of European Americans is pervasive among African Americans (Feagin, 2014; Gossett, 1998).

As a group, African Americans have historically avoided the use of professional helping services, including group work (Stark-Rose et al., 2012). Yet, group work is appropriate for counseling, psychoeducation, and working with African Americans in other ways because of their collectivist culture. Group work is especially relevant if it is "grounded in the African American worldview" (Williams, Frame, & Green, 1999, p. 260). Commonly shared positive values of that worldview include the importance of family, creative expression, and spirituality.

"African American culture has typically provided a network of support systems through community resources," which the group may parallel (Pack-Brown & Fleming, 2004, p. 183). African American culture is communalism that is manifest in strong kinship ties and an emphasis on social responsibility for others, even those outside of one's immediate family (Helm & James, 2010; Perrone & Sedlacek, 2000). A "'safety in numbers' principle makes it easier" for some African Americans to disclose before a group than before an individual professional helper (Merta, 1995, p. 574).

In groups, African Americans may share, cooperate, and have their personal experiences validated. "In addition, group counseling experiences may help African Americans increase their sense of hope and optimism, decrease their feelings of alienation, develop more effective coping techniques, and acquire more effective socialization skills" (Ford, 1997, p. 103).

"The African American community often presents a challenge to group leaders who are unfamiliar with the African American worldview and life experiences" (Pack-Brown & Fleming, 2004, p. 189). For instance, in group work, African Americans express themselves in various ways, such as displaying "their emotions in culturally specific language patterns or by displaying nonverbal behavior in a demonstrative manner" (Brinson & Lee, 1997, p. 48). Therefore, when leading a group composed of African Americans, a group leader who is not African American must be aware of both the verbal and the nonverbal traditions of members and not ascribe negative connotations to normal means of expression. Likewise, in leading groups whose membership contains only some African Americans, a non–African American not only needs to realize regular cultural ways of expression but also must help educate and sensitize other non–African Americans to these patterns. Steen has created the acronym **KOFFE** (Knowledge, Open Communication, Faith, Family, and Empowerment), as a group counseling model for working with African Americans (Steen, Shi, & Hockersmith, 2014).

Other ways of working with African Americans in counseling, psychoeducational, and therapeutic settings involve the creative arts. "Music, poetry, literature, folklore and graphic expression" may be useful aids in promoting group interaction (Brinson & Lee, 1997, p. 52). Gender issues are often unique, and because of discrimination, oppression, racism, historical hostility, and cultural stereotypes, getting African American men to participate in counseling or group work is a challenge (Muller, 2002). African American women are, as a group, more receptive, but they "must contend with long-standing negative, stereotypical image [too] of being Black and female" (Pack-Brown & Fleming, 2004, p. 188). Therefore, group workers must be sensitive and appropriate in involving this segment of the African American population in groups.

In work with African Americans, especially if the group workers are European Americans, care must be taken in setting up the group so that members will be able to share freely and benefit from the group. The process of setting up may therefore involve not only the topics of sessions but self-examination and input from professionals in the African American community as well (Muller, 2002). For African American women on predominantly White college campuses, an Afrocentric group counseling approach has been found to be beneficial (Brown, Lipford-Sanders, & Shaw, 1995). Such an approach centers on positive African values within a cultural context. Also, an African American Women's Spirituality Group has been found to be an effective intervention for African American women because it connects them with others around shared cultural experiences (Williams et al., 1999). Two resources that introduce models for group work with African Americans are the videos *I Am Because We Are! Afrocentric Approaches to Group Work* (Pack-Brown & Whittington-Clark, 2002) and *Images of Me: A Guide to Group Work with African American Females* (Pack-Brown, Whittington-Clark, & Parker, 1998).

Reflection

What other general characteristics are prevalent in African American men and women? In African Americans as a group? If you are not African American, how do you think you could build trust within a group that was composed of a number of African Americans? What would you do differently than you usually do? What would be the same?

Hispanic/Latino/a Americans

As with other ethnic and cultural groups, there is considerable variety in populations that are characterized as Hispanic/Latinos/as. There are four major Hispanic/Latino/a subgroups in the United States: Mexican Americans (65%), Central and South Americans (21%), Puerto Ricans (10%), and Cuban Americans (4%) (Diller, 2014; Rivera, Fernandez, & Hendricks, 2014). Shared values among these groups include the importance of family, interdependence and cooperation, the worth and dignity of the individual, and an acceptance of life as it exists (Diller, 2014). Differences include the use of language, religious rituals, and celebrations (Villalba, 2010). Therefore, if group workers are going to be effective leaders, they should be aware of different Hispanic/Latino/a groups and the cultural gulfs as well as bridges that separate and unite them (Altarriba & Bauer, 1998).

The professional literature notes that group work with Hispanic/Latino/a Americans can be beneficial. However, the number of individuals in a group should be limited to a maximum of 10, because many Hispanic/Latinos/as tend to speak all at the same time. Groups for this population take a number of forms and can be quite powerful. For instance, Gonzalez-Lopez and Taylor (1997) found that group therapy with Latinos and Latinas can transform their thinking.

In Hispanic/Latino/a groups, counselors should generally be active, validating, and supportive (Baca & Koss-Chioino, 1997). In addition, recommendations have been made regarding language, especially in groups in which members' first language is Spanish. For instance, Espin (1987) recommends that leaders of such groups be bilingual: For many members of Hispanic/Latino/a groups, Spanish is the language of emotions because it was in Spanish that affective meanings were originally encoded. Salgado de Synder (1987) also recommends that Spanish be used in Hispanic/Latino/a groups, along with English, to facilitate the emergence and discussion of taboo topics, such as sexuality, that may have been lost in the process of acculturation.

In working with Hispanic/Latino/a groups, sex-role socialization issues and cultural identity may affect the process, too. Hispanic women, as a group, tend to be more reserved than Hispanic men (Arredondo, Gallardo-Cooper, Delgado-Romero, & Zapata, 2014). Therefore, the group leader may need to use a skill such as drawing out to help Hispanic women—who have been most socialized in their cultural tradition—to voice their opinions and actively contribute to the group. One way to accomplish this goal is through the use of a "comadre or compadre" group approach where group members offer social support and a sense of community like extended family members (Rayle, Sand, Brucato, & Ortega, 2006). In such a group setting, stress may be reduced and depression modified while a sense of belonging, respect, and affirmation is enhanced. This effect may be especially notable in recently immigrated, monolingual Mexican women.

On college campuses, groups that support **Chicanas** (women of Mexican descent) may also be valuable and effective in helping them succeed. One such group, built around Yalom's 11 therapeutic factors, was found to help Chicanas "build personal and professional support systems, feel validated with respect to common experiences and educational concerns, develop skills and strategies to negotiate personal and educational difficulties, and discuss cultural values within a group context" (Gloria, 1999, p. 256). Likewise, Hispanic/Latino males may be reluctant to disclose information that they perceive as threatening their masculinity or machismo (Baruth & Manning, 2012). For this reason, group workers need to be encouraging and patient in conducting groups with Hispanic/Latino males.

Considerable anecdotal information is available about the effectiveness of Hispanic/Latino/a group work in such areas as academic skills, value clarification, problem solving, self-esteem, and pride in one's cultural identity (Merta, 1995). For instance, Baca and Koss-Chioino (1997) have presented a model for group counseling with Mexican-American adolescents specifically targeted toward teens in this population who have behavior problems, including substance abuse. Likewise, Villalba, Ivers, and Ohlms (2010) have found that Cuento therapy, a culturally relevant form of bibliotherapy using stories to convey morals or themes, is effective with middle school children living in rural emerging Latino/a communities to enrich the school experience of these children.

In preparing Hispanic/Latinos/as for a group, leaders are wise to consider minimizing resistance by avoiding such words as "counseling" or "psychotherapy," which are equivalent to the word "crazy" (Rivera et al., 2014). The leader also needs to be aware of the importance of rules and gender roles (e.g., marianismo and machismo) and the part each of them, and gender overall, plays in the functioning of the group.

Overall, Hispanic/Latino/a groups have proven quite productive, especially for Mexican Americans.

Case Example

Tanya Is Tempted to Betray Her Heritage

Tanya is the only person of Hispanic/Latina heritage in her psychoeducational group. Her parents immigrated to North America from Mexico when she was a child. Most of her life she has lived in a "White neighborhood" and played with children whose native language is English. As she learns in her group, there are many cultures within the United States, and her Hispanic/Latina one is strong and filled with many traditions.

At first Tanya is proud of her heritage, but she is teased outside the group for that. Therefore, she begins to speak up less in the group and her comments become more limited. It is obvious to the group leader, Hernando, that Tanya wants to say more than she is saying. He wants to help her own

her feelings, and yet he does not want her to create such a stir that there is a backlash.

Questions

What do you think Hernando could do to help Tanya and the group be more accepting and open? What do you think he should avoid doing?

Asian Americans

Asian Americans are one of the fastest growing groups in the United States, comprising over 18 million people or approximately 5.6% of the total U.S. population (Chung & Bemak, 2014). The demographic profile of Asian Americans includes an array of more than 43 disparate cultural groups. Each group has its own distinct historical and sociopolitical backgrounds, languages, identity, issues, cultures, and challenges (Chung & Bemak, 2014; Sandhu, 1999). Thus, although Asian Americans are often lumped into one main category, there are wide intergroup and intragroup differences that may make it difficult for group workers to deal effectively with unique issues of particular individuals (Chen & Han, 2001). Furthermore, the myth that members of this population are the "**model minority**" (i.e., highly successful with no serious problems) is exactly that—a myth. In actuality, Asians in the United States, not only face many of the same problems as other minorities, such as racism and stereotyping, but they also face pressure to be a model minority since many Asians have achieved so much. The model minority coverage that Asians receive in the press makes it very difficult for Asians who cannot meet the high achievement standards of this model. Therefore, for group workers, Asian Americans are a challenge. Members of this population must be understood and worked with beyond the myths that surround them.

One issue that must be addressed in working with Asian American culture groups is the disparity "between group work values (e.g., openness, expression of feelings, directness) and the cultural values of Asian Americans (e.g., verbal nonassertiveness, reluctance to display strong emotions in front of strangers, and unwillingness to disclose personal problems to strangers)" (Merta, 1995, p. 574). The importance of **saving face** (not embarrassing oneself or disgracing one's family) is also highly prized by many Asian Americans (Kim, Atkinson, & Umemoto, 2001; Singh & Hays, 2008). The means for preventing a clash in values and the loss of face may be demanding and require an adjustment in the ways leaders conduct groups, especially counseling and therapy groups. Many Asian Americans have been taught to respect authority and see a group leader as a person of authority (Chung & Bemak, 2014; DeLucia-Waack, 1996b). Because of this cultural introjection, they will not challenge the group leader even when such a challenge might be beneficial to everyone in the group.

One way to work with groups of Asian Americans, especially college students, is to offer "groups which focus on practical concerns to them rather than on forums which focus on more personal concerns" (Cheng, 1996, p. 10). For work with college students, groups that feature topics such as career choices, immigration, academic topics, and communication skills seem to be successful and well attended. Cheng (1996) also recommends that groups for Asian American students be short term (one to five sessions) in addition to theme centered.

Another successful way of conducting groups with Asian Americans is a stage-specific interactive approach (Chen & Han, 2001). In this model, group workers "carefully respond to specific tasks and challenges that arise in each stage" of the group (p. 113). For example, in the forming stage, group leaders need to realize that nonverbal messages from Asian American members, such as silence, may convey respect rather than resistance, and they must treat these behaviors accordingly. Similarly, in the working stage of the group, leaders need to realize that emphasizing Asian Americans' strengths, rather than their pathologies, helps them to move more toward a sense of choice and control.

An approach for Native Hawaiian adolescents in particular is culturally consonant group counseling using values, concepts, processes, and techniques of Ho'oponopono (an indigenous interpsychic and intrapsychic healing method) (Kim, Omizo, & D'Andrea, 1998). In this problem-solving approach, the emphasis is placed on values such as *aloha* (love and caring), *lokahi* (unity and harmony), and *ohana* (extended family). Although more research needs to be conducted using what the authors set up as a 10-week group, indications are that Hawaiian adolescents with low self-esteem may benefit from such an experience.

Overall, most kinds of groups that are well designed seem to work in a therapeutic way for Asian Americans. A particular population that may find group work beneficial is Southeast Asian refugees. "Several studies have pointed toward its effectiveness with this population" (Chung, Bemak, & Okazaki, 1997, p. 207). Highly traumatized refugees may especially find solace in group therapy (Chung & Bemak, 2014).

Reflection

What other general characteristics than those mentioned here are prevalent in Asian American men and women? In Asian Americans as a group? If you are not Asian American, how do you think you could build rapport within a group that was composed of a number of Asian Americans? What would you do differently than you usually do? What would be the same? If you are Asian American, what suggestions would you make about conducting a group for Asian Americans? Be as specific as you can, because there are numerous Asian American cultures.

Native American Indians

"Long before the notion of group counseling was a glimmer in the eyes of the early pioneers of the counseling profession, Native peoples throughout North and South America were using group approaches for therapeutic benefits of creating and maintaining harmony and balance in the personal, social, environmental, and spiritual realms of people's lives" (Garrett, Garrett, & Brotherton, 2001, p. 17). Native American Indians generally share some common values, such as an emphasis on cooperation, health, holism, sharing, spirituality, healing, and an extended-family orientation (Colmani & Merta, 1999; Dufrene & Coleman, 1992; McWhirter & Robbins, 2014). Thus, in work with Native American Indians, groups have been found to be more appropriate than individual counseling (Appleton & Dykeman, 1996). Four crucial elements relevant to wellness from a Native American Indian perspective are belonging, mastery, independence, and generosity (Garrett, Brubaker, Torres-Rivera, West-Olatunji, & Conwill, 2008). These variables are best discussed within a group setting in regard to balancing them for wellness, because they involve more than just a single person. Therefore, healers in Native American Indian society rarely treat individuals in isolation from their family, friends, and neighbors.

Of the approximately 5 million Native American Indians in the United States and Alaska, approximately 50% reside in urban areas, so it is important to consider the degree of traditionalism versus the degree of acculturation to mainstream American values and cultural standards before treating members of this population (Garrett, 2004). In general, Native American Indians' cultural values revolve around harmony, noninterference, and the balancing of dualities.

Yet, in spite of the strong tradition of groups in Native American Indian cultures, members of this population face barriers in participating in many mainstream group experiences. These barriers include a distrust of institutions because of European colonization, different perspectives on health and well-being, an aversion to the confessional nature of some groups, and logistic and practical considerations (McWhirter & Robbins, 2014).

However, several group approaches to working with Native American Indians seem to work well. Two approaches, for young men in particular, are vision quest and the sweat lodge ceremony. In **vision quest**, young men coming of age retreat to a secluded spot in nature and sit in a sacred circle where they deprive themselves of food, water, sleep, and shelter for a number of days, seeking an auditory or visual message about themselves, others, and the earth. After they return to society, they share their vision in a ritualized group setting. The quest is deeply spiritual, involving social support and interpersonal learning. It involves such group therapeutic factors as universality, cohesion, and acceptance (McWhirter & Robbins, 2014).

The **sweat lodge ceremony** is also a life transformation ceremony, but it may include individuals of any age. About 10 participants undergo a ritualized cleansing of the mind, body, and spirit through structured processes in a small turtle-shaped dwelling known as a *sweat lodge* (Colmani & Merta, 1999; Garrett & Osborne, 1995). The sweat lodge, where blasts of hot steam are created by pouring a special mixture of water and herbs over heated rocks, becomes "a type of counseling center and place for group therapy" (Lake, 1987, p. 8). The four-phase process of the sweat lodge ceremony is similar to other group process models in that it includes an entrance (exploration), a threshold (transition), purification (working), and an emergence (consolidation/closure). Within this process and in other gatherings is the **talking circle** tradition (Garrett, 2004). The group leader uses a go-round procedure, and all assembled use "I" statements to express their thoughts and feelings, in both prayer and conversation, about themselves, their families, their connections with others, and their future. The process itself includes the 11 therapeutic factors identified by Yalom, but it contains strong moral-cognitive development and cultural identity components for Native American Indians, too (Colmani & Merta, 1999).

Research also supports the use of art therapy in groups for Native American Indians. "Art media provide clients culturally sensitive avenues for expression through nonverbal forms" (Appleton & Dykeman, 1996, p. 225). In a group consisting of Native American Indians and people of other cultures, the arts can be an especially powerful form of communication because "American Indian group members may be reserved in their level of self-disclosure when they are among non-Indians" (Brinson & Lee, 1997, p. 48). Art therapies in groups overcome barriers of culture, socioeconomic status, and other surface differences while inspiring, directing, and healing intrapersonal and interpersonal rifts.

The **inner circle/outer circle approach** is a fourth way of working with Native American Indians in groups. Group members divide up and sit in two concentric circles. Inner circle members then describe what is painful or frustrating in their lives with their fists clenched so that they can feel the tension physically as well as emotionally (Garrett et al., 2001). They then turn around to the outer circle members, who sit with open palms. When the outer circle group has granted permission, the tensions of the inner circle are slowly released into their open hands. Each outer circle member in turn takes the opportunity to share with his or her inner circle member specific themes, key words, or underlying feelings. The outer circle member may request guidance or support from a community circle outside of the outer group and use the insight or action from the community circle with the inner circle group member. Much of the therapeutic value of this approach comes from the interaction of the circles and the bringing together of people physically, mentally, and spiritually through an interrelationship process.

Overall, Native American Indians tend "to value a group orientation and may find group work the preferred modality of treatment . . . [especially if the group leader is] perceived by the Native American group members as genuine, considerate, and nonmanipulative" (Merta, 1995, p. 576).

Arab Americans

Arab Americans are a fast-growing and mosaic group coming from 22 countries as diverse as Egypt, Lebanon, Morocco, Yemen, Tunisia, and Palestine. There are more than 3 million Arab Americans in the United States, most of whom are Christian (approximately 66%), with a sizable portion being Muslim (24%) (Nasser-McMillan, Gonzales, & Mohamed, 2014). However, "Arabic and Muslim cultures often overlap. Thus, although the majority of Arab Americans are Christian, Muslim traditions and values are often upheld by Muslim and Christian Arab Americans alike" (Nasser-McMillan & Hakim-Larson, 2003, p. 151).

Arab Americans vary among themselves. Potential differences include social class, level of education, language (Arabic has distinct dialects), relative conservatism of the country of origin, time of immigration, and level of acculturation (Abudabbeh & Aseel, 1999). Despite such cultural variations, sufficient commonalities exist that special attention from service providers is warranted.

Arab cultures tend to be of a high context rather than of a low context, such as in North American society. Therefore, Arab Americans as a group usually differ significantly from traditional Americans in that they emphasize social stability and the collective over the individual.

The family is the most significant element in most Arab American subcultures, with the individual's life dominated by family and family relations. Education is valued in Arab American households, with approximately 4 in 10 Americans of Arab descent having earned a bachelor's degree or higher (aaiusa.org, search for "demographics").

When working with Arab Americans, especially immigrants, it is crucial for group workers to remember that there is a sharp delineation of gender roles in such families. Furthermore, patriarchal patterns of authority, conservative sexual standards, and the importance of self-sacrifice prevail. There is also an emphasis on the importance of honor and shame because people in Arab cultures seek outside help from helpers such as group workers only as a last resort (Abudabbeh & Aseel, 1999). Complicating matters even more is the fallout, tension, and distrust from September 11, 2001 (Beitin & Allen, 2005; Nasser-McMillan et al., 2014).

Therefore, clinical recommendations for working with groups in this population include

- being aware of their cultural context,
- being mindful of the issue of leadership and the importance that authority figures play in their lives,
- being attentive to the part that the extended family plays in decision making,
- being sensitive to the large part culture plays as an active and tangible co-participant in treatment,
- being conscious of the fact that a strength-based approach to treatment is both desirable and works better, and
- being active as a group worker and balancing the role so as not to be seen as a rescuer or a threat.

Group workers can help Arab Americans by helping them access groups where they can find support and become members of a larger community that is dealing with issues as they are. Group counseling or therapy poses

> some potentially problematic issues for particular clients. This is especially true for the war refugees from Iraq, due to the paranoid symptoms that often accompany the diagnosis of PTSD [posttraumatic stress disorder] in clients who have experienced wartime trauma. On the other hand, parenting groups and 12-step programs seem to be effective with some nonrefugee Arab immigrant groups, perhaps due to the collectivist nature of the Arab culture in the countries of origin. (Nasser-McMillan & Hakim-Larson, 2003, p. 154)

Reflection

What general characteristics are prevalent in Arab American men and women whom you know that have not been cited here? In Arab Americans as a group? If you are not Arab American, how do you think you could conduct a group that was primarily composed of Arab Americans? What would you do differently than you usually do? What would be the same? If you are Arab American, what advice would you wish to give those who run groups for or that include Arab Americans?

European Americans

People descended from European ancestors comprise the largest number of people in the United States and make up what is known as the *majority culture*. Descendants of Germans, Irish, English, French, Italians, Poles, and Russians are among the most numerous of the European Americans. They all share some similarities, with the most obvious being their white skin color. This similarity has both positive and negative attributes. On the plus side, it provides an outer link of similarity and some assumptions of alikeness that bring people together. On the minus side, skin color may lead to some insensitivity about self or others. "White Americans often have difficulty perceiving themselves as members of a cultural group and often refer to themselves and others as 'American' or 'a person' without regard to race" (Brown, Parham, & Yonker, 1996, p. 510). Indeed, White racial identity theory argues not only that within-group differences exist among Whites but that these differences are based on the degree and type of identity people of white skin color have with White culture (Carter & Akinsulure-Smith, 1996).

Regardless of skin color or identity, European Americans differ dramatically among themselves, just as in other cultural groups (McMahon, Paisley, & Molina, 2010). Their values, religious traditions, and customs vary. For instance, historically, persons who came from northern European countries and arrived in the territory that would become the United States in the 1600s and 1700s discriminated against the ancestors of southern Europeans arriving in the late 1800s to the early 1900s. Thus, many second- and third-generation European Americans may share much more in common with minority culture populations, especially in regard to struggles against prejudice, than would seem likely or obvious. Recognizing these within-group differences can help group workers to avoid stereotyping, generalizing, and treating all European Americans the same. It can also help facilitate their linking of European Americans to other members of groups from outwardly different backgrounds.

Nevertheless, as a group, people of European origin in North America "have been in a position of social and cultural dominance with respect to other groups" (Lee, 1997, p. 19). European

Americans have generally defined the lifestyles, attitudes, and values of society. As a group, European Americans are time conscious and view nature as something to be conquered. Furthermore, collectively (but with notable exceptions), they are future-time oriented, competitive, individualistic, rational thinkers; are democratic; are driven by a strong work ethic; and generally live in nuclear families (Carter, 1991; Katz, 1985; McMahon et al., 2010). European Americans who understand their own world view, cultural values, and racial identity are more likely than not to have a positive influence on others in groups who both differ from and are similar to them.

There is very little professional literature on working with European Americans in groups. Until recently, it has been assumed that, unless otherwise stated, either groups include a majority of European American participants or they are conducted by a European American. That assumption is probably still more correct than not, because authors of groups that focus on cultural minorities identify their groups as such (e.g., African American, Hispanic). Therefore, it is difficult, if not impossible, to tease out guidelines for working with European Americans in groups, except maybe with recent European immigrants (McMahon et al., 2010).

Nevertheless, it is helpful to be aware of two factors in working with European Americans in groups. The first is to realize that, as with other cultural groups, there are more within-group differences than between-group differences among European Americans. Therefore, just as with other groups, it is important to focus on differences as well as similarities among participants.

Second, in working with European Americans in groups, it is crucial to address matters that affect members socially, such as the fact that American culture is becoming increasingly diverse. Social and cultural factors are probably of greatest concern to the group as a whole and cause members the most anxiety and difficulty. The reason is that collectively European Americans have had a history of racism coupled with **White privilege** (i.e., the positive ways Whites have benefited from racism, such as disproportionate access to social and economic resources) (Hays & Grimmett, 2014). Thus, changes occurring in demographics will most likely affect the way European Americans function.

GROUPS FOR GAYS, LESBIANS, BISEXUALS, TRANSGENDERS, QUEERS, AND QUESTIONING INDIVIDUALS

In recent years, gays, lesbians, bisexuals, transgenders, queers, and questioning individuals (GLBTQQs) have become increasingly visible in American society (Horne, Levitt, Reeves, & Wheeler, 2014). Empirical estimates have suggested that 6% to 10% of the American population identifies as lesbian or gay, with an unknown percentage of people in the bisexual, transgender, queer, and questioning categories (Goodrich & Luke, 2011). However, regardless of their visibility or their number, GLBTQQs are still discriminated against in many ways both in the public domain (Horne et al., 2014; Khng, 2001) and in other settings, such as their families of origin. Thus, as individuals, GLBTQQs have distinct concerns related to their lifestyles in particular and life problems in general. Some of these concerns, such as sexism and homophobia, are of special significance, but other matters include career, life development, and social justice issues. All of these issues just mentioned have to do with social justice.

The lifestyles of GLBTQQs vary from being hidden or invisible, to coming out, to openly acknowledging their sexual orientation. Groups devoted specifically to working with members of each group, who often have more in common than not, have proven useful and productive, at least according to anecdotal reports. Mixed groups, whose members have heterosexual, homosexual, bisexual, transgender, queer, and questioning identities, have also been successful (Firestein, 1999). In working with GLBTQQs in groups, it is important to remember that they are a diverse population. There are large within-group differences as well as between-group differences among members.

Groups have been used to work with GLBTQQs in adolescence as well as with more mature populations, although most of these groups have been "process/counseling groups at the exclusion of task or psychoeducational groups" (Goodrich & Luke, 2010, p. 144). Support groups for sexual minority youth have been found to be a means for members of this population to talk about their concerns with a counselor in school (Muller & Hartman, 1998). However, most school counselors feel ill-prepared to work with GLBTQQ and questioning adolescents in schools (Goodrich & Luke, 2010). Group work with members of GLBTQQ populations has also been employed with adults—for example, working with bisexual men who may link their self-worth to **accelerated aging**, the process of defining oneself as older than one's chronological age (Horne et al., 2014; Wolf, 1987). Such groups allow individuals in them to share their experiences and gain support from one another.

Regardless of members' age, the matter of confidentiality is of uppermost importance in groups for GLBTQQs. It is also critical that group workers who lead GLBTQQ groups explore their own sexuality (Hitchings, 1994) and understand how social influences affect the personal and interpersonal lives of group members (Cowie & Rivers, 2000). Furthermore, it is crucial that group workers receive proper supervision in working in GLBTQQ groups. Until recently, there were no models for supervision of group work specifically designed to address the needs of GLBTQQ persons in groups. However, Goodrich and Luke (2011) have developed a transtheoretical framework, the **LGBTQ Response Model for Supervision of Group Work (RMSGW)**, through which group leaders can plan and implement group interventions with members of this population.

Case Example

Gloria Joins a Group

Gloria has wrestled with her homosexual tendencies for years. Now, at 19, she has decided that she is a lesbian and she wants to "come out" to others. She joins a counseling group in order to work on this issue. The group comprises a number of individuals from various backgrounds and with diverse issues.

When Gloria brings up her wish to the group, some members are accepting and encouraging. Others seem horrified and intolerant. Fred, as the leader, tries to bring the group together to be supportive of

Gloria. He encourages members to ask Gloria questions and to help her explore herself to the fullest. Most members do so. However, there are two members who condemn Gloria and threaten to leave the group. Fred stops the group for the day and asks all members to explore their own sexuality and be ready to talk about it next session.

Questions

What do you think of Fred's plan? What are some other ways Fred could handle this situation?

Summary and Conclusion

In this chapter, group work has been examined from a diverse and multicultural perspective as well as a social justice lens. As Horne (1996) has stated in reviewing the literature on group work, "There is much greater diversity in the populations we now

serve" (p. 2). Groups are composed of individuals with all types of cultural backgrounds, and to ignore the cultural differences among members and treat everyone the same in a group is to negate the richness inherent in the group membership and to promote injustice. Yet, theoretically and pragmatically, diverse and multicultural group work, especially that which focuses on working with groups composed of members from different cultures, has been slow in its evolution. Even more discouraging has been the dearth of literature and practice on working positively in groups with differences.

The reasons for the lack of progress in diverse and multicultural group work can be attributed to myths and fears as well as the sheer complexity of developing an applicable multicultural group work theory. Yet, goals, assessments, and ways of working with specific minority and majority populations are coming to the forefront in ever-increasing numbers, along with social justice. Attention is now being paid to group leaders' awareness of cultural distinctions and appropriate actions they need to take in regard to these differences. Similarities between groups are being noted. Pedersen (1997b) suggests that a culture-centered perspective promotes understanding, freedom, health, and justice.

With information on different cultural groups being published more frequently in professional journals, there is hope that practical as well as theoretical and justice work in this area will increase. It is from reading this literature and studying general and specific information, as well as practice, that group leaders must mature in understanding the groups they assist. Along with this understanding must come direct contact with members of other cultures and experiences in cultures other than one's own. Finally, group workers must simultaneously explore their own cultural heritage and become aware of both the positive and negative aspects of their learned values. Through a lifelong commitment to learning about different cultures and the promotion of social justice, group workers can become effective in leading and participating in groups that are culturally heterogeneous.

Classroom Exercises

1. Make at least three visits to a naturally occurring culture group (e.g., club, church group). Observe how members of the group interact in similar and different ways. Describe for the rest of the class what this experience tells you about the group. What is your reaction to what you saw?

2. What general steps would you take in leading a task/work group composed of individuals from different cultural backgrounds? How would your steps be different if this group were a counseling/therapy group? Would leading a diverse psychoeducational group require that you do anything different from what you have already proposed?

3. Because literature on social justice is still relatively new, go to your library and find an article on the subject. Critique it. What new information not covered in this chapter did you find?

4. What myths do you think are prevalent about members of your cultural group? What reality (or kernel of truth) underlies these myths? How do you think a group leader should work with a group composed of members of your culture based on the truth as opposed to the myth?

CHAPTER 9

Specialty Groups and Creativity in Groups

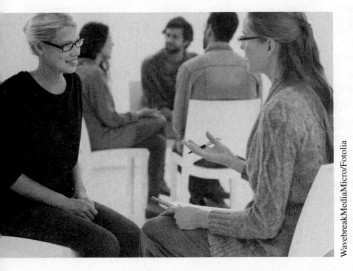

WavebreakMediaMicro/Fotolia

I am taken back by your words—
to your history and the mystery of being human
in an all-too-often robotic world.
I hear your pain
and see the pictures you paint
so cautiously and vividly.
The world you draw is a kaleidoscope
ever changing, ever new, encircling, and fragile.
Moving past the time and through the shadows
you look for hope beyond the groups you knew
as a child.
I want to say: "I'm here. Trust the process."
But the artwork is your own,
So I withdraw and watch you work
while occasionally offering you colors
and images of the possible.*

*From "Journey", *Journal of Humanistic
Education and Development, 28, p. 142 © 1990
by Samuel T. Gladding. Reprinted by
permission from Samuel T. Gladding.*

CHAPTER OVERVIEW

From reading this chapter, you will learn about

- What specialty groups are and different types of these groups
- What creativity is in a group setting and how deBono's six hats approach, Eberle's SCAMPER model, and Sawyer's zig zag idea can help group workers be more creative
- What creative exercises can be used in different stages of a group

AS YOU READ, CONSIDER

- What specialty groups you have participated in up to this point in your life and how they have affected you
- How easy or difficult it would be to implement the ideas of deBono, Eberle, or Sawyer
- What other creative exercises you are aware of that might be used at different group stages

When I was a novice group worker, I was asked to lead a marriage enrichment group. The only problem: I was single. However, somehow I was able to pull off the feat, although I am sure it will go down in history as one of the most cognitive marriage enrichment groups ever. A number of years later, my wife and I led a marriage enrichment group for just a night. The difference was dramatic. We had stories to tell to illustrate points and a lot of humor to go with the anecdotes. Specialty groups are just that—focused on a special topic the group leader should know something about before getting involved. It helps when the leader is also a bit creative and is not discussing a stage of life he or she read about in a book.

Specialty groups are groups that focus on one particular population or problem, such as military veterans, new mothers, or addiction. These groups require a great deal of knowledge and expertise from their leaders. They vary considerably in format and take many forms. Some are open and psychoeducational, whereas others are closed and psychotherapeutic. Just as Apple initially advertised its iPhones with the slogan that whenever there is a problem, "there's an app (application) for that," so it could be said of special situations or populations that "there's a group for that."

In setting up such groups and in conducting other groups, especially those that go through stages, creativity is often called for (Gladding, 2010). Trying to conduct a group mechanically or "by the numbers" is a formula for disaster, because group members and group moments are often unpredictable and filled with surprise. Knowing just the facts is usually not enough to move the group along or take care of members' concerns. Therefore, this chapter contains information not only on various specialty groups but also on three ways of helping groups be more creative in what they do and how they do it. Edward deBono's six hats, Robert Eberle's SCAMPER, and Keith Sawyer's eight-stage zig zag model are creative methods that group workers conducting any type of group can use to help themselves and their members overcome barriers or inertia. These ways of working with groups, whether specialized or not, can facilitate growth, development, and achievement.

SPECIALTY GROUPS

Specialty groups vary. They are designed for populations that have specific and unique concerns. There are literally hundreds of such groups, from those that are remedial to those that are preventive. These groups, which are more than the sum of their parts, have the potential to become **mutual aid support systems** where members of the group need each other and use each other as resources as well as using the leader (Shulman, 2014). In this section, 14 examples of specialty groups are given as representative of the kinds of groups that people join voluntarily or that they are required to attend. Realistically, there are about as many specialty groups as there are unique situations, so a description of the groups that follow will be more like a Whitman's Sampler box of chocolates than a chocolate factory or a cocoa plantation. It is important for group workers to be aware of the gamut of groups available for referrals. Specialty groups have always been needed and much appreciated by those with particular concerns and circumstances. They will continue to be needed in the future.

Groups for Health Care Providers and Health Care Consumers

Health care is a concern for almost everyone, from those who focus on providing services to persons who are motivated to stay healthy. With the increased emphasis on health, there are opportunities to apply group interventions to medical settings and the biopsychosocial model of well-being. Three group modalities are most relevant in the health care world: psychoeducational groups, psychotherapy groups, and theme groups (Drum, Becker, & Hess, 2011). "Psychoeducational interventions serve as a bridge to other resources and promote better self-care practices" (p. 259). They may be used to inform consumers of the symptoms and treatment of a disorder such as a stroke. For individuals with disorders that are exacerbated by stress stemming from interpersonal difficulties, psychotherapy groups may be best. Thus, individuals who are emotionally upset with their physical condition may benefit from talking with others about their anger rather than bottling it up or displacing it onto others. Finally, theme groups, which are a hybrid of the two previously mentioned groups, are relatively short-term as well as goal oriented and may be most appropriate for individuals in supporting a needed but difficult change. For example, individuals diagnosed with diabetes may use such time-limited groups to gather information and garner support from others who have the same disorder.

Besides being used with established health care professionals and patients, groups can be used in training aspiring practitioners. For example, Bayne (2011) reports that groups used to enhance empathy for third-year medical students appear to be promising in promoting empathic connections.

Groups for Military Personnel and Their Families

Individuals who sign up for the military face a number of challenges that are not apparent at first. In addition to living a regimented and disciplined life that is group oriented, military personnel must also cope with physical and psychological stress, loneliness, safety issues, and deployment for extended periods of time (Fenell, 2014). Movies and television dramas such as *American Sniper, Saving Private Ryan, Band of Brothers*, *The Pacific*, and *Unbroken* graphically illustrate some of the challenges military personnel face regardless of the era.

Those in the armed forces are one of the most likely groups to suffer from trauma and the stress, such as acute or posttraumatic stress disorder (PTSD), whether they have seen actual combat or not (Westwood, McLean, Cave, Borgen, & Slakov, 2010). In order to address and help decompress military personnel from active duty to civilian life, Westwood et al. set up a residential group-based program entitled the Veterans Transition Program (VTP) on a university campus (as opposed to a hospital). The purpose of the program was to serve as a life transition course designed "to assist the transition of military personnel back into Canadian society by aiding with their personal and career readjustment" (p. 44).

The program addressed the impact of trauma exposure through the reduction of symptoms by providing veterans and to some extent their families with the "necessary knowledge, skills and the social support to promote improved overall coping thereby facilitating successful re-entry into civilian life" (p. 47). The process involved peers, because of a lack of trust in mental and medical health professionals. Most participants described a "letting go" of emotional baggage, less depression, and increased self-esteem as a result of being in the group. They also reported benefiting from peer interaction.

Groups for spouses, children, and adolescents with family members who are deployed away from their home bases are important as well because of the strain such a separation puts on a family (Chandra et al., 2010; de Burgh, White, Fear, & Iverson, 2011). Groups offered to family members can be both preventive and remedial. They are best offered in settings where spouses, children, and adolescents regularly gather, such as community centers and schools. Rush and Akos (2007) describe one such group as a hybrid psychoeducational-counseling group designed to increase student knowledge (e.g., emotional cycles of deployment), build student competencies (e.g., coping skills, mastery of developmental tasks), and promote a safe environment to express emotions with connected peers. By providing such a group, children and adolescents who have mixed feelings (e.g., pride and loss) about a family member serving in a military zone overseas can freely express their sentiments as well as find support and gain new abilities.

Reflection

Who do you know who has been in the military? What thoughts and feelings has he or she expressed to you regarding their service and the challenges that went with it? How do you think a group could have helped this person and/or their family?

New Mothers' Groups

Motherhood is the highlight of many women's lives and brings them much joy and fulfillment. Infant and mother attachment is a protective factor for the future mental health of both. However, not every birthing experience ends happily. Postpartum depression and infant attachment issues are of special concern because they take a toll on the new mother, the infant, the family, and community in which the new mother lives.

Treatment for postpartum depression or attachment disorders has traditionally been carried out through individual interventions, but the demand for such services often overwhelms the ability of providers and is not successful. Groups can be especially valuable in such circumstances. Niccols (2008) used a group-based intervention for parents as an alternative method to individual work to enhance infant attachment security. The group involved 76 mothers in an eight-session attachment group called "Right from the Start" (RFTS) and was compared to home visits for such services. An analysis of results indicated no significant differences between RFTS and home visiting, with both groups showing small improvements in infant attachment security and maternal sensitivity. RFTS cost significantly less and was more cost effective than home visiting. Furthermore, it was not significantly different in terms of participation rates, client satisfaction, or follow-up service requests. Niccols concluded that RFTS is as effective as home visiting in improving infant attachment security and maternal sensitivity.

In another group counseling study using self-report and observational measures, Clark, Tluczek, and Brown (2008) worked with women who had moderate to severe depressive symptoms following birth. They found that women who had these symptoms during the postpartum period reported significantly less depression and experienced their infants as more reinforcing following treatment (the group experience) than did similar women on a wait-list control group. The counseling group operated for 12 weeks and used a standardized manual, with specific topics being focused on each session. Mothers in the postpartum depression group also were rated following treatment as exhibiting significantly more positive effective involvement and heightened communication in interactions with their infants than did mothers in the wait-list control group.

Involuntary and Mandated Groups

Sometimes because of inappropriate behaviors, individuals are mandated to attend groups. They usually do so reluctantly and are often unmotivated to change. Furthermore, many are angry and look for ways to not participate or even to sabotage the group and its leader. Thus, individuals who take on the role of leading such groups have their work cut out for them. Corey (2012) notes that leaders of involuntary groups need to be energetic, dynamic, patient, engaging, and thick-skinned. They should never take comments made by group members personally.

Schimmel and Jacobs (2011) propose that those who lead involuntary groups do so "using creative and multi-sensory interventions to insure that members are actively engaged in the group process" (p. 144). Specifically, they propose strategies such as doing something unexpected that is engaging and relevant to the purpose of the group—for example, starting the group with a vivid movie or television scenes. They also recommend using creative props as visual aids to illustrate points, such as bringing out strings to represent anger fuses and having group members identify how long their fuses are and how they could be lengthened. Movement, writing activities, and dyads are other ways of moving the group forward. The authors conclude, "A key to leading meaningful groups with involuntary members is not allowing the negative energy to consume the group" (p. 157).

Anger and Aggression Management Groups

The movie *Anger Management* staring Adam Sandler and Jack Nicholson is funny and was popular when it was released in 2003. However, out-of-control anger and aggression are not humorous and are problematic behaviors in American society. They catch the public's attention when they escalate into tragic and violent acts of murder involving innocent people, such as the children at Sandy Hook Elementary School, the adolescents at Columbine High School, and moviegoers in Aurora, Colorado. Yet lower-level acts of aggression, such as physical and emotional bullying, are much more prevalent and of daily concern to many children within educational institutions.

Attempts to decrease aggression have primarily been of two types—prevention and containment. Prevention is the most difficult of these strategies, but as important, if not more so, then remediation. Research has found that children who are highly aggressive during the elementary school years are at greatest risk of physical aggression during adolescence and adulthood (Mash & Wolfe, 2010). One way of helping children bond more socially with others and be less prone to aggression is through bibliotherapy (Shechtman, 2009). Bibliotherapy offers relevant, innovative, and flexible treatment—as a stand-alone intervention or as a preventive method in conjunction with other forms of treatment.

In the bibliotherapy approach, the group leader reads specially prepared stories or poems to the children in the group. The children then give their reactions to what happened, and the aggressive nature of a response by a character is discussed along with the circumstances surrounding it. The idea is to generate within the group alternative ways of behaving or to call to the attention of group members that the actions taken in the story were not appropriate. Thus, there are sensitizing as well as informational elements to this group process, and new ways of thinking and acting are generated.

In adulthood, many men deny their feelings and as a result are more likely than other segments of the population to have trouble managing negative emotions, especially in intimate relationships. Groups for men experiencing this problem can be helpful (Rabinowitz, 2005; Saunders, 2008). For example, psychodynamic group therapy can offer men opportunities to identify, understand, and change the underlying problems related to their emotional expression resulting in aggressive behavior. In addition, these groups help to improve these men's interpersonal relationships (Lanza & Schmidt, 2008). Likewise, groups for cultural minority men, such as Asian

American men, can be of help as a place where they may explore and be supported in expressing their anger and their passion without feeling inadequate or inferior (Wah, 2008).

Case Example

Andy and the Anger Management Group

Andy was not keen on conducting an anger management group, but his supervisor thought he needed the experience, so Andy reluctantly agreed. His group was small, only four, but they were very vocal. Andy could tell they had a lot of repressed feelings that they were airing each week. He closed every group by commending group members for their honesty.

Then one day a group member told Andy that if he used that "namby-pamby compliment routine again" to close the group that he was going to knock Andy off his rocker. At the end of the group Andy did not use the compliment, but told the rest of the group that he had been threatened. He then left abruptly.

Questions

What do you think of Andy's actions? What do you think he should have done? What would you have done in that situation?

Cancer Support Groups

Cancer is a prevalent and scary disease. It often strikes individuals unexpectedly and with a negative prognosis. Groups are helpful in generating hope in cancer patients as well as providing them with important information and support.

A group for men with prostate cancer is an example of a cancer support group. In such groups men are able to talk about their feelings and fears as well as learn about the disease and ways to combat it. In a review of 21 studies of such groups, Chambers and colleagues (Chambers, Pinnock, Lepore, Hughes, & O'Connoll, 2011) found that cognitive-behavioral and psycho-educational interventions, such as providing coping skills training for patient-spouse dyads, appeared helpful in promoting better psychological adjustment and quality of life for these men and their partners.

Likewise, research shows that group psychotherapy for women who undergo treatment for breast cancer is effective "in reducing depression, pain, distress, and hopelessness and improving mood, self-esteem, and social support" (Corwin, Wall, & Koopman, 2012, p. 254). Often women in such groups have multiple spiritual as well as psychological needs. To meet those needs, **Psycho-Spiritual Integrative Therapy (PSIT)**, an approach that defines spirituality as a subjective experience of the sacred, however the individual apprehends it, may be used. Initial research using PSIT in women's breast cancer groups has been encouraging (Garlick, Wall, Corwin, & Cooper, 2011).

Telephone Groups

Whether through landlines or cell phones, **telephone groups** are gaining popularity as a way of gathering information, providing support, and working with individuals on a variety of matters, especially in rural areas. An example of the use of a telephone group can be found in a study conducted by Fraizer and colleagues (2010) using four telephone focus groups and five face-to-face focus groups in which a single moderator used the same open-ended questions and discussion facilitation techniques. The comparison was part of a larger study to gain a better understanding of employment experiences after diagnosis of gynecologic cancer. Offering the telephone option made it easier to recruit women from rural areas and geographically distant cities. Interaction between participants occurred in both types of focus group.

Content analysis revealed that similar elements of the employment experience after cancer diagnosis were described by telephone participants and face-to-face participants. However, participants disclosed certain emotionally sensitive experiences only in the telephone focus groups. Thus, the telephone focus groups provided useful data and reduced logistical barriers to research participation. The researcher concluded that visual anonymity might help some participants feel more comfortable discussing certain personal issues.

Telephone support groups are an important modality for meeting the growing needs of a number of other individuals, too, including family caregivers and frail older adults (Toseland, Naccarto, & Wray, 2007). Studies suggest that these groups can provide information, support, and coping skills to caregivers. In addition, individuals with serious disorders can use telephone support groups as well. For instance, Social Anxiety Anonymous/Social Phobics Anonymous offers free telephone conference support groups each week (socialanxietysupport.com). Callers from around the world are given different times they may join this 12-step approach for aiding recovery from social anxiety problems. Likewise, telephone support groups and counseling using the telephone, sometimes referred to as **telecounseling**, is an effective treatment modality for adults adjusting to a physical disability (Dorstyn, Mathias, & Denson, 2011).

Online Groups

Online groups are those that use the internet and other technology to assist individuals communicate with each other. They usually take one of two forms. They may be either **asynchronous** (e.g., with an e-mail mailing list, "where messages formatted as typed text can be sent at any time whether or not the receiver is on-line") or **synchronous** (e.g., "where group members must be on-line and logged into the site of a group at a designated time") (Page, Delmonico, et al., 2000, p. 134). Both have advantages and disadvantages; synchronous discussions are more challenging because of technological limitations and scheduling problems (Romano & Cikanek, 2003). Yet, the use of Internet support groups for health and mental health concerns has grown and become a resource for groups of individuals with chronic pain, brain injuries, alcohol abuse, or depression, and for other underserved populations with severe problems (Page, 2010; Rath, Bertisch, & Elliott, 2014; Townsend, Gearing, & Polyanskaya, 2011).

Haberstroh and Moyer (2012), for instance, explored a private, open-enrollment, asynchronous online support group for adults who self-injure. Although they found that some of the group members would have preferred a chat room, they also found that the privacy of online information and interactive groups was attractive as members searched for help. Using ground theory, the investigators discovered six themes within the group. Among the implications they found was that Yalom's factor of universality is an important factor in such stigmatized groups. "Individuals may feel less ashamed or alone when they can connect authentically with others who share similar struggles" (p. 128).

In a synchronous research study, Golkaramnay, Bauer, Haug, Wolf, and Kordy (2007) discovered that group therapy delivered through a chat room as a follow-up after inpatient treatment can be effective, too. The group study consisted of 114 aftercare patients with mental disorders who were divided into groups of 8 to 10 patients each. They met with a group therapist in their chat room for 90 minutes at a time for 12 to 15 weeks. They were matched with a control group that received no treatment. Twelve months after discharge, chat participants showed a substantially lower risk (24.7%) for negative outcome than controls (38.5%). Furthermore, the low dropout rate and the high session attendance supported the expectation that this novel offer met patients' needs and thus opens a new avenue for the optimization of care for patients with mental disorders.

Because of the availability of new software programs, such as The Palace, visual, auditory, and spatial cues can be simulated and the group virtual room and experience can become more personal. PalTalk also has possibilities as a convenient format for online discussion groups (Page et al., 2003). The "cutting edge of current technology appears to be synchronous video groups" using Polycoms connected with high-speed Internet (Page, 2004, p. 615).

Furthermore, online learning is growing in training group leaders in a content area. For instance, Krieger and Stockton (2004) describe how a course on developmental theory and structuring therapy groups for younger populations was offered online. The 5-week course made it possible for a variety of school personnel to gain access to practical information while also offering them a chance to experience a different type of learning environment that fit into their schedules. Likewise, Facebook groups have become a popular tool for awareness-raising, fundraising, and support-seeking related to breast cancer, attracting more than 1 million users (Bender, Jimenez-Marroquin, & Jadad, 2011).

Case Example

Tom the Techie

Tom has always loved computers, and he works in an engineering company where he is constantly on the Web creating or modifying designs in products. His supervisor has just informed Tom that he will now become a member of an international group that will be charged with building the next generation of products the company hopes to introduce. Thus, Tom will be in a chat room with other engineers for at least 2 hours, 3 days a week.

Tom is introverted and has a difficult time relating to his fellow engineers in person. He wonders how he will do in the setting he is now being assigned to.

Questions

How do you think Tom needs to get ready for his upcoming experience? What do you think the drawbacks to this assignment are for Tom? What are the advantages?

Trauma Stress Groups

Trauma is a recognized disorder that has a negative lifetime impact on persons unless it is treated. Groups have been found to be valuable in that regard. For instance, the effectiveness and impact of a school-based, trauma/grief-focused group treatment program for war-exposed youth in Bosnia and Herzegovina were investigated by a team of researchers using semistructured focus groups. In their investigation, they conducted separate groups for students and their school counselor group leaders (Cox et al., 2007). Overall, students' and leaders' evaluations of the groups were generally positive. General themes of outcomes and impacts perceived by students and group leaders include acquisition of coping skills and attitudes, willingness to advocate for peers, improved interpersonal relationships, negative impacts, general positive impacts, impacts in the schools, impacts on the group and logistics of the program, and broader impacts on the perception of mental health in the community. The broad positive impacts of this program suggest that trauma/grief-focused group treatment intervention programs targeting trauma-exposed youth may be effective on multiple levels with war-exposed youth and their communities.

In another approach to using groups to work with trauma victims, Akinsulure-Smith (2009) implemented a psychoeducational group treatment program with high school students in New

York City who had a history of refuge trauma, war, and human rights abuses. The students involved had been further traumatized by the 9/11 attacks. The 60-minute closed group met for 7 weeks in a school setting. "Each session followed a similar format to provide coping skills and emphasize resilience and social support" (p. 143). Although the outcome of this group was not formally measured, Akinsulure-Smith points out that other research "has found group treatment to be an effective intervention with refugees and asylum seekers" (p. 148).

In a follow-up to her earlier trauma group, Akinsulure-Smith (2012) conducted a group for African male refugees and asylum seekers admitted to the United States. She found that an open-ended group of 90 minutes a week with therapeutic techniques drawn from African cultural traditions helped to reduce trauma symptoms and depressive symptoms in a statistically significant way after 6 months.

In addressing trauma and disaster, Bemak and Chung (2011, 2014) advocate for counselors working in groups with survivors of natural and people-made disasters. They classify their approach as the Disaster Cross-Cultural Counseling (DCCC) model. It has five phases: (1) creating a comfortable and safe environment, (2) developing new skills to deal with post-disaster realities, (3) combining newly developed skills with prior coping skills, (4) establishing psychological stabilization by accepting new circumstances and increasing a sense of hope, and (5) emphasizing and integrating social justice principles into postdisaster group counseling interventions. This last task is one of making sure that cultural minorities receive access and equity of resources and services.

Reflection

The Gulf Coast region of the United States has suffered two major disasters in recent years—Hurricane Katrina and the BP oil spill. What do you know about how individuals in that region have coped? What kind of ongoing groups do you think would be appropriate for people of the Gulf Coast? Why?

Disabled Persons Groups

Americans with disabilities are a large and diverse group. The Centers for Disease Control and Prevention (CDC) notes that 21.8% of adult Americans have a disability—approximately 47.5 million people. The term **disability** is not always easy to define (Weed & Berens, 2010). It usually refers to a mental, behavioral, or physical impairment that affects at least one of an individual's daily activities. However, it can have broader meaning depending on who is defining it. Nevertheless, some research studies show that those with disabilities are less likely to be satisfied with life as compared to individuals without disabilities, and unfortunately they are more likely to go without needed health or mental health care than are those without a disability (Ellis, Simpson, Rose, & Plotner, 2014).

Disabilities may be classified in a number of ways, including those who have physical, cognitive, and visible (versus invisible) disabilities (Ellis et al., 2014). Issues that are common sources of distress for people with disabilities are those related to educational, social, and intrapersonal domains. Thus, group leaders should have an awareness of these universal difficulties as well as an awareness of how specific disabilities affect a particular group member. In addition, group leaders should consider disabilities as a dimension of culture and realize that even those with the same disability may be at different places developmentally. Overall, the research seems to indicate that a variety of groups are directly and indirectly useful for those with disabilities.

Adventure Groups

Adventure groups are relatively short-term experiential psychotherapeutic approaches that use adventurous activities and being in natural environments to facilitate therapeutic change in clients. The idea for such groups grew out of the Outward Bound tradition, where individuals would leave a safe haven for a journey into the unknown. Like other psychotherapeutic groups, adventure groups are developmental—that is, they evolve from forming to adjourning. Furthermore, they can be useful for a variety of clients and can be thoughtfully integrated into clinical and hospital settings (Gillen & Balkin, 2006).

Adventure-based groups have been found to reduce feelings of hopelessness, guilt, and shame and to increase empathic responses among adults in psychiatric hospitalization. Part of their power comes from clients having to learn new skill and novel ways of relating interpersonally.

Fletcher and Hinkle (2002) have reported that the integration of an adventure component into group counseling results in enhanced self-confidence, self-concept, and well-being. Glass and Benshoff (2002) state that another benefit of using adventure groups is increased group cohesion. Adventure counseling groups also used a nonverbal therapeutic style, thereby facilitating communication among clients who struggled to respond orally in clinical group settings (Williams, 2000).

Prevention Groups

Prevention groups are groups set up to help avoid potential problems. They have their roots in public health and can take multiple forms such as child abuse prevention, eating disorder prevention, prediabetic care, and youth violence prevention (Merchant & Yozamp, 2014). "Prevention groups are designed to reduce the incidence of future harm and facilitate health-promoting and risk-reducing behaviors" (p. 6). They are needed because (1) there are simply not enough mental health professionals to offer remedial services, (2) mental disorders have a stigma attached to them that makes some individuals avoid seeking help and thus get worse, and (3) a wide variety of mental concerns can be avoided through careful planning (Conyne, 2014). In addition, health and wellness promotion is supported by the government and even some insurance companies. A great many prevention groups have positive outcomes because they help their members develop skills and are empowered to deal with potentially harmful situations. Psychoeducational groups are purported to be most suited for prevention purposes. For instance, Gerrity and DeLucia-Waack (2007) did a meta-analysis of sexual abuse prevention programs from 1985 to 1996 that were aimed at younger children and delivered mainly in large psychoeducational groups. They found through looking at outcomes as measured through behavioral observation, questionnaires, and interviews that these interventions for "preschool children were twice as effective as those for early elementary children and three times as effective as those for 8 to 12 year olds" (p. 102).

Because of an uptick in violence in Israeli society, Guez and Gill-Lev (2009) selected eight girls, 14 to 15 years of age, to participate in a psychoeducational group to explore egalitarian relationships, with the goal of reducing the likelihood that members would be as likely to enter a violent relationship. The group was part of a preventative intervention program for girls who were identified as being at high risk. The participants met for 12 sessions to discuss a range of different topics associated with egalitarian relationships and violence, from both theoretical and practical perspectives. After having completed the program, participants generally reported a high level of satisfaction. Most responded that participating in the group significantly enhanced their knowledge about egalitarian, nonabusive relationships, as well as their personal awareness of the implications of violent behavior.

Likewise, using an experimental research design, 81 Latino families were randomly assigned to two formats of Entre Dos Mundos/Between Two Worlds (EDM), a prevention group program for Latino adolescents. The prevention groups used identical session themes: 56 families attended action-oriented skill training and 25 attended unstructured support groups. When EDM was delivered in action-oriented family groups using psychodrama techniques, the program was associated with lower rates of oppositional defiant behavior, anxious depression, parent-adolescent conflict, and total problems in Latino immigrant adolescents. A follow-up 1 year after program completion showed that action-oriented groups maintained superior effects when compared to support groups (Smokowski & Bacallao, 2009).

Groups for Depression

Depression is an insidious and pervasive disorder. Depression does not respect a person's status in life and may be triggered by a number of factors including those that are situational, such as loss of a loved one, loss of a job, or loss of an opportunity. However, depression may also be prone to more physical factors such as the biological makeup of the person experiencing this malady. Usually depression is the result in a combination or confluence of genetic, biological, environmental, and psychological influences. Major depressive disorders, which are associated with feelings of worthlessness and a diminished interest or pleasure in most activities, affects approximately 6% to 7% of American adults each year (Anxiety and Depression Association of America; adaa.org).

Groups can be helpful in working with those suffering from depression (Bieling, Milosevic, & McCabe, 2014). Most major theoretical approaches, such as cognitive-behavioral therapy, self-management therapy, and mindfulness-based cognitive therapy, can be used in groups across a broad range of population with those who are depressed.

Achievement Groups

Groups can promote academic achievement for adolescents in a variety of ways. For instance, brief psychoeducational groups can be used to teach African American males self-advocacy skills, with the ultimate goal of improving their self-concept and academic motivation (Dowden, 2009).

Specific group interventions for high school students from all cultural and ethnic backgrounds can also be used. These groups, as described by Bailey and Bradbury-Bailey (2007), are dedicated to developing and nurturing academic and social excellence. One of the interventions employed in promoting achievement in such groups is the "exam lock-in" (ELI) that occurs from Friday afternoon to Sunday afternoon on the weekend before fall-semester and spring-semester final exams. In this setting, members of these achievement groups, known as the "Empowered Youth Program," are locked in a participating high school where they participate in both individual and small group study sessions. They are proctored by teachers and graduate students who are sensitive to culturally based learning styles and who simultaneously push them and nurture them. The focus of the small-group portion of the weekend is building on the strengths of the young people involved. Leaders involved in the small-group sections of this program take the time to build positive relationships with the group members, and that commitment results in a relationship of trust and respect, as well as higher grades.

Case Example

Pauline and the Preventive Group Adventure

Pauline is a newly minted group counselor who believes that an ounce of prevention is worth a pound of cure. She does not want to do remediation work. Yet, she has been assigned by her mental health agency to one of the poorest sections of the city in which she lives. Having studied other cultures, Pauline thinks an after-school study group would be helpful for kids in the neighborhood to prevent them from getting bad grades and to boost their self-images as achievers. Therefore, Pauline puts up signs at a local community center and even on telephone poles.

Her initial effort works as half a dozen preteens show up on the appointed day and appointed hour. Attendance is fine initially, but Pauline is a strict taskmaster, allowing no eating, drinking, or horseplay in her office. By the third week, no one comes.

Questions

What did Pauline do right in beginning her group? Where did she go wrong? What could she do to revive the group and get it going again?

Although it is not possible to highlight all the research on specialty groups in this brief overview, what is reported here is significant in indicating their power and importance for a variety of people and circumstances. Thus, groups for the incarcerated, those who work in aftercare, individuals who are recovering from human-made and natural disasters, people seeking enrichment, survivors of major diseases and disorders, persons going through grief, and those in community action programs are crucial and significant if run right.

As important as specialty groups may be in illustrating the breadth of group work, it is equally important to emphasize the depth of groups. That is where creativity comes in.

CREATIVITY IN GROUPS

A key factor in the development of any group, whether preventive or remedial, is **creativity**, which is essentially the ability to produce new and useful thoughts, behaviors, and feelings in a socially appropriate context (Csikszentmihalyi, 2013). Said another way, healthy group work is not a mechanical process. There is no formula or recipe. If there were, almost all groups would function well, and as with brownies that are baked at 350 degrees for 30 minutes, everyone would be delighted with the results. Rather, groups that work well depend on collaboration. Groups are innovative because of the combined input from their members and leaders (Paulus & Nijstad, 2003).

This section of the chapter examines the essence of creativity in groups looking at three models—the six hats approach of Edward deBono, the SCAMPER acronym model of Robert Eberle (1971), and the eight-step zig zag approach of Keith Sawyer. Different stages of the group process are then examined using each of these models.

DeBono's Six Hats Approach to Creativity

Edward deBono (1999) is the originator of what is popularly referred to as the **six hats approach to creativity**. When considering a problem, difficulty, challenge, or concern, deBono advocates that the situation be broken down using what he describes as six hats (six ways of thinking). Each hat is color coded and is to be employed before a decision is made as to what to do. The six hats are as follows:

With the white hat, questions are raised considering purely what information is available. The idea is to tease out as thoroughly as possible what the facts are. This type of thinking is neutral and objective.

The red hat focuses on emotions. The objective is to get at instinctive gut reaction or statements of emotional feelings in regard to the matter being discussed. There does not need to be any justification for the feelings.

The black hat is one people wear in looking at the bad points of the matter at hand. Judgment and logic are applied to identify flaws or barriers to the course of action being considered. Care and caution are dominant in this way of thinking.

The yellow hat is one where the good points of an idea are highlighted, benefits of the idea are identified, and harmony is sought. The yellow hat perspective could be considered sunny and positive, asking what might be the best thing that would happen if the idea under consideration was adopted.

The green hat is one that represents growth and looking at where a thought might eventually go.

Finally, the blue hat is one associated with thinking about thinking. It is the organizing hat, and one that is necessary so that thoughts are considered logically and sequentially.

As previously stated, each colored hat is used as a metaphor for a way of thinking. Switching to a different way of thinking is symbolized by the act of putting on a specifically colored hat. The hat metaphors allow for a more complete and elaborate segregation of ways of thinking than would otherwise be the case. All of these thinking hats help group members think more deeply and thoroughly, especially if everyone has on the same hat at the same time.

Reflection

How radical is deBono's hat concept to you? Do you think it would work with people you know in the groups you belong to? Why or why not?

DeBono (1973) states that in ordinary, unstructured thinking the process is unfocused. People leap from critical thinking to neutrality to optimism without a structure or a strategy. The six hats thinking process attempts to introduce **parallel thinking**, which is a thinking process where the focus is in specific directions. When done in a group, it effectively avoids the consequences of the adversarial approach, where the objective is to prove or disprove statements put forward by others. In parallel thinking, group members put forward as many statements as possible in the category they are focused on, such as feelings or optimism. This leads to exploration of a subject where all participants can contribute, in parallel, with knowledge, facts, cautions, and so forth.

The opposite of parallel thinking, where all members of the group are wearing specific hats at specific times, is **spaghetti thinking**, where one person is thinking about the benefits of an idea while another considers the facts. The strands of spaghetti may touch on the same subject, but they do not connect. The hats allow spaghetti thinking to be avoided so that everyone together considers the problems, or the benefits, or the facts, reducing distractions and supporting cross-pollination of thought. This process is achieved because everyone puts on one hat together, then the next hat together. In this way, everyone thinks in the same way at the same time. The only exception is the facilitator, who tends to keep the blue hat on all the time to make sure the group progresses. Evaluating the outcomes of thinking and what they should do next is the final stage in this group process.

Eberle's SCAMPER Model of Creativity

A different way of becoming more creative is represented by Robert Eberle's (1971) **SCAMPER model**. Each letter in this atheoretical mnemonic device stands for a different way of being creative.

The S stands for what can be substituted or put in place for what has been. In cooking, athletics, and the arts, substitution is common. For instance, applesauce may be substituted for butter. In everyday life, especially in the helping professions, the phrase "yes, and" may be substituted for the words "yes, but." Just as applesauce is healthier for individuals than butter, so are the words "yes, and": They open up conversation and dialogue, especially in interpersonal settings such as a group.

The C in SCAMPER is for what can be combined. Peanut butter and chocolate are among other foods that can be combined to make a tasty treat—Reese's Peanut Butter Cups. When ideas are combined, such as in a group setting, the result is often richer and better, too. Hence the saying "two heads are better than one."

Adapting or adopting is what the A in SCAMPER refers to. In motor sports, cars are adapted to run at high speeds around an oval track, whereas in romantic relations, couples often adopt a song that they consider theirs, or they adopt a child or pet to make their lives richer. In counseling, especially in a group, members can adapt to one another's style of communication or to the climate of the environment. Similarly, they can adopt an open and accepting attitude towards others.

M is the letter that represents "modifying" by making something either larger or smaller. Thus, people can magnify or minify their voices to gain attention. In a similar way, modification can be made in a group setting by extending time for sessions or increasing their number, or by members learning to speak more frankly or diplomatically.

The letter P stands for "put to other uses." Just as water, originally used to drink and bathe in, can be put to other uses such as generating electricity, so other elements in an environment can be used in new ways. For instance, words that have an inspirational meaning for individuals can be shared in a group to become line savers, such as the sentence used in Alcoholics Anonymous: "One day at a time." The line savers can, in turn, be used by members of a group in other ways than were originally intended. For instance, when facing a major performance, teams of dancers or athletes may pick up the phrase "One day at a time" to remind themselves that they must practice daily in order to be in the spotlight as time goes by.

E is a reminder to SCAMPER users to eliminate behaviors that are unproductive. For instance, excessive words or excessive behaviors might be dispensed with without any consequences. One way to think about elimination is to imagine oneself as a pest exterminator. Everyone has pesky behaviors—for example, repeating a point several times so that people in a group tire of hearing it.

Finally, the R in SCAMPER stands for what can be reversed or rearranged. Reversal might come in revisiting decisions made at an earlier time and talking with the group about regrets, or rejoicing in making the decisions one did. Rearranging is much like making bouquets of flowers, realizing that if one flower is shifted, the emphasis in the arrangement changes. However, the new arrangement—for example, of personal or professional habits—may have a healthy payoff.

Case Example

Sally Substitutes SCAMPER in Place of Her Usual Style

Sally has been a very directive group leader. She is sensitive, but she does not hold back from telling the group pertinent thoughts that cross her mind. Although this approach has worked well for her in her groups for people with addictions, she decides she will give the SCAMPER model a try.

In the next group session, Linda Rae rants about the fact that people do not listen to her. As far as she can see, she is unimportant. She then talks about taking drugs to relieve her pain of emptiness and escape her low self-esteem. Sally introduces the SCAMPER model to the group then and focuses in on how Linda Rae could substitute running or reading for drugs and how much healthier it would be.

Questions

What do you think of Sally's suggestion? Is Sally still being directive? Is her strategy too simple, and is it creative? What else might Sally do to help Linda Rae?

Sawyer's Zig Zag Model of Creativity

Keith Sawyer believes the creative process is a nonlinear set of behaviors and that it can be learned. As a researcher, he has read evidence-based studies on creativity and has come up with an eight-step process.

Step 1: Ask. According to Sawyer, creativity always starts with a penetrating and novel question no one has thought of before. Such questions are not impossible to answer, such as, "How many angels can dance on the head of a pin?" Rather, they are based in reality (sometimes stretched to the limit), such as that asked by Thomas Edison: "I wonder if a carbon filament will produce a light longer and stronger than a platinum filament?"

Step 2: Learn. To have a creative life, a person must be constantly learning, practicing, mastering, and becoming an expert (which usually takes about 10 years). The process of learning is lifelong and involves acquiring knowledge from any source available. Once a person has mastered a domain, he or she can make new discoveries. For instance, Jonas Salk had been a medical researcher for years before he discovered the vaccine that eliminated polio.

Step 3: Look. Active observation, or mindfulness, and being consciously aware of the environment is the secret to this step in the creative process. How people look at the world determines what they see and how creative they will be. A book may look boring from the outside and be a fascinating read once a person opens it up.

Step 4: Play. In order to free one's mind, play is essential. Physical activity, visualizing, pretending, t'ai chi, daydreaming, meditation, or letting one's mind wander are some of the ways to have fun in a carefree and relaxed way, thus letting the unconscious combine ideas that would not come together otherwise. After all, Archimedes discovered the water displacement method for determining the volume of objects with irregular shapes through taking a bath—that is, playing with the water.

Step 5: Think. Successful creativity is a numbers game, so generating a lot of ideas through thinking, and realizing most will not pan out, is essential. After all, if you don't know where you are going (having not thought it out), you will probably end up someplace else.

Step 6: Fuse. Creativity is a combination of ideas coming together. It is never just a single idea. For instance, a hamburger might represent a single idea, but combined with another hamburger and condiments, the result is a "Big Mac," or, as McDonald's put it in 1968: "Two all-beef patties, special sauce, lettuce, cheese, pickles, onions—on a sesame seed bun."

Step 7: Choose. The saying goes for marriage that "men ask; women choose." Whether that saying is right is not as important as realizing that critical examination of ideas and selecting the best is crucial if people are to be creative.

Step 8: Make. Good ideas become reality in the creative process. For example, Maya Angelou shaped her words into poems, stories, and songs, which she constantly revised by rewriting and refining them. Likewise, the cell phone keeps evolving as new ideas for it are generated.

THE SIX HATS, SCAMPER, AND ZIG ZAG WAYS OF WORKING WITH GROUPS AS A WHOLE

In order to see how the six hats, SCAMPER, and zig zag models work, I have highlighted five scenarios from the stages of group work—forming, storming, norming, performing, and adjourning. I also discuss ways of working with these models as a group leader and a group member in these stages.

FORMING SCENARIO

Jill joined an exercise group because she thought it would help her physically and psychologically. The group meets twice a week for a couple of hours. The first hour is spent exercising using various machines and weights as well as jogging. The second part of the hour is a "cool down" where group members talk about what they have done and are doing to improve themselves in both body and mind. Jill is thrilled with the group, and during this first week she became enamored with Anna and Donna, who are about her same age. She is less attracted to Ralph and Ida, whom she perceives as twice her age and who are in bad physical shape.

SCAMPER Approach

The challenge from the SCAMPER model is in regard to combining and eliminating. Jill needs to see that Ralph and Ida may be more like her than not in that they have a desire to become better physically and psychologically. Therefore, as a group member or leader your task is to help Jill connect with, and not disregard, these individuals. You might lead with comments such as, "So how is the group like you, Jill, in their desire to be better than they are?" When Jill acknowledges that everyone is there for the same reason, it would be appropriate to help her focus on the group as a whole (combining) and what each person has to offer (eliminating the idea that only those most like her, such as Anna and Donna, have anything to offer).

Six Hats Approach

As mentioned, this approach starts and ends with the blue hat (thinking and organizing). With Jill, it would be logical to organize her thinking initially around the red hat (feeling) and her negative reactions to Ralph and Ida. The focus might be: "Where does that feeling come from?" Then the conversation could proceed to the white hat (information that is neutral and objective), such as the fact that Ralph and Ida are older and overweight. Talk could then concentrate on the yellow and black hat in regard to what she might gain through associating with them as well as with Anna and Donna (such as knowledge about what not to do in the future) and what she has to lose by such a move (for example, becoming despondent in seeing how out of shape they are). Finally, returning to a logical order of thought again (blue hat), Jill might think and voice how she could be engaged creatively with these individuals (such as helping them reach their goals through coaching them) and still become better friends with the young women she identifies with most.

Zig Zag Approach

The zig zag approach is not linear. Any of the eight steps can play a role at any stage of creativity. Each step feeds the other seven. However, in the forming stage, I may ask as the group leader a "how" question, such as, "How can I get Jill more integrated into the group and help her see that everyone in the group has something to offer her, not just the ones that are most similar to her?" Likewise, I may ask Jill to play with the idea that she has come to the group at the same age and shape as Ralph and Ida: "What could she do in such a case to foster an identity more like the others in the group?"

STORMING SCENARIO

You are fed up! Meg has been dominating the group with useless chit-chat. She speaks anytime there is a moment of silence. It would not be so bad, except that she has nothing to say. She talks about her past a lot, and about her daily likes and dislikes. It is annoying, and it is getting on your nerves! The group seems content to let Meg chatter. You really wonder if you have been placed with a group of namby-pamby good-for-nothing wimps! Next time Meg opens her mouth, you are thinking of literally stuffing one of your socks into that open cavity and telling her to shut up. You realize that this kind of behavior is inappropriate. So you are deciding what to do.

SCAMPER Approach

Eliminating Meg's senseless chatter is obviously high on your list, but so is modifying the reaction of the group, which at this point is nil. Thus, the letters E and M are dominant in your thinking. One way you might eliminate senseless chatter is to have the group become focused on a theme and assign Meg readings in regard to the theme. Another way to help her and help the group is to have a time limit for everyone in regard to talking, such as 3 minutes. You can help the group modify its behavior this way, too, by encouraging some of the more thoughtful members of the group to maximize their behavior by speaking out more during sessions.

Six Hats Approach

Starting with the blue hat (organization), you want to help the group think about how they can be smooth rather than rough in talking about topics and feelings. You can get a gauge on feelings by using the red hat, and once you find that there is a high-energy feeling around being more efficient, you can help members concentrate on the green hat of "How could that happen?" and "What would be the advantages (yellow hat) and drawbacks (black hat) in doing things differently?" That will lead you back to the blue hat of setting up a structure that will change the group dynamics.

Zig Zag Approach

First, you look and become aware that you are not imagining that Meg is dominating the group with senseless chatter. With that reality confirmed, you choose a thinking strategy. Many ways to keep Meg from talking so much, such as extinction, reprimanding, and instructing, come quickly to mind. However, you do not want to embarrass Meg or set up a negative atmosphere in the group. Therefore, you decide to ask yourself: "What could I do to help modify Meg's behavior and include her into the group?" You come up with the answer that you will use rounds to make sure everyone gets a say in the group and to modify Meg's dominance. That should keep Meg from being scapegoated while moving the group along through this stage.

Reflection

From the two situations you have just read, what is your initial impression of the three models of creativity discussed? Which one impresses you most with its approach to the situations?

NORMING SCENARIO

Everyone appears to identify with being a member of your group's team. They high-five and greet one another enthusiastically every time the group meets. They really seem to like each other. However, you have noticed that the group seems to be stuck in a routine of talking to each other about trivial matters, such as what members did on the weekend. This behavior prevents the group from working on important matters in their lives until the final few minutes of the group. The result is almost zero growth in this growth group. You confront the group with their behavior, and they basically attack you, telling you that they do not need a "taskmaster." You collect your thoughts as to what to do, especially in regard to Don, who is the one who called you a taskmaster.

SCAMPER Approach

On the immediate horizon is to eliminate name calling and to substitute effective ways of working for those that are less productive. One way to do this would be to ignore the name calling initially and to focus with the group on what they could do to maximize time, rather than singling out Don. Could they agree to stop the ritual of high-fiving and discussing their weekends? If so, you could help them substitute a weekly ritual of discussing how they could reach the goals they set for growth when the group began. If they can make this adjustment and adopt a new way of behaving in the group, they will become more focused, which will be of benefit to them all.

Six Hats Approach

In this scenario, the beginning is with the blue hat of organization. The group is badly organized in regard to how it is operating. Very little growth is taking place. Confronting members about that fact is one way of getting to members' individual and collective feelings. The confrontation could come in a sentence such as: "I have heard all of you say you would like to grow personally and professionally, but I see that very little group time is devoted to that. Help me understand." Then the green hat of creativity could be handed to the group as a whole: "What could we do to be more productive?" From there would come the yellow hat: "If we did this, then we would . . ." and the black hat of "But can we realistically do this?" followed by the white hat of "Here is what we are doing" and "Here is what we could do." The end of the conversation would come back to the blue hat of "Okay, let's organize our group this way from now on."

Zig Zag Approach

You think initially that you are mad at the way the group is operating and especially at Don. However, you realize by looking around that the group is simply playing it safe in what they are doing and saying. You therefore ask yourself how you can get them to connect with one another on a deeper level. One idea that comes to you is to let the group play with this idea and then choose several scenarios where they are talking about common matters but not on such a superficial level. In other words, you decide to take yourself out of the role of problem solver and empower the group to be more efficient and effective. After group members think and generate a number of possibilities, you help them fuse their many ideas into ways of helping each other, and the group as a whole have deeper conversations.

PERFORMING SCENARIO

The group is erratic. It seems to make progress and then it seems to regress. You are concerned that the group will run out of steam before it completes the self-study that it has been asked to undertake. Members and subcommittees are not doing their assigned tasks, and your report is due within the month. As the group leader, you are perplexed. Everyone seems to get along—in fact, you wonder if everyone is getting along too well. Would it be helpful to stir up some controversy? Should you give the group a pep talk? What would happen if you "chewed them out?" Hmmm. You wonder.

SCAMPER Approach

There are several ways to be creative in helping the group from the SCAMPER perspective. One thing you could do is to rearrange membership in subgroups in hopes of breathing new energy into these groups and the group a whole. You could put the subgroups to other uses—that is, assign them new tasks. However, that might cause more chaos without resulting in anything productive. A third option would be to combine subgroups and see if that would help them focus better. Then there is the "chewing out" option. Chewing the group out would substitute being stern for being nice. Hmmm. . . . It might work—but it is risky!

Six Hats Approach

Objectively, as you put on your white hat (facts) or put it on with the group, nothing is happening as it should. Could it be that the organization for completing this task is flawed? If so, how could it be organized? (This is the blue hat combined with the green hat.) What would be the benefits to reorganization (yellow hat)? What would be the drawbacks (black hat)? What is your feeling about letting the group stay "as is" as opposed to making changes (red hat)? What does that tell you and the group about organization/reorganization (blue hat)?

Zig Zag Approach

First, you look and quietly become aware that the group is not making the progress it needs to. You sense that members do not seem to feel a sense of urgency, and thus you ask yourself, "Why? What's going on?" You then choose to make what has been written so far into a document and read it before the group. Obviously, there are many blank spots in this product. Thus, you ask your group members to start generating ideas that can be expanded on, fused, and combined into the document. Your approach brings new energy and enthusiasm to the group as they play with the empty space in the self-study and ask themselves what should go where as they play at envisioning a final product.

ADJOURNING SCENARIO

Robert is having a hard time letting go of his group experience. He is an athlete, but as the end of the group has gotten closer, he has become misty-eyed and his voice has cracked on several occasions as he has expressed his appreciation to those in the group who have helped him. He has asked the group today if they would like to keep going for 10 more sessions. His request has caught you completely by surprise, but you realize you need to say something to both Robert and the group.

SCAMPER Approach

At first glance it might seem that the SCAMPER approach would stress elimination and reversal, but it is impossible to eliminate or reverse what has been said. Therefore, the emphasis is on putting his request to another use, that is, what would happen if the group were extended? By focusing on this question, members may become more aware and can more objectively discuss Robert's request.

Six Hats Approach

Robert has surprised everyone, and it may be productive initially to take the temperature of the group and see how everyone is feeling (red hat). Then it would be helpful to talk about the benefits and drawbacks of extending the group (yellow and black hats). What are the facts and challenges facing the group if it continues (white hat)? How could members make the most of what they have now as opposed to extending the group (green hat)? How would an extension of the group function as opposed to how it is functioning now (blue hat)?

Zig Zag Approach

You initially ask yourself: "What is Robert doing and why does he think 10 more sessions would be helpful to him?" You have learned over the years that behavior like Robert's is consistent with individuals having had problems with loss. Thus, you look for something you might suggest to help Robert and the group bring closure to this session and the group. You think of your experiences as a group leader and other groups that have had trouble ending. You remember that reminding the group that there will be a follow-up in a few weeks has been helpful in the past because it reassures everyone they will meet again. Therefore, you make the suggestion that the group focus on when the follow-up to their experience will be instead of concentrating on whether they will consider 10 more sessions immediately. You tell them they can always re-form at another date, but for now they need to sum up their learning and prepare to meet again as a follow-up. You also assure everyone you will be around to talk to, if needed.

Case Example

Beau Balances a Counseling Group

Beau is working with underemployed adults in a community center. The group meets once a week at night. He is wedded to the deBono six hats method of working with the group and has found it to be effective in helping group members help each other. However, he does not like the red hat, because he does not think emotions have much to do with finding a better job. Therefore, he has dropped the red hat from his group's approach to finding better careers and the career decision process.

Questions

What do you think of Beau's strategy? Is the deBono hat strategy really dependent on using all six hats? What would you recommend to Beau?

CREATIVE EXERCISES FOR DIFFERENT GROUP STAGES

Creative approaches to working with groups require thought, knowledge, planning, and experience. There are no cookie-cutter ways of working with groups in different stages. However, there are some exercises that can be used in working with individuals and groups to make the most of their experiences. Here are some examples of the many ways group leaders and members can help a group at different stages during its development. As in the previous section, five distinct stages and exercises that go with these stages are delineated. In reality, some of the exercises may be used constructively in groups that do not go through stages. Furthermore, some of these exercises can be modified or adapted to unique aspects of a group in which a person may find himself or herself.

FORMING AND WARMING UP

Music Openings.　Music can be especially powerful in a group at its beginning. Selected music can help set an upbeat or sedate tone when clients first enter the group room. For example, beginning a group through drumming is a unique way to jump-start conversations about group dynamics and each person's role in them.

Milling Around.　In this exercise, individuals simply walk around and participate with others as instructed by the leader by making or not making eye contact, by touching or not touching each other with shoulders or elbows. The idea is to assess how comfortable each member feels moving in a certain manner. The entire exercise is brief (about 2 to 5 minutes) and is processed with the group leader for as long as needed afterwards.

Poems as a Group Catalyst.　This process, which can be used as an icebreaker, involves having the group leader read a nondidactic poem—such as those by Langston Hughes, Maya Angelou, James Dickey, or Billy Collins—to group participants after they have been through a series of warm-up exercises. Each person in the group is asked to identify with an image in the poem and then talk about this image in regard to how it represents them. For example, a person might identify with grass and talk about how his or her life is growing.

Train Station.　This movement exercise was originated by Playfair (e-mail Playfair1@aol. com). It is an icebreaking exercise used in an initial meeting of a group. In Train Station, the group is divided in two. Half of the group is designated to be the greeters and the other half the passengers. The group is then given the following instructions: Each greeter has just received a phone call from a best friend from early childhood. It has now been a number of years since they saw each other, but the former best friend is to arrive in a few hours at the train station in the city where the greeter now lives. The greeter is so excited that after agreeing to meet the friend, he or she hangs up the phone without thinking to ask what the person who called looks like. Lacking this information and the ability to trace the call, the greeter goes to the train station at the desig-nated hour and decides that the best strategy to employ in this situation is to move slowly but with enthusiasm toward the group of passengers now arriving. Thus, with arms waving, the greeters as a group move in slow motion toward the passengers, who all display similar behaviors. As each greeter gets to a passenger looks are exchanged, but then both realize the person who they are exchanging glances with is not the right person; thus, both look away and toward another person in the immediate area, who also turns out not to be the right person. This activity continues until all the greeters and passengers have passed each other, after which participants are given a chance to voice how they experienced the exercise. They are then informed by the leader of the group that nothing they ever do in the group will be as embarrassing.

Passive-Active.   This movement activity can be used with any age group as a warm-up exercise. It requires part of a group to be passive and the other part active. The active members make statues out of the passive members (within reason), but the passive members may come alive at any time, and likewise the active members may become passive at any time. The fun of this type of play activity lies in creating the statues and in the element of surprise. As a warm-up, this activity can go on for about 5 minutes. It is important for counselors to make sure that the entire group does not become active or passive all at once.

STORMING

Circles.   Group members are asked to draw a circle and then to color different parts of the circle to represent various feelings they have about themselves and the group, such as active or passive. Drawing in such a manner helps these individuals become more aware of how they see themselves and the group. It also opens up concrete avenues for them to use in talking about how they would like the group to be.

Home Spot.   In this exercise, members of a group stand up and huddle with arms around each other's shoulders as if they were a football team. Each member of the group is asked to pick out a spot in the room where he or she would like to take the group, but to keep it a secret. The leader then instructs the group members to take the group to his or her spot. Since there is no clear direction of where the group is going, there is a bit of tussling as each member tries to move the group to his or her designated spot. (Group leaders must be careful to instruct the group about excessive use of force and to prevent it.) After a minute or two of going nowhere, the leader stops the exercise and asks group members about their experience (which is usually one of frustration). Ways of finding direction and avoiding conflict are then discussed with the group as a whole.

Hamlet's Dilemma.   This approach works on an experiential and cognitive level for groups that are stuck or storming. It is used with group members who role-play in groups of three, in which one plays the protagonist such as Hamlet ("to be or not to be") and is flanked by the other two, whose roles are those of caution and action, respectively. In these role-plays, which last for 15 minutes, each of the flanking actors tries passionately to persuade the prince (or princess) to choose his or her point of view (i.e., "Be more than you have ever been before" or "Be safe, don't do anything"). After time is called, the protagonist shares with the others in the group thoughts and feelings that emerged during his or her decision making. The process is repeated until each of the trio (and ultimately everyone in a group) has an opportunity to actively participate as the protagonist.

Hamlet's Dilemma

Reflection

When have you ever been undecided about a course of action, such as whether to date someone or buy a certain item? How did you end up making a choice? What do you think of Hamlet's Dilemma as a way of making a decision? How might you modify it?

NORMING

Group Mural.   In this exercise, long pieces of paper are hung on walls and various art materials are distributed. Group members are instructed to draw themselves in the group and to draw the group itself. Group leaders then work with the group and the individuals in it on what they have drawn and how it relates to the mission of the group and to themselves as members of the group.

Clay Pieces.   In this exercise, group members work on individual clay pieces that represent who they are in the group and what the group is as a whole. This exercise is meant to show that everyone has a place in the group and contributes to the group as a whole. The group is more than the sum of its parts, but it is made up of many pieces.

PERFORMING

Locomotion.   The idea of the locomotion exercise is to have clients see how many different movements they can make to get from one place to another (e.g., jumping, running, and skipping). They can then combine movements and even do the same movements with a partner.

Afterwards, the feelings involved with these movements are processed. The idea that there are a number of ways to get from one point to another is discussed.

Adverbs. Group members form a circle with one designated person holding up a pen and letting the person to his or her right know that the pen is going to be passed by saying an adverb (for simplicity: a word ending in "ly," such as *slowly*) and combining it with an action that coincides with the word (in this example, moving slowly). The person who receives the pen passes it in turn to the next person on the right, doing the same thing, coordinating the adverb with the action. This process is continued through the rest of the group, and three to four rounds are conducted. Each person must give and demonstrate a different adverb, but if someone cannot think of a word, that individual is simply allowed to say "pass" and pass the pen to the next individual in the circle.

Areas. The group room is marked off literally or figuratively into different feeling areas such as *sad*, *bored*, *happy*, and *angry*. Each member of the group spends time in these areas and tries to embody that emotion. Then members reassemble under the feeling *content* and talk about how each experience felt. For example, what is your behavior like when feeling sad as opposed to feeling happy?

Case Example

Eileen Gets Hooked on Feelings

Eileen has been working with a group of middle schoolers who are not very aware, let alone sophisticated, in identifying their feelings. She is focused in her psychoeducational group on helping these students recognize their different emotional states. She decides one day to do an opening activity that involves a taste test. She prepares small portions of common foods for students to taste, from sugar to vinegar. She blindfolds the students before they taste the substances, but takes pictures of their reactions to the foods. She then has them talk about their experiences in small groups with the pictures before them. She thinks it is a great way to help students recognize their emotions and also learn about the pure taste of foods.

Questions

How well do you think emotions correlate with taste? How else might Eileen teach students to recognize their emotions? What are the upsides of Eileen's actions? What are the risks?

Common Object. In this fantasy exercise, members of a group are encouraged to imagine themselves as a common object, such as a piece of luggage or a ladder. They are then asked to describe what their lives would be like and how they would feel if they were indeed that object. For example, as a piece of luggage a group member might have an active life of travel and feel both exhilarated and exhausted. When talking about the common object, members are encouraged to stay in the present tense. They actually end up talking about themselves in many ways and seeing their lives differently as a result of projection and fantasy.

Acting "As If." In this Adlerian procedure, group members discuss how they would like to behave. Then they are simply instructed to act as if they were the persons they wish to be. The technique is one that is usually met with protests because members think they are being phony, but stress is lowered when individuals involved know they are simply acting and that their new behaviors in effect are no different from trying on new clothes to see how well they fit and feel.

Skits. Often overlooked as a way to creatively address issues, skits humorously broach subjects that group members have concerns about. At such a time, skits can be videotaped and shown to participants again. From skits, group members gain a sense of empowerment and empathy that gives them more freedom to constructively operate within the group.

Role-Plays.   A role-play activity is where a role, usually not one familiar to the group member, is assumed and actively acted out, such as being assertive. In the process, if the role-play is successful, the group member learns more about issues and challenges of being seen or cast in a certain way.

ADJOURNING (CLOSING)

Music Good-bye.   During termination, selected music or music activities can help instill in group members a sense of closure and can promote integration. Music such as "The Way We Were" is played, and then each group member is given the opportunity to say what he or she received from or added to the group and what he or she is taking away from the group as an insight or growth experience.

Saying "Good-bye" Through Imagery.   Imagery may be used to enhance the group process in almost any stage, but it may be especially powerful in the adjourning stage. For instance, during this stage, where the focus is on closure and anticipation, group members may give each other good-bye gifts in the form of future visions for themselves and others.

Balloons.   In this experience, each member of a group is given a sheet of paper with his or her name on it and a drawing of a bunch of balloons. Members of the group then pass their papers to the right around the group, and other members of the group write or draw a kindness or good quality about the person on one of the balloons, and continue passing the papers and writing or drawing on them until each sheet is returned to its owner. This is an excellent way to end a group.

Rainbow.   In this exercise, a brightly colored rainbow is made with everyone in the group's name on a stripe. The group leader then focuses on the fact that everyone in the group has strengths and gifts that contribute to the beauty and uniqueness of the group. As each group member's name is read, other group members call out strengths of that person that are written down or symbolically drawn on that person's stripe by the leader. This is an excellent multicultural exercise and a good way to end a group.

Closing Poems.   In this written exercise, group participants write couplets or lines about what they have learned in the group. The lines are then linked together in an interactive way that results in a collaborative poem. The poem may begin with the line: "Today I learned in the group" or "Through this group experience I learned." A good ending line is "Now I am moving on." When complete the poem might look like this:

> **Today I learned in the group**
> *I can speak and be heard*
> *I can take a risk and still be accepted*
> *I can remain silent and reflect*
> *I can try out a new idea*
> *I can let my feelings show*
> **Now I am moving on**

Such a procedure requires everyone's participation. It is usually an effective way to terminate a group experience permanently, or in the case of open-ended groups, to close the group for that session.

Summary and Conclusion

All groups are special, but there are specialty groups as well that focus on working with particular populations or problem sets. This chapter has covered some of these groups across the life span and has also examined groups that are dedicated to working with people who have specific problems, such as the unemployed, the angry, the disabled, and victims of trauma or reactions to birth. Specialty groups are not just about problematic situations, though, as can be seen in group examples that focus on achievement and prevention. Working with individuals in groups does not always have to be face-to-face, as the telephone and online group examples illustrate.

In addition, this chapter has looked at how three approaches to creativity—the six hats, SCAMPER,

and zig zag models—can be used in groups. The basics of these models have been explained, and they have been applied to the five major stages in a group's life. Various creative exercises that may be employed in distinct stages of groups complete this chapter. However, group members and leaders must realize that although there are literally dozens of books on group exercises, a group leader who tries to conduct groups simply using exercises may well feel inept and in the long run be inefficient, because exercises by themselves do not have enough depth to move the group forward. Rather, it is creativity, purpose, focus, and clarity, along with activities and the leadership qualities and employment of helping skills, that make groups function or fail.

Classroom Exercises

1. What do you see as the difference between specialty groups and "other groups"? Are not all groups special? What skills do you think you might especially need to focus on should you decide to lead a specialty group?

2. What groups are you most interested in? Do they exist in your community? If so, request permission to visit one or to talk with the leader of such a group. Report back to your class on how your expectations and reality differed and converged.

3. A group for people who are addicted is reported to be one of the most difficult types of groups to conduct. What do you think keeps leaders of these groups motivated? What are the benefits and drawbacks of working with addicted people in a group?

4. Creativity is often shrouded in mystery and misunderstood. How do the six hats, SCAMPER, and zig zag models help you in understanding this phenomenon? Which of these models appeals to you most? Why?

CHAPTER 10

Ethical and Legal Aspects of Working with Groups

The courtroom buzzes like a bee hive
with the rustling of papers
and the rush of people coming in and out.
I sit quietly collecting my thoughts
waiting to make my contributions.
There will be some sweetness today
but also some sadness and sorrow.
I can only do what I do best
in a group ruled by a hierarchy.*

From "Beehive" © 2010/2014 by Samuel T. Gladding. Reprinted by permission from Samuel T. Gladding.

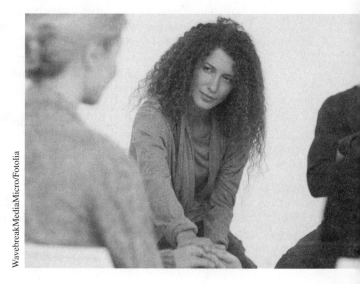

WavebreakMediaMicro/Fotolia

CHAPTER OVERVIEW

From reading this chapter, you will learn about

- Major ethical issues in group work and the making of ethical decisions
- Promoting ethical principles in groups and responding to complaints of unethical behavior
- Legal issues in groups and how they affect the functioning of a group

AS YOU READ, CONSIDER

- The ethical principles and codes you abide by and why they are important in your life
- If you think ethical codes are different in working with groups than with individuals and what unethical behaviors might be more prevalent in a group
- How your knowledge of the law and legal proceeding influences your life individually and in society

Many of the countries of the world have monarchs. They have different levels of power and prestige, but those who have authority serve as leaders in a group hierarchy. Such a position is for better or for worse. The betterment side can be seen in Catherine the Great (1762–1796) of Russia. During her 34 year reign she worked with the nobility of Russia as a group to expand its boundaries and become recognized as one of the great powers of Europe. On the opposite end of hierarchical powers in legal and ethical matters is another Russian tsar, Paul I (1796–1801), who was the son of Catherine the Great. During his 5-year reign, Paul reversed most of his mother's reforms, alienated the nobility with higher taxes, reintroducing corporal punishment for the nobility, and randomly sent people into exile to show off his unlimited power. He did nothing that would be considered progressive. Unfortunately, people became so angry with him that he was assassinated.

Group leaders are constantly making decisions. Much of what they decide is guided by the ethical guidelines of the professional organizations to which they belong and the legal codes of local, state, and federal governments (Remley & Herlihy, 2014). At times, practitioners are confused about whether their decision making is based on ethical guidelines, legal standards, or both. *Ethics* and the *law* are not one and the same. Rather, "they can probably be best conceptualized as two over-lapping circles which share a common intersection" (Kitchener, 1984a, p. 16). Ethical and legal opinions complement and contradict each other. "In some cases, an ethical decision may not be legal, and in other cases, a legal obligation may not seem ethical" (Rapin, 2014, p. 71). Group leaders who make the best and wisest decisions are those who are informed by as many sources as possible.

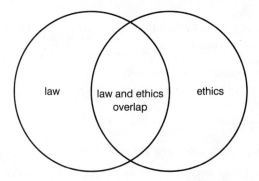

Information alone, however, is not enough. Knowledge in and of itself does not guarantee proper ethical behavior (Welfel, 2013). Group leaders and members must also practice what they learn (Mangione, Forti, & Iacuzzi, 2007). "Conduct and character are correlated," but not perfectly (Hayes, 1991, p. 24). It is only with practice that those who work in groups become skilled at discerning the rationale for their behaviors and the consequences of them (Foltz, Kirby, & Paradise, 1989). Therefore, ethical and legal decision making is a dynamic activity that needs careful attention if group leaders are to stay current and act in the best interest of their group members. "It becomes every group leader's responsibility to attempt to think ethically and behave professionally" (Gumaer & Scott, 1986, p. 149). "Ethical decision making is an ongoing process with no easy answers" (Moleski & Kiselica, 2005, p. 3).

In this chapter, the nature of professional and personal ethics is examined, along with some specific ethical guidelines for group leaders. Potential problems related to ethics in group work are examined, as are issues involving the training of group leaders in ethics. In addition, the nature of law and legal codes is explored, because they affect the field of group work. Potential legal problems in groups are also discussed. Although many ethical and legal matters are fairly straightforward and clear-cut, some are not. Group work is a complex process, and those who are most involved in it must be multifaceted.

THE NATURE OF ETHICS AND ETHICAL CODES

Ethics may best be defined as suggested standards of conduct based on a set of professional values (Gladding, 2011a). To behave in an ethical way is to act in a professionally acceptable manner based on these values. However, although ethics address what is right and correct and are deduced from values (Welfel, 2013), ethical conduct "is a matrix relationship involving numerous variables" (Rapin, 2010, p. 61).

All ethical issues involve values as grounds for decision making. Some of the dominant values underlying the practice of ethics are based on the virtues of autonomy, beneficence, non-maleficence, justice (fairness), fidelity, and veracity (truthfulness) (Kitchener, 1984b; Meara, Schmidt, & Day, 1996).

Autonomy is the promotion of self-determination, or the power to choose one's own direction in life. In groups, it is important that members feel they have a right to make their own decisions. For example, if Kathy is struggling in a counseling group about whether to marry, then she needs to feel she is not being pressured by the group to decide one way or the other.

Beneficence is promoting the good of others. It is assumed in groups that leaders and members will work hard for the betterment of the group as a whole. For example, in a career support group, members who find out information concerning employment opportunities will share those tips with others in the group.

Nonmaleficence means avoiding doing harm. To act ethically, members of groups must be sure the changes they make in themselves and the help they offer others are not going to be damaging. For instance, Yoko, a Japanese American, may not be helped if she takes a group leader's advice and becomes more assertive with her family of origin.

Justice (fairness) refers to the equal treatment of all people. This virtue implies that everyone's welfare is promoted and that visible differences in people, such as gender or race, do not interfere with the way they are treated. Thus, Mohammed is not made to feel apart from the group because he is the only Muslim in it.

Fidelity refers to loyalty and duty. It is keeping promises and honoring commitments. In group work, fidelity involves stating up front what the group will focus on and then keeping that pledge. In such situations, trust is established, and group members are able to accomplish what they set out to do. For example, a psychoeducational group basically deals with information. Therefore, if Mark joins such a group, he expects that the group leader will not ask him to disclose private concerns about himself that might be embarrassing, because the focus of the group is on the dissemination of facts.

Veracity is truthfulness. In group work, veracity is important in all phases of the group's development. Group members and leaders who are not truthful with themselves or others set up situations in which a good working relationship is impossible to achieve. For instance, in a therapy group, if Tosha tells the group she is not offended by a remark made by another member when she really is, then her behavior in the group may change and the group as a whole may deteriorate because of this untruthfulness. Generally, veracity in groups has to do with both interpersonal and intrapersonal honesty.

At first glance, the practice of ethics does not appear to be difficult. Indeed, individuals who are sheltered from complex interpersonal relationships may find it relatively easy to behave ethically. However, when behavior is considered in the multifaceted world of a group of diverse people, the matter of ethics and acting ethically may become complicated (Mangione et al., 2007). A uniform code of ethics is needed as a guide in such situations because a professional code of ethics "sets out norms and expectation for practitioners in order to collectively minimize the risk of harm to clients and the general public" (Francis & Duggar, 2014, p. 131).

Reflection

I once had a chapter of a book I had written plagiarized. To make the matter worse, it was done by someone who was prominent and whom I knew quite well. I realized that if I turned the person in, that person would most likely lose a lot, including a license to practice counseling as well as a reputation. However, not to turn the person in would be to accept the dishonesty of the act and enable the person to be deceitful again. If that situation happened to you, how would you respond? What would be the bases for your action?

A **code of ethics** is a set of standards and principles that organizations create to provide guidelines for their members to follow in working with the public and with one another. Codes of ethics are constantly evolving. Parts of ethical documents are aspirational in nature and not enforceable, whereas other sections require strict professional adherence. In short, ethical codes do not address all possible situations.

In a field such as group work, in which practitioners come from varied backgrounds, often some question arises as to which code of ethics to follow and when (Page, Mitchell, Olson, & Vernon, 2000). The reason is that within each specialty (e.g., counseling, medicine, nursing, psychology, social work), codes of ethics have been developed. Some do not deal with aspects of group conduct, and some contradict one another (Corey, Corey, Corey, & Callanan, 2015). In addressing the field of counseling specifically, Herlihy and Remley (1995) point out that "the existence of multiple codes of ethics creates a confusing situation both for professionals and for consumers" (p. 130). Their observation is pertinent to the field of group work.

One document that specifically addresses ethical issues in group work is the *Best Practice Guidelines* of the Association for Specialists in Group Work (ASGW) (2007; Thomas & Pender, 2008). This document provides "structure to the planning, performing, and processing tasks required for effective and ethical practice in counseling and psychotherapy groups" (Rapin, 2014, p. 75). It should be used along with the more general Codes of Ethics from one's professional association, such as the American Counseling Association (ACA), because together these documents give guidance for ethical interaction in groups. They are based on years of group experience and were developed in response to the need to outline proper behaviors and correct questionable practices within the group field. Two other documents, the ASGW's *Multicultural and Social Justice Competence Principles for Group Workers* (2012) and its *Professional Standards for the Training of Group Workers* (2000), are also important sources of ethical information, as they outline ways of working with diverse groups and the qualifications of group leaders in different types of groups.

It is important that group leaders be aware of these codes, standards, and guidelines as well as others like them from similar helping professions, such as social work and psychology.

Although codes of ethics, best practice guidelines, and professional training standards are not entirely satisfactory because in many situations no one behavior seems entirely ethical, ethical codes, guidelines, and standards such as those just mentioned give group workers a starting place to find answers and resolutions. Therefore, these documents should be studied and discussed throughout a professional's career. An advanced group leader is expected to operate much more ethically than one with less experience.

Case Example

Sunny's Sad Situation

The principal of her school asked Sunny, a classroom teacher, to lead a counseling group for elementary children. Sunny had no background in group work, but she did not want to disappoint her principal. Therefore, she consented.

Matters quickly went from bad to worse. Sunny invited acting-out kids to be in her group without getting their parents' permission or even notifying them. By the second session, Sunny found that she faced both a disorganized situation in her group and a bunch of angry parents. Being clueless, she moved quickly to seek advice from the school system's attorney.

Questions

How could Sunny have avoided this situation? What would you have advised her to do had she come to you before consenting to lead the group? Afterwards? What positive role could ethics have playing in this scenario?

MAJOR ETHICAL ISSUES IN GROUP WORK

A number of major ethical issues are involved in most kinds of group work. For some types of groups, such as task/work groups, a few of these issues will not be as prevalent as for other types, such as psychotherapy or counseling groups. Among the most important issues are those involving training of group leaders, screening of potential group members, the rights of group members, confidentiality, personal relationships between group members and leaders, dual relationships, personal relationships among group members, uses of group techniques, leaders' values, referrals, records, and closings and follow-up. All of these issues are discussed here.

Training of Group Leaders

Certain personal characteristics are vital for group leaders: self-awareness; genuineness; the ability to form warm, caring relationships; sensitivity and understanding; self-confidence; a sense of humor; flexibility of behavior; and a willingness to self-evaluate. Without these personal qualities, potential group leaders would have difficulty in their interpersonal relationships and would not be effective. Usually, individuals wishing to become group leaders will obtain specialized training in one of the four areas of group work specialization: psychoeducation, counseling, psychotherapy, or task/work. However, it is the responsibility of professional education programs, such as those accredited by the Council for the Accreditation of Counseling and Related Educational Programs (CACREP), to be sure that program graduates are personally integrated and have received the experiences and possibly therapy they need to work out biases and use strengths (Yalom & Leszcz, 2005).

In addition to personal qualities, the training of group leaders involves selected course work and experience in core group skills, such as being able to identify the basic principles of group dynamics (ASGW, 2000). It is also important for potential group leaders to be involved in different types of group experiences, both as participants and as leaders or co-leaders (Corey, Corey, Corey, & Callanan, 2015; Yalom & Leszcz, 2005). Just as the ASGW has published its professional standards, so has the American Group Psychotherapy Association (AGPA) (2002) and other professional group associations. Personal-growth experiences are seen by group associations as part of the total program for aspiring group leaders.

Regardless of the standards followed, group leaders must recognize their limitations (Welfel, 2013). Those who do not possess professional credentials in an area in which they wish to practice either must not practice or must be supervised by a professionally qualified person (ASGW, 2000). It is essential that leaders and members have a clear conception of the type of group to which they belong and the kind of goals they wish to achieve (Gumaer & Martin, 1990). One way for beginning group leaders to gain clarity and experience, in addition to those ideas mentioned previously, is to join a **training group** (Corey, Corey, & Corey, 2014). In such a group, beginning leaders can learn to recognize and work out major personal and professional issues that affect their ability to conduct groups—for example, criticism, anxiety, jealousy, or the need for control.

Screening of Potential Group Members

A second major issue in group work is screening potential members, which is more difficult than it seems. It becomes even more complicated when the group is composed of nonvolunteers.

Screening is actually a three-part process. It begins when group leaders formulate the type of group they would like, and are qualified, to lead. Next is the process of recruitment, in which the leader must make sure not to misrepresent the type of group that is to be conducted. In the recruiting process, potential members have a right to know the goals of the group, the basic procedures to be used, what will be expected of them as participants, what they can expect from the leader, and any major risks as well as potential values of participating in the group. Recruiting is often conducted in a number of ways, including the distribution of flyers as well as direct, personal contact with potential group members and helping professionals who may know individuals appropriate for such an experience.

Finally, the leader screens applicants on a one-to-one or small-group basis to be sure they are able to benefit from and contribute to the group (Riva, Lippert, & Tackett, 2000). This type of screening is valuable because it provides an opportunity for the group leader to establish rapport, clarify norms and expectations of group behavior, and answer any questions the individual may have about the group.

An important aspect of screening, besides the personal contact it provides, is finding out whether a potential group member is currently in any other kind of mental health treatment, such as individual counseling. If a person is, then it is essential for the group leader to contact the other mental health services provider and inform him or her about the potential member's desire to participate in the group. The potential group member ultimately must decide in collaboration with this professional whether to join the group. The potential member needs as much information as possible about the benefits and liabilities of such action. It is advisable at the end of the screening process, and before accepting a member into the group, that the leader obtain a member's signature on an **informed consent statement** (Welfel, 2013) (see Figure 10.1). Such a process acknowledges that the individual is aware of the group activity in which he or she is about to participate and is doing so voluntarily.

Informed Consent Statement
(for group counseling)

I, _____, acknowledge that group counseling is an activity that involves my being open, honest, and willing to participate with others as I strive, with them, to reach personal and group goals. I may experience negative, as well as positive, feelings in this process. I am entering this relationship voluntarily and pledge to work hard in the group in collaboration with the group leader and other members.

_____   _____
date   group member signature

                                _____
                                group leader signature

FIGURE 10.1   An informed consent statement.

Rights of Group Members

Group members have rights that must be respected and protected if the group is going to work well. These rights are similar to the rights of others who are consumers of professional services. Group members need to "understand what choices they have in participating and what consequences will occur if they refuse" (Rapin, 2014, p. 76). Overt ways of conveying this understanding are important in both voluntary and **involuntary groups** (where members are mandated to attend, such as those that are court ordered or conducted in an inpatient mental health facility). In some types of groups, such as counseling groups, recipients of services can be alerted to their rights through the distribution of prepackaged materials, such as those produced by Chi Sigma Iota (International Academic and Professional Counseling Honor Society) and the National Board of Certified Counselors. These materials, along with a verbal explanation of them, are crucial to fully informing individuals of their rights.

In addition, specific guidelines pertaining to rights and risks in particular group situations should be covered (Remley & Herlihy, 2014). Group members should be told before the group begins that their participation in the group is voluntary or involuntary accordingly and what the consequences will be if they choose not to participate, if they are disruptive, or if they leave the group. Furthermore, group members should be informed of their rights to resist following instructions or suggestions of leaders and other members. They should expect to be treated individually and respectfully and to be protected from physical and psychological threats and intimidation. They should also be informed as clearly as possible about what the group leader can and cannot do. Basically, group members have the right to know as realistically as possible what type of group procedures will be used, what members can and cannot do, and what the risks are in their participation.

Confidentiality

Confidentiality is the right of group members to reveal personal thoughts, feelings, and information to the leader and other members of the group and expect that information to not be disclosed to others outside the group. Not keeping confidences is like gossiping and is destructive to the group process. Underlying the keeping of confidence is the matter of trust. If groups of any kind are going to be productive, then members must trust one another.

Group leaders should deal with the importance and reality of confidentiality during the pregroup screening process. It should be stressed to potential group members that everyone in the group is expected to maintain confidentiality as a means of creating trust, cohesiveness, and growth (Corey et al., 2015; Cottone & Tarvydas, 2007). At the same time, the leader must acknowledge that he or she cannot guarantee confidentiality and that there may be certain cases in which ethical or legal considerations may force the leader to break confidentiality (Welfel, 2013). For example, Section B of the American Counseling Association's *Code of Ethics* (2014) deals with confidentiality and privacy and spells out as clearly as possible when confidentiality must be broken, such as when clients pose a danger to themselves or others or when legal requirements demand disclosure.

When group leaders find or suspect that members have broken confidentiality, they need to address the matter quickly and directly with the group as a whole. For instance, if Paul, as group leader, learns in a counseling group that Bonita has told her closest friends about Jill's reactions to her failed marriage, then Paul needs to raise the issue before the group for discussion and suggestions. The atmosphere surrounding such an experience will be tense and should be serious.

In efforts to prevent breaks in confidentiality, leaders need to reaffirm periodically to group members the importance of not discussing with others what occurs in the group (Corey et al., 2015). This approach keeps the matter of confidentiality constantly before the group and may serve a preventive function by increasing members' awareness so that they do not unintentionally discuss material outside the group. Unfortunately, leaders and members cannot prevent breaks of confidentiality after a group ends, and this reality must also be addressed.

Reflection

When have you had your own or a friend's confidentiality broken? What were the results of this breach? How did you feel? What did you do? What do you think you should do if this happens in a group now?

Personal Relationships Between Group Members and Leaders

The degree and kind of relationship between group members and leaders will vary from group to group. In task/work groups, for instance, casual contact between group members and leaders is usually unavoidable and may even be productive. However, in therapeutic groups, such contact is likely to be inappropriate and could be destructive to the persons involved as well as to the group as a whole. It is more likely that relationships between group members and leaders will be detrimental to the group as a whole if they are not carefully handled. Such relationships can lead to favoritism or to a failure to focus on important personal topics within the context of the group itself. Usually, outside personal contact between group leaders and members in therapeutic or counseling groups is discouraged or prohibited because this behavior may foster dependency or may lead to unhealthy dual/multiple relationships.

Dual/Multiple Relationships

Dual/multiple relationships occur when group leaders find themselves in two or more potentially conflicting roles with their group members, such as "professional (e.g., professor, supervisor, employer) or personal (e.g., friend, close relative, sexual partner)" (Herlihy & Remley, 2001, p. 80).

Although certain dual/multiple relationships may seem unavoidable and may even seem harmless, they carry the potential for harm because of the inherent vulnerability of the client and the imbalance of power between counselor and client (Neukrug, Milliken, & Walden, 2001). In a counseling training program, for instance, a group leader might be a member's teacher and have the responsibility of assigning grades. The fact that the group leader might come to know something about the member's background could potentially have a detrimental effect on the member's grade (Davenport, 2004). For example, Patricia, the group leader, might find out that Jessie, a group member, is a lesbian. If Patricia has unresolved issues or biases involving homosexuals, she will treat Jessie differently than before. Regardless of the exact setting, dual/multiple relationships can negatively affect the people involved in subtle and obvious ways. Therefore, they are best avoided.

In academic settings, Remley and Reeves (1989) advise counselor educators to avoid dual and multiple relationships such as requiring or allowing students to participate in a group experience led by the educators as a part of a course. Most of these situations usually involve a conflict of interest. Ways of resolving these circumstances include (a) using faculty-supervised post-master's students to lead groups for entry-level students; (b) using a blind-grading system; (c) requiring students to participate in externally supervised groups; (d) employing role-play techniques; (e) having students co-lead their own groups while the instructor observes; and (f) using a "fishbowl training" technique in which students co-lead their own groups alternating between an inner and outer circle, again with the instructor observing and helping the group process what occurs (Forester-Miller & Duncan, 1990; Kane, 1995). However, how to handle potentially dual or multiple relationships in either an academic or nonacademic setting is not as easy or as prescriptive as it may seem on the surface, for there is not a lot of research in this area (Goodrich, 2008).

In examining dual and multiple relationships, it is important to look at the difference between a dual relationship and a relationship with dual qualities (Aponte, 1994). For instance, a group leader may know about a member's personal issues and yet be able to treat the member fairly and appropriately. However, most relationships with dual or multiple qualities, such as conducting a group and grading participants or offering group counseling to a friend, are fraught with the potential to become contaminated. Therefore, if there is the slightest doubt about whether a group worker is about to enter into such a relationship, the leader should err on the side of caution.

If a potential dual or multiple relationship cannot be avoided, such as in a rural setting where there are limited services, then all parties concerned should carefully explore the potential benefits and pitfalls in the affiliation before entering it. If possible, it is wise to have an outside neutral party strictly monitor the relationship on a regular basis. This type of an arrangement is preventive and follows the ethical principle that "the professional should, at all cost, do no harm to the client" (Sklare, Thomas, Williams, & Powers, 1996, p. 265).

Personal Relationships Among Group Members

The matter of personal relationships among group members is another ethically gray area. Context is one of the major deciding factors. In some settings, for example, work environments, schools, or mental hospitals, group members will inevitably interact with one another outside the group. In other settings, such as outpatient treatment groups or special task forces, this type of interaction is unlikely to occur naturally. Most group leaders do not make hard and fast rules about personal relationships among group members because this type of rule is impossible to enforce (Jacobs, Schimmel, Masson, & Harvill, 2016). There are some cases, such as in self-help groups, in which contact with members outside the structured group may be therapeutic. However, in most counseling and psychotherapy groups, member-to-member contact outside the group results in the formation of subgroups or hidden agendas, which can be detrimental. Therefore, discouraging socialization in these types of groups is a prudent policy (Remley & Herlihy, 2014).

Overall, for most groups, the focus should be on open relationships within the group setting. There is a rich and subtle interplay between the group member and the group environment, and each member at once shapes and responds to his or her social microcosm. The more spontaneous the interaction is, the more varied will be the environment and the greater the likelihood that problematic issues will be touched on for all the members (Yalom & Leszcz, 2005).

Uses of Group Techniques

Group techniques or exercises are structured ways of getting members to interact with one another. They can have a powerful impact on group members and positively affect how people work together or change. However, when leaders misuse group techniques, they can also inhibit the natural ebb and flow of a group (Carroll & Krause, 2008). For instance, Meg may start each group counseling session with a structured exercise to avoid having to grapple with the hard job of focusing on group process and the difficult issues that have arisen in the group. In such a situation, Meg may accelerate the pace of the group, but at a cost. As Yalom and Leszcz (2005) state, "The group pays a price for its speed; it circumvents many group development tasks and does not develop a sense of autonomy and potency" (p. 472). Therefore, the use of group techniques as in Meg's case is ethically questionable.

Corey (2012) believes that structured exercises are best used when they are focused on group goals or group members' achievements. Group leaders face ethical problems when they lack the skill or sensitivity to use exercises properly or when they "de-skill" group members by making them overly dependent on the leader and less likely to help one another (Jacobs et al., 2016; Yalom & Leszcz, 2005). In such cases, leaders may generate more feelings or nonverbal expressions than they or the group can handle and ultimately may lead the group to a dead end (Carroll & Wiggins, 1997; Corey et al., 2015). In choosing an exercise for a group, the leader should always have a rationale and tailor the exercise to fit the particular needs of the group. Using techniques isolated from relationships and theories amounts to the employment of "gimmicks," which is an unprofessional and unethical way to work (Patterson, 1986).

Case Example

Jerry Puts Gimmicks into Gear

Jerry was leading a group for the first time. Not knowing exactly what to do to get the group moving, he used a warm-up exercise initially. It worked like a charm. Group members quickly started talking to one another, and Jerry noted that the group went well.

Because he was leading a psychotherapy group, Jerry believed it would be good to start each group with an exercise. He quickly learned the meaning of the term *diminishing returns*, as each week the activities he brought in seemed to be less powerful than the week before. Group members did not seem particularly interested in beginning the group that way, especially if they had unfinished business from the week before.

Questions

What would you tell Jerry to do at this point? What are other positive and negative aspects of beginning a group with an activity or gimmick?

Group leaders can employ at least 14 different kinds of exercises in the groups they conduct: written, movement, dyads and triads, rounds, creative props, arts and crafts, fantasy, common reading, feedback, trust, experiential, moral dilemma, touching, and group decision (Jacobs et al., 2016). Whenever an exercise is used in a group, it should be processed so that it allows group members to become better informed about themselves and the group. Therefore, at least twice as much time should be allowed for the processing of exercises as for completing them. Ways of processing include sharing in small groups, sharing in the group as a whole, sharing through writing, using rounds, or employing some combination of these methods.

Leaders' Values

Group leaders have values and, for better or worse, values influence the goals, methods, and ultimately the success of group work and counseling (Corey et al., 2015; Mitchell, 1993; Patterson, 1958; Williamson, 1958). Leaders who try to hide their values may actually do more harm than good in certain situations. For instance, if Jana dislikes the patronizing way Carolyn responds to other group members but does not voice her value about members leveling with one another, then the group may either avoid interactions with Jana or scapegoat her. However, leaders must be careful not to impose their values on group members. Such action short-circuits members' exploration, especially in counseling and psychotherapy groups, and results in confusion and chaos.

Group members have the ultimate responsibility to make their own decisions. However, leaders help members explore their values more thoroughly while maintaining their own. If group leaders and members have conflicts about values, then leaders are responsible for making referrals (Corey et al., 2015). Leaders must stay attuned and be aware of the impact of values in a group of any kind.

Referrals

Referrals (transfers of members to another group) are made when group leaders realize they cannot help certain members achieve designated goals or when a conflict between leaders and members has proven unresolvable. The group leader is responsible for making appropriate referrals when necessary because he or she cannot be all things to all people. The process of making a referral involves assessing one's own values and limitations as a group leader and listening to individual group members concerning their particular needs.

Group leaders should maintain an extensive and current list of referral sources. The referral process itself involves four steps: (1) identifying the need to refer; (2) evaluating potential referral sources; (3) preparing the client for the referral; and (4) coordinating the transfer (Hackney & Cormier, 2012). For instance, if Dot realizes in her psychotherapy group that she cannot help Mahalah, then she may first arrange to meet with Mahalah after a group session and discuss the situation with her. Before the meeting, Dot should prepare a list of potential referral sources and have these ready for Mahalah to see during their session together. If Mahalah is not ready for a referral, then Dot may have to meet with her again. After Mahalah has been persuaded of the wisdom of the referral, Dot should work with her on the arrangements.

Records

When conducting groups for counseling or therapeutic purposes, it is important that group workers keep records. Such documentation helps the group worker concretely review what happened in the group, when it occurred, and who was involved. By reviewing past events, issues and agendas that develop in the group can be better addressed, and the group worker can document for third parties, such as courts or managed care agencies, information that may be relevant to any ethical or legal issues that arise (Bond, 2011).

Written records should be kept in locked files in a secured area. The area also should be locked and have limited access. One way to keep records is to write them in a problem-oriented format. However, such a procedure "tends to transcribe clients' experiences into the official language of diagnostic labels" and can be dehumanizing (Chen, Noosbond, & Bruce, 1998, p. 405). Another possibility is to document the experiences of group members and the group as a whole in what Yalom and Leszcz (2005) describe as a *process summary*. Using this method, the group worker highlights group process, "reinforcing clients' understanding of the highly charged here-and-now experiences" of the group (Chen et al., p. 405). A third alternative is for the group worker to write a therapeutic document to the group using key phrases, responses, and descriptions of vivid nonverbal behaviors, thereby capturing the dynamics of a session (Chen et al.). Group members can then discuss the document and their reactions to it at the beginning of the next session. They can also use the document as a reflective tool outside of group sessions to evaluate themselves or the group and to make appropriate changes.

Closings and Follow-Up

Closings and follow-up "become ethical issues more because of errors of omission rather than errors of commission" (Gazda, 1989, p. 307). Groups need to reach some form of closure before ending. By doing so, they help promote and maintain changes members have made while in the group. For long-term groups, the closing process may mean several sessions devoted to winding down and tying up loose ends, whereas for short-term groups, a few hours devoted to this activity will be all that is necessary. Issues related to attachment, loss, and meaning are primarily dealt with in ending a group (Corey et al., 2015; Hackney & Cormier, 2012; Mangione et al., 2007). The important point is that these issues involving separation and consolidation be addressed.

Case Example

Lars and Loss

In a psychotherapy group, Lars, who lost his parents early in life, has become particularly upset and angry that the group is ending. He has unresolved issues in dealing with loss. Although he modified his behavior and thinking in the group, he fears he will revert back to his former style of retreating inward and becoming depressed if he is not helped by the group and the leader to come to an acceptable resolution about the group ending.

Questions

What might you as the group leader do to help Lars? What do you think the group as a whole could do in assisting Lars at this time of ending?

The ethical issue in follow-up usually centers on its neglect rather than its inclusion. Group leaders should make themselves available to group members for consultation as well as follow-up meetings after a group has ended. If group leaders are negligent about this important procedure, then group members may not adequately assess the impact the group has had on them and are unlikely to continue working on their goals as specifically as they would otherwise. Besides providing for the welfare of group members, follow-up after the ending of a group has the added benefit of helping group leaders evaluate the effectiveness of what they did in the group and improve their group leadership styles. "Perhaps the most meaningful evaluation material can be gained by a group leader 30 days or more after a group ends. At that time the members are more independent of the leader and perhaps can be more honest" (George & Dustin, 1988, p. 115).

Again, consider the case of Lars. If he receives follow-up, then he will most likely feel that he has not been abandoned. Furthermore, he can focus during follow-up on the improvements he has made since the group ended and be reinforced for this new behavior.

Reflection

Think of when you received follow-up from a professional (or even a nonprofessional) about a service or product you purchased. How did you feel when you received the contact? What were your impressions of the person and the service or product? Do you think members of counseling groups might have similar thoughts and emotions?

MAKING ETHICAL DECISIONS

Because group leaders face such a wide variety of issues, it is crucial that they know beforehand how they will make ethical decisions. Although such decisions can be made in many ways, some approaches to ethical decision making can make the process operate more smoothly. Two are discussed here.

The first is making ethical decisions according to both principle ethics and virtue ethics (Corey et al., 2015). **Principle ethics** are ethics based on obligations. They focus on finding "socially and historically acceptable answers to the question, 'What shall I do?'" (p. 10). Codes of ethics are based on principle ethics (actions stemming from obligations). **Virtue ethics** focus on "the character traits of the counselor [or group worker] and nonobligatory ideals to which professionals aspire rather than on solving specific ethical dilemmas. Simply stated, principle ethics asks 'Is this situation unethical?' whereas virtue ethics asks 'Am I doing what is best for my client?'" (p. 10). In a group, integrating principle ethics and virtue ethics becomes complex.

A second way of making ethical decisions is to use specific steps as a guideline. For example, in the case of promoting beneficence and enhancing ethical decision making, a mnemonic device that reminds group leaders and members of what they should do can be helpful. One device created for these situations is the **A-B-C-D-E Worksheet** (Sileo & Kopala, 1993). The letters stand for assessment, benefit, consequences and consultation, duty, and education. Some of the points are more applicable in certain situations than in others, but the device gives practitioners an idea of what they can use to enhance the group's good.

In addition to using this type of worksheet on a particular aspect of group ethical decision making, members can take general steps in the overall process. For example, in ethical decision making, Hill, Glaser, and Harden (1995) suggest a seven-step model to follow in a sequential fashion. This model begins with the recognition that a problem exists and ends with continuing reflection. It is one that involves client collaboration in the process, which Walden (1997) states empowers the client—in this case, the group. Thomas (1992) recommends a less elaborate model. First, she attempts to define a situation. Then she consults ethical codes for information and guidance. A continuum of alternative actions is generated next. At either end of the spectrum will be choices ranging from "take radical action" to "take no action," with more moderate suggestions in the middle part of the choice curve. The next part of the process is to evaluate all suggested actions in regard to other persons' welfare and professional responsibilities. After the consequence of each action is examined, some tentative decision is made and finally implemented. Records are kept, at least of the final outcome.

One unique psychoeducational group experience for ethics-based decision making is conducted through the Arizona courts with the adult criminal diversion programs. These programs offer alternatives to prosecution for persons formally charged with criminal offenses—usually first-time offenders with misdemeanors (Alexander, 1999). In this program (four sessions of 2 hours each), group members work to solve their own and other members' real problems. They do so through tapping into universal values that they already hold, such as goodness, thoughtfulness, tolerance, responsibility, and honesty, as well as learning how to make better decisions. In this program, ethics-based decision making "entails the following steps: (a) identify the problem, (b) research the facts, (c) identify all of the people who will be affected by this decision, and (d) list all of the solutions you can think of and evaluate each alternative" (Alexander, 1999, pp. 210–211). Homework is given, case studies are featured, and members are encouraged to think creatively, such as using brainstorming, metaphorical thinking, and generating unconventional ideas. In this way, opportunities for making choices (and making better decisions) are expanded.

PROMOTING ETHICAL PRINCIPLES IN GROUPS

The promotion and implementation of ethical conduct in groups occur on two levels: training and practice. There is an opportunity in educational settings to instill in prospective group leaders' knowledge of and a feel for ethics (ASGW, 2000; Hayes, 1991; Paradise & Siegelwaks, 1982). Indeed, such a procedure is crucial to the welfare of group leaders and other helping professionals in general. For individuals already in practice, training in the ethics of working with groups can best be achieved through continuing educational opportunities and peer supervision.

Training Group Leaders

Training group leaders to address ethical issues is a multidimensional process (Brabender, 2007). On one level, group leaders must become familiar with ethical codes and standards. On another level, they must get to know their own ethics and values. On a third level, prospective group leaders must practice recognizing ethical dilemmas and making ethical decisions. Finally, individuals must become aware of the development of ethical decision making over time so they can assess their own development as practitioners. Rapin (2010) actually puts ethical behavior in a group in the following formula: "(moral and ethical development + core knowledge and skills + specialty/ best-practice guidelines + legal parameters) × decision-making model(s)" (p. 61).

Regardless of how conceptual it may be, the different aspects of ethical behavior require integrating. Indeed, as Kitchener (1986) points out, the training of potential group leaders requires sensitizing them to ethical standards and issues, helping them learn to reason about ethical situations, developing within them a sense of being morally responsible in their actions, and teaching them tolerance of ambiguity in ethical decision making.

To become familiar with ethical codes, best practices, and standards in group work is initially as simple as reading pertinent documents and articles. This type of approach has often been used. Although it may expose persons to the basics of what are commonly accepted guidelines in the practice of group work at a particular time, it does not teach them that ethics are normative rather than factual (Wilcoxon, Remley, & Gladding, 2012). Ethics "inevitably change both as new scientific evidence dictates new approaches and as our culture changes" (Gazda, 1989, pp. 297–298). A prime example of the rapid change in ethics is the revision of the ASGW's *Ethical Guidelines for Group Counselors* (1989) and the decision by the ASGW not to use these guidelines after the mid-1990s and instead to use the ACA's code of ethics (2014) and the ASGW's own best practices document (Thomas & Pender, 2008) as standards for ethical conduct. Training group leaders in ethical decision making today thus involves the dynamic process of examining particular codes of ethics, guidelines, and standards while simultaneously exposing prospective group leaders to vignettes related directly to ethical cases. Casebooks and DVDs on ethics are helpful in this procedure (e.g., Corey, Corey, & Haynes, 2014; Herlihy & Corey, 2014), but they are never enough by themselves.

Reflection

Do you learn better from casebooks or DVDs? How does the learning differ for you? Which medium do you think would work best in teaching ethics? How could you make each more dynamic?

On a second level, ethical training requires individuals to examine and understand their own personal codes of ethics (Van Hoose & Kottler, 1977; Van Hoose & Paradise, 1979). Group discussion related to general dilemmas can increase ethical awareness and help individuals gain more self-understanding (Paradise & Siegelwaks, 1982). For example, in a classroom situation, a teacher may use a values scale, like those generated by Milton Rokeach (2001), to help class members assess the values they hold most closely. The teacher may present controversial group case histories to the class and ask members to focus on ways they would handle these situations.

A third way to emphasize ethics is on an integrated level. Prospective group leaders can gain a greater exposure to dealing with ethical dilemmas from a practical viewpoint through role-plays in simulated groups and direct participation in practitioner training groups (Conyne, Wilson, & Ward, 1997). Using these methods, leaders-to-be get a feel for decision making and group dynamics. This type of knowledge is crucial for potential group leaders who do not have a good understanding of making decisions within the dynamics of a group. It can help them learn to reason and risk as well as prevent them from becoming ineffective, harmful, and unethical.

Finally, as a last part of training, individuals who aspire to be group leaders should be exposed to developmental theories of ethical reasoning so they can gauge their own professional growth (Welfel, 2013). Models such as those developed by Van Hoose and Paradise (1979) hold promise for helping persons in training to gain a clearer understanding of their own level of functioning.

Continuing Education and Peer Supervision

For practitioners already in the field of group work, the matter of keeping up with ethical codes and growing as an ethically based professional can be met by taking continuing education courses and by undergoing peer supervision. Almost all professional associations offer programs on ethics at their national, regional, and state conventions. **Continuing education units (CEUs)** for participating in professional programs help group workers stay attuned to the latest developments in areas related to group work. For example, programs on group dynamics, group leadership, and group standards are frequently offered at conventions of the American Counseling Association and Association for Specialists in Group Work. Many professional associations require that their members participate in such activities.

Continuing education can be supplemented with **peer supervision**, in which practitioners meet regularly to consult with one another about particularly difficult group situations (Borders et al., 2014). Through this type of experience, practitioners, especially those in private practice, become more informed, establish support, avoid burnout, and stay more aware of the ethical dimension of working with clients in particular cases. It is interesting to note that peer supervision is conducted in a group environment, which can also provide information on dealing with, among other topics, issues in running groups (Greenburg, Lewis, & Johnson, 1985).

Both continuing education and peer supervision can be helpful in subtle as well as obvious ways to professionals who practice group work. In addition to giving them more knowledge and procedures to use in groups, these educational methods can create new awareness of even minor misconduct in the group leader or in the group. Through this awareness, such behavior can be eliminated. For example, in some groups, a promise is made that no pressure will be put on a participant, but then nonactive members are encouraged in subtle ways to be involved in the group (Kottler, 1994). In helping themselves and their groups make ethical decisions about incidents like this one, group workers increase the safety and efficiency of their groups as well as their own self-knowledge.

RESPONDING TO COMPLAINTS OF UNETHICAL BEHAVIOR

It is unusual for a group member to file an ethics complaint against a group leader. However, such incidents occasionally happen, especially in counseling and psychotherapy groups. When they do, the group leader, as a helping professional, needs to take appropriate actions. Two essential actions are to notify his or her professional liability insurance carrier and "ensure that an attorney is promptly retained" (Chauvin & Remley, 1996, p. 564). The reason is that allegations in an ethical complaint can be used as the basis for a lawsuit. Therefore, ethical complaints must be treated seriously.

If an ethics complaint is lodged against a group worker, it will usually be made with a group with which the worker has an affiliation, such as a professional association's ethics committee or a state licensing board. The group worker will have an opportunity to respond to the charges, and the committee or board will then act as a jury. Charges may be dismissed or upheld. If they are upheld, then the group worker may be disciplined through a reprimand, suspension, probation, or revocation of membership or licensure. Regardless, it is in the group worker's best interest to be discreet. If an emotional outlet is needed to handle the stress associated with such a process, then the group worker should seek professional counseling services. As with all matters pertaining to adversity, prevention is the first and best practice when dealing with ethical matters.

Overall, "ethical conduct results from a combination of didactic knowledge, an understanding of problem-solving approaches, a clear conception of philosophical principles . . . that underlie a formal code of ethics, and a basically sound character that leads one to respond with maturity, judgment, discretion, wisdom, and prudence" (Bersoff, 1996, p. 90).

Case Example

Hostile Henry Strikes Again

Although they were both in the same profession, Henry hated Fielding. He thought Fielding was a little too good and was too kind. Therefore, when Henry heard rumors that Fielding had said something outrageous as the leader of a psychotherapy group, he immediately filed an ethics charge against him with his national professional group and the state licensure board.

The information Henry received was wrong, and he later retracted his charge. Fielding had been hurt professionally and personally by then.

Questions

What would you advise Fielding to do? What would you do in regard to Henry if you were the national group or the state licensure board?

LEGAL ISSUES IN GROUPS

Ethics and the law are separate but sometimes overlap (Rapin, 2010; Remley, 1996). By their nature, ethical codes and laws tend to be reactive, emerging from what has occurred rather than anticipating what may occur (Corey et al., 2015). **Law** refers to a body of "agreed-upon rules of a society that set forth the basic principles for living together as a group. Laws can be general or specific regarding both what is required and what is allowed of individuals who form a governmental entity" (Remley & Herlihy, 2014, p. 4). Some ethical issues, such as telling the truth, have legal ramifications when violated. There are also situations regarding issues such as confidentiality and advertising in which conflicts may emerge between legal and ethical systems. Therefore, group leaders are well advised to have knowledge of both ethical codes and legal precedents.

Often, when persons feel wronged by professional helpers, the helpers' actions will be judged according to the standards of the group with which their services are most identified (Woody, Hansen, & Rossberg, 1989). The conduct of group leaders, for example, would likely be compared with the type of behavior considered appropriate in the ASGW's "Best Practice Guidelines" (2007) or a similar definitive document. Thus, group workers must keep up with professional and legal developments on a regular basis. This means staying abreast primarily of community, state, and national standards and knowing what to do in the case of legal action (Hartsell & Bernstein, 2013).

Community, State, and National Standards

Group leaders who function successfully are aware of "community standards, legal limitations to work, and state laws" governing the practice of groups, especially those that directly affect counseling or psychotherapy (Ohlsen, Horne, & Lawe, 1988, p. 391). This type of information may be best obtained from these sources:

1. Civic, religious, and business leaders of the community in which the group worker resides;
2. Professional state counseling boards;
3. State departments of education;
4. Persons involved in the state or national divisions of major professional counseling associations;
5. Liaison personnel in national professional associations;
6. Local attorneys; and
7. Members of the state attorney general's office.

It is not unusual for helping professionals, such as group workers, to fail in their practices because they have not paid enough attention to community, state, and national standards (Woody, 1988). Knowing theories and techniques of group work is not enough to make practitioners successful, especially those who operate in diversified settings or who wish to operate as private practitioners (Paradise & Kirby, 1990).

The best procedure to employ in preventing legal difficulties is to do one's professional "homework" beforehand. This means reading and studying major references on legal decisions that have an impact on conducting groups. For example, major sources explaining the relationship between the law and mental health practices include those by Wheeler and Bertrum (2015); Hartsell and Bernstein (2013); Hummel, Talbutt, and Alexander (1985); Sidley (1985); and Swenson (1997). The ACA's legal series, edited by Theodore P. Remley, Jr. (1996), is also excellent in this regard. Primary sources for researching legal opinions include the *United States Supreme Court Report* (for Supreme Court decisions), the *Federal Reporter* (for U.S. Courts of Appeals decisions), and the *Federal Supplement* and *Federal Rules* (for U.S. District Court decisions). An official state reporter, such as *Connecticut Reports* or *Alabama Reports,* usually disseminates state court decisions. A frequently used legal research source is *Shepard's Case Citations,* which follows "the judicial history of a targeted case" (Woody & Mitchell, 1984, p. 32).

Bibliographies on group work are a rich source of information on all professional aspects of groups. With the use of the Internet and computer technology, specialized bibliographies can be put together quickly and cost-efficiently. Reading journal articles, books, and monographs and attending workshops on trends and issues in human services all should be included in group workers' schedules. Consultation with professional peers on landmark legal decisions, such as *Tarasoff v. Board of Regents of the University of California* (1969), is also vital.

Legal Action

Legal action is most likely to be taken against a group worker, especially in a psychotherapy or counseling group, if members think they have suffered physical harm, emotional trauma, or psychological or financial damage as a result of participating in a group experience. Such legal action usually is in the form of a **malpractice** suit that implies the group leader has failed to render proper service because of either negligence or ignorance. "The word 'malpractice' means bad practice," and "the claim against the professional is made by a 'plaintiff' who seeks a monetary award based on a specific amount of damages: physical, financial, and/or emotional" (Gazda, 1989, p. 299). Practitioners can best avoid these suits by maintaining reasonable, ordinary, and prudent practices (Crawford, 1994). For example, keeping written records of groups under lock and key and securing electronically stored records are musts (Bond, 2011; Mitchell, 2007).

Specific practices that are most likely to prevent lawsuits include these:

1. Screening to reject inappropriate potential group members
2. Spending extra time at the beginning of the first group session to discuss group rules and group members' responsibilities
3. Following the ethical codes of professional organizations to which one belongs
4. Practicing only those theories and techniques in which one has actual expertise
5. Obtaining consent or contracts in writing from members (or, in the case of minors, their parents)
6. Warning members about the importance of confidentiality and the exceptions in which member confidentiality will have to be broken

7. Staying abreast of recent research, theory, and practice techniques within one's specialty
8. Empowering members to evaluate their own progress and be in charge of their own progress
9. Obtaining regular peer supervision of one's work
10. Following billing regulations and record-keeping practices to the letter of the law (Corey et al., 2015; Paradise & Kirby, 1990; Van Hoose & Kottler, 1985; Wheeler & Bertrum, 2015)

If a malpractice suit is filed, especially as a result of counseling or psychotherapeutic experiences, plaintiffs must show that

1. a therapist–client relationship was established,
2. the therapist's conduct fell below the minimal acceptable standard for the case,
3. the conduct of the therapist was the cause of injury to the client, and
4. an actual injury was sustained by the client (Schultz, 1982).

Although the therapist–client relationship may be established easily (e.g., through producing a bill or receipt for services), other criteria in malpractice suits are more difficult to prove. In suits charging that the group leader's conduct fell below minimum standards, the measure usually used in such cases is what other practitioners in the same geographical area would do under similar circumstances (Wilcoxon et al., 2013). Group workers who are in contact with and in line with other practitioners in their area are less likely to be affected by this criterion, although local standards are increasingly being replaced with those on a national level.

The question of whether the group leader's conduct caused injury to a person is easiest to prove if the acts and injury are closely related in time (Wilcoxon et al., 2013). Finally, in deciding whether a group member sustained an actual injury, one or more of the following effects must be shown:

- Exacerbation of a previous symptom
- Appearance of a new symptom
- Client misuse or abuse of therapy (e.g., increased intellectualization or dependency)
- Client overextension of self (e.g., taking on inappropriate tasks)
- Disillusionment with therapy (e.g., feelings of hopelessness and depression) (Strupp, Hadley, & Gomes-Schwartz, 1977).

Case Example

Phyllis Becomes a Plaintiff

Phyllis joined her therapist's psychotherapy group because she had issues revolving around unresolved grief from her childhood. About halfway through the group, the leader became demanding. He insisted that if group members were going to get better, they needed to "spill their guts" and "get on with life." Feeling pressured, Phyllis complied with the leader's demands. She later came to regret her actions, especially when she found out that information she had disclosed in the group was out in the public domain.

In response, Phyllis quit the group and sued the leader. She was visibly upset. The case was settled out of court, with the leader apologizing to Phyllis and returning the money he had charged her. Phyllis wanted to press the case further, but she could not prove she had been harmed in an irreparable way. Furthermore, the leader had kept careful records, which documented that Phyllis had asked him to "push her" to talk before the group.

Questions

Even though Phyllis was limited in what she could do legally, do you think she had some ethical recourses? If so, what would they have been?

Most malpractice suits in group work will center on **unintentional civil liability** (a lack of intent to cause injury). For example, Lilly may claim that a group leader caused her harm by not letting her fully express herself when he blocked her from verbally attacking another group member with whom she disagreed. However, in some cases, "intentional" harm becomes the issue in question. **Intentional civil liability** cases include situations in which there are issues regarding

> *battery* (the unconsented touching of a person),
>
> *defamation* (injury to a person's character or reputation either through verbal *[slander]* or written *[libel]* means),
>
> *invasion of privacy* (violation of the right to be left alone), or
>
> *infliction of mental distress* (outrageous behavior on the part of the therapist) (Wilcoxon et al., 2012).

These types of cases are usually more clear-cut than those involving unintentional actions. In all cases, group specialists, especially those who work in psychotherapeutic or counseling groups, are advised to study their professional standards and codes of ethics carefully before, during, and after group sessions. In all cases, professionals who work with groups should carry **professional liability insurance** (insurance designed specifically to protect a group worker from financial loss in case of a civil suit). Any court litigation can be costly, and even the most careful group leader may be the subject of legal action. Thus, purchasing liability insurance (usually available through professional associations) and carefully keeping up to date on ethical and legal matters may be two of the best practices that group leaders can employ in helping themselves operate on the highest possible level.

Reflection

Who have you known who has been in a civil court case? What did they have to pay their attorney? How much do you think malpractice insurance would cost? Check.

Summary and Conclusion

This chapter has covered various aspects of ethical and legal issues regarding group work. Many of the topics focus on group leaders' responsibilities to their members and themselves. However, some material in this chapter is specifically targeted toward the rights and responsibilities of group members. It is assumed by most individuals who join a group that their leaders will be ethical and professional. However, that is not always the case, and some group members become casualties of their experience. To ensure against this, most professional associations, particularly the Association for Specialists in Group Work and the American Group Psychotherapy Association,

have constructed best practice guidelines, ethical codes, and professional standards by which group leaders and groups should abide. These documents are probably more relevant to leaders of psychotherapy and counseling groups, but they also apply to those who work in psychoeducational settings and with task/work groups. By adhering to such guidelines, codes, and standards, group leaders tend to maximize the benefits and minimize the harm that a group can do to individuals.

Nevertheless, group leaders must pay attention to specific ethical issues, including their training and competence; screening potential members; informing members about the group and the rights they have; ensuring confidentiality to the greatest extent possible; establishing appropriate relationships among group members and between the leader and members; owning but not imposing their own values; using group exercises properly; making appropriate referrals; transcribing and keeping appropriate records; and employing termination and follow-up procedures correctly. Group leaders and members must also scrutinize how they make ethical decisions.

None of these are simple tasks that are easily accomplished on a one-time basis. Therefore, group leaders must constantly monitor their behavior and keep current on ethical matters. "A combination of good personal character and virtue with sound thinking and good decision-making skill . . . ensures the best solution to an ethical dilemma" (Sileo & Kopala, 1993, p. 90). Prospective group leaders may receive cognitive and experiential training in ethics while they are still in training, whereas more experienced leaders (who are supposed to be more knowledgeable about ethics) must rely more on continuing education experiences and peer supervision.

Legal aspects of group work are similar to those involving ethics in some ways, but there are differences. It is important for group specialists to do their homework in researching legal cases that affect human services professionals and consult with others about ways to behave within the limits and spirit of the law. Getting to know community, state, and national standards for the practice of their profession is a major way to do this. If practitioners encounter legal difficulties, then they need to know the difference between unintentional and intentional malpractice suits and what they need to do in such cases. It is crucial that all group leaders carry professional liability insurance.

Classroom Exercises

1. Compare the ethical codes of as many professional associations as you can in regard to the practice of group work. Once the codes are collected, have half of the class note the similarities within them and the other half of the class highlight the differences. Discuss your findings and their implications for working with groups.

2. Pretending you are a group leader, think of what you would do in the following two situations and then role-play these scenes with fellow classmates:

   a. A group member of the opposite sex, whom you find attractive, asks to meet with you outside the confines of the group. The member states the purpose of such a meeting in vague terms, but he or she assures you that it is important.

   b. You discover that several of the group members are talking about group activities and individuals to their friends. This is the fourth meeting of the group, and everyone is present.

   How did your thinking change or stay the same after these role-playing situations?

3. Have each member of the class write a potential ethical dilemma within a group context in which they are currently involved. Collect the situations and, as a class, discuss with your instructor some strategies that might be employed to deal with these situations.

4. As a class, visit the reference librarian of your library. Ask him or her to show you the resources most readily available for tracking down legal information on counseling cases. If possible, have the librarian follow a case through its introduction and appeals. Discuss with a classmate how you could make use of the resources you have at your disposal for keeping up with the legal aspects of group work.

CHAPTER 11

Monkey Business/Fotolia

Groups for Children

I watch the children line up like ducks
all in a row, except one.
Noisily they ramble past concrete walls
follow-the-leader style
behind a brown-haired woman
in a light yellow dress
who quietly talks to them through her motions.
Today is picture day in the school
with a jolly old man who says: "Cheese"
tossing tidbit compliments before boys and girls
as they fix their smiles at him.
In just a flash roles are caught,
a moment recorded, and lines form again.
Straight and precise the children walk
all except one, who in dimly-lit halls,
rapidly steps in a zigzag manner
defying a rule and defining himself.*

*From "Still Life", *North Carolina Personnel &
Guidance Journal, 4,* © 1975 by Samuel T.
Gladding. Reprinted by permission from
Samuel T. Gladding.

CHAPTER OVERVIEW

From reading this chapter, you will learn about

- Types of groups for children
- Setting up groups for children and the role of leaders in children's groups
- Studies on the outcomes of children's groups including strengths and limitations

AS YOU READ, CONSIDER

- What types of groups you most enjoyed as a child and why
- How effective you are in relating to and working with children
- What groups you think are most important for children to be a part of

In 1985, Lionel Richie and Michael Jackson gathered a diverse and all-star group of singers in the United States to record a song, "We Are the World," which became the fastest-selling record in American music history. The song was a fund-raiser for famine relief in Africa, with its proceeds going to charity. This historical event was noteworthy for at least two reasons. First, the group of artists assembled included many of the most popular singers of the day, who unselfishly gave of their time and talent in a cooperative group effort to raise money for the less fortunate. Second, the groups benefiting most from this altruistic endeavor were mothers and children who could not provide for themselves as a group.

Children, whether the initiators or recipients, may benefit from groups as much, if not more, than any other age group. The reason is that members of this population, although among the least empowered in society, are still growing in multiple directions. Thus, preventive or remedial interventions on any level with individuals in this age group can yield rich dividends for years to come.

Children are not miniature adults. They have specific needs, wants, wishes, frustrations, joys, and fears, some of which are best shared in a group. In growing up, developmental, emotional, and behavioral problems affect up to 22% of all children (Shechtman, 2014). Unless these situations are addressed, they will fester and will often plague the lives of these individuals. Therefore, it is best to work with children during times of development, pain, or crises. Groups are an ideal place for such work to occur.

However, group work with children, defined here as groups for children under age 14, requires a special knowledge of child development and group theory. "Children have shorter attention spans, are more likely to project their feelings onto others, tend to need more structure and direction, and have much less control over their situation and environment" (DeLucia-Waack, 2000a, p. 132). Thus, to be helpful to children, group workers must be attuned to children's issues and needs in a distinct way. For instance, unlike adults, children usually respond better to nonverbal techniques than they do to verbal exercises because of their limited vocabularies and their dispositions to display feelings through play instead of words (Henderson & Thompson, 2011). Group specialists must adapt their approaches to the social, emotional, physical, and intellectual levels of this population.

When children face natural age and stage developmental tasks together (e.g., learning how to work cooperatively, learning how to express emotions appropriately), they frequently master more than the specifically targeted skills. However, to benefit from groups, children "may need help in channeling their enthusiasm into meaningful and therapeutic interactions" (Nitza, 2014, p. 101). Being with other children and adults does not automatically promote a sense of well-being within children and lead to the prevention of present dilemmas or future problems. Rather, growth and maturity are enhanced on multiple levels in children, as they are shown new ways of handling situations and exposed to new people. In children's groups, timing as well as content is crucial, and learning occurs best at what Havighurst (1972) describes as a **teachable moment**, a time when children are ready and able to learn.

Since the late 1960s, small-group work, especially in school settings, has proven its efficacy and has become a major model by which children are helped (Akos & Milsom, 2007; Baker, Parks-Savage, & Rehfuss, 2009; Perusse, Goodnough, & Lee, 2009). This type of work concentrates on promoting life skills and correcting faulty assumptions. In elementary and middle schools (where most children under 14 are educated), psychoeducational and counseling groups are used to help children learn new skills and become aware of their values, priorities, and communities. Even task groups have been shown to promote children's social and emotional learning (Van Velsor, 2009).

Research shows that approximately 70% of children's groups take place in schools. Small groups give students the opportunity to "explore and work through their social and emotional challenges with others who are experiencing similar feelings" (Campbell & Bowman, 1993, p. 173). For example, group counseling is often employed with children who have special life event concerns, such as separation from a parent through divorce (DeLucia-Waack & Gellman, 2007; DeLucia-Waack & Gerrity, 2001), failing grades (Boutwell & Myrick, 1992), loneliness and shyness (Shechtman, 2014), or grief and bereavement issues (Falco & Bauman, 2014). Group counseling is also appropriate for children who have disruptive or acting-out behavior problems, such as violent outbursts, excessive fighting, defiance, maladjustment, and an inability to get along with peers and teachers (Brantley, Brantley, & Baer-Barkley, 1996; Nelson, Dykeman, Powell, & Petty, 1996).

In almost all their daily environments, children spend a great deal of time interacting in groups; therefore, these settings are ideal places to conduct preventive guidance work as well as remedial counseling, regardless of the type of group involved (Kulic, Horne, & Dagley, 2004; Van Velsor, 2009). Peer influences are especially powerful in middle school environments and can be used to promote development and achievement (Akos, Hamm, Mack, & Dunaway, 2007). The most basic underlying principle of dealing with children in groups stresses that groups are natural childhood environments. However, in working with children in group settings, care must be exercised to prevent harm and promote health. Readiness for group guidance, psychoeducational experiences, and task groups is determined by the developmental level of individuals and their corresponding needs. Readiness for group guidance and counseling is determined by the amount of dissonance children feel between how they are acting and what they see others their age doing. Overall, the key to working with children in groups is readiness on the part of both the leader and the children.

Case Example

Sabrina's Exhaustive Experience

As the new counselor at her school, Sabrina wanted to prove her worth to others. Thus, during her first month, she set up six groups ranging from a friendship group to a grief group. She was enthused at first and poured herself into working with the children in her groups. However, conducting six groups a week began to get old, and Sabrina found she was tired of the meetings she had set up.

When she tried to terminate some of the groups, both the children and their parents complained. They liked meeting, and everyone seemed to be getting something from the groups. Finally, over the protest of everyone, Sabrina ended the groups. She was simply too exhausted to continue. Clearly, she was not as ready for the experience as the children were.

Questions

If you had been Sabrina, how would you have handled your newness to the school and the setting up of groups? When she became overextended, what do you think Sabrina could have done besides shutting down the groups? What part do you think readiness had to do with this situation?

TYPES OF GROUPS FOR CHILDREN

Developmental and nondevelopmental factors determine what types of groups are set up for children. **Developmental factors** include variables such as the age, gender, and maturity level of those involved. **Nondevelopmental factors**, in contrast, encompass less predictable qualities, such as the nature of the problem, the suddenness of its appearance, its severity, and the present coping skills of children and their families.

As mentioned previously, groups for children generally take the form of guidance and psychoeducation (learning a new skill or experience) or counseling and psychotherapy (rectifying or resolving problematic behaviors, assumptions, or situations). All groups for children need to "include interventions to discuss feelings, connect with others, and identify potential solutions for their concerns, regardless of the theme or topic of the group" (DeLucia-Waack & Nitza, 2014, p. 39). The emphasis is on children's healthy development (Villalba, 2007). Interventions vary depending on the children (or parents and teachers) with whom the group worker is interacting. However, some generalizations can be made.

First, group guidance and psychoeducation usually involve the group worker in the role of an information giver with a large group of children. In such situations, the group worker functions as an instructor or a guide and may work directly with teachers. For example, a group worker and teacher may jointly present information on ways of dealing with grief and sorrow effectively. In this case, the teacher may read a short book, such as Judith Viorst (1971), *The Tenth Good Thing About Barney*. Then the group worker may use discussions and role-plays to help the class apply the lesson to their lives—for example, when a pet dies, it is okay to be sad and appropriate to talk about what the pet meant to you and how you loved it.

It is not easy to give individual attention to all members of a psychoeducational group. Consequently, the experience is usually less personal and more limited in scope than a counseling or psychotherapy group. However, psychoeducational groups, like group counseling and psychotherapy, can be an effective way to help children unlearn inappropriate behaviors and master new ways of relating more easily through interaction and feedback in a safe practice situation with their peers (Henderson & Thompson, 2011). For example, in a psychoeducational group, Chad may learn ways to be assertive in verbally asking for what he wants from Jane instead of being inappropriately aggressive by bullying or hitting. He may also learn constructive ways to deal with situations when he does not get what he wants.

Second, guidance and psychoeducational groups primarily focus on improving skills and awareness in personal and interpersonal areas, such as values, attitudes, beliefs, social maturity, and career development, but they are not limited to these general growth topics. Group counseling and psychotherapy, however, are more remediation based and deal with such personal and interpersonal concerns as "self-concept, social skills, interpersonal relationships, problem solving, academic skills, communication skills, and values" (Franks, 1983, p. 201). Therefore, when the fifth-grade class participates in a group psychoeducational experience, it is assumed they are generally healthy but uninformed about a subject area, such as boy–girl relationships.

Third, although there is often an overlap in the subject areas covered in the activities of the groups just mentioned, the number of children involved in psychoeducational groups and counseling and psychotherapy groups usually differs. The latter types of groups focus on more specific concerns and in greater depth. Not as many individuals can be included.

Finally, the amount of risk taking and the overall process of these ways of working with groups tend to be distinct. Greater personal risks are taken in group counseling and psychotherapy, and these groups are held in a less structured environment than is found in group guidance and psychoeducation. In addition, learning is usually more cognitively based in guidance and psychoeducational groups, whereas it is more emotionally based in counseling and psychotherapeutic groups.

Reflection

Think of skills you learned in groups growing up, from those in schools to those in religious or civic settings. What skills have stayed with you from those times? How did the presence of peers help or hinder your mastering of information or behavior?

Group Guidance for Elementary/Middle School Children

Group guidance for children of elementary and middle school age may be conducted in schools, community agencies, or both (Corey, Corey, & Corey, 2014). Thus, group work may involve student groups, classroom groups, school personnel, a whole school system, or even a school-community cooperative venture (Conyne & Mazza, 2007). **Preschool and early school-aged children** include ages 5 through 9, and **preadolescents** are defined as children in the latency period ranging in age from 9 to 13 years. Children below the age of 5 are usually not included in groups because of the egocentric nature of their development. However, exceptions can be made for more mature 3- and 4-year-olds, and children below age 5 may successfully be included in prosocial learning groups (Golden, 1987).

Group guidance in the schools is a preventive and wellness approach (Villalba, 2007). School counselors usually act as group leaders. Traditionally, they have presented their lessons to groups of children within a regular classroom environment. These offerings are varied and can range from a puppet show on friendship for preschoolers to realistic portrayals of preteen situations, such as those shown in the award-winning Canadian Broadcasting Corporation's *DeGrassi Junior High*, for older children. Other lessons focus on a variety of subject areas, such as personal or mental health, getting along with parents, and cooperation with peers. Career development and self-exploration are two particularly proactive topics often explored. Making the transition from elementary to middle school is another (Akos & Martin, 2003). This last type of group may be especially potent in reducing student anxiety, preventing negative outcomes associated with transition, establishing supportive networks among peers, and positively influencing the developmental paths and school success for preadolescents.

Two excellent resources for conducting group counseling activities with elementary students are:

Rosemarie Smead's (1994) *Skills for Living: Group Counseling Activities for Elementary Students*, where Smead not only describes how to conduct specialized groups for children but also provides readers with ways of working with parents, teachers, and principals; and

Ann Vernon's (2006) *Thinking, Feeling, Behaving: An Emotional Education Curriculum for Children Grades 1–6*, where Vernon provides a bevy of activities for this age population based on rational-emotive behavior therapy (REBT).

School guidance and counseling journals, such as *Professional School Counseling*, also contain a wealth of ideas. For instance, one interesting and classic group psychoeducational activity found in the predecessor of this publication is the "Get Along Gang" (Bond, 1993), an activity aimed at helping third-graders contain their anger. In this experience, the counselor presents name calling as a game. Name-callers win if another person gets angry at being called a name. To win the game, students who are called names must not get angry or show their anger.

Group guidance works best when counselors know what they want the group to achieve. One classic model for reaching this goal is known as SIPA (structure, involvement, process, and awareness) (Tyra, 1979). In *structuring,* counselors ask children to listen or do new activities according to certain guidelines. *Involvement* consists of getting the group to be active participants. (Even children who do not wish to participate may report back to the group as observers after an activity is over.) *Processing* is composed of sharing ideas, and *awareness* is consolidating what was learned in the guidance time. An example of a SIPA group is one Kizner (1999) offered in an elementary school setting to adopted children. The 12-session group consisted of presenting information about adoption, preparing an autobiography, fostering student's self-esteem, expressing feelings, and having discussions around adoption-related issues.

Many psychoeducational groups revolve around activities and are subsequently sometimes called **activity group guidance (AGG)** (Hillman & Reunion, 1978). These activities are developmental in nature and typically include coordinated guidance topics. For example, in promoting self-understanding and understanding of others, puppets, drawings, and music are often used (DeLucia-Waack, 2001b; Egge, Marks, & McEvers, 1987; Gladding, 2011b). These artistic activities are nonthreatening and enhance interaction and motivation in ways that language alone cannot do. For some children who are not in contact with their emotions, songs that they have written and sung to different tunes can give them an awareness of themselves not possible otherwise (Miles, 1993).

DeLucia-Waack and Gellman (2007) used music as an intervention in a study they did on efficacy of a children-of-divorce group. They compared their approach to a more traditional psychoeducational children-of-divorce group. They found after the groups ended and after a 3-month follow-up that both interventions significantly decreased cognitive and social anxiety and all irrational beliefs about divorce, except hope of reunification. Depression did not decrease for all participants, but when the relationship between depression and irrational beliefs was examined, irrational beliefs were found to be mediators of depression for children of divorce. These results suggest that current interventions for children of divorce decrease anxiety and irrational beliefs in general, but specifically addressing irrational beliefs may also decrease depressive symptoms.

Because of the inherent power of active developmental media, they are often packaged in commercial classroom guidance programs, such as **Developing Understanding of Self and Others—Revised (DUSO–R)** (Dinkmeyer & Dinkmeyer, 1982). A typical AGG session has three stages:

1. A 10-minute warm-up in which the group and leader discuss an appropriate guidance principle
2. A planned activity that attempts to implement the guidance principle for the day
3. A follow-up discussion, lasting about 5 to 10 minutes, in which the group reviews the impact of the guidance principle activity on themselves (Hillman & Reunion, 1978)

At other times, group workers implement group activities on their own, sometimes in various formats. For example, they may decide to have the group express a variety of feelings through making rhythmic sounds on their knees to represent the emotions at different times of the day or in different situations. Such an activity can help build empathy and foster prosocial behavior. In these cases, children may sound out in a group a variety of feelings, such as sad, mad, unsure, happy, and satisfied. Then, as in the more structured methods, group discussions take place (Gladding, 2011b).

In guidance and psychoeducational groups, a variety of techniques work well, and group workers should move developmentally from more simple activities to those that are more complex. For example, learning or becoming aware of one's emotions should be followed by activities that promote the recognition of feelings in others. Such a process could be achieved by having children participate in a game that Akos (2000) calls "Referential Communication." This activity requires children to sit in a circle with paper and crayons. They are asked to draw a green triangle in the middle of their paper. Then each child takes turns giving a command as to what to draw next. When the activity is over, the children show their drawings and talk about the differences as well as how easy or hard it is to understand the perspective of other group members.

Campbell (1991) gives four techniques for working with undermotivated children in psychosocial groups: (a) using guided fantasy, (b) focusing on specific behaviors to be improved, (c) creating positive affirmations (positive statements about oneself), and (d) employing visualizations. One or more of these techniques may not work with some children, but probably some will. The point is that variety is the essence of group guidance and psychoeducational lessons.

A relatively new model for offering group guidance and psychoeducational material in elementary schools, especially to preschoolers on sensitive subjects such as child sexual abuse, is to involve parents as teachers who work with counselors (Kenny, 2009). In middle schools, counselors may train teachers to provide needed psychoeducational services. Through such arrangements, the productivity of school counseling personnel can be increased while reducing the need for staff (Rolland & Neitzschman, 1996). After mastering core individual and group counseling skills, parents, teachers, and counselors work together even more closely than they might otherwise.

Case Example

Abdul's Activity

As a new elementary school counselor, Abdul thought he should use group work as a way of delivering services to the children he served. Unsure about what concerns were of highest value, he developed a needs survey and had the children fill it out. The response rate was good, but the results were troubling, because the children had listed a lot of concerns about computer games and some very shallow ways of relating to one another.

Abdul decided he needed more input and formed two groups of advisors: a teachers' group and a parent group. After meeting with both, he found they each had different opinions about what he should do.

Questions

What do you think Abdul did well? What do you think he could have done better? If you were Abdul, what would you do now?

Group Counseling Within the Schools

Group counseling within schools is essential to the healthy growth of elementary and middle school students. It "provides a structure for students to give and receive feedback from peers, practice new skills in a safe place, and an opportunity for students to talk and express feelings with others who may share common experiences" (Falco & Bauman, 2014, p. 320). Psychoeducational and counseling groups, "where a counselor works with a group of 6 to 8 students, greatly increases the number of students who can benefit from working with a school counselor" (DeLucia-Waack, 2000a, p. 131). Such groups are becoming the preferred method of counselor intervention because they enable "a counselor to see more students and to use counselor time to its maximum" (Boutwell & Myrick, 1992, pp. 65–66). In small group settings, the effective, cognitive, and behavioral domains of students are explored.

Sometimes group counseling is focused. In such cases, there is an emphasis on a particular ethnic, social, or achievement group. For instance, on two different occasions, Steen (2009, 2011) set up a group counseling intervention to promote academic and personal development for fifth-grade African American elementary students. His rationale was that group counseling is a logical venue in which to capitalize on the collectivism of African American youngsters. He found that integrating culturally relevant literature into the group counseling format had a positive effect on the identity of the children. The group counseling intervention he used was one he devised: Achieving Success Everyday (ASE). Likewise, Khattab and Jones (2007) formed a psychoeducational and counseling group for preadolescent girls to actively help them in developing habits of resiliency and perceptions of self-worth and had positive results.

In another focused group counseling activity, Cercone and DeLucia-Waack (2012) conducted 12 eight-week psychoeducational groups of 45 minutes each for children of divorce (kindergarten through sixth grade) with each group having a range of four to six members. In six of the groups, music on divorce by singer/songwriter Dan Conley (1994) was used to introduce the topic for the day, while the other six groups used the exact same format but without the music. Both treatment conditions were effective in reducing depression, anxiety, and irrational beliefs about divorce.

Group counseling usually takes one of three approaches in dealing with persons and problems: (a) crisis centered, (b) problem centered, and (c) growth centered. **Crisis-centered groups** are formed because of some emergency, such as conflict between student groups. These groups usually meet until the situation that caused them to form has been resolved. Group counseling provides individuals with a means to examine their situation and to think together about some possible solutions (Myrick, 2011). Sometimes, groups formed because of a crisis continue meeting after the crisis has passed and develop into either problem-centered or growth groups. For example, after a fight between some fourth- and fifth-graders, children in one school formed a "peace group." The purpose of the group was originally to promote ways to resolve problems among the children who had been in open conflict. As the group continued to develop, however, its purpose was enlarged to finding ways to spot problematic situations in the school and correct them in a productive way.

Problem-centered groups are small groups set up to focus on one particular concern—for example, coping with stress or developing social skills. They are useful to students who have one major difficulty, such as being under too much pressure—for instance, children who have demanding parents who insist they excel in school and extracurricular activities, such as athletics or dance. Like the members of crisis-centered groups, those involved with problem-centered groups are usually highly motivated and committed to working on their situations and themselves.

To illustrate a problem-centered group, Clark and Seals (1984) describe a three-phase open group counseling approach for ridiculed children that provides support "to children who long for acceptance" (p. 161) and who have a problem getting it. In the initial phase of the group, the focus is on establishing a relationship based on trust and encouragement. Children who get involved in the group feel a sense of **universalization**, realizing that they are not the only ones who face being ridiculed. In the second phase, erroneous thoughts and distorted cognitions are challenged. The final phase of the group serves to promote positive behaviors, including the working out of strategies to deal with peers who ridicule. Role-plays are often used in this phase, and interpersonal interaction and cooperation are encouraged.

Another problem-centered group is the *friendship group* (Coppock, 1993). This group is for students who have been referred to a school counselor for specific problems, such as misbehavior, lack of social skills, or poor academic performance. It is closed ended, lasting from 6 to 8 weeks. In it, students are invited to "develop and practice friendship skills" (p. 152). These skills revolve around nonthreatening activities, such as introducing oneself to another, playing games (e.g., receiving compliments), making up adventures (e.g., imagining oneself in a new place and time), and solving problems, especially those that are of a personal nature. This last part of the group is done only if students are developmentally ready to work with the group on a problem and only after problem-solving skills have been discussed and demonstrated in the group.

Growth-centered groups focus on the personal and social development of students. Their purpose is to enable children to explore their feelings, concerns, and behaviors about a number of everyday subjects and to make changes if they wish. An excellent example of a growth-centered and preventative group is an educational/guidance group Waliski and Carlson (2008) conducted with a preschool class. In the eight-session group, preschool children were taught social and emotional skills and given the opportunity to practice these new skills. The overall result was an increase in social skills and a decrease in aggressive behavior.

In two studies with older children, ages 6 to 12, groups were used to promote social competence (Rose, 1987; Ware, Ohrt, & Swank, 2011). The groups used a number of behavioral principles, such as rehearsal, instruction, modeling, feedback, coaching, assignments, and rewards/prizes, to help their members gain social skills, such as introducing oneself, dealing with mistakes, cooperating, taking turns, and waiting. Group members improved their interpersonal skills, their understanding of others' perspective, their management of emotions, and specific social functioning abilities.

As a way of helping children, growth-centered groups allow group workers, such as school counselors, to add a personal touch to the learning process by getting to know children more deeply. These groups are preventative in that more children are able to display prosocial skills at the end of them and disruptive behaviors are decreased.

Reflection

Which of the small group formats—problem-centered, crisis-centered, or growth-centered—appeals to you most as a potential leader of groups for children? When have you seen any of these types of groups run? What were the results?

Group Guidance and Counseling in Community Settings

The basic dynamics of group guidance and counseling for children in settings outside school environments do not differ substantially from those conducted within schools. Community settings with groups for children, such as churches, clubs, and mental health centers, basically structure and run their groups in a manner similar to that used in educational institutions. A major difference, however, between schools and community agencies is the populations of children served. Community organizations will usually have more homogeneous groups than will schools. This difference occurs because children group themselves in organizations according to their interests and because mental health professionals in agencies often start groups for certain "types" of children—for example, shy low achievers, those who have witnessed domestic violence, or those with conduct disorders.

Nevertheless, this lack of diversity can be overcome through group exercises. For example, structured technique, such as the *Human Rainbow,* makes it possible for children to recognize unique as well as universal qualities in themselves and others. In this structured activity, children first create masks and then form a circle—a human rainbow—around the room. Afterward, they discuss similarities and differences among people and address areas in human relations in which they have a major concern (Buban, McConnell, & Duncan, 1988).

It is important in community settings, as well as educational institutions, that group guidance or counseling activities be presented in an appealing way. One means to do so is to advertise groups as "clubs." By forming clubs instead of guidance or counseling groups, children avoid any stigmas attached to mental health activities. In the process, they can become more involved in the group and, thereby, get more from the experience.

Case Example

Sadie's Seasonal Affective Disorder Group

Sadie identified three girls in her school who were affected by seasonal affective disorder (SAD). She thought if she formed a group for them that focused on good things in their lives, she might suppress their sadness. Therefore, she formed a theme group that she called a club named "Glad" (Great Lassies and Dames). The idea behind the club was to study the lives of girls and women who had overcome obstacles and achieved fame.

The club got off to a great start. Everyone read inspirational stories and talked about the remarkable girls and women who could serve as role models for them. The third week, Kari asked if she could invite a friend. Because the group had not been advertised as closed, Sadie was unsure what to do.

Questions

Would another person without the characteristics of the first three be detrimental to what Sadie was trying to accomplish? What do you think? What would you do in this case?

SETTING UP GROUPS FOR CHILDREN

In designing group experiences, group workers must consider the maturity of the children with whom they are working and the purpose of the group. Assessing children's maturity is most frequently accomplished by establishing regular contacts with them. Determining topics for the group to explore can be accomplished through the use of "sociograms, self-concept inventories, incomplete sentence activities, and children's drawings" (Gerler, 1982, p. 87). Decisions can also be made when counselors conduct needs assessments with students, teachers, parents, and other related school personnel or when counselors hear several students voicing similar concerns over a short period. Regardless of how the decision is made, many questions must be answered before the group begins, including these:

1. What medium will be most used in group communication?
2. What structure will be employed?
3. What materials will be used in the group?
4. How will group members be recruited and screened?
5. How long will group sessions meet?
6. How many children will be in the group?
7. What will the gender mix be?

Nonverbal Versus Verbal Communication

Gazda (1989), in concurrence with other authorities in the field of children's group counseling, such as Dinkmeyer and Muro (1979), Keat (1974), and Slavson (1945, 1948), states that children under 12 years of age should participate primarily in groups that involve play and action, using techniques such as sociodrama, child drama, and psychodrama. Ginott (1968) also recommends the use of active play therapy for young children (under age 9) in groups—specifically, water-colors, finger paints, clay, and sand—and Jones (2002) advocates group play therapy with sexu-ally abused preschool children. Bratton, Ceballos, and Ferebee (2009), in describing the integration of creative activities in a humanistic play group for preadolescents, state that expres-sive activities in such groups encourage preteens "to reach more deeply into their own resources, enabling them to handle future challenges more effectively" (p. 251).

In support of play therapy and expressive activities in such groups are practitioners who, in the words of Campbell (1993), state that toys and activities are "the words children use to express emotions" (p. 10). Opposed to this **action-centered view of groups** are professionals such as Ohlsen, Horne, and Lawe (1988), who believe that children can be taught the proper ways to express themselves verbally and that verbally oriented groups are viable with even very young children.

In practice, most counselors combine a mixture of verbalization and activity in their group sessions in a manner that is most helpful to their participants. In doing so, those who most favor verbal interaction hold onto the belief that the interplay of words and roles will "change the cog-nitive map and action patterns of a group member," whereas those who are activity oriented "believe that personality modifications occur through activity" (Kaczkowski, 1979, p. 45). There is some truth in both points of view.

Group Structure and Materials

In addition to deciding on the primary way of obtaining information from children, professionals who conduct groups must formulate how groups will be structured. **Highly structured groups** have a "predetermined goal and a plan designed to enable each group member to reach this identified goal with minimum frustration" (Drum & Knott, 1977, p. 14). Such groups are usually used for teaching skills that may be transferred to a wide range of life events. Often, groups are highly structured at their beginning and become less structured as group members get to know one another better. Unstructured groups, in contrast, are used in more experientially based situations in which process is emphasized rather than product. It is rare for a children's group of any kind to be totally unstructured.

Group workers must also decide how materials used in the groups will be employed. If the emphasis of the group is on completing a project (e.g., drawing a figure) as opposed to experienc-ing a feeling (e.g., freehand drawing), then the materials that are distributed and instructions given should reflect this. There are basically four approaches to using materials and structure: (a) unstructured material, unstructured approach; (b) unstructured material, structured approach; (c) structured material, unstructured approach; and (d) structured material, structured approach (Kaczkowski, 1979). Each approach has its advantages and limitations.

The key to making the group a productive vehicle for helping children is for the group worker to use a leadership style that will enable him or her to blend meaningful materials with an appropriate degree of verbalization and activity. For instance, in group counseling, a leader may employ a democratic style that encourages sharing and openness. By creating such an atmos-phere and modeling appropriate behaviors, group leaders establish trust within the group and set concrete examples of how change can be accomplished.

Reflection

When have you seen a leader relate well to a group of children? What did the leader do that made him or her attractive to the children? Which of those same traits or techniques could you employ if working with a group of children?

Recruiting Members and Screening

Once preliminary decisions about form, structure, and materials are made, the group worker begins the task of recruiting members. One of the best ways to accomplish this task is to provide parents, teachers, and students with an **information statement** that describes what the group is about and what is expected of its members (Ritchie & Huss, 2000). Flyers, bulletin boards, newsletters, and word of mouth may be used in various ways in this effort. Children who are potential group members, especially for topic-focused group counseling, will often ask to join a group.

Assuming that counselors have taken appropriate precautions, the next step after recruitment is screening. Not all children who volunteer or who are referred are appropriate for a group. Therefore, a pregroup screening process must be used. Prescreening has special importance with children's groups because of the ethical and legal responsibilities involved in conducting groups for minors. "Issues such as the client's right to privacy, informed consent, and parental involvement take on special significance when treating minors in groups" (Ritchie & Huss, 2000, p. 147). For instance, in regard to privacy, "counselors in schools or community agencies should be careful that their recruitment process does not label potential group members and violate their right, and the right of their parents to privacy" (p. 148). Thus, it would be unwise to form a group for "antisocial boys." Although a label of this nature may seem absurd, it has happened, and group workers need to be careful in describing and advertising their groups. In an extreme case, parents might sue the counselor for slander or damages caused by associating their child with a negative label.

One way to screen potential participants is through pregroup assessment methods. These methods may be informal or formal. An informal method is having a child write out what he or she wishes to get from a group. A more formal method is using instruments specifically designed for this purpose, such as the *Group Psychotherapy Evaluation Scale* or the *Group Assessment Form* (DeLucia-Waack, 1997a). Individual or small-group intake interviews can also be employed by group workers to talk with children about the group and its purpose.

If, based on relevant inclusion criteria, the counselor thinks certain children can benefit from the group and these children display an interest, then the children are invited to join. Selection is crucial to the group's success because group member satisfaction and identity with the group will influence group cohesion and ultimately affect personal outcomes.

When group workers and children decide that the group is appropriate, letters requesting permission for participation must be sent to parents. Children must sign consent forms, too, so that everyone is in agreement before the group begins about the purpose of the group and the procedures involved. Overall, group work with children is more difficult to set up than group work with adults because of the many considerations involved in protecting children's rights (Corey, Corey, Corey, & Callanan, 2015).

Group Session Length and Number in Group

Opinions vary on how long group sessions should last and how many children should be included in a group. One general guideline is the younger the children, the shorter the session and the smaller the group (Myrick, 2011). When groups become too large (e.g., nine or more), members do not get an opportunity to participate as much with one another, and the dynamics of the group change. In such situations, subgroups may form, or "in-groups" and "out-groups" may develop.

The number who can be included in large group guidance activities is virtually unlimited. However, most counselors think in terms of 25 to 30 students. This enables the group to be conveniently subdivided into five or six small working teams with about 5 or 6 students each. Small groups within the group can be further subdivided, if necessary, into triads and dyads.

In group counseling, numbers are of concern. Group size should always be determined after examining the purpose of the counseling group, the developmental needs of the students, and the time available (Posthuma, 2002). When working with children ages 5 to 6, sessions may be held for only 20 minutes each two or three times a week, and the number of children allowed to participate may be limited to 3 or 4 (Henderson & Thompson, 2011). As children mature, the time allotted for each session and the numbers included go up (Dagley & English, 2014). For example, preadolescent children (ages 9 to 13) may meet in groups of 5 to 7 for as long as a regular classroom period (45 to 50 minutes), although the time allotted usually is around 30 minutes.

Gender and Age Issues

A final consideration in setting up a group is a decision regarding the sex and age range of the participants. On the issue of gender, there is considerable disagreement (DeLucia-Waack & Nitza, 2014). For example, Ginott (1968) and Benson (2010) believe that children of different sexes should be mixed in preschool group settings but that school-age children should be separated. Gazda (1989) also believes that school-age children should be segregated by sex, but not until the ages of 9 or 10. He contends that around the time of puberty, girls begin to mature more rapidly than boys, and the two genders do not mix well in groups. By contrast, Ohlsen (1977) advocates that groups include both girls and boys because he feels that group counseling is the safest place for girls and boys to learn to cope with each other regardless of social or sexual development. This same point of view is held by Henderson and Thompson (2011), who stress a balance of both sexes in a group unless the problem to be discussed is such that the presence of the opposite sex would hinder discussion—sex education topics, for example.

In regard to age, a general rule of thumb is to group children with those who are within about 1 chronological year of one another. Exceptions are made when more aggressive children are grouped with older children and less mature children are grouped with younger children. Some children with severe problems may do best with individual counseling.

Case Example

Fred Tries to Form a Children's Group for Victims of Bullies

As the only counselor in an elementary school of 500, Fred was overwhelmed in his first year of work. He tried everything, including blocking out much of his day to see individual children. This school year, though, he is determined to work smarter and set up a number of groups to see children with common concerns. He realizes that in his school there are four main groups of children needing his services: children who are experiencing their parents divorcing, children who are being bullied, children who are underachieving, and children who are lacking social skills and who have low self-esteem. Fred is fine in forming groups for children who have the just-mentioned difficulties, except that he is unsure about what to do with the children being bullied. There does not seem to be a good way to advertise this group so that those so affected will want to join it.

Questions

Would you try to establish a group for children who are being bullied? Why or why not? If you did, how would you go about recruiting them? What would be the emphasis of such a group?

ROLE OF THE LEADER IN CHILDREN'S GROUPS

The leader's role in children's groups varies. In group guidance, the leader is a teaching facilitator who encourages self-exploration. Guidance lessons are planned in cooperation, and often participation, with classroom teachers. Sometimes a counselor and a teacher will co-lead a group and map out their developmental curriculum far in advance. At other times, they will make use of **timely teaching**, when a particular event stimulates thinking and discussion among students (Faust, 1968). Many group guidance leaders operate from an atheoretical base in regard to the process of change. They stress developmental learning. Others are more integrative or holistic. Yet a third group of leaders concentrate solely on a single area of change.

In relation to the approach taken, leaders of children's guidance and psychoeducational groups influence what happens in the groups by the way they arrange chairs. Myrick (2011) states that students can be seated in five basic arrangements. When the classroom is arranged in a **row formation**, attention is focused toward the front. This arrangement is good for making a presentation, but it limits, and even inhibits, group interaction. In the second formation, a circle, student eye contact is increased and equality is promoted, but if the class group is too large (e.g., more than 20), students may lose a sense of connectedness with others. In the **semicircle arrangement**, students can see one another. Discussion involves everyone. However, if the group is too large (e.g., more than 20), students may not feel that they are a group.

The fourth arrangement, **in and out circles**, is referred to as a **fishbowl**. The inner circle promotes a sense of closeness, but those in the outer circle may feel left out and become bored. To help promote participation by everyone, group leaders can assign tasks for the outside group members to do (e.g., taking notes on group interactions) while they observe the inside group. They can also rotate groups in and out of the inner circle on a regular, timely basis. Another way to encourage participation by everyone is for leaders to leave an empty chair in the inner circle where those in the outer circle can sit and observe directly on a one-by-one basis what is happening in the inner circle.

Finally, the group guidance leader can use another structured arrangement known as **discussion teams** to promote involvement in guidance and psychoeducational activities. In this arrangement, students are divided into teams that are then seated in semicircles around the room. This formation has the advantage of getting students involved with one another and raising the level of excitement among the children. The disadvantage is that interaction is mainly limited to a small number of individuals, and other group members get to participate in only one group.

In group counseling, leaders have more of a tendency than in group guidance to have a theoretical orientation and act accordingly. For example, the Adlerian group leader functions as an open, democratic individual who is based in the here and now. These leaders vary in their techniques, but in working with children's groups, they are prone to emphasize encouragement and the law of natural consequences (Dinkmeyer & Sperry, 2000). In contrast, group counselors who take a Rogerian approach in their group work with children "put far greater emphasis on the facilitative quality of the counselor as a person. . . . The counselor's personhood [is] the basic catalyst that prompts group participants to make progress or not" (Boy & Pine, 1982, p. 179).

Leaders in rational-emotive behavior therapy groups with children stress the teaching of rational thinking (Ellis, 1974a; Weinrach, 1996). However, leaders in transactional analysis (TA) prefer to work with children in groups to promote the confrontation of games and help children learn basic TA concepts by seeing them demonstrated in themselves and others (Harris, 1967; Henderson & Thompson, 2011). In a similar way, leaders who adhere to Gestalt theory work in groups to promote awareness and support personality change from within (Corey, 2012). Finally, leaders of behavioral and cognitive-behavioral groups, which are the most popular for the treatment of children (Shechtman, 2014), focus on teaching children appropriate prosocial skills and helping them eliminate dysfunctional behavior.

Case Example

Claire Chooses an Approach

Claire wants to help her fourth-graders become more team oriented. She thinks that will help them become more academically accomplished as a group. She thinks an Adlerian approach would work best because of its social emphasis. She finds that the class becomes closer as a result of her theory selection and implementation. Yet, she is not sure what another theory might produce.

Questions

What would you advise? What would be the advantages and limitations of your choice?

STUDIES ON THE OUTCOMES OF CHILDREN'S GROUPS

Because psychoeducational and counseling groups have been conducted with elementary and middle school children for years, numerous studies have been made on them. Unfortunately, only a few of those studies have been research based (Shechtman, 2014, 2007). Nevertheless, as Bowman (1987) discovered in a national survey, counselors, especially school counselors, consider groups to be vital in reaching some students whom they would otherwise miss. Furthermore, DeLucia-Waack and Gerrity (2001) point out that "groups provide elements of support, altruism, universality, and cooperation that individual counseling cannot provide" (p. 281). The following are some examples of outcomes from group counseling with children over the years.

In a study investigating the impact of a psychoeducational group for social anxiety, Vassilopoulos and associates (Vassilopoulos, Brouzos, Damer, Mellou, & Mitropoulou, 2013) found that after an 8-week program using cognitive restructuring, anxiety management techniques, and social skills training, elementary children had a significant decrease on scales measuring social anxiety and negative interpretation of anxiety. There was also a significant increase in children's self-reported likability. Similarly, in regard to fourth- and fifth-graders who were children of alcohol abusers. Riddle, Bergin, and Douzenis (1997) found that they benefited in a number of ways from group counseling. In particular, the self-concepts of these children, as measured by the *Piers-Harris Children's Self-Concept Scale,* improved. In addition, these children increased their social skills and lowered their anxiety over the 14-week period of the groups. They also acquired information about the disease of alcoholism and learned strategies to employ to cope with parental alcoholism. Without the use of a group, these benefits, which applied to 40 students in the public elementary schools in southeast Georgia, would not have been realized on such a scale.

In another elementary school research project, Allan and Bardsley (1983) found group counseling to be helpful for **transient children** (those children who have moved to a new community and a new school) as they adapt to their environments. They describe a six-session group counseling format that positively affected students, teachers, parents, and a principal.

In working with fourth- and fifth-graders whose parents divorced, an 11-session support group for elementary school children was found to be beneficial (Tedder, Scherman, & Wantz, 1987). In this group, a developmentally appropriate introductory activity, the *caterpillar,* was used. Students filled in the eight sections of their caterpillar by drawing an expressive face in the first segment, writing three words that described themselves in segment 2, listing two of their hobbies in segment 3, writing three present feelings in segment 4, identifying where they were born in segment 5, describing where they would like to be at the present time in segment 6, listing an activity they would like to do in segment 7, and writing about a unique special personal quality in segment 8. The most important outcome of this research was its use of objective instruments to verify positive outcomes. Parents especially noted the impact of the group on their children's behavior.

Other research also shows the effectiveness of groups for elementary school-age children whose parents are divorcing. Furthermore, DeLucia-Waack and Gerrity (2001) suggest a framework for leading counseling and psychoeducational groups for children of divorce in school, agency, and court-based programs. They stress the use of the creative arts, such as music, bibliotherapy, puppets, and drama, in such groups to help children express their feelings and practice new behaviors and skills in a safe and supportive environment.

A Disruptive Child's Play Group (DCPG) for third-grade children in an elementary school has also produced positive results (Bleck & Bleck, 1982). After children participated in this 10-session program, their self-concept scores improved significantly compared with those for a control group. In another study on self-concept in the same year, Durbin (1982) found that self-concept for a sixth-grade girls' group improved significantly at the end of nine 35-minute sessions. Durbin's group followed a multimodal format based on Keat's (1979) **HELPING** framework—health, emotions, learning, personal interactions, imagery, need to know, and guidance. HELPING is an alternative model to Lazarus's (1976, 1989) **BASIC ID** approach—behavior, effect, sensation, imagery, cognition, interpersonal relations, drugs/diet. The HELPING model has also been found to be a motivator for increasing daily school attendance of third-grade boys (Keat, Metzgar, Raykovitz, & McDonald, 1985). It includes developmentally stimulating activities within it, such as "Feelings Bingo," in which participants use "I" messages after a feeling is called and "win" by filling out their feeling card horizontally, diagonally, or any way the caller decides beforehand.

In two studies involving children with learning disabilities, a population that comprises 2% to 10% of the school-age population, group counseling was found to improve self-concept, social behavior, and locus of control (Omizo, Cubberly, & Longano, 1984; Omizo & Omizo, 1988). The 1988 study included participants from varied ethnic backgrounds in grades 4 to 6 and compared the 10-session treatment group with a control group. The other study, which also included a control group, was conducted with predominantly White middle-class children from ages 8 to 11 years and lasted for eight sessions. Both studies have significant implications for educators in helping children with learning disabilities to learn.

One of the most promising research studies on groups with children is a replication study conducted by Lee (1993) of the effect of classroom guidance on student achievement. In her work, Lee followed the **Succeeding in School lessons** created by Gerler and Anderson (1986). This series of 10 lessons deals with modeling after successful people in school while learning to feel comfortable and responsible. It focused on promoting cooperative efforts; enhancing student self-concept; and learning appropriate school skills, such as listening and asking for help. Although Lee's research had some flaws, she found that fifth- and sixth-graders who took part in this experience significantly improved their academic achievement in mathematics over a control group. The group also made gains in language and conduct.

In addition to the studies cited here, many others, either statistically or qualitatively, report positive results on the use of groups with elementary and middle school children (e.g., Daniels, D'Andrea, Omizo, & Pier, 1999 on counseling groups with homeless children and their mothers; Huss & Ritchie, 1999 on support groups for parentally bereaved children, and Singh, 2013 on the use of popular opinion leader groups to reduce "gay bullying" in middle schools). Research by Shechtman (2007) and her colleagues in Israel has been particularly strong in reporting the effectiveness of counseling groups on friendships of latency-age children lacking in social efficacy. These researchers have found such groups to lead to significant gains in intimacy, particularly in boys (Shechtman, Vurembrand, & Hertz-Lazarowitz, 1994). Research (Brannigan, 2007) has also found that psychoeducational groups that identify sixth-graders' learning styles and strengths assist them in increasing their academic performance.

Some studies are now investigating the strengths and weaknesses of specific packaged types of groups. One of the most promising of these is the Student Success Skills (SSS) model (Campbell & Brigman, 2005), a group intervention for elementary and middle school students related to school success in academic and social performance. Twenty-five school counselors who trained in this structured small group counseling approach worked with midrange to low-performing students and saw them improve in both academic performance and behavior compared to a control group. Overall, research is making strides in informing potential group workers with children about which types of groups and experiences are effective with certain populations and when.

Reflection

When have you seen children do better in a group, such as a learning group or a team sport, than they did by themselves? What do you think made the difference—for example, peers, structure, setting?

STRENGTHS AND LIMITATIONS OF USING GROUPS WITH CHILDREN

Using guidance, psychoeducational, counseling, and psychotherapy groups with children poses a number of advantages and limitations. How successful a particular group will be depends on many variables, such as how well prepared the leader and members are, the composition of membership, the amount of time allotted, and the group's focus.

Children who profit most from group counseling and psychotherapy share the following characteristics: They volunteer, are committed to discussing what genuinely concerns them, are focused on learning new behaviors, are interested in helping other group members learn new behaviors, and believe that their counselor or group leader and parents (and even teachers) have confidence in their ability to learn and implement new behaviors. The opposite may be said for children who do not benefit.

Myrick (2011) lists a number of advantages and limitations for both group guidance and group counseling with children. Among the advantages of group guidance and psychoeducational activities are the following:

1. It allows the counselor/group leader to see a large number of students in a brief amount of time and work in a preventive fashion.
2. It allows the counselor/group leader to use inside (teachers) and outside (community personnel) resources to help children learn to help themselves.
3. It promotes security and comfort in children, promotes peer interaction, and enhances learning of practical ways to handle problem situations.

Among the limitations of group guidance and psychoeducational activities are the following:

1. It may be too impersonal at times and fail to help children in a practical way.
2. It may include too many individuals and prohibit general discussion or the exploration of certain subjects.
3. It may stereotype the counselor as a presenter of knowledge and inhibit the counselor from being more spontaneous.

Group counseling with children has advantages and limitations, also. Among the advantages listed by Myrick (2011) are the following:

1. It is more efficient than individual counseling because more children can be seen at any one time.
2. It is more realistic than individual counseling. Because of its social interaction base, it allows group members to share with one another frequently and learn through peer modeling and feedback.
3. It promotes support, acceptance, relaxation, risk taking, and resources for involved members.
4. It may free the counselor/group leader to make strategic intervention with members of the group.

Limitations of group counseling with children are:

1. It takes more time to develop trust and closeness because of the increased number of individuals involved in the counseling process.
2. It is more difficult to safeguard confidentiality and to include all members actively in group discussions and activities.
3. It is more difficult to organize group counseling activities than it is to see select children on a one-to-one basis—that is, group counseling formats require school system and/or parental permission/approval.
4. It requires leaders and members to be sensitive to topics that are inappropriate for the group and to be aware of, and counteract, nonproductive behavior of select group members.

Gumaer (1986) states that experienced middle school counselors can implement group work by recognizing its value; improving their involvement with teachers; discussing the rationale for more group work with their principals; obtaining additional training if necessary; and becoming self-motivating through initiating groups in cooperation with principals, faculty, and students. Ways in which new counselors in schools can begin group work include selling the principal on its value and explaining that it is an integral part of counseling. They should also offer in-service training to teachers, set up a time to conduct a group, implement one group at a time, publicize groups, lead growth-centered groups initially, and evaluate all group experiences.

Reflection

How would you go about selling the merits of group guidance and group counseling to school personnel, especially principals and superintendents? What kind of campaign would you run if you were in charge of making such a pitch? Why do you suppose that as a group, upper administrators in schools have not funded more counselors in elementary settings?

Summary and Conclusion

This chapter has examined the use of guidance/psychoeducation, counseling, and psychotherapy groups with elementary and middle school children. Group workers, both inside and outside schools, frequently conduct these types of groups for children in this age range (under 14 years). To be effective, leaders must have knowledge of group dynamics, group process, and human development. They must target their activities either toward guidance and psychoeducational groups, in which learning and prevention are the chief targets, or toward group counseling and psychotherapy, in which resolution and growth are the primary concerns. Developmental and nondevelopmental situations are dealt with in these groups.

Setting up groups for children is contingent on many factors. Certainly the matter of structure is of central concern. Structure involves how much control the group leader allows members to have and how materials are used. Another important aspect is related to how long the group will meet and with whom. A general rule of thumb seems to be that the younger the children, the shorter the time of the meeting, although frequency of meetings may be

increased. The debate about including both genders in groups is fairly evenly split. Conducting groups for just one gender and for both genders poses some advantages and disadvantages. The maturity and developmental readiness of the boys and girls involved is a key factor in whether to have a one-gender group or a mixed group.

The leader's role will vary in children's groups depending on the purpose of the group and the theoretical model advocated. Generally, leaders will be more active at first. Leaders use both nonverbal and verbal ways of learning, depending on the maturity of the children involved. Research supports the employment of groups in many settings with children, including those who have suffered loss, need support, or lack social skills. Multimodal group counseling and guidance seem especially appropriate because children respond to a number of stimuli at different times in their lives. Although group guidance, counseling, and psychotherapy are not without limits, counselors or group leaders often limit the effectiveness of group work by failing to use their resources sufficiently. Thus, various ways of advocating for and implementing groups have been discussed.

Classroom Exercises

1. One way to begin a group on an elementary/middle school level is to have children engage in activities that focus on their strengths. For example, children may be asked to draw something they do well and share it in a group. Pretend you are under age 14, and try this activity. Discuss with your group, and then the class as a whole, your reaction to this exercise. As a class, devise five other activities to use in group guidance and counseling with children. List the pros and cons of each.

2. In a group of four, create an activity for a group guidance class in each of the areas listed by Keat et al. (1985) in the HELPING model. Discuss the advantages and limitations of multimodal guidance and counseling as developed by Keat and Lazarus.

3. Compare problem-centered group counseling with growth-centered group counseling. Discuss with another student in class how problem-centered group counseling might become more growth oriented. Continue the discussion by listing strategies that a group leader could use in keeping a growth-oriented group from becoming problem centered. Share your ideas with the class as a whole.

4. Find a current research article on using groups with children. Share the results with the class as a whole in a reaction report giving the strengths and limitations of the study as you see them and how you might use this information later in working with a children's group.

Groups for Adolescents

BlueSkyImages/Fotolia

Out of the depth of your mind come the secrets
rough diamond-shaped forms
slowly pressured in pain and cut with hope.
With inner strength
you mine repressed memories
and change your expression
as feelings are released.
Privately, I wish for more of your story
but the struggle is deep
and the thoughts are too heavy
to be quickly lightened with insight.
So with the group I patiently listen
and silently applaud your emergence.*

*From "Secrets—Revised" © 1990 by
Samuel T. Gladding. Reprinted by permission
from Samuel T. Gladding.*

CHAPTER OVERVIEW

From reading this chapter, you will learn about

- Types of groups for adolescents
- Setting up groups for adolescents and the role of leaders in adolescent groups
- Studies on the outcomes of adolescent groups, including problems, strengths, and limitations

AS YOU READ, CONSIDER

- Your own experiences as an adolescent and what formal and informal groups you joined
- The difficulties and potential of working with adolescents in groups, and how you can minimize negatives and promote positives in members of this population
- What groups you think are most important for adolescents to be a part of and why

Groups for adolescents can be life saving and life changing. Take the South Shore Drill Team of Chicago, for instance. This team, made up of 350 young men and women from ages 8 to 21, is a highly disciplined, choreographed, and increasingly stylized alternative to the street.

Team members use wooden mock rifles, hip-hop music and modern dance moves in their performances, which have taken them all over the world, from Morocco to Walt Disney World to the annual back-to-school Bud Billiken Parade down Chicago's Martin Luther King Drive. In 2009, the team performed at over ten dozen events in nine states. Although many on the drill team come from struggling families and from schools where many pupils fail or drop out before graduation, 99 percent of the members of this team graduate from high school and many go on to college. (Terry, April 11, 2010, n.p.)

The group, in this case a team, is the difference between academic success and failure in most cases, and the difference between life and death in some situations.

Adolescence (defined here as the age span from 13 to 19 but extended to include some individuals as old as 25) is a challenging period in life. It is a time of both continuity and discontinuity marked by extensive personal changes (Graber & Brooks-Gunn, 1996; Hamburg & Takanishi, 1989; Henderson & Thompson, 2011). Young adults during this time grow up physically and mature mentally, but they struggle with psychological and social issues related to their growth and development (Bailey & Bradbury-Bailey, 2007). "Between 17% and 22% of children and adolescents have serious developmental, emotional, or behavior problems" (Shechtman, 2014, p. 586). Among other challenges they face, adolescents must learn to cope with crises in identity, delinquency, sexual concerns, peer and friendship pressures, dramatic physical changes, career and college decisions, and movement into greater independence. They do so in an environment that, despite all outward appearance, is often filled with loneliness, anger, turmoil, frustration, and self-doubt. Life events, both positive and negative, affect their lives (Wasielewski, Scruggs, & Scott, 1997).

Adolescents are expected to behave maturely in their relationships with their peers and adults. They are given some adult privileges, such as obtaining a driver's license and registering to vote. However, most adolescents experience frustration and stress in being independent, on one hand, and yet dependent on their parents and school or community authorities, on the other. Some of their turmoil may also be exacerbated because teens are officially denied some of the most tempting status symbols of adulthood, such as sanctioned sex and the legal consumption of alcohol. Often, adolescents "seem to have to wait for circumstances to make their decisions for them, because they are not really free to decide for themselves" (Harris, 1967, p. 176). At other times, adolescents are pressured into adult roles too soon, such as facing combat in the military. Little wonder that the world, for many adolescents, is uneven and confusing.

Yet, despite frustrations, adolescents reach out for growth and change and become the "cultural pioneers" of each generation. In their search for identity, they frequently create new fashions and trends. Many adolescent identities are relatively short lived and discarded—for example, wearing one's hair long or not trusting adults. Yet, the fads in clothing, music, language, and dance, while isolating some adolescents from general society, unite them with peers and in many cases help them constructively break away from their families of origin and establish a sense of individuation from others (Santrock, 2013).

Overall, *adolescence* (a term originated by G. Stanley Hall) is a time of rapid changes. It is characterized by some or all of the following: "storm and stress" (Hall, 1904), heightened emotionality, experimentation, and a desire for independence. The rapidity of transition associated with adolescence helps explain why many individuals in this category have difficulties in adjustment. Girls as a group appear to experience more stress than boys do, especially after age 14 (Yeaworth, McNamee, & Pozehl, 1992).

Groups of all kinds can be helpful to adolescents in making a successful transition from childhood to adulthood. They are valuable because they allow members to experience a sense of belonging, to share common problems, to find and provide support, to facilitate learning, to help ease internal and external pressures, and to offer hope and models for change (Malekoff, 1997; Nims, 2002). A group context allows open questioning or modification of values and an opportunity to practice communication skills with peers and adults. Often, through groups, adolescents find out more about their "vertical attachments (parents) and horizontal attachments (peers)" (O'Malley & Allen, 1993, p. 266). In a group setting, adolescents can safely experiment with reality, test their limits, express themselves, and be heard. By participating in groups, they may develop a greater sense of identity and intimacy (Erikson, 1963, 1968). One way to capitalize on behavioral and emotional strengths is to offer group counseling that promotes mindfulness skills (Wisner & Norton, 2013). Using the processes of increased self-awareness and self-disclosure to others in the group (Jourard, 1971), along with having the opportunity to prove that they can translate their ideas into actions in the context of a community, enables adolescents to achieve new or refined personal and interpersonal skills. Within groups, adolescents often find "genuine acceptance and encouragement" from peers and "a trustworthy adult who seems to trust and respect" them (George & Dustin, 1988, p. 142).

Reflection

Society has multiple portrayals of what adolescence is like through plays such as *Grease* and *West Side Story*. What was your adolescence like? How do you think it differed from adolescence today? How was it the same?

TYPES OF GROUPS FOR ADOLESCENTS

On a typical day, adolescents spend a great deal of their time in groups. There is the family group at home; the learning group at school; possibly a work group; and, of course, a social group. Peers are especially important to adolescents (Santrock, 2013), influencing the developing young person for better or worse. Society labels such groups as the "right" or the "wrong" crowd, and adolescents strongly identify with the values generated by their primary peer groups. In addition to these natural groups, there are at least two other main types of groups to which adolescents may belong and to which adults may have input. One is the developmental psychoeducational group, which is primarily voluntary and self-focused; the other is the nondevelopmental counseling or psychotherapy group, which can be voluntary or nonvoluntary and focuses on either oneself or oneself with others. Both can have a powerful impact on adolescents who participate in them and have been found to be effective (Gerrity & DeLucia-Waack, 2007).

Developmental Psychoeducational Groups

Developmental psychoeducational groups usually focus on common concerns of young people, such as identity, sexuality, self-management, self-advocacy, depression, parents, achievement motivation, peer relationships, career goals, and educational or institutional problems (Dagley & English, 2014; DeLucia-Waack, 2006). Individuals join these groups out of a sense of need and a desire to gain knowledge and experience that will help them better handle their concerns. Such groups are conducted in schools, community agencies, or both. Traditionally, they have an adult leader.

In schools, "research evidence has consistently demonstrated the value of group counseling. . . . Working with students in a small group format is an effective way to address developmental, situational, and academic issues" (Steen, Bauman, & Smith, 2008, p. 253). Some of the top group topics for adolescents, according to high school counselors, are career exploration, college plans, communication skills, peer helping, decision making, study skills, and self-concept (Bowman, 1987; Dansby, 1996). Most of the counselors surveyed by Bowman believed that small-group psychoeducational and counseling services are "vital and practical to implement in their programs" (p. 261). However, both Bowman and Dansby found that high school counselors believe setting up groups with adolescents is unrealistic because of a lack of time and scheduling problems. Other barriers secondary school counselors encountered included being underappreciated and dismissed, as well as feeling outside their comfort zone (Williams, McMahon, McLeod, & Rice, 2013). Consequently, counselors in schools do not lead groups that often, and only about 8% to 12% of their time is spent in this activity (Akos, 2004).

When developmental psychoeducational groups are offered to adolescents, however, they seem to have positive results. For example, Milsom, Akos, and Thompson (2004) found in a pilot study that adolescents with learning disabilities who participated in a psychoeducational group increased their disability self-awareness as well as their postsecondary education knowledge while becoming better advocates for themselves. Psychoeducational group discussions can also facilitate the process of examining careers that adolescents may not have considered previously (Glaize & Myrick, 1984) and increase their understanding of how to effectively handle conflict even if there is no initial effect on their proclivity toward violence (Lancaster, Lenz, Meadows, & Brown, 2013). In addition, structured groups for high school seniors can help them make the transition from school to college, the military, or a career (Goodnough & Ripley, 1996). Such groups may be especially pertinent at the end of the senior year (April and May), when peer groups are beginning to break down and adjustments in regard to the future must be made.

The Goal Wheel, a group developmental counseling model based on both Navajo philosophy and the medicine wheel, is a unique way of helping adolescents in schools conceptualize goals and plan steps they may take to achieve such goals in a meaningful and balanced life (Garner, Bruce, & Stellern, 2011). Each student makes a wheel, divided into four quadrants: imagine, planning, action, and enjoy (reflecting positively on what has happened). They also set short-term, achievable goals that can be accomplished from week to week. The overall effect of the group, where members and leaders encourage one another, is to help foster or restore direction, hope, and self-worth to adolescents involved.

Related types of psychoeducational groups—for example, cognitive restructuring groups—can also help students learn and grow. In these groups, adolescents are taught skills related to resolving problematic situations before they arise. They thereby avert major crises. For example, the *Solving Problems Together* psychoeducational group counseling model (SPT) is designed to help students discover positive strategies for responding to negative peer pressure. In SPT groups, students are active problem solvers, and as they work through problems, group members "develop knowledge, strategies, and communication skills for effective problem solving" that can serve as tools for lifelong success (Hall, Rushing, & Khurshid, 2011, p. 98). Likewise, Chong (2005) found that socio-cognitive groups for adolescents in Singapore facilitated attitudinal change and helped students become "responsible learners." Overall, communication skills groups have been found to effectively help high school students improve their interpersonal relationships with peers in terms of sending and receiving verbal and nonverbal messages. This improvement is especially likely if role-playing exercises are included as a part of the small-group experience (Hudson, Doyle, & Venezia, 1991).

In addition to improving communication skills, Kit and Teo (2012) have found evidence that an 8-week, psychoeducational therapy group can be effective in a smoking cessation program for at-risk and delinquent adolescents (ages 13 to 18) in Singapore. The group, "Quit Now!," revolved around six themes from "My journey here" to "Living my new life" and used structured expressive art activities as key motivators to keep participants engaged in group activities. Results from a 6-month follow-up found that 25% of the adolescents in a high school setting and 100% of those in a residential rehabilitation setting were able to stop smoking using the skills they had learned.

Small-group work in adolescent sexuality education has proven effective, too, both in and out of school settings. "Some adolescents' lives will be immediately and dramatically improved by sexuality education" in a group setting, whereas for others the impact will be more subtle (McMurray, 1992, p. 389). The actual and potential results for employing developmental psychoeducational groups with adolescents are great. These groups are not only efficient, effective, and important as school counseling interventions "but they also provide opportunities for students to support and learn from each other" (Milsom et al., 2004, p. 395).

Phillips and Phillips (1992) have summarized an exemplary school district's model of offering structured developmental groups. The groups set up in this model focused on the personal concerns of students. Groups of 8 to 16 met for 50 minutes (one class period) a week. They were conducted for 10 weeks during school hours, with the periods being rotated each week. All groups were co-led, with some teachers serving as co-leaders with counselors and other mental health staff. During the sessions, the group leaders used basic group counseling skills, such as reflecting content and feeling, clarifying messages, helping members recognize their own strengths and outside resources, and encouraging members to take actions that could help them resolve situations by themselves. During each session, students were reminded of group rules, such as confidentiality, but otherwise were allowed to talk freely and openly about their concerns. The outcome was both personal growth and prevention.

Finally, in relation to personal growth and prevention, intergroup dialogues among racially diverse high school students have been found to foster understanding of others and help students, especially Whites, grapple with complex issues, such as race, power, and privilege, often for the first time. This type of intergroup dialogue starts with affinity groups where members share similar social status, common goals, or are perceived and responded to similarly by other groups. Once commonality of an in-group context is established, group members are able to speak nondefensively to out-groups (i.e., those different from themselves) in a comfortable and productive way (Tauriac, Kim, Sarinana, Tawa, & Kahn, 2013).

Case Example

Oscar's Career Exploration Group

As a community volunteer, Oscar gives 2 hours of his time each week to work with Hugh, the high school counselor. Instead of focusing on individual students, Oscar and Hugh decide to lead an after-school group for students who are interested in exploring careers. The group will be psychoeducational. Seventeen students show up for the group, and Oscar and Hugh structure it so that topics include careers that vary in their educational requirements. They bring in outside speakers to talk about their careers and how they decided to follow their chosen paths. The 10-week course is a big success.

Questions

If you were Oscar or Hugh, how might you follow up this group? What careers would you include in a group like the one just described? Why?

Nondevelopmental Counseling/Psychotherapy Groups

In contrast to developmental psychoeducational groups, which focus on life skill issues for adolescents in particular, **nondevelopmental counseling and psychotherapy groups** tend to concentrate more on concerns adolescents have with adults and society, such as drug or alcohol use, school problems (e.g., poor grades, truancy), or deviant behavior. Usually, schools, agencies, or courts establish these groups, and troubled adolescents may either volunteer or be forced to attend (Jacobs, Schimmel, Masson, & Harvill, 2016). An excellent resource for finding experiential exercises to use with young adolescents in groups is Smead's (1996) *Skills and Techniques* *for Group Work with Children and Adolescents*, which covers topics pertinent to the needs of this age population, such as developing self-esteem, managing stress, making friends, and coping with grief and loss.

An exemplary program for helping volunteer adolescents who experience high levels of stress and lack support is "Teachers as Counselors" (TAC), which was designed and implemented by the Spring Independent School District (Houston, Texas) (Wasielewski et al., 1997). In the TAC program, teachers who interact with students in mature, effective, and nurturing ways are selected and trained to work with adolescents. The concerns of these adolescents may be situational or developmental, such as having trouble making new friends, failing courses, having problems with physical size, or hassling with parents. The groups are composed of 6 to 10 members and meet for 50 minutes a day, 1 day a week for 10 weeks. The teachers are supervised each week when they lead student groups (usually once or twice a year) for 2 hours at a time in a group of fellow teachers. Thus, students, teachers, counselors, and the school as a whole benefit from this experience. All students who participate are free to discuss any topic that causes them stress.

Reflection

The TAC model just described is one that depends on delegation and supervision to ensure that it works well. What has been your experience in delegating or supervising someone else? How do you think that experience would affect you should you decide to start a group program similar to TAC?

Not all counseling and therapy groups for adolescents are voluntary, of course. When potential members are not given a choice whether to participate, the result is usually resistance and reluctance. Although some of the hostility of these members may be overcome before the beginning of the group by talking to the participants and inviting them to share their thoughts and feelings, leaders of such groups face an uphill battle to create cohesion. They must be creative and innovative to turn around the negative energy. Starting with a formal presentation of the rules is not the way to begin a nonvoluntary group of adolescents. Just listening to the adolescents' complaints about having been referred to the group is a good place to start. After such feelings have been vented, members and leaders can begin to talk about common concerns and goals. Several constructive ways of handling participants' negative feelings and resistance are suggested by Corey, Corey, and Corey (2014):

1. ***Meet with these adolescents individually before the group starts***—This pregroup meeting gives the counselor/group leader and the adolescents a chance to explore feelings connected with participation in a required group and alternatives connected with the choice of nonparticipation. Such a meeting also provides the counselor/group leader with an opportunity to explain the nature of the group and how it will be conducted and to find out whether the adolescents have had any previous therapy experiences. Rapport may be established at this time, too. In summarizing such a pregroup meeting, an adolescent group leader may find himself or herself saying, "A lot of emotions are coming into this group, many of them associated with anger. However, the way the group is set up should give everyone a chance to express themselves and explore areas in their lives that may be problematic. I look forward to working with you as we begin our group next week."

2. ***Work with the resistance that uncooperative adolescents bring rather than fighting it***—Working with resistance includes listening in an understanding, nondefensive way to adolescents' stories about the reasons they have been forced to come to a group. For example, SueAnn may say that she feels like a "victim" of a teacher conspiracy, whereas Ray may describe his situation as one in which Mr. Cardwell "really has it in for me." In these cases and others like them, the experience of being heard is helpful in breaking down hostility and building up trust. The group leader may also work with resistance by inviting certain adolescents to try the group for a few sessions and then decide whether they will continue. This type of option gets adolescents into the group and yet gives them a choice.

If this technique does not work, then an adolescent may be invited to the group as an observer for a session. Thus, Jack, as the group leader, may say to Kate, a rebellious 15-year-old, "Although I would like for you to be a member of this group, I would first like to invite you to see how it works. You can come for three sessions as an observer. Then we can talk about what you have seen and your thoughts about the group, at which time you can join or withdraw from observing." After seeing the group in action, the adolescent can then decide whether to participate or choose another consequence imposed by others.

3. ***Respond to adolescents' sarcasm or silence with honest, firm, and caring statements***—By being simultaneously firm and caring, group leaders can help nonvoluntary adolescents become less emotionally upset in regard to the group, the leader, and the process. For example, leaders may tell adolescents who call them names, "I really care about you as a person, but I care about myself, too, and name calling will not be permitted in this group. I would like for you to be able to talk about your anger and other feelings, but in a direct and clear manner. That will mean using 'I' when you make a statement." Responding in this manner shows concern and care. It also establishes rules that are clear and firm. It helps the group leader and the group take care of themselves and function in a direct and nondefensive way.

Overall, developmental psychoeducational and nondevelopmental counseling/psychotherapy groups are two of the primary ways adolescents receive constructive help from adults and one another. Although such groups are found in both schools and agencies, the ways in which they are conducted may differ because schools have more internal control than most agencies. Developmental psychoeducational groups are almost always choice oriented, whereas developmental counseling/psychotherapy groups are usually geared toward both choice and change. As a rule, leaders of nondevelopmental counseling/psychotherapy groups face more of a challenge in helping participants get involved if the groups are nonvoluntary.

Case Example

Pete's Pregroup Preparation

Pete knows that the kids he is working with in juvenile detention do not want to be a part of a group. They have been mandated to come. Rather than start out looking at a group of angry young teenagers, he decides to visit them a day or two before the group actually starts. When he sits down with each person, he explains to them what is going to happen and what their options are. He has them read and sign a statement to that effect, too. Thus, when the group begins everyone has had the same pregroup preparation.

Questions

What do you think of Pete's strategy? What else might he do?

SETTING UP GROUPS FOR ADOLESCENTS

Determining how a group will be set up is based on the type of group. In some groups, the material to be presented may have general applicability to a wide range of individuals. In other groups, the focus of the group is narrow and deals with specific and sometimes troublesome aspects of life, such as sexuality (McMurray, 1992) or grief (Moore & Herlihy, 1993). Cultural, situational, and developmental aspects of group content and context must always be kept in mind.

Regardless of the topic and the level at which it is aimed, group leaders still need to be careful in selecting group members. They must make sure that adolescents who are chosen are mature and motivated enough to benefit from the group and be of benefit to the group. Various factors that must be considered in working with adolescents in groups include the use of verbal versus nonverbal behavior, group structure and materials, recruiting members and screening, group session length, number of members, and gender and age issues.

Nonverbal Versus Verbal Communication

Whereas groups for elementary and middle school children are activity focused, groups for adolescents are more verbally oriented. The reason is that the majority of individuals ages 13 and older are developmentally ready and prefer to interact through speech (Santrock, 2013). Sometimes adolescents, out of fear of being rejected or ridiculed, will withdraw or hold back on topics they wish to discuss. In such cases, **nonverbal cues**, such as body posture or facial expression, will take on added significance. For instance, if Paula begins to frown when the subject of group rules comes up but does not say anything, then the group leader may say, "Paula, you are frowning. I wonder if it is in connection to what we are now discussing?" Structured exercises may be introduced into adolescent groups, especially at the beginning, to facilitate trust, cohesion, and eventually more open and honest verbal communication (Carroll, Bates, & Johnson, 2004). For example, in the introductory session of a counseling group, members might be asked to begin by comparing themselves to an animal, body of water, or machine (Paisley, Swanson, Borders, Cassidy, & Danforth, 1994). Participants could first make a drawing and then talk about their ideas, or they could just discuss their comparisons in a go-round warm-up experience. For example, if group members are asked to compare themselves to bodies of water, then statements might be made as follows:

JULIE:	I am like a babbling brook. I flow in an even way most times.
DERRICK:	I am a raging stream. I have a lot of anger that spills over into my life and interactions with others.
ROSS:	I am a lake. I seem placid on the top but there is a lot that waits to be discovered underneath.
ALLISON:	I am a mountain river, flowing hard but as yet undiscovered.

In groups for adolescents, just as in groups for adults, members should be free to decide whether to talk, but the leader should work at setting up conditions that promote positive exchanges. Sometimes these conditions involve teaching basic communication skills in a structured manner.

Certain theories, such as Gestalt and psychodrama, focus on the congruence between verbal and nonverbal messages. Yet even leaders from primarily talk-oriented traditions, such as existentialism, will be more efficient when they concentrate on noticing how congruent members' words and behaviors are. Nonverbal behavior, such as inattentiveness, conveys a great deal and may be as important as verbal messages for all adolescent groups, even task/ work groups.

Another way to help adolescent group members unify their thoughts and actions is to use **action-oriented group techniques**, such as role playing and "I" statements (Corey, Corey, & Corey, 2014). For example, a leader may say to Joey, "I want you to show the group what happens when you are being rejected by Pal. By role playing this situation, I think both you and the group can get a better handle on it. Would you pick someone in the group to help us all see what is happening in the situation you just described?" Appropriate behaviors that are modeled by the counselor and prestigious peers may also be useful in showing members other options that are available to them.

Reflection

When have you learned a skill best from observing how someone else did it? When have verbal instructions been the best way for you to master a subject? What do you think the nonverbal to verbal ratio is in most psychoeducational groups? In most psychotherapy groups?

Group Structure and Materials

Many adolescent groups work best when they are structured around themes. **Themes** center around the genuine interests of participants. They hold group members' interest and invite their participation. Themes can vary from those that are serious, such as dealing with loss, to those that are pragmatic, such as explaining how to lead a class discussion. Flexibility can be built into theme structures, too. In a flexible theme format, the group decides week by week on the topic to be addressed. Too much choice can result in the group becoming bogged down and members losing interest. Therefore, limited flexibility is recommended. One way to achieve this goal is to have adolescents check off a list of the interests/problems on which they would like to work.

The materials needed in a group for adolescents vary according to the type of group to be led and the personalities of the members and leaders. For some highly verbal groups, few, if any, materials will be needed. For other, less motivated and primarily nonverbal groups, many materials, in the form of activities or stimuli, will be crucial (Carroll et al., 2004). **Structured activities** (planned group exercises and activities) and associated materials will generate discussion and participation, help the group to focus, promote experiential learning, provide the group leader with useful information, increase group comfort, and facilitate fun and relaxation (Jacobs et al., 2016). Some materials in these activities are used passively—for example, having members imagine themselves as certain objects or animals. Other materials are employed in a more active fashion, such as having group members cut out pictures or paste decorations on lunch bags that symbolically represent themselves and then using the bags in introductions to the group.

One particular type of adolescent activity group that requires considerable planning and materials is sand tray group counseling with adolescents. In this type of group, "members build small worlds with miniature figures in individual trays of sand and share their worlds as they are willing" (Draper, Ritter, & Willingham, 2003, p. 244). With adolescents, the typical miniature collection of realistic and fantasy people, animals, plants, structures, and transportation items must almost always be supplemented with "leisure, sport, and hobby items, such as miniature

Introduction of Personal Interests Bag

basketballs, skateboards, radios, and items that symbolize academic endeavors" (p. 247). The sand tray approach to group work with preadolescents has also proven effective. For instance, Flahive and Ray (2007) found that compared to a wait-list control group, the behaviors of 56 fourth- and fifth-graders who participated in a 10-week sand tray group were rated significantly better.

The creative arts are a natural means also for helping to attract and retain adolescents in a variety of structured groups in insightful ways (Gladding, 2011b; Rambo, 1997). Music may be especially powerful because of adolescents' general love for and familiarity with it. In addition, the power of the lyrics in certain music can help adolescents to convey thoughts that they would not be able to do otherwise (Saroyan, 1990).

Case Example

Lydia's Lyrics

Lydia knew the importance of music in the lives of adolescents, so when she set up her agency's group counseling program, she was sure she had done the right thing. When the teens came in, they heard music with lyrics that carried a message. As they were leaving, they heard another CD. Lydia was genuinely pleased with her planning and how the group went until the second session, when Ali came in early and said: "So are we going to listen to some more moldy oldies today?" Although he did not mean to insult Lydia, she was horrified and realized her music was not current.

Questions

How do you think Lydia could rectify this situation? What music might you suggest? What does this brief encounter tell you about the transient nature of adolescence?

Regardless of how materials are used, it is crucial that groups for adolescents not focus on the materials to the exclusion of the meaningful process. For example, if a group uses video feedback, then the emphasis should be on how viewing certain segments of the video is helpful to members in planning alternative behaviors, not on how everyone looked or how the equipment worked.

Recruiting Members and Screening

As has been previously mentioned, not all members of groups for adolescents are recruited. For example, the members of mandatory groups may be assigned to, or drafted into, a group whether or not they wish to be involved. However, in voluntary groups for adolescents, recruitment is of major importance. Leaders wishing to reach as many potential members as possible should publicize the group by posting announcements on bulletin boards and making contact with students, organizations, and teachers. Members for groups can also be recruited through using questionnaires and making informal contacts.

Public relations is a crucial part of the recruitment process. Potential members and referral sources must be courted and sold on the idea that what the group is designed to do can be effective, if properly supported. Thus, the group leader must include as much information as possible on material sent to key individuals, such as administrators. However, it is also important that the group not be oversold (Deck & Saddler, 1983).

Once a pool of potential members is recruited, screening takes place as it would with any other age group. Leaders look for members who will fit together well in regard to maturity, purpose, and background. A key component of the screening interview is to keep it from becoming too formal (Jacobs et al., 2016). Leaders must develop systems that help them screen potential candidates in a minimum amount of time and yet promote two-way interaction so that the potential group members become more informed about the leader and the structure of the group. One way to establish such an interaction process is to discuss a potential situation in a group with a group member candidate. The situation could be about any subject related to the type of group for which he or she is being screened: task, psychoeducational, counseling, or psychotherapy. For example, for a task/work group, a member might be questioned about a situation in which the group strayed from its task and did not seem willing or able to get back to it. The potential member could then be asked what he or she would do to help get the group back on track.

Ohlsen, Horne, and Lawe (1988) state that attraction is a key component to the final selection of adolescents for a group. **Attractiveness** is a multidimensional concept, but basically it refers to members positively identifying with others in the group. Leaders must be careful in selecting members who can relate well to one another, not just to the leader. For example, Steve may have interests that are similar to the group leader's, but in his peer group, he is unpopular and considered to be abrasive. Unless the group is to focus on improving peer relationships, Steve would probably not be a good choice as a group member.

Group Session Length and Number in Group

Sessions with adolescents usually last between 60 and 90 minutes. They may be extended, however, and even include minimarathons lasting all day (Corey, Corey, & Corey, 2014). Task/work groups that are charged with completing an assignment, such as decorating for a social event or coordinating a teen walkathon for funding cancer research, may especially benefit from longer group meetings. However, longer is not necessarily better, and a group for adolescents that lasts more than 90 minutes probably will not be productive.

In educational settings, the number of group sessions is usually dictated by divisional times in the school year, such as quarters or semesters. For instance, if a semester lasts 16 weeks, then a psychoeducational group might be geared toward a similar timetable, such as 14 weeks. Yet "the frequency of the group sessions and also the duration of the . . . sessions are directly related to the intensity of group involvement and growth" (Gazda, 1989, p. 153). If group members have major problems or deficits, then the sessions may last longer and be more frequent. Psychotherapeutic groups may especially benefit from these enlarged parameters.

The number in a group ultimately affects its outcome and rate of progress. With increased size, member interaction and relationships decrease, and the group becomes more leader centered. Therefore, small groups of 5 to 10 members may be ideal in working with adolescents. Gazda (1989) states that the number of adolescents he includes in a group is based on duration and frequency. When both are brief (e.g., 3 months), he prefers to work with a group of from 5 to 7. If both are longer (e.g., 6 months), then the group may include from 7 to 10 members. He notes that "as a rule, the smaller the group, the more frequently it meets, and the longer it meets, the greater the opportunity for intensity of group involvement and growth" (p. 152).

Gender and Age Issues

Whether to include both males and females in a group for adolescents depends on its purpose. Sometimes one-gender groups will be more appropriate. For instance, in a counseling or psychotherapy group dealing with the trauma and recovery from rape, it may be in the best interest of the group that only girls be included. Likewise, in a structured psychoeducational group for aggressive girls, a one-gender group with a female leader works best (Cummings, Hoffman, & Leschied, 2004). In one-gender groups, a key to the success of the group is the identity associated with gender and the topic. This type of identity comes through early socialization patterns. In summing up the research on the socialization of boys and girls in groups, Gigliotti (1988, p. 277) states that the most reliable differences show that boys play in large groups, whereas girls play in small ones. In addition, boys' friendship groups are more extensive or broadly accepting; girls' friendship groups are more stable and exclusive. Furthermore, boys in a group show more outwardly competitive behavior than girls do.

Although not dismissing gender socialization differences, Jacobs et al. (2016) believe the value of a coed group is that "there is a lot to learn about the opposite sex during the adolescent years, [and thus] a coed group can be beneficial" (p. 421). Myrick (2011) also does not think gender makes a difference in how groups run unless a boy and a girl who are "going together" are in the same group or unless a topic related to physical growth or other sensitive sex-related issues are to be discussed.

In running **mixed-gender groups** (those that include boys and girls), especially if the focus is on social relationships and dating, it may be necessary for group leaders to develop methods to get young adolescent males involved so they will get the maximum benefit from the experience. Adolescent boys, as compared with adolescent girls, are usually less comfortable, less involved, and less likely to achieve as positive an outcome in groups that emphasize interpersonal relationships. Adolescent girls as a group are more interested in social relationships and are more at ease in sharing. "Adolescent females also perceive counselors and counseling 'as significantly more attractive and trustworthy,' than do adolescent males" (LeCroy, 1986, p. 505).

In regard to age, Kymissis (1993) recommends that certain adolescent ages not be mixed. For example, high school freshmen and sophomores do not mix well with juniors and seniors.

However, he reports that there is little difficulty in mixing college undergraduates, although undergraduates and graduate students are not easily combined. Age in the adolescent years may not be quite as sensitive a variable as during childhood. Nevertheless, it appears that older adolescents are less affected by age differences than are younger adolescents.

Case Example

Agnes's Adolescent Group

Agnes is an experienced group counselor. She knows boys are more reluctant as a group to speak up once a group begins. Therefore, in selecting kids for her latest group, one of the screening devices Agnes used was a basketball. She threw each potential member a basketball and noticed how comfortable he felt with it. Based on this criterion and a few others, Agnes began the group by having her group go outside and shoot baskets. They all seemed to enjoy it and they loosened up with one another rather quickly.

Questions

What do you think of Agnes's screening method? What else might she have used? What should she have avoided?

ROLE OF THE LEADER IN ADOLESCENTS' GROUPS

The role of leaders in groups for adolescents is multidimensional. In addition to keeping up with the interpersonal and intrapersonal dynamics of group members, leaders must be extremely self-aware. They must be willing and courageous enough to explore, and perhaps relive, much of their own adolescent experience so that it will not interfere with their work and result in countertransference. Adolescents respond well to leaders who are open with them, enthusiastic, and caring. These types of leaders are true to themselves first and are good role models for those whom they lead. They personify congruence and are able to laugh at themselves and joke with others in a productive way—for example, noting how the palms of their hands sweated when, as a teen, they danced with a member of the opposite sex.

The roles of leaders are determined by the types of groups they lead, too. In evaluating the literature on child, preadolescent, and adolescent groups, Denholm and Uhlemann (1986) have devised a three-dimensional model with several components under each dimension. The first dimension, *developmental level*, includes three age groupings: children, preadolescents, and adolescents. The second dimension is *approach*, which is composed of four approaches to group work: activity, discussion, counseling, and therapy. The third dimension, *inquiry theme*, includes three components: theory, research, and practice.

The classification scheme that Denholm and Uhlemann (1986) have devised has a utilitarian as well as a conceptual function. From it, the authors have classified select journals so that leaders can consult these periodicals to learn more about the types of groups they are conducting. For example, by using the Denholm and Uhlemann model, a leader looking for ideas for a counseling group for adolescents would find that issues of *Professional School Counseling* and the *Journal of Counseling and Development* provide some of the best information. This classification system saves the leader time and energy in finding practical ideas.

In general, group leaders for adolescents in high school are active. Both activity level and structure are related to the group's maturity. The theoretical persuasion of leaders also plays a vital part, as does whether the group is voluntary.

One way in which leaders can promote group cohesiveness and the acquisition of skills in adolescent groups is through modeling the types of behaviors they wish to encourage. "Good models have a tremendous impact on adolescents and can teach them how to relate openly and to help others" (Ohlsen et al., 1988, p. 279). By matching the gender between leaders and adolescents, the acquisition of modeled social skills may be enhanced. Leaders can also use influential peers in modeling. Thus, in an assertiveness group for girls, a female leader who is assertive can be extremely helpful in showing the girls how they can adopt and adapt an assertive approach to their unique situations. Peer leaders in adolescent groups are usually more persuasive than adult leaders in bringing about change. Therefore, adult group leaders may work well by training mature adolescents to lead groups and then supervising the adolescent leaders.

Reflection

The family therapist Carl Whitaker claims that as a child he was a misfit. So in moving to a new school he sought out a couple of boys who were popular and hung out with them and their friends. According to Whitaker, it helped him adjust and do well. When have you seen such a phenomenon happen? Why do you think this type of grouping is so rare? How as a secondary school counselor could you make it happen more?

As in groups for other special populations, it is the leader's responsibility to stress the importance of confidentiality. Adolescents may use personal information gathered in a group for gossip or simply to be vindictive. In either case, the information is harmful, and such action must be prevented. One preventive measure is for leaders to state rules about confidentiality during the first session and every session thereafter. Leaders must also deal immediately with any potential breach in confidentiality and determine what has occurred. Finally, if confidentiality is broken, then leaders must either enforce rules or have the group itself deal with the problem. In any case, leaders' responsibility must be exercised.

Overall, leaders of groups for adolescents face a number of challenges. Some of these include being understanding, yet firm; facilitative, yet controlling; and active, yet trusting of the group process. How the group leader acts will depend on the composition, focus, and maturity of the group, as well as the background of the leader. Myrick (2011) states that six basic responses make leaders more effective facilitators:

1. Using feeling-focused responses (e.g., "You seem to have some real feelings about what happened in this situation.")
2. Clarifying or summarizing responses (e.g., "So instead of responding to Laura's words, you found yourself getting depressed and withdrawing from the group.")
3. Employing **open-ended questions** (e.g., questions that invite more than one- or two-word responses, such as questions that begin with "What" or "How")
4. Giving **facilitative feedback** (telling another person the effect he or she had on you as a compliment or a confrontation (e.g., "Julius, I find you easy to talk with.")
5. Providing a simple acknowledgment (e.g., "Thanks" or "All right")
6. Presenting **linking** (when the leader identifies similarities and sometimes differences that are occurring among group members to help them join together, for example, "I notice that Willie and Buffy are the only ones who have taken a risk tonight.")

Leaders of adolescent groups must be skilled and flexible in the use of these responses to avoid what Myrick (2003) describes as **low facilitative responses**:

1. *Advice/evaluation*—telling people how to behave or judging them, for example: "Jody, you should sit up straight when you are in this group."
2. *Analyzing/interpreting*—explaining the reasons behind behavior without giving the person an opportunity for self-discovery, for example: "Ginger, I am sure you are tired and worn out, but I am not excusing you from participating in this exercise."
3. *Reassuring/supportive*—trying to encourage someone, yet dismissing the person's real feelings; for example: "You can do it, Matthew. I know you feel like you can, too."

Leaders of groups for adolescents may help themselves and their groups even more if they also make use of peer counselors or parents as consultants, when appropriate. In either case, leaders receive information and feedback they might not get otherwise.

PROBLEMS IN ADOLESCENTS' GROUPS

As with other types of groups, problematic areas that leaders must address can arise in groups of adolescents. McMurray (1992) discusses these difficulties in regard to an educational group, but these problematic behaviors are not limited to just one type of group. Among the possible problems are outright disruptiveness, a hesitancy or reluctance to engage with others, polarization, attempting to monopolize, inappropriate risk taking, and overactivity or giddiness. Each of these behaviors is briefly discussed here, along with a corrective response.

Outright Disruptiveness

Cases of outright disruptiveness in adolescent groups are more common than in adult groups because of the level of group member maturity. Disruptiveness can range from verbally yelling at other group members to attempting to pick a fight. For example, Juan may challenge another sensitive Hispanic boy in a group to be "macho" and call him names when he does not act so.

Ways of combating disruptive behavior include going over the rules of the group so that the inappropriate behavior does not occur because members are informed or warned of consequences. Having the group leader talk with a disruptive member directly before, during, or after a group meeting can be beneficial. Likewise, allowing members of the group to discuss the situation and decide what to do with the disruptive member can also be helpful. Finally, as a last resort, the disruptive person can be dropped from the group. However, taking this radical step will affect the group's dynamics and its ability to work because members will feel less secure and trusting (Donigian & Malnati, 1997). Dropping or removing a member from a group of any kind is an extreme measure that is used only if nothing else can be done.

Hesitancy to Engage with Others

A reluctance or hesitancy to engage with others can be a result of underdeveloped verbal or social skills. Sometimes, members want to act productively but simply do not know how. In such cases, engaging the problematic member either within the group context or in a leader–member conference can help to correct the situation. During these encounters, the motivation of the member can be determined. For members who wish to become more appropriate and productive, modeling and encouragement are recommended.

Polarization

Polarization occurs when a group becomes divided into different and opposing subgroups. Such divisiveness may be caused by accidental circumstances, such as chance encounters of members outside the group setting, or by premeditated plans. Polarization is more easily corrected in the first case because the group and its leader can help members understand how their behavior outside the group affects the functioning of the group. However, if polarization is a result of planned actions, then a member or members may have to be dismissed for the group as a whole to work well again. This is why extra caution and time should be spent in setting up a group.

Monopolizing

Monopolizing is not unique to adolescent groups. Reasons for it, which have been discussed previously, are related to anxiety of a group member or members. Monopolizing may also be used as an attention-getter or a way of avoiding people or situations. In task/work groups, monopolizing may be handled by delegating tasks or asking for limited responses. In other types of groups, timed methods may help cut down or eliminate monopolizing behaviors. For example, the leader may ask members to respond to something occurring in the group in 25 words or less. If the monopolizer tends to exceed the word limit, then the leader or the group as a whole can use the technique of a cutoff to keep the group on task and on time.

Inappropriate Risk Taking

Sometimes group members share information too soon or reveal inappropriate information. This type of behavior is not unusual with adolescents, especially those who have limited awareness of themselves and others. For example, an adolescent boy might brag of taking drugs before fellow group members to impress them. In such cases, structured group exercises that help individuals understand themselves better in relation to others may be helpful. Reviewing group rules, talking privately with the person involved, cutting off the person's behavior, or redirecting the group as whole may be appropriate strategies for handling such a situation.

Overactivity or Giddiness

When adolescents are overactive or giddy in a group, it is attributable to several factors: the natural energy of individuals in this age group, embarrassment, the leader's or the group's failure to set limits, or boredom with the group or the topic being discussed. For example, Marsha and Suzanne may giggle and pass notes to each other constantly because of their inability to identify with the matters being raised in the group.

To respond to this type of behavior, leaders can simply acknowledge it and continue with group activities. Leaders can also discuss their feelings about the behavior with the group, or they can talk privately and individually with the member(s) most responsible for it. Another corrective action that can be taken in such a situation is to process with the group what is happening and how they as a group would like to handle the matter.

Overall, groups of adolescents have unique problem behaviors that those who work with such groups need to know about to be effective. Such information is helpful, if not vital, for leaders who plan to enter group work with adolescents. A good leader of adolescents' groups will use the power of the group as well as his or her skills.

Reflection

What adolescent behaviors do you think are most disruptive in a group? When have you seen a group correct disruptive behavior in its midst?

STUDIES ON THE OUTCOMES OF GROUPS FOR ADOLESCENTS

Even though groups are not as widely used with adolescents as with younger children, numerous studies have been done on their impact. Some of these reports are in the form of case studies, but others have used well-controlled research designs. Groups have been found to be effective with adolescents in promoting exploration of participants' lifestyle patterns and relationships with parents (Dinkmeyer & Sperry, 2000). Group work has also been used in helping adolescents deal with major changes in their lives, such as moving to a new school as freshmen or transfer students (Deck & Saddler, 1983; Strother & Harvill, 1986), and in reducing conflict among students in racially tense situations.

Groups are important ways to help adolescent refugees from other cultures to learn about customs and to prevent adjustment difficulties or psychological disturbances related to the resettlement experience (Tsui & Sammons, 1988). In addition, groups have a long tradition of being helpful experiences for students trying to make career decisions (Anderson, 1995; Gibson & Mitchell, 2006). Groups may also be used in school settings to attract and hold students in school through graduation (Blum & Jones, 1993). For instance, Sonnenblick (1997) reports forming a group as a club for high-risk middle-school girls that helped them mature and take more responsibility for themselves by participating in community service activities. In five schools cited by the American School Counselor Association as being exemplary in practice, counselors made deliberate attempts to achieve specific goals through group work (Carroll, 1981).

Likely candidates for group counseling among adolescents are potential high school dropouts (Krivatsy-O'Hara, Reed, & Davenport, 1978), high-risk adolescents with divorced parents (Coffman & Roark, 1988), adolescents who are substance abusers or delinquents (Dryfoos, 1990, 1993; Nims, 2002), and adolescents with unhealthy lifestyles and poor peer relationships (Zinck & Littrell, 2000). The group approach for all of these populations can take a systems perspective and consider the problematic behavior in its environmental context. For adolescents with divorced parents, taking a systems perspective involves focusing on helping these adolescents to realize they are not alone in their experience and that a change in the family structure, such as a divorce, has an impact on many facets of their lives. A triangle represents the three dimensions in the divorce system: the person ("I"), others ("We"), and the divorce ("It") (see Figure 12.1).

In a group for adolescents with divorced parents, information about the effects of divorce ("It") is highlighted first. For instance, the legal, adversarial, and prolonged nature of divorce might be discussed, along with the stages most people go through in coming to terms with a divorce. After the group leader provides enough information, "I" and "We" interaction is focused on. Discussion of these areas may include such topics as dealing with friends, extended family members, and the separating parents, as well as strategies for coping with depression, anger, and grief. In general, Omizo and Omizo (1988) have found that young adolescents who participate in divorce groups have higher self-esteem and possess a more internally based locus of control than those who do not.

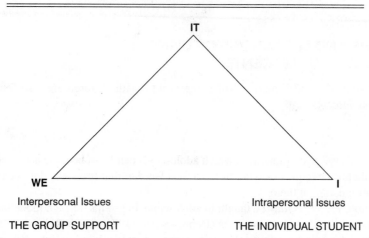

THE DIVORCE
Extrapersonal Issues the Group Has Formed to Address

IT

WE

I

Interpersonal Issues   Intrapersonal Issues

THE GROUP SUPPORT   THE INDIVIDUAL STUDENT

FIGURE 12.1   Conceptual model of divorce.   *Source:* From Albert E. Roark, Shirley Gwinn Coffman (1988). "Likely Candidates for Group Counseling: Adolescents with Divorced Parents", *School Counselor,* 35 p. 250. Copyright © 1988 by American School Counselor Association. Reprinted with permission.

In addition to a systems perspective, groups for adolescents in danger of experiencing major crises can take a skills approach. Such an approach can be seen in regard to groups for adolescents who have low motivation for learning. Thompson (1987) formulated the "Yagottawanna" ("you have to want to") group. The group relied heavily on the following concepts: "positive thinking, positive reinforcement, modeling, shaping, skill development, self-responsibility, self-discipline, and cognitive restructuring" (pp. 134–135). It consisted of nine 45-minute sessions spread over 9 weeks. The sessions were both didactic and experiential, and students were followed up on individually 2 months after the group ended. When pre- and posttest results were compared for the group, participants were found to view the group favorably and their abilities more positively.

In the area of juvenile delinquency, Zimpfer (1992a) found group treatment for this population to be international in scope. "By far the most frequently reported treatment approach involves the delinquents' peers for therapeutic leverage" (p. 117). Treatment groups for juvenile delinquents seem to fall most often into the category of long-term psychotherapy. However, cognitive, behavioral, psychoeducational, psychodrama, family, and even music therapy have been employed in working with this population.

Bringing about change in the treatment of juvenile delinquents in groups seems to be most productive with youth who are first-time offenders, those who were less abused as children, and those who are from stronger social and economic backgrounds. The use of moral discussion groups has also been found to be helpful in rehabilitating juvenile offenders (Claypoole, Moody, & Peace, 2000). Such groups consist "of dilemma discussions, anger control, and social skills training as well as implementation of a positive peer culture into the institution" in which the juveniles live (p. 396).

Overall, it appears that groups have powerful potential for helping many adolescents to change and develop new social and academic skills (DeLucia-Waack, 2006). Studies with these groups need to use control groups more and refine their research methods. Nevertheless, the use of groups with adolescents in preventive and remedial ways is promising, especially in the schools.

STRENGTHS AND LIMITATIONS OF USING GROUPS WITH ADOLESCENTS

Many of the strengths and limitations of using groups with children are also found in using groups with adolescents.

Strengths

Groups are a "natural" environment in which adolescents can learn because adolescents spend a great deal of their time in groups. Therefore, groups feel familiar to many adolescents, who look forward to participating in them.

In addition, life skills may be taught to adolescents in groups through modeling, role playing, group discussions, and brief lectures (Dennis-Small, 1986; Zinck & Littrell, 2000). Many adolescents have behavioral deficits. Through groups, they can learn important ways of coping and dealing with life stressors.

A sense of belonging is also created in groups, and adolescents are given opportunities to learn through direct interaction with or observation of other group members and the leader (Trotzer, 2007). Often this learning is carried over (**generalization**) from the group experience to the adolescent's daily life.

Groups provide for multiple feedback that can help adolescents in their personal growth and development. In addition to having the advantage of the leader's input, adolescents in groups also receive peer feedback. Many times, the power of the peer group can be used constructively to promote needed change.

A final strength of groups for adolescents is the opportunity they provide for members to help one another. It is often through helping others that an individual's own self-esteem and self-confidence are increased.

Limitations

Unless potential members are carefully screened, a group may not have enough appeal to motivate the participants. For example, the most common reason for adolescents discontinuing 12-step programs is boredom and lack of fit (Kelly, Myers, & Rodolico, 2008). In addition, many adolescents deny they have any type of problem and believe there is a stigma associated with discussing problems with others. Adolescent boys, especially, may feel this way.

Another limitation is the pressure that some adolescents may feel to conform to behaviors in which they do not believe. Peer group pressure is extremely strong in the adolescent years and may be misused in a group of adolescents unless it is carefully monitored (Corey, Corey, & Corey, 2014).

Individuals in groups may not be given enough attention. Because of their backgrounds or maturity levels, some adolescents need individual counseling or programmed learning. The group is not a suitable environment initially for some troubled young adults (e.g., those who are suicidal).

Another limitation that can develop if a group is not screened carefully is poor group communication and interaction. Often adolescents tend to "scapegoat" (blame) others for their problems. At other times, they will disrupt, criticize, or ignore others because they are so engrossed in themselves. Properly run adolescent groups screen out adolescents who are not ready to work on themselves or who are too self-centered, immature, or unhelpful.

A final limitation of doing group work with adolescents concerns legal and ethical issues (Corey, Corey, Corey, & Callanan, 2015). To work with minors, group leaders almost always have to obtain parental consent. In addition, if leaders want their groups to succeed, they must get the consent of the adolescent as well. Leaders may need to consult professional colleagues and associations more when working with adolescents than when working with adults. This process is time consuming and may slow down progress.

Summary and Conclusion

In conducting groups for adolescents, group workers must consider a number of variables. For instance, the age and developmental stage of the adolescents must be appreciated and understood before they are gathered into groups. Adolescence is a period of life filled with rapid changes and many paradoxes. It is a time of transition in which the developing young person's focus is on achieving a solid sense of identity. There is much experimentation and periods of progression and regression during this time. Adolescents often look more mature than they are and get themselves into situations for which they are not developmentally ready. In screening adolescents for groups, each potential member must be considered individually.

However, because adolescents spend a great deal of their lives in groups, working with them in a group setting is usually beneficial. Voluntary, developmental psychoeducational groups include adolescents who are concerned about particular situations. Individuals in these groups are generally quite motivated. Adolescents in nonvoluntary counseling/psychotherapy groups, which often focus on issues that are of lower priority to them, are usually less motivated and involved. In setting up either type of group, leaders must remember to pay attention to the verbal and nonverbal behavior of participants, to focus the group structure around themes, and to make sure that participants, regardless of how they are recruited, find the group to be attractive.

When working with adolescents who are forced into a group situation, leaders are wise to spend time talking with them about their feelings on an individual level before the group begins. Regardless of which type of group is led, the number of sessions, length of sessions, and other ground rules for the

group experience should be spelled out before the group begins. Potential problematic behaviors should also be kept in mind.

The leader of a group for adolescents, although a facilitator, is also an authority figure because of his or her adult status. Therefore, effective group workers make the most of peers within the group and model behaviors frequently. They also make themselves sensitive to age and gender issues that may affect the group's development. They even train adolescents to be peer group leaders.

When conducted properly, groups for adolescents can help them become more aware of their values and lifestyles. Groups can also help these young people overcome or cope with situational concerns, such as moving, dealing with divorce, choosing a career, handling unplanned pregnancies, overcoming substance abuse, and becoming motivated to learn. More long-term problems involving adolescents, such as juvenile delinquency, can be handled through group work, although with limited success.

Among the strengths of groups for adolescents is that groups are a natural way for adolescents to relate to one another. Furthermore, groups emphasize the learning of life skills, focus on generalizing behaviors practiced in the group to real-life situations, and provide multiple feedback and an increase in self-esteem that comes about through helping others. The drawbacks to working with adolescents in groups include legal and ethical considerations (e.g., obtaining parental consent), the stigma of talking to others about one's problems (especially for boys), the lack of attraction a group may have for some, and the pressure of the group to force some of its members to conform to behaviors that are against their beliefs.

Classroom Exercises

1. Reflect on your own life as an adolescent. What were your major concerns? List the top five. Compare your list with those of the other class members. Which items are similar, and which are different? To what do you attribute the commonalities and differences? Discuss how working in a group was (or would have been) helpful to you at this stage of life. Be specific and note cultural influences in using or not using a group.

2. Discuss with another class member how you would go about setting up a nonvoluntary group for adolescents in a school or an agency in which you work or hope to work. How would this procedure differ from setting up a voluntary group for adolescents? Focus particular attention in your assessment on screening processes, motivational issues, verbal/nonverbal exchanges, and results.

3. Critique a recent journal article on group work with adolescents. How did the group leader set up the experience? What made it successful or unsuccessful? Discuss your results in a group of four. As a group, make a list of factors that you obtained from reading these articles that promote or inhibit the success of groups for adolescents.

4. Pair up with another class member and talk about the different types of groups you participated in as an adolescent (e.g., Scouts, clubs, athletic teams). Discuss how you think each group affected your development as a person and what carryovers from these experiences still have an impact on you.

CHAPTER 13

Groups for Adults

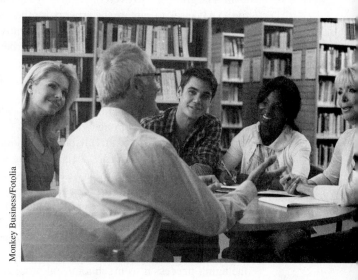

Now matured to adulthood
embers from our past times glow
waiting to burst forth in the presence of others
like kindling and feelings
when heated and flamed.
As we grow, so does our light,
a spark that spreads like friendship in a circle,
a blaze that brightens but does not consume.
So in the warmth and reality of a group we become
stronger in reflection,
people who are openly aware of the gift
that is life
and the bittersweet insight that cycles,
like fires, have ending. . . .*

*From "Circles" in ASGW Newsletter, 14, p. 3
© 1986 by Samuel T. Gladding. Reprinted by
permission from Samuel T. Gladding.*

CHAPTER OVERVIEW

From reading this chapter, you will learn about

- Types of groups for adults
- Setting up groups for adults and the role of leaders in adult groups
- Studies on the outcomes of adult groups including strengths and limitations

AS YOU READ, CONSIDER

- What issues you think are most important to adults, at what ages, and why
- The differences in group dynamics in groups for adults over the life span
- Your level of comfort in working with adults as opposed to other age levels

In the movie *The Monuments Men*, an American unit of seven art experts at various stages of life seeks to rescue art masterpieces from the Nazis and return them to their rightful owners. The group is led by Lieutenant Frank Stokes (George Clooney), who coordinates them as a team. The group has to overcome not only the Nazis but American combat units and Soviet armed forces who seek to capture the artwork for themselves. The age-diverse unit suffers casualties but is largely successful because of their cooperative nature and well-defined mission, showing the power of a task/work group of adults at their best.

Adulthood is a somewhat nebulous term. It implies that a person has reached physical, mental, social, and emotional maturity. Yet, as numerous researchers note, adulthood is a multi-dimensional stage of growth often characterized by a certain unevenness and unpredictability (Santrock, 2013). There is little uniformity to adulthood. Indeed, as Allport (1955) states, human beings are "always becoming."

For the purposes of this chapter, adulthood is conceptualized as the age period between 20 and 65 years. It includes individuals in **young adulthood** (20 to 40 years), in which identity and intimacy are two intense primary issues, as well as adults in **midlife** (40 to 65 years), in which needs related to **generativity** become the main focus (Erikson, 1963). Men and women experience this stage of life differently (Kimmel & Messner, 2013; Kirk & Okazawa-Rey, 2009), as do individuals with special needs and developmental concerns.

Wrenn (1979) advises counselors to "learn to work more effectively with adults" (p. 88). Understanding life stages and transitional experiences is a must. As Nichols (1986) points out, the **aging process** is as much a mental process of considering oneself older as it is a biological phenomenon composed of physiological changes. Responses to being an adult and grappling with issues related to it may be facilitated in groups. In such settings, people may talk with, understand, identify with, and learn from others in similar situations.

TYPES OF GROUPS FOR ADULTS

There are probably more types of groups available and run for adults than for any other age or stage of the population. Indeed, "group research has shown that nearly all group training experiences occur with adults" (Goodrich & Luke, 2010, p. 144). Work and task groups are a primary type of group conducted for adults because many adults work outside of the home and many more are involved in volunteer civic and community activities (Hulse-Killacky, Killacky, & Donigian, 2001). Often groups at workplaces are focused on team building and the production of services, whereas volunteers attend groups whose purposes and activities are psychoeducational in nature and are devoted to accomplishing a goal for a special cause.

Counseling groups are also used for exploring the personal issues of adulthood and for helping adults deal with transitions relevant to their life-cycle changes. For instance, adjusting to marriage, parenthood, or single life are three areas on which counseling groups for adults might focus.

Likewise, group psychotherapy is employed in mental health facilities for adults whether on an inpatient or an outpatient basis (Yalom & Leszcz, 2005). Group therapy on this level is quite important because of its implications for society. Eliminating mental disorders and excessive stress, which impairs the functioning of adults, is crucial to well-being. Support and self-help groups for adults are also quite popular and encompass almost any specific problematic area, especially coping with addiction, abuse, and grief.

In short, adults have greater opportunities than other age groups to participate in groups on all levels. Specific examples of groups for adults are covered in this chapter.

Reflection

What types of groups for adults are you aware of in your community? Which of these groups have you or do you belong to? Which ones are you familiar with because a friend or family member has participated in them?

SETTING UP GROUPS FOR ADULTS

Many of the factors that go into setting up a group for adults were covered in previous chapters and are not repeated here. It should be noted, however, that although it is artificial to divide adult groups based simply on the obvious characteristics of the populations involved, such as age, gender, status, and concerns, it is sometimes helpful or necessary to form adult groups on the basis of such dominant factors. For instance, the primary concerns of young adults (e.g., intimacy, beginning careers) are quite different from those of adults in midlife (e.g., generativity, advancement in careers). If there are specific developmental or situational matters that dominate a group, then these two different age populations may not mix well. Two universal issues to consider in setting up adult groups are themes and needs.

A theme is an important device used in establishing a group. Many groups for adults revolve around issues related to particular interests or concerns in life (themes). For example, psychoeducational, theme-oriented groups for college and university young adults may focus on anything from choosing a career to dealing with loneliness or disabilities (McWhirter, 1995). To be successful, the topic for a theme-based group must reflect a real-life situation that is of interest to participants, include some personalization of information, and teach some behavioral life skills connected with the subject area. In a business or a family group, cohesiveness and the value of teamwork may be important to everyone. It can be taught through adventure-based activities where participants cooperate in order to win games and experience some real or perceived risks in an outdoor setting (Gillis, Gass, & Russell, 2014). Theme groups can also be psychotherapeutic and deal with such matters as chemical dependency or grief (Andrews, 1995).

A second guideline for establishing groups for adults focuses on needs, that is, necessities or obligations. For instance, many adults, such as women who work outside the home, need assistance in overcoming circumstances that limit them. A group that concentrates on overcoming barriers to advancement, such as sexism or gender discrimination, may be particularly useful for such women (Giordano, 1995; Sullivan, 1983b; Szymanski & Owen, 2009). Likewise, for women who work primarily as homemakers, a support group centering on common concerns such as taking care of necessary tasks, raising children, and finding meaning in life may be useful (Olson & Brown, 1986). Groups for other populations with special needs and concerns, such as those with autism, may also prove beneficial to members (Howlin & Yates, 1999).

Overall, in setting up groups for adults, the purpose of the group should be made clear, potential participants should be screened, rules governing the life of the group should be explained, members' rights and expectations should be noted, and the leader's qualifications should be communicated. Furthermore, groups for adults should be sensitive to the diversity within this population, and techniques used in such groups should be appropriate for the life experiences of the members without being forced on them.

Case Example

Lee Lets the Rules Slide By

When he was in the process of setting up an anger management group for men, Lee became busy with other projects as well. Although he screened each potential participant, he did not inform everyone of the rules. Ernesto was one of those. Therefore, when Ernesto lashed out at Greg in a threatening way, he was surprised to be called on the carpet for his actions. He protested to Lee that he had not been told that such behavior would not be tolerated in the group. Lee thought for a moment and realized he had not conveyed the group rules to Ernesto, so he met with him immediately after the group ended to go over this information.

Questions

Given these circumstances, what would you have done differently, if anything, with Ernesto? What are some ways to be sure that vital information is given to all members of a group before the group begins?

ROLE OF THE LEADER IN GROUPS FOR ADULTS

As with other age-span groups, the role of the leader in groups for adults varies according to type, membership, and format (open ended or closed ended) of the group. Leaders of psycho-educational and prevention groups, such as **marriage enrichment** groups (Waring, 1988), must plan carefully what they are going to do and have a solid rationale behind their actions. Their goal is to instruct and help members learn new skills. In counseling and psychotherapy groups, theory must be the driving force behind the behavior of leaders. What leaders do and how they do it come from both a philosophical and a research base connected with the theory they embrace. Task/work groups usually do not have clear expectations of the leader except that he or she will focus on both the process and the outcome of the group (Hulse-Killacky et al., 2001).

In any type of group, the activities used by the leader may be either sequential or non-sequential. Most leaders prefer to work following a sequential pattern because this approach is both developmental and logical. However, when there is a crisis in a group or the group regresses, the leader may appropriately employ nonsequential activities to move the group forward.

The skills leaders will use in groups have been covered previously. Before beginning a group for adults, group workers should make sure that they are familiar with such skills and have mastered them.

STUDIES ON THE OUTCOMES OF GROUPS FOR ADULTS

Just as there are more groups for adults than for any other age or stage, there have been more studies conducted on groups for adults than on any other type of group. In fact, the research on groups for adults is so extensive that it is impossible to generalize the findings. Therefore, for the purposes of this chapter, select groups in the adult age range are singled out as representative of some of the groups in which adults participate. Specific groups covered here are those for college students, for people in midlife, for specific concerns of men and women, for couples and families (both preventive and therapeutic groups), for adult offenders and abusers, and for persons with life-threatening illnesses.

Groups for College Students

Formal and informal groups are found many places on college campuses. Formal and therapeutic groups have consistently been a part of college counseling centers standard practice for decades (Whittingham, 2014). They are usually specialized in regard to the concerns they are set up for, such as eating disorders or anxiety. They are invaluable in helping young adults and continue to be used to reach a large number of students who are struggling with difficult situations in their lives. Because of demand and need, these groups are often time limited, topical, and process oriented (Kincade & Kalodner, 2004). Many issues that college students struggle with, such as a fear of failure, mild depression, self-esteem, weight control, and interpersonal relationship concerns, are well suited for the types of help groups can offer and "are best addressed via group work" (Damer, Latimer, & Porter, 2010, p. 10). The research shows that the most effective groups for college students are those that last from 10 to 12 sessions and that are closed (Keats, 2009).

Millennial students tend to use college counseling centers more frequently and for more severe problems than previous generations. Their top three complaints, however, are similar to the past: anxiety, depression, and relationship problems, in that order (Barr, Rando, Krylowicz, & Reetz, 2011). Groups are well suited for dealing with these issues and can be used in a number of ways for promoting better mental health and adjustment in students with these concerns. For example, Damer and Melendres (2011) found that a 4-week psychoeducation group helped reduce test anxiety. Likewise, Newsome, Waldo, and Gruszka (2012) found that a 6-week mindfulness group with college students planning to entering helping professions (e.g., counseling, teaching, or social work) significantly reduced stress while significantly increasing mindfulness and self-compassion. Groups in higher education institutes have also been used with students as a means of building a stronger sense of community on campus (Taub, 1998a).

Another way groups have been used in higher education environments, which is both preventive and remedial, is to assist young people in separating from their families and in becoming independent adults. Studies show that group counseling based on Virginia Satir's model of treatment has proven effective in enhancing "college students' positive and definite family roles" and improving their relationships with family members (Pan, 2000, p. 316). In addition, family-of-origin groups have been found to help students "leave home" and become more self-sufficient (Mathis & Tanner, 2000; Valdes & McPherson, 1987). The tasks for college students in leaving home for membership in larger communities include "accepting new responsibilities for decision making and caring for physical needs; and mourning the losses in leaving home, for example, parents, friends, and support networks" (Vinson, 1995, p. 240). In family-of-origin groups, students explore the family context from which they came by drawing a type of family tree (a **genogram**) (see Figure 13.1).

Ideally, a genogram will represent three generations in the student's life, but in this case only two generations are represented. By examining the vocational, intergenerational, marital, and relationship patterns of men and women in their families, students can gain insight into the actions of others as well as their own behaviors. In Wendy's situation, she is clearly not measuring up to the standards of her mother and is much less successful in college than her brother. She felt guilt and anxiety about being "less than" the rest of her family. Through construction of her genogram, Wendy was able to see how she was being upset by comparing herself to other family members. Through role playing, rehearsal, feedback, and self-disclosure in a group of other college students who had also constructed genograms, Wendy was able to make positive changes based on her present needs rather than her perceived patterns of inferiority.

Psychoeducational groups may also be helpful to college students. Some of the most common topics include enhancement or building of self-esteem, speech anxiety, depression management,

Dan (father) age 62
Former athlete, successful businessman

Emily (mother) age 59
Former college beauty queen, entrepreneur

Matt (son) age 21
Academic All-American football player

Wendy (daughter) age 19
Average-looking, struggles with math

FIGURE 13.1   Genogram of Wendy's family.

stress management, eating disorders, and academic probation support (Kincade & Kalodner, 2004). Psychoeducational groups have also been used to help freshman student athletes adjust to college life (Harris, Altekruse, & Engels, 2003). In these groups, participants have been able to discuss relevant topics in a safe environment.

For nontraditional adult college students (those outside the 18- to 24-year-old range), psychoeducational groups may be used to help them find information and resources about academic life, obtain emotional support from peers, interact socially, and meet developmental and remedial needs. Such groups are longitudinal in nature and provide both an emphasis on topics of particular concern to these students and emotional support and growth. More limited groups for adult college students can focus on other concerns, such as reentry problems, dealing with spouses or family, and competing successfully in the classroom. At the end of the college experience, a job support group can help these individuals become more easily launched into the job market and find a proper fit between their skills and employers' needs (Arp, Holmberg, & Littrell, 1986). These types of groups meet for a limited time, for example, six sessions, but provide older students a wealth of information about how to set goals, evaluate their assets, use placement centers, write résumés, and conduct themselves in interviews.

Another important and popular topic among college students is becoming more aware of careers and more decisive about an after-college occupation (Niles & Harris-Bowlsbey, 2005).

In career awareness and self-exploration groups, McWhirter, Nichols, and Banks (1984) have found that brief lectures on particular subjects, such as self-disclosure, trust, self-esteem, and communications, combined with small-group interaction, give undergraduates an opportunity to evaluate more carefully what they wish to do vocationally. Transition-to-work groups, a psychoeducational type of group, may also be used with university students who have learning disabilities (McWhirter & McWhirter, 1996). In this five-session group, resources available to group members are emphasized, including ways to communicate about disability issues, marketing oneself, legal issues regarding employment, and practical ways of compensating for one's disabilities.

Phelps and Luke (1995) have reported that a structured counseling group for excessively self-critical university and college students works well. This type of group is set up to meet for 2 hours each week for 6 weeks and to include between 8 and 12 participants. Each session builds on the one before it and is interactive in nature, combining a mini-lecture with a group activity. Co-leaders are recommended for such groups. Group workers who wish to use such a format should be familiar with both cognitive strategies and Gestalt therapy because many of the activities for helping in this group are based on these two approaches.

Another group that has been found to be effective is for college students who are shy. This group was advertised as a "clinic" to minimize any implication of psychopathology. The 14-week, behavioral/cognitive-oriented group emphasized learning to be more relaxed in social situations; developing new behaviors (social skills) in a safe, supportive setting; identifying and changing self-defeating habits of thinking; understanding the dynamics of shyness; and realizing that a person can be both shy and happy (Martin & Thomas, 2000).

Psychotherapeutic types of groups for college students that have been found useful are groups for adult children of alcoholics (ACoAs). These students are more prone than other students to suffer anxiety, depression, substance abuse, and psychosomatic disorders as a result of growing up in a home in which one or both parents were alcoholics (Harman & Withers, 1992). These types of groups are usually structured so that potential group members will feel safe and be able to address issues readily.

Yet, other types of groups commonly found in college environments include those for students who are survivors of sexual abuse, homesick, suffering grief or loss, or concerned about their sexual orientation, or for those who wish to explore health issues more deeply. Yet, other counseling and therapy groups found in college environments are those focused on various cultural/ethnic heritages, general personal growth, health/wellness issues, and sexual assault recovery. Generally, there seems to be a group for most concerns students bring to campus (Kincade & Kalodner, 2004; Niles & Harris-Bowlsbey, 2005).

To assess the needs of all persons in campus communities, college officials may use a *nominal-group technique* (a structured small-group process). In such a procedure, five to nine people from different campus settings identify specific issues related to the mental health and personal needs of students, faculty members, and staff (Skibbe, 1986). Ideas are written down and discussed in a round-robin format with minimal attention devoted to relationships among group members. Ideas are then prioritized and sometimes discussed, reranked, and even voted on. The session takes 45 to 90 minutes, after which the group is disbanded and the members are thanked for their participation. Although this group procedure does not lend itself to statistical analysis and may not yield a representative sample of opinion, it is an enjoyable process for those involved and a fairly quick and efficient way for counselors to obtain a good idea of major issues within the campus community.

Reflection

How did you adjust to college as either a traditional or nontraditional student? What groups, on a formal or informal basis, helped you, such as resident life hall meetings or friends with similar interests? Were you to go through the experience again, what types of groups would you recommend to the administration of your university?

Groups for Adults in Midlife

Many types of groups are available for adults in midlife (ages 40 to 65). Most, outside of task/ work groups, are psychoeducational and preventive (geared toward learning and wellness) or counseling and psychotherapeutic (focused toward making choices or changes). Some of the groups mentioned in this section may be used by individuals of almost any age, but they especially tend to attract midlife adults. Brown (2011) notes that adults are much more prone than children or adolescents to participate in psychoeducational groups (and other types of groups). The reason is because adults more often have specific objectives or learning that they expect from groups. In addition, they have life experiences that add to the richness of groups, and they are task focused. Some examples of the impact that groups have made in the lives of adults are as follows.

Bisio and Crisan (1984) used a 1-day group workshop with adults to focus on nuclear anxiety and hidden stress in life. They emphasized principles of Viktor Frankl's (1962) logo- therapy and helped participants create a renewed sense of hope and purpose in life. Members of this group did not desire or need counseling, yet the group was therapeutic in addressing an area of immediate concern.

Historically, all types of experiential activity groups have reported a wide range of specific gains for adult participants in such areas as increased self-esteem, self-efficacy, and social com- petence (Hatch & McCarthy, 2003). An interesting, interdisciplinary, long-term, positive-wellness model of such a group for self-selected adults (16 weeks) is the **jogging group** (Childers & Burcky, 1984). This approach is based on the premise that physical exercise is an important ele- ment that contributes to people's abilities to perform better in all areas of life. In the jogging group, an hour of exercise in the form of walking, jogging, or running is combined with another hour of group process. The group is co-led by a counselor and a health facilitator (a physician or an exercise physiologist) and follows Lazarus's (1976, 1981) multimodal *BASIC ID* concept, which focuses on behavior, affect, sensation, imagery, cognition, interpersonal relationships, and drugs/biological factors. Jogging seems to speed up the group's developmental growth just as other active outdoor experiences often do. The result is a greater awareness of self, a lowering of defenses, and a transfer and investment of physical and psychological energy into the group.

Case Example

Janelle Takes Her Group on a Hike

Janelle was charged by her supervisor to set up a group for depressive adults. She knew something about the effects of depression and how people who suffer with it are often lethargic. Janelle was aware,

too, that a traditional group format might not be ideal for such a group.

Therefore, Janelle decided to alter the format of her group from one that was predominantly talk oriented to one that was a combination of walk and talk focused. Because all of her members were mobile, she greeted them each week in tennis shoes (and they were instructed to wear the same). They then took a half-hour walk in a nearby park. Janelle altered the pace and route of the walk each time so that it was different. Her members at first groused a bit, but as the group progressed they seemed to not only grow accustomed to the format but look forward to it. Best of all, most reported progress in coping with their depression, and some put themselves on a regular exercise routine.

Questions

When have you seen exercise be helpful and how? What other activities might be incorporated into groups for depressives? In groups for the overly anxious?

A common developmental and situational reality for adults in all walks of life is loss and grief. In working through loss, adults must accomplish four tasks related to the mourning process. Initially, they must accept the reality of the loss and then experience the pain that comes with loss. Next, they must adjust to their new environment while withdrawing emotionally from the lost relationship and reinvesting their emotional energy elsewhere (Worden, 1991). In facilitating a grieving and loss group, a closed-ended group counseling or group psychotherapy model that lasts for 2-hour sessions over 16 weeks is recommended by Price, Dinas, Dunn, and Winterowd (1995). In such a group, participants have enough time to work through their sorrow and display what Yalom describes as a therapeutic factor—"altruism" (support, reassurance, suggestions, and insight)—to other group members. In grief groups, members who keep a journal of their experiences work through their situations best.

For adults who have grown up in families in which at least one parent abused alcohol, heterogeneous groups can be empowering, especially if they are based on Yalom's therapeutic factors of altruism, imitative behavior, and corrective recapitulation of the family dynamic (Corazzini, Williams, & Harris, 1987; Harris, 1996). Such psychotherapeutic groups allow **adult children of alcoholics (ACoAs)** to question and change any of the four common behavioral roles (hero, scapegoat, lost child, and mascot) that they tended to play out to survive the instability, confusion, and fear they experienced growing up (Wegscheider, 1981). These roles are based on general systems theory and served as protection and defense against perceived and emotional or physical threat when the ACoA was young. Harris (1996) has developed a model based on interpersonal theory that depicts ACoA role behavior along two dimensions: control and affiliation. In this model, which can be informative for group leaders, two levels of behavior are depicted through the use of adjectives and descriptors. Level 1 behavior is the most healthy and flexible, being essentially nonpathological. Level 2 behavior is extreme and rigid. It is the type of behavior most written about in the ACoA literature and is diagnosable. By understanding this model, group leaders are less likely to stereotype and more likely to play to the strengths of ACoA members.

Because families with addicts tend to be rather isolated (Conyers, 2003; Steinglass, Bennett, Wolin, & Reiss, 1993), an extended system of group support is invaluable for ACoAs who wish to continue their growth toward more functional behavior. These individuals need help in learning to break the three rules that Black (1981) has identified as being universal for them: (a) do not trust, (b) do not talk, and (c) do not feel. Corazzini et al. (1987) recommend that groups of this nature work best when they are conducted in an open-ended versus a closed-ended format. Whitfield (1987) further notes that "many clinicians who work with ACoAs or other troubled or dysfunctional families believe that group psychotherapy is the major choice for recovery work" (p. 142). Such work should be combined with a psychoeducational approach to the dynamics related to addiction, dysfunction, and recovery as well as individual and family counseling.

Groups may also be used to help grown-ups who were abused as children (Courtois & Leehan, 1982; Gitterman & Shulman, 2005). *Victims of abuse* (whether physical, psychological, sexual, or neglect) have a number of common characteristics, such as low self-esteem, self-blame, unresolved anger, and an inability to trust. Groups help them share their stories with others and feel emotional relief. In addition, group members can help one another focus on resolving present, problematic behaviors that would be difficult to do individually. "The sharing and empathy derived from common experiences and reactions, as well as the analysis of the interactions between members, are of great therapeutic value" (Courtois, 1988, p. 244). In short, **groups for victims of abuse** help them break the cycle of isolation so common to this population and interrelate in a healthy, dynamic way. "Many survivors come to view the group as a new family in which they are reparented as they help to reparent others" (Courtois, 1988, p. 247). No more than six members should be included in such groups to give everyone adequate "airtime."

Another counseling group that helps adults break out of isolation and resolve grief issues is a **group for survivors of suicide** (Gross & Shakespeare-Finch, 2013; Robinson, 2001). The process of grieving is more difficult for survivors of a suicide death "because death in these cases is usually sudden, unanticipated, untimely, often violent, and subject to stigmatization by the community" (Moore & Freeman, 1995, p. 40). A group for survivors of suicide emphasizes the importance of universality, imparting information and instilling hope, catharsis, and self-disclosure, as well as broader meaning-making processes surrounding acceptance or adjustment. The group comprises feeling normal within the group, providing a sense of permission to feel and to express emotions and thoughts and to bestow meaning. A group of this type is recommended to include 8 to 10 participants, selected after prescreening. It should be structured, closed-ended, and time limited. Groups for survivors of suicide can be conducted on a self-help and support group basis as well as a formal basis.

Two other types of trauma groups are **critical incident stress debriefing (CISD) groups** (Mitchell & Everly, 1993; Tuckey & Scott, 2014) and **solution-focused debriefing (SFD) groups** (Juhnke & Osborne, 1997). The purpose of both of these groups is to help victims of violence deal with its repercussions, such as feelings of helplessness, anxiety, depression, and disorganization. The CISD is "a structured, one-session small group experience comprising seven stages: introduction, fact, thought, reaction, symptom, teaching and reentry" (Mitchell & Everly, 1993, p. 67). It usually lasts 1 to 3 hours and is led by a minimum of three trained group members. Psychoeducational information is given to group participants about posttraumatic stress disorder (PTSD) symptoms so that they can recognize and get treatment for this disorder if necessary. Before and after the CISD, group members and facilitators mingle together informally for light refreshment so that they can get to know one another better and assess any areas that might need more attention.

The SFD group is similar to the CISD in its emphasis on a specific distressing incident, focus on the here-and-now, seven-stage format, inclusion of only persons who have witnessed the same violent episode, and the expertise of its leaders in postcrisis symptoms. However, the SFD is conducted over 3 weeks and enhances recovery through an extended group process. Also, following solution-focused theory, the SFD asks its participants to identify times when they are not encountering symptoms or reacting to the violence they witnessed. In addition, group members are encouraged to continue seeing themselves improving and identify what they need to do to keep improving.

Three final types of groups for adults in midlife that are psychoeducational and psychotherapeutic in nature are those that center on careers (Brown, 2012). Such groups give direct emotional support to their members, providing them with a place to release feelings and educating or reeducating them for a career. For example, in a qualitative research study, Kondo (2009) compared the experiences of two groups of executive job seekers—job club members and nonmembers. His findings indicated that job club members "benefited from group learning, increased accountability, networking opportunities, emotional support, helping other members, and enhanced understanding of the context of their experiences. Job club members also enjoyed lower levels of frustration with the search process, used a wider range of outplacement firm services, and devoted more time on average to job search activities" (p. 27).

Groups may also be a viable option for relatives of the jobless (Bauman, 2009). Often family members of the unemployed do not realize or understand the dynamics surrounding the loss or search for employment. They may feel isolated and embarrassed as well. Groups that specialize in working with this population go a long way in alleviating intrapersonal and interpersonal stress and conflict in regard to career searches and employment dynamics.

Three types of career groups are especially prominent: career change groups (Zimpfer & Carr, 1989), career support groups (Giordano, 1995), and job support or career transition groups (Dagley & Calhoun, 2014; Riordan & Kahnweiler, 1996). **Career change groups** help participants sort out the reasons for pursuing a new career and whether some alternative course of action may be healthier for them. These groups are especially relevant for middle-aged adults, particularly those at the middle-management level, who are thinking of the best ways to advance in their careers by changing their jobs. Persons who usually consider such a strategy have a number of personal characteristics such as an elevated motivation to achieve; a steady and successful work record; a high need for advancement, career challenge, and individual satisfaction; a positive self-image; a high energy level; and a sense of limited chances for advancement in their present position (Campbell & Cellini, 1980). They may also face increased pressure for different behavior from their spouses (McCullough & Rutenberg, 1988). An effective career change group is holistic in nature, exploring personal as well as professional aspects of individuals' lives.

Likewise, **career support groups** are geared toward life-span issues of work, particularly women's work issues. "In general, women often find themselves in work situations in which they believe that their skills and abilities are underused, their pay and status are low, and few opportunities for advancement seem to exist" (Giordano, 1995, p. 5). In these situations, a support group that helps women develop successful coping mechanisms for the difficulties they encounter in their work environments is appropriate. Such a group is aimed at increasing women's feelings of self-efficacy by offering them "information to develop more effective self-care skills, offering them opportunities to perceive their qualities and strengths, and offering them validation of their current experiences" (p. 6).

Finally, there are a variety of **job support groups**, or career transition groups, as they are sometimes called (Riordan & Kahnweiler, 1996). These groups, which are proactive and developmental, are set up for people who have lost their jobs and need emotional support, who want to learn how to achieve career goals, or who are unemployed and are emotionally struggling with the stigma, shame, and isolation of their situations. They "can serve each member as a vehicle for acquiring new information, for developing job-hunt strategies, and for developing new interpersonal and interview skills" (Dagley & Calhoun, 2014, p. 545). In addition, at their best, career transition groups provide each person with opportunities to observe role models and with individualized test interpretation.

In all of these types of groups, clients' experiences are likely to be positive because the specific kind of support offered is geared toward their needs.

Groups for Men and Women

Men and women share many common concerns and objectives as adults. For example, "autonomy and attachment are functional adult goals, in love and work, for both men and women" (Aylmer, 1988, p. 192). Both genders also share some general experiences such as learning how to balance life demands. Thus, in some cases mixed-gender groups are not only appropriate but productive. For instance, a psychoeducational group for male and female survivors of childhood abuse and neglect, during the later stages of their recovery, may benefit both men and women as they learn different perspectives and insights from opposite-gender members (Choate & Henson, 2003).

Yet, socialization patterns dramatically influence the ways men and women perceive themselves and how they function in society (Bata, 2006; Eaves & Sheperis, 2011). Prescribed roles dictated by society often affect men and women negatively. Therefore, in many cases gender-specific groups may be more appropriate and give men and women a safe place to explore new frontiers of their personal, economic, and social development (Gonzalez-Lopez & Taylor, 1997; Singh & Hofsess, 2011).

GROUPS FOR MEN

> From hunting parties in early civilization to Cub Scouts, Little League, fraternities, and work in modern life, men have often found themselves in the company of each other. In these same-sex groups, they have competed as well as supported and worked with each other toward common goals such as hunting for food, winning a game, bringing success to a company, or fighting a war. (Rabinowitz, 2005, p. 264)

However, there is a dearth of materials and research on working in groups with men, especially among racial minorities (Stark-Rose, Livingston-Sacin, Merchant, & Finley, 2012). It has only been since the 1970s that groups for men have developed as a useful treatment modality to address their needs.

One of the first types of groups specifically for men was the all-male **consciousness-raising (C-R) group** (Garfield, 2010). The C-R groups became popular at a time of turmoil and rapid change and paralleled one of the peaks of the women's movement. These groups did not maintain their popularity, yet variations of them remain today in other forms of men's groups that are theme related. In essence the C-R group "broke the ice" in making it more acceptable for men to work in groups. Thus, today's groups for men are a viable way of helping men begin to see how they have been affected by limited culturally prescribed roles and how they have inhibited their own growth by following these roles, suppressing their emotions, and avoiding taking care of themselves medically and mentally (Evans, 2013; Kiselica & Kiselica, 2014).

The result is that a diverse set of group formats are now applicable for helping men with their specific needs (Heppner, 1981; Rabinowitz, 2005). For instance, support and psychoeducational groups for single, custodial fathers have been implemented and found to be effective. One study (Tedder, Scherman, & Sheridan, 1984) revealed that men who participate in *custodial father support group* meetings make more changes in the desirable direction of learning how to take better care of their children and themselves than those who do not. A commonality of experience and purpose unites these individuals and leads to greater cohesion more quickly than is usually the case in groups for men.

Groups can help men in identifying personal and general concerns of being male and ways of constructively dealing with issues and problems they face. For example, through groups, men can learn to resolve gender role conflicts and manage **polarities** (two interrelated, interdependent, opposite poles, such as career and family) instead of inappropriately trying to solve them through either–or choices or partner abuse (Hurst & Vanderveen, 1994; Schwartz & Waldo, 2003). Groups can also help men become more attuned to the realities of their worlds, such as problems ranging from stress to self-denial (Kiselica & Kiselica, 2014; Rabinowitz, 2005; DeAngelis, 1992). Furthermore, groups can help men integrate and appreciate both their masculine and feminine sides and realize more fully the transformational aspect of their lives. As O'Neil and Egan (1992) have shown, at least 30 gender role transitions arise for some men over their life span. These "role transitions are interactive and not mutually exclusive. This means that changes in one may affect the other" (p. 312).

> ### Reflection
>
> Not all men go through the same stages in life. Do men, as a group, have common stages regardless of lifestyle? If so, what are they? If not, why not?

Getting men to participate in groups, although usually beneficial, has often been difficult. One hindrance involves myths and misconceptions about men, groups, and men in groups (Garfield, 2010). For instance, some men and some group workers believe that "men don't emote," "all men's groups are really anger groups," "men are too competitive to be supportive of each other in a group," "men aren't interested in meeting with other men," and "only male liberals have a need to express their feelings with other men." Another drawback is the belief that traditional sex-role stereotypes keep men from even thinking about being in a group. For instance, "most men still feel the pressure of fulfilling the three P's: Provider, Protector, and Procreator" (Andronico & Horne, 2004, p. 457) and fall back on their traditional roles as being independent, self-reliant, competitive, achievement oriented, and loners. Therefore, they do not think of joining a group outside of one that they may already be in, such as a team or a service group.

However, men are likely to participate in groups if the myths and sex role limitations can be addressed productively and if they are sure the group will be a safe experience. It also helps if groups for men are set up in certain ways, such as being theme oriented and psychoeducational at least initially. For example, Gearing, Colvin, Popova, and Regehr (2008) designed a theme group for men wanting to improve their fathering experience. The starting point for the group was the idea that fathers have a valuable and nurturing role to play in the lives of their children. Rather than teaching a specific set of parenting skills, the group relied on members' own resources and the collected wisdom of the group on what it meant to be a father. The result as demonstrated by standardized measures was a significant improvement for fathers and their participation within their families on a number of roles and an increased sense of self-esteem, competence, and decreased stress in parenting. Likewise, Smiley (2004) describes a group for gay men newly diagnosed with HIV/AIDS. Such a specialized group negates the social isolation of those afflicted and offers them support, a sense of family, and a source for healing. Groups centered around themes such as work, marriage, aging, and retirement are attractive to men as a group because they do not expose them to expressing their feelings before other groups of men, they are usually time limited, and they may involve rituals.

Other approaches to working with men in groups include using mixed-sex groups to help men receive more varied input on who they are and what they are experiencing as males (DeAngelis, 1992). This information is compared with other group members, especially females. Groups contribute to the interpersonal growth of men, too, and help sanction the employment of unused skills, such as emotions. For instance, Garfield (2010) has found that when men's groups emphasize core attributes of friendship (connection, communication, commitment, and cooperation) that contribute to emotional intimacy in men's relationships, the behaviors associated with these attributes spill over into other domains such as marriage.

Men often participate in groups through telling stories or using humor and metaphors (Kilmartin, 2014; McKelley, 2014). Therefore, group leaders may need to encourage some men to tell their stories, use their humor, or talk in metaphors to help them to interact with others (A. Horne, 1999). The men's movement, exemplified in the mythopoetic approach of Bly (1990), can be a powerful adjunct to traditional therapeutic groups for men because it encompasses the telling of stories. As a movement, "**mythopoetic** refers to a process of ceremony, drumming, storytelling/poetry reading, physical movement, and imagery exercises designed to create a 'ritual process.' Through this process, the participants explore individually and in groups their intuitive sense of masculinity, which differs from socially mediated male gender roles" (Williams & Myer, 1992, p. 395). They strive first to be personally authentic and to nurture society with their integrity. One way of conceptualizing these groups is as support groups that emphasize both the psychological and the spiritual aspects of growth (Guarnaschelli, 1994).

Overall, groups for men help participants observe new role models and practice what they learn within a safe environment. When leaders use social learning principles, men in groups increase their levels of effective expressiveness and ultimately their flexibility and overall functioning. Many men do best in groups when they have a chance to participate in a physical or mental exercise before the group's work actually begins. Therefore, specific exercises for this population have been developed. Overall, "working with men in groups has been identified as one of the most powerful and effective means of addressing the issues being faced by men today" (Andronico & Horne, 2004, p. 456).

GROUPS FOR WOMEN

"The evolution of women's groups in the United States can be traced to the consciousness-raising groups of the 1960s and 1970s" (S. Horne, 1999, p. 232). At first, all-women groups were controversial. However, women's groups have become an increasingly popular therapeutic avenue to help women with issues that confront them, such as substance abuse, domestic partner violence, sexual assault, and poverty (Kees & Leech, 2014). The formats vary from support and general therapy groups to groups that focus on specific concerns (McManus, Redford, & Hughes, 1997, p. 2). Nevertheless, "there is not a 'typical' women's group, nor are there 'typical' women's issues" (Leech & Kees, 2005, p. 367).

When working with diverse groups of women, counselors must understand their own and their clients' unique characteristics, experiences and beliefs, the beliefs and influences of the groups of which they are members, and the universal aspects of being human (Kees & Leech, 2014). For example, when doing group counseling with South Asian women in regard to intimate partner violence, group leaders must realize that these women may be treated as outcasts once they divulge what has happened to them because of the cultural emphasis on maintaining the primacy of the family image (Singh & Hays, 2008). However, the same is not true with women who are European American and who have experienced intimate domestic violence. Instead, they may be open to a number of different types of interventions including joining a group designed to foster career development (Chronister & Davidson, 2010).

There are some issues, such as dealing with chemical dependency or empowerment, in which women do better in women-only treatment groups (Kauffman, Dore, & Nelson-Zlupko, 1995; Singh & Hofsess, 2011). Evidence also supports that group psychotherapy and online peer support groups are effective in improving the quality of life of women with physical conditions most commonly found in women, such as breast cancer (Gore-Felton & Spiegel, 1999; Lieberman, 2007). Support groups for women who have particular concerns, such as issues facing working mothers, may be beneficial, too (Morgan & Hensley, 1998). Although women's groups have addressed topics as diverse as spirituality and community change, some of the most focused issues in groups for women center around sexual abuse, relationships, healthy self-concept, anger, and work. Each is briefly explored here with two considerations in mind: (1) "there is considerable room for improvement in the research process for women's groups" (Leech & Kees, 2005, p. 371), and (2) groups can provide "a special environment in which women may resocialize themselves" (Sullivan, 1983a, p. 4).

In regard to sexual abuse, women who are victims of sexual assaults can form or join sexual abuse or **rape survivors' groups** to help them recover from sexual trauma. These groups take several forms but often are conducted as group psychotherapy and counseling (Bass & Davis, 2008; Eaves & Sheperis, 2011). In a psychotherapy or group counseling setting, survivors of sexual abuse can vent their feelings and construct a new cognitive framework or gain a new perception of the abuse. The social interaction of the group can also reduce their feelings of isolation, aloneness, and shame. The results of such groups have been positive and encouraging. For example, Sprei and Goodwin (1983) found that women from ages 18 to 60 who had been raped were able to decrease their sense of isolation and stigma while learning to model effective coping strategies. The group they set up was open ended and addressed issues related to information, anger, feelings of helplessness, and rape trauma. The group offered support to these women in the midst of crisis and helped them "explore behaviors, attitudes, and life choices" (p. 45). A variation of this type of group, combining rape and incest victims, has also worked well over an 8-week, 2-hour session format (Sharma & Cheatham, 1986). In both cases, learning new coping behaviors was stressed. Likewise, a closed, highly structured, adventure-based group for women who self-identified as having been abused in any way proved effective (Kelly, 2006). Although the group purported to be psychoeducational, it had a healing and growth component that came through processes connected with wilderness survival.

Another survivor's group based on feminist principles was found to be effective as well. In this group, each woman was treated as an expert regarding her own life, and egalitarian relationships between members and the group leader were fostered (Rittenhouse, 1997). In comparing group therapy for incest survivors, Randall (1995) found that "incest group members consistently value cohesiveness and self-understanding" (p. 237). The reason is probably that cohesiveness is associated with trust, belonging, and connectedness, whereas self-understanding has to do with historical and situational relationships with one's family of origin. In line with these two top factors, incest groups consistently ranked Yalom's therapeutic factors of identification, guidance, altruism, and interpersonal learning as low. The reason may be the self-absorbed perspective that most incest survivors take in a group.

Regardless, the success of abuse and particularly sexual abuse, psychotherapy, and counseling groups has had a positive spillover effect in society at large. For example, from these groups have sprung psychoeducational groups for young women to prevent date violence (Rosen & Bezold, 1996). To bring the subject of incest and rape before the general public's attention, both women and men have formed task/work groups. In these groups, programs have been developed on local community levels to combat demeaning and dehumanizing sexual behaviors. The impact has been pervasive, and such public figures as cartoonist Mort Walker, the creator of the comic strip "Beetle Bailey," have done something positive in regard to sexual abuse and harassment. Walker, for example, no longer draws General Halftrack chasing Miss Buxley. He has concluded that such behavior is inappropriate and should not be condoned, even in jest.

Relationship groups for women have also been found to be useful (Kees, 1999; McManus et al., 1997; Pearson, 1988). In relationship groups, the focus is on breaking out of the dependency and caretaking roles in which women often find themselves and connecting with oneself and others in a healthy and growth-producing way (Maass, 2006). Emphasis is placed on being in relationships where one's own needs as well as others' needs are met. The groups are often short term and goal oriented but can be long term and continued for the purpose of support and friendship. They sometimes revolve around themes, such as creating a better self-concept, boundary setting, and enhancing communication and relationship skills. The benefits of participation include forming new friends, expressing emotions, and changing destructive patterns.

People with eating disorders present a unique challenge to group workers. Participants must be prepared properly before their group experience, or they will drop out because of "their feelings of shame, their poor communication skills, and their avoidance of intimacy or commitment" (Cummins, 1996, p. 8). Attention to the composition and the establishment of healthy norms are important to group success and client growth as well, for "eating disorder groups often gravitate toward the needs of the 'sickest' member" (Wanlass, Moreno, & Thomson, 2005, pp. 64–65).

Eating disorders groups for women who have obsessive and distorted ideas in regard to thinness and body image may take several forms (Cook-Cottone, Beck, & Kane, 2008; Cummins, 1996; Gerstein & Hotelling, 1987; Kalodner, Coughlin, & Seide, 2014). They may be geared toward self-help or support, or they may be manually instructed. Each form of eating disorders group has strengths and limitations in regard to dynamics and recovery. Self-help groups by themselves, however, do not seem to deal adequately with the complex nature of eating disorders (Enright, Butterfield, & Berkowitz, 1985).

Participation in any of these groups can assist individuals in demystifying the nature of eating disorders. Often, relatively short-term treatment (4 months) can alter participants' behaviors and help them develop more effective coping mechanisms. "A group therapy program combining therapeutic orientations (psychodynamic, group process, and feminist)" can increase "the independence, ego strength, degree of personal control, and ability of bulimic women to form healthy interpersonal relationships" (Gerstein & Hotelling, 1987, p. 172). In addition, recent research indicates that an integrative mind, body, and relationship group intervention is powerful in the treatment of both bulimia and anorexia eating disorders (Gerrity & DeLucia-Waack, 2007; Cook-Cottone et al., 2008; Wanlass et al., 2005).

Groups dealing with women's anger have taken a number of forms throughout the years. Many have explored the nature of anger and focused on controlling it. In a women and anger group, Juntunen, Cohen, and Wolszon (1997) used a short-term (eight-session), structured, **theme group** (a psychoeducational, counseling, or psychotherapy group that focuses on a particular problem or theme) to help women understand and acknowledge the role anger has played in their lives and "to develop broader choices" in how they express anger (p. 98). The researchers found that the format for the group and its length were not satisfactory for women who wanted quick help for explosive or acting-out types of anger. However, women who had difficulty acknowledging or identifying anger seemed to benefit from the group experience, especially in hearing other women talk about anger in ways to which they could relate and in going through structured role-play activities that assisted them in recognizing, understanding, and working with their anger.

Case Example

Amy Confronts Her Anger

Having been abused throughout her life and into her marriage, Amy decided to join a counseling group. She was not sure what to do, though. She had always stuffed her feelings inside, and letting them out she found to be easier said than done. Gloria, the leader of her all-women's group, encouraged her to not sit passively by but to model after some of the other women in the group whom she saw getting better.

Amy did just that. She saw that Jeanette seemed to be getting better and that Jeanette was vocal in expressing her emotions without going overboard.

Jeanette was not afraid to cry, either. Thus, through modeling Amy became more comfortable in expressing her feelings about the abuse she had received from a number of sources. After the group ended, she joined another similarly focused group because she felt she still had issues with which she needed to deal.

Questions

What does Amy's behavior tell you about the developmental nature of people and groups? What else might you have done to help Amy had you been her leader, Gloria?

Groups for Couples, Families, the Divorced, the Widowed, and the Remarried

Couples, families, and those who are divorced, widowed, or recently remarried face many stresses. Psychoeducational, counseling, and psychotherapy groups are especially popular for persons in these circumstances.

PARENT EDUCATION GROUPS

One of the major concerns of many adults is parenting. Most adults who become parents do not receive any training in how to parent and have to learn how to work with children on a trial-and-error basis (Campbell & Palm, 2003). In addition, "today's parents are raising children under social conditions decidedly different from those that the parents experienced as children" (White & Mullis, 1997, p. 47). To help parents acquire knowledge and evaluate their beliefs and attitudes, **parent education groups** were organized beginning in the late 1800s by the Child Study Association of America (Resnick, 1981). These groups initially focused on a discussion-oriented format about the needs of parents (usually mothers) and children. However, parent education groups are now considered "a form of consultation in which the consultant (leader) is assisting the consultee (parent) by teaching effective child-rearing techniques" (White & Riordan, 1990, p. 201).

Literally dozens of parenting program groups operate around the world (Li, 2009). In these groups, single parents or couples work to develop healthy strategies for dealing with each other and their children as the family develops. Some of these parenting programs include those for abusive and neglectful parents, adoptive parents, foster parents, minority group parents, single parents, and parents of children with special needs (LeMasters & DeFrain, 1989). Most take an eclectic approach and train their leaders to understand and promote positive group dynamics to bring about constructive changes in parent–child and family interactions.

Regardless of the approach followed, White and Riordan (1990) state that there are common aspects to all parent education groups. For instance, parents are "usually sensitive to almost any issue that relates to their relationship with their child" (p. 205). They are also initially resistant to change. When directing a parent education group, a leader is wise to anticipate issues that parents might raise and to be prepared to address these concerns in a productive manner. For example, parents will frequently inquire about the use of physical punishment (spanking), the importance of heredity in determining behavior, gender role appropriateness, religious beliefs as a basis for parenting, peer influences, guilt over parental decisions, and feelings about school. Effective parent education group leaders use nontechnical language in working with parents. They also thoroughly explain and demonstrate suggested interventions and accept differences in participants' backgrounds and values (Miller & Hudson, 1994). Overall, parents are best served in parenting groups when they are listened to, helped to sort through their options, and newly empowered to make decisions regarding their children. Innovative methods, such as the use of sand trays, may be used with parents who have major therapeutic concerns such as coping with adolescent substance abuse or depression (James & Martin, 2002).

Reflection

What do children and parents have to learn to cope with today that was not true 20 years ago? What community or virtual groups either help or hinder the development of relationships in parent–child interactions? If you were going to start a group for parents today, what would be its emphasis? Explain.

COUPLES AND FAMILY GROUP THERAPY

Couples group therapy began in the 1970s and has had an uneven history (Gladding, 2015; Piercy, Sprenkle, & Wetchler, 1996). Proponents of couple group therapy list its many advantages, including (a) identification by group members of appropriate and inappropriate behaviors and expectations by others, (b) development of insight and skills through observing other couples, (c) group feedback and support for the ventilation of feelings and changed behavior, and (d) reduced cost.

Framo (1981) recommends that couples group therapy be used when preparing couples to do family-of-origin work, in which they meet with their families and work through difficulties not resolved in childhood. Couples groups are limited to three couples in this approach, all of whom have some similarity in background. Ohlsen (1979) includes five couples in his groups, as does Abraham (2010). The belief is that having this number of couples makes the group easier to handle and provides an enriched learning environment for members.

Hendrix (1988) also uses five or more couples in his workshops, which are known as **imago (image) relationship therapy**, an eclectic approach that includes elements of psychoanalysis, transactional analysis, Gestalt psychology, cognitive therapy, and systems theory. Hendrix's approach, popularized in his book *Getting the Love You Want,* is the most structured of the couples group therapies and has revived interest in psychotherapy workshops for couples. Hendrix suggests that couples go through specific exercises in a uniform manner and encourages observation of others and participation by the individual couple.

Multiple-family group therapy (MFGT) involves treating several families together at the same time with an explicit focus on problems or concerns shared by all of the families in attendance (Baltimore, 1997; Homrich & Horne, 1997). Among other aspects of MFGT is that it has been proven as an evidence-based intervention for treating persons with severe mental illness, particularly schizophrenia, and their families. It integrates psychoeducation and behavioral family therapy together (Stuart & Schlosser, 2009). MFGT is probably the most demanding form of group work and requires its leaders to have a solid working knowledge of both group and family theories. MFGT approaches usually use co-leaders to handle the complex dynamics associated with working with so many individuals at once.

This approach has many of the same advantages that couples group therapy has, including the fact that families can often serve as co-therapists for each other (Piercy et al., 1996). "Multifamily group counseling models are becoming more popular because they enable counselors to address the concerns of many people of various developmental levels in a time-efficient process" (Sayger, 1996, p. 81). **High-risk families** (e.g., those prone to violence) and **families in high-risk environments** (e.g., those living in neighborhoods prone to violence) may especially benefit from such groups. The reason is that these groups provide "an opportunity to build a sense of community and social support, to create conditions that aid in the development of resilient children, and to empower families to use more functional strategies in their lives" (Sayger, 1996, p. 81). Another benefit of multiple-family group models is that they may function in many ways (e.g., psychoeducational, task-oriented, counseling/psychotherapeutically focused).

GROUPS FOR THE DIVORCED AND THE WIDOWED

The divorced and the widowed can best make use of groups in the process of working through their pain and the challenges they face living alone (Davidson, 2006). In groups specifically designed to deal with their situations, the divorced and the widowed can share experiences with one another as well as obtain emotional support, receive feedback on their perceptions and behaviors, gain advice and information on dealing with problems, and get tangible assistance

(Addington, 1992; DiGiulio, 1992). One model of a specific group for those who have separated has been devised by Addington (1992), who focuses the group on both the emotional impact and the emotional response of such an experience. The **emotional impact of separation** includes dealing with loss, putting the separation in perspective, becoming aware of the limited value of searching for causes of the separation, becoming more cognizant of systems interactions (e.g., family, work, social network), using the past as a guide to the future, and moving from a dyadic to a monadic identity. The **emotional response of separation** focuses on continuing relationships with an ex-spouse; recognizing the influence of the separation on family, friends, and children; working and dating; and sexual adjustment.

Outside of structured groups offered by professionals, most *groups for the divorced and the widowed* tend to be of a psychoeducational or self-help nature. **Parents Without Partners (PWP)** is probably the best known and most organized of such groups on a national level. PWP offers a variety of activities to its members, including interest groups, educational presentations and discussions, and recreational and social activities. Members and their children become linked to one another through these formal and informal group activities.

Case Example

David Deals with His Divorce

David was seeing Walter for the pain he was continuing to incur even though he had been divorced for 2 years. Walter suggested he join a divorce group that Walter led, in the hope that the group would be of more help to him than Walter could be alone.

David was skeptical, but he agreed to try the group for four sessions. What happened amazed him. He found out that others were having similar struggles even though they had been divorced

longer. He also found out that there were informal support groups he could join if he wanted. In short, David found out he was not alone. The more he talked in the group, the better he felt.

Questions

Why do you think David was skeptical of the group at first? What do you think happened that helped David begin to move on in his life? What other things not mentioned in this brief case do you think might be helpful for David?

GROUPS FOR REMARRIEDS

Remarrieds, that is, stepfamilies, are one of the three most common types of families in North America (nuclear and single-parent families being the other two). Yet, blended families are especially vulnerable during their first 3 years. Therefore, a psychoeducational, closed, multicouple group intervention that focuses on enrichment is an excellent way to help such families stabilize, grow, and constructively face future challenges. Michaels (2006) has proposed a six-session group for these families using a format that emphasizes developmental, nurturing, and strengthening bonds in these families through didactic and experiential methods. Group problem solving is used, as well as couples-focused activities.

Groups for Adult Offenders and Persons with Life-Threatening Illnesses

Adult offenders and persons with life-threatening illnesses may seem quite different, but they share some common characteristics. Both categories of people are often isolated from others and struggle internally. Groups can help individuals in these circumstances, although in different ways.

GROUPS FOR ADULT OFFENDERS

The term *offender* refers to "people involved in the criminal justice system and includes both incarcerated (housed in a secure correctional environment) and nonincarcerated (i.e., parole, probation) offenders" (Morgan, Romani, & Gross, 2014, p. 441). In examining the literature on adult offenders, Zimpfer (1992b) found that group work in prisons for those who have committed a crime has been around since the late 1950s.

Regardless, working with offenders is a challenge. Potential problematic areas include offenders' low level of trust and high levels of anger, frustration, and sense of deprivation. Therefore, a number of approaches and types of groups have been reported in the professional literature (Morgan et al., 2014). Some have focused on helping inmates adjust to prison life, and others on helping them readjust to the outside world. Zimpfer and Morgan point out that research in the area of treating adult offenders is growing and that group work in this area appears to be effective in producing positive outcomes. The importance of improved self-images of offenders who participate in various groups is a variable in treatment that is increasingly being noted.

Among the specific types of adult offenders targeted for treatment in groups have been those found guilty of sex offenses, people driving while intoxicated, shoplifters, domestic violence perpetrators, and crack cocaine users. Success for specific populations in this mix varies, but there is some consensus that group psychotherapy and group counseling for sex offenders is much more effective than individual treatment for this population (DeAngelis, 1992). The reasons have to do with the manipulative nature of such offenders and the power of the group to prohibit seductive or illusive behavior. Likewise, abusive men may benefit from groups, even those that are psychoeducational and open ended (Schwartz & Waldo, 1999). In such groups, they may not only find out information concerning the nature of abusive relationships but also develop healthy socializing techniques. Likewise, psychoeducational groups are helpful to other offenders in such areas as anger or stress management, problem-solving skills, life skills, cognitive restructuring, or criminal thinking errors (Morgan et al., 2014). Out-of-group homework exercises, regardless of the type of group employed, can also help.

Grief counseling groups may be appropriate for a variety of male prison inmates who are *disenfranchised grievers*, that is, persons removed from their natural support systems (Olson & McEwen, 2004). Through grief counseling groups, these inmates are able to give voice to their feelings, especially the loss of family, friends, freedom, privacy, and even past pain. In the process they are able to express their emotions, find connections with others who have had similar circumstances, and experience relief as well.

A cognitive, psychotherapeutic group technique for assessing offenders' (and involuntary clients') "private logic" (way of thinking) and helping them change is **sophistry** (Evans & Kane, 1996). This method enables group workers to get beyond offenders' resistance. It employs paradox (telling resistant clients not to change), hidden reasons in a group debate, and a reorientation phase to get offenders to examine defects in their thinking and to learn to practice appropriate thought processes. Sophistry basically cuts through offenders' excuses and makes covert logic overt so that it can be challenged and corrected.

Reflection

What experiences have you had with persons who have gone to prison, are still in prison, or are on probation? How would you feel about leading a group of prisoners in a psychoeducational group? In a counseling group? Would the nature of their crime make a difference in the way you interacted with them?

GROUPS FOR PERSONS WITH LIFE-THREATENING ILLNESSES

The concept of group work for persons with life-threatening illnesses originated from Joseph Hersey Pratt's idea of treating tuberculosis outpatients in a group context in 1909. More recently, psychotherapeutic groups have also been employed as a way of treating persons with other life-threatening diseases. In a review of the literature on groups for cancer patients, Harman (1991) notes the results of outcome studies with this population.

One of the most interesting of Harman's findings is that groups are still a preferred method of working with cancer patients and their families. Such groups offer education, support, and release from stress and emotion that has built up. Furthermore, groups help all involved in experiencing the therapeutic factors described by Yalom (Yalom & Leszcz, 2005) as essential to good psychotherapeutic groups: universality, cohesiveness, and the instillation of hope. Groups for those with terminal illnesses are a way to impart information in a quick and efficient manner. Finally, some forms of group work, specifically existential groups for cancer patients and those with other life-threatening illnesses, can assist such individuals in better coping with their diagnosis and living more fully in the time they have left (Spira, 1997).

STRENGTHS AND LIMITATIONS OF USING GROUPS WITH ADULTS

Strengths

One strength of using groups with adults is cost savings. Many adults have similar concerns, and it is more effective to address these common matters in a group setting than individually. Time and money are saved in using a group to convey information or treat individuals with similar problems.

Effectiveness is another advantage connected with groups for adults. For example, groups have been used to help undergraduate and graduate students master course material. These **study groups**, a type of task group, typically involve three to four students who meet at least on a weekly basis to "share information, knowledge, and expertise about a course in which they are all enrolled" (Ender, 1985, p. 469). The idea is that each group member will support and encourage the others and will obtain insight and knowledge through the group effort.

Nonproductive behavior (e.g., perfectionism) may be altered or eliminated through group work with adults. Furthermore, groups often play a key role in helping individuals in adulthood maximize their efforts and focus their energy on appropriate developmental tasks. In the process, members may form a stronger identity.

A final strong point of working with adults in groups is that adults may be motivated to work on concerns with others and may also have an idea of outcomes they would like to achieve. Therefore, the group process may be enhanced by their presence, and results may be quite positive.

Limitations

A limitation of doing group work with adults is scheduling. Offering appropriate groups at a time and a place where potential members can attend may be a challenging endeavor. Adults are busy people, and setting up a group for them takes organizational skills and patience.

A second drawback of conducting groups with adults is a kind of passive-aggressive behavior by some members. For instance, many men are hesitant to enter groups because of past socialization patterns. Likewise, college students may resist group counseling because they believe it is "unpredictable, less effective than individual counseling, and detrimental to participants" (Carter, Mitchell, & Krautheim, 2001, p. 67).

Yet a third weakness associated with offering groups to adults is screening and assembling group members who have a common focus. Practitioners in both public and private settings often find they have a variety of individuals with whom they are working on individual concerns but that the overlap is not sufficient to justify beginning a group.

Finally, group work with adults may be difficult because of past beliefs and behavioral patterns. Adults have had longer to practice certain interactions and may take longer to change them or learn new ways of behaving.

Case Example

Carl and the Cancer Group

At age 52, Carl was diagnosed with prostate cancer. The prognosis was good, and after a number of radiation treatments, Carl's cancer was virtually wiped out. Carl realized he was fortunate, and he wanted to give back to the hospital and physicians who had helped him. He was able to get the names of some other men who recently had successfully undergone radiation treatment for cancer and decided he would form an aftercare group. He wrote and called all the men on his list but found that only one was willing to commit to being in the group. He knew men are not as prone as a group to share their feelings as women, but he was amazed that his response was so low.

Questions

Why do you think most of the men Carl contacted did not wish to join the group? What else do you think Carl could have done to recruit members to his group?

Summary and Conclusion

The period of adulthood ranges from the early 20s to the mid-60s. Such a wide span in life is filled with many problems and possibilities. In young adulthood (ages 20 to 40), major concerns center on identity and intimacy, whereas in midlife (ages 40 to 65), attention is focused on generativity and fulfillment. Group work can help individuals in all stages of adulthood to clarify their focus and maximize their potential. In this chapter, groups for different ages and stages of adulthood and the gender problems that go with them have been considered.

College students and young adults, for example, are faced with major decisions involving learning, relationships, and career choices. Groups for them, especially on college campuses, are relatively short term and focus on specific agenda items. Groups can help college students and young adults become better oriented toward their environments and tasks in life, facilitate growth, and prevent problems. However, when members of this population become stuck, they may also use groups for psychotherapy purposes.

Adults in midlife sometimes struggle coming to grips with the reality of their age and the aging process. Groups are especially helpful to midlifers in evaluating themselves in regard to family and career. Many individuals do not fully realize how their childhood influences their adulthood until midlife. For people who have grown up in families with alcohol addiction or other forms of abuse, groups can be supportive, educational, and therapeutic. Many self-help groups, such as those sponsored by Adult Children of Alcoholics, can help them break out of isolation and learn how to change dysfunctional behavioral patterns. Groups for midlifers may also focus on positive wellness, such as jogging groups, or potential change, such as those that emphasize careers and job changes.

Because men and women are socialized differently, and because biological differences often result in unique concerns, groups for one gender or the other are sometimes helpful. A process of mutual identification can be facilitated when the leader of the group and group members are all of the same sex.

Role modeling is also enhanced in such groups (Gonzalez-Lopez & Taylor, 1997). Through group work, men may realize the strict limitations of traditional roles for males and make changes that allow them greater flexibility and growth. Particular problems related to work and stress may be dealt with from a psychotherapeutic and psychoeducational perspective. The mythopoetic movement is an appropriate adjunct to working in groups with men. Likewise, women may use groups to deal with career and workplace issues (Giordano, 1995). Women may also use groups to help free themselves from socialized roles that are not productive for them as adults, such as always being dependent or passive. Furthermore, they may work in groups to overcome traumatic events in their lives, such as rape, or to concentrate on self-concept issues, such as those involved in eating disorders or careers inside or outside the home.

Groups are also helpful for adults in midlife who are married or unmarried. Couples and family groups are another type of group work for midlife married adults in need of a psychotherapeutic or psychoeducational group. Groups for the divorced and the widowed, especially self-help groups such as Parents Without Partners, can offer much for this population. Parent education groups, which focus on skill development, support, and discussion, are useful for parents of all types. In these groups, parents learn to concentrate on their own behaviors as well as those of their children.

Classroom Exercises

1. In groups of three, investigate the number of groups that operate on your college campus. These groups may vary from those that emphasize learning to those that are psychotherapeutically oriented. Have each class group report back to the class as a whole and discuss what they have found out about the campus community and group work.
2. The transition to midlife is sometimes filled with apprehension. Have each member of the class draw a picture depicting himself or herself at young adulthood and midlife. In dyads, talk with another class member about the differences you anticipate or have experienced. What are the advantages and drawbacks of aging as you perceive them? How might a group be helpful in this process?
3. Divide the class into two groups based on gender. Each group will review articles from professional periodicals published within the past 3 years on the use of groups with men and women. The men will review only articles on women in groups; the women in the class will do the opposite. Each group will then tabulate the results of its findings and present this information to the whole class. After the presentation, discuss what has been found and how it might be used.
4. Interview a panel of parents (of other class members, if possible) about parenthood. List top concerns and explore how a parent education group leader might address these difficulties. Consult your parent panel about which interventions seem most constructive for them and why. Then discuss as a class the merits and limitations of parent education groups.

CHAPTER **14**

Groups for Older Adults

When you wake up one morning
and feel you've grown old
Take this poem down from your shelf
and slowly read its well-wrought lines
which fade like memories of our youth.
Those were the days on the knolls of Reynolda
when times were measured in looks not words,
Those were the moments we wrote in our memories
and now, like fine parchment,
though faded they remain
clear impressions in the calmness of age
of excitement, adventure, and love,
bringing warmth and smiles
to the chill of the season . . .
and brightness to a world full of grey.*

From "A Poem in Parting" by Samuel T. Gladding, © 1968/1989/2006. © Samuel T. Gladding. Reprinted by permission from Samuel T. Gladding.

CHAPTER OVERVIEW

From reading this chapter, you will learn about

- Types of groups for older adults
- Setting up groups for older adults, including the role of the leader in such groups
- Studies on the outcomes of groups for older adults and their caregivers, including strengths and limitations

AS YOU READ, CONSIDER

- How you think groups for older adults differ from those of other age groups and how they are similar
- The importance of the leader in groups for older adults and how it is different and similar to that of other leaders in age-specific groups
- Why it is critical to have groups for caregivers for older adults as well as for members of this population

Aging is an inevitable process, although many individuals and skin beauty creams deny or openly fight it. Despite mythical and historical searches for the fountain of youth, such as the legendary stories associated with Ponce de León, everyone who lives grows older. No one "youths" with age. But aging has its advantages. As the poet Robert Browning wrote in *Rabbi Ben Ezra*:

> *"Grow old along with me!*
> *The best is yet to be,*
> *The last of life, for which the first was made. . . ."*

Late adulthood begins in the 60s and extends up to approximately 120 years of age. It is the longest span of any period of human development—50 to 60 years (Santrock, 2013). Aging is an individualized process with a heterogeneous population. Many people begin to acknowledge the inevitable decline in their physical powers somewhere between ages 35 and 50. Others continue to deny that they are getting older or even do not display many mental or physical changes until quite late in life.

In previous generations, working in groups with older adults was not a priority. The reason was that the number of individuals over the age of 65 years (a traditional time of retirement in the past) was relatively small (e.g., 3 million in 1900). However, the percentage of those over age 65 continues to rise and in 2014 stood at 13.7% of the population, or 43 million. By 2060, the number is projected to more than double and will be 92 million, representing nearly 20% of the people in the United States (AgingStats.gov, at www.agingstats.gov/Main_Site/Data/2012_Documents/Population.aspx).

Although older adults (age 65 and up) are of interest to mental health professionals, existing services for this population have not kept up with demand (Knight, 2004; Persky, n.d., at www.mhaging.org/info/olus.html). Many reasons account for this deficiency. One is that the number of people in this category has grown dramatically, whereas the supply of mental health workers has not risen as rapidly (Bartels & Naslund, 2013). For instance, since 1900, the number of persons above age 85 has increased eightfold, whereas the population in general has increased only threefold (Hern & Weis, 1991). Another reason older adults are underserved is that mental health services have traditionally been geared toward those in middle age and younger. Further complicating the situation are the limitations some helpers place on themselves and older adults by accepting many of the myths, misconceptions, and stereotypes about the aged. For example, some may believe that older people cannot change or be creative (Cohen, 2000; Corey, Corey, & Corey, 2014; Greene, 1986). Acceptance of these myths leads to an "attitude bias" against working with older adults. This bias is known as **ageism** (discrimination against older people). In actuality, many characteristics of those who are older make them excellent candidates for numerous helping services, especially group work.

Benefits and liabilities come with any age, and growing older is no exception. On the positive side, most people past the traditional retirement age of 65 (used as a marker event to separate midlife from old age) still enjoy a high quality of life and have many years to live (about a quarter of their lives) (Cowley, 1997; Skinner & Vaughan, 1997). Often they exemplify what Erikson (1963) describes as **wisdom**—the ability to make effective choices among alternatives— and **integrity**—the total integration of life experiences into a meaningful whole. If married, older people frequently experience increased marital satisfaction and intimacy (Walsh, 1988). There is also an increase in the religious and spiritual life of many older people and with it an associated sense of well-being and meaningfulness (Levin, Taylor, & Chatters, 1994). In addition, many individuals create some of their best works after 65. Examples include Goethe completing *Faust* at 80; Titian painting masterpieces at 98; Toscanini conducting at 85; and Benjamin Franklin helping to frame the American Constitution at 80.

Because approximately 70% of persons over age 65 are grandparents, they often find enrichment and pleasure through interacting with their grandchildren (Mead, 1972; Streib & Beck, 1981). Others find significance in their lives through becoming foster grandparents or doing volunteer work. Most keep in contact with their children, if they have any, and are able to resolve some issues of earlier family life. A significant percentage of older adults (95%) maintain their own households and seem to value their independence. Until age 75, the majority of individuals in this age group are, as a rule, relatively free from disabling physical impairments, view themselves as basically middle-aged, grow emotionally and mentally, and generally enjoy a variety of physical exercises and activities, including sex (Cohen, 2000; Luke, 2010; Okun, 1984). Persons in this age range are known as the **young-old**.

On the negative side, older adults as a group share many common psychological and physiological concerns. For instance, loneliness, loss, fear, and hopelessness are often prevalent among members of this group (Corey, Corey, & Corey, 2014; France, 1984). "Feelings of worthlessness may develop as older individuals internalize their devalued social position and lose control over their lives" (Thomas & Martin, 1997, p. 43). Individuals over the age of 75 are considered the **old**, and those over 85 years are viewed as the **old-old**. Collectively, older age groups are more likely than others to experience declines in health and overall functioning and eventually to have chronic health problems that require increased attention (Myers, 1989; Walsh, 1988). In addition, numerous individuals, especially older men, have difficulty adapting to retirement and mourn the loss of meaningful roles outside of the household. Sometimes this adjustment can lead to conflict and dysfunction. The poor and those who are cultural minorities usually have more trouble in old age, a continuation of discrimination and need they have suffered through their lives for the most part (Himes, Hogan, & Eggebeen, 1996).

Widowhood is another downside to aging. Because women have traditionally married older men and live longer than men, this possibility is of special concern to them. Ageism may be a painful societal force that tarnishes one's sense of pride in age. Finally, there is the prospect of facing one's own mortality. The inevitable end of life is an event some individuals in old age have difficulty accepting.

Changes required of most individuals at the older stages of life include making adjustments for declining physical strength, retirement, death of friends or spouse, and declines in income and health (Anderson, Goodman, & Schlossberg, 2012; Cox, 2009; Santrock, 2013). New social roles, such as being a grandparent, must be learned; different relationships must be established with peers and children. The requirements of older adults, although not as numerous as those in adolescence, are still demanding. Not everything happens at once, however, and older individuals have time to make the transition gradually. The "'**density of time**'—its fullness and eventfulness—seems to lessen with age" (Schlossberg, 1981, p. 13).

Many of the problems associated with living more than 65 years are the result of limited socialization and interpersonal activities. Others involve damaged self-image and self-esteem. Almost all of these difficulties can be constructively addressed through some form of group work. In fact, just the interpersonal nature of groups can be therapeutic for older adults, especially those who are isolated and lonely (Brandler, 1985; Henderson & Gladding, 2004; Zimpfer, 1987).

Reflection

What has been your relationship with people above the age of 65? How do you feel about being that age one day? What do you think could be done to counter ageism?

TYPES OF GROUPS FOR OLDER ADULTS

Groups for those ages 65 and over are geared toward the needs of the persons involved and the expertise of the group leader(s) (Corey, Corey, & Corey, 2014; Haight & Gibson, 2005). On the psychoeducational and task/work side of the ledger are groups for older adults run by the **Gray Panthers** and **AARP** (formerly the American Association of Retired Persons) that focus on advocating issues important to members of this population. In addition, there are national, as well as local, religious and civic organizations that provided psychoeducational and task/work groups for older adults and which may not be as political. Counseling and psychotherapy groups for this population include an additional seven types of groups: (a) reality oriented, (b) remotivation therapy, (c) reminiscing and life review, (d) psychotherapy and counseling, (e) topic- and theme-focused, (f) member specific, and (g) eGroups. All eight of these types of groups are covered here.

Psychoeducational and Task/Work Groups

Many individuals, both young and old, are unaware of the issues and challenges facing people over age 65. Two main advocacy groups for older adults in the United States, the Gray Panthers and AARP, address these matters in the groups they run, which have both unique and overlapping functions. The Gray Panthers run groups that focus on issues dealing with universal health care, jobs with a living wage, preservation of Social Security, affordable housing, access to quality education, economic justice, the environment, peace, and challenging ageism, sexism, and racism (www.graypanthers.org). Gray Panthers groups are organized nationally and at local levels. AARP (www.aarp.org) is the country's largest nonprofit organization dedicated to the interests of mature Americans. It conducts groups on different levels for its membership and others who are interested in legislative initiatives affecting the lives of senior citizens. Issues covered include education, health care, advocacy, and community involvement. Both the Gray Panthers and AARP are headquartered in Washington, DC.

Because of the power of these two groups and the fact that numerous individuals grew up with them, many older adults join them and find both meaning and services through participating in them. However, other older adults join local religious or civic groups within their communities that are not as politically active. They also benefit from the interactive psychoeducational and task/work groups such organizations sponsor, especially if they stay actively involved (Skinner & Vaughan, 1997).

In addition, there are psychoeducational groups for older adults who are not as physically able and who require long-term care. Currently there are around 9 million people over age 65 in the United States in this category with an expected rise to more than 12 million by 2030 (Vacha-Haase, Archibald, Brescian, Martin, & Fitzpatrick, 2009). In such group settings, socialization and cognitive stimulation occur and increase the well-being of individuals in these environments. Vacha-Haase and colleagues have given extensive details about how to set up and run a current events group in long-term care facilities. Among the recommendations they make are that such groups should be small (8 to 12 at most and usually smaller), homogenous (with people who have similar cognitive abilities), and conducted in an optimal environment (such as a warm and comfortable room). Groups may be open or closed, and open-ended questions are optimal. Leaders of such groups may have to paraphrase often as well as reflect emotions to let members know that their feelings have been heard. However, these groups are effective in helping residents move into a higher state of functioning than would otherwise be possible.

Counseling and Psychotherapy Groups

In addition to psychoeducational and task/work groups, there are seven counseling and psychotherapy groups for older adults that are covered here. All differ in both purpose and scope from the psychoeducational and task/work groups just described. They are aimed at helping mentally impaired older adults through psychotherapeutic means. The groups in this cluster are reality oriented, remotivation therapy, reminiscing and life review, and therapy. The last three groups in the counseling and psychotherapy category—topic- and theme-focused, member-specific, and eGroups—are more preventive and educational in nature.

Reality-oriented groups are set up for older individuals who have become disoriented to their surroundings. (Reality-oriented theory is unrelated to the theory of reality therapy developed by William Glasser.) These groups, although educationally focused, are therapeutically based in that they emphasize helping group members become more aware of their present surroundings in terms of time, place, and people (Burnside, 1986; Thomas & Martin, 2010). Group membership is limited to three or four participants when the circumstances are severe, but groups for less disoriented individuals may involve seven or eight people. Groups meet daily and, if basic information is mastered, members progress to more creative and practical activities (Capuzzi & Gross, 1980). Because reality-oriented groups are conducted at such a low level, helping professionals with minimal training in human relationship skills are able to lead them.

Initially, these types of groups were established in institutional settings, but now they are found in outpatient and day-care groups (Thomas & Martin, 2010). Regardless, they meet every day and follow a set schedule. Group sessions include sensory training, group exercises, and practical skills on a 24-hour-a-day basis (Taulbee, 1978; Thomas & Martin, 2010).

Remotivation therapy groups, in contrast to reality-oriented groups, are aimed at helping older clients become more invested in the present and future. Their membership is composed of individuals who have "lost interest" in any time frame of life except the past. The groups were originally set up in mental hospitals and nursing homes in the early 1950s by Dorothy Smith, a hospital volunteer. Participation in such groups is usually limited to 15 members who are selected for their ability to relate to others, willingness to join the group, and lack of distorted memories (Dennis, 1978). Sessions focus on nonpathological topics, such as gardening, art, or holidays. Participants are encouraged to respond to others and to materials presented in an appropriate verbal or nonverbal manner. The goals of this process are for participants to become more cognitively organized and to increase socialization skills through interacting with others.

According to Beaver (1983, p. 240), remotivation therapy groups follow five basic steps:

1. "The climate of acceptance"—establishing a warm, friendly relationship in the group
2. "A bridge to reality"—reading literature, keeping up with current events, investigating ideas
3. "Sharing the world"—developing a specific topic through leading questions, use of props, planned activities
4. "An appreciation of the work of the world"—stimulating the participants to think about themselves in relation to work or vocational interests
5. "The climate of appreciation"—finding joy through getting together

Often remotivation groups are preliminary to other types of group experiences, such as those involving family problems or individual concerns. Studies show positive empirical results for remotivation therapy groups (Burnside, 1986; Stotts & Dyer, 2005; Zimpfer, 1987), although they have been criticized for being too rigid and disallowing feelings.

Case Example

Betty and the Books

Betty was interested in starting a remotivation group because she thought that older people, especially in group facilities, do not get enough outside stimulation. Because of the harsh weather where she lived, she thought a remotivational group centered on great books would be ideal. She solicited a list of interesting books from a local reference librarian and brought it to the group's first meeting. The first book went over well and the second almost as well. However, by the third book she could sense that the enthusiasm for the group was waning. One of the members even said: "All we do is read books. Isn't there something else we can do that would be stimulating?" Betty's feelings were hurt, but instead of shutting the group down, she sought professional help.

Questions

What would you advise Betty to do in regard to the group? What else could she do with the group besides read books? How might she keep members' interest?

Reminiscing and life review groups "are generally considered to be synonymous, defined as a naturally occurring, universal process whereby experiences and unresolved conflicts are revived, surveyed, and reintegrated into people's views of their lives" (Thomas & Martin, 2010, p. 511). Reminiscing in a group can be therapeutic because the process of sharing memories helps individuals achieve a sense of integrity and self-worth. Reminiscence is not just to recall the past events or experiences. "Reminiscing serves several functions for the older person including:

- promoting self understanding;
- preserving personal and collective history;
- transcending the material world and physical limitations;
- allowing for identification of universal themes of humanity; and
- reinforcing coping mechanisms" (Texas A&M AgriLife Extension Service, 2013).

Reminiscing groups help individuals retrieve memories from the past, work through unresolved conflicts, reintegrate remembered experiences, assess former adaptive coping responses, and find a deeper sense of identity and connectedness with the world (Chen, Li, & Li, 2012;

Thomas & Martin, 2010, p. 511). Overall, these groups are aimed at increasing life satisfaction rather than improving social skills (Kennedy & Tanenbaum, 2000).

There are a number of ways reminiscing and life review groups can be structured, but DeVries, Birren, and Deutchman (1995) suggest guiding themes, such as looking at people's family histories, careers, health, love/hate, values, and sexuality.

Westwood and Ewasiw (2011) recommend a similar approach which they call a "**guided autobiography**" (GA). In this process, individuals doing the autobiography reflect, organize, and write on the assigned theme of the week, then rehearse what they are going to share and have control during a session over their experience and emotions. Westwood and Ewasiw add a component to this life review though, a **therapeutic enactment** (TE) where individuals are asked to enact critical stage events in their lives that are unresolved, limited, or blocked. The TE experience may be on several levels: emotional, cognitive, physical, or behavioral. The result is a deeper level of learning and changes within the self that the GA by itself does not provide. Insight gained from this process helps these older adults realize more deeply their finiteness and prepare for death.

A major therapeutic value of the reminiscing and life review group process lies in the sense of affiliation it creates among its members. These groups provide both a chance to be introspective and "an opportunity for social intimacy with others" (Singer, Tracz, & Dworkin, 1991, p. 167). Further beneficial aspects include a more positive mood among members, increased self-esteem, and enhanced life satisfaction (Thomas & Martin, 1997, 2010). Members feel more competent and in greater control of their lives because of participating in the group. Their memories give them a vehicle for communicating with others who are at their same age and stage. Isolation and loneliness are eliminated in group interactions. Through sharing, the processes of creativity and pleasure are enhanced as the individual, the group, and the group leader gain insight into a person's psychological history (Christensen, Hulse-Killacky, Salgado, Thornton, & Miller, 2006). In short, the reminiscing and life review group can be the springboard for conducting other groups or be an end in itself.

Reminiscing and life review groups are usually conducted once or twice a week for about an hour and consist of six to eight members. They may be relatively long term (more than a year) or short term (10 weeks or fewer) (Beaver, 1983; Christensen et al., 2006). The content of the group sessions is structured and often chosen by group members; however, it may be selected at times by the group leader(s) (Haight & Haight, 2007). Popular, but not always pleasant, topics in one all-female reminiscing group of women 65 years of age and older were favorite holidays, first pet, first job, first day of school, first date, first toy, first playmate, and first memory (Burnside, 1993).

Topics and themes for women and men in such groups vary. Whatever the case, content is often highlighted through the use of poetry, music, visual aids, and other memorabilia. Music may be the key to encouraging the discussion of past or present feelings and thoughts about events, such as learning, romance, loss, and family life (Duffey, Somody, & Clifford, 2006/2007). Typically, music is initially played that revolves around a particular theme, such as the importance of home or family. Such an activity usually takes place after the group as a whole has warmed up by participating in a brief sing-along of familiar songs that include their own accompaniment of clapping and foot tapping. This approach has been found to be effective in helping reduce depressive symptoms in older people (ages 73 to 94 years) with dementia (Ashida, 2000) and has value in other older group settings as well. Music may also involve activities such as group rhythms and drumming (Reuer, Crowe, & Bernstein, 2007). This percussion-based approach requires no musical training and is interactive, allowing older adults the experience of fun, socialization, stimulation, and a sense of belonging.

As the group comes to a close, feelings of separation must be dealt with. Leaders of reminiscing groups may disclose their own sense of loss. They may emphasize that they will cherish memories of each individual and that they appreciate the sharing that has taken place.

Reflection

What songs remind you of home and memories of your family? Compare your list to that of someone else. What overlaps and differences do you have?

Leaders for such groups must be skilled in group dynamics and interpersonal communication responses. They should be inquiring but not intrusive. Other helpful qualities include "delving into the daily existence of . . . group members, getting to know them as people, and overcoming pre-set notions about who elderly people are and how they experience the world" (Christensen et al., 2006, p. 86). Patience and flexibility are key ingredients that leaders need to master as well.

Singer et al. (1991) provide a model of a reminiscing and life review group in an adult day-care center. In establishing their group, leaders decided on a closed-ended, voluntary group format. They screened their prospective members beforehand to ensure they were mentally alert as well as motivated for the experience. Goals for the group included decreasing social and emotional isolation, depression, and loneliness; increasing social skills and self-esteem; and enabling members to develop a social network by the end of the group. After 10 weekly 1-hour sessions, the staff of the center and members themselves noticed significant advancements in the achievement of the group's goals. Life for participants became more meaningful and enjoyable because of the respect and understanding they found in the group. The main drawback to this particular group was that 10 sessions did not provide enough time for the members to process fully all of the material they wanted to discuss.

Therapy groups for older adults are geared toward the remediation of specific problems this population faces, such as role changes, ageism, social isolation, loss, physical decline, and fear of the future (Altholz, 1978; Henderson & Gladding, 2004; Weisman & Schwartz, 1989). Sometimes persons "who are referred to group psychotherapy are . . . depressed, highly agitated and disruptive, or unable to do reality testing" (Maynard, 1980, p. 232). Others have fewer ongoing unresolved, serious personal problems, but they are still in need of help.

There are a number of theoretical approaches to working with older adults therapeutically in groups. O'Leary, Sheedy, O'Sullivan, and Thoresen (2001) found that older adults responded well to Gestalt therapy groups. Participants in these groups were less antagonistic and more agreeable with others than were nonparticipants.

Generally, therapy groups for older adults are composed of between 6 and 12 members. They are usually long term (a year or more), although some groups tend to be briefer. These groups may be highly structured or relatively unstructured, but leaders need a background in gerontology as well as experience in group work with older persons. It is advisable for group leaders to screen potential members carefully, assessing their competencies to process conflict and emotional issues (Thomas & Martin, 2010). That way, as in other groups, they do not get themselves into situations where they find a group member who is disruptive or unable to function well. Leaders of therapy groups for older adults must be knowledgeable about and skilled in the treatment of major mental disorders. It is likewise vital that they recognize and be able to deal with developmental and transitional factors connected with aging. In addition, leaders must also be encouraging of group members and willing to self-disclose when appropriate. Overall, therapy groups help their members gain a greater appreciation of themselves and where they are developmentally.

Case Example

Thelma Sets Up a Group for Therapy

Thelma has worked with older adults all her life. She has usually done so on a one-to-one basis. However, her facility now has a number of older adults who are socially isolated and facing physical decline. Therefore, Thelma decides to run a therapy group.

To her credit Thelma screens members, chooses eight, finds a room that is appropriate, and sets up a time for the group to begin. Then, she is in a bit of a bind. She is not sure exactly how to start the group, although she has explained the purpose of the group to its members.

Question

How would you advise Thelma to get the group going? Be as specific as you can.

Topic- and theme-focused groups are centered on a particular topic or theme, such as widowhood, bibliotherapy, sexuality, health, parenting grandchildren, current events, spirituality, or the arts. They are psychoeducational in nature and "are designed ultimately to improve the quality of daily living for older people" (Beaver, 1983, p. 241). These groups also assist the aging to find more meaning in their lives and to establish a support group of like-minded people. Their leaders must have topic-specific knowledge of the issues being covered (Myers, 1989). For instance, in groups for bereaved spouses, leaders must assist the members to cope with the pain of grief and mourning (including the "holding on" and "letting go" processes), help combat the social isolation that is so pervasive for this population, provide "consensual validation" for spouses regarding their bereavement experiences, and support members as they begin to understand the changes facing them as they begin to fashion a new future for themselves (Walter, 2005). Membership in such groups is voluntary, and the groups may be conducted in a variety of settings. The size, composition, duration, and frequency of the group depend on the group goals and member competencies (Thomas & Martin, 2010). Significant social interaction often results from such experiences.

Member-specific groups are related to topic- and theme-focused groups, but they focus more on particular transitional concerns of individual members, such as grief, hospitalization, or institutionalized day care. Basically, member-specific groups may be conducted for older adults or members of their families. When these types of groups are conducted for the aging, they are aimed at helping all participants recognize and face particular concerns that are common to people who grow older, such as loss of physical strength or the effects of physical illnesses. In a similar way, member-specific groups that concentrate on families assist them in dealing with common themes related to how a group member's well-being and adjustment will affect each person in the family (Sullivan, Coffey, & Greenstein, 1987).

The same leadership skills required to lead a topic- and theme-focused group are necessary in conducting a member-specific group, but leaders must focus more on individual concerns than those of the group as a whole. For example, members of a family group with a relative who has Alzheimer's disease all may have different areas on which they wish to concentrate (Glosser & Wexler, 1985; Hinkle, 1991). There is no simple way to personalize a member-specific group.

eGroups are what their name implies. They are Internet-based groups for older persons (and others) who are homebound (Thomas & Martin, 2010; Thomas, Martin, Alexander, Cooley, & Loague, 2003). They may be used in multiple ways, from a life review group using **eMemories and eStories** (memories and stories that are shared online with an eGroup) to various types of support groups. Nearly half of North Americans above age 58 have access to computers and the Internet. Thus, this type of group has great potential. With ethical standards in place for online counseling from the American Counseling Association and from the National Board for Certified Counselors, the potential use of eGroups in a professional and effective way is quite possible.

Thomas and co-workers (2003) recommend that potential members of such groups be referred by a professional counselor and not recruited through advertisements. In addition, they recommend that members of the group be screened. Furthermore, security and confidentiality should be maintained, and potential members who cannot guarantee security of their Internet access should be allowed to participate only in limited types of groups. Finally, each eGroup should have a counselor and a backup counselor accessible to each group member in case of a concern or emergency.

Overall, if ethical concerns and technological skill barriers can be overcome, eGroups can help older people be connected with cohorts in other geographical areas and "build a supportive and healing community for older people who otherwise would be more isolated," thereby producing "the feeling of personal control that is so important for the empowerment and psychological and physical well-being of older people" (Thomas & Martin, 2010, p. 517).

Case Example

Inez Goes on the Internet

Inez self-describes herself as "a little older than a baby-boomer." She is a widow and a computer wiz. "I buy everything online," she tells you. Because she is located in a rural area and cannot drive, she asks you about joining an eGroup. You investigate and find one that would fit her.

Inez is enthused. She signs on but does not give her real name. Then she starts describing herself and her situation in unrealistic ways. You are monitoring the group, and finally you confront Inez with what she is doing. Her response: "I'm just having a little fun."

Questions

What might you say next? Is Inez really hurting anyone? What might you recommend that she do?

SETTING UP GROUPS FOR OLDER ADULTS

Just as with other groups, those involving older adults must be carefully and thoughtfully proposed. This means that goals should be clearly established before the group begins. Older adults generally need a clear, organized explanation of the specific purpose of a group and why they can benefit from it. The establishment of any group for older adults involves pregroup screening, especially if the group is counseling or therapeutically oriented.

Most groups for older adults are conducted on an outpatient or outreach basis, but in some cases, they are carried out in institutional settings. In outreach environments, task-oriented psychotherapy groups are beneficial because of a sense of accomplishment that these groups foster among their members through the achievement of tangible products (Zimpfer, 1987). Regardless of the setting or the focus, certain procedures should be followed when preparing to work with a group of individuals age 65 and older.

The first consideration is the physical environment in which the group will be conducted. The meeting room should be functional, geared for comfort, and in a quiet area. The ideal location is a ground-floor room with upholstered chairs, good lighting, and space for wheelchairs; it should be near a bathroom, away from steps, and with a constant temperature of about 75 degrees with no drafts. Unfortunately, this kind of environment is usually hard to find (Henderson & Gladding, 2004). Once a good setting is found, a tight circle works best for accommodating the hearing impaired and creating a sense of cohesiveness (Stone & Waters, 1991).

A second matter of importance is scheduling. Certain times of the day do not work well for meetings; for example, early evening is not good for many older group members who may have difficulty with night driving or like to go to bed early. Therefore, the group should be set up to maximize participation. This usually means finding out the schedules of potential participants and building time for group meetings around them. Once a good time is established, most groups for older adults are set up to be closed ended to build trust and develop empathy (Capuzzi & Gross, 1980; Hendrix & Sedgwick, 1989). The major exceptions to this procedure are psychotherapy groups in institutional settings or support groups such as those for the widowed that may benefit from an open-ended format (Folken, 1991; Yalom & Leszcz, 2005).

A third matter that must be considered is the physical ability of group members. Physical disabilities and sensory impairment can contribute to a feeling of social isolation in older adults and also inhibit their participation in a group (Myers, 1990). Some members who have lost sensory and mobility functions may require special treatment. One way to take care of their needs is to employ a **multimodal method** (using verbal and nonverbal means) for conveying information (Erwin, 1997). A warm-up activity or brief informational presentation before the group actually gets to work can help members understand the group's focus for the day.

Burnside (1978) lists a number of other factors that make groups for the aged distinct from other types of groups. These factors must be considered when setting up such groups:

- As a rule, groups for older adults tend to be smaller in size (e.g., four to eight members) than groups with other age populations, except for elementary school children. Remotivation therapy groups, which may be as large as 15 members, are a notable exception to the rule of having small groups for older adults.
- The physical environment is more important to the well-being of the group and its members than is true with other age groups. Older adults have greater difficulties with physical body systems than do other age groups because of lifestyle factors such as **hypokinesis** (physical inactivity) (Burlew, Jones, & Emerson, 1991). For some groups, physical exercise along with group activities is an excellent combination.
- Unlike the norms for some other groups, older group members are encouraged to socialize with one another outside the group setting. This type of socializing helps break down barriers that isolate older adults and is, therefore, therapeutic.
- Growth and enhancement are meaningful themes for groups for older adults. Encouragement is more appropriate than confrontation in working with this population.
- Older adults take longer to build trust than do those in other age groups (Waters, McCarroll, & Penman, 1987). The reasons for this gap vary, but they often reflect socialization patterns, such as believing that negative secrets should be kept private or feeling that no one will really understand them.

> ### Reflection
>
> What are some characteristics of older adults not mentioned here? How might they have an impact on a group?

ROLE OF THE LEADER IN GROUPS FOR OLDER ADULTS

Almost all major theoretical approaches can be used to work with older adults (Henderson & Gladding, 2004; Storandt, 1983). Therefore, the role of the leader in groups for older adults depends on his or her knowledge of theory, the type of group to be led, the leader's previous experience and abilities, and participants' level of readiness. Hawkins (1983) suggests the following steps for prospective leaders, especially those with little experience:

1. *Read*—It is critical to separate fact from fiction when working with members of an older population. Reading books and articles specifically geared toward the developmental and nondevelopmental issues of the aged will help leaders be more objective. Excellent reviews of the literature on groups for older adults are often published in scholarly journals (e.g., Myers, Poidevant, & Dean, 1991). A humorous yet insightful book on a wide range of topics related to aging is *It's Better to Be over the Hill Than Under It: Thoughts on Life over Sixty* (LeShan, 1990).
2. *Examine*—Along with reading, leaders need to examine their own prejudices and stereotypes of the old. Some leaders who grew up in a culture or subculture that stressed youth or staying young, such as the "baby boom generation," may have particular difficulty in dealing with older adults and their concerns (Folken, 1991). Leaders with negative ideas about older adults will probably be detrimental to the group and should be replaced.
3. *Meet*—It is crucial to the group's success that leaders become aware of their own perspectives on the lives of older individuals. One place such an encounter can occur is through remembering major exchanges with older adults within the leaders' families of origin. Other opportunities for such meetings are found in present settings, such as retirement homes, where leaders visit older individuals and learn more about them as persons.
4. *Fantasize*—Leaders should imagine their own lives in the future and become more aware of what their wishes, hopes, and fears might be then. For instance, leaders may envision themselves as lonely or economically destitute after retirement. Then they can empathize more with actual group members they may meet in these circumstances. By fantasizing, leaders can face their future and avoid projecting any undesirable characteristics onto those with whom they work.
5. *Learn*—Those who lead groups for older adults need to learn what social, educational, and political organizations, such as AARP and the Gray Panthers, are available on the national, state, and local levels. These groups are often rich resources for group members.
6. *Care*—It is important, and indeed critical, that older adults realize that others, such as group leaders, sincerely care about them. Such caring adds to the self-esteem of everyone. It promotes rapport and enriches the process of being in a group.

In addition, leaders need to realize that the pace of a group for older adults is usually slower and the goals are more limited than for most other groups. To compensate for this slower pace and to reduce frustration, group leaders need to be accepting, remind members of positive changes, and encourage continued participation (Haight & Gibson, 2005).

Likewise, leaders need to be cognizant that common themes in groups for older adults are loss and loneliness, death and dying, concern about physical changes, increased dependency, relationships with adult children, grandparenting, and finding meaningful and enjoyable activities in which to participate (Corey, 2012; Myers, 1989). With these themes in mind, it is understandable that certain words and processes that are normally used in groups for other populations are not usually appropriate in groups for older adults. *Long-term goal* and *termination,* for instance, are two that should be avoided (Ekloff, 1984; Waters et al., 1987). These words have a tendency to arouse anxiety in some older persons, especially those who are frail or sick. Members may become fearful that they will not be able to attain goals or that they may suffer yet another loss. In general, a less stringent criterion for success is appropriate when working with groups for older adults. A relaxed atmosphere is also important.

Leaders also need to share impressions and experiences in their lives within the groups they conduct to keep them focused and moving. One of the most significant mistakes new group leaders make when working with older adults is not self-disclosing.

Overall, group leaders for older adults must be verbally and nonverbally active and personally and professionally concerned, as well as clear and direct. By performing in such a fashion, leaders can help move their groups away from self-centeredness to a healthy group-centeredness (Henderson & Gladding, 2004; Hendrix & Sedgwick, 1989). Group leadership skills in such cases do not differ significantly from those used with other populations, but the emphases of leaders vary. Their alertness to certain key issues—such as religion, economics, intergenerational conflict, or loss—is usually greater than would be the case in other age groups.

In summary, leaders working with older persons in groups must be sensitive to relevant issues, such as concerns with aging and death, as well as to real constraints, such as waning physical health and vitality and fewer social outlets (Jacobs, Schimmel, Masson, & Harvill, 2016). A major issue that most group workers face in dealing with older adults is their inexperience in knowing what their members' stage of life is like. Therefore, group workers must accept this reality and be open to being a learner, as well as a facilitator, within these groups. They must come to terms with their own aging and eventual death as well in a way that enables them to face life energetically and realistically. Personal integration of one's own life, professional knowledge of aging, and familiarity with psychoeducational and psychotherapeutic processes that will best help them relate to the aged are the key factors in becoming an effective group leader for older adults.

Case Example

Dora Confronts Death

Dora has a master's degree and 5 years of experience at her agency. She is from a close-knit family that is healthy and often engages in games of touch football during the holidays. In her late 20s, Dora is dedicated to the mental health of all of her clients. She always acts professionally.

As the co-leader of a group for older adults at a retirement center, Dora notices that Mr. Smoak has missed the last two sessions of the group. When she inquires about this, she is told that Mr. Smoak became ill about 10 days ago and died yesterday.

Dora is shocked. She lets her co-leader, Brian, know, and they discuss the matter. Dora really liked Mr. Smoak, and she feels guilty that she did not visit with him during his recent illness. She is not sure she can continue as the co-leader of the group.

Questions

How would you approach Dora if you were Brian? How could you involve other members of the group in handling this situation, or would you? Do you think Dora should continue as a co-leader of the group? Why or why not?

STUDIES ON THE OUTCOMES OF GROUPS FOR OLDER ADULTS

Studying groups for older adults is complicated at times because, along with the inclusion of a group experience, some individuals, especially in counseling and psychotherapy groups, receive individual and medical treatments that affect how they function. Nevertheless, there are some clear-cut studies that indicate the effectiveness of groups for older adults.

In regard to reality-oriented groups, the empirical evidence for their success is not strong. The reason is possibly because of the limited nature of the clients who compose the groups or the low level of leadership skill required of facilitators (Zimpfer, 1987).

Counseling groups for dealing with the problems of the aged have been studied also. Two such examples were given in this chapter—one focused on expressing anger and alleviating depression (Johnson & Wilborn, 1991) and the other concentrated on ways of handling stress and promoting the mental health of older adults (Stone & Waters, 1991).

In the group dealing with anger, Johnson and Wilborn (1991) found that a 6-week group counseling experience did not significantly decrease anger in a group of older women. However, they found that the women seemed to value the opportunity to talk about the expression of anger and its importance in their lives. They suggested a longer period be allocated for anger-management groups for older adults in replication studies.

In the group set up to help older adults manage stress, Stone and Waters (1991) used peer facilitators in a format of four sessions, each lasting 2 hours. They emphasized the importance of personal sharing, participant control, and enhancement of self-esteem. The peer counselors who worked with this small group of 8 to 10 individuals had instant credibility because of their age, and they were perceived as strong role models and reinforcers of group members' actions. Although no formal measures of change were taken in this group, members and the peer counselors reported that the group was helpful in increasing members' abilities to handle stress, change perceptions, and realize that others shared their concerns.

Anecdotal results have also been reported from an open-ended, topic-specific support group for widowed persons in Orange County, Florida, called "The Talk Group." The idea behind this group, which started in 1983, is that a *therapeutic alliance* is formed between individuals in grief and those who are helping them. The result is that "bereaved individuals who enjoy a high level of social support suffer fewer depressive symptoms and somatic complaints than those who are not so well supported" (Folken, 1991, p. 173). Thus, The Talk Group appears to benefit both the newly widowed and the group volunteers who work in it.

Another topic-specific group that is primarily psychoeducational in nature is for grandparents who are raising grandchildren (Vacha-Haase, Ness, Dannison, & Smith, 2000). The group, based on the curriculum *Second Time Around—Grandparents Raising Grandchildren* (Dannison & Nieuwenhuis, 1996), has initially been found to help custodial grandparents establish "contact with others who face similar life challenges" and as a result to "decrease feelings of isolation" and to "increase the use of positive coping strategies" (Vacha-Haase et al., 2000, p. 76).

Therapeutic writing groups for older adults have yielded promising results, too. For instance, Schuster (1998) found that, in nursing homes, residents who worked with her in a writing group took on a more positive identity and changed their familial and social relationships for the better. In this group, members wrote and then shared their writings as a way to reveal information about their thoughts and feelings.

In a nationwide study of group work in nursing homes, Mazza and Vinton (1999) found that most of the 304 respondents offered three types of groups for elderly residents—educational, support, and therapy/counseling. Most also provided educational and support groups for family members, but only 40% of the nursing homes offered therapy/counseling groups for family members. "The results of this study offer evidence that group work is generally an established part of the services offered in skilled nursing facilities" (p. 68).

GROUPS FOR CAREGIVERS FOR OLDER ADULTS

Caregivers are crucial in the daily care and well-being of older adults who may not be able to take care of themselves completely (Thomas & Martin, 2010). It has been estimated that more than 65 million Americans serve as caregivers for their sick, disabled, or infirm relatives, which include a number of older adults (Vacha-Haase, 2014). As demographics change, the ratio of available caregivers for older adults is declining (Redfoot, Feinberg, & Houser, 2013). The phenomenon of groups for caregivers for older adults is a relatively recent development (Santrock, 2013). It stems from the "advancements in medical science, technology, and health care" that enable human beings to live longer (Dobson & Dobson, 1991, p. 178). With this increased life span, middle-aged adults—the children of older adults—are often finding themselves as caregivers for older adult populations, although they have limited information and few role models to emulate. As a group, they "experience problems with confinement, infringement on lifestyle, restricted social life, work and family conflicts, and emotional and physical stress" (Thomas & Martin, 1997, p. 44). The result is often frustration, resentment, and physical and emotional strain. To address these concerns, groups for caregivers have been formed.

A number of different kinds of caregiver groups are available, ranging from those for direct relatives to those for nursing home staff members. The common denominator of these groups is that they primarily attempt to provide their members with information and support (Kennedy & Tanenbaum, 2000). Therefore, caregiver groups are mainly psychoeducational and psychotherapeutic in nature. Often they are short term, closed-ended, and meet at nontraditional hours, such as early evening. Through the caregiver group, a bond is formed among participants that helps them realize the universal nature of their situations (Dobson & Dobson, 1991; Hinkle, 1991; Vacha-Haase, 2014). For nonrelative caregivers, especially those concerned with providing services to the dying, groups help them ventilate their feelings and revitalize themselves and their efforts (Smith & Maher, 1991). In a group for dementia caregivers in Taiwan, depression level for participants in a 12-week experimental support group was significantly decreased, showing that the support group was effective for reducing caregivers' depression although not effective for relieving their burden of care (Chu et al., 2011).

Overall, groups for caregivers are preventive in nature. They affirm, support, and educate. They help link caregivers with others who can help them handle both unique and universal problems. They provide a means for participants to renew their own mental health and to concentrate on the interactional tasks ahead of them. As the older adult population increases, groups for caregivers for older adults will become more necessary and more prevalent.

> **Reflection**
>
> Who do you know who has looked after an older relative? What are some of the difficulties and concerns they have had? How do you think a group for caregivers could be or could have been of help to them?

STRENGTHS AND LIMITATIONS OF GROUPS FOR OLDER ADULTS

Strengths

Being a member of a group has numerous benefits for older people. The strengths are related to both the quantity and the quality of interpersonal relationships that older adults have (Haight & Gibson, 2005; Horswill, 1993). Group members become more aware of their needs, commonalities, unique traits, and possibilities through sharing in a group. They are also able to find support for and resolution to their problems and concerns. Gaining a sense of the universality of their concerns may be especially key in such groups (Hawkins, 1983). Belonging to a group, especially with people who are around the same age, assists participants in realizing that they are not alone in their focus on "body image, physical ailments, and fear of mental deterioration" (p. 187). Through sharing, they come to develop a sense of community and a feeling of belonging (Thomas, 1991). This type of atmosphere contributes to their overall wellness.

Another strength of a group for older adults is that it gives its members an opportunity to try out different responses and initiate new behaviors. Older persons often engage in **growing times**, when fresh learning occurs on an individual and interpersonal level (Wrenn, 1989). This process may involve merely a better appreciation of what they encounter or where they have been, or it may entail a physical action, such as talking or taking on a different life role. Within a group, especially if it is psychoeducationally oriented, older individuals can experiment with behaviors they never had an opportunity to try when they were younger. Doing so can help them fulfill their sense of what is ideal and give them a more positive view of themselves.

A third positive aspect of group membership involves the process of formal and applied learning. A popular movement in the United States since the 1970s is **Road Scholar** (formerly known as Elderhostel), in which older individuals live and study together for a time, often on a college campus. This way of learning helps elders gain new knowledge and reinforce one another as achievers, and it promotes social cohesion. Often an older person's life experience allows him or her to become the teacher as well as the student. Learning groups are not just for the young (Johnson & Johnson, 2013).

Groups for older adults can also enhance self-concept (O'Brien, Johnson, & Miller, 1979). Through groups, older adults can be helped to focus on some of the advantages of growing old. For instance, many older individuals find comfort in integrating different aspects of their lives. Such reflection and ongoing involvement foster hope and ward off depression. Persons in such situations become contributors to society.

Finally, groups for older adults provide a series of checks and balances for those who participate in them. They shift responsibility for growth and development from caregivers or relatives to the persons in the group (Mardoyan & Weis, 1981). Participants in groups are empowered to take control of their present lives and to resolve past difficulties as best they can. This type of emphasis promotes growth in a way not usually possible in other one-to-one relationships because more ideas are shared and processed. For instance, through meeting with peers, older adults may learn to focus more in their lives on what they select to do, how they optimize their opportunities, and how they compensate for factors related to aging, such as slowing down (Baltes & Baltes, 1990). The late Arthur Rubinstein, an admired concert pianist who performed well into his 80s, used many of these factors, such as selecting pieces that were difficult but not dependent on speed.

Case Example

Joe and the Gym

Joe used to be a bodybuilder. He loved lifting weights and working out at the various stations in the gym he belonged to. However, at age 70, Joe realized he could not work out as he once had. He initially thought he should give up his gym membership, buy a rocking chair, and sit. However, he was approached one day by the owner of the gym and asked if he would start an exercise group for seniors. Joe was delighted by the invitation but did not know exactly what he should do. Then it occurred to him that he could have group members go through a series of exercises for half an hour and then cool down by talking to one another for another half an hour. That way they would get to exercise their bodies and their minds.

Questions

What do you think of Joe's idea? How realistic is it? What else might he do?

Limitations

One limitation of groups for older adults is they are labor intensive. Finding an environment that is suitable and setting it up in a way that is conducive to good communication takes time and effort.

Groups for older adults also require their leaders to have specialized skills that may be anxiety producing at best. A leader of a group of this nature must face his or her mortality and be sensitive to the life and death issues of those in the group. Such understanding is not easily achieved.

In groups for older adults, especially the old-old, group members and leaders have to face real loss. The death of a member may occur during the group or shortly thereafter. Dealing with loss and death is never easy, and group members and even leaders may be hesitant to invest as much in the group or its members because of this possibility.

A fourth constraint of groups for older adults is that they often have more limited goals than other groups, and members tend to be more limited in accomplishing them. Group workers who like to see dynamic progress and outcomes may be disappointed in conducting groups for older adults.

Finally, while working with a group for older adults, group workers and even members of the group itself will most likely have to deal with the caregivers for other members (Thomas & Martin, 2010). Although many of these encounters will be positive, they can also be a source of stress to the leader and members because of the energy they require.

Reflection

How do you deal with minor personal losses, such as less elasticity in your skin or wrinkles around your eyes? How do you deal with major losses such as death? What do your reactions to these questions tell you about how you might function in a group for older adults?

Summary and Conclusion

Aging and the aged have been rigorously studied in the United States only since the late 1950s. With a growing number of individuals reaching age 65 and older, however, the importance of studying and working with this population has increased rapidly. Older adults have unique concerns and potentials that are frequently denied or overlooked. They bring to any situation a wealth of experience and talent as well as life circumstances unique to their time and informative to others.

Group work with older adults is still basically in its infancy. Before 1980, there was almost no professional literature on working with groups of older people (Myers, 1989). Now, research and approaches are more refined (Corey, 2012; Haight & Gibson, 2005; Henderson & Gladding, 2004; Thomas & Martin, 2010). However, questions still remain about what works best with which populations and when, even though Zimpfer (1987) has stated that, when an older adult "client's needs are diagnosed correctly, the treatment often seems to work no matter what it is" (p. 91). Seven major types of groups, outside psychoeducational and task/work groups, are frequently used therapeutically with older adults: reality orientation, remotivation therapy, reminiscing and life review, therapy and counseling, topic- and theme-focused, member specific, and eGroups. Psychoeducational and task groups that involve older adults, such as the Gray Panthers and AARP, are groups in which those over 65 may actively participate. Such groups offer social connections and support seldom found in other groups for older adults. Local religious and civic groups also offer support for some. Each of these types of groups has advantages and limitations.

In general, groups are quite appropriate and useful for older adults because groups may help them to integrate their lives more fully, find support, and develop a sense of universality. Furthermore, groups help older people combat loneliness and a sense of isolation. They may also give older adults a sense of orientation in time and place and an opportunity to continue to grow and develop.

Setting up a group for older adults depends on the leader's background and the participants' needs. Basically, many of the procedures for establishing groups are those required when working with other populations. However, group leaders need to be sensitive to time factors, foci, and themes that are especially appropriate for older adults. It is crucial that the needs and interests of both men and women be considered in setting up groups. For example, activities that center around both social and task-related opportunities should be included. This may mean setting up groups that focus on quilting bees, crafts, dances, and woodwork as well as seminars on travel, Social Security policies, and health insurance benefits.

When leaders direct their attention to these matters and come to terms with their own prejudices about age and their own sense of aging, they can promote positive interactions and development within groups of elderly people. As the qualitative and quantitative aspects of groups for older adults grow, so will other activities connected with them. Among the most important of these related occurrences will be groups for caregivers for the aged. Through psychoeducational and psychotherapeutic means, such groups can help relatives and professionals of older adults maintain their own mental health and give optimal care.

Classroom Exercises

1. Divide into teams and investigate the most recent professional literature on any of the primary types of groups mentioned in this chapter. Report back to the class as a whole on your findings and which approaches seem to work best with which populations of older adults.
2. Draw a picture of yourself at age 70. Then work backward and make a drawing of yourself for each

preceding decade until you reach your present age decade. After you have finished the drawings, role-play one of the ages you have drawn with a classmate and talk about how it feels to be that age and what concerns you have.

3. Collect data for a week from popular media, such as television, magazines, and newspapers, that demonstrate ageism or a lack of ageism. Share your findings with classmates. Make recommendations to the class on three ways that ageism can be positively countered.

4. Think of your experiences with older people when you were a child. Talk with other classmates in a group of three about what your experiences taught you about the aged and what impressions they still make on your life. How would your past affect your present performance as a leader for an elderly group?

CHAPTER 15

Transactional Analysis, Reality Therapy, Adlerian, and Person-Centered Groups

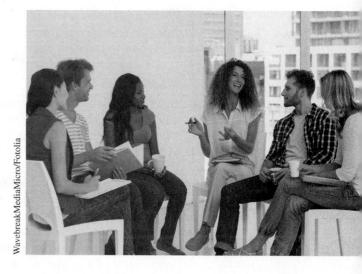

WavebreakMediaMicro/Fotolia

We sit like strangers in hard-backed chairs
at right angles from each other—
On the corners our sentences meet
reflecting our thoughts and lives.
Slowly, messages in our minds
make a move, a personal process
whose destination is undetermined
But develops as we detect
a crowd of quick-passing, open questions
That linger in our conversations
after the sights of people
have vanished with the fading light
And self-understanding has broken through
as we travel from dusk into night.*

From "In the Midst of the Puzzles and Counseling Journey" by Samuel T. Gladding, 1978, Personnel and Guidance Journal, 57, p. 148. © Samuel T. Gladding. Reprinted by permission from Samuel T. Gladding.

CHAPTER OVERVIEW

From reading this chapter, you will learn about

- The premises and practices of transactional analysis, reality therapy, Adlerian, and person-centered groups
- The role of leaders and desired outcomes in theoretically run groups
- How the effectiveness of the groups listed is evaluated

AS YOU READ, CONSIDER

- Which theoretical perspective you are most drawn to in conducting a group
- The different roles leaders play in helping a group evolve
- The unique and universal criteria used in evaluating the effectiveness of a theoretically led group

In 1543, Nicolaus Copernicus, a Renaissance mathematician and astronomer, formulated a heliocentric model of the universe that placed the Sun, rather than the Earth, at the center. He further proposed that the Earth revolves around the Sun, as do other planets. His theory was radical for his day when the prevailing thought was that the universe revolved around the Earth. It began the Copernican revolution and contributed importantly to the scientific revolution that followed. His work proved that a good theory can change the world (or at least the way we look at it!).

Because theory is so important, professional helpers and especially group leaders need to be steeped in counseling theories that are applicable to working with groups. The aftereffects of groups are often long lasting, and the theories used to run them make a difference because individuals usually leave groups at their conclusion with a different understanding of themselves and others. These changes may be positive or negative but are rarely neutral. Groups that are influenced for the better, especially counseling or therapy groups, have leaders who are skilled in promoting interactive activities from a theoretical position. These leaders are guided by the theories they use as to what they need to do next. Theories also offer techniques that group members can master and use after the group has ended (Schimmel & Jacobs, 2014). In this chapter, four theoretical models for conducting group work are examined: transactional analysis (TA), reality therapy, Adlerian, and person-centered.

Transactional analysis (TA) has been oriented toward groups since its inception. Eric Berne, the founder of the theory, believed that groups are more efficient than individual counseling in helping individuals understand their personal life scripts (Barnes, 1977; Berne, 1966; Stewart & Joines, 2012). In TA groups, the emphasis is on understanding intrapersonal and interpersonal dynamics. Participatory learning is through interactions in sessions and homework assignments. TA theorists and practitioners have also explored cultural frames of reference and intergroup encounters (James, 1994). However, to participate in a group, individuals must learn basic TA concepts (Lapworth & Sills, 2011; Newell, 2002). They must also be willing to work on past experiences in a present context.

For the **redecision school of TA**, in which the emphasis is on intrapsychic processes, groups are the main choice of treatment (Goulding, 1987). Groups provide a living experience in which members are able to examine themselves and their histories, which allows individuals to change their life scripts. For the other two schools of TA—*classical*, which emphasizes present interactions (Berne, 1964; Widdowson, 2010), and *cathexis,* which emphasizes reparenting (James, 2002)—groups are also frequently employed. The emphasis of TA groups is both interpersonal (i.e., the classical model) and intrapersonal (i.e., the cathexis and redecision models). In addition, TA is geared toward working on task/work group communication processes, such as those between employer and employee and among co-workers (Nykodym, Ruud, & Liverpool, 1986).

Reality therapy, founded by William Glasser, developed in the 1950s and 1960s and has since evolved. In the 1980s, **control theory**, a complete system for explaining how the brain works, was added. Choice theory replaced control theory as the base of reality therapy in the 1990s. The latest developments regarding reality therapy can be found on the William Glasser Institute Web site (wglasser.com). Like TA, reality therapy was initially employed more in groups than with individuals.

Originally, reality therapy "had no systematic theory, only the empirical idea that individuals are responsible for what they do" (Glasser, 1984, p. 320). However, Glasser developed and employed his approach in educational settings, where it is still quite popular (Glasser, 1999). In such settings, raising the self-esteem of low-achieving students and helping them alter their behaviors and attitudes are emphasized in and out of groups (Comiskey, 1993; Williamson, 1992). In addition, reality therapy has been applied to many populations seeking mental health services (Glasser & Breggin, 2001; Roy, 2014). Reality therapy has also gained a foothold in task/work environments, such as the **total quality movement (TQM)**, in which an emphasis is placed on working cooperatively and productively in small groups. It has also been examined in groups for its sensitivity to cultural issues of clients (Cunningham, 1995) and has been found to be effective in multiple cultures (e.g., In & Hwang, 1997; Peterson, Chang, & Collins, 1998).

Adlerian theory has always had a group focus. It concentrates on the inherent social interest of persons and emphasizes social development, cooperation, and education. Alfred Adler was an early user of groups for psychotherapeutic and psychoeducational purposes (Manaster & Corsini, 1982). He used groups to counsel parents as early as 1922; however, Adler never developed a theory of group work beyond the major principles he advocated in his approach to individual psychology. It was left to one of Adler's followers, Rudolph Dreikurs, to develop a group approach based on Adler's principles. Dreikurs introduced group therapy into private practice in 1929 in Vienna and then again in the United States in the late 1930s.

The growth and development of **person-centered group work** is linked to the theory and personal influence of Carl Rogers. In the 1960s, Rogers expanded his focus to the small group as well as to the individual. Rogers adapted some of the T-group (training group) structure and combined it with his own clinical approach and positive humanistic views into what he called the **basic encounter group**, in which "individuals come into much closer and direct contact with one another than is customary in ordinary life" (Rogers, 1967, p. 270).

In the 1970s, variations of these types of groups went by many names—for example, *personal growth groups, sensory awareness groups, sensitivity groups,* and *human relations groups.* Rogerian-based groups rapidly spread across the country and gained wide acceptance, especially among college students and the middle class. "In its heyday, the decade between 1962 and 1972, a reasonable estimate would be that several million people participated in some form of encounter group" (Bebout, 1978, p. 323). Rogers also became interested in large-group phenomena in the 1970s and initiated a new group format—the **community for learning**—in which about 100 people lived and worked together for 2 weeks at a time.

TRANSACTIONAL ANALYSIS GROUPS

Premises of Transactional Analysis Groups

TA theory has multiple aspects (Hargaden & Sills, 2002; Stewart & Joines, 2012). The basic concepts revolve around the development and interaction of what Berne (1964) called an **ego state**—"a system of feelings accompanied by a related set of behavior patterns" (p. 23). Three basic ego states—Parent, Adult, and Child—exist and operate within every individual and can be observed in the dynamic interactions of individuals (see Figure 15.1).

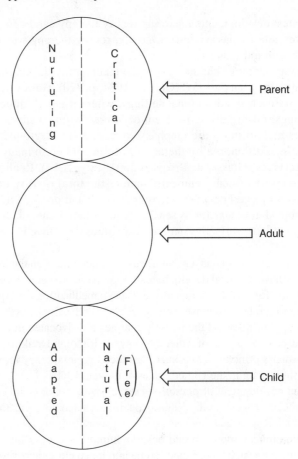

FIGURE 15.1 TA ego states.

Each ego state functions in its own special way, as follows:

1. The **Parent ego state** is dualistic—both nurturing and critical (or controlling). "The function of the *Critical Parent* is to store and dispense the rules and protection for living. The function of the *Nurturing Parent* is to care for, to nurture" (Grimes, 1988, p. 53). Typical statements from the Critical Parent are "Be home by seven" and "Watch what you are doing." Typical statements from the Nurturing Parent are "Rest for a while" and "Here, let me take your coat."

2. The **Adult ego state** functions like a computer in that it receives and processes information from the Parent, the Child, and the environment. It then makes the best decision possible. The Adult is the realistic, logical part of the person. A typical statement coming from the adult is "The appointment is this afternoon. I need to be on time."

3. The **Child ego state** is divided into two parts. The *Adapted Child* conforms to the rules and wishes of Parent ego states within the self and others. It is compliant and easy to get along with. A typical Adapted Child statement would be "I'm going to do what you ask because I am a good boy/girl." The *Free Child* (or *Natural Child*) reacts more spontaneously; it has fun and is more curious and playful. It takes care of its needs without regard for others while using its intuition to read nonverbal cues. For instance, the Free Child might say, "Come on, let's have fun!"

There are four basic ways to identify which ego state individuals are in at a particular moment: behavioral, social, historical, and phenomenological (Woollams, Brown, & Huige, 1977). It is important to be aware of the ego states of people, for it affects the manner in which they interact with themselves and others; a person who is operating from a Parent ego state is more likely to be critical or supportive than is a person who is operating from a Child ego state. Likewise, if an individual uses one ego state exclusively—for example, the Adult—then he or she is less likely to be flexible in thought and action than is a person who uses all three ego states.

Knowledge of their own ego states empowers individuals and those working with them to assess which types of transactions they are most likely to have and to take corrective measures, if needed (Hargaden & Sills, 2002). This type of information helps these persons avoid playing **games**, which Berne (1964) defined as "an ongoing series of complementary ulterior transactions progressing to a well-defined, predictable outcome" (p. 48). Games are played on three levels, and almost all of them are destructive and result in negative payoffs (i.e., *rackets*). *First-degree games* are the least harmful and may even be considered socially acceptable (e.g., "Blemish"). In these games, minor faults are highlighted, such as when Pat says to Suzanne, "You look great except for your hair." *Second-degree games* are more serious and usually result in some physical confrontation (e.g., "Uproar"). The interactive process in second-degree games leaves the people involved feeling negative, such as when Jim is called names by Marco. *Third-degree games* are deadly and often played for keeps (e.g., "Cops and Robbers"). There is nothing socially redeemable about third-degree games—for example, if Ed is caught stealing from the elderly and tries to fight his way free from the police.

People who play games operate from three distinct positions: (a) the *victim* (who appears to be innocent), (b) the *persecutor* (who appears to cause problems), and (c) the *rescuer* (who appears to solve the problem for the victim). Individuals who play games often switch between these roles as the *drama triangle* (Karpman, 1968) illustrates (see Figure 15.2). Games have a social as well as an individual dynamic, and they are often played on a group or organizational level on either an intra- or intergroup basis (Summerton, 1993).

TA also emphasizes several other beliefs about human nature; for instance, it holds that persons are born with positive tendencies to grow and develop, but this potential must be nurtured to become a reality (Dusay & Steiner, 1971). It likewise stresses that individuals structure their time to obtain **strokes** (i.e., physical or psychological recognition) in six major ways: (a) withdrawal, (b) ritual, (c) pastimes, (d) work, (e) games, and (f) intimacy (Berne, 1972). These ways of interacting can be represented through the use of an **egogram** (i.e., a bar graph) and will not change unless a person actively decides to change the amount of time spent engaging in certain behaviors (see Figure 15.3).

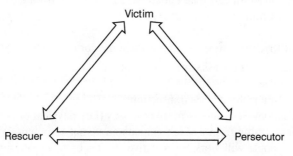

FIGURE 15.2 Drama (Karpman) triangle.

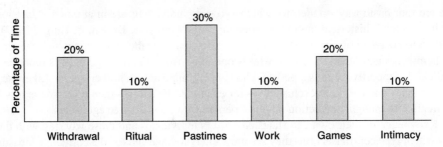

FIGURE 15.3 An egogram.

Over their life span, people gradually develop **scripts**, or habitual patterns of behavior, that influence how they spend their time—for example, as losers, nonwinners, or winners (Berne, 1972; Capers, 1975). Most people initially script their lives as a Child in the *I'm Not OK—You're OK* stance (a powerless one) but change to an Adult stance in later life as they affirm an *I'm OK—You're OK* position (characterized by trust and openness) (Harris, 1967). Other options open to them are *I'm OK—You're Not OK* (projection of blame onto others) and *I'm Not OK—You're Not OK* (hopeless and self-destructive).

Scripts include **transactions** (i.e., social action between two or more people). These transactions are manifested in social (overt) and psychological (covert) levels (Dusay & Dusay, 1989). Clear transactions with no hidden agenda are *complementary transactions*. For example,

PERSON 1:   What time is it?

PERSON 2:   It is 3 o'clock.

Crossed transactions are those in which a response is returned from an unexpected or inappropriate ego state. When this occurs, the person initiating the conversation often feels hurt and withdraws.

PERSON 1 (ADULT EGO STATE):   What time is it?

PERSON 2 (CRITICAL PARENT):   You are always in a hurry.

Ulterior transactions (which are often represented by dotted lines) occur when a message appears to be sent on one level but is actually transmitted on another level. Such transactions will often seem to be from an Adult ego state but are actually coming from the Child, represented by the designation "Adult/Child."

PERSON 1 (ADULT/CHILD MESSAGE):   Want some coffee at my place?

PERSON 2 (ADULT/CHILD MESSAGE):   I'd really like that.

Figure 15.4 illustrates these three transactions.

Through transactions, individuals receive strokes (i.e., physical or psychological recognition). Strokes can be anything from a quick glance to a verbal comment. When positive strokes are not forthcoming, people will work for negative strokes by using ulterior means. Games are the result and bad feelings the payoff in such cases.

1. *Complementary* (both persons are operating from the same ego state)

2. *Crossed* (an inappropriate ego state is activated)

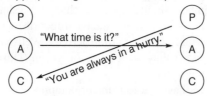

3. *Ulterior* (two ego states operate simultaneously, one disguises the other)

FIGURE 15.4 Three types of interpersonal transactions.

Reflections

When have you seen people operating from the Parent, Adult, Child TA ego states? In examining your own life, from which ego states do you see yourself operating frequently? What do you think about the concepts of games? When have you seen them being played in a group?

Practice of Transactional Analysis in a Group

TA is preferably used in groups that serve as a setting in which people can become more aware of themselves, the structure of their individual personality, the transactions they have with others, the games they play, and the scripts they act out. Such awareness enables persons to see themselves more clearly so that they can change what they want to change and strengthen what they want to strengthen (James & Jongeward, 1971). TA is especially appropriate in classroom settings to help children move into the OK position, especially when combined with behavioral approaches (Newell, 2002).

According to Berne (1966), the objective in group treatment settings is to "fight the past in the present in order to assure the future" (p. 250). The Child and Parent ego states represent the past, whereas the present is embodied in the Adult. Appropriate relations among these three ego states are necessary for people to function productively, and ultimately the Adult needs to be dominant in deciding which ego state will be displayed.

THERAPEUTIC CONTRACTS

All TA groups are based on the participants' ability and willingness to make and work on **therapeutic contracts** (Stewart, 2014). Contracts are specific, measurable, concrete statements of what participants intend to accomplish during the group. They place responsibility on members for clearly defining what, how, and when they want to change. Contracts can be made in all types of groups: task/work, psychoeducational, counseling, and psychotherapeutic. From the beginning of groups, members should learn that change is a shared responsibility; they cannot passively wait for the group leader to assume the direction of work in a group. In short, the contract establishes the departure point for group activity. Well-written contracts make it clear that participants are getting what they want from the group (Dusay, 1983), and are based on decisions made by the Adult ego state.

Generally, "TA contracts have the four major components of a legal contract" (Dusay & Dusay, 1989, p. 428). These aspects include (a) *mutual assent*—clearly defining a goal from an adult perspective and joining with the therapist's Adult as an ally, (b) *competency*—agreeing on what can realistically be expected, (c) *legal object*—an objective, and (d) *consideration*—a fee or price for services. An example of a group contract is an agreement by members of an industrial group to remain together long enough to complete a mutually agreed-on activity, such as eliminating discriminatory language from company contracts. Group members usually meet weekly to assess the progress made in pursuing their goals.

CLASSICAL CONTRACTS

Classical school contracts are carried out with an emphasis on one or more of the following: (a) structural analysis, (b) transactional analysis, (c) game analysis, and (d) life script analysis. "To achieve the most complete treatment, all four need to be accomplished; each one is built upon the previous level and must be completed in order" (Donigian & Hulse-Killacky, 1999, p. 116). In *structural analysis*, all group members become aware of the structure of their ego states and how they function. Members are encouraged to "decontaminate" any ego state that is not operating properly, such as when a person who appears to speak from the Adult ego state is instead speaking from the Parent ego state: "Children should be seen and not heard."

TA involves the diagnosing of interactions among group members to determine whether they are *complementary* (i.e., from appropriate and expected ego states), *crossed* (i.e., from inappropriate and unexpected ego states), or *ulterior* (i.e., from a disguised ego state, such as the Child speaking as if it were an Adult).

Game analysis includes an examination of destructive and repetitive behavioral patterns and an analysis of the ego states and types of transactions involved. Because games prevent intimacy, it is crucial that they be eliminated (Berne, 1964). The classical TA group devotes considerable time to helping members become aware of the games they initiate and participate in. With this knowledge, they can come to develop intimate and nonmanipulative relationships.

Finally, on the deepest level, classical TA school groups perform **life script analyses**, which are people's basic plans involving transactions and games (Steiner, 1974). Typically, scripts are made on an unconscious level when individuals are children (before age 5) and determine life plans, such as living a tragic or happy existence (Berne, 1961). As a general rule, script analysis is difficult to do in a group.

REDECISION CONTRACTS

Groups have within them curative factors because of their social nature. Properly conducted TA groups give their members knowledge and insight into their lives. A special form of TA, **redecision theory**, helps clients make redecisions while they are in their Child ego state (McCormick, 1995). This task is accomplished by having these individuals reexperience a past event as if it were now present. This process usually involves combining TA and Gestalt approaches and may be geared toward individuals or couples in a group (Tyler, 1995). Persons who engage in the redecision process first make a contract to address significant symptoms they wish to change, then they take actions that focus on rackets and games they have experienced. They are taught that they are responsible for both their feelings and their actions (Goulding, 1975).

The next step of this process is for group members to explore the sources that led them to make a particular life decision. Accountability is stressed, as is power for changing, because help-less or so-called cop-out words, *can't, perhaps,* and *try,* are not accepted. Once group members redecide and make a change by actually reliving an early scene from their past psychologically, they are reinforced and encouraged to continue. Group leaders help such individuals focus on how they will conduct themselves in a new way outside the group and develop a needed support system to continue the changes they have made. Fantasizing what lies ahead and how they will cope is also a part of this process (Goulding, 1987).

Role of the Transactional Analysis Group Leader

TA group leaders are more than just group members. They stand apart as "primarily listeners, observers, diagnosticians, and analysts—and, secondarily, process facilitators" (Donigian & Hulse-Killacky, 1999, p. 115). TA groups are leader centered and, although member–member transactions occur, they do not have the same effect as a leader–member interaction.

Overall, transactions in TA groups that are between the group leader and a member are considered major; those that occur among group members are minor. A group is functioning optimally when major and minor transactions involving all members take place and when attitu-dinal and behavioral changes occur. By staying detached, the leader is able to see more clearly than group members the games that are occurring and is thereby able to analyze and intervene dynamically.

It is vital that TA group leaders understand themselves well from a TA perspective and that they adopt an "I'm OK" life position because they are teachers within the group. They must have a thorough understanding of how TA concepts operate in their own lives before they try to help others apply these concepts. Also, if TA leaders are going to be able to establish rapport with group members and help them change, then they must think well of themselves most of the time.

The leader has four specific roles within the TA group (Corey, 2012). **Protection** involves keeping members safe from psychological or physical harm. **Permission** centers on giving group members directives to behave against the injunctions of their parents. (**Injunctions** are Parent commands recorded by the Child that call for the Child to adopt certain roles, such as "Do as you are told.") **Potency** is the use of appropriate counseling techniques in certain situations. For example, making a contract for change and active listening are two appropriate and potent coun-seling techniques. Finally, **operations** are specific techniques employed by TA group leaders that include interrogation, specification, confrontation, explanation, illustration, confirmation, inter-pretation, and crystallization (Berne, 1966; Gladding, 2013). For instance, a group leader may confront a member about the inconsistencies shown between the member's speech and behavior.

Desired Outcome of Transactional Analysis Groups

If a TA group is successful, then members will learn about themselves through their analysis of structures, transactions, games, and scripts. The knowledge they acquire from this process will enable them to think, feel, and behave differently if they choose, freeing them from old Parent messages (injunctions) and early, self-defeating scripts made by their Child. They may adopt an "I'm OK—You're OK" position in life and "get on" with themselves in a positive way (Newell, 2002).

Woollams and Brown (1978) view the process that leads to this desired outcome as going through seven steps: (a) trust in the other, (b) trust in self, (c) moving into group, (d) work, (e) redecision, (f) integration, and (g) termination. These steps are usually intertwined and can rarely be distinguished from one another. At the end of the group, however, members should have accomplished what they set out to do or have a contract for finishing their goal(s) (Tudor, 1995). TA promotes the integration of the person in multimodal ways; however, the outcome in TA is not likely to be accomplished unless its practitioners borrow behavioral and affective techniques and procedures from other theories.

Case Example

Thomas and the TA Group

Thomas was tired of always being put down by his peers. Therefore, when a chance came for him to join a TA counseling group, he jumped at it. He thought that through the use of TA in a group he could gain a greater perspective on both himself and those with whom he associated.

He was not disappointed. He signed a contract to work on the way he presented himself to others and got down to work immediately. Through the group he realized that he often spoke from his Child ego state and that he invited criticism and putdowns in his life from the Parent ego state of many of his acquaintances. Therefore, Thomas made modifications in his speech patterns. He learned to speak more often from the Adult ego state, and he stopped himself from getting hooked into playing games with others.

Questions

Why do you think Thomas would be a typical or atypical member of a TA group? Besides modifying his ego state speech, what other tools do you think a TA group could use to help Thomas learn, and how else might they help him?

Evaluation of Transactional Analysis Groups

TA groups are potentially powerful ways of helping individuals work together for the good of themselves and others. However, they have limitations as well as strengths.

STRENGTHS AND CONTRIBUTIONS

There are a number of strengths associated with the TA theory of group work. First is the cognitive clarity of the language used to explain TA concepts (Grimes, 1988; Yalom & Leszcz, 2005). TA works in groups by helping members to understand how they function intra- and interpersonally and how they came to make the decisions in life they did. The clarity of TA concepts is also useful in helping group members realize what they need to do to change. This approach stresses intellectual insight as the initial basis for doing things differently.

Another strong aspect of TA is its simplicity. TA concepts can be readily grasped. The theory can be used in its most elementary form in just a few hours. The almost immediate applicability of TA makes it popular with group leaders who want their members to gain intellectual understanding quickly and make practical strides in resolving difficult relationships (Sigmund, 1995).

A third benefit of using TA in groups is that individuals "move faster toward getting well" (Harris, 1967, p. 204). Group members who make progress toward achieving their goals reinforce others in the group to do the same. This dynamic occurs in both subtle and overt ways and helps group members achieve results not possible in individual treatment formats.

A final strength of using TA in groups is that it can be used in task/work, psychoeducational, counseling, and psychotherapy settings. It can also be combined effectively with other more action-centered approaches, such as Gestalt or behavioral, to produce a dynamic method of change (Goulding & Goulding, 1979; Newell, 2002). Such combinations help group members put their contracts and thoughts into achievable forms.

LIMITATIONS

A major drawback of TA is its restrictive interpretation of the complexities of human nature by categorizing them into a limited number of games, ego states, and scripts (Yalom & Leszcz, 2005). People are more complex than the concepts of TA, and group members may find themselves restricted in dealing with complicated situations because of a shortage of TA concepts to describe what is happening. It is also difficult to use TA language uniformly and correctly.

A second limitation of TA in groups is its strong emphasis on understanding. This cognitive focus is further complicated because some TA leaders use the structure and vocabulary of TA to "avoid genuine contact with their clients or to keep them from revealing their reactions" (Corey, 2012, p. 343). These types of behaviors set up barriers and constitute a misuse of TA theory while lessening the impact of the approach on participants. "If the group becomes immersed in analysis to the exclusion of spontaneous interaction and emotional expression, it has the potential to become merely an intellectual exercise" (Vander Kolk, 1985, p. 66).

Another shortcoming of TA in groups is its neglect of emphasizing group process (Yalom & Leszcz, 2005). TA centers largely on member–leader interaction and does not effectively use other group dynamics, such as interpersonal learning, cohesiveness, and universality. Future research in TA needs to focus on controlled research designs that will allow investigators to contrast and compare TA techniques in groups uniformly (Kapur & Miller, 1987).

A final weakness of the use of TA in groups is the lack of empirical evidence to support its effectiveness. Although Dusay and Dusay (1989) cite "hard data gain" as an outcome of TA treatment, little research has been done on TA groups per se. The *Transactional Analysis Journal* is interested in publishing such studies but so far has received relatively few.

Learning More

TA is akin to psychoanalysis in its emphasis on ego states. However, TA is much more cognitive in nature and is less concerned with the unconscious. There are hundreds of certified transactional analysts throughout the world. Most TA group practitioners belong to the ITAA:

> International Transactional Analysis Association (ITAA)
> Web site: itaaworld.org

The ITAA publishes material on TA theory and practice. Especially noteworthy is its professional periodical, the *Transactional Analysis Journal*. The ITAA also provides workshops and educational training in the practice of TA.

REALITY THERAPY GROUPS

Premises of Reality Therapy Groups

Reality therapy, as a theoretical approach, differs from other common-sense ways of working in groups by emphasizing that "all behavior is generated within ourselves for the purpose of satisfying one or more basic needs" (Glasser, 1984, p. 323). Unlike most other helping theories, reality therapy claims that human behavior is a reaction not to outside events but rather to internal needs. **Reality therapy's four human psychological needs** are belonging (involvement with people, the need to love and be loved), power (the need to be in charge of one's life, to accomplish and achieve), freedom (the need to make choices), and fun (the need to laugh, experience humor, and enjoy life) (Vernon, 2011b). These needs originate is the "new" human brain. There is also one physiological need, survival, which originated in the "old" human brain (Glasser, 1985). "No matter what the presenting problem, all clients seen in counseling are struggling unsuccessfully to satisfy one or more of these basic needs" (Glasser, 1986b, p. 3) (see Figure 15.5).

Glasser (1965, 1999, 2001, 2003) states that reality therapy differs from other psychotherapeutic systems in the following ways:

1. It rejects the concept of mental illness. People choose to act psychotically or neurotically in an attempt to control the world to some extent and to satisfy their needs. The only behavior we can control is our own.
2. It emphasizes the present as the "cutting edge" of people's lives and focuses on how individuals can effectively control the world they live in and choose behaviors that are best for them. Such behavior is especially important in the four major personal relationships that cause problems: husband–wife, parent–child, teacher–student, and manager–worker.
3. It does not deal with transference but relates to clients' perceptions.
4. It does not consider the unconscious or dreams but rather concentrates on present awareness in an attempt to make that awareness even greater.
5. It stresses that persons must judge their own behaviors in light of personal and societal values.

FIGURE 15.5 Reality therapy as a theoretical therapy.

6. It attempts to teach people a better way of fulfilling their needs and taking responsibility for themselves. In essence, Glasser sees all psychotherapy as teaching and all psychoeducation as psychotherapeutic.

A main emphasis of reality therapy is cognitive and behavioral in nature. Wubbolding (1992, 2001, 2011) has created an acronym, WDEP, as a pedagogical tool, that summarizes reality therapy and provides a memory peg for retaining, applying, and implementing the principles of reality therapy. In WDEP, W = wants, D = direction and doing, E = evaluation, and P = planning.

Practice of Reality Therapy in a Group

The practice of reality therapy in a group setting is basically a rational and pragmatic process. It emphasizes observable behavior in a here-and-now setting (Glasser, 1992, 2000). For example, what is someone in the group doing now in regard to personal and relationship difficulties? If the process goes smoothly, then group members will give up unproductive and self-defeating behaviors, such as trying to control others and making themselves miserable in the process, and instead will commit to new action patterns that they have mutually agreed on with the group leader. One such choice might be to give up the belief that others are responsible for the ways they feel and to choose to accept the personal freedom they have to control their own thoughts, feelings, and behaviors.

Group leaders apply reality therapy concepts in many different ways. The main focus, however, is to help clients take responsibility for their actions, find better ways to meet their needs, and change inappropriate or destructive ways of behaving (Glasser & Breggin, 2001). Wubbolding (2011) is one of the masters of applying the theory to groups. He stressed that there are two main components involved in using reality therapy in groups: setting up the environment and applying proper procedures using the WDEP framework.

Setting up the environment involves establishing an atmosphere in which work within the group can take place. Wubbolding (1999, 2001) suggests a list of ABCDE dos and don'ts: **A**lways **b**e **c**ourteous and **d**etermined as well as **e**nthusiastic (i.e., look for the positive). Don't **a**rgue, **b**elittle, **c**riticize, **d**emean, or get lost in **e**xcuses. In many ways, Wubbolding's suggestions for setting up the environment are similar to steps 1, 6, and 7 of **reality therapy's original eight basic steps** (Glasser, 1984; Glasser & Zunin, 1973). All of the steps in the process are listed here, although reality therapy has evolved a great deal since its debut:

1. *Make friends/establish a meaningful relationship.* In this first step, the reality therapist attempts to establish rapport with each group member. People are usually involved in groups because of a need to connect with others. Therefore, the group leader can take the initial step in fulfilling this need. This process is achieved by having the group leader screen applicants and then engage them in conversation or activity soon after they come to the group. In doing so, the leader determines, with the help of the group member, what he or she pictures as a way of meeting his or her basic needs. This picture comes from within the internal world of the group member (Glasser, 1986b) and is drawn out by the leader through skillful questioning and interactions.

2. *Emphasize present behaviors/Ask, "What are you doing now?"* This second step focuses in on the process of choice. Reality therapists stress the importance of using thinking and acting, rather than feeling or physiology, to bring about change (Glasser, 1986a). Group members are asked to concentrate on behaviors they can control in the present. For example, members have choices in the ways they think about and interact with other group

members and the group leader. For instance, Willie can choose to avoid Florence and Jamie in the group, or he can face them and share with them his perceptions.

3. ***Stress whether clients' actions are getting them what they want.*** The emphasis here is on group members' judging their behaviors and learning that their behaviors are within their control. A part of this process focuses on personal values, whereas a second part underlines reasonable rules by which societal systems live. Persons with difficulties may be acting against their own best judgment or the collected wisdom of society (Glasser, 1986b). For example, if Tess becomes upset every time someone ignores her but her actions do not bring about changes, then she may be confronted with the fruitlessness of what she is doing.

4. ***Make a positive plan to do better.*** This is a critical stage in the group process. It involves "planning, advising, helping, and encouraging" (Glasser, 1984, p. 336). It is based on the accomplishment of the first three stages. The plan of action is the individual's, but group members and the leader can be effective in providing input and suggestions that will make the plan even more potent. Wubbolding (1988) suggests that an effective plan has the following components: (a) ties in closely with a member's needs; (b) is simple and easy to understand; (c) is realistic and attainable; (d) includes positive actions; (e) is independent of others' contributions; (f) is practiced regularly; (g) is immediately doable; (h) is process oriented; and (i) is open to constructive input by group members by being written down and well formulated.

5. ***Get a commitment to follow the positive plan.*** It is not enough to formulate a plan of action; group members must follow through. In making a commitment, group members take responsibility for their lives and, in the process, gain more control. For example, if George commits himself to 15 minutes of exercise a day, then he achieves control of his body and time in a new way.

6. ***No excuses.*** At times, group members will not succeed in their plans of action. In such cases, the group leader and members simply acknowledge that the person failed. The past is not brought up, and excuses are not discussed. Accepting excuses gives persons in the group the idea that they are weak, cannot change, and are, in effect, unable to control their lives (Wubbolding, 1988, 1991). Instead, individuals are helped to formulate another plan (usually a modification of the original one) and are encouraged to try again. Sometimes the plan is broken down into smaller steps than previously for, as Glasser and Zunin (1973) point out, "It is much better to have client success in small stages than to try to effect a large change and experience failure" (p. 301).

7. ***No punishment.*** "Punishment is the infliction of pain with no reasonable way to reduce or end the pain no matter what the wrongdoer does" (Glasser, 1984, p. 337). It is the opposite of choice and control and often leads to individuals acting in negative or self-defeating ways. Therefore, reality therapy stresses that persons who do not follow their plans of action must live with the natural consequences. This usually means they do not get what they want, and such a response, along with the group's encouragement, often motivates them to try again.

8. ***Never give up.*** Change takes time, especially if the client has a long history of failure. Group leaders persevere with group members who are slow to change. This consistency begins to become internalized by clients as they realize that the leader is like a good friend who does not give up easily. With this realization, they often become more willing to try new behaviors, and the process of change can begin. For example, Betsy may internally remind herself that her group leader still believes she can lose the weight she committed to dropping. Therefore, she renews her commitment and effort.

In addition to this eight-step procedure, Wubbolding (2011) suggests four special techniques that are applicable to setting up the environment of a reality therapy group: (a) skillful use of questioning, (b) self-help procedures, (c) use of humor, and (d) use of paradox.

Skillful *questioning* is crucial. The group leader asks open-ended and inviting questions to help members become more explorative. For example, the leader might say, "Clarence, what do you hope to get out of this group?"

Self-help procedures focus on the positive. Behaviors that members would like to change are targeted. A real effort is made by group members to implement actions that will lead to success, such as learning new social skills.

Glasser advocates the use of *humor*, too. Wubbolding's emphasis on this procedure is to stress its timing, focus, and importance in building trust. Humor should be used to help individuals gain an awareness of a situation not easily obtainable in another way. For example, in regard to self, the group leader might say, "Whenever I think I've learned all the answers about groups, the groups change the questions."

Finally, in regard to using **paradox**, Wubbolding (1999) stresses that with some group members, change is best brought about indirectly rather than directly. To be successful, group leaders may employ paradox (asking members to do the opposite of what they want) so that the message they give, such as "go slowly," is taken seriously and disobeyed for the good of the group member. Most reality therapy group leaders are not initially able to use paradox successfully.

Applying proper procedures in working with groups using the WDEP framework revolves around specific behaviors. In the "W" part of this process, group members are asked what they want. The question is geared toward cultural considerations and the commitment of the person in the group. The leader presses for both specifics of the answer and a level of commitment indicating that the person is fully dedicated to achieving the want and will do what it takes to reach a goal. The "D" part of the procedure is focused on what the person is doing but extends to where he or she is going. If a camera could take a picture of both the doing and the going aspects of the person's life, then the person, group members, and the group leader would have a clear idea of the person's present reality and direction.

"E" represents self-evaluation. A self-evaluation can take a behavioral, emotional, or cognitive form—the important thing is that this evaluation must be realistic and honest. Finally, there is the "P" part of Wubbolding's way of working in groups, which stands for a direction based plan of action. A good plan is **s**imple, **a**ttainable, **m**easurable, **i**mmediate, and **c**ontrolled by the planner. Wubbolding (1999) combines the first letters of the words describing a good plan to form the acronym SAMIC. He believes group leaders must be persistent and never give up on their clients.

Reflections

One of the major tenets of reality/choice therapy is to never give up on a person. When have you seen that idea work? What made it work? Are there circumstances where it would be best to give up on a person?

Role of the Reality Therapy Group Leader

Reality therapy group leaders are active and involved. They strive to be warm, confronting individuals who keep pointing out reality to group members in a direct, caring manner. For example, as the group leader, George, may say to Jana, "Is what you are doing now working?"

Glasser (1965) lists four criteria for effective reality therapy leaders. First, they must be responsible persons who are able to fulfill their own needs. Next, they must be mentally strong and able to resist group members' pleas for sympathy and excuses for nonproductive behavior. A third quality is acceptance of group members for who they are. Finally, group leaders must be emotionally involved or supportive of group members. Overall, leaders must be mentally and emotionally mature and comfortable with themselves before they can work with group members.

Corey (2012) states that reality therapy practitioners must strive to carry out other functions, too. Among the most prevalent is serving as a personal model of responsible behavior. Group members are likely to emulate leaders whether leaders wish them to or not. In addition, reality therapy group leaders must foster the process of self-evaluation in their members. They may do this through modeling the self-evaluation process in themselves. Furthermore, leaders need to establish a structure and limits for group sessions. They must assist group members in understanding the scope of the group process and the need to apply what they have learned in the group to their own daily lives.

Desired Outcome of Reality Therapy Groups

If the reality therapy group process is successful, then members realize several benefits. Among the most important is the change they will experience in moving past self-defeating patterns of behavior, that is, being stuck in repetitive and nonproductive activity. Instead, they will engage in new behaviors designed to help them achieve responsible, present-oriented goals. They will realize that, just as the group leader did not give up or punish them when they were not successful with their positive plans of action, they do not have to become discouraged, defeated, or punitive when they do not initially achieve what they want.

Group members come away from the reality therapy experience with a greater awareness of their values. Through the group, they realize they have a choice in what they do. Outside events and past histories lose much of their power.

Case Example

Raquel Becomes a Reality Therapy Leader

Raquel is a school counselor and has been involved as a reality therapist for years. In starting a group she chose 10 adolescent, acting-out boys from her school and screened them. Nine expressed interest in her group for learning new behaviors and were chosen. Each week Raquel worked with the boys to make a plan and to stick with it. No excuses for failure were allowed, and she did not give up even on Burt, who had 5 straight weeks of not following through on

what he proposed. When the 12-week group ended, the boys had bonded and were reluctant to end the experience. However, they all agreed that they were more successful than previously with their teachers, families, friends, and even themselves.

Questions

Do you think reality therapy is more successful with those on whom others have given up? Does the background of group members really make a difference? Why?

Evaluation of Reality Therapy Groups

Reality therapy has been used in a number of different kinds of groups and is very versatile. Nevertheless, it has limitations as well as strengths.

STRENGTHS AND CONTRIBUTIONS

Several strengths of reality therapy make it an attractive and productive method to use in groups. First, reality therapy emphasizes accountability. Individuals are responsible for deciding what they value and wish to change in their lives; therefore, responsibility is placed squarely on the shoulders of group members. They may act on the seven deadly habits that destroy relationships: "criticizing, blaming, complaining, nagging, threatening, punishing, and bribing or rewarding to control," or they may improve their relationships through enacting the seven caring habits of relationships: "supporting, encouraging, listening, accepting, trusting, respecting, and negotiating differences" (Glasser, 2005, p. 21).

A second strength of this approach is its emphasis on action and thinking, as opposed to feeling and physiology (Glasser, 1986a, 2000). By highlighting that group members make plans and carry them out, reality therapy breaks the inertia of the past and makes it more likely that clients will change. Part of this action/thinking process involves refusing to accept excuses and not punishing (Glasser, 1984; Wubbolding, 2011).

A third valuable dimension of a reality therapy group is its viability with people in society on whom others have given up (Glasser & Breggin, 2001). For example, delinquents, prisoners, and addicts are groups that are often neglected or ineffectively served (Dugan & Everett, 1998). Reality therapy groups make it possible to work productively with populations that are viewed as incorrigible or difficult. This approach is also effective in crisis counseling and long-term group counseling, such as with victims of rape (McArthur, 1990).

A fourth asset of this approach is its emphasis on definable procedures for working with individuals in groups (Glasser, 1986b; Wubbolding, 1987, 1999). Reality therapy is straightforward in emphasizing what group leaders need to do and when. It has become more flexible through the years, with practitioners adding new techniques to its repertoire, such as paradoxical methods and teaching metaphors and stories (Wubbolding, 1991).

A final selling point of reality therapy in groups is that the treatment continues only until participants are able to resolve difficulties. Reality therapy is a relatively brief approach (Wubbolding, 1999, 2011). Most individuals have only limited time to work on their difficulties. Reality therapy is geared to that reality and helps group members become involved with others and reinforce each person's successful plans.

LIMITATIONS

One drawback of reality therapy is its emphasis on the exchange of communication, either verbal or written (Glasser, 1984). Many reality therapists use contracts in their groups to have members clarify exactly what their goals are. Individuals who cannot or will not communicate in this way do not benefit much from this approach.

A second limitation of reality therapy is its simplicity. Glasser's eight-step method of conducting a group or Wubbolding's WDEP model may be misapplied by "mechanical" group leaders who do not understand or appreciate the complexity of human nature and change. These individuals are likely to be too controlling or rigid so that group members do not get the opportunity to struggle with their own issues.

A third weakness of reality therapy is its extreme position on some issues. For instance, Glasser denies that there is genetically based mental illness and insists that people choose to behave in mentally ill ways (Glasser, 1984, 1986a; Glasser & Breggin, 2001). Also, reality therapy refuses to deal with the unconscious and denies the importance of past events.

A fourth problem of this theory in groups is its lack of proven effectiveness. Glasser argues that reality therapy is one of the most popular theories in educational, correctional, and substance abuse programs (Evans, 1982), but the validity of this theory has not been researched thoroughly.

A final restriction of reality therapy is its emphasis on conformity and utility. Group members are expected to conform to the reality of those with the most power (Glasser, 1986a). This emphasis is pragmatic, but it may discourage creative and independent behaviors. It also takes the emphasis away from changing one's environment. The drawback is that attention to larger and important issues may be bypassed or ignored.

Learning More

Reality therapy is a dynamic approach to working with groups. The theory and its treatment were originally developed by William Glasser, but reality therapy has been popularized and explained in depth by both Glasser and Robert Wubbolding. Both run institutes where training and educational materials may be obtained. Their addresses are as follows:

William Glasser International, Inc.
wglasserinternational.org

Center for Reality Therapy
realitytherapywub.com.

ADLERIAN GROUPS

Premises of Adlerian Groups

Chief among the major tenets of Adlerian theory is that people are primarily motivated by social interest (Corsini, 1988; Simpson, Vernon, & Erford, 2011). **Social interest** has been defined as "not only an interest in others but an interest in the interests of others" (Ansbacher, 1977, p. 57). "From the Adlerian point of view the essence of normality is having a feeling of concern for others" (Corsini, 1988, p. 10). This concern is expressed as a positive attitude toward people (Sonstegard, Bitter, & Pelonis, 2004) that can be and is developed in a group context.

Other major concerns that undergird Adlerian theory are as follows:

1. *The purposefulness of all behavior*—Adlerians believe that individuals do not act randomly. They act with a goal in mind, and although they are sometimes not aware of their goal, the general direction of life is from minus (inferiority) to plus (perfection, i.e., completeness) (Dreikurs, 1950). For instance, if Beverly lashes out at Carmen, her intent may be to protect her privacy, although she may say afterward, "I'm not sure why I just did that."

2. *The subjective nature of perception*—Adlerians emphasize the phenomenological nature of human behavior. People perceive the world based on their experiences, not objectively. Therefore, if Eric has known only abuse in his life, he may perceive the world and his group as hostile.

3. *The holistic nature of people*—For Adlerians, people are a unified whole, not a collection of parts. People are more like trees, which grow from seeds and branch out, than they are like machines, which are a collection of parts (Corsini, 1988). From this perspective, one answer is usually inadequate to explain even a simple act.

4. *The importance of developing a healthy style of life*—A **style of life** is the way one prefers to live and relate to others. Adlerians stress that a faulty lifestyle is based on competitiveness and on striving to be superior to others. Lifestyles are not noticed when a

person is in a favorable situation but manifest themselves when difficulties arise (Adler, 1956). Lifestyles are developed early in a person's development (around age 5), but they are open to change.

5. *The self-determinism of the individual to chart a future based on expected consequences of behavior* (Corsini, 1988; Hawes, 1985)—Adlerians stress that people are creative and can choose from among a wide range of possible behaviors (Manaster & Corsini, 1982; Sonstegard et al., 2004). All behavioral disorders are based on failures to choose wisely.

Reflections

When, in either public or private life, have you ever seen someone fail to choose wisely? What do you think was going on in that person's mind? Do you think facts or emotions are predominant in an unwise decision?

Practice of Adlerian Theory in a Group

Adlerian groups are primarily psychoeducational in nature, although some of these groups are therapeutically oriented and are conducted in a counseling context. The groups are "heterodox with respect to procedures" (Corsini, 1988, p. 19) but have many unifying aspects. The idea in Adlerian groups is that people can learn from one another. As Dreikurs (1969) points out, "Since . . . problems and conflicts are recognized in their social nature, the group is ideally suited not only to highlight and reveal the nature of a person's conflicts and maladjustments but to offer corrective influences" (p. 43).

Some groups are more didactic than others. For example, in **Adlerian parent education** groups, developmental and preventive aspects of parenting are explained. These groups focus on empowering parents to consider the dynamics and purposes of their children's behaviors. They encourage group members' discussion and interaction. Change in parental behaviors is expected before a change will occur in their children. These groups also stress cooperation among family members as a goal. They emphasize the use of logical and natural consequences to avoid power struggles. The Adlerian approach promotes parent discussion groups with a trained leader and a set curriculum. This orientation is democratic, and regular family council meetings are encouraged as a forum where all members in a family voice concerns and needs.

One variation of an Adlerian psychoeducational group is the **C group** (Dinkmeyer, 1973). The name is based on each component of the group: collaboration, consultation, clarification, confrontation, concern, confidentiality, and commitment. All aspects of the group begin with a *c*. The C group approach has now been updated and is currently packaged as **Systematic Training for Effective Parenting (S.T.E.P.)**. Another Adlerian parent education program is *Active Parenting Today in 3: Your Three Part Guide to a Great Family* (Popkin, 2006).

At least three unifying factors link Adlerian groups together regardless of their form. One is the emphasis on an **interpretation of a person's early history**. To promote change, it is helpful for group members to recognize and understand how they created their own lifestyles. Thus, if Eleanor is miserable, she had an active part in becoming this way. A second similarity in Adlerian groups is the practice of stressing individual, interpersonal, and group process goals during the duration of the group. **Individual goals** may involve developing insight into the creation of a mistaken lifestyle and taking corrective measures. **Interpersonal goals** may entail becoming more socially oriented and involved with others. **Group process goals** may center on promoting and experiencing a cooperative climate in the group. Thus, Shuford can come to realize he has isolated himself and reach out to people in the group, as well as the group itself.

After an initial screening of members, an Adlerian counseling group begins with an emphasis on the leader's part to promote cooperation and an egalitarian spirit. Group members may contract to work on areas that have personal meaning to them. After the proper participatory atmosphere has been created, participants are invited to explore their own life-styles and understand how their present behavior promotes or deters their current functioning in life tasks (Maniacci, Sackett-Maniacci, & Mosak, 2014). Some of the ways this second phase of the group is conducted include exploring family constellations, early recollections, and basic mistakes.

After this analysis, group members are ready to move into the **insight and reorientation phases of the group**. The insight phase involves helping individuals understand why they made the choices they did in the past. It often is accompanied by the group leader's use of interpretation which is offered as a tentative hypothesis, such as "Could it be. . . ?" or "I wonder if. . . ?" For example, "Joan, I wonder if there is a connection between your sister's success and your pattern of abandoning projects just when you are doing well in them?"

In the final phase, **reorientation**, counseling group members are encouraged to act differently and take control of their lives. Such a procedure means taking risks, such as acting "as if" they were the people they wished to be. For example, Damany may resolve to act as if he does not need the backing of his parents to make a successful career choice.

Role of the Adlerian Group Leader

Although co-leading groups is common in the Adlerian approach (Maniacci et al., 2014), a number of qualities characterize effective individual Adlerian group leaders. The ideal leader is a well-balanced person who possesses certain characteristics: adaptability, courage, humor, sincerity, an acceptance of others, and an openness that promotes honest interchange with group members. Adlerian group leaders need a positive attitude that instills hope in others (Sonstegard et al., 2004). In addition, group leaders must have good knowledge of their members and be active in attacking in a timely manner the **faulty logic** (i.e., irrational ideas) their members hold.

Corsini (1988) states that the personality of Adlerian group leaders is as important as the techniques they employ. Maniacci et al. (2014) agree that the personhood of the leader is crucial. For leaders to be effective, they must feel free to share opinions and feelings. Therefore, group leaders are collaborative participants in the group process. Leaders model the behavior that group members should demonstrate and create the proper attitude in the group.

Overall, Adlerian group leaders focus on understanding present behavioral patterns of group members and challenging them to change. Although they are reassuring and caring, effective leaders use group dynamics to help groups help themselves. Leaders may encourage group members to confront one another about specific behaviors they are displaying and basic life assumptions behind their behaviors with the realization that, in so doing, members learn something about their own beliefs. Thus, goals in life and modifications members may need to make in order to change can be made more completely and thoroughly (Fehr, 2003).

In working with groups of children, Adlerian leaders may primarily use **encouragement** (wherein leaders imply faith in the child by stating their belief that behavior change is possible), **natural consequences** (living with the results of a particular behavior, such as getting lost because one did not follow directions), and **acting "as if"** (wherein children act as if they are the ideal person they wish to be). With adult groups, more systematic plans may be employed. Leaders may use the three techniques just mentioned plus others, such as **task setting** (members set short-range, attainable goals and eventually work up to long-term, realistic objectives) and **push button** (members are helped to realize they have choices in their lives about which stimuli they pay attention to and remember). In either case, Adlerian leaders strive to stay true to the theory behind the process yet be inventive.

Case Example

Alicia Acts "As If"

When Alicia joined the Adlerian parents' group, she was uncertain about herself and the roles she played in the lives of her children. She married young and immediately had two children, now 5 and 7. They seemed to run wild. She did not get much help from her husband.

Through the group, she began to get ideas on what she could do to improve her life and those of her children and husband. One such idea was to act "as if." Using this technique, Alicia acted as if she

were confident in properly disciplining her children and instructing her husband on ways he could be helpful. The result was that Alicia now feels better about herself and what is happening with her children and husband, too.

Questions

What other Adlerian-based techniques would you advise Alicia to use? What is the rationale for your choice?

Desired Outcome of Adlerian Groups

The outcomes of Adlerian group practice focus primarily on the growth and actions of the individual within the group rather than the group itself. On a global level, members of an Adlerian group should be socially oriented, personally integrated, and goal directed when the group ends. They should have corrected faulty beliefs, eliminated competitive behavioral stances, and become more in contact with family-of-origin issues. Children in Adlerian groups should recognize more clearly the logical consequences of their actions and who they can be; adults who work with children should be more cognizant of children's faulty belief systems (i.e., that they must be superior, helpless, powerful, or deficient) and corrective measures to take in helping them eliminate misguided thoughts and behaviors (Dreikurs, 1968). Children in Adlerian groups are worked with more directly than any other ages.

Adolescents in Adlerian groups are specifically helped to deal better with their own and others' perceptions of themselves and to realize they do not have to engage in competitive behaviors to be accepted. There are a number of ways to promote cooperative behaviors among adolescents (see Table 15.1).

With families and adults, Adlerian groups are directed toward social adjustment. Members of these groups are helped to understand that the basic problems in families and social relationships are people oriented and that relationships built on democratic principles work best.

Although little literature is available on Adlerian task/work groups, the outcome from these groups should emphasize social cooperation and teamwork (Larson & LaFasto, 1989). Task/work group members may realize how much more they can accomplish when working together rather than separately.

Table 15.1 Typical faulty goals of adolescents.

Faulty Beliefs	Goals	Examples	Adult Reactions	Peer Group Reactions	Reactions to Corrective Feedback	Alternative Corrective Methods
I am worthwhile and belong only:						
When I am best at everything	Superiority	Super striving for best grades, most honors, first in the class, etc.	Approval	Admiration	Justifies striving	Avoid blanket approval Promote courage to be imperfect Encourage social cooperation
When I have widespread peer social acceptance	Popularity (social climbing)	Constantly attempting to obtain widespread peer social acceptance	Approval	Acceptance Subgroup envy or annoyance	Superficial compliance Friendly disagreement	Avoid blanket approval Encourage independent activity
When I live up completely to all standards of established adult society	Conformity	Constantly tries to please, particularly adults rather than peers, with good behavior, grades, etc.	Approval	Annoyance (with some) envy	Superficial compliance	Avoid blanket approval Encourage peer social activities Encourage individuality
When I am in complete control or free from outside control	Defiance: Independence struggle	Arguments over hair, dress, etc.	Annoyance Irritation Anger	Acceptance Approval	Continue to argue Defiant compliance	Avoid arguing Suggestions at other times
	Aggression	Vandalism Fighting Delinquency	Anger Hurt Revenge	Rejection by most Subgroup acceptance	Strike back	Avoid hurt and anger Don't strike back Reasonable limits and use of consequences
	Withdrawal	Runaway Truancy Suicide	Fear Alarm	Indifference Some sympathy	Passive response No improvement	Avoid hysterical reaction Encourage social participation
When I prove and enjoy myself sexually	Sexual promiscuity	High level of intimate sexual activity with others	Disgust Shock Disapproval	Rejection by most Subgroup acceptance	Defiant rejection	Avoid shock and disgust Encourage desire for self-respect and respect of others

Table 15.1 (Continued)

Faulty Beliefs	Goals	Examples	Adult Reactions	Peer Group Reactions	Reactions to Corrective Feedback	Alternative Corrective Methods
When I am completely supported and consoled in my shortcomings	Inadequacy	Gives up easily Displays dependence	Pity Hopelessness	Pity Indifference	Meager effort, then gives up again	Avoid discouraged reaction or pity Provide opportunities for small successes and encouragement
When others find me completely charming and pleasing	Charm	Fascinating and pleasing with smooth talk and behavior	Charmed and flattered, sometimes mixed with annoyance	Charmed Flattered Pleased Envious	Steps up charm Pouting Withdrawal	Be unimpressed but friendly Remain courteous and insist on effort
If I am physically beautiful or strong	Beauty Strength	Excessive attention to and dependence on physical appearance	Admiration sometimes mixed with envy or irritation	Admiration sometimes mixed with envy	Ignoring	Avoid praise Encourage nonphysical pursuits, e.g., reading, art, music
When I am "superman" or "superwoman"	Sexism	Boys: Macho behavior Girls: Clinging-vine behavior	General approval Some annoyance	General approval Some annoyance	Rejection	Avoid blanket approval Encourage contrasting "feminine" or "masculine" attitudes and behaviors
When I am completely involved in learning or discussing ideas	Intellectualizing	Very bookish	Approval	Indifference Subgroup acceptance	Argument	Avoid blanket approval Encourage social leisure activities
When I am fully involved in religious ideas and activities	Religiosity	Deep involvement in religious ideas and activities Regular and frequent attendance at church	Approval sometimes mixed with concern or annoyance	Ignored by most Subgroup acceptance	Pity Defensiveness	Avoid blanket approval or arguments Encourage exploratory thinking and talking

Source: From E. W. Kelly and T. J. Sweeney (1979). Typical Faulty Goals of Adolescents, *The School Counselor, 26*(4), pp. 239–241. Copyright © 1979 by American School Counselor Association. Reprinted with permission.

Evaluation of Adlerian Groups

The theory and practice of Adler's ideas have distinct strengths and limitations.

STRENGTHS AND CONTRIBUTIONS

A strength associated with Adlerian groups is that they are usually nonthreatening. Adlerian groups are also generally helpful to participants because of their educational emphasis, and most are based on a healthy operational model (Maniacci et al., 2014). In these groups, members often enjoy the experience and feel they come out with concrete ways to handle specific everyday problems.

A second advantage of Adlerian group theory and practice is that methods associated with this approach are logical and based on "common sense" (Sweeney, 2009). Most group participants do not feel put off by the terms or procedures. In addition, most group leaders are able to learn and use Adlerian concepts in a relatively short time. This approach encourages democratic participation, which is useful for both the members and the leader in promoting openness and dialogue.

A third attractive feature of Adlerian groups is that they are holistic. Most Adlerians will typically employ a cognitive method to help participants understand the materials being presented. They will also address behavioral and affective aspects of the person.

A fourth strength of Adlerian group work is its eclectic nature. Adlerians are not tied to rigid procedures and methods. For instance, Adlerian group leaders may make use of psychodrama and other active therapeutic techniques (Maniacci et al., 2014). In addition, Adlerian groups stress common concepts of the Adlerian approach such as the value of social interests, goal-directed behavior, and individual indivisibility.

Another strong point of the Adlerian approach is its flexibility in working with varied populations. Different forms of Adlerian groups are used with children (Sonstegard & Bitter, 1998b), adolescents (Sonstegard & Bitter, 1998a), parents (Croake, 1983), and families (Lowe, 1982). Furthermore, Adlerian group work has been found to be successful with such diverse clients as those seeking relief from loneliness (Brough, 1994) and those enrolled in outpatient substance abuse programs (Prinz & Arkin, 1994).

LIMITATIONS

A drawback of Adlerian group work is the leader's style. Adlerians are unified in respect to their philosophy of equality and theory of personality development, but they follow their own style in regard to procedure. They "have no guidelines other than their experience" (Corsini, 1988, p. 14). The emphasis placed on different aspects of the approach is left entirely to the group leader. Therefore, if the group leader deviates somewhat from Adlerian principles, the group may have difficulty.

Another limitation of the groups derived from Adlerian theory is the narrowness of their scope. The Adlerian approach assumes that all problems are socially based. Many difficulties are, but some problems have different causes that are not addressed in Adlerian groups. For example, in a work group, the processes set up to produce a product may be at fault rather than the people involved. Likewise, an impoverished environment may contribute to friction between people whether they wish to be social or not.

A third weakness of Adlerian groups is their lack of uniformity. Most notable Adlerian theorists have achieved success because of their individual ability to translate Adlerian principles into practice. Although some followers of Adler (e.g., Dinkmeyer & Sperry, 2000) have translated Adlerian principles into more unified practice techniques, the Adlerian approach still lacks concreteness of techniques in group work.

Finally, the research on which Adlerian group work is based is relatively weak. If Adlerian groups are to achieve prominence, more data must be generated to document their effectiveness.

Learning More

Adlerian theory is practiced worldwide. Its emphasis on social living makes it a popular approach to group work. For more information on Adlerian organizations and institutes, contact NASAP:

> The North American Society of Adlerian Psychology (NASAP),
> Telephone: 1-260-267-8807, Web page: alfredadler.org

NASAP also publishes a newsletter and a scholarly periodical, the *Journal of Individual Psychology.*

PERSON-CENTERED GROUPS

Premises of Person-Centered Groups

Basic encounter groups, as defined by Rogers, are built on several premises. The first is a trust in the inner resources of persons. As Rogers (1980) put it, "Individuals have within themselves vast resources for self-understanding and for altering their self-concepts, basic attitudes, and self-directed behavior; these resources can be tapped if a definable climate of facilitative psychological attitudes can be provided" (p. 115).

A second underlying facet is a sense of trust in the group to help members develop their potential without being directed by a leader. This is a belief that encounter groups will promote a positive growth tendency that resides within individuals. Rogers (1970) emphasized that movement in encounter groups will be positive, even when initially ill defined. "The group will move—of this I am confident—but it would be presumptuous to think that I can or should direct that movement toward a specific goal" (p. 45).

A third major tenet of Rogers's approach is the idea that certain conditions must be created within the group for group members to maximize their full potential (Rogers, 1970). *Communication*—for example, the expression by the group leader and group members of empathy, genuineness (congruence), and acceptance (unconditional positive regard)—is necessary. In addition, group members must engage in **active listening** (hearing meanings behind words and nonverbal gestures); self-disclose and unmask pretensions and façades; deal with immediate issues of concern; and, when needed, **confront** (challenge incongruencies in thoughts and actions).

Finally, encounter groups are based on the understanding that a qualified person with special training and experience will facilitate them. Group leaders must be skilled in allowing group members to struggle to express themselves. They must be integrated personally as well as educated professionally.

As opposed to a T-group, basic encounter groups are less structured, theoretical, here-and-now slanted, and task oriented while being more process based and confrontational in feedback. Members are free to talk about their past and present because encounter groups do not make a distinction between "growth and development goals and psychotherapy goals" (Shaffer & Galinsky, 1989, p. 211). As a rule, basic encounter groups are more open to allowing a wider range of expressible behaviors than are T-groups. Those who join them are usually more focused on broadening their own **personal growth** (a global emphasis that stresses development as a result of experiences, such as travel or encounter) as opposed to working on personal growth issues (an individual emphasis that springs from a perceived deficit or need).

Overall, basic encounter groups are established on the premise that individuals who participate in them are relatively healthy. They were initially referred to as **group therapy for normals** (Yalom & Leszcz, 2005). It is assumed that these individuals (usually 8 to 18 in number and strangers to one another) will voluntarily commit to attend a select number of group sessions and work on developing a greater sense of awareness and acceptance of themselves and others. They will help themselves and others become more skilled in using personal and interpersonal assets as the group continues.

Reflections

One of the factors that hurt the encounter group movement was the variations of it that were tried by untrained group leaders. Do you still see groups of any type, from teams to task forces, in your community that are led by individuals who appear not to know what they are doing? How does that affect the perception of groups where you live?

Practice of Person-Centered Theory in a Group

Certain procedures (i.e., techniques and processes) are common to all encounter groups. One of the most crucial is the creation of a psychological climate in which group members can risk being themselves. To achieve such a therapeutic climate, Rogers (1970) uses an **unstructured group** format in which members freely express their thoughts and feelings once trust is established. Group leaders facilitate the development of trust by disclosing their own negative and positive feelings.

Feedback and communication are also critical components in encounter group experiences, because no real contact can occur between individuals without the expression of feedback and communication. *Feedback* involves one person giving another his or her perception of a behavior. For example, Claudia may say to Karl, "I really like the way you were honest in telling me how you felt about what I suggested to you." *Communication of thoughts and feelings* is best conveyed when clearly understood language and gestures are used. For instance, Matthew may say to Henrique in a serious manner, "It's frustrating when you close up when I ask you to say more."

The process in which these basic techniques are employed, the **Rogerian-oriented encounter group 15-stage process** (Rogers, 1970), is well defined, although the stages do not always occur in a clear-cut sequence and may vary from group to group:

1. *Milling around*—In the initial stage of the group, members are often confused about who is responsible for conducting the group and what they are supposed to be doing. This confusion results in frustration, silence, and a tendency to keep conversations on a superficial level. Milling around is largely a warm-up activity that prevents members from getting down to business.
2. *Resistance*—Group members enter the group with both public and private selves. They tend to avoid exposing their private selves until they have built trust in other members.

3. *Revealing past feelings*—As trust begins to develop, group members start to talk about their feelings, but only those that are safe to expose (e.g., the past). The talk at this point is on there-and-then experiences (i.e., those that are historical) and those that are nonthreatening to expose.

4. *Expression of negative feelings*—As the group develops, initial here-and-now feelings are expressed, but generally in a negative manner. Most of these feelings are directed toward the leader, and they are generally in the form of blame for not providing enough structure. For example, Ralph may say to Kevin, the group leader, "I wish you would either become more active in this group or find us a new leader." Rogers hypothesizes that negative feelings occur first because members (a) want to test the trustworthiness of the group and (b) are less vulnerable to rejection if they are negative rather than positive.

5. *Expression of personally meaningful material*—At this stage, real trust in the group is established. Group members feel free to explore and talk about important meaningful events in their lives. They usually start off being more negative than positive but change as other group members accept them more. For instance, Peggy may say to the group, "I want to tell you more about myself than you have heard so far," and then begin to talk about some experiences in her life that she has made known to only very few people.

6. *Communication of immediate interpersonal feelings*—At this point in the group, members begin to be affected by and respond to other group members. They indicate to others how their comments and actions are perceived. Thus, Charles may say to Steve, "Your comments about your life decisions strike me as those of a man with deep regret." Genuine encounter occurs at this point.

7. *Development of a healing capacity in the group*—After members have expressed personal feelings about themselves and others, they begin to reach out to one another. This is accomplished after members offer warmth, compassion, understanding, and caring to others in the group who have shared their concerns. It is the caring attitude of group members more than the expertise of the group facilitator that Rogers believes is of the utmost importance. Therefore, when Tommy tells Jean that he cares about her as a person regardless of her past, Jean can begin to take risks.

8. *Self-acceptance and the beginning of change*—As members are accepted more, they become increasingly aware of their own behaviors and feelings and are consequently less rigid. They open themselves to changes that will lead to more changes. For instance, when Freddie realizes that other members like him even when he is not perfect, he begins to open up in what he says and to whom he directs his words.

9. *Cracking of facades*—Encounter group members tend to drop the masks they have been wearing and become more genuine in this stage. Group members become less tolerant of façades as the group develops. They often demand, rather than ask, that individuals stop relating in a polite or superficial way.

10. *Feedback*—Through feedback, group members become more self-aware. For instance, Mark may not realize that he is considered to be authoritarian unless other members of the group tell him. Feedback is primarily constructive and greatly enhances the ability of members to perceive how others see them.

11. *Confrontation*—Confrontations of group members become more pronounced as members realize the group is reaching a climax. Confrontation is in the form of both positive and negative feedback.

12. *Helping relationships outside the group*—Stage 12 is a parallel to stage 7, but group members experience healing and helping relationships with one another outside the formal group experience. This process helps them resolve any misunderstandings and develop new relationships.

13. *The basic encounter*—Genuine person-to-person contact is the overriding characteristic at this point in the group. Members come to realize how satisfactory and meaningful it is to relate to one another in such a way. Therefore, George seeks to become closer to Brenda, Betty, and Barry than previously because he realizes how much he learns from them about himself and human interaction patterns.

14. *Expressions of closeness*—As the group nears completion, group members express positive feelings about their experience and about one another. A sense of group spirit develops more strongly. Thus, Todd may say to the group as a whole, "I feel as if each of you is a member of my family."

15. *Behavior changes*—Behavior changes, the result of increased congruence, are more pronounced toward the end of a group. Members tend to act in a more open, honest, caring manner, and they carry these behaviors into everyday life experiences after the group terminates. For example, Mickey may be more open with strangers after the group than he ever thought about being before.

Role of the Person-Centered Group Leader

Group leaders of person-centered groups derive their direction from group members. Usually, such leaders view the groups with which they work as being capable and having the inner resources to direct and develop themselves as individuals and as a group (Raskin, Rogers, & Witty, 2014). The leadership style of such persons is generally less active than in many other approaches to group work, although Rogers tends to be more confrontive in groups than in individual counseling sessions. Research indicates that effective facilitators confront their clients more frequently in a positive way, using empathy and positive regard, than do noneffective leaders (Bates & Goodman, 1986).

Generally, leaders of Rogerian-based groups are paradigms "for interpersonal effectiveness, modeling the therapeutic norms of openness, congruence, warmth, genuineness, and acceptance" and for creating a climate within the group that promotes the development of relationships (Ohlsen, Horne, & Lawe, 1988, p. 68). Group leaders, who are known as **facilitators**, do not use gimmicks and planned procedures. Interpretation and other expert-oriented procedures are ignored. Instead, a person-centered group leader participates as a member of the group and shares struggles with the group. In doing so, the leader attempts to understand each person in the group on a more personal basis and accept himself or herself and others genuinely (Bozarth, 1981).

Overall, person-centered group leaders carry out five distinct functions: (1) conveying warmth and empathy, (2) attending to others, (3) understanding meaning and content, (4) conveying acceptance, and (5) linking (Posthuma, 2002). These functions are expressed through such basic group skill techniques as listening, supporting, reflecting, sharing, affirming, clarifying, summarizing, engaging, and, of course, encountering. Overall, leaders use themselves as instruments of change. They convey the core conditions of empathy, congruence, and acceptance (Thorne, 1992). Their attitude toward the group helps create a climate that makes a difference in the growth of group members.

Case Example

Carey Experiences the Climate

When Carey entered the person-centered group, she was as tight as a clam. She did not make eye contact and she did not speak up. Other members wondered why she was there, and initially Carey did, too. She had come out of a desire to break her old habits of being withdrawn, but because she immediately retreated into a shell, she had second thoughts about whether she should have come to the group session or not.

Interestingly, no one pressed her to talk or do anything. They seemed comfortable with Carey the way she was. The same atmosphere prevailed during the second meeting of the group and continued to prevail thereafter.

As Carey became more comfortable, she opened up more at first with brief comments and later with well-thought-out statements. She seemed to be enjoying the group when it ended, and 3 months later when the group had a reunion, Carey actually arrived early.

Questions

What does Carey's experience in the group tell you about the power of acceptance and openness? Do you think Carey would have fared as well in some other theory-oriented group(s)? If so, which one(s) and why?

Desired Outcome of Person-Centered Groups

Person-centered encounter groups are intended for group members to develop self-awareness and awareness of others and to grow. The goal of personal growth is connected to what Rogers describes as **self-actualization** (becoming all that one can be) (Day & Matthes, 1992). Another goal is openness to experience, especially as it relates to intimacy and meaningfulness with others. Behavior change is hoped for as group members alter their physical gestures and become relaxed. Finally, there is the goal of becoming less alienated from oneself and others (Donigian & Hulse-Killacky, 1999).

Rogers (1970) reports that the desired outcomes of his approach and actual results have been consistent. In a systematic follow-up study he conducted, questionnaires were sent to 500 participants of small groups led by him and his associates 3 to 6 months after the group ended. Only two individuals felt the group experience had been damaging to them. Most surveyed reported that the group had a positive and long-lasting impact on their behavior. Although there are some problems in doing survey research, it appears that person-centered encounter group members felt that they benefited from their experiences.

Other researchers, notably Lieberman, Yalom, and Miles (1973), found less positive results, stating that almost 10% of the participants they researched reported that marathon person-centered encounter groups were damaging to them. It should be noted that Rogerians do not prefer group experiences that last more than 12 hours (Landreth, 1984). More research needs to be conducted on the overall impact of basic encounter groups.

Evaluation of Person-Centered Groups

Person-centered groups have factors that are beneficial for some individuals in some situations, but they also have limitations.

STRENGTHS AND CONTRIBUTIONS

The basic encounter group movement has helped traditional group leaders, especially those working from a psychotherapeutic perspective, to become aware of the importance of enhancing the development of the total individual. Until the 1960s, the focus of group psychotherapists was on reduction, rather than expansion, of group participants' experiences. After encounter groups gained popularity, group psychotherapists were inclined to stress clients' assets as well as try to alleviate their deficiencies.

A second strength of the person-centered approach has been its emphasis on the group leader. The heart of the basic encounter group is the group facilitator (Yalom & Leszcz, 2005). The facilitator's task is to have a genuine interest in others and to set up conditions for personal growth. Few other group approaches concentrate as much on the leader as a person. However, most group models have been positively influenced by the person-centered emphasis on the importance of the leader.

A third positive contribution of the basic encounter group model is the emphasis on improving personal communication skills. Maliver (1973) notes that after an encounter group experience, participants are more aware of irritating mannerisms in their communication patterns and may change their behaviors. The change may lead to enhanced personal development (Hall et al., 1999; Raskin et al., 2014).

A fourth advantage of basic encounter groups has been in the area of research technology. Before the basic encounter group movement, research of group psychotherapy sessions was rather crude and unimaginative. Since then, empirical research has become more sophisticated and is rooted in the encounter group tradition of investigation (e.g., Bates & Goodman, 1986; Hayashi, 1990; Yamamoto, 1995).

Another contribution of the Rogerian group model is its influence on other educational models. For instance, some parent education programs are based on this group theory, such as Thomas Gordon's (1970) **Parent Effectiveness Training (PET)**.

Finally, person-centered encounter groups have made group work acceptable for "normals." Because group participants are not seen as "sick," the group can work with individuals on personal development without the stigma of negative labeling.

LIMITATIONS

A weakness of encounter groups is that they may be dangerous to participants who need therapy or structure and who try to use these groups as they would more organized psychotherapy groups (Lieberman et al., 1973). Persons with intellectual disabilities, severe brain damage, or severe emotional disturbances need greater structure and guidance than basic encounter groups provide. These individuals are not ready for the openness of encounter groups and may regress as a result of such an experience.

A second limitation of basic encounter groups is the way in which members and leaders are chosen. There are generally no rules for the selection of encounter group members (Wood, 1982). Some individuals may talk their way into such groups by convincing group leaders they can benefit from the experience. Group leader training is also not stressed in this tradition, so encounter group facilitators may end up being too passive or too caught up in a **crash-program mentality** in which group experiences are carried out to excess (Yalom & Leszcz, 2005).

A third criticism of the person-centered approach is that it may not lead anywhere. Rogerians as a group have "had little interest in directing the group's conscious attention to its own processes" (Shaffer & Galinsky, 1989, p. 211). Although the qualities espoused by basic encounter group leaders are quite appropriate for beginning a group, the group's movement may come to a halt because there is no reliance on techniques to motivate members or stir members in a particular direction (Corey, 2012). The emphasis on the personhood of the facilitator and the lack of emphasis on technique may not be productive for some groups (Cain, 1993).

A fourth drawback of basic encounter groups is their history. In the 1960s and 1970s, basic encounter groups became so popular that they were nearly a fad. As a result, they lost some of their influence and power. Some skepticism about these groups still exists. Indeed, as Yalom and Leszcz (2005) point out, it is difficult to find a basic encounter group experience now, although much of the structure and technology of this type of group survive in large group awareness programs, such as est and Lifespring.

A final limitation of basic encounter groups centers on the research methods used to evaluate them. The **self-report research format** used by Rogers, where participants write out or check off how they are different as a result of the group, has been found to be inadequate. This type of research does not measure the complexity of personal change in a group of this type. Thus, the claims of success for basic encounter groups are questionable. There were, and still are, variations of person-centered encounter groups throughout the world, so it is hard to determine exactly which variables have contributed to the success of which groups and how.

Learning More

Although person-centered theory began as an individually based way of helping, it evolved into a powerful way to work with groups. A primary source for finding out more on person-centered group programs is the following:

Center for Studies of the Person
Web site: centerfortheperson.org

One of the best films on person-centered group work is a classic titled *Journey into Self* (McGaw, Farson, & Rogers, 1968). The film shows Rogers and Richard Farson leading a basic encounter group and demonstrating the basic qualities important to Rogerian group leaders: empathy, genuineness, caring, and spontaneity.

Summary and Conclusion

Since its inception, transactional analysis has often been used in groups. It is frequently thought of as a group treatment and group work approach. The major thrust of the transactional analysis group is to concentrate on analyzing ego states (Parent, Adult, Child) that individuals within the group are using. The group leader helps group members become aware of how they are functioning and how they might change their patterns of interaction. Cognitive understanding is emphasized initially in this process.

When the group is functioning properly, group members interact with one another (*minor transactions*). However, the major focus of the group is on leader–member interactions (*major transactions*). Thus, the transactional analysis group is leader centered and does not take advantage of group dynamics. Practitioners of this approach are still in the process

of validating the effectiveness of transactional analysis groups. However, the theory is simple, clear, and can easily be used by members of groups in coming to better understand their structure, transactions, games, and life scripts.

Reality therapy is unique in that it has some similarities to behaviorism and phenomenology. These similarities include its emphasis on perception and action and its deemphasis of the past, the unconscious, and emotions. Yet, reality therapy is distinct. It has incorporated choice theory into itself. At its core, it stresses the employment of action and thoughts.

Reality therapy groups used to follow a fairly well-formulated eight-stage approach, and some still do. As a result of being in a reality therapy group, members should become more aware of their values and more focused on changing their behaviors instead of trying to change others. It is hoped they will make choices in their lives and be responsible and accountable. Many group leaders, such as those working in education, mental health, and business, find reality therapy to be effective with the populations they serve. Although popular, reality therapy still needs a more solid research base.

Adlerian group work is a social, democratic, relationship-oriented approach. It emphasizes the importance of change in the present while understanding the development of past faulty beliefs and behaviors. Many Adlerian concepts, such as inferiority complex, encouragement, and empathy, have been absorbed into other helping theories. Nevertheless, Adlerian theory is still a viable way of assisting groups of individuals in a wide range of group settings. A major strength of the Adlerian groups is their flexibility in working with children, adolescents, adults, parents, and families. The application of Adlerian theory to different groups is psychoeducationally based.

Adlerian groups need a stronger base of research support in the future if they are going to continue to prosper. More uniformity and concreteness of methodology also have to be employed. For now, however, Adlerian groups offer a viable and positive alternative to other types of groups. By leading groups that are shorter in length, more health focused, and more socially oriented, Adlerians have carved out a unique niche.

Person-centered groups, especially the basic encounter group, are both a historical footnote in the group work movement and a present reality. The influence of these groups lives on in these people's memories as well as in some groups that are still conducted according to the encounter group model. Carl Rogers introduced the concept and format of basic encounter groups. They caught on quickly and were widely imitated. As a scientist-practitioner, Rogers investigated the impact of these groups and generally found them to make a positive contribution to the lives of individuals participating in them. True to his theory and belief about human nature, he set up the groups in a largely unstructured way, believing that the goodness and growth within people would emerge.

Today, encounter groups survive primarily in a less formal format but are the basis of several religious and self-help groups. The bad publicity and negative findings associated with these groups in the past probably mean that they will probably not emerge as a widespread popular movement again; yet, their legacy in the group field is noteworthy. They contributed to new expectations of members and leaders in groups, and they fostered attention on how communication patterns change in a group setting.

Classroom Exercises

1. Read a recent article (published in the past 5 years) on a TA, Reality Therapy, Adlerian, or person-centered group. Discuss the content of the article with three other classmates. What were the major findings?
2. What is your favorite part of each of the group theories presented in this chapter? Which aspect did you like least? Discuss your thoughts and feelings concerning these theories with another class member.
3. With another classmate, compare the Adlerian approach to group work with TA emphasis. Keep your remarks focused on the comparisons between the approaches you choose. Share your remarks with another pair.
4. With which groups of people do you think a person-centered group would work best? With which group of people do you think a reality therapy group would be a good fit? Explain your answer as it relates to the philosophy and pragmatics of each approach, and if possible the research that supports your view.

CHAPTER 16

Existential, Gestalt, Rational-Emotive Behavior Therapy, and Psychodrama Groups

I remember doing role plays in your group
trying to look cool, while my palms sweated
and my heart beat as fast as a hummingbird's wing.
You were supportive . . . giving me a part of the
   warmth
you brought with you that summer
while encouraging me to explore the universe
that was myself.
Other classes, other seasons came as quickly as
   the sound
of laughter and as silently as sorrow.
With you I traveled the roads to becoming a
   competent clinician
and engaged in counseling conversations late
   into the night
Sharing all the light and darkness of those moments
as I came to be.*

From "In the Midst of the Puzzles and
Counseling Journey" Personnel and Guidance
Journal, 57, p. 148 © 1978 by Samuel T.
Gladding. Reprinted by permission from
Samuel T. Gladding.

WavebreakMediaMicro/Fotolia

CHAPTER OVERVIEW

From reading this chapter, you will learn about

- The premises and practices of existentialism, Gestalt, rational-emotive behavior therapy (REBT), and psychodrama groups
- The role of leaders and desired outcomes in the theoretical group noted above
- How groups like those just mentioned are evaluated regarding their effectiveness

AS YOU READ, CONSIDER

- Which theoretical perspective you are most drawn to in conducting a group
- The different roles leaders play in helping a group evolve
- The unique and universal criteria used in evaluating the effectiveness of a theoretically led group

Trephining (aka: trepanning) first occurred in Neolithic times, or the New Stone Age, about 5,000 years ago. During this procedure, a hole, or trephine, was chipped into the skull using crude stone instruments to set free what was believed to be evil spirit(s) that were inhabiting a person's head and causing psychopathology. There is no evidence the procedure worked and much to prove it did not. However, in the late 19th century, a new approach for working with those with mental disorders was formulated: moral therapy. It was based on humane psychosocial care and praised for freeing those suffering from mental disturbances from shackles and barbaric physical treatments. Instead, such things as emotions and social interactions were considered. Much of today's treatment for helping is based on this latter enlightened approach. We know feelings, thoughts, and behaviors play numerous roles in people's lives for better or for worse and the theory of evil spirits being responsible for mental disorders is wrong. The four theories examined in this chapter (existentialism, Gestalt, REBT, and psychodrama) all deal with how thoughts, feelings, and behaviors can be expressed productively in groups and help individuals, and the groups they belong to, be as healthy as possible.

Existentialism is a philosophy that addresses what it means to be human, including thoughts, feelings, and anxieties (Simpson & Diambra, 2011). This philosophy has been applied to the helping professions only since the mid-1940s (Tamm, 1993). Existentialists stress the importance of beliefs, such as values, freedom, and responsibility. The nature of discovering meaning in the midst of everyday life, as well as in absurd and tragic events, is emphasized. In existential thought, life is full of angst as well as joy. There is a paradox to human existence that the more fully one lives life, the more strongly one is aware of death. This paradox highlights the fine line in life between being and not being (Mullan, 1992).

Existential groups in the United States have become popular since the 1960s because of two factors: the rapid change in lifestyles among Americans and an increase in literature relating to existential groups. Increases in technology, the breakdown of the family, and the accelerated pace of work have caused many people to seek a deeper understanding of who they are and what life means. The writings and media presentations of Irvin Yalom, Rollo May, and Viktor Frankl have also helped people focus on applying existential philosophy to everyday life as well as counseling and group environments.

Gestalt therapy is an experiential and humanistic approach to change founded by Fritz Perls, along with Laura Perls and Paul Goodman. In Gestalt environments, there is an emphasis on the teaching of awareness skills. Gestalt groups are experiential in nature and stress interpersonal interactions and learning through awareness and enactment.

In the original Gestalt workshops, "Perls and his immediate disciples preferred to focus on the group solely as a backdrop for individual work" (Shaffer & Galinsky, 1989, p. 121). They concentrated on one individual at a time. The person who wanted to "work" would sit in the **hot seat** with his or her chair facing the therapist. The rest of the group served as a kind of **Greek chorus** in the background, where they resonated and empathized with the one who was working, thereby gaining insight into themselves and others. Work sessions lasted from 10 to 30 minutes and ended with a mutually decided closure. The initial ideas and processes generated by Perls, combined with those of Kepner (1980) and Zinker (1977), evolved into the *Gestalt group process.*

Rational-emotive behavior therapy (REBT) was founded by Albert Ellis. The focus is on behaviors as well as cognitions. REBT groups originated in 1958 when Ellis noticed that working in groups was beneficial and economical (Vernon, 2011a; Weinrach, 1980). From the beginning, REBT groups have varied. At times the groups are as large as 100 and meet for the purpose of demonstrating REBT principles, a skills-learning approach. In such cases, the emphasis is on psychoeducational and psychotherapeutic principles regarding a specific topic, such as dealing with anxiety, depression, or interpersonal relationships.

Other types of groups conducted by REBT practitioners are open-ended and closed-ended psychotherapy and counseling sessions that may include group marathons (Ellis & Dryden, 1997). Most REBT groups of this nature usually meet weekly, with open-ended ones being conducted on an indefinite basis over a number of months and closed-ended ones seldom meeting more than 10 to 12 sessions. Marathons are conducted on a 12- to 36-hour basis depending on the leader and setting.

Regardless of form, the number of members in REBT groups is usually limited to a dozen. This arrangement allows group members the chance to interact with other people, to take verbal and nonverbal risks, to receive maximum feedback, to learn from others' experiences, and to make contributions to the group as a whole (Ellis, 2011).

Psychodrama is one of the oldest and most dynamic theories devised for working with groups (Fox, 2008). Its originator, Jacob L. Moreno, initially experimented with his theory in the streets of Vienna after World War I with an enactment procedure known as "The **Living Newspaper**." He spent the rest of his life developing and refining the concepts and practice of psychodrama both in Austria and in the United States (Moreno, 1984; Nolte, 1989). Although psychodrama gained notoriety in the United States as a therapeutic intervention at Moreno's psychodrama theater in Beacon, New York, and at St. Elizabeth's Hospital in Washington, DC, it is applicable in a number of settings and is practiced worldwide (Blajan-Marcus, 1974; Moreno, 1949). One of the most productive spin-offs of this approach is the use of role-play within psychoeducational, psychotherapeutic, and management groups (Blatner, 1996, 2005).

Psychodrama explores the human psyche through dramatic action (D'Amato & Dean, 1988; Goldman & Morrison, 1984). The idea evolved out of Moreno's creativity, which was fostered by his encounters with children and his love for spontaneity and the theater. In essence, psychodrama became an extension of Moreno's personality (Fox, 2008). He advocated a group approach in an era of intrapersonal emphasis. Therefore, many of his contributions to the field of group work (e.g., his emphasis on action and his focus on the here and now) have never been properly acknowledged.

Moreno found that those who played nonscripted and unrehearsed parts, as well as members of audiences, experienced an emotional **catharsis** (a release of pent-up feelings) as a result of participating in or observing dramatic enactment. Shortly thereafter, psychodrama as a formal system was conceptualized, with Moreno stressing the uniqueness of the approach by having clients relive, instead of retell or analyze, conflicts.

EXISTENTIAL GROUPS

Premises of Existential Groups

Existential groups are based on several premises, among them the belief that people form their lives by their choices. Human beings, unlike other living creatures, are aware of their existence and their own mortality. They have freedom to make choices and the freedom of responsibility for what they do (Frankl, 1997): People are the authors of their lives. They can make their lives meaningful, according to Frankl (2000), in one of three ways: (a) doing a deed, or achieving or accomplishing something; (b) experiencing a value, such as the intrinsic worth of a work of nature, culture, or love; and (c) suffering, by finding a proper attitude toward unalterable fate.

A person who does not actively seek meaning in life chooses despair or psychopathology. Therefore, existentialism is a process of evaluating and simultaneously releasing and incorporating objects and events in life's quest for meaning. This demand to discard and obtain so that life can be lived to the fullest creates tension and anxiety. The result can be that persons refuse to take risks or become spurred on to make positive choices for their lives. For example, Grant may be inspired by an existential view to overcome his natural shyness and decide to speak up in class. Taking this risk may result in Grant being recognized for his scholarship and developing new friendships. In contrast, Pearl may give in to her shyness and not be responsive. The result may be that she depreciates herself and becomes more estranged from her classmates.

Practice of Existential Theory in a Group

Existential groups are usually conducted with an emphasis on psychotherapy, counseling, and psychoeducation. Each group member is seen as starting out on an equal footing with the others. Each gradually shapes a particular life space in the group (Yalom & Josselson, 2011). In the process it is crucial that members come to realize their potential and their responsibilities for making healthy and self-directed choices (May, 1983). One of the first goals is to increase **self-awareness**. Corey (2012) refers to this increase as helping group members discover their unique "being-in-the-world." Such a discovery comes through questions, such as "Who am I?" and "Where am I going?" Thus, Darlene may constantly compare and contrast her understanding of herself in reference to others in the group. By doing so she may raise her consciousness and discover new possibilities.

It is hoped that with awareness comes an increase in **personal responsibility**, especially as it relates to interpersonal modes of behavior. Responsibility is the keystone of the group therapeutic process (Yalom & Josselson, 2011). People cannot live unto themselves without contracting what existential philosopher Soren Kierkegaard described as a "sickness unto death." Significance is found only by constantly being responsible for making meaning out of what we do or what occurs to us. In a group situation, it is not enough that Andy relates information about what has happened to him. Instead, he must take responsibility for assigning meaning to events by experiencing them as thoroughly as possible interpersonally. For Jorge's descriptions of his childhood to have relevance for Andy, he must think about the meaning of events in this period of his own life.

In combination with awareness and responsibility is the productive handling of **anxiety** (Deurzen-Smith, 1997). Being anxious is unavoidable; it is connected with facing new challenges and decision making. People can deny they are anxious, but doing so makes their lives less fulfilling. Therefore, group members must face their anxiety by seeing their lives as journeys that never stop changing and that will end. Therefore, when Gene tells the group he is nervous about his new relationships at work, he has made a positive step in handling himself and the anxiety that might otherwise paralyze him.

Along with handling anxiety is a struggle to **search for meaning**—something people must do for themselves. Searching for meaning in even simple events, such as the sharing of food, constitutes a choice between being and nonbeing (death). Death and nonbeing take many forms, from traumatic experiences, such as having a life-threatening illness, to more mundane times, such as boredom (Greenstein & Breitbart, 2000). Thus, when Gus recognizes that he is dying professionally because he does not take continuing education courses, he has made progress in reclaiming and renewing his life.

Reflection

When have you felt most alive in your life? What were you doing? How would you relate that feeling to existential theory? How do you relate your experience to being in a group?

Role of the Existential Group Leader

"Group leaders who work from within an existential framework find that leading a group is an intensive and personal experience" (Carroll, Bates, & Johnson, 2004, p. 15). This leadership carries with it a responsibility to be active and reflective. Existential group leaders are always thinking and taking risks. They are aware and sensitive to the concerns of others and do not take the role of an expert but rather the role of a fellow traveler (Tamm, 1993). They use anxiety and other uncomfortable emotions in a productive way to help group members realize that these feelings will lead them toward deeper awareness.

Group leaders work hard to develop close relationships with all group members. In existential groups, meaningful change occurs only when there is personal contact and interaction. These encounters are ones in which information can be carefully considered. Another job of existential group leaders is confrontation, pointing out discrepancies between what group members say they want and what they are doing. For example, a group leader might say to Edna that she talks about inventing ways to process foods but she has stopped cooking. The leader would ask, "How do these two facts interrelate?"

In addition, leaders use themselves in existential groups as a source of knowledge and a model in regard to human experience. Leaders are calm in the presence of the turmoil that may go on within a group. They relate how they have faced difficulties and how they have made choices that were enabling. They talk about the meaning they have experienced and how they have overcome obstacles. Through self-disclosure, members become more aware not only of the leader but of themselves.

Desired Outcome of Existential Groups

If the existential group process is successful, members will benefit. First, they will become more aware of themselves and the choices they have. Thus, Christopher will come to realize that when he decides to postpone a decision, he is making a decision. Members of existential groups will become more self-determining, too. They will refuse to be one of a crowd unless they consciously make that choice. They will realize that their feelings, even painful ones, can be motivational (Greenstein & Breitbart, 2000).

Another outcome of an existential group experience may be that members find new meaning in all aspects of their lives. They no longer take matters for granted but realize that much can be learned from their encounters in the world, even if some of their interactions are initially disconcerting. Related to this emphasis on meaningfulness is highlighting present, here-and-now experiences. The paradox of the human experience is that we are both alone and connected. We are alone in having to decide what to do or how to interpret the world, but there is a connectedness to life through relationships. Those in an existential group ideally come to appreciate contact more (Greenstein, 2000).

A third outcome of an existential group is an emphasis on becoming authentic. **Authenticity** is the ability to affirm oneself and to make the most of discovering and using personal talents and creativity (Tillich, 1952). Like other qualities people strive to develop, the process of being true to oneself and of developing abilities is a lifelong challenge. Thus, DiAnna may claim her talent as a dancer, thereby dedicating herself to go to dance rehearsals regularly and participate in recitals to maximize her potential.

Finally, in an existential group, a desired outcome is increased interpersonal responsibility (Yalom & Josselson, 2011). In the group, members learn how others view their behaviors, how their behaviors make others feel, how their behaviors create the opinions others have of them, and how their behaviors influence their opinions of themselves. Thus, Jack may come to realize that, when he interrupts and tries to focus the group on himself, other members see his behavior as egotistical.

Overall, as the result of being in an existential group, members better understand themselves, interpersonal relationships, and their immediate worlds. The group becomes a microcosm of how members are seen and function in their environments. Members come to realize that life is a journey both shared and solitary.

Case Example

Mason and the Meaningfulness

Mason is a drifter. He has wandered in and out of educational institutions and work environments. He has been divorced twice. With a menial job and little hope, he attended a free lecture on existentialism at the public library. He was taken by the concepts and asked the lecturer for additional reading. Several books were recommended, which Mason devoured. He then joined an open-ended existential discussion group.

He has been attending the group now for 3 months. He seems pleased with the content that is being delivered and the discussions that follow. He thinks he is finding some direction in his life. He wonders if what he is experiencing is group therapy.

Questions

Do you think Mason's group is therapeutic? Would you consider it group therapy or something else? If "something else," what would you call it? Why?

Evaluation of Existential Groups

Existential groups have strengths and limitations. Some of these qualities are inherent in the philosophy of existentialism; others are specific to individual and group concerns.

STRENGTHS AND CONTRIBUTIONS

A strength of existential groups is that they deal with ultimate issues in life and present their members with opportunities to explore values and lifestyles. It is difficult to be in an existential group and not question how you are living and the meaning of life. The realities of death and loss, for instance, become more significant factors and concerns (Yalom & Josselson, 2011; Viorst, 1986). After participating in an existential group, participants often let go of past patterns, customs, and beliefs and focus differently.

A second benefit of existential groups is that they provide a framework for other forms of group work. For instance, "the existential concepts of encounter and responsibility are . . . essential factors in psychodrama" (Avrahami, 1995). Likewise, the approach of Alcoholics Anonymous is consistent with existential philosophy for groups (Page & Berkow, 1998). Meaning-of-life groups, using a logotherapy existential protocol, have been used in substance abuse treatment as an approach for examining the purpose of recovery, especially a person's values, attitudes, and motivation (Somov, 2007).

A third positive feature of existential groups is that they deal with group members holistically (Lowenstein, 1993). Concerns about specific behaviors or past events are not the focus. Therefore, existentialist group members cannot blame others or shirk responsibility for who they are and what they are presently doing.

The versatility of existential theory in groups is also a strong point. In working with cancer patients in groups, existential theory has been combined with cognitive theory (Kissane et al., 1997) as well as with experiential activities (van der Pompe, Duivenvoorden, Antoni, & Visser, 1997) to produce positive results.

Finally, existential groups are applicable to individuals from a wide range of cultures: for example, African American women who have suffered because of prejudice and discrimination (Pack-Brown, Whittington-Clark, & Parker, 1998). The philosophy and emphasis of the existential approach is open. Overall, existential group work has a wide appeal because the theory behind it focuses on a person's reason for being in life.

LIMITATIONS

One limitation of existential groups is that they only really benefit members who are verbal, communicative, and unafraid to confront painful issues (Lowenstein, 1993).

Another minus associated with existential groups is that the theory that supports them has limited applicability outside of counseling and psychotherapy settings. Psychoeducational and task/work groups are seldom based on this approach.

A third drawback of existential groups is that it takes maturity, life experience, and close supervision to practice this approach (Deurzen-Smith, 1997). The nature of existentialism theory and practice presents problems in training existential group leaders.

Finally, existentialism and existential groups are broadly based and do not generally deal with specific behaviors or concerns. Group members who need information or immediate answers are not good candidates for these groups.

Learning More

Existential theory is practiced in groups in a number of countries. The following is the most prominent professional organization devoted to existential issues in counseling:

> The Society for Existential Analysis
> Web site: existentialanalysis.org.uk

This society publishes the *Journal of the Society of Existential Analysis* and provides courses and advanced training in the field.

An excellent Web site for exploring existential psychotherapy and joining another professional therapy association for existentialism is the International Society for Existential Psychology and Psychotherapy (ISEPP) (existentialpsychology.org). It publishes the *International Journal of Existential Psychology and Psychotherapy*. For individuals interested in seeing an existential therapist conduct a group, Irvin Yalom's DVD series, *Understanding Group Psychotherapy* (1990), is recommended.

GESTALT GROUPS

Premises of Gestalt Groups

Four basic assumptions underlie Gestalt groups (Davis-Gage, 2011). First is the **principle of holism** (integration). Often individuals will carry around **emotional debris** ("unfinished business") from their past. These concerns are usually linked to resentment and incomplete separation from a lost love object. Through a series of prescribed exercises (e.g., an empty chair technique), integration occurs. The person becomes more complete—that is, more than the sum of his or her individual experiences.

A second assumption involves the **principle of awareness** (Leung, Leung, & Ng, 2013). People are free to choose only when they are *self-aware:* in touch with their existence and what that means (Hagedorn & Hirshhorn, 2009). The concept of awareness includes the sensations, thoughts, and behaviors that individuals experience. It is the "what" of existence and is focused in the **here and now** (the present). Awareness often results in insight when persons "own" their control and responsibility over a situation. Awareness and **dialogue** (talk between others and oneself or between different aspects of oneself) are two primary therapeutic tools in Gestalt therapy.

Third is the **principle of figure/ground**. The *figure* in life is composed of experiences that are most important, such as deciding how to approach a person. *Background* is experiences that are less pressing, such as what to do after dinner. Healthy persons take care of their figural (most important) needs first. As figural needs are met, these individuals become more aware of and take care of background needs.

The fourth principle of the Gestalt approach is the **principle of polarities**. If people are to meet their needs, they must differentiate their perceptual field into opposites/poles—for example, active/passive. The idea is for clients to express both sides of a polarity or conflict and then integrate this experience holistically. Often people fail to resolve conflicts within themselves and with others because they are not in contact with the opposite sides of situations. For example, if Fran sees her father as only good, she will not be able to deal with her relationship with him realistically.

Overall, Gestalt group process is complex and is based on the assumption that groups are multidimensional systems that operate on several levels at once. Groups, and people, are holistic, with all of their functions interrelated. It is impossible to understand the person in the group outside of the context of the group. Another assumption is that people are **proactive** (they take the initiative) in making choices, especially if they are self-aware and living in the present (Passons, 1975). As an approach, Gestalt theory views individuals as **intrinsically neutral**—that is, without a predetermined set of responses.

In addition, Gestalt therapy is premised on the idea that individuals will experience a certain amount of "elasticity." **Elasticity** is the ability to move from one set of needs to another and back. It is the elasticity of the figure/ground formation on which selfhood is rooted. Another way of explaining this phenomenon is to say that people perceive themselves changing in an expanding and contracting way depending on their needs.

A final major idea of the Gestalt approach is that awareness (a total organism response) gives people self-cohesiveness and enables them (Hagedorn & Hirshhorn, 2009). If individuals are healthily aware of themselves and their environments, they choose an active way of dealing with life's polarities. This usually means they integrate the opposite aspects of polarities and make a choice based on the information available. Therefore, Gestalt group process stresses increasing awareness, choice, meaningfulness, integrative wholeness, and closure.

Reflection

When have you been most aware of needs in your life? When have you noticed changes from figure/ground to ground/figure in your development? How has this awareness and the changes that come with it contributed to your interactions with others and yourself?

Practice of Gestalt Theory in a Group

Gestalt group process is sometimes misperceived as individual "hot seat" psychotherapy in a group setting. Actually, Gestalt groups function in several ways.

One way is for the Gestalt leader to focus on one person in the presence of other members. This is more of a traditional West Coast practice, according to Latner (1973), in which Gestalt practitioners who have been heavily influenced by Perls pay attention to the issues of self-awareness, centering, and responsibility (Corey, 2012).

In contrast, the traditional East Coast style of Gestalt group work is more interactive, involving direct, here-and-now group member communication. This model is interpersonal, similar to Yalom's model for existential group therapy (Earley, 2000).

A third model is a mixture of the two models just described with a balance between interaction and one-on-one focus (Yontef, 1990). It is sometimes referred to as **dual-focused Gestalt group work** (Harman, 1988). One older variation of this model is the so-called **floating hot seat** (Yontef & Jacobs, 2014) in which interaction is promoted by encouraging group members to work on exploring their personal issues when someone in the group touches on a subject that has personal relevance for them. A newer form of this approach is Kepner's (1980) **trilevel model of Gestalt group work**, where attention is systematically focused on (a) the individual at the intrapersonal level, (b) two or more people at the interpersonal level, and (c) the group as a systematic unit. This model illustrates how dynamic Gestalt group work can be.

Despite diversity in operating procedures, Gestalt group practitioners share many common beliefs and practices. First, they stay centered on the here and now (present experiences). They do this by asking *how* and *what*, instead of *why*, questions. This focus allows the most pressing needs of people to surface and to be addressed (Westwood, Keats, & Wilensky, 2003). Second, Gestalt group practitioners ask group members to work on a specific problem to help foster greater awareness. Sometimes, group members may be actively involved in helping other members process what is happening in their work. At other times, the interaction is between the group leader and the group member, with the rest of the group functioning as a background. Regardless, the focus is on individual responsibility and integration (Perls, 1969).

A third quality that Gestalt practitioners share is their emphasis on behavioral processes. Finally, Gestalt practitioners use a series of experiments and exercises to help their members achieve greater awareness and growth (Resnikoff, 1988). **Experiments** are nonplanned experiences that occur spontaneously. For example, if a group member starts waving her arms when talking about how she wishes to be free of present life circumstances, the group leader might say to her, "Melody, develop that," at which time the member might begin to exaggerate the movement into a wing-like flapping motion. In response to this motion, the leader might encourage the member to "fly," at which point the member might pretend to do so. The experience would then be processed. Exercises, in contrast, are planned activities that have been used previously to help group members become more aware. For example, having Tom, a group member, role-play a situation is a type of exercise.

Both experiments and exercises revolve around five main themes: (a) enactment, (b) directed behavior, (c) fantasy, (d) dreams, and (e) homework (Polster & Polster, 1973). They all occur in the present and are chosen for the specific purpose of promoting growth. Some of the better-known exercises are explored here.

Making the rounds is a warm-up game in Gestalt groups in which confrontation is heightened by asking group members to say something they usually do not verbalize. For example, Anita might say to the group "I am afraid to tell you about myself . . . because. . . ." She then makes the rounds with other members telling each her fear and becoming more aware in the process. As she goes from member to member she hopefully works through some unfinished materials of the past, in which case rounds are suspended.

Two other types of enactment are rehearsal and role reversal. In a *rehearsal*, group members are invited to say what they are thinking. For example, they may voice how much they struggle to please others. They are then free to decide whether they wish to spend their time and energy in this manner. In a *role reversal*, people act the opposite of what they feel. For instance, Craig, who is feeling inadequate, will act adequate, even bold. By doing so, he gets a feel for an area he previously denied.

Body language is another group member exercise. The emphasis is placed on what a person's body is doing, such as finger tapping or leg kicking. The leader asks, "What are your fingers saying?" or "What is your leg doing?" Participants may then emphasize what their behaviors mean. They do this through exaggerating the behavior or simply noting its present movement. The result is an integration of mind and body awareness.

A fourth technique used in Gestalt groups is **changing questions to statements**. This procedure requires a member who raises a question to make it into a statement. For instance, "Do you really think that is why you did not succeed?" would be changed to "I do not think that is why you were unsuccessful." Changing questions to statements helps group members become more aware of their feelings. It also helps eliminate **condemning questions** that put people down, such as "Don't you think you should feel differently?"

The **empty chair technique** is designed to help group members deal with different aspects of their personalities. This technique is used in individual Gestalt sessions but is effective in group settings. There are two variations. In both, an empty chair is placed in front of the group member who wishes to work. In the first variation, the participant is asked to put into the chair all of the feelings that are opposite of the way he or she usually feels, such as anger, aggression, and impulsiveness. The individual then switches seats and becomes the feelings put into the chair. A dialogue is promoted between the polar parts of the individual, with the person changing chairs every time he or she switches feelings. The idea is to promote an integration of feelings and thoughts.

In the second variation, *unfinished business* (the tendency of a person to relive past thoughts and feelings in the present) is the focus. Unfinished business centers on unacknowledged grief, anger, or loss and remains in the background of people's lives, inhibiting their ability to function in the present. Participants who have unfinished business are asked to put the object, feeling, or person in the empty chair and say good-bye. Sometimes another group member can play the part of whatever was placed in the chair and say good-bye in return.

A variation of the integrative empty chair technique is the **top dog/underdog dialogue**. In this method, group members are asked to examine the *top-dog introjections* they have taken from parents (usually represented by "should" and "you") and their feelings about situations (represented by "I" statements). For example, "You should always be polite, but sometimes I do not feel that way." Then they carry on a dialogue between these two aspects of themselves before the group or with another group member and try to become aware of their self-identity and ways to act that would be appropriate.

Fantasy exercises are another popular Gestalt group method. Corey (2012) notes that fantasy can be employed to help group members (a) be more concrete in assessing their feelings, (b) deal with catastrophic experiences, (c) explore and express feelings of guilt and shame, and (d) become more involved in the group. It is not necessary that group members live out their fantasies. Just the fact that they are acting as if they were doing what they have hoped for is helpful.

Dream work to Perls (1969) is "the royal road to integration." It is used in groups by having those who dream recreate and relive the dream in the present. By doing so, these individuals become all parts of the dream. They may do this through working alone in the group setting or having others in the group act out different parts of the dream. The latter idea is known as *dream work as theater* (Zinker, 1977). It assumes basic archetypal themes exist that group members share and benefit from by experiencing.

Dreams are expressions of the polarities within individuals in Gestalt theory. Therefore, it is important to act out the different parts and become conscious of the forces within. Rainwater (1979) suggests that people explore their dreams by asking themselves certain questions, such as "What am I feeling?" "What do I want?" "What am I doing?" and "What is my dream telling me?" By questioning and enacting with others, individuals become more aware, integrated, and empowered to act.

Provost (1999) has described a 6-week growth group based on Gestalt, Jungian, and humanistic theories that helped participants process and understand their dreams. The group, including the leader, used the **energy field** (the sum total of individual members' energies and attention in the group) to help a group member expand the dialogue and action within the original dream. As a result, the dream became a means for understanding oneself and the group better.

Coven (2004) found that Gestalt Group Dreamwork could be effective with an Asian population, specifically Taiwanese. Contrary to cultural stereotypes, "participants readily enacted roles, were personally open, and expressed intense feelings" (p. 175). However, Coven cautioned that his experience may be atypical. Nevertheless, it seems clear that "dream work facilitates group cohesion and is fun, stimulating, and powerful in assisting with the development of personal insight" (Berube, 1999, p. 98).

Homework is a technique that primarily involves group members practicing outside the group what they have learned inside the group. For example, Carole may learn through homework assignments to make statements to her colleagues, such as "This room feels cold to me," instead of asking them condemning questions such as "Aren't you aware that you have the thermostat set too low and that people are freezing in this room because of your actions?" Homework helps group members achieve closure on unresolved issues as well. For instance, Ishu may speak to his parents about how he felt neglected as a child and bring the results of this discussion back to the group to process.

Case Example

Gerard Has a Gestalt Experience

Gerard has lived a lonely life drifting in and out of jobs and relationships. He is depressed and has been having a hard time lately defining himself as anything other than a "loser." He recently heard of a professor who was offering a group experience for depressives. Gerard applied, was screened, and joined the group.

His first day he was surprised to find that instead of introducing everyone verbally, the professor, who was the group leader, had members cut out pictures and words from magazines and either place them in a bag (if they were not ready to share) or paste them on a bag if the pictures and words represented aspects of the person that the individual was willing to

reveal. Gerard found he put more of his material in the bag than on it. As the weeks went by, he occasionally pulled words out of his bag and shared them.

The group was active for 14 sessions, and through it Gerard was able to voice his concerns by relating his dreams, reversing roles, and rehearsing new ways of relating to others. He felt energized at the end of each session.

Questions

How do you think Gerard's experience would have differed had he enrolled in a person-centered group? The fact that Gerard was energized seemed helpful to him. What might he have done to maximize this energy with the group?

Role of the Gestalt Group Leader

The leader is central to the functioning of the Gestalt group, for the leader is usually the person who determines what takes place, with whom, and when such interaction will occur. One of the leader's jobs is to help group members locate their **impasses** (the places in which they get stuck) and work through them to awareness and growth. To achieve this goal and promote a therapeutic breakthrough, the leader may intentionally frustrate group members by refusing to play their manipulative games, such as being helpless. Perls (1969) puts it this way: "My function as a therapist is to help you to the awareness of the here and now, and to frustrate you in any attempt to break out of this" (p. 74). The leader balances challenging group members with supporting them.

Zinker (1977) sees the leader's role as that of an artist. It is up to the leader to create an atmosphere that promotes growth within the group. To do so, the leader self-discloses and allows things to happen. He or she must be "agenda free" and block off attempts by group members or the group as a whole to desert the "now." This may mean that the leader asks group members or the group, "What is happening to you (us) now?" It also means that the leader makes sure everyone speaks for himself or herself by using "I" messages instead of "you" messages: for example, "I feel happy when dancing" rather than "You feel happy when dancing." Whenever possible and appropriate, "should" messages are changed to "want to" messages.

Overall, Gestalt group leaders play several roles during the group's life span: (a) expert-helper; (b) seer, communications expert; (c) frustrator; (d) creator; and (e) teacher (Levin & Shepherd, 1974). Leaders must balance these roles with personal integrity and have the strength to withstand pressures from the group to desert the present. They must not rely on gimmicks to try to promote the growth of group members, yet they cannot be passive. They must trust their intuition and play hunches. Competent Gestalt group leaders are "catalysts" who keep group members focused on "now" issues and help them increase awareness and find personal/interpersonal resolutions for issues that emerge.

Desired Outcome of Gestalt Groups

As a result of a Gestalt group, members should be more aware of themselves in the here and now and change (Flores, 1988). It is hoped they will shed **layers of neurosis** (the *phony*—being unauthentic; the *phobic*—being afraid to really see themselves as they are; and the *impasse*—where their maturity is stuck). Then they can come to realize self-growth through *implosiveness*—feeling their deadness—and *explosiveness*—releasing pent-up energy to be authentic and alive to feelings (Perls, 1970). The bottom line is that members become congruent on personal and interpersonal levels and do not get mired down in the past. The experiential quality of Gestalt groups is especially beneficial for persons who are cognitive. It forces them to use other ways of relating.

Numerous people have experienced favorable results through participating in Gestalt groups. Lieberman, Yalom, and Miles (1973) found that Gestalt group members rated their experience first among 17 different groups in regard to pleasantness and constructiveness. They felt they had learned a great deal and were enthusiastic. They rated their group leader highly. In a more recent study, Shen (2007) found Gestalt-play groups with Taiwanese seventh and eighth graders to be helpful in strengthening family involvement. Shen concluded from this research that "using a short-term developmental model, group counseling may benefit Chinese youth who are raised in a culture that values academic achievement and family life" (p. 303). Likewise, Leung et al. (2013) found that Chinese helping professionals reported better emotional well-being and more hopefulness after participating in an interactional Gestalt marathon group for 18 hours over 2 days.

Evaluation of Gestalt Groups

Strengths and limitations of Gestalt groups must be recognized before individuals decide to enroll in such groups. Otherwise they will have difficulties.

STRENGTHS AND CONTRIBUTIONS

One strength of Gestalt groups is their particular suitability to group leaders "who have a humanistic, existential approach to helping others" (Vander Kolk, 1985, p. 82). Gestalt group work lends itself well to leaders who are creative and who strive to bring out the creativity in others. It emphasizes the effective dimension of human existence. When people's emotional arousal is raised, they are often more persuadable (M. Young, 2013).

A second strength of Gestalt groups is that their focus is on working through impasses and becoming more integrated. Members help one another feel more connected and less alone. As Frew (1983) points out, there is power in the group that comes from member–group interaction as well as from leader–member interaction.

A third strength of Gestalt groups is the variety of exercises and experiences they foster. Gestalt group work is usually intense and active (Day & Matthes, 1992). By participating in planned and spontaneous activities, group members come to realize different aspects of themselves than they might through just talking. The group is influential in forcing members out of previously unproductive patterns of interacting.

Gestalt groups are also quite powerful in working with a variety of difficulties, from addiction (Browne-Miller, 1993) to couple communication (Curman & Curman, 1994). The versatility of

Gestalt groups make them popular with clinicians, especially those who work in settings where talking is not as effective as movement.

A final strength of the Gestalt groups is the abundance of training institutes available to professionals for learning this approach. Several publications are devoted to this theory, including *The Gestalt Journal*. Group leaders have a reservoir of rich resources.

LIMITATIONS

The limitations of Gestalt theory and practice in groups mirror its strengths. First, the Gestalt approach tends to eschew the cognitive side of human nature. Gestalt theorists are often accused of being anti-intellectual and concerned only with effective and bodily experiences. Perls's famous statement "Lose your mind and come to your senses" is sometimes quoted in support of this criticism.

A second limitation of Gestalt groups is that leaders may not be able to help the group work through impasses. When this occurs, there is individual leader–member interaction, or there is uncontrolled group pressure on individuals to take steps they are not ready to do. Such action is usually nonproductive and can be destructive.

A third limitation of the Gestalt approach is the potential danger of abusing techniques and people. Unless leaders are sensitive to the needs of group members, they may become mechanical in showing off techniques and not really helpful. Ethical questions are of major concern if the group leader opens up members' feelings and does not help them resolve these emotions in an integrative fashion.

Finally, Gestalt groups are difficult to research. There are few empirical data on them. Although Simkin (1975) may be correct in saying, "Most Gestalt therapists are busy practicing their art rather than evaluating it" (p. 283), more research must be conducted if this approach is to continue within the mainstream of group work (Rudestam, 1982). Yalom (1985), for instance, has already dismissed some aspects of Gestalt group work by saying, "I feel that Perls's group therapy technique is ill-founded and makes inefficient use of a group's therapeutic potential" (p. 453).

Learning More

A number of centers support and encourage the practice of Gestalt theory in group work and in counseling and therapy. One of the most productive of these centers is:

> The Association for the Advancement of Gestalt Therapy (AAGT)
> aagt.org

The Gestalt Therapy Network (gestalttherapy.net) is another informative link and provides a forum where Gestalt therapists on all levels can discuss their experiences and learn from others.

The Gestalt Therapy Page (gestalt.org), a project sponsored by The Gestalt Journal Press, also provides good information. It annually publishes *The Gestalt Directory,* which includes information about Gestalt practitioners and training programs, and produces *The Gestalt Journal,* a periodical devoted to publishing articles on Gestalt theory and practice.

RATIONAL-EMOTIVE BEHAVIOR THERAPY GROUPS

Premises of Rational-Emotive Behavior Therapy (REBT) Groups

The underlying premises of REBT are stoic and humanistic. Rational-emotive behavior therapy is based on the idea that thinking about events, not external circumstances, produces feelings and behaviors (Fehr, 2013). "Ellis believes that emotional troubles are rooted in personal perceptions

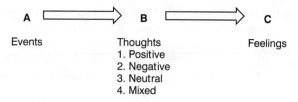

FIGURE 16.1 The ABC model of human interaction.

of unchangeable facts, such as another person's unkindness" (O'Connor, 2001, p. 32). Individuals who have negative, faulty, or irrational thoughts become emotionally disturbed or upset. Their **self-talk** (the messages people give themselves internally) influences their mental health and actions in nonproductive ways. This phenomenon is as true for leaders of groups as for people in general (Browne, 2005). Therefore, to behave rationally, individuals need first to control their thoughts and behaviors (Ellis, 1962, 1995, 2011). If people can change their irrational beliefs and behaviors to rational ones, they will suffer less and actually enjoy life.

The process of change is built on an **A-B-C model of human interaction** (see Figure 16.1). "A" is the event, "B" is the thought process, and "C" is the feeling state resulting from thoughts. To change negative or nonproductive feelings, individuals must think differently. According to Ellis, there are **four types of thoughts: negative, positive, neutral, and mixed**. Negative thoughts concentrate on painful aspects of an event; positive thoughts focus on just the opposite. Neutral cognitions are those that are neither positive nor negative. Those that are mixed contain elements of the other three.

Although people are entitled to feel as much emotion as they want about events, Ellis's approach allows individuals to control their effect by switching the focus of their thoughts (Ellis, 1988; Harper & Ellis, 1975). For example, if Paige does not speak to Carmen at a meeting, then Carmen may think that she was slighted or that Paige was preoccupied with another task. If Carmen makes the second choice, she will not get upset, whereas the first way of thinking will result in anger. In switching thoughts from negative to neutral or positive, people often make better-informed decisions.

Rational-emotive behavior therapy stresses the **dual nature of human beings**. Individuals have both rational and irrational beliefs that can be modified through disputation (Ellis, 1976). Self-rating is discouraged in this approach because no one can live up to a label, such as "good," and individuals tend to become discouraged when they act differently from what they believe is perfect behavior for themselves. Therefore, Ellis advocates that individuals see themselves as "fallible human beings" who act in certain ways in specific circumstances. By avoiding labels and forms of the verb *to be* (e.g., *am, are, was*), people are able to live more rational lives (Harper & Ellis, 1975).

Overall, REBT can be thought of as a philosophy of life as well as a treatment for changing behaviors (Weinrach, 1996). If individuals learn to think more rationally, they are likely to stop inappropriately evaluating themselves, others, and events in the world over which they have no control (Ellis, 2011). They can also quit **making wishes into demands**—for example, using *should, ought,* and *must* in regard to an action.

Practice of Rational-Emotive Behavior Therapy in a Group

Rational-emotive behavior therapy groups vary (Fehr, 2013) but over a number of years, Vernon (2011a) has identified three types of REBT groups. The first is an open-ended problem-solving group where members learn the basics of REBT and apply them to current problems members are having. The second is a topic-specific group where all members share the same problem such as stress, procrastination, or perfectionism and work on it together. The third and final type of group is preventive. It is typically psychoeducational and is structured around a specific activity or lesson. It introduces REBT concepts and application of the ideas to the group, which members use accordingly.

Regardless of the format, REBT groups tend to be more didactic, philosophical, and skills oriented than most other types of groups. The leader consistently introduces REBT theory to the group, and group members are asked to apply the theory to troublesome personal problems or concerns. These situations are analyzed using the A-B-C theory (i.e., activating event, belief, consequences) of therapeutic intervention (Dryden, 1999). Then group members, as well as the leader, give feedback and suggestions (Ellis, 2011). The feedback is in the form of disputation, "D," which takes three forms: cognitive, imaginal, and behavioral. The process is most effective if all three forms are used (Walen, DiGiuseppe, & Wessler, 1980).

Cognitive disputation involves direct questioning, reasoning, and persuasion. It may involve asking the question "Why?"—an inquiry seldom employed in helping relationships. For example, group members might ask one another, "Why must that occur?" Cognitive disputation also involves monitoring one's self-talk in regard to giving oneself irrational or absolute messages. Sichel and Ellis (1984) have developed a self-help form to assist clients in identifying irrational beliefs.

Imaginal disputation has participants seeing themselves in stressful situations and examining their self-talk (Maultsby, 1984). Then they go through the sequence again, but in the process modify their self-talk so it is more rational. For example, individuals might imagine themselves taking a major test while initially telling themselves they did not have a chance to pass. The same scene would then be envisioned in which group members would tell themselves positive or neutral statements, such as "I have studied hard and I am ready" or "I will think each question through before answering."

Behavioral disputation involves many forms, from reading (bibliotherapy) to role playing in the group. Enactment of the problem in the group setting and possible ways of handling it are used. Homework may be assigned in the form of emotive-dramatic exercises, such as a **shame attack** (in which the person actually does what he or she dreaded and finds that the world does not fall apart regardless of the outcome). For example, a shame attack for Shirley might involve speaking to Ned and confirming in her mind that her self-worth is not based on whether he responds. Ellis actually used such a behavioral exercise in his early adulthood (Dryden, 1989). Being shy around women, he forced himself to speak to literally 100 women one day, none of whom he knew. Ellis went a step farther by asking these women he did not know out for a date. Many of the women did not reply to him, and none of them went out with him. Through this experiment, he found that his world did not come unraveled when he was ignored or rejected.

Reflection

When have you ever had a disappointment and realized that your world did not end? How did your thinking help or hurt you in putting the situation into perspective?

Little attention is paid to past events in an REBT group. The focus is on the here and now. REBT groups, which are primarily focused on counseling and psychotherapy, use a "no holds barred approach" (Hansen, Warner, & Smith, 1980, p. 243). Virtually no restrictions are placed on the types of subjects that can be discussed. Members of the group learn to handle themselves better in a variety of difficult situations by thinking and behaving rationally. In many ways, REBT groups can be conceptualized as psychoeducational, where members learn a new way of life.

The REBT approach to group work is not limited to just intellectually bright individuals. It is appropriate for persons functioning at all levels (Ellis, 1997). Most often, the approach stresses remediation. However, at some institutions of education, the emphasis is on prevention (Ellis & Bernard, 1983). For example, the teacher of the ABCs of REBT may illustrate through drawings and other graphic means how emotions develop and what children can do to stay in control of themselves at potentially emotional times.

Regardless of where they participate in an REBT group, members are exposed to a wide variety of cognitive and behavioral methods. Among the best known of these techniques are actively disputing clients' thoughts, persuading them to work from an REBT viewpoint, teaching clients the ABCs of REBT, and giving clients feedback on the rational outcomes of their thoughts. Disputing clients' thoughts has already been covered, so the other three techniques are briefly discussed here.

THE REBT VIEWPOINT

Persuading clients to work from an **REBT viewpoint** involves getting them to believe the premises on which REBT is based. Many REBT group specialists spend at least half of their time in initial group sessions highlighting studies that show that the ideas on which REBT was founded are valid. For instance, as a group leader, Laurie may talk to group members at length about ancient wisdom as well as modern research on the power of thought to affect a person's way of living.

TEACHING CLIENTS THE ABCs OF REBT

The *ABCs of REBT* involve group leaders outlining to members how feelings are derived from thoughts. It is a way of persuading clients to work from a rational-emotive behavior viewpoint and teaching them a valuable tool.

GIVING CLIENTS FEEDBACK

Giving feedback on rational outcomes of thoughts requires that the group leader and members suspend judgment and function cognitively. Feedback refers to the final results of rational thinking. Sometimes this feedback is worded in the present; on other occasions, it is projected into the future. For example, Bart may say to Lindsey, "If you keep thinking rationally about your studies, I expect you'll be a logical candidate for medical school in the future."

In addition to the techniques previously mentioned, group members are encouraged to role-play and to find appropriate models to emulate. The focus is to teach skills and promote and foster a way of life. Ellis (1979) stated this view as follows: "Just as skill training enables clients to change their perceptions of their abilities, so does helping them to perceive themselves differently enable them to acquire better skills" (p. 133).

Role of the Rational-Emotive Behavior Therapy Group Leader

"The Rational-Emotive group is leader-centered. It is the leader's task to make sure that the group is philosophically and cognitively based" (Hansen et al., 1980, p. 246). In REBT groups, the leader encourages rational thinking in a number of ways (Ellis, 1974a, 1974b), including the following: (1) teaching group members about the origins of emotions; (2) being active in the group process by challenging and probing; (3) encouraging group members to help one another to think rationally; (4) using activity-oriented experiences in the group and homework assignments outside the group; and (5) allowing the expression of feelings previously hidden by group members that are then dealt with in a practical, rational way.

In psychotherapeutic and counseling groups, the group leader encourages members to work as **auxiliary counselors**. When they do, participants benefit from multiple inputs. The group leader also serves as a model for the group and reveals how he or she practices REBT in daily life. "The leader's objective is to help participants give up their demands for perfection" (Vander Kolk, 1985, p. 108). Techniques used by the group leader do not vary much from other group approaches and are usually a combination of cognitive, behavioral, and effectiveness-based interventions, such as confrontation, challenging, persuasion, role playing, and imagining.

Case Example

Carlos Learns to Calm Down

Carlos has always been emotional. Traditionally, he has not thought through problems but has reacted to situations with feelings ranging from anger to delight. Although he loves the highs, he loathes the lows. Therefore, his goal in the REBT group he joined was to be more level in his emotional responses—that is, to calm down.

Initially, becoming calmer was hard for Carlos. It took him awhile to master the ABCs of REBT. He was used to going to either positive or negative ways of reacting to events instead of to neutral or mixed ways of responding. Therefore, he asked members of the group to role-play with him. They put him in situations that were prone to have a lot of emotion attached to them, such as winning the lottery or being in an accident. Eventually, Carlos learned to respond in a neutral or mixed way to events with the option that he could choose to feel as much or as little emotion as he wanted.

Questions

What do you think of Carlos's strategy for becoming more rational? What else could he have done?

Desired Outcome of Rational-Emotive Behavior Therapy Groups

A desired outcome of an REBT group is for group members to learn how to think rationally. If they can learn how to control their thought processes, they will be able to deal effectively with a wide variety of problems. For example, insurance representatives who reduce their type A behavior (e.g., aggressive, hostile, impatient) do a better job in relating to their customers, their product, and themselves (Moller & Botha, 1996).

A second objective is for group members to achieve particular goals in their own lives connected with using REBT to overcome an irrational belief such as anxiety (Cowan & Brunero, 1997). Knowing how to implement the theory is not enough; it must be practiced, both inside and outside of the group context. For instance, if Dottie knows REBT theory but does not apply the process to her life, then she is limiting herself.

A third expected result of an REBT group is that members should have a better knowledge of how REBT can be employed in situations with which they have no firsthand experience. Knowing this will allow them to be helpful in addressing novel, nondevelopmental problems.

A final payoff from participating in an REBT group is that members gain the experience of personally understanding the process of change. For example, victims of childhood sexual abuse who overcome their depression through group rational-emotive behavior therapy understand the difficulties of changing their thoughts, emotions, and behaviors (Rieckert & Moller, 2000). Thus they empathize more with others who are in the process of self-modification.

Evaluation of Rational-Emotive Behavior Therapy Groups

REBT groups have inherent strengths and limitations. These groups are primarily psychoeducationally, psychotherapeutically, and counseling focused.

STRENGTHS AND CONTRIBUTIONS

A strength of employing REBT theory in group work is its focus on the importance of cognition in influencing people's emotions and actions (Weinrach, 1996). Rational-emotive behavior therapy is one of the few integrative theories used in a group that places primary importance on cognitions, and cognitive-based group therapy has proven effective in the remediation and prevention of disorders such as major depressive episodes (Pearson & Burlingame, 2013).

A second strong point of the REBT group approach is how Ellis has demystified the process of using REBT in a group setting. The essentials of REBT can be taught quickly. It is relatively easy for everyone involved in the group process to learn (Ellis, 1997).

Another positive associated with REBT groups is that they are excellent environments for clients who are phasing out of individual therapeutic counseling (Wessler & Hankin, 1988). These groups help persons in transition see themselves more clearly and equip their members with skills in rational thinking.

A fourth strength of using REBT theory in groups is versatility. REBT theory is geared toward working with large segments of the population. It is broad based and stresses a multitude of specific treatments. Wolfe (1995), for instance, reports that REBT women's groups, including those focused on sexuality, aging, authority, dependency, power, and risk taking, all have had positive results.

A final positive of REBT groups is the opportunities they provide for members to do homework assignments, take verbal and nonverbal risks, and learn from the experiences of others, both inside and outside the group context (Ellis, 2011). Such groups emphasize action as well as talk (Rieckert & Moller, 2000). Books such as *A New Guide to Rational Living* (Harper & Ellis, 1975), *How to Stubbornly Refuse to Make Yourself Miserable About Anything—Yes, Anything!* (Ellis, 1988), and *The Practice of Rational Emotive Behavior Therapy* (Ellis & Dryden, 2007) are assigned reading between sessions.

LIMITATIONS

One limitation of REBT is its traditional focus on the individual, not the group. Although group members learn a lot about their ability to control thoughts, emotions, and behaviors, they do not usually learn a lot about group dynamics.

Another limitation of the REBT approach is its confrontive and directive stance. Group leaders and members may push members to get rid of faulty beliefs and adopt new thought patterns before they are ready. This trade-off may not be in the best interests of participants because it has not been personalized. Hence, faulty beliefs may not really be discarded, and rational ones may not really be adopted.

A third drawback of REBT groups is that borderline-disturbed members may get worse. Some individuals who require a great deal of individual attention or those who have a low intellectual capacity may do better in individual sessions. Because the emphasis in REBT is not on a close client–counselor relationship, these individuals may receive more of the personal and professional attention they need in non-REBT settings.

A final negative of REBT groups is the lack of rigorous research specifically on them. Ellis (1982) claimed that REBT groups are effective, but his research was based more on cognitive groups in general than on REBT groups. A review of outcome studies of REBT by McGovern and Silverman (1986) is more convincing, and Solomon and Haaga (1995) suggest that methodological limitations of REBT research have caused researchers to underestimate REBT's effectiveness. However, greater uniformity in regard to methodology is needed in REBT research. Studies such as those by Rieckert and Moller (2000), where control and treatment groups were used in measuring the effectiveness of REBT groups for adult victims of childhood sexual abuse, hold promise.

Learning More

REBT deals with changing emotions and has been found to be an effective treatment in group work for a number of problems. Its founder, Albert Ellis, was especially prolific and influential in counseling and psychology circles. The best-known training facility for learning more about REBT is:

> The Albert Ellis Institute
> Web site: albertellis.org

The institute offers a variety of material on REBT, including programs of study. The *Journal of Rational Emotive and Cognitive Behavior Therapy* is a primary source of articles on REBT.

PSYCHODRAMA GROUPS

Premises of Psychodrama Groups

Psychodrama is sometimes viewed as "nothing more than a grand extension of the clinical interview" (Greenberg, 1974, p. 13), but it is much more. Psychodrama emphasizes a freeing of individuals from the irrational forces that bind them into dysfunctional behavior patterns. The goals of psychodrama emphasize action (Carnabucci, 2014). Group members are removed from the usual one-to-one relationship with counselors and are given an opportunity to act out and experience various aspects of their problem(s). Personal interaction and encounter, focus on the here and now, spontaneity and creativity, full expression of feelings, and reality testing are stressed.

A focused emphasis of psychodrama is on the holistic interaction of protagonists in their dramas. The group leader is the producer of the dramas. Protagonists rework their lives as both players and playwrights (Blatner, 2000). "Habitual verbal defenses are circumvented" (Blatner, 2005) and new realizations occur. For instance, a psychodrama leader might say to a group member, "Show the group how your interactions with your father affected your view of work." The member would then enact alone, or with others, scenes that came to mind of early memories. Such enactments would be shown in dramatic form rather than discussed. The result would be a new awareness by the group member that he or she could then discuss, and observations from group members of what they noticed in the enactment(s). Basically, psychodrama is predicated on the assumption that humans in society are continually evolving and can become aware of matters pertaining to their lives at any developmental stage. Persons who are open to themselves begin to realize their strengths as well as their liabilities. Such realizations make them more capable of meeting external demands in creative ways.

At the heart of psychodrama is the **encounter**, an existentialist concept that involves total physical and psychological contact among persons on an intense, concrete, and complete basis in the here and now. The encounter can relate to past events, anticipated ones, or present circumstances, but it always involves taking a moment or a particular situation in one's life and expanding it in various dimensions (Leveton, 2001). One particular dimension that the encounter deals with is **surplus reality**—"psychological experience that transcends the boundaries of physical reality" (Blatner, 2005, p. 429). These experiences, which include relationships with those who have died or were never born, or with God, are often as important to people as actual occurrences. For example, Jodie may still grieve for the child she lost in childbirth. In the encounter, she can express her feelings through dramatically reliving the scene of loss and the ways she might have handled or dealt with the tragedy at that time. Overall, the encounter is the experience of identity and total reciprocity, summed up by Moreno (1914) in the following poetic way:

> A meeting of two: eye to eye, face to face. And when you are near I will tear your eyes out and place them instead of mine, and you will tear my eyes out and will place them instead of yours, and I will look at you with your eyes and you will look at me with mine. (p. 3)

The main concepts that emphasize Moreno's premise on experiencing one's situation fully in the here and now are spontaneity and creativity, situation, tele, catharsis, and insight (Greenberg, 1974; Horvatin & Schreiber, 2006). **Spontaneity** is the response people make that contains "some degree of adequacy to a new situation or a degree of novelty to an old situation" (Moreno, 1945, p. xii). The purpose of spontaneity is to liberate oneself from scripts and stereotypes and gain new perspectives on life. Responding in new creative ways is part of this process. For example, Mildred, instead of panicking when she is given a math test, now begins to sit calmly and study the whole exam before making a response.

Situation is the emphasis on the present, where "natural barriers of time, space, and states of existence are obliterated" (Greenberg, 1974, pp. 16–17). Under these circumstances, clients are able to work on past problems, future fears, and current difficulties in a here-and-now atmosphere. For instance, Lucas plans for his high school graduation, college, and an entry-level job by confronting his fear of success and his present lack of self-confidence.

Tele is the total communication of feelings between people, "the cement which holds groups together" (Moreno, 1945, p. xi). It is experienced most when it occurs between two people. At its best, it involves complete interpersonal and reciprocal empathy. In a tele, Mitch and Sandy tell each other which qualities they most admire in the other and how it makes them feel when they think they have expressed one or more of these qualities, such as empathy and poise.

Catharsis and insight are the "end products" of spontaneity and tele (Greenberg, 1974). *Catharsis* involves an emotional purging, such as when Delilah screams out in regard to her mother, "All I ever wanted you to do was love me!" Although it is one of the end products of spontaneity and tele, catharsis is "the beginning of reparation and healing" because what was disowned, such as suffering and grief, is now personally accepted, expressed, and integrated (Westwood et al., 2003, p. 123). **Insight** is a related concept, consisting of immediate new perceptions and understandings about one's problems that occur during or after the experience of catharsis. For instance, in the preceding example, Delilah might say after her cathartic experience, "I never realized I was so angry."

Practice of Psychodrama in a Group

The practice of psychodrama is multidimensional. First, physical and personal factors must be considered, such as a stage, a protagonist, actors, a director, and an audience (Blatner, 1996, 2005; Haskell, 1973) (see Figure 16.2). Second, techniques must be employed in a methodological manner (Holmes & Karp, 1991; Moreno & Moreno, 1959).

The **stage** is the area where the action takes place. It may be a platform, or simply be a part of a room. The stage is wherever the participants want it to be. For instance, Jason may say, "The

FIGURE 16.2   The psychodrama stage.   *Source:* Republished with permission of Springer Pub. Co., from *Acting In: Practical Applications Of Psychodramatic Methods,* Adam Blatner MD, 2e. Permission conveyed through Copyright Clearance Center, Inc.

corner of the room will be my stage this time." Most groups find it beneficial to have the stage in a separate place from where the group meets to remind members that the enactments are different from verbal interchanges (Blatner, 1996).

The **protagonist** is the person who is the subject of the psychodrama enactment (Blatner, 2005). He or she may play many parts. For example, in a psychodrama, Laurel as the protagonist played different parts of herself, from being sweet and innocent to being mean and spiteful. At times, the protagonist may step out of a scene and observe. Regardless, the goal of the protagonist is to express the thoughts, feelings, and issues relevant to the role being played. A key element to being a protagonist is spontaneity.

Actors are those who play the parts of other important people or objects in the play. They are called "auxiliaries" and, with prompting from the protagonist, they can play the protagonist's double, an antagonist, or even a piece of furniture. An auxiliary can play more than one part, such as being the protagonist's best friend and worst enemy.

The **director** is the person who guides the protagonist in the use of psychodramatic methods to help that person explore his or her problem (Blatner, 1996). The director is roughly equivalent to the group leader in other theoretical approaches.

Finally, the **audience** describes others who may be present during the psychodrama. The purpose of the audience is to give feedback regarding what they saw, heard, and felt during the psychodrama. Sometimes the audience becomes involved while the psychodrama is being conducted and makes sound effects or comments at the request of the director. For example, the audience might be directed to repeat to Rhonda when she gets angry and makes a mistake, "Keep cool. Use your head. Keep cool. Use your head." In such cases, the audience becomes a *chorus*.

The techniques employed in psychodrama are dependent on many variables. Among the most important factors that influence which techniques will be used are the situation of the protagonist, the skill of the director, the availability of actors, the size of the audience, the goals of the session, and the phase in which the psychodrama is operating. Special situations will require different skills. For example, Blatner (1996) states that some psychodrama techniques are best employed when the objective is to clarify the protagonist's feelings (e.g., monodrama, soliloquy, the double). Others are used to facilitate the expression of emotion (e.g., amplification, asides, exaggeration of nonverbal actions). Yet other techniques (e.g., role reversal, audience feedback, nonverbal interaction exercises) are completed in self-awareness situations. The psychodrama process generally goes through three phases: warm-up, action, and integration.

1. *Warm-up phase*—The warm-up phase is characterized by the director making sure he or she is ready to lead the group and that members are ready to be led. This process may involve both verbal and nonverbal activities designed to put everyone in the right frame of mind to conduct the psychodrama and establish trust and an atmosphere of spontaneity (Blatner, 2005; Moreno, 1940). For instance, the director may walk around arranging furniture while speaking to participants. Then he or she may lead the group in some get-acquainted exercises. After these activities, the group may engage in **action exercises** (e.g., sensory awareness methods, guided imagery), which help members discover common themes within the group as well as focus on individual concerns. Overall, the warm-up is experiential and allows members to process some of the technical procedures they will experience in the actual psychodrama (Leveton, 2001). At the end of the warm-up, the action phase of psychodrama begins.

2. *Action phase*—This part of the psychodrama process involves the enactment of protagonists' concerns. The director helps each protagonist who chooses to work "set the stage" for a specific scene in the here and now. Group participants are assigned auxiliary ego roles of significant others or things in the protagonist's life. Then the opening scene is portrayed, and the protagonist and auxiliary egos are given an opportunity to refine their roles and gear their interaction from the surface to significant events. The director may encourage the protagonist at this point to do a role reversal so that he or she can feel more empathy or projection of feelings. Other techniques that are often employed are the use of soliloquy, the double technique, and asides. All are targeted toward helping the protagonist elaborate on feelings.

Finally, the protagonist is helped to work through the situation by developing other adaptive attitudes and behavioral responses. *Working through* may mean repeating a scene using new behavioral strategies. It may also involve role reversals or the use of modeling. The crucial thing in the action stage is that protagonists express repressed emotions and find a new, effective way to act.

3. *Integration phase*—The last phase of psychodrama involves discussion and closure. After the action phase, a protagonist is off balance, vulnerable, and in need of support. The director encourages the group to give the protagonist as much personal, supportive, and constructive feedback as possible during this time. Feedback focuses initially on the effective, rather than the intellectual, aspects of the enactment. Toward the end of the group, it is appropriate to express some cognitive aspects of what has been experienced (Blatner, 1996; Corey, 2012). At the completion of this phase, an emphasis is placed on understanding and integration so the protagonist can act differently if any similar situations arise. Figure 16.3 illustrates how the intensity of emotions in these three phases of psychodrama changes over time.

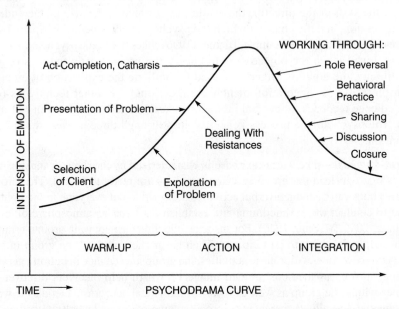

FIGURE 16.3 Psychodrama curve. *Source:* Republished with permission of Springer Pub. Co., from *Acting In: Practical Applications Of Psychodramatic Methods*, Adam Blatner MD, 2e. Permission conveyed through Copyright Clearance Center, Inc.

There are hundreds of psychodrama techniques with many variations, so only a few major techniques (creative imagery, magic shop, sculpting, soliloquy, monodrama, double and multiple double, role reversal, and mirror) are considered here. Their use varies and is dictated by the circumstances within a particular psychodrama.

1. **Creative imagery**—This warm-up technique consists of inviting psychodrama participants to imagine neutral or pleasant objects and scenes. The idea is to help participants become spontaneous. For instance, Del realizes he can create a picture of a sunrise from a mountaintop although he lives on a coastal plain.

2. **The magic shop**—This warm-up technique is especially useful for protagonists who are ambivalent about their values and goals. It involves a storekeeper (an auxiliary ego) who runs a magic shop filled with special qualities. The qualities are not for sale but may be bartered for (Verhofstadt & Leni, 2000). Thus, if Leroy, the protagonist, wants better relationship skills with others, he may have to give up irrational anger in exchange.

3. **Sculpting**—In this exercise, group members use nonverbal methods to arrange other group members into a configuration like that of significant persons with whom they regularly deal, such as family members or social peers. The positioning involves body posturing. It assists members in seeing and experiencing their perceptions of significant others in a dynamic way. For example, by arranging family members with their backs toward her, Regina realizes how shut out of her family she felt when growing up.

4. **Soliloquy**—This technique involves the protagonist giving a monologue about his or her situation, as he or she is acting it out. For instance, the person who is driving home from work alone may give words to the thoughts that are uppermost on his or her mind, such as "I feel life is unfair." A variation on this activity is the *therapeutic soliloquy* technique, in which private reactions to events in the protagonist's life are verbalized and acted out, usually by other actors. For example, other group members may push and tug at each other, showing Helena her ambivalence about going on to graduate school.

5. **Monodrama** or **autodrama**—In this technique, the protagonist plays all the parts of the enactment; no auxiliary egos are used. The person may switch chairs or talk to different parts of the self. The monodrama is a core feature of Gestalt therapy. For instance, Walt becomes the significant thoughts he has about his upcoming marriage and has a dialogue between these expressions in different chairs arranged in a circle.

6. **Double and multiple double**—The double is an important technique in psychodrama. The group member designated by the director takes on the role of the protagonist's alter ego and helps the protagonist express inner feelings. The double follows the lead of the director but can also make feeling statements to guide the director in case he or she misses a cue (Monterio-Leitner, 2001).

   In cases in which the protagonist has ambivalent feelings, the multiple double technique is used. In these situations, two or more actors represent different aspects of the protagonist's personality. The doubles may speak at once or take turns. Through their input, the protagonist should gain an idea of what his or her thoughts and feelings are.

   Doubles can emphasize or **amplify** statements made by the protagonist in a number of ways. Speaking to the protagonist in the first person, doubles may verbalize nonverbal communications, question themselves, interpret what is being said and not said, contradict feelings, make a self-observation, or engage in denial (Blatner, 1996, 2000). For instance, referring to Irene's changing jobs, her double says, "I wonder for whom I am doing this, myself or my children?" An effective double will reach the core of the protagonist's experience, and the protagonist will feel confirmed and understood.

7. **Role reversal**—In this technique, the protagonist switches roles with another person on stage and plays that person's part. For instance, Zelda becomes Claudia and acts like her. Zerka Moreno (1983) states that role reversal encourages the maximum expression of conflict; Blatner (2005) and Hagedorn and Hirshhorn (2009) maintain that role reversal is a core part of psychodrama.

8. **Mirror**—In this activity, the protagonist watches from offstage while an auxiliary ego mirrors the protagonist's posture, gesture, and words. This technique is used in the action phase of psychodrama to help the protagonist see himself or herself more accurately. For instance, Rufus learns through watching Buster mirror him that he is not the clearheaded, decisive person he imagined himself to be.

Role of the Psychodrama Group Leader

The director is the leader of a psychodrama and as such wears many hats. Moreno (1953, 1964) suggests that the *director* serves as a producer, a facilitator, an observer, and an analyzer. The director sets norms and models skills that ensure safety and personal control (Brown-Shaw, Westwood, & DeVries, 1999). The director builds his or her skills in three areas:

1. knowledge of methods, principles, and techniques,
2. understanding of personality theory and its relationship to developing an evolving philosophy of life, and
3. his or her own personality development and maturity. (Blatner, 1996)

In addition to a broad general knowledge of life and human nature, a director is expected to have completed specific course work in subject areas such as general psychology, group process, communication theory, and nonverbal communications.

The director's function is to conduct such tasks as leading the warm-up experience, encouraging the development of trust and spontaneity, establishing a structure so that protagonists can identify and work on significant issues in their lives, protecting members from abuse by others, and bringing some type of closure to group sessions. Potential directors should have experienced many psychodramas and have received direct supervision from experienced directors. Overall, Corsini (1966) concludes that effective group directors possess three qualities: creativity, courage, and charisma.

Case Example

Monique Delivers a Monologue

Monique has wrestled with the impulsive side of herself for years. She idealizes calmness and can see herself being poised. Sometimes she achieves this demeanor, but often she becomes flustered in her dealing with others and impulsively fires off an email or blurts out a sentence that she later regrets. Her inability to control herself in frustrating situations

has cost her promotions and raises. Therefore, when someone suggested that Monique try psychodrama, she was ready. She thought it would help and doing psychodrama would allow her to learn how she might control her actions better.

During the warm-up phase of her first psychodrama session, Monique was led through a guided imagery exercise by her director, Sharon. She found herself emotionally charged from the experience. During the action phase of the session, Monique volunteered to be the protagonist and while in that role, she delivered a monologue while acting out her problem with impulsivity. She was surprised by her words and actions and found comfort in help from other actors. During the integrative phase of the psychodrama, members of the group gave Monique constructive feedback, such as the comment: "When you seemed to think about your behaviors, you were able to talk yourself into acting calmer." Monique left the session feeling supported and stronger.

Questions

Although you may not have been in a psychodrama session, when have you found yourself supported by others as you told or showed them a situation with which you were dealing? How do you connect that experience to psychodrama?

Desired Outcome of Psychodrama Groups

The desired outcome of psychodrama can be described as the creation of catharsis, insight, and emotional resolution (Horvatin & Schreiber, 2006; Moreno, 1964). Yablonsky (1976) states that Moreno's goal in psychodrama is "to develop a 'theatrical cathedral' for the release of the natural human spontaneity and creativity that he believed existed naturally in everyone" (p. 274). Through psychodrama, individuals should be able to experience and work through past, present, or anticipated events that have caused them distress. When they have gained emotional and cognitive insight by acting out their difficulties, they will reach a stage of renewed self-awareness, readjustment, integration, acceptance, control, and prevention.

It is essential that participants in psychodramas be willing to take risks and be open to constructive feedback. One of the desirable spinoffs from psychodrama is the learning that takes place when one is not the main protagonist. A definite **spillover effect** from this approach is watching a main character reach resolution on important issues.

Evaluation of Psychodrama Groups

Psychodrama groups can be powerful and have much to commend them as ways of working with others. However, they are not without limitations.

STRENGTHS AND CONTRIBUTIONS

A major strength of psychodrama is its diversity. Psychodrama is appropriately used in psychotherapeutic environments as well as in psychoeducational and business settings. For example, the Harvard Law School uses certain aspects of psychodrama to help students practice interpersonal skills they have difficulty performing (Bordone, 2000). Furthermore, psychodrama can be employed with individuals of all age, educational, and socioeconomic levels. For instance, Amatruda (2006) helped 10- to 13-year-old elementary school children in a special education program communicate more positively with one another and improve their status with peers by using action techniques and psychodrama methods. Students' negative behaviors in the classroom decreased, interactions with one another were more positive, and attitudes toward their own potential improved as a result of the psychodrama-based conflict resolution and skill-building training. Other forms of psychodrama have been used in family therapy, addiction treatment, the training of theologians, the sensitizing of leaders, and the supervision of counselors (Gendron, 1980; Wilkins, 1995). A unique use of psychodrama is in middle school to help teachers and counselors demonstrate the concept of roles (Shaffer, 1997) and to describe and prevent bullying behavior (Beale & Scott, 2001). A novel form of psychodrama is a structured "guided autobiography," which is used with older people as an educational and therapeutic exercise (Brown-Shaw et al., 1999).

Another positive aspect of psychodrama is its teaching potential. Group members learn a great deal about themselves through their active participation (Kranz & Lund, 1993). As Zerka Moreno (1983) points out, professionals in various mental health specialties can use psychodrama to learn how they interact and resolve matters with difficult clients. Psychodrama gives these professionals a feeling for situations.

A third strength of a psychodrama group is its fostering of creativity and spontaneity within leaders and members (Coven, Ellington, & Van Hull, 1997). A major problem that people have is their inability to find resolutions to stressful or harmful situations. Psychodrama promotes new ways to help people find solutions to problems. By acting on a difficulty in the confines of a safe environment, the protagonist gets a feel for how things can be different (Moreno, 1987). For example, Peter realizes in the calm atmosphere of the group that he can respond to a negative statement by ignoring it, using humor, becoming negative himself, or using confrontation.

A fourth positive aspect of psychodrama is its integrative and vicarious effect. Psychodrama emphasizes action coupled with emotional release. A by-product of this process is the change in thoughts that accompanies changes in behavior and emotion (Coven et al., 1997). This change is not limited to just the protagonist but can extend to members of the audience. As the psychodrama concludes, a good psychodrama director "shifts the focus to the audience and discusses the impact of their experiences, parts of the psychodrama with which they identified, issues they got in touch with, and what they learned from the psychodrama in general" (Ohlsen, Horne, & Lawe, 1988, p. 105).

A final strength of psychodrama is the input and feedback the audience and actors give the protagonist and each other (Moreno, 1964). Psychodrama promotes interaction and experiential learning among group members.

LIMITATIONS

A major limitation of psychodrama is the danger of overexposing the protagonist to him- or herself as well as to the audience. A sense of timing and knowledge of what hidden factors need to be exposed are crucial. The ability of a psychodrama director to know when and what to emphasize is one that takes years to develop. First attempts at helping are not as polished as later efforts.

Another area of concern to professional group workers is the quantity and quality of the research underlying psychodrama. Role playing has the potential to change individual attitudes and behaviors (Mann, 1967), but psychodrama is more than role playing. As D'Amato and Dean (1988) point out, there is a need for controlled research on the factors that make up the approach. Even the "taproot of the theory," that is, that when problems are acted out, the client's mindset becomes more spontaneous, has never been empirically verified (p. 312).

A third constraint of psychodrama is connected with the availability of training. There are few training centers for directors. Needed qualities of directors go beyond experience with observing/participating and studying to include intuition and charisma. There is the danger that some psychodrama groups may differ radically from others because of the self-awareness and knowledge of the director. Since 1975, the American Board of Examiners in Psychodrama, Sociometry and Group Psychotherapy has tried to ensure uniformity in professional standards for directors.

A final criticism of psychodrama is that it may focus too much on expression of feelings rather than change in behavior. A lot of emphasis in psychodrama is placed on effect and present experiences. If the group is not carefully constructed, then the emotional part of the theory and the here-and-now emphasis will override the integrative aspect of the approach.

Learning More

Psychodrama is an interesting and active form of group work. Professionals who wish to practice it must undergo extensive training. One of the most prominent organizations devoted to the study and furtherance of psychodrama is:

> American Society of Group Psychotherapy and Psychodrama (ASGPP)
> Telephone: 609-737-8500; Web site: asgpp.org

The ASGPP publishes an excellent professional periodical, the *Journal of Group Psychotherapy, Psychodrama, and Sociometry*. It also holds conferences and provides training opportunities for its members.

Summary and Conclusion

Four active group approaches have been examined in this chapter: existentialism, Gestalt, REBT, and psychodrama.

Existential groups, like Adlerian and person-centered groups, focus on relationships. A predominant belief underlying these groups is that techniques follow understanding within the groups between members and the leader. Therefore, the existential approach in group work can incorporate other major theoretical perspectives and even borrow techniques from them (Vontress, 1996). The flexibility of existential group work is one of its strengths. Its use in multicultural groups reflects the appropriateness of this theory of group work as one of the universal ways of working with people in groups.

The influence of Gestalt groups was most prominent in the 1960s and 1970s, when they were perceived as exciting and active. The processes within these groups, when properly conducted, helped group members become self-aware and integrated.

Gestalt group processes have received favorable reviews from their participants, but controversy still surrounds the use of these groups. Part of the controversy is based on a lack of empirical evidence to support their effectiveness. The perception still exists that the groups are all action and no thought.

REBT is frequently used in group settings, particularly group counseling and psychotherapy. It makes use of a number of effective, behavioral, and cognitive methods to help its group members bring about change. A primary aspect of this approach is the initial teaching needed to educate group members that feelings are derived from thoughts. After this information is clearly understood, the group proceeds with the leader being in charge but with other participants acting as "auxiliary counselors."

REBT groups stress role playing and homework assignments as well as recognition of thoughts. Disputations are usually employed to get rid of faulty, irrational thinking and help participants take better control of their lives. Overall, REBT groups enable their members to learn from one another. These groups are highly structured and didactic but do not stress group dynamics. In many ways, REBT groups function in a psychoeducational format even when they are emphasizing psychotherapeutic changes.

Psychodrama continues to be one of the most exciting forms of group work. Although it has been widely used in psychotherapy and counseling settings (Davis-Gage, 2011), aspects of it are quite appropriate in psychoeducational and task/work environments. This approach to groups requires a great deal of action or participation. Within the psychodrama, protagonists work out their problems, release feelings, and try new behaviors. Psychodrama goes through stages and needs an expert and experienced director to work properly.

Classroom Exercises

1. Which of the Gestalt exercises listed in this chapter do you think would be effective if you were leading a counseling group? Would they be the same if you were leading a psychoeducational group or a task group? Discuss your answer with the class.

2. What do you find most appealing about Gestalt groups? What is the least appealing aspect of these groups? In what way is the action-oriented philosophy of this approach a strength or a weakness compared to the other group approaches with which you are now familiar?

3. Discuss in groups of three how psychodrama has influenced other forms of group work. Which techniques have other group approaches borrowed from psychodrama? How do they use these techniques differently?

4. Have a class debate between two teams on the pros and cons of using the theories covered in this chapter. Poll the class after the debate on which points they remember each side making and why they remember those emphases.

History of Group Work

The history of groups is as old as the history of people. From the beginning of humankind, individuals have gathered together to create, achieve, and resolve matters not possible otherwise. Groups are a natural way for people to communicate and interrelate with one another. No written history indicates when or where the first groups were formed, but all cultures have made use of groups in their growth and development.

USES OF GROUPS BEFORE 1900

Before 1900, organized groups were generally formed for functional and pragmatic reasons. Most were large. Their primary emphasis was on distributing information. Immigrants, the poor, and the mentally ill were among those populations receiving special attention in large groups. Social workers and physicians used group structure to help individuals gain knowledge about themselves, their surroundings, resources, and others.

An example of how groups were used at the time can be found in the work of Jane Addams at Hull House in Chicago. Addams formed groups of new immigrants and the poor to help them understand their environments better and to assist each other in breaking down barriers that impeded them. What she did would be classified now as the beginnings of **social group work**. She organized individuals into purposeful and enriching groups that engaged in reading, crafts, and club activities. In addition, she discussed with group participants matters such as hygiene and nutrition, which helped them make needed personal changes.

The group movement developed not because of one individual or discipline but rather because of the need for social reform and education. The use of large groups for instructional purposes evolved into the use of small groups for various purposes. By the beginning of the twentieth century, a group movement had begun that would slowly emerge and grow in scope, size, and impact.

GROWTH OF WORK WITH GROUPS: 1900 TO THE PRESENT

1900 to 1909

Joseph Hersey Pratt is credited with having organized the first formal group experience that was not primarily educational or task/work oriented. He started a psychotherapy group for tuberculosis outpatients in 1905 at the Massachusetts General Hospital in Boston. He was one of the first to write about the dynamics that occur within group settings, and his work served as a model for other leaders exploring processes within their groups. Pratt started his group primarily for humane and economic reasons. The group served as a source of support and inspiration for tuberculosis patients whose conditions were chronic and cyclical and whose circumstances often led to personal discouragement and depression. Pratt noticed that the people in the group not only became more concerned with one another over time but had a positive influence on one another.

In 1907, Jesse B. Davis, principal of Grand Rapids High School in Michigan, directed that one English class per week would be devoted to "Vocational and Moral Guidance." Unlike Pratt,

Davis did not emphasize the dynamics of the group process. Rather, he stressed the functionality of a group as an environment in which to learn life skills, values, and the importance of citizenship. The groups formed from his directive were psychoeducational.

1910 to 1919

The initial progress in group work slowed from 1910 to 1919, although educational and task/work groups were used to a considerable extent. For instance, soldiers were instructed in groups during World War I, and teamwork was emphasized during the war for both civilians and military personnel. During this conflict, psychological group tests, such as the Army Alpha and Beta intelligence tests, were developed and administered. Groups were also used in a limited way to treat combat-fatigued soldiers.

In Europe, Jacob L. Moreno published a significant, philosophical paper on group methods in 1914, written under the name of J. M. Levy. It stressed the psychoanalytic and social psychological perspectives of individuals working together.

1920 to 1929

Several important events in the development of groups occurred in the 1920s. First, in 1922, Alfred Adler initiated a new and systematic form of group guidance and counseling that became known as **collective counseling**. Adler employed his treatment method with both prison and child guidance populations. In the child guidance clinics, he established a team of helping specialists, such as psychiatrists, psychologists, and social workers, to interview children. Parents and children were helped by the team to realize that problems with children usually are related to problems in the family. Adler and his associates devised family group meetings, or **family councils**, as a means of getting input from everyone in the family on how to resolve difficulties and improve family relations.

A second major event in the 1920s was Jacob L. Moreno's formulation in 1921 of the **Theater of Spontaneity** (*Stegreiftheatre*), a first step in his creation of psychodrama. Moreno's ideas influenced later theorists, such as Fritz Perls in his founding of Gestalt technology and William Schutz in his formation of encounter techniques. Some of the ideas stemming from psychodrama, such as role playing, the taking of "stage center," the emphasis on here-and-now interaction, the promotion of catharsis, the focus on empathy, and the encouragement of group members helping one another, are incorporated in many forms of groups today.

Related to Moreno's work, although entirely independent from it, was Trigant Burrow's focus on the interpersonal relationships of individuals. Burrow thought that interpersonal relationships play a crucial role in the formation and enactment of psychotherapy. He believed that isolation was detrimental to mental health.

A final significant occurrence during the 1920s was the investigation of small groups. Researchers began to learn which types of interactions were the norm in small-group settings and how groups influence individuals. Individual versus group performances were evaluated. Because of this scientific approach, the concept of groups gained respect, and the power of groups became more recognized.

1930 to 1939

The 1930s are noted in group work history for five major events.

- First, group guidance and educational publications and practices increased.
- Second, Jacob Moreno continued to write and make creative presentations.

- Third, there was an increase in the number and quality of fieldwork studies by sociologists, such as Muzafer Sherif, Theodore Newcomb, and W. F. Whyte.
- A fourth event during the decade was the founding of the first major self-help group in America, **Alcoholics Anonymous (AA)**.
- A final noteworthy phenomenon of the 1930s was the movement of psychoanalytic treatment into the group domain and the discovery of several dynamics that operate in group psychotherapy.

Group guidance and education in schools centered on vocational and personal themes. Initially, these activities were the responsibility of homeroom teachers. Some schools even referred to homeroom as "the '**guidance hour**' or 'guidance room'." In this arrangement, the teacher's responsibilities were "to establish friendly relationships, to discover the abilities and needs, and to develop right attitudes toward school, home, and the community."

Jacob Moreno's most productive writings and presentations started in the 1930s and continued for several decades. He introduced the terms *group therapy* and *group psychotherapy* into the vocabulary of helping professionals in 1931 and 1932. He also devised one of the earliest forms of group treatment: *psychodrama*. Psychodrama is an interpersonal approach in which participants act out their feelings regarding past or present events and attempt to clarify conflicts. This type of therapy and the emergence of therapy in small groups, which became more prevalent, opened the way for the theoretical conceptualization of group counseling.

The third major event of the decade—studies of groups in natural settings—used various investigative methods to gather data. Sherif, for instance, studied the influence of groups on the establishment of social norms by charting the response of individuals inside and outside a group setting to a particular stimulus called the *autokinetic movement*. He found that individuals who had been a part of a group tended to view this light phenomenon within the range established by their group. Likewise, Newcomb found that students from politically conservative homes tended to become more liberal because of the prevailing norms of their peer groups. Finally, Whyte studied larger social systems by moving into the slums of Boston in 1937 for $3\frac{1}{2}$ years. He found that gangs, clubs, and political organizations had a dramatic impact on individuals' lives.

In the late 1930s, AA was established by founders who came to realize the potency of individuals meeting together and interacting in a supportive way to produce change. It evolved into an organization that continues to help alcohol abusers gain and maintain control of their lives by remaining sober. Many of the techniques used in AA are similar to those found in other self-help groups—for example, listening, empathizing, supporting, and teaching.

Psychoanalytic **group analysis** also emerged in the 1930s. One of the leaders of this movement was Trigant Burrow, who studied how social forces affect behavior and stressed the biological as well as the interactive principles of group behavior. He described the biological principles as a process called **phyloanalysis**. Other pioneers of psychoanalytic group analysis were Louis Wender and Paul Schilder. Wender's work resulted in interventions for inpatient groups from a psychoanalytic perspective. He was one of the first group workers to describe group therapeutic factors, such as intellectualization, person-to-person transference, and catharsis in the family. Schilder's efforts focused on the interactions among individual group members.

1940 to 1949

The 1940s are often seen as the beginning of modern group work. Two major directions in the formal development of groups took place during this time: (1) the theoretical writings and practices of Kurt Lewin and Wilfred Bion and (2) the establishment of group organizations. The climate in which group work developed during this time reflected the reaction of American and British societies against authoritarian dictatorships and for democracy.

Kurt Lewin is generally recognized as the most influential founder and promoter of group dynamics during this era. A refugee from Nazi Germany, Lewin worked tirelessly to research and refine group dynamics and surrounded himself with energetic and brilliant people. He began writing in the 1930s, but the major impact of his work emerged in the 1940s. Lewin's approach, **field theory**, emphasizes the interaction between individuals and their environments. It is based on the ideas of Gestalt psychology. For Lewin, the group is a whole that is different from and greater than the parts that compose it.

Lewin was instrumental in establishing a workshop on intergroup relations in New Britain, Connecticut, in 1946. The workshop led to the formation of the **National Training Laboratories (NTL)** in Bethel, Maine, and the growth of the **basic skills training (BST)** group, which eventually evolved into the **training group (T-group)** movement. Lewin discovered through his collaborative research that group discussions are superior to individual instruction in changing people's ideas and behaviors. His emphasis on a here-and-now orientation to the environment and his point that changes in a group's behavior depend on an "unfreezing" and "freezing" process of human behavior were major contributions to understanding groups. Lewin first applied the concept of *feedback* to group work.

Wilfred Bion, a member of the **Tavistock Institute of Human Relations** in Great Britain, also stressed the importance of group dynamics. Bion stated that group phenomena may be radically different from those within a family. His focus was on group cohesiveness and forces that foster the progression or regression of the group-as-a-whole. Bion found that he could characterize the emotional pattern of a group as either a **"W" (work) group** or a **"BA" (basic assumption) activity**, which was an antiwork group. BA groups could be broken down further into three subpatterns: *BA Dependency* (where members are overdependent on the group leader), *BA Pairing* (where members are more interested in being with one another than in working on a goal), and *BA Fight–Flight* (where members become preoccupied with either engaging in or avoiding hostile conflict).

During the 1940s, two major group organizations and publications were founded. The first organization was the **American Society of Group Psychotherapy and Psychodrama (ASGPP)**, which Moreno established between 1941 and 1942. The second was the **American Group Psychotherapy Association (AGPA)**, a psychoanalytically oriented organization established by Samuel R. Slavson in 1943. Two pertinent journals started during the 1940s were *Sociatry* in 1947, which was retitled *Group Psychotherapy* in 1949, and the *International Journal of Group Psychotherapy* in 1949. Each journal reflected the philosophy of its founder, Moreno and Slavson, respectively.

1950 to 1959

The 1950s were characterized by a greater refinement in group work and more emphasis on research. For example, in regard to group behavior, Bales noted that, in most groups, stereotyped roles tend to emerge over time. He listed 12 broad categories, from positive reactions (e.g., shows solidarity) to negative reactions (e.g., shows antagonism).

Group procedures also began to be applied to the practice of family counseling. Among the pioneers in this area was Rudolph Dreikurs, who began working with parent groups. Dreikurs employed Adler's theory and ideas in setting up these groups, which were primarily educational in nature. Another clinician, John Bell, also started using groups in his work in family therapy. Beginning as early as 1951, he conducted family therapy sessions like group counseling sessions.

Bell treated families as if they were strangers in a group. He relied on stimulating open discussions to solve family problems and, as in group counseling, he encouraged silent members to speak up and share ideas. Nathan Ackerman, Gregory Bateson, and Virginia Satir were significant professionals during this decade. Their independent but similar focus was on modifying the psychoanalytic model of group therapy for working with families. Ackerman and Satir were more clinically oriented and developed techniques for treating dysfunctions in families. Bateson concentrated more on research, especially group dynamics within families.

The last major development in groups during the 1950s was the implementation of new group concepts. A group "vocabulary" was developed to describe phenomena within group sessions. For example, Richard Blake and Jane Mouton initially used the term *developmental group* during this decade. The first textbook in group work was published in 1958: *Counseling and Learning through Small-Group Discussion* by Helen I. Driver. Terminology for working with groups mushroomed in the 1950s.

As language and terms for groups increased, a shift occurred in the types of groups that were created. Group guidance began to wane in the late 1950s and was replaced by group counseling as a major way to bring about behavioral changes, especially in educational settings. Group psychotherapy increased in popularity as tranquilizing drugs made working with groups in mental health settings viable. The Japanese implemented a new type of group called the **total quality group** under the direction of work group master W. Edwards Deming. This type of group, which focused on problem solving related to consumer satisfaction and quality issues in business, would later influence American industry.

1960 to 1969

Group work, especially group counseling and psychotherapy, was popular in the 1960s. Part of the reason for the flourishing of groups during this time was the result of events occurring in society. The Vietnam War, hippie movement, racial strife, and social activism increased public awareness of the power that groups can have to promote community change.

Some of the most creative leaders in the history of group work came into prominence during this time. Group practice became so popular that the *New York Times* designated 1968 as "the year of the group." Many forms of group work were initiated or refined during the 1960s, including encounter groups, sensory awareness groups, growth groups, marathons, and minithons. It seemed to be a decade in which there was a group for everyone and everyone was in a group. The increased interest in and respect for group counseling and psychotherapy marked the beginning of the reversal of the negative attitude toward the efficacy of group work that was strongly adhered to by most of the psychoanalytic community at the time.

Two of the most popular groups were encounter groups and marathon groups. Carl Rogers coined the term *basic encounter group*, which was later shortened to *encounter group*, to describe his approach to group work, an extension of his theory of individual counseling. Encounter groups are often known as *personal growth groups* because the emphasis in these groups is on personal development. Encounter groups are sometimes also referred to as **sensitivity groups**, a term that focuses on individuals' awareness of their own emotional experiences and the behaviors of others. In encounter groups, emphasis is placed on the exploration of intrapsychic and interpersonal issues, and a feeling of community and connectedness is promoted.

Marathon groups were devised by George Bach and Fred Stoller in 1964 as a way of helping people become more authentic with themselves and switch from the marketing stance of role-playing and image making. Marathon groups are usually held for extended periods, such as

24 hours, and group members are required to stay together. Fatigue is an important factor in these groups, as members become tired and experience a breakdown in their defenses and an increase in their truthfulness, resulting in self-growth. Bach devised creative ways to help people in these groups (and in marriages) resolve interpersonal conflict by learning how to fight fairly.

With the popularity of groups came abuses. Many well-intentioned individuals and some charlatans established groups with no clear ideas about how to run them. As a result, some individuals became casualties of the group movement. They were instructed to do such things as yell at others, physically attack those they disliked, or simply disrobe and lay all their defenses aside. The publicity seekers and entrepreneurs who set up these groups received reams of publicity, most of which was bad. By the end of the 1960s, the group movement was under attack, and the field had been set back considerably. Many individuals made cults out of groups and impaired the functioning of those who participated in their activities.

However, positive and important events occurred during this period as well, especially in the development of group theory and practice. Among the most popular theorist-practitioners of this decade were those who took a humanistic-existential orientation. In addition to Rogers and Bach, four were important:

- Fritz Perls, who conducted numerous workshops at the Esalen Institute in California demonstrating his Gestalt theory through the use of a group setting;
- Eric Berne, who highlighted his therapeutic approach, transactional analysis (TA), in group settings;
- William C. Schutz, who illustrated through group work that individuals can take care of their interpersonal needs for inclusion, control, and affection through groups and stressed the use of nonverbal communication, such as touching or hugging, in groups; and
- Jack Gibb, who studied competitive versus cooperative behavior in groups and discovered, among other things, that competitive behavior in one person fosters competitive behavior, as well as defensiveness, in others.

1970 to 1979

In the 1970s, group work continued to grow, but not without controversy. Jane Howard's book *Please Touch* was an attempt in the early '70s to answer some critics of group work, who basically characterized sensitivity groups as antidemocratic and morally degrading. Howard's description of her movement from one encounter group to another debunked some popular misconceptions of these groups as "hotbeds" for junkies and addicts, but her book raised other issues, such as the importance of group leadership and the screening of group members. The controversy surrounding groups in the 1970s was due to their rapid, almost uncontrolled, growth in the late 1960s and the fact that guidelines for leading and conducting group experiences themselves were not well defined.

Irving Janis created the term *groupthink* to emphasize the detrimental power that groups may exert over their members to conform. He showed that a groupthink mentality can be devastating to the growth of individuals and the problem-solving ability of the group itself.

In partial answer to this need for more professionalism in the conducting of groups, the **Association for Specialists in Group Work (ASGW)** was formed in 1973 by George Gazda and Jack Duncan as a divisional affiliate within the American Personnel and Guidance Association (now the American Counseling Association). The association grew rapidly during the 1970s and was active throughout the decade in promoting responsible group leadership and setting up standards under which group leaders should operate.

Group research also came into prominence during the 1970s, with the percentage of research articles on groups rising to 20% as compared to only 5% in the 1950s. Irvin Yalom and George Gazda conducted particularly important work. Yalom published the first edition of his classic book, *The Theory and Practice of Group Psychotherapy*. In it he analyzed group methods and processes and described 11 curative (therapeutic) factors within groups, the most central and necessary of which are group cohesiveness and interpersonal learning. In addition, Yalom and Lieberman found that leadership style in groups influences how individuals fare in such settings. Aggressive, authoritarian, and confrontational leaders and those who are most distant and cool produce the most group casualties. Gazda was largely responsible for collecting primary accounts of how different group workers, especially psychotherapists and counselors, conceptualized and practiced their approaches. He helped link group leaders together.

1980 to 1989

In the 1980s, the popularity of group work for the masses increased, as did the continued professionalism of the group movement itself. The AGPA was one of the associations that continued to refine group theory and practice. For instance, the AGPA published a collection of articles edited by James Durkin that examined how **general systems theory**, which emphasizes circular causality as opposed to linear causality, could be used in groups.

In addition to the expansion of theory, the number of different types of groups grew. Self-help groups, in particular, mushroomed. It was estimated in 1988 that between 2,000 and 3,000 self-help groups operated in the United States. These mutually supportive groups usually did not include professional leaders but were led by paraprofessionals or group members. Examples of such groups then and now are Alcoholics Anonymous, Narcotics Anonymous, Weight Watchers, and Compassionate Friends. Educational groups also received increased attention during this decade. Noted leaders in the group work area, such as George Gazda, proposed the use of **developmental group counseling** with multiple populations for teaching basic life skills.

A code of ethics for group workers was published by the ASGW in 1980 and revised in 1989. (Ethical standards for working with groups have now been incorporated into the American Counseling Association *Code of Ethics*.) Standards for training group leaders were proposed by the ASGW during the decade and adopted in 1991. By the end of 1989, the ASGW had attracted more than 5,000 members. The AGPA and other group organizations also grew.

By the end of the 1980s, group work was recognized as a viable means of helping individuals in a variety of settings. More types of groups were available, with a new emphasis on self-help, social skills, development, and ethics. More care was being focused on evaluating the effects of group experiences, and the number of research articles on group work was increasing.

1990 to 1999

In the 1990s, group work continued to flourish. In 1991, the Group Psychology and Group Psychotherapy (GPGP) division of the American Psychological Association was established. It began publishing its own journal, *Group Dynamics*, in 1997.

More mature group organizations continued to prosper, too. For example, the AGPA celebrated its 50th anniversary in 1992 and set up a certification for group psychotherapists, the Clinical Registry of Certified Group Psychotherapists, in 1994. A number of new books and a plethora of scholarly articles were published in the decade as well. Group work was increasingly used in school settings, especially as a way of influencing educational endeavors and social skills. However, group work also focused on groups for special populations, such as those in the midst of divorce, adult offenders, people from different cultures, and people with disabilities. A particularly innovative specialized type of group for the treatment of Borderline Personality Disorders, *dialectic behavior therapy*, was developed in the early 1990s by Marsha Linehan and her research team. The approach, based on cognitive-behavioral therapy, uses a psychosocial method that teaches coping skills to group members during a weekly 2.5-hour session. Such skills as interpersonal effectiveness, distress tolerance, reality acceptance skills, emotion regulation, and mindfulness are taught. The clinical effectiveness of DBT has empirical support.

The number of individuals interested in working with groups increased in the 1990s for almost all group associations. More emphasis was placed on specialty groups, for example, groups focusing on depression, bulimia, or sexual abuse. In 1991, the ASGW approved and published professional standards for the training of group workers in four main areas: psychoeducational, task/work, counseling, and psychotherapy groups. A distinction in these standards was made between core group competencies and group work specialties, with specialists already having mastered core skills. Furthermore, research from a variety of sources on different types of groups supported their effectiveness and cost efficiency. In addition to these activities, professional associations offered more training and educational opportunities in groups. For example, the ASGW and the AGPA held annual national conferences on group work and sponsored continuing education courses.

Furthermore, the 1990s were filled with a wide variety of self-help groups and support groups. Parenting groups became more popular, and the number of **cooperative learning groups** increased. In addition, **focus groups**, composed of representative samples of individuals concerned with issues, products, or outcomes, came into wider use and provided important information for businesses, politicians, and policy makers. Probably the greatest growth in the use of groups, at least in North America in the 1990s, was in work settings. In these environments, the use of task/work groups grew dramatically as organizational hierarchies began flattening out and workers became more collaborative in achieving goals.

2000 TO THE PRESENT: GROUP WORK NOW

In the early years of the twenty-first century, groups continued to be popular in multiple settings. Generally, groups work for an ever-increasing number of client concerns. Counselors, coaches, teachers, politicians, and corporate researchers have made groups more a part of their personal and professional lives than ever before. Books on the therapeutic aspects of groups, such as Paul Solotaroff's *Group*, sell well. Small groups are now well accepted as a method of providing support, as well as promoting change, effective decision making, problem solving, team building, and social skill building.

Other trends affecting group work outside of what has already been mentioned are: (1) social justice, (2) training and education, (3) technology, (4) research, (5) the development of brief solution-focused ways of delivering group services, and (6) standards. Each is discussed here.

Social Justice

Kiselica and Robinson define social justice as using all the methods of counseling and psychology to confront injustice and inequality in society. The concept has been further refined into a description that is both a process and a goal. Although there is still much discussion and debate over social justice and group work, it is clear that the concept and practices that go with it will continue. Topics both now and for the future surrounding social justice and group work will include consciousness raising, group empowerment, community organizing, definition of social justice, attribution theory, and sociopolitical identity development.

Training and Education

The training and educating of group leaders has become more sophisticated recently as the dynamics within groups have become better understood. For instance, instructors can intentionally model effective group leader behaviors and use these behaviors and the students' responses to them as powerful ways to augment the didactic material being taught about group dynamics and theory. Instructors can use different techniques during the initial, middle, and final stages of a group, such as providing a high degree of structure in early group meetings to increase cohesion and reduce anxiety.

In addition to modeling, group training now focuses on presenting skills in steps. No longer are novice group leaders told that they must observe the dynamics in a group and help group members understand what is going on within themselves and their interpersonal relationships.

Likewise, in introducing graduate students to the dynamics within a group, the simulated group counseling model has been developed. For this model to be effective, students role-play different group members in an ongoing group experience lasting 8 weeks. The advantages of this model are that students are provided with a safe and realistic experience for learning how groups develop. Furthermore, dual-relationship ethical concerns are reduced because professors are not dealing with actual self-disclosures from students in personal growth groups. Thus, professors do not find themselves in the ethical bind of being an evaluator of students academically while also gaining intimate personal knowledge about those students.

A related simulation model for group work training is known as process-play. In this procedure, students participate in a here-and-now focused, process-oriented training group, but their interactions are guided by superficial characteristics specified as the mask (e.g., responding differently to persons who are tall or who are wearing green) rather than interpersonal dynamics. The masks stimulate group conflict resolutions in and of themselves without relying on member self-disclosures or traditional role playing. Thus, student privacy is protected.

Technology

The use of technology worldwide ranges from a minimal encounter constituting information exchange or referral to resources, to more interactive exchanges constituting the dissemination of information, provision of support, and offerings of electronic counseling. Computers, cell phones, computer simulation, and other forms of technology have altered the ways people interact individually and in groups. Whereas electronic course tools, such as the "bulletin board" of WEB-CT, have been used to deliver group theory in rural areas, technology has been used in a number of other ways also, such as teaching social skills to children in a multiuser virtual environment (MUVE). As technology becomes more advanced, easier to use, and more affordable, opportunities for enhancing traditional group activities with technological approaches continue to grow. This technology has taken numerous forms, including the use of chat rooms, computer conferencing, electronic mailing lists, virtual environments, and newsgroups.

Collectively, the computer support for a group activity is referred to as **groupware**. For instance, groupware is used to set up chat rooms at various Web sites, allowing people who are physically separated to have in-depth discussions on subjects of common interest. Likewise, computers provide a means for class discussion outside of regular meetings. In one case a psychotherapeutic group intervention was delivered for 4 years via the Internet to three groups of spousal caregivers of persons with dementia. Additional uses of groupware include electronic mail systems, keypad voting systems, and computer support for group decision making. Group use of computers holds promise for the future, especially for learning and helping group members stay in contact with one another and exchange information. Computer-mediated support groups are a growing phenomenon.

Research

Research shows that group work is an effective method for providing services to others. It has proven efficacious across a variety of settings and populations. Meta-analyses have been published that make it possible to more clearly compare outcomes of different group formats and individual versus group treatments. Yet, group research is in its infancy compared with research in other social sciences. There is still much that is not understood about the intricacies of complex interactive variables found in groups. Research into psychoeducational groups, as well as prevention groups, is relatively minuscule. In other words, research is yet to be conducted on which variables in which combinations lead to effectiveness in various types of groups.

In order for this situation to be rectified, researchers are devising more sophisticated techniques to measure change. Clinicians and researchers are being encouraged to interact more. Overall, increased concern and attention are being devoted to group research, including an exploration of group forms that have fallen out of favor, such as marathon groups.

In addition to research in these areas, professional group associations are giving awards and grants for group research and recognizing major researchers in special ways. For instance, the entire September 2005 edition of the *Journal for Specialists in Group Work* was devoted to the contributions of Rex Stockton, especially his writing and research on group counseling over a 30-year period. Finally, qualitative, as well as quantitative, methods of conducting research on groups are emerging. This more phenomenological approach holds promise for exploring dynamics within groups. Specifically focusing on the evaluation process in groups is also being emphasized.

Brief Group Work

Brief group work began as an alternative to long-term group therapy. Today it is especially valued as a response to managed care and other health management programs that have imposed the expectation of quick results on the health care and mental health communities and limit the number of sessions they reimburse for treatment. In addition, brief group therapy has been found to be efficient, cost-efficient, and the treatment of choice for certain types of problems (e.g., adjustment, trauma reaction).

Solution-focus theory and therapy was one of the first forms of brief group work practiced. The importance of brief treatment in group work cannot be overstressed, as it appears to meet the requirements of managed care companies and of many clients, the vast majority of whom come for eight or fewer sessions regardless of the services offered.

Standards

In addition, there is an emphasis on the refinement of standards needed to conduct groups. For instance in 2008, the AGPA produced a document entitled *Clinical Practice Guidelines for Group Psychotherapy* for members of its association who practice dynamic, interactional, and relationally based group psychotherapy. Likewise the ASGW updated its 1999 document *Principles for*

Diversity-Competent Group Workers into a more comprehensive and relevant document, *Multicultural and Social Justice Competence Principles for Group Workers*.

THE FUTURE OF GROUP WORK

Group work has come a long way in its short formal history. Undoubtedly, it will be robust and permeate almost all segments of society on a global level in the future. However, predicting where group work will go in the future is difficult. Nevertheless, trying to map the direction of group work is important to the health and well-being of the profession. The more accurately professionals can anticipate where groups are going, the better they can train themselves and others to meet needs. After all, counselors of the twenty-first century will be expected to provide a variety of group work applications.

One direction group work appears to be going is becoming more concrete and structured in regard to treatments for precise diagnoses. There is an increased emphasis on group systems theory as well and how it can provide a variety of directions for innovations in group research and practice. Furthermore, a greater variety of groups are being created, including approaches that are more educational and growth inducing than ameliorative or adjustment focused. In relation to the greater breadth of groups offered, participants are now conceived as collaborators in treatment rather than as passive receivers. In addition, groups are being offered for a wide variety of populations, such as male inmates, people with multiple sclerosis, victims of intimate partner violence, survivors of childhood sexual abuse, people with depression, homeless adults, substance abusers, and those in grief.

Linked to the area of specialization is the challenge for group workers to use the power of the group more fully in the future. Groups that are able to harness the resources within themselves and work for the betterment of those within them and in the larger world are more constructive and effective in promoting change and fostering support.

History of Group Work Chart

Prior to 1900—Jane Addams, Hull House in Chicago, beginning of social group work (forerunner of social justice) to help new immigrants and the poor; large groups used for instruction

1905—Joseph Hersey Pratt organizes the first formal psychotherapy group at Massachusetts General Hospital in Boston for tuberculosis patients

1907—Jesse B. Davis, principal of Grand Rapids High School in Michigan, directs that one English class per week will be devoted to "Vocational and Moral Guidance," start of psychoeducational groups/group guidance in the schools

1914—Jacob L. Moreno published a significant, philosophical paper on group methods in 1914, written under the name of J. M. Levy

1916/1918—U.S. Army administers psychological group tests, such as the Army Alpha and Beta intelligence tests

1921—Jacob L. Moreno forms Theater of Spontaneity (Stegreiftheatre), a first step in his creation of psychodrama

1922—Alfred Adler initiates a new and systematic form of group guidance and counseling with prisoners and children, known as collective counseling, forerunner of group counseling

1928—Trigant Burrow focuses on the interpersonal relationships of individuals

1931/1932—Jacob L. Moreno introduces the terms *group therapy* and *group psychotherapy* into the vocabulary of helping professionals; refines psychodrama

1935—founding of Alcoholics Anonymous, one of the first large-scale national support groups

1935—Trigant Burrow studies how social forces affect behavior and stresses the biological as well as the interactive principles of group behavior, a process he calls *phyloanalysis*

1936—Louis Wender describes group therapeutic factors such as intellectualization and transference

1939—Paul Schilder focuses on the interactions among individual group members

1934/1939—Muzafer Sherif, Theodore Newcomb, and W. F. Whyte study groups in their natural settings. Sherif studies the influence of groups on the establishment of social norms; Newcomb studies peer groups; Whyte studies gangs and political organizations

1940—Kurt Levin founder and promoter of group dynamics, emphasizes the interaction between individuals and their environments, based on ideas of Gestalt psychology; approach is known as *field theory*

1942—American Society of Group Psychotherapy and Psychodrama (ASGPP) founded by Jacob Moreno

1943—American Group Psychotherapy Association (AGPA), a psychoanalytically oriented organization, established by Samuel R. Slavson

1946—Kurt Levin instrumental in formation of National Training Laboratories in Bethel, Maine, and growth of basic skills training groups, which evolves into the training group (T-group) movement

1947—Jacob Moreno creates the journal *Sociatry*, which changes its name to *Group Psychotherapy* in 1949

1948—Wilfred Bion stresses the importance of group dynamics as a member of the Tavistock Institute of Human Relations. Bion characterizes emotional pattern of a group as either a W (work group) or a BA (basic assumption) activity

1949—Samuel Slavson establishes the *International Journal of Group Psychotherapy*

1950—Rudolph Dreikurs applies Adlerian theory and group procedures to the practice of family councils

1951—John Bell conducts family therapy sessions like group counseling sessions. Nathan Ackerman, Gregory Bateson, and Virginia Satir later in the decade will modify the psychoanalytic model of group therapy for working with families

1955—Richard Blake and Jane Mouton coin the term *developmental group*

1958—Helen I. Driver publishes the first textbook on group work: *Counseling and Learning Through Small-group Discussion*

1959—W. Edward Deming and the total quality group emerge into prominence

1960—Group counseling and psychotherapy become more popular as the Vietnam War, racial strife and social activism increase public awareness of the power that groups have to promote community change

1961—Jack Gibbs studies competitive versus cooperative behavior in groups; finds competitive behavior in one person fosters competitive behavior, as well as defensiveness, in others

1964—Marathon groups are devised by George Bach and Fred Stoller

1964—Eric Berne highlights his therapeutic approach, transactional analysis in group settings, publishes *Principles of Group Treatment* in 1966

1965—Carl Rogers instrumental in the forming of basic encounter group, an extension of his theory of individual counseling; encounter groups, as they are later called, become known also as personal growth groups and sensitivity groups

1967—Fritz Perls conducts numerous Gestalt therapy groups at the Esalen Institute in California

1967—William C. Shutz illustrates through group work how individuals can take care of their interpersonal needs for inclusion, control, and affection through groups

1968—*New York Times* designates 1968 as "the year of the group"

1970—Jane Howard publishes *Please Touch*, an attempt to answer the critics of group work who characterize sensitivity groups as antidemocratic and morally degrading; she highlights the importance of professional leadership and member selection

1970—*Carl Rogers on Encounter Groups* is published

1971—Irving Janis creates term *groupthink* to emphasize detrimental power that groups may exert over their members to conform

1971—Yalom and Lieberman find that leadership styles in group influence how individuals fare in such settings; aggressive, confrontive, distant leaders produce the most group casualties

1970— Irvin Yalom publishes first edition of his classic book *The Theory and Practice of Group Psychotherapy*, describes the 11 curative (therapeutic) factors within groups

1973—The Association for Specialists in Group Work is founded by George Gazda and Jack Duncan as a division of the American Personnel and Guidance Association (i.e., American Counseling Association)

1980—A code of ethics for group workers is published by ASGW in 1980; it is revised in 1989

1981—James Durkin examines how circular causality, as opposed to linear causality, can be used in groups

1988—Self-help groups in the United States mushroom to between 2,000 and 3,000

1989—George Gazda proposes the use of developmental group counseling for teaching basic life skills

1990s—Parenting groups, cooperative learning groups, and focus groups become popular

1991—ASGW adopts standards for training group leaders in four main areas: psychoeducational, task/work, counseling, and psychotherapy

1991—Group Psychology and Group Psychotherapy is established as a division of the American Psychological Association

1992—ASGW holds its first national conference in St. Petersburg, Florida

1992—AGPA celebrates its 50th anniversary

1993—Marsha Linehan and her research team develop dialectic behavior therapy

1994—AGPA sets up a certification for group psychotherapists, the Clinical Registry of Certified Group Psychotherapists

1997—*Group Dynamics*, the journal of Group Psychology and Group Psychotherapy, begins publication

1998—*Principles for Diversity-Competent Group Workers* developed by ASGW

1999—Paul Solotaroff's *Groups* is published, on the therapeutic aspects of groups

2000s—Group work in the 2000s has focused on the following:

1. Social justice—confronting injustices and inequality in society through groups
2. Training and education—more emphasis on modeling effective group leader behavior by instructors, presenting skills in steps, using simulated group counseling models such as process-play
3. Technology—use of computers, cell phones, computer simulation, electronic course tools, groupware, computer support for group activities, online groups
4. Research—meta-analysis of studies comparing different group formats and individual versus group treatment; renewed exploration of groups such as marathons; recognition of group researchers, such as Rex Stockton, by the *Journal for Specialists in Group Work* (2005) for his writing and research on group counseling
5. Brief ways of delivering group services—brief group work, such as that based on solution-focused therapy has become more popular as an alternative to long-term group therapy; it is cost effective and meets the requirements of managed care companies
6. standards—AGPA document, *Clinical Practice Guidelines for Group Psychotherapy (2008)*, for members of its association who practice dynamic, interactional, and relationally based group psychotherapy; ASGW document *Multicultural and Social Justice Competence Principles for Group Workers* (2012)

2015 and beyond—More concrete and structured groups are being developed for treating precise diagnoses and for a wider variety of populations; more educational and growth groups are being created

Challenge for group workers is to use the power of group more fully in the future

Some Prominent Self-Help Group Organizations

Adult Children of Alcoholics (ACoA): Offers group-based support and information for adults who grew up in homes with alcoholic or otherwise dysfunctional parents. Groups are based on the 12-step program.

Address: PO Box 3216; Torrance, CA 90510
Phone: 310-534-1815
Web site: adultchildren.org

The AGS Foundation for Health in Aging (FHA): Created to bridge the gap between research and aging adults and caregivers. Education, advocacy, providing referral support for the aging are the primary activities of FHA.

Address: 350 Fifth Ave., Suite 801; New York, NY 10118
Phone: 212-755-6810   Fax: 212-832-8646
Web site: healthinaging.org

AIDS.ORG: Dedicated to the prevention of the HIV virus and the improvement of life for those affected by HIV and AIDS. The Web site serves as the forum for disseminating information and facilitating discussion to inform the public, professionals, and people with HIV/AIDS.

Address: 7985 Santa Monica Blvd. #99; West Hollywood, CA 90046
Phone: 323-656-6036
Web site: aids.org

Al-Anon/Alateen: A voluntary mutual-help group based on the 12-step model for relatives and children of alcohol abusers. Members meet regularly to offer support and discuss common problems.

Address: 1600 Corporate Landing Pkwy.; Virginia Beach, VA 23454
Phone: 757-563-1600   Fax: 757-563-1655
Web site: al-anon.alateen.org

Alcoholics Anonymous (AA): An organization that helps alcohol abusers gain and maintain control of their lives by attaining and maintaining sobriety, through total abstinence. The 12-step model of recovery was first developed for AA.

Address: PO Box 459; New York, NY 10163
Phone: 212-870-3400
Web site: aa.org

ALS Association: An organization promoting research, education, and public policy to support people with ALS (Lou Gehrig's disease) and their families. Local chapters also provide support group meetings and clinics to coordinate medical care for ALS patients.

Address: 27001 Agoura Rd., Suite 250; Calabasas Hills, CA 91301-5104
Phone: 818-880-9007   Fax: 818-880-9006
Web site: alsa.org

Alzheimer's Association: A national organization with the mission of providing better care for Alzheimer's patients, supporting the advancement of research, and promoting brain health.

Address: 225 N. Michigan Ave., Floor 17; Chicago, IL 60601
Phone: 312-335-8700   Fax: 866-699-1246
Web site: alz.org

American Foundation for Suicide Prevention (AFSP): The leading national organization dedicated to the prevention of suicide. AFSP focus its efforts on research, providing information to the public, and advocacy for social and policy change.

Address: 120 Wall St., 22nd Floor; New York, NY 10005
Phone: 212-363-3500   Fax: 212-363-6237
Web site: afsp.org

Anxiety and Depression Association of America (ADAA): An organization dedicated to furthering prevention and treatment of anxiety disorders and depresssion, as well as helping better the lives of persons with such disorders.

Address: 8730 Georgia Ave., Suite 600; Silver Springs, MD 20910
Phone: 240-485-1001   Fax: 240-485-1035
Web site: adaa.org

Autism Society: Connects parents of children with autism and professionals to improve the quality of life and to provide a representative voice for those with autism.

Address: 7910 Woodmont Ave., Suite 300; Bethesda, MD 20814-3067
Phone: 301-657-0881   Fax: 301-657-0869
Web site: autism-society.org

Caregiver Action Network (CAN): A support organization for family caregivers, providing education and empowerment to work for their own well-being and that of their loved ones.

Address: 10400 Connecticut Ave., Suite 500; Kensington, MD 20895-3944
Phone: 800-896-3650   Fax: 301-942-2302
Web site: caregiveraction.org

Celebrate Recovery: A Bible-based recovery group for individuals seeking freedom from addictions, hurts, and habits, based on eight principles.

Address: 1 Saddleback Parkway; Lake Forest, CA 92630
Phone: 949-609-8000
Web site: celebraterecovery.com

CFIDS and Fibromyalgia Self-Help: Dedicated to providing education and group support for persons dealing with Fibromyalgia and Chronic Fatigue Syndrome. The organization provides online self-help courses and facilitates support group meetings.

Web site: cfidsselfhelp.org

Children and Adults with Attention-Deficit/Hyperactivity Disorder (CHADD): The leading national organization helping those affected by AD/HD, through activities such as education, research, public awareness, and working with government agencies.

Address: 8181 Professional Pl., Suite 150; Landover, MD 20785
Phone: 301-306-7070   Fax: 301-306-7090
Web site: chadd.org

Clutterers Anonymous (CLA): A self-help organization based on the 12-Step model for persons suffering from clutter in their lives and personal space.

Address: PO Box 91413; Los Angeles, CA 90009-1413
Phone: 310-281-6064
Web site: http://sites.google.com/site/clutterersanonymous/Home

Co-Anon: Family groups for family members and friends of persons addicted to cocaine, who meet to discuss common problems.

Address: PO Box 12722; Tucson, AZ 85732-2722
Phone: 520-513-5028, 800-898-9985
Web site: co-anon.org

Co-Dependents Anonymous (CoDA): Promotes the development of healthy relationships for persons, using the 12-step model.

Address: PO Box 33577; Phoenix, AZ 85067-3577
Phone: 602-277-7991
Web site: coda.org

Co-Sex and Love Addicts Anonymous (CO-SLAA): A 12-step support group for family members and friends who are seeking healthy relationships and boundaries with loved ones affected by a sexual addiction.

Phone: 860-456-0032
Web site: coslaa.org

Cocaine Anonymous (CA): A fellowship of individuals seeking recovery and sobriety from addiction to cocaine and other drugs.

Address: 3740 Overland Avenue, Suite C; Los Angeles, CA 90034
Phone: 310-559-5833   Fax: 310-559-2554
Web site: ca.org

COSA: Self-help groups for those whose lives have been affected by sexual addiction or sexually compulsive behavior.

Address: PO Box 14537; Minneapolis, MN 55414
Phone: 763-537-6904
Web site: cosa-recovery.org

Crystal Meth Anonymous (CMA): A fellowship of people recovering from addiction to methamphetamines. The organization operates as independent 12-step meetings, which promote shared understanding, encouragement, and support among members.

Address: 4470 West Sunset Blvd.; Los Angeles, CA 90027-6302
Phone: 877-262-6691
Web site: crystalmeth.org

Debtors Anonymous: A self-help group designed to help men and women recover from incurring compulsive, unsecured debt.

Address: PO Box 920888; Needham, MA 02492-0009
Phone: 800-421-2383   Fax: 781-453-2745
Web site: debtorsanonymous.org

Depression and Bipolar Support Alliance (DBSA): Formerly known as the National Depressive and Manic Depressive Association, this organization seeks to educate and provide peer support for people with mood disorders, including depression, bipolar disorder, and anxiety disorders.

Address: 730 N. Franklin St., Suite 501; Chicago, IL 60654-7225
Phone: 800-826-3632   Fax: 312-642-7243
Web site: dbsalliance.org

Emotions Anonymous: A supportive fellowship of people working together to recover from emotional difficulties. The issues faced by members may include depression, anger, fears, loneliness, grief, anxiety, and low self-esteem.

Address: PO Box 4245; St. Paul, MN 55104-0245
Phone: 651-647-9712   Fax: 651-647-1593
Web site: emotionsanonymous.org

Epilepsy Foundation: An organization dedicated to the welfare of those with epilepsy, working to ensure their ability to participate fully in life experiences and to prevent and treat seizures.

Address: 8301 Professional Place; Landover, MD 20785
Phone: 800-332-1000   Fax: 301-577-4941
Web site: epilepsyfoundation.org

Families Anonymous: A support group made up of people who have been affected by the substance addiction of family members and friends and who share common concerns about how best to help them and help themselves in the process of offering assistance.

Address: PO Box 3475; Culver, CA 90231-3475
Phone: 800-736-9805   Fax: 310-815-9682
Web site: familiesanonymous.org

Gam-Anon: A support group based on the 12-step model for friends and family members who are affected by the gambling addiction of a loved one.

Address: PO Box 157; Whitestone, NY 11357
Phone: 718-352-1671   Fax: 718-746-2571
Web site: gam-anon.org

Gamblers Anonymous (GA): A mutual help group, based on the 12-step model, composed primarily of compulsive gamblers who have a desire to get help for their gambling problem.

Address: PO Box 17173; Los Angeles, CA 90017
Phone: 213-386-8789
Web site: gamblersanonymous.org/ga

International OCD Foundation (IOCDF): An international organization that supports people with Obsessive Compulsive Disorder and their family and friends, in addition to supporting research and education about OCD and related disorders.

Address: PO Box 209006 Yale Station; New Haven, CT 06520
Phone: 203-432-2400   Fax: 203-432-7425
Web site: iocdf.org

Marijuana Anonymous (MA): A self-help group based on the 12-step model designed to help individuals recover together from a marijuana addiction and to bring help to those still struggling with this addiction.

Address: PO Box 2912; Van Nuys, CA 91404
Phone: 800-766-6779
Web site: marijuana-anonymous.org

Mental Health America (MHA): An organization devoted to educating the public about the realities of life with mental illness and to advocate for those with mental health disorders. Founded over 100 years ago by Clifford Beers, MHA was formerly known as the National Mental Health Association.

Address: 2000 N. Beauregard St., Floor 6; Alexandria, VA 22311
Phone: 703-684-7722   Fax: 703-684-5968
Web site: mentalhealthamerica.net

Nar-Anon Family Groups: A support group organization that seeks to help people who are affected by an addiction of a family member or close friend. Nar-Anon also has an Internet-based support forum, which can be accessed via the organization's Web site.

Address: 22527 Crenshaw Blvd., Suite 200B; Torrance, CA 90505
Phone: 310-534-8188   Fax: 310-534-8688
Web site: nar-anon.org

Narcotics Anonymous (NA): An international, community-based fellowship of men and women seeking recovery and sobriety from drug addiction. The NA program is based on the 12-step model of AA.

Address: PO Box 9999; Van Nuys, CA 91409
Phone: 818-773-9999   Fax: 818-700-0700
Web site: na.org

National Alliance on Mental Illness (NAMI): An organization working toward eradicating mental illness, with focused efforts on advocacy, education, research, and support for people with mental illness.

Address: Colonial Place Three; 2107 Wilson Blvd., Suite 300; Arlington, VA 22201-3042
Phone: 703-524-7600   Fax: 703-524-9094
Web site: nami.org

National Association of Anorexia Nervosa and Associated Disorders (ANAD): This organization works to relieve problems associated with eating disorders, raise public awareness, and provide support for those who suffer. Support services include support groups, a telephone hotline, and an e-mail referral service linking individuals with mental and medical professionals.

Address: PO Box 7; Highland Park, IL 60035
Phone: 847-831-3438   Fax: 847-433-4632
Web site: anad.org

National Anxiety Foundation (NAF): An organization focused on educating and providing medical information on anxiety disorders and treatment for individuals suffering from these disorders.

Address: 3135 Custer Dr., Lexington, KY 40517-4001
Web site: lexington-on-line.com/naf.html

National Eating Disorder Association (NEDA): An organization providing eating disorder information, resources, and support to those struggling with an eating disorder and to their close friends and family members. NEDA also maintains an information and referral phone service, Helpline (800-931-2237).

Address: 603 Stewart St., Suite 803; Seattle, WA 98101
Phone: 206-382-3587   Fax: 206-829-8501
Web site: nationaleatingdisorders.org

National Federation of Families for Children's Mental Health: Provides support services, resources, and leadership for families with children with emotional, behavioral, and mental health challenges.

Address: 9605 Medical Center Drive, Suite 280; Rockville, MD 20850
Phone: 240-403-1901   Fax: 240-403-1909
Web site: ffcmh.org

National Hospice and Palliative Care Organization (NHPCO): A national organization of hospice providers and volunteers dedicated to improving end-of-life care.

Address: 1700 Diagonal Rd., Suite 625; Alexandria, VA 22314
Phone: 703-837-1500   Fax: 703-837-1233
Web site: nhpco.org

National Mental Health Consumers' Self-Help Clearinghouse: An association providing consumers updated information and access to mental health issues and service providers.

Address: 1211 Chestnut St., Suite 1207; Philadelphia, PA 19107
Phone: 800-553-4539
Web site: mhselfhelp.org

National Parkinson Foundation, Inc. (NPF): The NPF works to support persons with Parkinson disease and caregivers and to promote research and education for the treatment and cure of the disease. The organization also seeks to meet needs through regional community-based support centers.

Address: 1501 NW 9th Ave./Bob Hope Rd.; Miami, FL 33136-1494
Phone: 800-327-4545   Fax: 305-243-5595
Web site: parkinson.org

Nicotine Anonymous (NicA): A support group based on the 12-step model designed to help all who desire to stop using nicotine. Nicotine Anonymous supports many approaches to stop using tobacco, including cessation programs and withdrawal aids.

Address: 419 Main St., PMB #370; Huntington Beach, CA 92648
Phone: 415-750-0328; 877-879-6422
Web site: nicotine-anonymous.org

North American Council on Adoptable Children (NACAC): Promotes permanent family placements for children, especially those in foster care. NACAC focuses its efforts on advocacy, parent leadership building, education, and support for adoptions.

Address: 970 Raymond Ave., Suite 106; St. Paul, MN 55114
Phone: 651-644-3036   Fax: 651-644-9848
Web site: nacac.org

Overcomers in Christ: A Christian support group for those struggling with addiction, including substance abuse and sexual addiction.

Address: PO Box 3446; Omaha, NE 68134
Phone: 402-573-0966   Fax: 402-573-0960
Web site: overcomersinchrist.org

Online Gamers Anonymous (OLGA): A self-help recovery group, based on the 12-step program, that helps individuals experiencing negative consequences from excessive online and video game playing. OLGA also offers help and support for friends and family members of gamers. Meetings and forums take place in face-to-face settings, as well as by Internet chatrooms and message boards.

Address: 104 Miller Ln.; Harrisburg, PA 17110
Phone: 612-245-1115
Web site: olganon.org

Overeaters Anonymous (OA): A self-help group offering a 12-step recovery program for people seeking freedom and health from a problem with overeating. OA focuses on physical and emotional wellness, not dieting or weight loss.

Address: PO Box 44020; Rio Rancho, NM 87174-4020
Phone: 505-891-2664   Fax: 505-891-4320
Web site: oa.org

Parents and Friends of Lesbians and Gays (PFLAG): A coalition of family and friends of gay, lesbian, bisexual, and transgendered persons that works to promote diversity and equality for people of all sexual orientations. Primary efforts include advocacy, providing community and support resources, and educating the society.

Address: 1726 M Street NW; Suite 400; Washington, DC 20036
Phone: 202-467-8180   Fax: 202-467-8194
Web site: community.pflag.org

Parents Anonymous: A child abuse prevention agency that works to strengthen families by providing support and training for parents. The organization also partners with community agencies to promote safe, nurturing home environments.

Address: 675 W. Foothill Blvd., Suite 220; Claremont, CA 91711-3475
Phone: 909-621-6184   Fax: 909-625-6304
Web site: parentsanonymous.org

Rape, Abuse & Incest National Network (RAINN): This leading organization works to help prevent sexual assault, provide assistance to victims, and to achieve justice for perpetrators. The organization also runs the National Sexual Assault Hotline (800-656-HOPE).

Address: 2000 L Street NW, Suite 406; Washington, DC 20036
Phone: 800-656-HOPE   Fax: 202-544-3556
Web site: rainn.org

Rational Recovery: A recovery program providing instruction and materials for individuals to achieve permanent abstinence from any type of addiction. The program is an individual-focused program, and individuals work on their own toward their recovery.

Address: PO Box 800; Lotus, CA 95651
Phone: 530-621-2667   Fax: 530-621-4374
Web site: rational.org

Recoveries Anonymous (RA): A 12-step solution focused recovery group for persons with any problem or behavior, as well as family and friends of those seeking recovery.

Address: PO Box 1212; East Northport, NY 11731
Web site: r-a.org

Recovery International (Recovery, Inc.): A self-help organization, based on cognitive behavioral techniques, that offers peer-led support groups and a recovery method for those seeking healing from mental and behavioral disorders.

Address: 802 N. Dearborn St.; Chicago, IL 60610
Phone: 312-337-5661   Fax: 312-337-5756
Web site: recovery-inc.org

S-Anon: Family support groups for individuals affected by another person's sexual addiction, based on the 12-step recovery model.

Address: PO Box 111242; Nashville, TN 37222-1242
Phone: 800-210-8141, 615-833-3152
Web site: sanon.org

Save Our Selves/Secular Organizations for Sobriety (SOS): A network of support groups that help individuals work toward sobriety from an addiction. SOS is an alternative to spiritually based and 12-step recovery approaches, respecting unique individual approaches to recovery.

Address: 4773 Hollywood Blvd.; Hollywood, CA 90027
Phone: 323-666-4295   Fax: 323-666-4271
Web site: sossobriety.org

Schizophrenia and Related Disorders Alliance of America (SARDAA): A national organization supporting and offering hope to persons with schizophrenia and related disorders and their families. SARDAA supports Schizophrenics Anonymous, operates a telephone hotline, and provides education to this population and the general public.

Address: PO Box 941222; Houston, TX 77094-8222
Phone: 240-423-9432
Web site: sardaa.org

Sex Addicts Anonymous (SAA): A 12-step organization helping men and women overcome sexual addiction.

Address: PO Box 7094; Houston, TX 77270
Phone: 800-477-8191
Web site: saa-recovery.org

Sex and Love Addicts Anonymous (SLAA): A 12-step fellowship for individuals with seeking recovery from sexual and love addiction, which can include compulsive sexual activity, overdependence on others, or obsession with romance, fantasy, or relationships.

Address: 1550 NE Loop 410, Suite 118; San Antonio, TX 78209
Phone: 210-828-7900   Fax: 210-828-7922
Web site: slaafws.org

Sexaholics Anonymous (SA): Mutual help group for those who want to cease self-destructive sexual thoughts and behavior.

Address: PO Box 3565; Brentwood, TN 37024-2565
Phone: 615-370-6062   Fax: 615-370-0882
Web site: sa.org

Sexual Compulsives Anonymous (SCA): An organization of 12-step recovery groups dedicated to helping people who desire recovery from sexually compulsive behaviors.

Address: PO Box 1585, Old Chelsea Station; New York, NY 10011
Phone: 800-977-HEAL (4325)
Web site: sca-recovery.org

SMART Recovery: A self-management and recovery training program that provides recovery materials to help individuals gain freedom from addictions. SMART facilitates group meetings and online forums for the recovery process.

Address: 7304 Mentor Ave., Suite F; Mentor, OH 44060
Phone: 866-951-5357   Fax: 440-951-5358
Web site: smartrecovery.org

Solve ME/CFS Initiative: A research and education-based organization, whose mission is to promote understanding and prevention of myalgic encephalomyelitis, Chronic Fatigue Syndrome, and related disorders.

Address: PO Box 220398; Charlotte, NC 28222-0398
Phone: 714-365-2343
Web site: solvecfs.org

Suicide Prevention Advocacy Network (SPAN): Now part of the American Foundation for Suicide Prevention, SPAN is a community-based organization that works to prevent suicide by promoting public policy initiatives and education. The organization is composed primarily of persons who have survived suicide attempts or are affected by the suicide of a loved one.

Address: 1010 Vermont Ave., NW, Suite 408; Washington, DC 20005
Phone: 202-449-3600   Fax: 202-449-3601
Web site: afsp.org; select "Become an Advocate"

Survivors of Incest Anonymous (SIA): A self-help organization based on the 12 steps, providing support for adult survivors of childhood incest. Incest is defined loosely by the organization, including sexual and other unwanted touching activity by family, extended family, or other trusted adults.

Address: PO Box 190; Benson, MD 21018-9998
Phone: 410-893-3322
Web site: siawso.org

The Balanced Mind Parent Network: Works to help families with children and teens with bipolar disorder. Seeks to educate the public and connect families to resources, primarily using the network's Web site.

Address: 1000 Skokie Blvd., Suite 570; Wilmette, IL 60091
Phone: 847-256-8525   Fax: 847-920-9498
Web site: thebalancedmind.org

Tourette Syndrome Association (TSA): An international group offering resources and referral support for persons with Tourette syndrome and their family members. TSA also works to understand the disorder more fully and to promote accurate public perceptions of the disorder.

Address: 42-40 Bell Blvd., Suite 205; Bayside, NY 11361-2820
Phone: 718-224-2999   Fax: 718-279-9596
Web site: tsa-usa.org

Women for Sobriety: A self-help program designed specifically for women with alcohol addiction. The program specifically addresses the unique issues women face in recovery.

Address: PO Box 618; Quakertown, PA 18951-0618
Phone: 215-536-8026
Web site: womenforsobriety.org

Workaholics Anonymous: A recovery fellowship based on the 12-step group format, designed for men and women who desire to stop compulsive working. Meetings are available in person, online, and over the phone.

Address: PO Box 289; Menlo Park, CA 94026-0289
Phone: 510-273-9253
Web site: workaholics-anonymous.org

GLOSSARY

AARP a leading group for those age 55 and above to learn which social and political events affect them most

A-B-C model of human interaction "A" is the event, "B" is the thought process, and "C" is the feeling state resulting from one's thoughts. To change negative or nonproductive feelings, individuals need to think differently (i.e., positive or neutral).

A-B-C-D-E worksheet an approach to ethical decision making that uses a mnemonic device to remind group leaders and members of what they should do. The letters of this worksheet stand for Assessment, Benefit, Consequences and Consultation, Duty, and Education.

accelerated aging the process of defining oneself as older than one's chronological age

acting "as if" an Adlerian therapeutic technique wherein someone acts "as if" he or she were the person he or she wishes to be

action-centered view of groups the view that groups for children under 12 years of age should involve play and action

action exercises sensory awareness methods or guided imagery used in the psychodrama warm-up phase to help members discover common themes within the group as well as focus more on individual concerns

action-oriented group techniques techniques that require group members to behave in an active manner (e.g., role playing, using "I" statements)

action phase the second part of the psychodrama process, which involves the enactment of protagonists' concerns

active listening to hear the tone and meanings behind verbal communication and to pick up on messages in nonverbal behaviors

activities verbal and nonverbal undertakings a group and its members participate in such as expressing themselves in different ways and interacting with others.

activity group guidance (AGG) group guidance involving activities that are developmental in nature; typically includes coordinated guidance topics

actors those who play the parts of other important people or objects in a psychodrama play. They are called *auxiliaries*. With prompting from the protagonist, they can play the protagonist's double, an antagonist, or even a piece of furniture. In the same psychodrama, an auxiliary could play more than one part, such as being the protagonist's best friend and worst enemy.

Adlerian theory an approach founded by Alfred Adler that concentrates on the inherent social interest of persons and emphasizes social development, cooperation, and education.

Adlerian parent education stresses cooperation among family members as a goal and emphasizes the use of logical and natural consequences to avoid power struggles. There is a democratic emphasis to this orientation, and regular family council meetings are held for all members to voice concerns and needs. The Adlerian approach stresses parent discussion groups with a trained leader and a set curriculum.

adolescence the age span from 13 to 19, although it can be extended to include some individuals up to age 25; a time of unevenness and paradoxes marked by extensive personal changes

adult children of alcoholics (ACoAs) adults who grew up in families in which one or both parents abused alcohol. These individuals developed coping mechanisms for dealing with their alcoholic family system, such as denial or overcompensation, that are usually not functional for a mature lifestyle. Dealing with feelings about the past as well as learning behaviors for coping and life skills are therapeutic foci for these persons.

Adult ego state (TA) the realistic, logical part of a person, which functions like a computer in that it receives and processes information from the Parent, the Child, and the environment

adulthood a somewhat nebulous term implying that a person has reached physical, mental, social, and emotional maturity

adventure groups (aka, adventure group counseling) a type of counseling group that is relatively short-term and experiential and uses adventurous activities and being in natural environments to facilitate therapeutic change in clients

advice giving instructing someone what to do in a particular situation. It is seldom appropriate or needed in most groups. It prevents members from struggling with their own feelings and keeps advice givers from having to recognize shortcomings in their own lives.

ageism discrimination against older people based on their age

aging process a biological phenomenon composed of physiological changes as well as a mental process of considering oneself older

airtime the amount of time available for participation in the group

Alcoholics Anonymous (AA) an organization that helps alcoholics gain and maintain control of their lives by remaining sober; established in the late 1930s

alternated a form of group co-leadership; one leader takes responsibility for a specific time or session, and the other leader provides support

American Group Psychotherapy Association (AGPA) a psychoanalytically oriented organization established by Samuel R. Slavson in 1943

American Society of Group Psychotherapy and Psychodrama (ASGPP) a professional group association established by Jacob L. Moreno between 1941 and 1942

amplify to emphasize statements made by the protagonist in psychodrama. Examples include verbalizing nonverbal communications, questioning one's self, interpreting statements based on what is being said and not said, contradicting feelings, self-observing, and engaging in denial.

anxiety tension; an uneasy feeling that accompanies decision making or performance

apprehension anxiety; a moderate amount helps group members key in on what they are experiencing and what they want to do

apprenticed a form of group co-leadership in which the more experienced leader takes charge of the group to demonstrate for a novice leader how to work with a group

assessing members' growth and change a technique similar to personal reviews but, in assessment, the emphasis is on individuals' memories of themselves at the beginning of the group and now. The idea of such an exercise is to have members see and share significant gains with themselves and others.

Association for Specialists in Group Work (ASGW) formed in 1973; a division within the American Counseling Association

asynchronous a type of online group, such as an e-mail listserv; messages can be formatted as typed and sent at any time, whether or not the receiver is online, too

attack on the group leader when members of the group become hostile or rebellious in regard to a leader's authority or conduct of the group. Underlying reasons for such attacks are subgrouping, fear of intimacy, and extragroup socializing.

attractiveness a multidimensional concept that basically refers to members positively identifying with others in the group

audience a term used to describe others who may be present during the psychodrama. Some may become auxiliaries.

authenticity the ability to affirm oneself and to make the most of discovering and using one's talents and creativity

authoritarian group leaders leaders who envision themselves as experts. They interpret, give advice, and generally direct the movement of the group much as a parent controls the actions of a child. They are often charismatic and manipulative. They feed off of obedience, expect conformity, and operate out of the wheel model.

autodrama see *monodrama*

authoritative power power predicated on social position or responsibility in an organization

autonomy the promotion of self-determination or the power to choose one's own direction in life. In groups, it is important that group members feel they have a right to make their own decisions.

auxiliary counselors group members who act as cocounselors once someone has presented a problem; occurs when a rational-emotive behavior therapy group leader encourages it to help participants benefit from multiple input

avoiding conflict when the group ignores areas of tension or silences or discounts members who expose the group's disagreements

awareness Gestalt term for a total organismic response to the environment so that a person gains insight and control over situations and becomes responsible in achieving a healthy response to life events

"BA" (basic assumption) activity a classification devised by Wilfred Bion for the emotional pattern of an antiwork group (as opposed to a "W" [work group]). BA groups can be broken down further into three subpatterns: *BA Dependency* (where members are overdependent on the group leader), *BA Pairing* (where members are more interested in being with one another than in working on a goal), and *BA Fight–Flight* (where members become preoccupied with either engaging in or avoiding hostile conflict).

band-aiding the misuse of support; process of preventing others from fully expressing their emotional pain

basic encounter group also known as *encounter group*; first established by Carl Rogers to describe his approach to group work; focuses on individuals' awareness of their own emotional experiences and the behaviors of others; emphasis is placed on the awareness and exploration of intrapsychic and interpersonal issues. Encounter groups are often known as *personal growth groups* because the emphasis in these groups is on personal development.

BASIC ID A. Lazarus's multimodal model for helping; includes the components of behavior, effect, sensation, imagery, cognition, interpersonal relations, and drugs

basic skills training (BST) approach to groups developed at the National Training Laboratories in the 1940s; predecessor of the *T-group* movement

behavioral disputation rational-emotive behavior therapy treatment that involves many forms, from reading (bibliotherapy) to role playing in the group. Often enactment of the problem within the group setting and possible ways of handling it are used. Homework may then be assigned in the form of *shame attacks* (in which the person actually does what he or she dreaded and finds that the world does not fall apart regardless of the outcome).

beneficence promoting the good of others. It is assumed in groups that leaders and members will work hard for the betterment of the group as a whole.

blind quadrant information originally unknown to oneself but known to others when the group began

blocking role an anti-group member role. Individuals who take this role act as aggressors, blockers, dominators, recognition seekers, and self-righteous moralists.

body language a Gestalt concept in which emphasis is placed on what a person's body is doing, such as a hand tapping

boundaries physical and psychological parameters under which a group operates, such as starting and ending on time

brainstorming a way to stimulate divergent thinking; requires initially generating ideas in a nonjudgmental manner. The premise of this approach is that creativity and member participation are often held back because of the critical evaluation of ideas and actions by other group members.

burnout a state of physical and emotional exhaustion

C group a type of Adlerian parent education group; each component of the group—collaboration, consultation, clarification, confrontation, concern, confidentiality, and commitment—begins with a *c*. The group is primarily psychoeducational. It emphasizes developmental and preventive aspects of parenting.

capping the process of easing out of emotional interaction and into cognitive reflection; especially useful during termination

career change groups groups for adults in midlife that are both psychoeducational and psychotherapeutic in nature

career support groups groups geared to life-span issues of work

caring genuine concern for others

catharsis a release of pent-up feelings, such as anger or joy; a psychoanalytic concept

chain in this group arrangement, people are positioned or seated along a line, often according to their rank. Communication is passed through others from a person at one end of the configuration to a person at the other end. The chain is a popular way to run some group organizations, such as the military. Disadvantages of the chain include indirectness of communication, lack of direct contact with others, and frustration in relaying messages through others.

changing questions to statements Gestalt procedure that requires a group member who has raised a question to rephrase it as a statement

Chicanas women of Mexican descent

Child ego state (TA) divided into two parts (a) *Adapted Child* conforms to the rules and wishes of Parent ego states within the self and others; (b) *Free Child* (or natural child) reacts more spontaneously, has fun, and is curious and playful. It takes care of its needs without regard for others while using its intuition to read nonverbal cues.

circle in this group configuration, all members have direct access to one another, and there is implied equality in status and power. The disadvantage of this arrangement is the lack of a perceived leader in the structure unless the identified leader is active and direct. Overall, the circle is probably the best structured way to ensure that group members have an opportunity for equal airtime.

clarify the purpose when group leaders remind members and the group as a whole what the appropriate behavioral interactions or foci in the group are and why

clarity of purpose the first step in the preplanning process; determining what the group is set up to accomplish

closed-ended groups that do not admit new members after the first session

code of ethics a set of standards and principles that organizations create to provide guidelines for their members to follow in working with the public and one another

cognitive disputation a process in REBT that involves direct questioning, reasoning, and persuasion

cognitively restructure to think of and perceive oneself differently

cohesion the togetherness of a group; "we-ness"

cohesiveness (see *cohesion*)

co-leader a professional or a professional-in-training who undertakes the responsibility of sharing the leadership of a group with another leader in a mutually determined manner.

The use of co-leaders in groups occurs often when membership is 12 or more.

collaboration sharing facts and feelings with other members in a group; helping a member obtain a personal goal when there is no observable reward for the other members of a group

collective counseling Alfred Adler's form of group counseling

commitment when participants begin to evaluate their performances and the performances of others in terms of accomplishment of the group's goals

communication facilitator a group leader who reflects the content and feeling of members and teaches them how to do likewise. This process focuses on both the expression of words and the emotion behind these communications. In addition, the leader stresses the importance of speaking congruently—that is, using "I" messages to state what one wants or thinks.

community for learning a large-group phenomenon in the 1970s initiated by Carl Rogers in which about 100 people live and work together for 2 weeks at a time

condemning questions questions that put people down and prevent them from seeing situations more honestly and openly (e.g., "Don't you think you should feel differently?")

confidentiality the explicit agreement that what is said within a group will stay in the group; the right of group members to reveal personal thoughts, feelings, and information to the leader and other members of the group and expect that nonmembers of the group will not learn of it in any way. Not keeping confidences is like gossiping and is destructive to the group process.

conflict management an approach premised on the belief that conflict can be positive. Thus, the focus in conflict management is on directing conflict toward a constructive dialogue.

conflict management orientations ways of handling conflict in a group (e.g., competing, accommodating, collaborating, sharing, avoiding)

conflict resolution based on the underlying notion that conflict is essentially negative and destructive, with the primary focus on ending a specific conflict

confront to challenge incongruencies in thoughts and actions

confrontation challenging group members to look at the discrepancies and incongruencies between their words and their actions

consciousness-raising (C-R) group a group set up to help its participants become more aware of the issues they face and choices they have within their environment

contact-focused group theory a conceptualization of groups in which the purpose of groups is highlighted; three primary contact groups described in this model are group guidance, group counseling, and group psychotherapy

continuing education units (CEUs) credits for participating in professional educational programs

contract an agreement, verbal or written, of what group members or the group as a whole will do and when

control theory a complete system for explaining how the brain works; added to base of reality therapy in the 1980s to make it more complete

cooperation group members working together for a common purpose or good

cooperative learning groups study groups established so that assigned tasks can be divided and accomplished; members are responsible for meeting regularly and teaching one another what they have learned

core mechanisms of group leadership core skills of group leadership (i.e., emotional stimulation, caring, meaning attribution, and executive function)

corrective emotional experience a hallmark of the working stage of a group; a group member is helped by others to interact interpersonally in an appropriate way through reality testing responses

counseling groups see *counseling/interpersonal problem-solving groups*

counseling/interpersonal problem-solving groups groups that focus on each person's behavior and growth or change within the group in regard to a particular problem or concern

countertransference a leader's emotional responses to members that are a result of the leader's own needs or unresolved issues with significant others

couples group therapy proponents of couples group therapy list many advantages for it, including (a) identification by group members of appropriate and inappropriate behaviors and expectations by others, (b) development of insight and skills through observing other couples, (c) group feedback and support for the ventilation of feelings and changed behavior, and (d) lower cost

crash-program mentality when group experiences are carried out to excess

creative imagery a warm-up technique consisting of inviting psychodrama participants to imagine neutral or pleasant objects and scenes. The idea is to help participants become more spontaneous.

creativity the act of taking elements from the environment and arranging or rearranging them in such a way that something new and useful is formed

crisis-centered groups groups formed because of some emergency, such as conflict between rival groups

critical incident in the life of the group an event that has the power to shape or influence the group positively or negatively

critical-incident model a training model focusing on a number of critical incidents in the life of a group of any type. The trainee, after studying group dynamics, watches a video of his or her instructor handling a number of different situations in a group. Then the trainee co-leads a group under the instructor's supervision and makes strategic interventions geared to the incidents in the particular group. Trainees are taught self-management skills as well as ways to deal with specific group situations.

critical incident stress debriefing (CISD) groups groups that help victims of violence deal with its repercussions, such as feelings of helplessness, anxiety, depression, and disorganization, lasting one 1- to 3-hour session.

culturally encapsulated holding stereotyped views of others who differ from oneself and acting accordingly.

culture the set of attitudes, values, beliefs, and behaviors shared by a group of people, communicated from one generation to the next via language or some other means of communication

culture-specific groups groups that focus on a specific cultural population where members are of the same or a similar background

curative (therapeutic) factors within groups eleven group factors (instillation of hope, universality, imparting of information, altruism, corrective recapitulation of the primary family group, development of socialization techniques, imitative behavior, interpersonal learning, group cohesiveness, catharsis, and existential factors) that contribute to the betterment of individuals in the group; first researched by Irvin Yalom

cutting off another term for blocking; defined two ways: (a) making sure that new material is not introduced into the group too late in the session for the group to adequately deal with it; (b) preventing group members from rambling

cyclotherapy process the idea that after the group first meets, it continues to evolve and can be conceptualized as forever forming, with certain issues returning from time to time to be explored in greater depth

democratic group leaders group-centered leaders who trust group participants to develop their own potential and that of other group members. They serve as facilitators of the group process and not as directors of it. They cooperate and collaborate with the group and share responsibilities with group members.

denial acting as if an experience does not exist or will never end

density of time the fullness of time and eventfulness; both seem to lessen with age

dependency group members who present themselves as helpless and incapable but refuse to listen to feedback. They are help-rejecting complainers and encourage the behavior of advice givers and band-aiders in a group.

Developing Understanding of Self and Others–Revised (DUSO–R) a commercial classroom guidance program based on Adlerian theory

developmental factors variables such as the age, gender, and maturity level of those involved in a group

developmental group counseling psychoeducational groups often used for teaching basic life skills

developmental psychoeducational groups groups that focus on common concerns of adolescents, such as identity, sexuality, parents, peer relationships, career goals, and educational/institutional problems. Individuals who join these groups do so out of a sense of need.

devil's advocate procedure procedure in which one or more members in the group are asked to question group decisions with a firm skepticism before the group reaches a conclusion

dialogue talk between others and oneself or between different aspects of oneself; one of the two primary therapeutic tools in Gestalt therapy (along with *awareness*)

director the person who guides the protagonist in the use of the psychodramatic method to help that person explore his or her problem. The director is roughly equivalent to the group leader in other theoretical approaches but serves as a producer, a facilitator, an observer, and an analyzer.

disability a mental, behavioral, or physical impairment that affects at least one of an individual's daily activities

discussion teams small groups used to promote involvement in guidance activities. In this arrangement, a large group is divided into four or five teams that are then seated in semicircles around the room. This formation has the advantage of getting members involved with one another and raising the level of excitement among them. The disadvantages are that interaction is mainly limited to a small number of individuals and that other group members do not get the advantage of participating in all the groups.

diversity a concept in groups applicable to the uniformity or nonuniformity of matters such as race, ethnicity, language, culture, gender, socioeconomic class, sexual orientation, religion, ableism, and disability

double and multiple double important techniques in psychodrama. The *double* consists of an actor taking on the role of the protagonist's alter ego and helping the protagonist express true inner feelings more clearly. In cases in which the protagonist has ambivalent feelings, the *multiple double* technique is used. In these situations, two or more actors represent different aspects of the protagonist's personality. The doubles may speak at once or take turns, but, through their input, the protagonist should gain a better idea of what his or her thoughts and feelings are.

drawing out the opposite of cutting off or blocking; a process in which group leaders purposefully ask more silent members to speak to anyone in the group, or to the group as a whole, about anything on their minds or a specific subject

dream work seen by Fritz Perls as "the royal road to integration." It is used by having those who dream recreate and relive the dream in the present. By doing so, these individuals become all parts of the dream. They may do this through working alone in the group setting or having others in the group act out different parts of the dream (i.e., *dream work as theater*).

dual-focused Gestalt group work a Gestalt approach in which attention is concentrated on group process, with the power of individual work within the group

dual nature of human beings an REBT concept that individuals are both rational and irrational

dual/multiple relationships when group leaders find themselves in two or more potentially conflicting roles with their group members

dyads groups of two

eating disorders groups professionally led psychotherapeutic and support groups for individuals who have obsessive and distorted ideas in regard to thinness and body image

eclectic a composite of theoretical approaches

educational and developmental procedure a group training model consisting of four components: (a) content, (b) decision making, (c) eventual leadership style, and (d) dual process

educational groups see *psychoeducational groups*; another name for such groups

ego state (TA) a system of feelings accompanied by a related set of behavior patterns; the three basic TA ego states are Parent, Adult, and Child

egogram (TA) a bar graph showing how people structure their time in six major ways: (a) withdrawal, (b) ritual, (c) pastimes, (d) work, (e) games, and (f) intimacy

eGroups Internet-based groups. These groups are often set up for older adults and those who are homebound

eMemories and eStories memories and stories that are shared online with an eGroup

elasticity a Gestalt term describing the ability to move from one set of needs to another and back

emotional ambivalence feelings of loss, sadness, and separation mixed with those of hope, joy, and accomplishment

emotional debris unfinished business

emotional impact of separation includes dealing with loss, putting the separation in perspective, becoming aware of the limited value of searching for causes of separation, becoming more cognizant of systems interactions (family, work, social network), using the past as a guide to the future, and moving from a dyadic to a monadic identity

emotional response of separation focuses on continuing relationships with an ex-spouse; recognizing the influence of the separation on family, friends, and children; working and dating; and making sexual adjustments

emotional stimulation sharing on an affective level as well as an intellectual level

empathizing putting oneself in another's place in regard to subjective perception and emotion and yet keeping one's objectivity. It demands a suspension of judgment and a response to another person that conveys sensitivity and understanding.

empty chair technique a Gestalt technique designed to help group members deal with different aspects of their personalities (e.g., a person is given an opportunity to role-play and speak to a missing person with whom he or she has unfinished business)

encounter an existentialist concept that involves total physical and psychological contact between persons on an intense, concrete, and complete basis in the here and now; a psychodrama concept

encouragement an Adlerian technique of having group members examine their lifestyles in regard to mistaken perceptions and take note of their assets, strengths, and talents. Encouragement is one of the most distinctive Adlerian procedures.

energy field the sum total of individual members' energies and attention in a group

ethics suggested standards of conduct based on a set of professional values

evaluation questionnaire serves the purpose of helping group members be concrete in assessing the group in which they have participated. This questionnaire can take many forms but is best if kept brief. An evaluation questionnaire should cover at least three aspects of the group: the leadership of the group, the facilities in which the group was held, and the group's effectiveness in achieving its objectives.

excursions a part of synectics in which members actually take a break—a vacation—from problem solving and engage in exercises involving fantasy, metaphor, and analogy. The idea is that the material generated in these processes can later be reintegrated back into the group.

executive function the role of the leader to manage the group as a social system that allows the group and its members to achieve specific goals

exercises planned activities that have been used previously to help group members become more aware; structured activities that the group does for a specific purpose

existentialism a philosophy that addresses what it means to be human

existential variables immediate feelings and interactions, such as conflict, withdrawal, support, dominance, and change

experiments nonplanned experiences that occur spontaneously in the group session

facilitating as done by group leaders, helping open up communication among group members

facilitative feedback telling another person the effect he or she has on you as a compliment or confrontation

facilitative/building role a role that adds to the functioning of a group in a positive and constructive way. Members who take on such a role may serve as initiators of actions and ideas, information seekers, opinion seekers, coordinators, orienters, evaluators, or recorders.

facilitators term for Rogerian group leaders

families in high-risk environments families living in neighborhoods prone to violence

family councils a form of family group meetings originated by Alfred Adler

fantasy exercises a method used in Gestalt group work to help group members (a) be more concrete in assessing their feelings, (b) deal with catastrophic experiences, (c) explore and express feelings of guilt and shame, and (d) become more involved in the group. It is not necessary for group members to live out their fantasies.

farewell-party syndrome a dynamic in which group members emphasize only the positive aspects of what has occurred in the group, instead of what they have learned. This type of focus tends to avoid the pain of closure.

faulty logic irrational ideas that clients hold

feedback involves one person giving another his or her perception of a behavior, sharing relevant information with other people, such as how they appear to others, so they can make decisions about whether they would like to change. Feedback information should be given in a clear, concrete, succinct, and appropriate manner.

fidelity loyalty and duty; keeping one's promise and honoring one's commitment. In group work, fidelity involves stating up front what the group will focus on and then keeping that pledge.

field theory Kurt Lewin's approach to groups, which emphasizes the interaction between individuals and their environments. It is based on the ideas of Gestalt psychology, in which there is an interdependence of part–whole relationships.

fishbowl the use of in and out circles in conducting a group

floating hot seat Gestalt technique in which interaction is promoted by encouraging group members to work on exploring their own personal issues when someone else in the group touches on an issue that has personal relevance for them

focus groups temporary groups composed of representative samples of individuals concerned with issues, products, and/or outcomes; increasingly used by businesses and politicians

focusers on others those who become self-appointed group "assistant leaders" by questioning others, offering advice, and acting as if they do not have any problems

follow-up reconnecting with group members after they have had time to process what they experienced in the group and work on their goals/objectives

formal feedback structured; may be set up through use of a *time-limited round*

forming, or orientation, stage of the group a stage characterized by initial caution associated with any new experience. During this time, group members try to avoid being rejected by others, the leader, or even themselves.

four types of thoughts: negative, positive, neutral, and mixed an REBT concept: (a) negative thoughts concentrate on painful or disappointing aspects of an event, (b) positive thoughts focus on just the opposite, (c) neutral cognitions are those that are neither positive nor negative, and (d) mixed thoughts contain elements of the other three thought processes

game analysis (TA) an examination of destructive and repetitive behavioral patterns and an analysis of the ego states and types of transactions involved

games (TA) an ongoing series of complementary ulterior transactions progressing to a well-defined, predictable outcome. Games are played on three levels, and almost all of them are destructive and result in negative payoffs (i.e., *rackets*). *First-degree* games are the least harmful; minor faults are highlighted. *Second-degree* games are more serious; the interactive process in second-degree games leaves the people involved feeling negative. *Third-degree* games are deadly and often played for keeps; there is nothing socially redeemable about third-degree games. People who play games operate from three distinct positions: (a) the *victim* (who appears to be innocent), (b) the *persecutor* (who appears to cause problems), and (c) the *rescuer* (who is seen as a problem solver or hero to the victim). Individuals who play games often switch among these roles.

GAP matrix for groups the "goals and process" model of group types; originated by Waldo and Bauman

general systems theory a theory that emphasizes circular causality as opposed to linear causality

generalization the display of behaviors in environments other than where they were originally learned

generativity a goal of midlife, according to Erik Erikson, in which people seek to be creative in their lives and work for the benefit of others and the next generation

genogram a type of family tree

Gestalt therapy an experiential and humanistic approach to change founded by Fritz Perls, along with Laura Perls and Paul Goodman. It emphasizes teaching of *awareness* skills and stresses interpersonal interactions and learning through enactment.

goals specific objectives that individuals in the group or the group as a whole wishes to accomplish

go-rounds also known as *rounds*; a procedure in which every group member comments briefly (usually a sentence or two) as his or her turn comes up around the circle

Gray Panthers a psychoeducational and advocacy task group for older adults

Greek chorus (see *hot seat*)

group a collection of two or more individuals, who meet face-to-face or virtually in an interactive, interdependent way, with the awareness that each belongs to the group and for the purpose of achieving mutually agreed-on goals

group analysis a term first applied to the treatment of individuals in psychoanalytically oriented groups by Trigant Burrow. He emphasized that social forces affect individuals' behaviors.

group as a whole one of three levels of a group where the focus is on the development, dynamics, and experiences of the entire group

group-as-a-whole approach a psychotherapy group approach where the therapist makes comments directed to the whole group that reflect processes operating in the group in the here and now that seem to be out of the group's current awareness

group-based training In this model, specific skills used in groups are first identified and defined by trainers. Examples are given in which this skill might be used. The flexibility of using various skills is stressed in this presentation. Next, both videos and role-plays are used to show trainees how a particular skill is employed. The third step in this procedure is structured practice in which each trainee demonstrates how he or she would use the skill that has been demonstrated. This enactment is then critiqued. Finally, group leader trainees, after learning all the group skills, are asked to demonstrate their group facilitation skills in 20-minute unstructured practice sessions. They are observed leading a group and given feedback on the use of skills they implemented during this time as well as those that they did not use.

group-centered perspective focuses on members and interpersonal processes

group cohesion a sense of "we-ness"

group collusion involves cooperating with others unconsciously or consciously to reinforce prevailing attitudes, values, behaviors, or norms. The purpose of such behavior is self-protection, and its effect is to maintain the status quo in the group.

group-conducted pregroup screening process a way of screening potential group members by placing them in a group and observing how they interact

group content information discussed within a group

group dynamics a term originally used by Kurt Lewin to describe the interrelations of individuals in groups

Group Emotional Intelligence Individual Regulation test (GEI-IR) an instrument devised by Christina Petersen with three scales: group efficacy, group trust, and group cohesiveness. It measures group emotional intelligence, a key component of effective group work.

group exercises (see *exercises*)

group for survivors of suicide group for adults that helps them break out of isolation and resolve grief issues specific to suicide; can also be conducted on a self-help and support group basis

group generalist model a training model entailing five steps: (a) the trainer models leader behavior for the total group; (b) the group is broken into subgroups of five or six, and each subgroup member practices leading a small-group discussion; (c) after each discussion, some aspect of the subgroup's behavior is processed (e.g., anxiety); (d) the subgroup critiques the leader's behavior; and (e) following practice by each trainee, the total group shares observations and conclusions about the activity

group interaction the way members relate to one another with nonverbal and verbal behaviors and the attitudes that go with them. Group interaction exists on a continuum, from extremely nondirective to highly directive.

Group Leader Self-Efficacy Instrument (GLSI) a 36-item scale for measuring group leader self-efficacy

group norming (see *norming*)

group observing group when a group breaks into two smaller groups and each observes the other function (as outsiders) for a set amount of time; sometimes called a *fishbowl procedure*

group process the interactions of group members as the group develops

group process goals in Adlerian groups, goals center around promoting and experiencing a cooperative climate within the group

group processing when a neutral third party observes and offers feedback to the group about what is occurring among members and in the group itself

group psychotherapy [also called group therapy. It is a group that addresses personal and interpersonal problems of living among people who may be experiencing severe and/or chronic maladjustment]

group setting the group's physical environment

group structure the way a group is set up physically as well as how the group members interact or structure themselves in relationship to others

Group Systems Theory a theory that states that there are three levels of a group: the intrapersonal, the interpersonal, and the group as whole. A group leader can implement an intervention that targets any of the three levels depending on the objective.

group techniques exercises that are structured so that group members interact with one another

group therapy for normals premise of basic encounter groups: individuals who participate are relatively healthy

group work According to the Association for Specialists in Group Work, "a broad professional practice involving the application of knowledge and skill in group facilitation to assist an interdependent collection of people to reach their mutual goals, which may be intrapersonal, interpersonal, or work related. The goals of the group may include the accomplishment of tasks related to work, education, personal development, personal and interpersonal problem solving, or remediation of mental and emotional disorders."

groups for victims of abuse groups set up to help victims of abuse break the cycle of isolation so common to this population and to interrelate in a healthy, dynamic way

groupthink a group situation in which there is a deterioration of mental efficiency, reality testing, and moral judgment that results from in-group pressures

groupware the collective name of computer support for something a group does

growing times when fresh learning occurs on an individual and interpersonal level

growth-centered groups groups that focus on the personal and social development of people and are set up to explore feelings, concerns, and behaviors about a number of everyday subjects

guidance groups see *psychoeducational groups*; another name for such groups

guidance hour also called *guidance room*; the term used for a homeroom at school in the 1930s; responsibilities of the teacher were to establish friendly relationships with students, discover their abilities and needs, and develop right attitudes within them toward school, home, and the community

guided autobiography in this process, individuals write their autobiography, reflect, organize, and write on the assigned theme of the week, then rehearse what they are going to share and, during a session, have control over their experience and emotions

Hawthorne effect changes in behavior as a result of observation/manipulation conditions under which a person or group works

HELPING D. B. Keat's multimodal framework for helping: Health, Emotions, Learning, Personal Interactions, Imagery, Need to Know, and Guidance

here and now the present

heterogeneous groups groups composed of dissimilar persons. Such groups can broaden members' horizons and enliven interpersonal interactions.

heuristic discovering, usually through research and investigation

hidden quadrant in the Johari Window, contains undisclosed information known only to oneself initially

highly structured groups groups with a predetermined goal and a plan designed to enable each group member to reach an identified goal with minimum frustration. Such groups are usually used in teaching skills that may be transferred to a wide range of life events.

high-risk families families prone to violence

homework working outside the group itself, members implement behaviors they have addressed or practiced within the group. These real-life situations help them realize more fully what they need to work on in the group.

homogeneous groups groups composed of similar persons

hope both a cognitive and an emotional experience in groups. Cognitively, the belief that what is desired is also possible and that events will turn out for the best; emotionally, the feeling that what one wishes for will occur. The importance of hope is that it energizes group members and the group as a whole.

hot seat the place in Gestalt group therapy where the person who wants to work sits with his or her chair facing that of the therapist or leader; the rest of the group serves as a kind of "Greek chorus" in the background of the encounter, where they resonate and empathize with the one who is working and gain insights into themselves and others through the process of identification

humor the ability to laugh at oneself and the group in a therapeutic and nondefensive manner; an especially important quality during the working stage of the group

hypokinesis physical inactivity

I/We/It a conceptualization of the group process in which attention is given to personal, interpersonal, and product outcomes

icebreaker an activity designed to promote communication between two or more people in a group

ice-breaking exercises introductory activities that link people together. Such exercises increase the group members' awareness of one another and/or remind members of what they did in previous sessions.

identification a "normal" developmental process in which individuals see themselves as being similar to one another

imaginal disputation a technique that has participants see themselves in stressful situations and examine their self-talk

imago (image) relationship therapy image therapy; an eclectic approach to working with couples that includes elements of psychoanalysis, transactional analysis, Gestalt psychology, cognitive therapy, and systems theory

impasses in Gestalt theory, the places where group members get stuck

in and out circles often referred to as the *fishbowl*. The inner circle promotes a sense of closeness, but those in the outer circle may feel left out and become bored. To help promote participation by everyone, group leaders can assign tasks for the outside group members to do while they observe the inside group.

incorporation personal awareness and appreciation of what the group has accomplished both on an individual and a collective level

individual goals in Adlerian groups, involves developing insight into the creation of a mistaken lifestyle and taking corrective measures

individually conducted pregroup screening procedure intake interview used to determine who will join a particular group

influential power based on the idea of persuasion and manipulation of others through convincing them that a certain course of action is correct

informal feedback reactions solicited of members by the group leader; provided in an unstructured way at any time. Such an invitation is likely to increase spontaneity and sensitivity.

information statement a written description of what a group is about and what is expected of its members

informational power premised on the idea that those who know more are able to exert control over situations, including those involving people

informed consent statement a document a group member signs acknowledging that the individual is aware of the group activity in which he or she is about to participate and is doing so voluntarily

injunctions (TA) Parent commands recorded internally by a Child that call for the individual to adopt certain roles

inner circle/outer circle approach a Native American group approach in which members are organized into two concentric circles. Inner circle members release their pain and frustrations, expressed as clenched fists, into the open palms of the outer circle members.

interpersonal learning groups groups that are designed to promote greater understanding across cultural groups and contain members from different cultural backgrounds

insight consists of immediate new perceptions and understandings about one's problems; often occurs during or after the experience of catharsis

insight and reorientation phases of the group in Adlerian groups, involves helping individuals understand why they made the choices they did in the past, often accompanied by the use of interpretation on the group leader's part that is offered as a tentative hypothesis

integration phase last phase of psychodrama; involves discussion and closure

integrity one of Erikson's virtues; the total integration of life experiences into a meaningful whole

intellectualization behavior characterized by an emphasis on abstraction with a minimal amount of affect; the use of thoughts and a sophisticated vocabulary to avoid dealing with personal feelings

intentional civil liability cases include situations such as (a) *battery* (the unconsented touching of a person); (b) *defamation* (injury to a person's character or reputation either through verbal *[slander]* or written *[libel]* means); (c) *invasion of privacy* (violation of the right to be left alone); and (d) *infliction of mental distress* (outrageous behavior on the part of the therapist or the group leader)

interactional catalyst occurs when group leaders promote interaction among group members without calling attention to themselves. It is a functional process that continues throughout the group and can take various forms, such as questioning whether two or more group members have something to say to each other and then being silent to see what happens.

interactive journal writing the process wherein group members keep logs of their thoughts, feelings, impressions, and behaviors within a group and exchange them in all directions—member–leader, member–member, and leader–member

interpersonal goals in Adlerian groups, involves becoming more socially oriented and involved with other individuals experiencing life difficulties

interpersonal style of group leadership leadership that focuses on transactions between individuals in the group

interpretation of a person's early history in Adlerian groups, group members' recognition and understanding of the ways they created their own lifestyles

intervention cube concept model for training group leaders (see *critical-incident model*)

intrapersonal style of group leadership leadership that concentrates on the inward reactions of individual members of the group

intrinsically neutral as an approach, Gestalt theory views individuals as neither positive nor negative (i.e., without a predetermined set of responses)

involuntary groups members are mandated to attend, such as those that are court ordered or conducted in an inpatient mental health facility

involvement group members' active participation with one another and investment of themselves in the group

job support groups groups for people who have lost their jobs and need emotional support; who want to learn how to achieve career goals and are willing to spend a good deal of time in doing so; and who are unemployed and are emotionally struggling with the stigma, shame, and isolation of their situations

jogging group approach built on the premise that physical exercise is an important element that contributes to people's abilities to perform better in all areas of life. The jogging group itself combines an hour of exercise, in the form of walking, jogging, or running, with another hour of group process.

Johari Awareness Model also known as *Johari Window*; a representative square with four quadrants that is often used to show what happens in group interactions when the group and its members are working or not working

joining the process by which leaders and group members connect with one another psychologically and/or physically

journal letters a way of ending a group; members and the leader write about their experiences in the group and give their letters to one another

journals also known as *logs*; in this experience, group members are required to write their reactions to the events of each session. This process enables them to spot inconsistencies in their reactions more quickly than if they simply talked about them.

justice fairness; refers to the equal treatment of all people. This virtue implies that everyone's welfare is promoted and that visible differences in people, such as gender or race, do not interfere with the way they are treated.

KOFFE (Knowledge, Open Communication, Faith, Family, and Empowerment) a group counseling model highlighting important concepts for working with African Americans

laissez-faire leaders leaders in name only. They do not provide any structure or direction for their groups. Members are left with the responsibility of leading and directing.

law a body of rules recognized by a state or a community as binding on its members

Law of Triviality the time a group spends discussing any issue is in inverse proportion to the consequences of the issue

layers of neurosis in Gestalt theory, those aspects of people that keep them from being healthy: the *phony*—being unauthentic; the *phobic*—being afraid to really see themselves as they are; and the *impasse*—where their maturity is stuck

leader-centered group autocratic; the leader instructs the followers in the "right" way. The leader-centered group is based on obedience from followers.

leaderless groups groups that rotate the leadership role among members (e.g., self-help groups)

leveling a process in which group members are encouraged to interact freely and evenly with one another. In leveling, group members who are underparticipatory are drawn out and those who are excessively active are helped to modify their behavior.

LGBTQ Response Model for Supervision of Group Work (RMSGW) a model of supervision created by Goodrich and Luke (2011) applicable to all group leaders so they can plan and implement group interventions with members of the gay, lesbian, bisexual, transgender, and questioning populations regardless of the group setting or context

life script analyses (TA) an examination of people's basic life plans involving transactions and games

life-skills group a type of guidance/psychoeducational group, especially designed for those who have a deficit of behavior. Emphasis is on a "how-to" approach to learning new behaviors; may include the use of films, plays, demonstrations, role-plays, and guest speakers (see *developmental group counseling*).

life-skills training focuses on helping persons identify and correct deficits in their life-coping skills and learn new appropriate behaviors

limits the outer boundaries of a group in regard to behaviors that will be accepted within the group

linear a cause-and-effect explanation

linking the process of connecting persons with one another by pointing out to them what they share in common. Linking strengthens the bonds between individuals and the group as a whole.

Living Newspaper a dramatic technique devised by Jacob Moreno in psychodrama in which recent happenings— sometimes local incidents, sometimes developments in world politics—were spontaneously dramatized

logs (see *journals*)

low facilitative responses (a) *advice/evaluation* (telling people how to behave or judging them); (b) *analyzing/ interpreting* (explaining the reasons behind behavior without giving the person an opportunity for self-discovery); (c) *reassuring/supportive* (trying to encourage someone yet dismissing the person's real feelings)

magic shop a warm-up technique in psychodrama that is especially useful for protagonists who are undecided or ambivalent about their values and goals. It involves a storekeeper (the director or an auxiliary ego) who runs a magic shop filled with special qualities. The qualities are not for sale but may be bartered.

maintenance role a person who contributes to the social-emotional bonding of members and the group's overall well-being. When interpersonal communication in the group is strained, there is a need to focus on relationships. Persons who take on such roles are socially and emotionally oriented. They express themselves by being encouragers, harmonizers, compromisers, commentators, and followers.

making the rounds a warm-up technique in which each member is given a chance to speak about a particular topic. In Gestalt groups, confrontation is heightened as group members are asked to say something they usually do not verbalize.

making wishes into demands using *should, ought,* and *must* in regard to a desired action

malpractice bad practice; implies the group leader has failed to render proper service because of either negligence or ignorance

manipulators group members who use feelings and behaviors to get their way regardless of what others want or need. Often they are angry.

marathon groups originated by George Bach and Fred Stoller in 1964 as a way of helping people become more authentic with themselves; usually held for extended periods, such as 24 or 48 hours; group members are required to stay together. As time passes, members become tired and experience a breakdown in their defenses and an increase in their truthfulness.

marriage enrichment a psychoeducational and growth group for married couples aimed at helping them have healthier relationships

meaning attribution refers to the leader's ability to explain to group members in a cognitive way what is occurring in the group

mediation having a third party hear arguments about a situation and then render a decision

member-specific groups related to topic-specific groups; focus on particular transitional concerns of individual members, such as grief, hospitalization, or institutionalized day care. Basically, member-specific groups may be conducted for older adults or for members of their families.

memory decay where more frequent life events of group members overshadow previous group experiences

midlife ages 40 to 65 years

mirror in this psychodrama activity, the protagonist watches from offstage while an auxiliary ego mirrors the protagonist's posture, gestures, and words. This technique is often used in the action phase of psychodrama to help the protagonist see him- or herself more accurately.

mixed-gender groups groups composed of both males and females

mixed groups groups that defy fitting any category. They encompass multiple ways of working with their members and may change their emphasis frequently. For example, some groups that are instructive are also simultaneously or consequentially therapeutic. The prototype for a mixed group is a *self-help group.*

model minority the myth that some groups, such as Asian Americans, are all high achievers, model citizens, and successful as measured by income and education, with no serious problems

modeler of appropriate behavior when group leaders consciously pick and choose actions they think group members need to learn through passive and active demonstrations; can include deliberate use of self-disclosure, role-plays, speech patterns, and acts of creativity

modeling a social behavioral method used to teach group members complex behaviors in a relatively short period by copying/imitating

monodrama also known as *autodrama*; in this technique, the protagonist plays all the parts of the enactment; no auxiliary egos are used. The person may switch chairs or talk to different parts of the self.

monopolizers group members who, because of their own anxiety, dominate conversation by not giving other persons a chance to participate verbally

monopolizing when a person or persons within the group dominate the group's time through talking

multimodal method using verbal and nonverbal means for conveying information

multiple-family group therapy (MFGT) involves treating several families together at the same time. It requires the use of co-leaders and has many of the same advantages that couples group therapy has, including the fact that families can often serve as cotherapists for one another.

mutual aid support systems groups where members of the group need each other and use each other as resources as well as use the leader

mutual help groups see *self-help groups*

mythopoetic refers to a process of ceremony, drumming, storytelling/poetry reading, physical movement, and imagery exercises designed to create a "ritual process"; a process often used in men's groups

narcissistic groups groups that develop cohesiveness by encouraging hatred of an out-group or by creating an enemy. As a result, regressive group members are able to overlook their own deficiencies by focusing on the deficiencies of the out-group.

National Training Laboratories (NTL) a group training facility in Bethel, Maine, established by Kurt Lewin and associates in the late 1940s

natural consequences living with the results of a particular behavior, such as not following instructions (an Adlerian concept)

negative group variables group action that includes, but is not limited to, avoiding conflict, abdicating group responsibilities, anesthetizing to contradictions within the group, and becoming narcissistic

nominal-group technique (NGT) a six-step process involving the generation both verbally and in writing of a number of ideas/solutions connected with a problem statement. This exercise does not require the open exposure of members as much as brainstorming and ends with a vote, discussion, and revote on priorities for resolving a situation. The time period for the group is 45 to 90 minutes, after which the group, composed of people from diverse settings, is disbanded and the members thanked for their participation.

nondevelopmental counseling and psychotherapy groups adolescent groups that tend to focus mainly on concerns of adults and society, such as drug use, school problems (e.g., poor grades, truancy), or deviant behavior. Usually, these groups are set up by a school, agency, or court, and troubled adolescents are forced to attend.

nondevelopmental factors unpredictable qualities such as the nature of a problem, the suddenness of its appearance, the intensity of its severity, and the present coping skills

nonmaleficence avoiding doing harm. To act ethically, leaders and members of groups must be sure the changes they make in themselves and help others to make are not going to be damaging.

nonverbal behaviors behaviors that make up more than 50% of the messages communicated in social relationships, such as in groups, and are usually perceived as more honest and less subject to manipulation than verbal behaviors. Four categories of nonverbal behavior are body behaviors, interaction with the environment, speech, and physical appearance.

nonverbal cues such behaviors as body posture and facial expression

norming process in which members form an identity as a group and a sense of "we-ness" prevails; there is enthusiasm, cooperation, and cohesiveness at this time. In many ways, the norming stage parallels the forming stage in regard to its emphasis on positive feelings. Norming, like storming, lasts for only a few sessions; it sets the pattern for the next stage: performing (i.e., working).

norms rules and standards of behavior. Groups typically accept both *prescriptive* norms, which describe the kinds of behaviors that should be performed, and *proscriptive* norms, which describe the kinds of behaviors that are to be avoided.

old individuals over the age of 75

old-old individuals over the age of 85; they are likely to experience declines in health and overall functioning

online groups groups that use the Internet and other technology to assist individuals in communicating with each other. They usually take one of two forms. They may be either asynchronous (e.g., with an e-mail mailing list, where messages formatted as typed text can be sent at any time whether or not the receiver is online) or synchronous (e.g., where group members must be online and logged into the site of a group at a designated time).

open quadrant in the Johari Window, contains information that is generally known to self and others

open-ended groups that admit new members at any time

open-ended questions questions that invite more than a one- or two-word response

operations specific techniques employed by transactional analysis group leaders, such as interrogation, specification, confrontation, explanation, illustration, confirmation, interpretation, and crystallization

other-content-focused groups groups that mainly focus on other topics than diversity, for example, substance abuse, but at the same time pay attention to the diversity of their members as an important group issue

paradox asking members to do the opposite of what you want in the hope they will disobey

parallel thinking a thinking process where the focus is in specific directions

parent education groups primarily psychoeducational groups focusing on the raising of children. Rudolph Dreikurs began setting up these groups in the 1950s using Alfred Adler's theory and ideas.

Parent Effectiveness Training (PET) a Rogerian-based parent education program. In PET, there is an emphasis on communication skills, and parents are encouraged to recognize their positive and negative feelings toward their children

and come to terms with their own humanness. A major hypothesis of this approach is that *active listening* (i.e., hearing what is implied as well as what is actually said) and *acceptance* (acknowledging what is happening as opposed to evaluating it) will decrease family conflicts and promote individual growth.

Parent ego state (TA) dualistic in being both nurturing and critical (or controlling). The function of the *Critical Parent* is to store and dispense the rules and protection for living. The function of the *Nurturing Parent* is to care for (i.e., to nurture).

Parents Without Partners (PWP) a popular national organization whose groups for the divorced and widowed tend to be psychoeducational or self-help

PARS model (Processing: Activity, Relationship, Self) a model for examining processing in an individual, group, or family situation

pat on the back a closing exercise in which members draw the outline of their hand on a piece of white paper that is then taped on their back. Other group members then write closing comments that are positive and constructive about the person on the hand outline or on the paper itself.

peer group supervision see *peer supervision*

peer supervision practitioners meeting on a regular basis to consult with one another about particularly difficult group situations

permission (TA) centers on giving group members directives to behave against the injunctions of their Parents

person-centered group work see *basic encounter group*

personal growth Rogerian term; a global emphasis that stresses development as a result of experiences, such as travel or encounter

personal power a strategy often used in mature relationships. Personal power's source is from the individual and his or her ability to persuade others to follow a selected course of action.

personal responsibility an existentialist concept, being responsible for making meaning out of what one does or what occurs

personalization skills using one's own personal attributes, such as openness or humor, to full advantage in a group setting

phyloanalysis the biological principles of group behavior

physical structure the arrangement of group members in relationship to one another

polarities two interrelated, interdependent, opposite poles, such as career and family

polarization when a group becomes divided into different and opposing subgroups or camps

position power a strategy often used when there are immature relationships between individuals. Position power is derived from the status of people's titles, such as "group leader" or "group facilitator."

positive group variables a collection of favorable group factors, such as member commitment; readiness of members for the group experience; the attractiveness of the group for its members; a feeling of belonging, acceptance, and security; and clear communication

potency the use of appropriate counseling techniques in certain situations to bring about change

preadolescents children in the latency period with an age range from 9 to 13 years

premature termination when individuals quit a group abruptly or when the group experience ends suddenly because of actions by the leader. There are three types of premature termination: the termination of the group as a whole, the termination of a successful group member, and the termination of an unsuccessful group member.

preschool and early school-aged children ages 5 through 9

pretraining orienting members of a group on what to expect of the group before it meets

prevention groups groups set up to help avoid potential problems

primary affiliation groups groups to which people most identify as belonging, such as a family or peers

primary tension awkwardness about being in a strange situation

principle ethics ethics based on obligations. They focus on finding socially and historically acceptable answers to the question "What shall I do?" Codes of ethics are based on principle ethics (i.e., actions stemming from obligations).

principle of awareness Gestalt assumption that people are free to choose only when they are *self-aware*—that is, in touch with their existence and what it means to be alive; awareness includes all sensations, thoughts, and behaviors of the individual

principle of figure/ground Gestalt principle. The *figure* in one's personal life is composed of experiences that are most important; the *ground* (or background) is composed of experiences that are less pressing.

principle of holism Gestalt term for *integration*

principle of polarities Gestalt belief that if people are to meet their needs, then they must first differentiate their perceptual field into opposites/poles—for example, active/ passive, good/bad. People fail to resolve conflicts because they are not in contact with the opposite sides of the situation.

proactive taking the initiative in making choices

problem-centered groups small groups set up to focus on one particular concern (e.g., coping with stress)

process observer a professional human services person who is neutral in regard to the group agenda and personalities; as part of the procedure of group processing, observes and gives feedback to the group on what and how they are doing

process skills observable behaviors used to run groups, such as summarization, immediacy, and confrontation. By improving these skills, group leaders become more versatile in their interactions with group members and the group as a whole.

processing an activity that helps group members and the group identify, examine, and reflect on their behaviors and what occurred in a group in order to increase understanding, extract meaning, integrate knowledge, and improve their functioning and outcomes

professional liability insurance insurance designed specifically to protect a group worker from financial loss in case of a civil suit

professional skills actions such as behaving appropriately in a crisis, safeguarding confidentiality, and turning in reports connected with the group in a timely manner

projecting the future asking group members to imagine what changes they would like to make in the short term and long term

promoting hope one of the basic "therapeutic" factors described by Irving Yalom. If members believe that their situations can be different and better, then they are likely to work harder in the group.

promoting a positive interchange a condition that, when created, can help members become more honest with themselves and others and promote cohesion in the group

protagonist the person who is the subject of the psychodrama enactment; may play many parts

protection involves a group leader keeping members safe from psychological or physical harm

pseudo-acceptance false acceptance; harmony is stressed over everything; prevents anxiety but also progress in a group

psychic numbing members anesthetizing themselves to contradictions in the group

psychodrama an interpersonal group approach in which participants act out their emotions and attempt to clarify conflicts; a way of exploring the human psyche through dramatic action; created and developed by Jacob Moreno; psychodrama process generally goes through three phases: (a) warm-up (preaction), (b) action, and (c) integration

psychoeducational groups groups originally developed for use in educational settings. They are premised on the idea that education is about changing perceptions as well as acquiring knowledge.

Psycho-Spiritual Integrative Therapy (PSIT) an approach that defines spirituality as a subjective experience of the sacred however the individual apprehends it

publicizing a group the way a group is announced; an appropriate activity in the planning substage of forming

push button an Adlerian technique wherein individuals are helped to realize that they have choices in their lives regarding which stimuli they pay attention to and remember

questioning a query that is sometimes a disguise for a statement. If group members are constantly questioning one another, then they are safe from exposing their true selves. Questions keep the group focused on why something occurred and prevent members from concentrating on what is happening now.

quiet storming when group members avoid one another without voicing their frustrations during the storming stage of a group

rape survivors' group a group for victims of rape aimed at helping them decrease their sense of isolation and stigma while learning to model effective coping strategies

rating sheet an evaluation form members fill out and return before they terminate a group or a group session. Members can rate themselves, other members, and the leader on a number of dimensions, including involvement, risk taking, goals, emotional involvement, feedback, and productivity.

rational-emotive behavior therapy (REBT) based on the idea that it is one's thinking about events that produces feelings, not situations themselves. Individuals who have negative, faulty, or irrational thoughts become emotionally disturbed or upset and act in nonproductive ways, whereas those with more neutral or positive thoughts feel calmer and behave constructively.

reality-oriented groups set up for older individuals who have become disoriented to their surroundings. These groups, although educationally focused, are therapeutically based in that their emphasis is on helping group members become more attuned to where they are with respect to time, place, and people.

reality therapy founded by William Glasser, this theory emphasizes that all behavior is generated within ourselves for the purpose of satisfying one or more basic needs

reality therapy's original eight basic steps (a) Make friends; establish a meaningful relationship. (b) Emphasize present behaviors; ask, "What are you doing now?" (c) Stress whether clients' actions are getting them what they want. (d) Make a positive plan to do better. (e) Get a commitment to follow the positive plan. (f) No excuses. (g) No punishment. (h) Never give up.

reality therapy's four human psychological needs belonging, power, freedom, and fun; one physiological need: survival

REBT viewpoint involves convincing group that the premises on which REBT is based are valid and applicable to their situations

recycling when individuals who have not benefited from a group experience go through a similar group to learn lessons missed the first time

redecision school of TA emphasis is on intrapsychic processes; groups provide a living experience in which members are able to examine themselves and their histories in a precise way. Individuals can then change their life scripts.

redecision theory a special form of transactional analysis; helps clients make redecisions while they are in their Child ego state. This task is accomplished by having these individuals reexperience a past event as if it were now present.

referrals transfers of members to another group; made when group leaders realize they cannot help certain members achieve designated goals or when there is an unresolvable conflict between leaders and members. The group leader should make appropriate referrals, because he or she cannot be all things to all people. The referral process itself involves four steps: (a) identifying the need to refer, (b) evaluating potential referral sources, (c) preparing the client for the referral, and (d) coordinating the transfer.

reframing conceptualizing potentially negative actions in a positive way

rehearsal (a) when members show others in the group how they plan to act in particular situations; (b) in Gestalt groups, when members are invited to say out loud what they are thinking

relationship groups groups that focus on helping women break out of the dependency and caretaking roles they often find themselves in and connecting with themselves and others in a healthy, growth-producing way. In such groups, the emphasis is on being-in-relation, where one's own needs as well as others' needs are met. The groups are short term (6 weeks) and goal oriented.

reminiscing and life review groups originated in the 1960s; based on the importance of "life review." They help individuals who are not yet at the older life stage to comprehend and appreciate more fully who they are and where they have been. Persons in these groups share memories, increase personal integration, and become more aware of their lives and the lives of those their age. Insight gained from this process helps these persons realize more deeply their finiteness and thus prepare for death.

remotivation therapy groups groups aimed at helping older clients become more invested in the present and future. Their membership is composed of individuals who have "lost interest" in any time frame of life except the past.

reorientation in Adlerian groups, when members are encouraged to act differently and take more control of their lives. Such a procedure means taking risks, acting "as if" they were the person they wished to be, and "catching themselves" in old, ineffective patterns and correcting them.

resistance any behavior that moves the group away from areas of discomfort or conflict and prevents it from developing; works in overt and covert ways (e.g., rebellion by group members against the leader; getting bogged down in details; becoming preoccupied with the unimportant)

reviewing and summarizing the group experience a procedure during termination in which group members recall and share special moments they remember from the group

Road Scholar a nonprofit program in which older individuals live and study together for a selected period

Rogerian-oriented encounter group 15-stage process (1) milling around; (2) resistance; (3) revealing past feelings; (4) expression of negative feelings; (5) expression of personally meaningful material; (6) communication of immediate interpersonal feelings; (7) development of a healing capacity in the group; (8) self-acceptance and the beginning of change; (9) cracking of facades; (10) feedback; (11) confrontation; (12) helping relationships outside the group; (13) the basic encounter; (14) expressions of closeness; (15) behavior changes

role a dynamic structure within an individual (based on needs, cognitions, and values) that usually comes to life under the influence of social stimuli or defined positions. The manifestation of a role is based on the individual's expectation of self and others and the interactions one has in particular groups and situations.

role collision when there is a conflict between the role an individual plays in the outside world (e.g., being a passive observer) and the role expected within the group (e.g., being an active participant)

role confusion occurs when a group member (or members) simply does not know what role to perform. This often happens in leaderless groups where members do not know if

they are to be assertive in helping establish an agenda or to be passive and just let the leadership emerge.

role incompatibility when a person is given a role within the group (e.g., being the leader) that he or she neither wants nor is comfortable exercising

role playing assuming an identity that differs from one's present behavior. Role playing is a tool for bringing a specific skill and its consequences into focus. It is vital for experiential learning in the group.

role reversal a psychodrama technique in which the protagonist literally switches roles with another person on stage and plays that person's part; group members act the opposite of what they feel

role transition when a person is expected to assume a different role as the group progresses but does not feel comfortable doing so

rounds also known as *go-rounds*; the process of giving members of a group an equal chance to participate in the group by going around the circle in which they are sitting and asking each person to make a comment on a subject that is presently before the group

row formation a group in which attention is focused toward the front. This arrangement is good for making a presentation, but it limits, and even inhibits, group interaction.

rules the guidelines by which groups are run

sarcasm masked feelings disguised through the use of clever language, such as biting humor

saving face the cultural value, often found in Asian and Asian-American cultures, of not embarrassing oneself or disgracing one's family

saying good-bye the final words members exchange with others at the end of a group that wraps it up, at least on an effective/cognitive level. Members are encouraged to own their feelings and express their thoughts at this time, especially in regard to what others in the group have meant to them.

SCAMPER model an atheoretical mnemonic word originated by Robert Eberle where each letter in the word stands for a different way of acting and thus being potentially creative in a group—substitute, combine, adapt/adopt, modify, put to other uses, eliminate, reverse/rearrange

scapegoat to blame others for one's own problems

screened when potential group members are interviewed before the group in regard to their suitability for the group

screening a three-part process that begins when group leaders formulate the type of group they would like to lead. Next is the process of *recruitment*, in which the leader must make sure not to misrepresent the type of group that is to be conducted and to publicize it properly. Finally, there is the task of interviewing applicants by the leader to determine whether they will benefit from and contribute to the group.

scripts (TA) patterns of behavior that influence how people spend their time. Most people initially script their lives as a Child in the *I'm Not OK—You're OK* stance (powerless) but change to an Adult stance in later life as they affirm an *I'm OK—You're OK* position (characterized by trust and openness). Other options open to them are *I'm OK—You're Not OK* (projection of blame onto others) and *I'm Not OK—You're Not OK* (hopeless and self-destructive).

sculpting an exercise in which group members use nonverbal methods to arrange others in the group into a configuration like that of significant persons with whom they regularly deal, such as family members, office personnel, or social peers. The positioning involves body posturing and assists group members in seeing and experiencing their perceptions of significant others in a more dynamic way.

search for meaning the search to find significance in one's life, even in the mundane events

secondary affiliation groups groups with which people least identify

secondary tension intragroup conflict

self-actualization realistically living up to one's potential; being the best one can be

self-awareness a state of being in touch with one's existence and what it means to be alive; includes all sensations, thoughts, and behaviors of an individual

self-disclosure revealing to the group personal information of which the group was previously unaware. It involves listening and receiving feedback as well as speaking. One of the strongest signs of trust in a group is self-disclosure.

self-efficacy a person's judgment of his or her capacity to organize and execute a course of action required to attain a designated type of performance

self-help groups groups that usually do not include professional leaders but are led by paraprofessionals or group members. Examples of such groups are Alcoholics Anonymous (AA) and Compassionate Friends.

self-report research format research method used by Rogers and nonbehaviorists in which participants write out or check off how they have changed as a result of the group experience

self-talk the messages people give themselves internally

semicircle arrangement a half-circle group structure in which members can see one another; discussion is likely to involve almost everyone. However, if the group is too large (e.g., more than 20), persons may not feel that they are a group.

sensitivity groups (see *basic encounter group*)

setting up the environment establishing an atmosphere in which work within the group can take place

settling-down period a time when members test one another and the group collectively before the group unifies

shame attack an REBT technique in which a person actually does what he or she dreaded and finds the world does not fall apart regardless of the outcome

shared a form of group co-leadership in which each leader takes charge of the group momentarily as he or she sees fit

silent members group members who are reticent to speak in the group owing to anger, nonassertiveness, reflection, shyness, or slowness in the assessment of their thoughts and feelings

situation a psychodrama technique in which an emphasis is placed on the present; natural barriers of time, space, and states of existence are obliterated

six hats approach to creativity an approach to creative thinking originated by Edward DeBono where a group uses lateral thinking to get all members to focus in the same direction when considering an option. The six hats and their corresponding foci are: blue (organization), red (emotion), white (facts), yellow (advantages/optimism), black (drawback), and green (growth).

Skilled Group Counseling Scale 18 skills organized into three stages: (a) counseling and exploration, (b) understanding, and (c) action

Skilled Group Counseling Training Model a model for helping beginning group workers learn and transfer group counseling skills to actual group counseling sessions

social group work organizing individuals into purposeful and enriching groups; first begun by Jane Addams at Hull House in Chicago for immigrants and the poor

social influence how interaction in groups exerts an influence on actions, attitudes, and feelings of people

social interest an Adlerian term defined as not only an interest in others but also an interest in the interests of others

social justice using all the methods of counseling and psychology available to confront injustice and inequality in society. Social justice emphasizes empowerment, self-determination, advocacy, and change.

sociogram a tool of sociometry that plots out group interactions

sociometry a phenomenological methodology for investigating interpersonal relationships

soliloquy a psychodrama technique that involves the protagonist (i.e., the client) giving a monologue about his or her situation as he or she is acting it out. A variation on this activity is the therapeutic soliloquy technique, in which private reactions to events in the protagonist's life are verbalized and acted out, usually by other actors (i.e., auxiliary egos).

solution-focused debriefing (SFD) groups groups that help victims of violence deal with its repercussions, such as feelings of helplessness, anxiety, depression, and disorganization, spanning seven stages in 3 weeks for enhanced recovery. These groups emphasize a specific distressing incident, focus on the here and now, and include only persons who have witnessed the same violent episode.

sophistry a cognitive, psychotherapeutic group technique for assessing offenders' (and involuntary clients') "private logic" (i.e., way of thinking) and helping them change. This method helps counselors get beyond offenders' resistance. It employs paradox (i.e., telling resistant clients not to change), use of hidden reasons in a group debate, and a reorientation phase to get offenders to examine their thinking.

spaghetti thinking thinking in a group where one person is thinking about the benefits of an idea while another considers the facts. The strands of spaghetti may touch on the same subject, but they do not connect.

specialty groups groups that focus on one particular population or problem, such as military veterans, new mothers, addiction, or unemployment

specialty/standards model an approach to conceptualizing groups in which they are defined according to their purpose, focus, and needed competencies. The ASGW has defined standards for four types of groups: psychoeducational, counseling, psychotherapy, and task/work.

spillover effect the impact for others who are helping or watching a main character in a psychodrama reach resolution on important issues; they see themselves as interacting in a new and better way.

spontaneity in psychodrama, the response people make that contains some degree of adequacy to a new situation or a degree of novelty to an old situation. The purpose of spontaneity is to liberate one's self from scripts and stereotypes and gain new perspectives on life.

stage in psychodrama, the area in which the action takes place

storming a time of conflict and anxiety in a group when it moves from primary tension (awkwardness about being in a strange situation) to secondary tension (intragroup conflict). It is a period when group members and leaders struggle with issues related to structure, direction, control, catharsis, and interpersonal relationships.

strokes (TA) physical, verbal, psychological, or nonverbal recognition

structured activities (see *exercises*)

structuring the group running the group according to a preset prescribed plan or agenda

study groups types of task groups, typically involving three to four students who meet at least weekly to share information, knowledge, and expertise about a course in which they all are enrolled. The idea is that each group member will support and encourage the others and will obtain insight and knowledge through the group effort.

style of life Adlerian term; the way one prefers to live and relate to others. Adlerians stress that a faulty lifestyle is based on competitiveness and striving to be superior to others.

subgrouping occurs when a large group breaks down into several smaller groups, each with its own identity and each existing as part of the larger group. Groups do not function well as a whole when subgrouping develops.

subgroups cliques of group members who band together, often to the detriment of the group as a whole

Succeeding in School lessons a series of 10 lessons created by Gerler and Anderson (in 1986) that deal with modeling after successful people in school while learning to feel comfortable and responsible. Succeeding focuses on promoting cooperative efforts; enhancing student self-concept; and learning appropriate school skills, such as listening and asking for help.

summarizing reflections by group members that recall significant events or learning experiences in the group

support groups types of self-help groups in which members share a common concern and have a professional group leader

supporting the act of encouraging and reinforcing others. Its aim is to convey to persons that they are perceived as adequate, capable, and trustworthy. Through the act of supporting, group members feel affirmed and are able to risk new behaviors because they sense a backing from the group.

surplus reality psychological experience that transcends the boundaries of physical reality. These experiences, which include relationships with those who have died or were never born, or with God, are often as important to people as their actual experiences with physical entities; a psychodrama concept.

sweat lodge ceremony a type of Native American group ceremony and ritual that leads to explanation, transition, purification, and emergence

SYMLOG System for the Multiple Level Observation of Groups

synchronous a type of online group; members must be online and logged in to the site of a group at a designated time to receive messages

synectics from the Greek; means the joining together of different and apparently irrelevant elements. Synectics theory applies to the integration of diverse individuals into a problem-stating, problem-solving group.

system a set of elements standing in interaction

systematic group leadership training involves the teaching of basic skills to beginning group leaders. It is a six-step method that includes the video recording of trainees leading a group before being introduced to the skill they are to learn (steps 1 and 2). Then the trainees read about and see a new skill demonstrated (steps 3 and 4). Finally, trainees critique their original videos and then make new videos demonstrating the skill they have just been taught (steps 5 and 6).

Systematic Training for Effective Parenting (S.T.E.P.) an Adlerian-based parent education program

systemically in a circular manner

systems theory a theory that focuses on the interconnectedness of elements. From this perspective, a group as an organism is composed of other organisms, commonly called members and a leader, who over time relate to each other face to face, processing matter, energy, and information (see *general systems theory*).

talking circle a sweat lodge ceremony tradition in which participants express their thoughts and feelings in both prayer and conversation with themselves and others

task processing ways of accomplishing specific goals in a group

task setting an Adlerian therapeutic technique wherein individuals set short-range, attainable goals and eventually work up to long-term, realistic objectives

task/work groups groups whose emphasis is on accomplishment and efficiency in completing identified work goals. They are united in their emphasis on achieving a successful performance or a finished product through collaborative efforts. Task/work groups take the form of task forces, committees, planning groups, community organizations, discussion groups, and learning groups.

Tavistock Institute of Human Relations a group research facility in Great Britain

teachable moment a time when people are ready and able to learn

team a number of persons associated together in work or activity, such as in athletic or artistic competition, in which members of a group act and perform in a coordinated way to achieve a goal. Teams differ from basic groups in four main ways: (a) They have shared goals, as opposed to individual goals in most groups. (b) They stress an interdependency in working more than do groups. (c) They require more of a commitment by members to a team effort. (d) They are by design accountable to a higher level within the organization than are groups.

team building effective development of a team through managing conflict, promoting interpersonal relationships, and achieving consensus

Team Player Inventory (TPI) a 10-item assessment instrument that denotes the degree to which individuals are predisposed toward organizational team-working environments

teamwork all members of a group working together cooperatively

tele the total communication of feelings among people; involves complete interpersonal and reciprocal empathy; a psychodrama concept

telecounseling a method for offering counseling and support groups using the telephone

telephone groups groups set up where members meet over the telephone because of an inability to meet in person or a preference not to do so. These groups provide information, support, and coping skills suggestions to their members.

Theater of Spontaneity a forerunner of psychodrama formulated by Jacob L. Moreno in 1921

theater style a type of group structure in which members are seated in lines and rows

theme group a group that focuses on a particular problem or theme

themes specific topics or subjects related to the genuine interests of the participants, thereby holding their interest and inviting their participation. Many adolescent groups work best when they are structured around themes.

theory a way of organizing what is known about some phenomenon to generate a set of interrelated, plausible, and, above all, refutable propositions about what is unknown. A theory guides empirical inquiry and is useful in testing hypotheses.

Theory X leader an autocratic and coercive leader who basically believes people are unambitious and somewhat lazy

Theory Y leader a nondirective and democratic leader who thinks that people are self-starters and will work hard if given freedom

Theory Z leader a facilitative leader who helps encourage group members to participate in the group and trust that individual and collective goals will be accomplished through the process of interaction

therapeutic contracts in transactional analysis groups, specific, measurable, concrete statements of what participants intend to accomplish during the group. They place responsibility on members for clearly defining what, how, and when they want to change. TA contracts have the four major components of a legal contract: (a) *mutual assent*—clearly defining a goal from an adult perspective and joining with the therapist's Adult as an ally; (b) *competency*—agreeing to what can realistically be expected; (c) *legal object*—an objective; and (d) *consideration*—a fee or price for services.

therapeutic enactment an action oriented technique where individuals are asked to enact critical stage events in their lives that are unresolved, limited, or blocked. The experience may be on several levels: emotional, cognitive, physical, or behavioral. The result is a deeper level of learning and changes within the self.

therapeutic fairy tale a projective group activity meant to help persons focus on the future and renew their effort in the group. In this process, individuals are asked to write a fairy tale in a 6- to 10-minute time frame. They are to begin their story with "Once upon a time," and in it they are to include (a) a problem or predicament; (b) a solution, even if it appears outlandish; and (c) a positive, pleasing ending. The tale is then discussed in regard to personal and group goals.

time limit for the group the number of times that the group will meet, usually announced in advance

timely teaching when a particular event stimulates thinking and discussion among students

top dog/underdog dialogue Gestalt method in which group members are asked to examine the *top-dog introjections* they have taken in from parents (usually represented by *shoulds* and *you*) and their own real feelings about situations (usually represented by "I" statements). They then are asked to carry on a dialogue between these two aspects of themselves before the group or with another group member and try to become more aware of their true self-identity and ways to act that would be appropriate.

topic- and theme-focused group a psychoeducational group centered around a particular topic, such as widowhood, bibliotherapy, sexuality, health, or the arts. Such a group is designed ultimately to improve the quality of daily living for older people. It may also assist the aged to find more meaning in their lives and to establish a support group of like-minded people.

total quality group implemented by the Japanese under the direction of task/work group master W. Edwards Deming; focus on problem solving related to consumer satisfaction and quality issues in business

total quality movement (TQM) in task/work environments, an emphasis on working cooperatively and productively in small groups

toxic effect (of counseling) a term used to describe the cumulative effect of working with people in pain. Specifically, it refers to the physical and psychic isolation, repeated feelings of loss in regard to client termination, and interpersonal distancing from family and friends who may perceive counselors as interpreting their words and actions

TRAC model of groups a model of groups known by the acronym TRAC (tasking, relating, acquiring, and contacting). Each letter represents an area in the total picture of group work. *Tasking* groups are focused on task achievement. *Relating* groups achieve objectives to increase the options for movement within the life of each person. *Acquiring* groups are directed toward learning outcomes that members can apply to others. In contrast, *contacting* groups are focused on the individual growth of members.

traditional leader a person who is controlling and exercises power from the top down as an expert; may be appropriate in running a hierarchical group that is diverse and whose members are physically separated

traffic director when the group leader helps members become aware of behaviors that open communication channels and those that inhibit communication

training group a group for beginning leaders designed to help them recognize and work out major personal and professional issues that affect their ability to conduct groups (e.g., criticism, anxiety, jealousy, need for control)

training group (T-group) approach to groups developed at the National Training Laboratories in the 1940s; primary attention to theory, group dynamics, and social material involving groups

trait approach the idea that some persons emerge as leaders because of their personal qualities

transactional analysis (TA) TA involves the diagnosing of interactions among group members to determine if they are *complementary* (from appropriate and expected ego states), *crossed* (from inappropriate and unexpected ego states), or *ulterior* (from a disguised ego state)

transactions social actions between two or more people, manifested in social (overt) and psychological (covert) levels

transference the displacement of affect from one person to another; the projection of inappropriate emotions onto the leader or group members

transformational leader a person who empowers group members and shares power with them in working toward the renewal of a group; may be needed when a group is floundering

transient children children who have moved to a new community and a new school

transition period the time after the forming process and the working stage; it includes the storming and before norming stages

trilevel model of Gestalt group work attention is systematically focused on (a) the individual at the intrapersonal level, (b) two or more people at the interpersonal level, and (c) the group as a systematic unit

unfinished business emotional debris from a person's past

unintentional civil liability a lack of intent to cause injury

universality a sense of commonness that group members feel in regard to their experiences when compared with others

universalization one's realization that others may have the same concerns

unknown quadrant in the Johari Window, contains material hidden from self and others because of lack of opportunity

unstructured group used in experientially based situations and employed where process rather than product is emphasized

users of sarcasm persons who mask their feelings through the use of clever language that has a biting humor

veracity truthfulness. In group work, veracity is important in almost all phases of the group's development. Group members and leaders who are not truthful with themselves or others set up situations in which a good working relationship is impossible to achieve.

verbal behavior when group members speak to one another. The content of speech between people along with its tone and emphases.

virtue ethics focus on the character traits of the counselor (or group worker) and nonobligatory ideals to which professionals aspire rather than on solving specific ethical dilemmas

vision quest a Native American ritual in which young men coming of age retreat to a secluded spot in nature and sit in a sacred circle where, self-deprived of food, sleep, and shelter for a number of days, they seek auditory or visual messages about themselves, others, and the earth. They share these visions once they return to society.

"W" (work group) (see *task/work groups*)

warm-up phase in psychodrama, characterized by the director making sure he or she is ready to lead the group and that group members are ready to be led

we/they mentality when practitioners of other points of view are seen as "uninformed," "naive," or "heretical"

wheel in this group arrangement, there is a center spoke, a leader, through which all messages go. Members have the advantage of face-to-face interaction with the leader, but they may become frustrated by the inability to communicate with another group member directly.

White privilege the positive ways Whites have benefited from racism such as disproportionate access to social and economic resources

wisdom one of Erikson's virtues; the ability to make effective choices among alternatives

working (performing, action) stage most unified and productive group stage that focuses on the achievement of individual and group goals and the movement of the group itself as a system

written projections a process whereby members are asked to see themselves or their groups in the future as having been successful and to describe what the experience is like. They are able to play with their fantasies at times as well as be realistic.

Y this group arrangement combines the structural elements of the wheel and the chain—there is a perceived leader. The efficiency of the unit is second only to that of the wheel in performance. Like a chain, the Y may frustrate group members who wish to have direct contact and communication with one another. Information is not equally shared or distributed.

yearbook feedback saying nice but insignificant things about a person, as high school students do when they write in annuals

young adulthood ages 20 to 40 years, in which identity and intimacy are two intense primary issues

young-old individuals between ages 65 and 75

REFERENCES

Abraham, L. (2010). *The husbands and wives club: A year in the life of a couples therapy group.* Austin, TX: Touchstone.

Abudabbeh, N., & Aseel, H. A. (1999). Transcultural counseling and Arab Americans. In J. McFadden (Ed.), *Transcultural counseling* (2nd ed., pp. 283–296). Alexandria, VA: American Counseling Association.

Addington, J. (1992). Separation group. *Journal for Specialists in Group Work, 17,* 20–28.

Adler, A. (1956). *The individual psychology of Alfred Adler.* New York, NY: Basic Books.

Agazarian, Y. M. (1997). *Systems-centered therapy for groups.* New York, NY: Guilford.

Akinsulure-Smith, A. M. (2009). Brief psychoeducational group treatment with re-traumatized refugees and asylum seekers. *Journal for Specialists in Group Work, 34,* 137–150.

Akinsulure-Smith, A. M. (2012). Using group work to rebuild family and community ties among displaced African men. *Journal for Specialists in Group Work, 37,* 95–112.

Akos, P. (2000). Building empathic skills in elementary school children through group work. *Journal for Specialists in Group Work, 25,* 214–223.

Akos, P. (2004). Investing in experiential training appropriate for preservice school counselors. *Journal for Specialists in Group Work, 29,* 327–342.

Akos, P., Hamm, J. V., Mack, S. G., & Dunaway, M. (2007). Utilizing the developmental influences of peers in middle school groups. *Journal for Specialists in Group Work, 32,* 51–60.

Akos, P., & Martin, M. (2003). Transition groups for preparing students for middle school. *Journal for Specialists in Group Work, 28,* 139–154.

Akos, P., & Milsom, A. (2007). Introduction to special issue: Group work in K-12 schools. *Journal for Specialists in Group Work, 32,* 5–7.

Alexander, V. (1999). Ethics-based decision-making: A psychoeducational workshop for adult diversion programs. *Journal for Specialists in Group Work, 24,* 208–219.

Allan, J., & Bardsley, P. (1983). Transient children in the elementary school: A group counseling approach. *Elementary School Guidance & Counseling, 17,* 162–169.

Allport, G. W. (1955). *Becoming: Basic considerations for a psychology of personality.* New Haven, CT: Yale University Press.

Altarriba, J., & Bauer, L. M. (1998). Counseling the Hispanic client: Cuban Americans, Mexican Americans, and Puerto Ricans. *Journal of Counseling & Development, 76,* 389–396.

Altholz, J. A. S. (1978). Group psychotherapy with the elderly. In I. M. Burnside (Ed.), *Working with the elderly: Group process and techniques* (pp. 354–370). North Scituate, MA: Duxbury.

Amatruda, M-J. (2006). Conflict resolution and social skill development with children. *Journal of Group Psychotherapy, Psychodrama & Sociometry, 58,* 168–181.

American Counseling Association. (2014). *Code of ethics and standards of practice.* Alexandria, VA: Author.

Anderson, D. (2007). Multicultural group work: A force for developing and healing. *Journal for Specialists in Group Work, 32,* 224–244.

Anderson, K. J. (1995). The use of a structured career development group to increase career identity: An exploratory study. *Journal of Career Development, 21,* 279–291.

Anderson, M., Goodman, J., & Schlossberg, N. K. (2012). *Counseling adults in transition: Linking Schlossberg's theory with practice in a diverse well* (4th ed.). New York, NY: Springer.

Anderson, W. (1982). A training module for preparing group facilitators. *Journal for Specialists in Group Work, 7,* 119–124.

Andrews, H. B. (1995). *Group design and leadership: Strategies for creating successful common-theme groups.* Needham Heights, MA: Allyn & Bacon.

Andronico, M. P., & Horne, A. M. (2004). Counseling men in groups: The role of myths, therapeutic factors, leadership, and rituals. In J. L. DeLucia-Waack, D. A. Gerrity, C. R. Kalodner, & M. T. Riva (Eds.), *Handbook of group counseling and psychotherapy* (pp. 456–468). Thousand Oaks, CA: Sage.

Ansbacher, H. L. (1977). Individual psychology. In R. J. Corsini (Ed.), *Current personality theories.* Itasca, IL: Peacock.

Aponte, H. J. (1994). How personal can training get? *Journal of Marital and Family Therapy, 20,* 3–15.

Appleton, V. E., & Dykeman, C. (1996). Using art in group counseling with Native American youth. *Journal for Specialists in Group Work, 21,* 224–231.

Armstrong, S. A., & Berg, R. C. (2005). Demonstrating group process using *12 Angry Men. Journal for Specialists in Group Work, 30,* 135–140.

Arp, R. S., Holmberg, K. S., & Littrell, J. M. (1986). Launching adult students into the job market: A support group approach. *Journal of Counseling and Development, 65,* 166–167.

Arredondo, P., Gallardo-Cooper, M., Delgado-Romero, E. A., & Zapata, A. L. (2014). *Culturally responsive counseling with Latinas/os.* Alexandria, VA: American Counseling Association.

Asch, S. E. (1951). Effects of group pressure upon the modification and distortion of judgment. In H. Guetzkow (Ed.), *Groups, leadership, and men* (pp. 177–190). Pittsburgh: Carnegie.

Ashida, S. (2000). The effect of reminiscence music therapy sessions on changes in depressive symptoms in elderly persons with dementia. *Journal of Music Therapy, 37,* 170–182.

Association for Specialists in Group Work. (1991). *Ethical guidelines for group counselors and professional standards for the training of group workers.* Alexandria, VA: Author.

Association for Specialists in Group Work. (2000). Professional standards for the training of group workers. *Journal for Specialists in Group Work, 25,* 327–342.

Association for Specialists in Group Work. (2007). Best practice guidelines. *Journal for Specialists in Group Work, 33,* 111–117.

Association for Specialists in Group Work. (2012). *Multicultural and Social Justice Competence Principles for Group Workers.* Retrieved from http://asgw.org/pdf/ASGW_MC_SI_Principles_Final_ASGW.pdf

Atkinson, D. R. (2004). *Counseling American minorities: A cross cultural perspective* (6th ed.). New York, NY: McGraw-Hill.

Avrahami, E. (1995). Elements of relinquishment in psychodrama: Choice-relinquishing junctions in the psychodramatic process of the protagonist. *Journal of Group Psychotherapy, Psychodrama and Sociometry, 48,* 96–112.

Aylmer, R. C. (1988). The launching of the single young adult. In B. Carter & M. McGoldrick (Eds.), *The changing family life cycle* (2nd ed., pp. 191–208). New York, NY: Gardner.

Azar, B. (1997, July). Teambuilding isn't enough: Workers need training, too. *APA Monitor, 28*(7), 14–15.

Baca, L. M., & Koss-Chioino, J. D. (1997). Development of a culturally responsive group counseling model for Mexican American adolescents. *Journal of Multicultural Counseling and Development, 25,* 130–141.

Bach, G. R. (1954). *Intensive group psychotherapy.* New York, NY: Ronald.

Bailey, D. F., & Bradbury-Bailey, M. E. (2007). Promoting achievement for African American males through group work. *Journal for Specialists in Group Work, 32,* 83–96.

Baker, J., Parks-Savage, A., & Rehfuss, M. (2009). Teaching social skills in a virtual environment: An exploratory study.

Journal for Specialists in Group Work, 34, 209–226.

Bales, R. F. (1951). *Interaction process analysis.* Reading, MA: Addison-Wesley.

Bales, R. F. (1980). *SYMLOG: A case study kit.* New York, NY: Free Press.

Bales, R. F., Cohen, S. P., & Williamson, S. A. (1979). *SYMLOG: A system for the multiple level observation of groups.* New York, NY: Free Press.

Baltes, P. B., & Baltes, M. M. (Eds.). (1990). *Successful aging: Perspectives from the behavioral sciences.* New York, NY: Cambridge University Press.

Baltimore, M. L. (1997). Multifamily group psychotherapy: Implementation and process. In S. T. Gladding (Ed.), *New developments in group counseling* (pp. 55–57). Greensboro, NC: ERIC.

Bandura, A. (1986). *Social foundations of thought and action: A social cognitive theory.* Upper Saddle River, NJ: Prentice Hall.

Barker, R. A. (1997). How can we train leaders if we do not know what leadership is? *Human Relations, 50,* 343–362.

Barnes, G. (1977). Introduction. In G. Barnes (Ed.), *Transactional analysis after Eric Berne* (pp. 1–31). New York, NY: Harper & Row.

Baron, R. A. (1974). The aggression-inhibiting influence of nonhostile humor. *Journal of Experimental Social Psychology, 10,* 23–33.

Barr, V., Rando, R. A., Krylowicz, B., & Reetz, D. (2011). *The Association for University and College Counseling Center director's annual survey monograph.* Denver, CO: AUCCCD.

Bartels, S. J., & Naslund, J. A. (2013). The underside of the silver tsunami—older adults and mental health care. *New England Journal of Medicine, 368,* 493–496.

Baruth, L. G., & Manning, M. L. (2012). *Multicultural counseling and psychotherapy: A lifetime perspective* (5th ed.). Upper Saddle River, NJ: Prentice Hall.

Bass, B. M. (1995). The meaning of leadership. In J. T. Wren (Ed.), *The leader's*

companion (pp. 37–38). New York, NY: Free Press.

Bass, E., & Davis, L. (2008). *The courage to heal.* New York, NY: HarperCollins.

Bata, E. J. (2006). Men, aging, and environmental trends. *The Advocate, 29*(1), 1, 10–11.

Bates, B., & Goodman, A. (1986). The effectiveness of encounter groups: Implications of research for counselling practice. *British Journal of Guidance and Counseling, 14,* 240–251.

Bates, M., Johnson, C. D., & Blaker, K. E. (1982). *Group leadership: A manual for group counseling leaders* (2nd ed.). Denver, CO: Love.

Bauman, S. (2009). Group work in the economic downturn. *Journal for Specialists in Group Work, 34,* 97–100.

Bauman, S., & Waldo, M. (1998). Improving the goals and process (GAP) matrix for groups: Incorporating feedback from the field. *Journal for Specialists in Group Work, 23,* 215–224.

Bayne, H. B. (2011). Training medical students in empathic communication. *Journal for Specialists in Group Work, 36,* 316–329.

Beale, A. V., & Scott, P. C. (2001). "Bullybuster": Using drama to empower students to take a stand against bullying behavior. *Professional School Counseling, 4,* 300–305.

Beaver, M. L. (1983). *Human service practice with the elderly.* Upper Saddle River, NJ: Prentice Hall.

Bebout, J. (1978). Basic encounter groups: Their nature, method, and brief history. In H. Mullan & M. Rosenbaum (Eds.), *Group psychotherapy: Theory and practice* (2nd ed., pp. 305–329). New York, NY: Free Press.

Becvar, D. S. (1982). The family is not a group—Or is it? *Journal for Specialists in Group Work, 7,* 88–95.

Bednar, R. L., & Kaul, T. J. (1985). Experiential group research: Results, questions, and suggestions. In S. L. Garfield & A. Bergin (Eds.), *Handbook for psychotherapy and behavior change* (3rd ed.). New York, NY: Wiley.

Bednar, R. L., & Lawlis, G. F. (1971). Empirical research in group psychotherapy. In S. L. Garfield & A. Bergin (Eds.), *Handbook of psychotherapy and behavior change* (pp. 812–838). New York, NY: Wiley.

Beitin, B. K., & Allen, K. R. (2005). Resilience in Arab American couples after September 11, 2001: A systems perspective. *Journal of Marital and Family Therapy, 31,* 251–267.

Bemak, F., & Chung, R. C-Y. (2004). Teaching multicultural group counseling: Perspectives for a new era. *Journal for Specialists in Group Work, 29,* 31–41.

Bemak, F., & Chung, R. C-Y. (2011). Post-disaster social justice group work and group supervision. *Journal for Specialists in Group Work, 36,* 3–21.

Bemak, F., & Chung, R. C-Y. (2014). Post-disaster group counseling. In J. L. DeLucia-Waack, C. R. Kalodner, & M. T. Riva (Eds.), *Handbook of group counseling and therapy* (2nd ed., pp. 571–584). Thousand Oaks, CA: Sage.

Bemak, F., & Epp, L. R. (1996). The 12th curative factor: Love as an agent of healing in group psychotherapy. *Journal for Specialists in Group Work, 21,* 118–127.

Bender, J. L., Jimenez-Marroquin, M-C., & Jadad, A. R. (2011). Seeking support on Facebook: A content analysis of breast cancer groups. *Journal of Medical Internet Research, 13,* 16.

Benson, J. (2010). *Working more creativity with groups* (3rd ed.). New York, NY: Routledge.

Berg, R. C., Landreth, G. L., & Falls, K. A. (2013). *Group counseling: Concepts and procedures* (5th ed.). New York, NY: Routledge.

Bernard, H., Burlingame, G., Flores, P., Greene, L., Joyce, A., Kobos, J. C., Leszcz, M., MacNair-Semands, R. R., Piper, W. E., Slocum McEneaney, A. M., & Feirman, D. (2008). Science to Service Task Force, American Group Psychotherapy Association. Clinical practice guidelines for group psychotherapy. *International Journal of Group Psychotherapy, 54,* 455–542.

Bernard, J. (1979). Supervisor training: A discrimination model. *Counselor Education and Supervision, 19,* 60–68.

Bernard, J., & Goodyear, R. (2013). *Fundamentals of clinical supervision* (5th ed.). Upper Saddle River, NJ: Pearson.

Berne, E. (1961). *Transactional analysis in psychotherapy.* New York, NY: Grove.

Berne, E. (1964). *Games people play: The psychology of human relationships.* New York, NY: Grove.

Berne, E. (1966). *Principles of group treatment.* New York, NY: Grove.

Berne, E. (1972). *What do you say after you say hello?* New York, NY: Grove.

Bersoff, D. N. (1996). The virtue of principle ethics. *The Counseling Psychologist, 24,* 86–91.

Bertalanffy, L. von (1968). *General systems theory: Foundations, development, application.* New York, NY: Braziller.

Berube, L. (1999). Dream work: Demystifying dreams using a small group for personal growth. *Journal for Specialists in Group Work, 24,* 88–101.

Bieling, P. J., Milosevic, I., & McCabe, R. E. (2014). Groups for depression. In J. L. DeLucia, C. R. Kalodner, & M. T. Riva (Eds.), *Handbook of group counseling and psychotherapy* (2nd ed., pp. 367–380). Thousand Oaks, CA: Sage.

Bieschke, K. J., Gehlert, K. M., Wilson, D., Matthews, C. R., & Wade, J. (2003). Qualitative analysis of multicultural awareness in training groups. *Journal for Specialists in Group Work, 28,* 325–338.

Bion, W. R. (1959). *Experiences in groups.* New York, NY: Basic Books.

Bisio, T. A., & Crisan, P. (1984). Stress management and nuclear anxiety: A structured group experience. *Journal of Counseling and Development, 63,* 108–109.

Black, C. (1981). *It will never happen to me.* Denver, CO: M.A.C.

Blajan-Marcus, S. (1974). Psychodrama and its diverse uses. In I. A. Greenberg (Ed.), *Psychodrama: Theory and therapy* (pp. 47–55). New York, NY: Behavioral Publications.

Blatner, A. (1988). *Acting in: Practical applications of psychodramatic methods* (2nd ed.). New York, NY: Springer.

Blatner, A. (1996). *Acting in: Practical applications of psychodramatic methods* (3rd ed.). New York, NY: Springer.

Blatner, A. (2000). *Foundations of psychodrama: History, theory, and practice* (4th ed.). New York, NY: Springer.

Blatner, A. (2005). Psychodrama. In R. J. Corsini & D. Wedding (Eds.), *Current psychotherapies* (7th ed., pp. 405–438). Belmont, CA: Thompson.

Bleck, R. T., & Bleck, B. L. (1982). The disruptive child's play group. *Elementary School Guidance & Counseling, 17,* 137–141.

Blocher, D. H. (1987). On the uses and misuses of the term theory. *Journal of Counseling and Development, 66,* 67–68.

Blum, D. J., & Jones, L. A. (1993). Academic growth group and mentoring program for potential dropouts. *School Counselor, 40,* 207–217.

Bly, R. (1990). *Iron John: A book about men.* Reading, MA: Addison-Wesley.

Bond, K. (1993). Classroom guidance: The get along gang. *Elementary School Guidance & Counseling, 27,* 303–304.

Bond, T. (2011). *Confidentiality and record keeping in counseling and psychotherapy.* Thousand Oaks, CA: Sage.

Borders, L. D., Glosoff, H. L., Welfare, L. E., Hayes, D. G., DeKruyf, L., Fernando, D. M., & Page, B. (2014). Best practices in clinical supervision: Evolution of a counseling specialty. *The Clinical Supervisor, 33,* 26–44.

Bordone, R. C. (2000). Teaching interpersonal skills for negotiating and for life. *Negotiation Journal, 16,* 377–385.

Borgers, S. B., & Koenig, R. W. (1983). Uses and effects of modeling by the therapist in group therapy. *Journal for Specialists in Group Work, 8,* 133–138.

Bormann, E. G. (1975). *Discussion and group methods: Theory and practice* (2nd ed.). Glenview, IL: Addison Wesley Longman.

Boutwell, D. A., & Myrick, R. D. (1992). The go for it club. *Elementary School Guidance & Counseling, 27,* 65–72.

Bowman, R. L., & Bowman, V. E. (1998). Life on the electronic frontier: The application of technology to group work. *Journal for Specialists in Group Work, 23,* 428–445.

Bowman, R. P. (1987). Small-group guidance and counseling in schools: A national survey of school counselors. *School Counselor, 34,* 256–262.

Bowman, V. E., & Boone, R. K. (1998). Enhancing the experience of community: Creativity in group work. *Journal for Specialists in Group Work, 23,* 388–410.

Boy, A. V., & Pine, G. J. (1982). *Client-centered counseling: A renewal.* Boston: Allyn & Bacon.

Bozarth, J. D. (1981). The person-centered approach in the large community group. In G. Gazda (Ed.), *Innovations to group psychotherapy* (2nd ed.). Springfield, IL: Thomas.

Brabender, V. (1985). Time-limited inpatient group therapy: A developmental model. *International Journal of Group Psychotherapy, 3,* 373–390.

Brabender, V. (2007). The ethical group psychotherapist: A coda. *International Journal of Group Psychotherapy, 57,* 41–47.

Brabender, V. (2010). Group dynamics. In R. K. Conyne (Ed.), *The Oxford handbook of group counseling* (pp. 182–204). New York, NY: Oxford University Press.

Brammer, L. M., Abrego, P. J., & Shostrom, E. L. (1993). *Therapeutic psychology.* Upper Saddle River, NJ: Prentice Hall.

Brammer, L. M., & MacDonald, G. (2003). *The helping relationship* (8th ed.). Boston: Allyn & Bacon.

Brandler, S. M. (1985). The senior center: Informality in the social work function. In G. S. Getzel & M. J. Mellor (Eds.), *Gerontological social work practice in the community* (pp. 195–210). New York, NY: Haworth.

Brandstatter, H., & Farthofer, A. (1997). Personality in social influence across tasks and groups. *Small Group Research, 28,* 146–163.

Brantley, L. S., Brantley, P. S., & Baer-Barkley, K. (1996). Transforming acting-out behavior: A group counseling program for inner-city elementary school pupils. *Elementary School Guidance & Counseling, 31,* 96–105.

Bratton, S. C., Ceballos, P. L., & Ferebee, K. W. (2009). Integration of structured expressive activities within a humanistic group play therapy format for pre-adolescents. *Journal for Specialists in Group Work, 34,* 251–275.

Bridbord, K., DeLucia-Waack, J. L., Jones, E., & Gerrity, D. A. (2004). The nonsignificant impact on an agenda setting treatment for groups: Implications for future research and practice. *Journal for Specialists in Group Work, 29,* 301–315.

Brinson, J. A., & Lee, C. C. (1997). Cultural responsive group leadership: An integrative model for experienced practitioners. In H. Forester-Miller & J. A. Kottler (Eds.), *Issues and challenges for group practitioners* (pp. 43–56). Denver, CO: Love.

Brough, M. F. (1994). Alleviation of loneliness: Evaluation of an Adlerian-based group therapy program. *Individual Psychology, 50,* 40–51.

Brown, B. M. (1996, Fall). A time for unity. *Together, 25*(1), 1, 6.

Brown, B. M. (1997, March). Psychoeducation group work. *Counseling and Human Development, 29,* 1–16.

Brown, D. (2012). *Career information, career counseling, and career development* (10th ed.). Upper Saddle River, NJ: Pearson.

Brown, N. A. (2011). *Psychoeducational groups: Process and practice* (3rd ed.). New York, NY: Routledge.

Brown, N. W. (2014). *Facilitating challenging groups.* New York, NY: Routledge.

Brown, S., & Beletsis, S. (1986). The development of family transference in groups for adult children of alcoholics. *International Journal of Group Psychotherapy, 36,* 97–114.

Brown, S. P., Lipford-Sanders, J., & Shaw, M. (1995). *Kujchagulia*—Uncovering the secrets of the heart: Group work with African American women on predominantly white campuses. *Journal for Specialists in Group Work, 20,* 151–158.

Brown, S. P., Parham, T. A., & Yonker, R. (1996). Influence of a cross-cultural training course on racial identity attitudes of white women and men: Preliminary perspective. *Journal of Counseling & Development, 74,* 510–516.

Browne, F. R. (2005). Self-talk of group counselors: The research of Rex Stockton. *Journal for Specialists in Group Work, 30,* 289–297.

Browne-Miller, A. (1993). *Gestalting addiction: The addiction-focused group therapy of Dr. Richard Louis Miller.* Stanford, CT: Ablex.

Brown-Shaw, M., Westwood, M., & DeVries, B. (1999). Integrating personal reflection and group-based enactments. *Journal of Aging Studies, 13,* 109–119.

Buban, M. E., McConnell, S. C., & Duncan, B. L. (1988). Children's fears of nuclear war: Group intervention strategies. *Journal for Specialists in Group Work, 13,* 124–129.

Burlew, L. D., Jones, J., & Emerson, P. (1991). Exercise and the elderly: A group counseling approach. *Journal for Specialists in Group Work, 16,* 152–158.

Burlingame, G. M., Fuhriman, A., & Johnson, J. (2004). In J. L. DeLucia-Waack, D.A. Gerrity, C. R. Kalodner, & M. T. Riva (Eds.), Process and outcome in group counseling and psychotherapy: A perspective. *Handbook of group counseling and psychotherapy* (pp. 49–61). Thousand Oaks, CA: Sage.

Burnes, T. R., & Ross, K. L. (2010). Applying social justice to oppression and marginalization in group process: Interventions and strategies for group counselors. *Journal for Specialists in Group Work, 35,* 169–176.

Burns, J. M. (1978). *Leadership.* New York, NY: Harper.

Burnside, I. M. (1978). Responsibilities of the preceptor. In I. M. Burnside (Ed.), *Working with the elderly: Group processes and techniques* (pp. 88–100). North Scituate, MA: Duxbury.

Burnside, I. M. (1986). *Working with the elderly: Group processes and techniques* (2nd ed.). Monterey, CA: Wadsworth.

Burnside, I. M. (1993). Themes in reminiscence groups with older women. *International Journal of Aging and Human Development, 37,* 177–189.

Butler, L. (1987). Anatomy of collusive behavior. *NTL Connections, 4,* 1–2.

Cain, D. J. (1993). The uncertain future of client-centered counseling. *Journal of Humanistic Education and Development, 31,* 133–138.

Campbell, C., & Bowman, R. P. (1993). The "fresh start" support club: Small group counseling for academically retained children. *Elementary School Guidance and Counseling, 27,* 172–185.

Campbell, C. A. (1991). Group guidance for academically undermotivated children. *Elementary School Guidance & Counseling, 25,* 302–307.

Campbell, C. A. (1993). Play, the fabric of elementary school counseling programs. *Elementary School Guidance & Counseling, 28,* 10–16.

Campbell, C. A., & Brigman, G. (2005). Closing the achievement gap: A structured approach to group counseling. *Journal for Specialists in Group Work, 30,* 67–82.

Campbell, D., & Palm, G. F. (2003). *Group parent education: Promoting parent learning and support.* Thousand Oaks, CA: Sage.

Campbell, R. E., & Cellini, J. V. (1980). Adult career development. *Counseling and Human Development, 12,* 1–8.

Capers, H. (1975). Winning and losing. *Transactional Analysis Journal, 5,* 257–258.

Capuzzi, D., & Gross, D. (1980). Group work with the elderly: An overview for counselors. *Personnel and Guidance Journal, 59,* 206–211.

Capuzzi, D., Gross, D. R., & Stauffer, M. D. (2011). *Introduction to group work* (5th ed.). Denver, CO: Love.

Carkhuff, R. (1971). *Helping and human relations* (Vols. 1 & 2). New York, NY: Holt, Rinehart & Winston.

Carnabucci, K. (2014). *Show and tell psychodrama: Skills for therapist, coaches, teachers, and leaders.* Racine, WI: Nusanto Publishing.

Carroll, M., Bates, M., & Johnson, C. (2004). *Group leadership* (4th ed.). Denver, CO: Love.

Carroll, M. R. (1981). End the plague on the house of guidance—Make counseling part of the curriculum. *NASSP Bulletin, 65,* 17–22.

Carroll, M. R. (1986). *Group work: Leading in the here and now* [Film]. Alexandria, VA: American Counseling Association.

Carroll, M. R., & Krause, K. (2008). *Elements of group counseling* (4th ed.). Denver, CO: Love.

Carroll, M. R., & Wiggins, J. D. (1997). *Elements of group counseling* (2nd ed.). Denver, CO: Love.

Carter, E. F., Mitchell, S. L., & Krautheim, M. D. (2001). Understanding and addressing clients' resistance to group counseling. *Journal for Specialists in Group Work, 26,* 66–80.

Carter, R. T. (1991). Cultural values: A review of empirical research and implications for counseling. *Journal of Counseling & Development, 70,* 164–173.

Carter, R. T., & Akinsulure-Smith, A. M. (1996). White racial identity and expectations about counseling. *Journal of Multicultural Counseling and Development, 24,* 218–228.

Castore, G. (1962). Number of verbal interrelationships as a determinant of group size. *Journal of Abnormal and Social Psychology, 64,* 456–457.

Cercone, K., & DeLucia-Waack, J. (2012). The effect of music and group stage on group leader and member behavior in psychoeducational groups for children of divorce. *Journal for Specialists in Group Work, 37,* 29–55.

Chambers, S. K., Pinnock, C., Lepore, S. J., Hughes, S., & O'Connoll, D. L. (2011). A systematic review of psychosocial interventions for men with prostate cancer and their partners. *Patient Education and Counseling, 85,* 75–88.

Champe, J., Okech, J. E. A., & Rubel, D. J. (2013). Emotion regulation: Processes, strategies, and applications to group work training and supervision. *Journal for Specialists in Group Work, 38,* 349–368.

Champe, J., & Rubel, D. J. (2012). Application of focal conflict theory to psychoeducational groups: Implications for process, content, and leadership. *Journal for Specialists in Group Work, 37,* 71–90.

Chandra, A., Lara-Cinisomo, S., Jaycox, L. H., Tanielian, T., Burns, R. M., Ruder, T., & Han, B. (2010). Children on the homefront: The experience of children from military families. *Pediatrics, 125,* 16–25.

Chauvin, J. C., & Remley, T. P., Jr. (1996). Responding to allegations of unethical conduct. *Journal of Counseling and Development, 74,* 563–568.

Chen, M., & Han, Y. S. (2001). Cross-cultural group counseling with Asians: A stage-specific interactive approach. *Journal for Specialists in Group Work, 26,* 111–128.

Chen, M., Noosbond, J. P., & Bruce, M. A. (1998). Therapeutic document in group counseling: An active change agent. *Journal of Counseling and Development, 76,* 404–411.

Chen, T. J., Li, H-J, & Li, J. (2012). The effects of reminiscence therapy on depressive symptoms of Chinese elderly: study protocol of a randomized controlled trial. *BMC Psychiatry, 12,* 189.

Chen, Z., Lawson, R. B., Gordon, L. R., & McIntosh, B. (1996). Groupthink: Deciding with the leader and the devil. *Psychological Record, 46,* 581–590.

Cheng, W. D. (1995, Fall). Pacific perspective. *Together, 24*(1), 8.

Cheng, W. D. (1996, Winter). Pacific perspective. *Together, 24*(2), 10.

Cheng, W. D., Chae, M., & Gunn, R. W. (1998). Splitting and projection identification in multicultural group counseling. *Journal for Specialists in Group Work, 23,* 372–387.

Childers, J. H., Jr. (1986). Group leadership training and supervision: A graduate course. *Journal for Specialists in Group Work, 11,* 48–52.

Childers, J. H., Jr., & Burcky, W. D. (1984). The jogging group: A positive-wellness strategy. *AMHCA Journal, 6,* 118–125.

Childers, J. H., Jr., & Couch, R. D. (1989). Myths about group counseling: Identifying and challenging misconceptions. *Journal for Specialists in Group Work, 14,* 105–111.

Chiu, T. L. (1997). Problems caused for mental health professionals worldwide by increasing multicultural populations and proposed solutions. *Journal of Multicultural Counseling and Development, 24,* 129–140.

Choate, L. H., & Henson, A. (2003). Group work with adult survivors of childhood abuse and neglect: A psychoeducational approach. *Journal for Specialists in Group Work, 28,* 106–121.

Chong, W. H. (2005). The role of self-regulation and personal agency beliefs: A psychoeducational approach with Asian high school students in Singapore. *Journal for Specialists in Group Work, 30,* 343–361.

Christensen, T. M., Hulse-Killacky, D., Salgado, Jr., R. A., Thornton, M. D., & Miller, J. L. (2006). Facilitating reminiscence groups: Perceptions of group leaders. *Journal for Specialists in Group Work, 31,* 73–88.

Christensen, T. M., & Kline, W. B. (2001). The qualitative exploration of process-sensitive peer group supervision. *Journal for Specialists in Group Work, 26,* 81–99.

Christmas, C., & Van Horn, S. M. (2012). SPARC groups: A model for incorporating spiritual psychoeducation into group work. *Journal for Specialists in Group Work, 37,* 170–201.

Chronister, K. M., & Davidson, M. M. (2010). Promoting distributive justice for intimate partner violence survivors with group interventions. *Journal for Specialists in Group Work, 35,* 115–123.

Chu, H., Lang, C-Y., Liao, Y-H., Chang, L-I., Chen, C-H., Lin, C-C., Chou, K-R. (2011). The effects of a support group on dementia caregivers' burden and depression. *Journal of Aging and Health, 23,* 228–241.

Chung, R. C.-Y., & Bemak, F. (2014). Group counseling with Asians. In J. L. DeLucia-Waack, C. R. Kalodner, & M. T. Riva (Eds.), *Handbook of group counseling and psychotherapy* (2nd ed., pp. 231–241). Thousand Oaks, CA: Sage.

Chung, R. C.-Y., Bemak, F., & Okazaki, S. (1997). Counseling Americans of Southeast Asian descent. In C. C. Lee (Ed.), *Multicultural issues in counseling* (2nd ed., pp. 207–231). Alexandria, VA: American Counseling Association.

Claiborn, C. D. (1987). Science and practice: Reconsidering the Pepinskys. *Journal of Counseling and Development, 65,* 286–288.

Claiborn, C. D., Goodyear, R. K., & Horner, P. A. (2001). Feedback. *Psychotherapy, 38,* 401–405.

Clark, A. J. (1992). Defense mechanisms in group counseling. *Journal for Specialists in Group Work, 17,* 151–160.

Clark, A. J. (1995). Modification: A leader skill in group work. *Journal for Specialists in Group Work, 20,* 14–17.

Clark, A. J., & Seals, J. M. (1984). Groups counseling for ridiculed children. *Journal for Specialists in Group Work, 9,* 157–162.

Clark, R., Tluczek, A., & Brown, R. (2008). A mother-infant therapy group for postpartum depression. *Infant Mental Health Journal, 29,* 514–536.

Claypoole, S. D., Moody, E. E., Jr., & Peace, S. D. (2000). Moral dilemma discussions: An effective group intervention for juvenile offenders. *Journal for Specialists in Group Work, 25,* 394–411.

Coche, E. (1984). Group psychotherapy for group therapists. In F. Kaslow (Ed.), *Psychotherapy with psychotherapists.* New York, NY: Haworth.

Coffman, S. G., & Roark, A. E. (1988). Likely candidates for group counseling: Adolescents with divorced parents. *School Counselor, 35,* 246–252.

Cohen, A. M., & Smith, R. D. (1976). *Critical incidents in growth groups: Theory and techniques.* La Jolla, CA: University Associates.

Cohen, G. (2000). *The creative age: Awakening human potential in the second half of life.* New York, NY: Harper.

Colmani, S. A., & Merta, R. J. (1999). Using the sweat lodge ceremony as group therapy for Navajo youth. *Journal for Specialists in Group Work, 24,* 55–73.

Comiskey, P. E. (1993). Using reality therapy group training with at-risk high school freshmen. *Journal of Reality Therapy, 12,* 59–64.

Comstock, D. L., Duffey, T., & St. George, H. (2002). The relational-cultural model: A framework for group process. *Journal for Specialists in Group Work, 27,* 254–272.

Conley, D. (1994). *If you believe in you.* New York City, NY: Treehouse Music.

Connors, J. V., & Caple, R. B. (2005). A review of group systems theory. *Journal for Specialists in Group Work, 30,* 93–110.

Conyers, B. (2003). *Addict in the family: Stories of loss, hope, and recovery.* Center City, MN: Hazelton.

Conyne, R. K. (1996). The Association for Specialists in Group Work Training Standards: Some considerations and suggestions for training. *Journal for Specialists in Group Work, 21,* 155–162.

Conyne, R. K. (1998). Personal experience and meaning in group work leadership: The views of the experts. *Journal for Specialists in Group Work, 23,* 245–256.

Conyne, R. K. (2014). Prevention groups. In J. L. DeLucia-Waack, C. R. Kalodner, & M. T. Riva (Eds.), *Handbook of group counseling & psychotherapy* (2nd ed., pp. 531–543). Thousand Oaks, CA: Sage.

Conyne, R. K., & Bemak, F. (2004). Teaching group work from ecological perspective. *Journal for Specialists in Group Work, 29,* 7–18.

Conyne, R. K., Crowell, J. L., & Newmeyer, M. D. (2008). Group techniques: How to use them more purposefully. Upper Saddle River, NJ: Pearson.

Conyne, R. K., & Diederich, L. T. (2014). *What is group work?* Thousand Oaks, CA: Sage.

Conyne, R. K., & Mazza, J. (2007). Ecological group work applied to schools. *Journal for Specialists in Group Work, 32,* 19–29.

Conyne, R. K., & Silver, R. (1980). Direct, vicarious, and vicarious-process experiences. *Small Group Behavior, 11,* 419–429.

Conyne, R. K., & Wilson, F. R. (1998). Toward a standards based classification of group work offerings. *Journal for Specialists in Group Work, 23,* 177–184.

Conyne, R. K., Wilson, F. R., & Tang, M. (2000). Evolving lessons from group work involvement in China. *Journal for Specialists in Group Work, 25,* 252–268.

Conyne, R. K., Wilson, F. R., & Ward, D. E. (1997). *Comprehensive group work.* Alexandria, VA: American Counseling Association.

Cook-Cottone, C., Beck, M., & Kane, L. (2008). Manualized-group treatment of eating disorders: Attunement in mind, body and relationship (AMBR). *Journal for Specialists in Group Work, 33,* 61–83.

Coppock, M. W. (1993). Small group plan for improving friendships and self-esteem. *Elementary School Guidance & Counseling, 28,* 152–154.

Corazzini, J. G., Williams, K., & Harris, S. (1987). Group therapy for adult children of alcoholics: Case studies. *Journal for Specialists in Group Work, 12,* 156–161.

Corey, G. (2012). *The theory and practice of group counseling* (8th ed.). Belmont, CA: Brooks/Cole.

Corey, G., Corey, M. S., Callanan, P. J., & Russell, J. M. (2014). *Group techniques* (4th ed.). Belmont, CA: Cengage.

Corey, M. S., Corey, G., & Corey, C. (2014). *Groups: Process and practice* (9th ed.). Belmont, CA: Cengage.

Corey, G., Corey, M. S., Corey, C., & Callanan, P. (2015). *Issues and ethics in the helping professions* (9th ed.). Belmont, CA: Cengage.

Corey, G., Corey, M. S., & Haynes, R. (2014). *Ethics in action.* Belmont, CA: Cengage.

Corsini, R. J. (1966). *Roleplaying in psychotherapy.* New York, NY: Free Press.

Corsini, R. J. (1988). Adlerian groups. In S. Long (Ed.), *Six group therapies* (pp. 1–43). New York, NY: Plenum.

Corwin, D., Wall, K., & Koopman, C. (2012). Psycho-Spiritual Integrative Therapy: Psychological intervention for women with breast cancer. *Journal for Specialists in Group Work, 37,* 252–273.

Cottone, R. R., & Tarvydas, V. M. (2007). *Ethical and professional issues in counseling* (3rd ed.). Upper Saddle River, NJ: Prentice Hall.

Couch, R. D. (1995). Four steps for conducting a pregroup screening interview. *Journal for Specialists in Group Work, 20,* 18–26.

Couch, R. D., & Childers, J. H., Jr. (1987). Leadership strategies for instilling and maintaining hope in group counseling. *Journal for Specialists in Group Work, 12,* 138–143.

Coulson, W. R. (1972). *Groups, gimmicks and instant gurus.* New York, NY: Harper & Row.

Coulson, W. R. (1974). *A sense of community.* Columbus, OH: Merrill/Prentice Hall.

Courtois, C. A. (1988). *Healing the incest wound.* New York, NY: Norton.

Courtois, C. A., & Leehan, J. (1982). Group treatment for grown-up abused children. *Personnel and Guidance Journal, 60,* 564–566.

Coven, A. B. (2004). Gestalt group dreamwork demonstrations in Taiwan. *Journal for Specialists in Group Work, 29,* 175–184.

Coven, A. B., Ellington, D. B., & Van Hull, K. G. (1997). The use of Gestalt psychodrama in group counseling. In S. T. Gladding (Ed.), *New developments in group counseling* (pp. 17–18). Greensboro, NC: ERIC.

Cowan, D., & Brunero, S. (1997). Group therapy for anxiety disorders using rational emotive behaviour therapy. *Australian and New Zealand Journal of Mental Health Nursing, 6,* 164–168.

Cowie, H., & Rivers, I. (2000). Going against the grain: Supporting lesbian, gay and bisexual clients as they "come out." *British Journal of Guidance & Counseling, 28,* 503–513.

Cowley, G. (1997, June 30). How to live to 100. *Newsweek,* 56–67.

Cox, H. G. (2009). *Later life: The realities of aging* (6th ed.). Upper Saddle River, NJ: Prentice Hall.

Cox, J., Davies, D. R., Burlingame, G. M., Campbell, J. E., Layne, C. M., & Katzenbach, R. J. (2007). Effectiveness of a trauma/grief-focused group intervention: A qualitative study with war-exposed Bosnian adolescents. *International Journal of Group Psychotherapy, 57,* 319–345.

Cox, J. R. (1999). *A guide to peer counseling.* New York, NY: Jason Aronson.

Crawford, R. L. (1994). *Avoiding counselor malpractice.* Alexandria, VA: American Counseling Association.

Croake, J. W. (1983). Adlerian parent education. *Counseling Psychologist, 11,* 65–71.

Csikszentmihalyi, M. (2013). *Creativity: The psychology of discovery and invention.* New York, NY: Harper.

Cummings, A. L. (2001). Teaching group process to counseling students through the exchange of journal letters. *Journal for Specialists in Group Work, 26,* 7–16.

Cummings, A. L., Hoffman, S., & Leschied, A. W. (2004). A psychoeducational group for aggressive adolescent girls. *Journal for Specialists in Group Work, 29,* 285–299.

Cummins, P. N. (1996). Preparing clients with eating disorders for group counseling: A multimedia approach. *Journal for Specialists in Group Work, 21,* 4–10.

Cunningham, L. M. (1995). Control theory, reality therapy, and cultural bias. *Journal of Reality Therapy, 15,* 15–22.

Curman, M., & Curman, B. (1994). The Gestalt couples group. In G. Wheeler & S. Backman (Eds.), *On intimate ground: A Gestalt approach to working with couples* (pp. 229–242). San Francisco, CA: Jossey-Bass.

Dagley, J. C., & Calhoun, G. B. (2014). Career and transition counseling in groups. In J. L. DeLucia-Waack, C. R. Kalodner, & M. T. Riva (Eds.), *Handbook of group counseling and psychotherapy* (2nd ed., pp. 544–559). Thousand Oaks, CA: Sage.

Dagley, J., & English, E. (2014). *Group work in schools.* Thousand Oaks, CA: Sage.

D'Amato, R. C., & Dean, R. S. (1988). Psychodrama research—therapy and theory: A critical analysis of an arrested modality. *Psychology in the Schools, 25,* 305–314.

Damer, D. E., Latimore, K. M., & Porter, S. H. (2010). "Build your self-confidence": A social anxiety group for college students. *Journal for Specialists in Group Work, 35,* 7–22.

Damer, D. E., & Melendres, L. T. (2011). "Tackling Test Anxiety": A Group for College Students. *Journal for Specialists in Group Work, 36,* 163–177.

Daniels, J., D'Andrea, M., Omizo, M., & Pier, P. (1999). Group work with homeless youngsters and their mothers. *Journal for Specialists in Group Work, 24,* 164–185.

Dannison, L., & Nieuwenhuis, A. (Eds.). (1996). *Second time around—Grandparents raising grandchildren.* Kalamazoo: Western Michigan University.

Dansby, V. S. (1996). Group work within the school system: Survey of implementation and leadership role issues. *Journal for Specialists in Group Work, 21,* 232–242.

Davenport, D. S. (2004). Ethical issues in the teaching of group counseling. *Journal for Specialists in Group Work, 29,* 43–49.

Davidson, K. (2006). Flying solo in old age: Widowed and divorced men and women in later life. In J. A. Vincent, C. R. Phillipson, & M. Downs (Eds.), *The future of old age* (pp. 172–179). Thousand Oaks, CA: Sage.

Davis-Gage, D. (2011). Gestalt and psychodrama approaches to counseling and psychotherapy groups. In B. Erford (Ed.), *Group work: Processes and application* (pp. 249–257). Upper Saddle River, NJ: Pearson.

Davies, D., & Kuypers, B. (1985). Group development and interpersonal feedback. *Group and Organizational Studies, 10,* 184–208.

Day, B., & Matthes, W. (1992). A comparison of Jungian, person-centered,

and Gestalt approaches to personal growth groups. *Journal for Specialists in Group Work, 17,* 105–115.

DeAngelis, T. (1992, November). Best psychological treatment for many men: Group therapy. *APA Monitor, 23,* 31.

de Burgh, H. T., White, C. J., Fear, N. T., & Iversen, A. C. (2011). The impact of deployment to Iraq and Afghanistan on partners and wives of military personnel. *International Review of Psychiatry, 23,* 192–200.

deBono, E. (1973). *Lateral thinking: Creativity step by step.* New York, NY: Harper & Row.

deBono, E. (1999). *Six thinking hats.* New York, NY: Little, Brown, and Company.

Deck, M. D., & Saddler, D. L. (1983). Freshmen awareness groups: A viable option for high school counselors. *School Counselor, 30,* 392–397.

Delbecq, A. L., & Van de Ven, A. H. (1971). A group process model for problem identification and program planning. *Journal of Applied Behavioral Science, 7,* 466–492.

Delbecq, A. L., Van de Ven, A. H., & Gustafson, D. H. (1975). *Group techniques for program planning.* Glenview, IL: Scott, Foresman.

DeLucia, J. L., Coleman, V. D., & Jensen-Scott, R. L. (1992). Cultural diversity in group counseling. *Journal for Specialists in Group Work, 17,* 194–195.

DeLucia-Waack, J. L. (1996a). Multicultural group counseling: Addressing diversity to facilitate universality and self-understanding. In J. L. DeLucia-Waack (Ed.), *Multicultural counseling competencies: Implications for training and practice* (pp. 157–195). Alexandria, VA: American Counseling Association.

DeLucia-Waack, J. L. (1996b). Multiculturalism is inherent in all group work. *Journal for Specialists in Group Work, 21,* 218–223.

DeLucia-Waack, J. L. (1997a). Measuring the effectiveness of group work: A review and analysis of process and outcome measures. *Journal for Specialists in Group Work, 22,* 277–293.

DeLucia-Waack, J. L. (1997b). The importance of processing activities, exercises, and events to group work practitioners. *Journal for Specialists in Group Work, 22,* 82–84.

DeLucia-Waack, J. L. (1998). What is the relationship between therapeutic factors and group work effectiveness really? *Journal for Specialists in Group Work, 23,* 235–236.

DeLucia-Waack, J. L. (1999b). Supervision for counselors working with eating disorders groups: Counter-transference issues related to body image, food, and weight. *Journal of Counseling & Development, 17,* 379–388.

DeLucia-Waack, J. L. (1999c). What makes an effective group leader? *Journal for Specialists in Group Work, 24,* 131–132.

DeLucia-Waack, J. (2000a). Effective group work in the schools. *Journal for Specialists in Group Work, 25,* 131–132.

DeLucia-Waack, J. L. (2000c). The field of group work: Past, present, and future. *Journal for Specialists in Group Work, 25,* 323–326.

DeLucia-Waack, J. L. (2001a). Mentoring future group workers. *Journal for Specialists in Group Work, 26,* 107–110.

DeLucia-Waack, J. L. (2001b). *Using music in children of divorce groups: A session-by-session manual for counselors.* Alexandria, VA: American Counseling Association.

DeLucia-Waack, J. L. (2002). A written guide for planning and processing group sessions in anticipation of supervision. *Journal for Specialists in Group Work, 27,* 341–357.

DeLucia-Waack, J. L. (2004). Multicultural groups. In J. L. DeLucia-Waack, D. A. Gerrity, C. R. Kalodner, & M. T. Riva (Eds.), *Handbook of group counseling and psychotherapy* (pp. 167–168). Thousand Oaks, CA: Sage.

DeLucia-Waack, J. L. (2006). *Leading psychoeducational groups for children and adolescents.* Thousand Oaks, CA: Sage.

DeLucia-Waack, J. L., & Fauth, J. (2004). Effective supervision of group leaders.

In J. L. DeLucia-Waack, D. A. Gerrity, C. R. Kalodner, & M. T. Riva (Eds.), *Handbook of group counseling and psychotherapy* (pp. 136–150). Thousand Oaks, CA: Sage.

DeLucia-Waack, J. L., & Gellman, R. A. (2007). The efficacy of using music in children of divorce groups: Impact of anxiety, depression, and irrational beliefs about divorce. *Group Dynamics: Theory, Research, and Practice, 11,* 272–282.

DeLucia-Waack, J. L., & Gerrity, D. (2001). Effective group work for elementary school-age children whose parents are divorcing. *The Family Journal: Counseling and Therapy for Couples and Families, 9,* 273–284.

DeLucia-Waack, J. L., & Nitza, A. (2014). *Effective planning for groups.* Thousand Oaks, CA: Sage.

Denholm, C. J., & Uhlemann, M. R. (1986). Organizing the child, preadolescent, and adolescent group literature: A pragmatic teaching tool. *Journal for Specialists in Group Work, 11,* 163–173.

Dennis, H. (1978). Remotivation therapy groups. In I. M. Burnside (Ed.), *Working with the elderly: Group processes and techniques* (pp. 219–235). North Scituate, MA: Duxbury.

Dennis-Small, L. (1986). *Life skills for adolescents.* Ann Arbor, MI: ERIC/CAPS (ED 278883).

DeRoma, V. M., Root, L. P., & Battle, J. V. (2003). Pretraining in group process skills: Impact on anger and anxiety in combat veterans. *Journal for Specialists in Group Work, 28,* 339–354.

Deurzen-Smith, E. van. (1997). *Everyday mysteries: Existential dimensions of psychotherapy.* London, England: Routledge.

DeVries, B., Birren, J. E., & Deutchman, D. E. (1995). Methods and uses of the guided autobiography. In B. K. Haight & J. D. Webster (Eds.), *The art and science of reminiscing* (pp. 165–177). Philadelphia, PA: Taylor & Francis.

Dies, R. R. (1983). Clinical implications of research on leadership in short-term group psychotherapy. In R. R. Dies & K. R. MacKenzie (Eds.), *Advances in group psychotherapy: Integrating research and practice* (pp. 27–78). New York, NY: International Universities Press.

DiGiulio, J. F. (1992). Early widowhood: An atypical transition. *Journal of Mental Health Counseling, 14,* 97–109.

Diller, J. V. (2014). *Cultural diversity: A primer for the human services* (5th ed.). Belmont, CA: Cengage.

Dinkmeyer, D. C. (1973). The parent "C" group. *Personnel and Guidance Journal, 52,* 252–256.

Dinkmeyer, D., & Dinkmeyer, D., Jr. (1982). *Developing understanding of self and others, D-2* (rev. ed.). Circle Pines, MN: American Guidance Service.

Dinkmeyer, D., & Muro, J. J. (1979). *Group counseling: Theory and practice* (2nd ed.). Itasca, IL: Peacock.

Dinkmeyer, D., Jr., & Sperry, L. (2000). *Adlerian counseling and psychotherapy* (3rd ed.). Upper Saddle River, NJ: Merrill/Prentice Hall.

Dobson, J. E., & Dobson, R. L. (1991). Changing roles: An aging parents support group. *Journal for Specialists in Group Work, 16,* 178–184.

Donigian, J., & Hulse-Killacky, D. (1999). *Critical incidents in group therapy* (2nd ed.). Pacific Grove, CA: Brooks/Cole.

Donigian, J., & Malnati, R. (1997). *Systemic group therapy.* Pacific Grove, CA: Brooks/Cole.

Dorstyn, D. S., Mathias, J. L., & Denson, L. A. (2011). Psychosocial outcomes of telephone-based counseling for adults with an acquired physical disability: A meta-analysis. *Rehabilitation Psychology, 56,* 1–14.

Dowden, A. R. (2009). Implementing self-advocacy training within a brief psychoeducational group to improve the academic motivation of black adolescents. *Journal for Specialists in Group Work, 34,* 118–136.

Downing, T. K. E., Smaby, M. H., & Maddux, C. D. (2001). A study of the transfer of group counseling skills from training to practice. *Journal for Specialists in Group Work, 26,* 158–167.

Draper, K., Ritter, K. B., & Willingham, E. U. (2003). Sand tray group counseling with adolescents. *Journal for Specialists in Group Work, 28,* 244–260.

Dreikurs, R. (1950). *Fundamentals of Adlerian psychology.* New York, NY: Greenberg.

Dreikurs, R. (1968). *Psychology in the classroom* (2nd ed.). New York, NY: Harper & Row.

Dreikurs, R. (1969). Group psychotherapy from the point of view of Adlerian psychology. In H. M. Ruitenbeek (Ed.), *Group therapy today: Styles, methods, and techniques.* New York, NY: Adline-Atherton.

Drum, D., Becker, M. S., & Hess, E. (2011). Expanding the application of group interventions: Emergence of groups in health care settings. *Journal for Specialists in Group Work, 36,* 247–263.

Drum, D. J., & Knott, J. E. (1977). *Structured groups for facilitating development: Acquiring life skills, resolving life themes, and making life transitions.* New York, NY: Human Science Press.

Dryden, W. (1989). Albert Ellis: An efficient and passionate life. *Journal of Counseling and Development, 67,* 539–546.

Dryden, W. (1999). *Rational emotive behavior therapy: A training model.* New York, NY: Springer.

Dryfoos, J. G. (1990). *Adolescents at risk: Prevalence and prevention.* New York, NY: Oxford University Press.

Dryfoos, J. G. (1993). Schools as places for health, mental health, and special services. In R. Takanshi (Ed.), *Adolescence in the 1990s.* New York, NY: Teachers College Press.

Duffey, T., Somody, C., & Clifford, S. (2006/2007). Conversations with my father: Adapting a Musical Chronology and the Emerging Life Song with older adults. *Journal of Creativity in Mental Health, 2,* 45–63.

Dufrene, P. M., & Coleman, V. D. (1992). Counseling Native Americans: Guidelines for group process. *Journal for Specialists in Group Work, 17,* 229–234.

Dugan, J. R., & Everett, R. S. (1998). An experimental test of chemical dependency for jail inmates. *International Journal of Offender Therapy and Comparative Criminology, 42,* 360–368.

Duncan, D. M., & Brown, B. M. (1996). Anxiety and development of conceptual complexity in group counselors-in-training. *Journal for Specialists in Group Work, 21,* 252–262.

Dunphy, D. (1968). Phases, roles, and myths in self-analytic groups. *Journal of Applied Behavioral Science, 4,* 195–225.

Durbin, D. M. (1982). Multimodal group sessions to enhance self-concept. *Elementary School Guidance & Counseling, 16,* 288–295.

Dusay, J. M. (1983). Transactional analysis in groups. In H. I. Kaplan & B. J. Sadock (Eds.), *Comprehensive group psychotherapy* (2nd ed.). Baltimore: Williams & Wilkins.

Dusay, J. M., & Dusay, K. M. (1989). Transactional analysis. In R. Corsini & D. Wedding (Eds.), *Current psychotherapies* (4th ed., pp. 404–453). Itasca, IL: Peacock.

Dusay, J., & Steiner, C. (1971). Transactional analysis in groups. In H. I. Kaplan & B. J. Sadock (Eds.), *Comprehensive group psychotherapy* (pp. 198–240). Baltimore: Williams & Wilkins.

Dye, A. (1997). The multiple T: A procedure for teaching group counseling skills. In S. T. Gladding (Ed.), *New developments in group counseling* (pp. 125–127). Greensboro, NC: ERIC.

Earley, J. (2000). A practical guide to fostering interpersonal norms in a Gestalt group. *Gestalt Review, 4,* 138–151.

Eaves, S. H., & Sheperis, C. J. (2011). Group work with adult populations. In B. T. Erford (Ed.), *Group work: Process and applications* (pp. 277–291). Upper Saddle River, NJ: Pearson.

Eberle, R. F. (1971). *SCAMPER games for imagination development.* Buffalo, NY: DOK.

Edelwich, J., & Brodsky, A. (1992). *Group counseling for the resistant client.* New York, NY: Lexington.

Egge, D. L., Marks, L. G., & McEvers, D. M. (1987). Puppets and adolescents: A group guidance workshop approach. *Elementary School Guidance & Counseling, 21,* 183–192.

Ekloff, M. (1984). The termination phase in group therapy: Implications for geriatric groups. *Small Group Behavior, 15,* 565–571.

Ellis, A. (1962). *Reason and emotion in psychotherapy.* New York, NY: Stuart.

Ellis, A. (1974a). Rational-emotive therapy in groups. *Rational Living, 9,* 15–22.

Ellis, A. (1974b). Rationality and irrationality in the group therapy process. In D. S. Milman & G. D. Goldman (Eds.), *Group process today* (pp. 78–96). Springfield, IL: Thomas.

Ellis, A. (1976). The biological basis of irrational thinking. *Journal of Individual Psychology, 32,* 145–168.

Ellis, A. (1977). Fun as psychotherapy. In A. Ellis & R. Grieger (Eds.), *Handbook of rational-emotive therapy* (Vol. 1, pp. 262–270). New York, NY: Springer.

Ellis, A. (1979). Rational-emotive therapy. In A. Ellis & J. M. Whitely (Eds.), *Theoretical and empirical foundations of rational-emotive therapy.* Pacific Grove, CA: Brooks/Cole.

Ellis, A. (1982). Rational-emotive group therapy. In G. M. Gazda (Ed.), *Basic approaches to group therapy and group counseling* (3rd ed.). Springfield, IL: Thomas.

Ellis, A. (1986). Rational-emotive therapy approaches to overcoming resistance. In A. Ellis & R. Grieger (Eds.), *Handbook of rational-emotive therapy* (Vol. 2, pp. 246–274). New York, NY: Springer.

Ellis, A. (1988). *How to stubbornly refuse to make yourself miserable about anything—Yes, anything!* Secaucus, NJ: Lyle Stuart.

Ellis, A. (1995). Changing rational-emotive therapy (RET) to rational emotive behavioral therapy (REBT). *Journal of Rational Emotive and Cognitive Behavioral Therapy, 13,* 85–89.

Ellis, A. (1997). REBT and its application to group therapy. In J. Yankura & W. Dryden (Eds.), *Special applications of REBT: A therapist's casebook* (pp. 131–161). New York, NY: Springer.

Ellis, A. (2011). Rational-emotive behavior therapy. In R. J. Corsini & D. Wedding (Ed.), *Counseling psychotherapies* (9th ed., pp. 196–234). Belmont, CA: Brooks/Cole.

Ellis, A., & Bernard, M. E. (Eds.). (1983). *Rational-emotive approaches to the problems of childhood.* New York, NY: Plenum.

Ellis, A., & Dryden, W. (2007). *The practice of rational emotive behavior therapy* (2nd ed.). New York, NY: Springer.

Ellis, S. K., Simpson, C. G., Rose, C. A., & Plotner, A. J. (2014). Group counseling services for persons with disabilities. In J. L. DeLucia-Waack, C. R. Kalodner, & M. T. Riva (Eds.), Handbook of group counseling & psychotherapy (2nd ed., pp. 264–275). Thousand Oaks, CA: Sage.

Emerson, S. (1995). A counseling group for counselors. *Journal for Specialists in Group Work, 20,* 222–231.

Ender, S. C. (1985). Study groups and college success. *Journal of College Student Personnel, 26,* 469–471.

Enright, A. B., Butterfield, P., & Berkowitz, B. (1985). Self-help and support groups in the management of eating disorders. In D. M. Garner & P. Garfinkel (Eds.), *Handbook of psychotherapy for anorexia nervosa and bulimia* (pp. 419–512). New York, NY: Guilford.

Epstein, N. B., & Bishop, D. S. (1981). Problem centered systems therapy of the family. *Journal of Marital and Family Therapy, 7,* 23–31.

Erikson, E. H. (1963). *Childhood and society* (2nd ed.). New York, NY: Norton.

Erwin, K. T. (1997). *Group techniques for aging adults: Putting geriatric skills enhancement into practice.* Philadelphia, PA: Routledge.

Espin, O. M. (1987). Psychological impact of migration on Latinas. *Psychology of Women Quarterly, 11,* 489–503.

Evans, D. B. (1982). What are you doing? An interview with William Glasser. *Personnel and Guidance Journal, 60,* 460–465.

Evans, M. P. (2013). Men in counseling: A content analysis of the *Journal for Counseling & Development* and *Counselor Education and Supervision*, 1981–2011. *Journal of Counseling and Development, 91,* 467–474.

Evans, T. D., & Kane, D. P. (1996). Sophistry: A promising group technique for the involuntary client. *Journal for Specialists in Group Work, 21,* 110–117.

Falco, L. D., & Bauman, S. (2004). The use of process: Notes in the experiential component of training group workers. *Journal for Specialists in Group Work, 29,* 185–192.

Falco, L. D., & Bauman, S. (2014). Group work in schools. In J. L. DeLucia, C. R. Kalodner, & M. T. Riva (Eds.), *Handbook of group counseling & psychotherapy* (2nd ed., pp. 318–328). Thousand Oaks, CA: Sage.

Fall, K. A., & Wejnert, T. J. (2005). Coleader stages of development: An application of Tuckman and Jensen (1977). *Journal for Specialists in Group Work, 30,* 309–327.

Faust, V. (1968). *The counselor-consultant in the elementary school.* Boston: Houghton Mifflin.

Feagin, J. R. (2014). *Racist America* (3rd ed.). New York, NY: Routledge.

Fehr, S. S. (2013). *Introduction to group therapy: A practical guide* (2nd ed.). New York, NY: Routledge.

Fenell, D. L. (2014). Counseling stoic warriors: Providing therapy to military men. In M. Englar-Carlson, M. P. Evans, & T. Duffey (Eds.), *Working with men in groups* (pp. 227–246). Alexandria, VA: American Counseling Association.

Fernando, D. M. (2009). Group work with survivors of the 2004 Asian tsunami: Reflections of an American-trained counselor. *Journal for Specialists in Group Work, 34,* 4–23.

Festinger, L. (1954). A theory of social comparison processes. *Human Relations, 7,* 117–140.

Fine, G. A. (1977). Humour in situ: The role of humour in small group culture. In A. J. Chapman & R. Grieger (Eds.), *Handbook of rational-emotive therapy* (Vol. 2, pp. 246–274). New York, NY: Springer.

Finn, C. A. (2003). Helping students cope with loss: Incorporating art into group counseling. *Journal for Specialists in Group Work, 28,* 155–165.

Firestein, B. A. (1999). New perspectives on group treatment with women of diverse sexual identities. *Journal for Specialists in Group Work, 24,* 306–315.

Flahive, M-W., & Ray, D. (2007). Effect of group sandtray therapy with preadolescents. *Journal for Specialists in Group Work, 32,* 362–382.

Fletcher, T., & Hinkle, J. S. (2002). Adventure based counseling: An innovation in counseling. *Journal of Counseling and Development, 80,* 277–285.

Flores, P. J. (1988). *Group psychotherapy with addicted populations.* New York, NY: Haworth.

Folken, M. H. (1991). The importance of group support for widowed persons. *Journal for Specialists in Group Work, 16,* 172–177.

Foltz, M.-L., Kirby, P. C., & Paradise, L. V. (1989). The influence of empathy and negative consequences on ethical decisions in counseling situations. *Counselor Education and Supervision, 28,* 219–228.

Ford, D. (1997). Counseling middle-class African Americans. In C. C. Lee (Ed.), *Multicultural issues in counseling* (pp. 81–108). Alexandria, VA: American Counseling Association.

Forester-Miller, H., & Duncan, J. A. (1990). The ethics of dual relationships in the training of group counselors. *Journal for Specialists in Group Work, 15,* 88–93.

Forsyth, D. (2013). *Group dynamics* (6th ed.). Belmont, CA: Cengage.

Forsyth, D. R., & Diederich, L. T. (2014). Group dynamics and development. In J. L. DeLucia-Waack, C. R. Kalodner, & M. T. Riva (Eds.), *Handbook of group counseling & psychotherapy* (2nd ed., pp. 34–45). Thousand Oaks, CA: Sage.

Fox, J. (Ed.). (2008). *The essential Moreno: Writings on psychodrama, group method, and spontaneity.* New Paltz, NY: Tusitala.

Framo, J. L. (1981). The integration of marital therapy with family of origin sessions. In S. Gurman & D. P. Kniskern (Eds.), *Handbook of family therapy,* pp. 133–158. New York, NY: Brunner/Mazel.

France, M. H. (1984). Responding to loneliness: Counselling the elderly. *Canadian Counsellor, 18,* 123–129.

Francis, P. C., & Duggar, S. M. (2014). Professionalism, ethics, and value-based conflicts in counseling: Introduction to the special section. *Journal of Counseling and Development, 92,* 131–134.

Frankl, V. (1962). *Man's search for meaning: An introduction to logo-therapy.* New York, NY: Washington Square Press.

Frankl, V. E. (1997). *Viktor Frankl—Recollections: An autobiography.* New York, NY: Plenum.

Frankl, V. E. (2000). *Man's search for meaning: An introduction to logotherapy.* New York, NY: Beacon.

Franks, J. C. (1983). Children. In J. A. Brown & R. H. Pate, Jr. (Eds.), *Being a counselor: Directions and challenges* (pp. 195–206). Pacific Grove, CA: Brooks/Cole.

Fraizer, L. M., Miller, V. A., Horbelt, D. V., Delmore, J. E., Miller, B. E., & Paschal, A. M. (2010). Comparison of focus groups on cancer and employment conducted face to face or by telephone. *Qualitative Health Research, 20,* 617–627.

Freeman, B., & McHenry, S. (1996). Clinical supervision of counselors-in-training: A nationwide survey of ideal delivery, goals, and theoretical influences. *Counselor Education and Supervision, 36,* 144–158.

French, J. R. P., Jr., & Raven, B. (1960). The bases of social power. In D. Cartwright & A. Zander (Eds.), *Group dynamics* (2nd ed., pp. 607–623). Evanston, IL: Row, Peterson.

Freud, S. (1949). *Group psychology and the analysis of the ego.* New York, NY: Hogarth.

Frew, J. E. (1983). Encouraging what is not figural in the Gestalt group. *Journal for Specialists in Group Work, 8,* 175–181.

Friedman, W. H. (1989). *Practical group therapy*. San Francisco, CA: Jossey-Bass.

Fry, W. F., & Salameh, W. A. (Eds.). (1993). *Advances in humor and psychotherapy*. Sarasota, FL: Pro Resources.

Furr, S. R. (2000). Structuring the group experience: A format for designing psychoeducational groups. *Journal for Specialists in Group Work, 25*, 29–49.

Gardner, J. W. (1990). *On leadership*. New York, NY: Free Press.

Garfield, R. (2010). Male emotional intimacy: How therapeutic men's groups can enhance couples therapy. *Family Process, 49*, 109–122.

Garlick, M., Wall, K., Corwin, D., & Koopman, C. (2011). Psycho-Spiritual Integrative Therapy for women with primary breast cancer. *Journal of Clinical Psychology in Medical Settings, 18*, 78–90.

Garner, H., Bruce, M. A., & Stellern, J. (2011). The Goal Wheel: Adapting Navajo philosophy and the medicine wheel to work with adolescents. *Journal for Specialists in Group Work, 36*, 62–77.

Garrett, M. T. (2004). Sound of the drum: Group counseling with Native Americans. In J. L. DeLucia-Waack, D. A. Gerrity, C. R. Kalodner, & M. T. Riva (Eds.), *Handbook of group counseling and psychotherapy* (pp. 169–182). Thousand Oaks, CA: Sage.

Garrett, M. T., Brubaker, M., Torres-Rivera, E., West-Olatunji, C., & Conwill, W. L. (2008). The medicine of coming to center: Use of the Native American *centering* technique—Ayeli—to promote wellness and healing in group work. *Journal for Specialists in Group Work, 33*, 179–198.

Garrett, M. T., Garrett, J. T., & Brotherton, D. (2001). Inner circle/outer circle: A group technique based on Native American healing circles. *Journal for Specialists in Group Work, 26*, 17–30.

Garrett, M. T., & Osborne, W. L. (1995). The Native American sweat lodge as metaphor for group work. *Journal for Specialists in Group Work, 20*, 33–39.

Gazda, G. M. (1989). *Group counseling: A developmental approach* (4th ed.). Boston: Allyn & Bacon.

Gazda, G. M., Ginter, E. J., & Horne, A. M. (2001). *Group counseling and group psychotherapy: Theory and practice*. Boston: Allyn & Bacon.

Gearing, R. E., Colvin, G., Popova, S., & Regehr, C. (2008). Re:Membering fatherhood: Evaluating the impact of a group intervention on fathering. *Journal for Specialists in Group Work, 33*, 22–42.

Gendron, J. M. (1980). *Moreno: The roots and the branches and bibliography of psychodrama, 1972–1980; and sociometry, 1970–1980*. Beacon, NY: Beacon House.

George, R. L., & Dustin, D. (1988). *Group counseling: Theory and practice*. Upper Saddle River, NJ: Prentice Hall.

Gerler, E. R., Jr. (1982). *Counseling the young learner*. Upper Saddle River, NJ: Prentice Hall.

Gerler, E. R., Jr., & Anderson, R. F. (1986). The effects of classroom guidance on success in school. *Journal of Counseling and Development, 65*, 78–81.

Geroski, A. M., & Kraus, K. L. (2002). Process and content in school psychoeducational groups: Either, both or none? *Journal for Specialists in Group Work, 27*, 233–245.

Gerrity, D., & DeLucia-Waack, J. L. (2007). Effectiveness of groups in the schools. *Journal for Specialists in Group Work, 32*, 97–106.

Gerrity, D. A. (1998). A classification matrix using goals and process dimensions: Issues for therapy groups. *Journal for Specialists in Group Work, 23*, 202–207.

Gerstein, L. H., & Hotelling, K. (1987). Length of group treatment and changes in women with bulimia. *Journal of Mental Health Counseling, 9*, 162–173.

Gibbs, J. (1965). Norms: The problems of definition and classification. *American Journal of Sociology, 70*, 586–594.

Gibson, R. L., & Mitchell, M. H. (2006). *Introduction to career counseling in the 21st century*. Upper Saddle River, NJ: Pearson.

Gigliotti, R. J. (1988). Sex differences in children's task group performance. *Small Group Behavior, 19*, 273–293.

Gillam, S. L., Hayes, R. L., & Paisley, P. O. (1997). Group work as a method of supervision. In S. T. Gladding (Ed.), *New developments in group counseling* (pp. 133–135). Greensboro, NC: ERIC.

Gillen, M. C., & Balkin, R. S. (2006). Adventure counseling as an adjunct to group counseling in hospital and clinical settings. *Journal for Specialists in Group Work, 31*, 153–164.

Gillis, H. L., Gass, M. A., Russell, K. C. (2014). Adventure therapy with groups. In J. L. DeLucia-Waack, D. A., Kalodner, & M. T. Riva (Eds.), *Handbook of group counseling and psychotherapy*, (2nd ed., pp. 560–570). Thousand Oaks, CA: Sage.

Ginott, H. (1968). Group therapy with children. In G. Gazda (Ed.), *Basic approaches to group psychotherapy and group counseling*. Springfield, IL: Thomas.

Giordano, F. G. (1995). The whole person at work: An integrative vocational intervention model for women's workplace issues. *Journal for Specialists in Group Work, 20*, 4–13.

Gitterman, A., & Shulman, L. (Eds,). (2005). *Mutual aid groups, Vulnerable and resilient populations, and the life cycle*. New York, NY: Columbia University Press.

Gladding, S. T. (1968/1989/2006). *A poem in parting*. Unpublished manuscript, Wake Forest University, Winston-Salem, NC.

Gladding, S. T. (1975). Still life. *North Carolina Personnel & Guidance Journal, 4*, 28.

Gladding, S. T. (1978). In the midst of the puzzles and counseling journey. *Personnel and Guidance Journal, 57*, 148.

Gladding, S. T. (1979). *A restless presence: Group process as a pilgrimage*. School Counselor, 27, 126–127.

Gladding, S. T. (1986). Circles. *ASGW Newsletter, 14*, 3.

Gladding, S. T. (1989a). First thoughts . . . A reflection on professional friendship.

Journal of Humanistic Education and Development, 27, 190–191.

Gladding, S. T. (1989b). *Group dynamics.* Unpublished manuscript, University of Alabama, Birmingham.

Gladding, S. T. (1989c). *In anticipation.* Unpublished poem, University of Alabama, Birmingham.

Gladding, S. T. (1990a). Journey. *Journal of Humanistic Education and Development, 28,* 142.

Gladding, S. T. (1990b). Secrets—Revised. *Journal of Humanistic Education and Development, 28,* 141.

Gladding, S. T. (1993a). *Beginnings.* Unpublished manuscript, Wake Forest University, Winston-Salem, NC.

Gladding, S. T. (1993b). *In reflection.* Unpublished manuscript, Wake Forest University, Winston-Salem, NC.

Gladding, S. T. (1994a). *Effective group counseling.* Greensboro, NC: ERIC/CASS.

Gladding, S. T. (1994b). *Transitions.* Unpublished manuscript, Wake Forest University, Winston-Salem, NC.

Gladding, S. T. (1997). *Rainbow.* Unpublished manuscript, Wake Forest University, Winston-Salem, NC.

Gladding, S. T. (2010). Creativity and spontaneity in groups. In R. K. Conyne (Ed.). *The Oxford handbook of group counseling* (pp. 383–396). New York, NY: Oxford University Press.

Gladding, S. T. (2011a). *The counseling dictionary* (3rd ed.). Upper Saddle River, NJ: Pearson.

Gladding, S. T. (2011b). *The creative arts in counseling* (4th ed.). Alexandria, VA: American Counseling Association.

Gladding, S. T. (2013). *Counseling: A comprehensive profession* (7th ed.). Upper Saddle River, NJ: Merrill/Prentice Hall.

Gladding, S. T. (2015). *Family therapy: History, theory, and practice* (6th ed.). Upper Saddle River, NJ: Prentice Hall.

Glaize, D. L., & Myrick, R. D. (1984). Interpersonal groups or computers? A study of career maturity and career decidedness. *Vocational Guidance Quarterly, 32,* 168–176.

Glaser, B. A., Webster, C. B., & Horne, A. M. (1992). Planning a group: An instructional project for graduate students. *Journal for Specialists in Group Work, 17,* 84–88.

Glass, J. S., & Benshoff, J. M. (1999). PARS: A processing model for beginning group leaders. *Journal for Specialists in Group Work, 24,* 15–26.

Glass, J. S., & Benshoff, J. M. (2002). Facilitating group cohesion among adolescents through challenge course experiences. *The Journal of Experiential Education, 25,* 268–277.

Glasser, W. (1965). *Reality therapy: A new approach to psychiatry.* New York, NY: Harper & Row.

Glasser, W. (1984). Reality therapy. In R. J. Corsini (Ed.), *Current psychotherapies* (3rd ed., pp. 320–353). Itasca, IL: Peacock.

Glasser, W. (1985). *Control theory: A new explanation of how we control our lives.* New York, NY: Harper & Row.

Glasser, W. (1986a). *The basic concepts of reality therapy* (chart). Canoga Park, CA: Institute for Reality Therapy.

Glasser, W. (1986b). *The control theory–reality therapy workbook.* Canoga Park, CA: Institute for Reality Therapy.

Glasser, W. (1992). Reality therapy. *New York State Journal for Counseling and Development, 7,* 5–13.

Glasser, W. (1999). *Choice theory: A new psychology of personal freedom.* New York, NY: HarperCollins.

Glasser, W. (2000). *Reality therapy in action.* New York, NY: HarperCollins.

Glasser, W. (2001). *Counseling with choice theory.* New York, NY: HarperCollins.

Glasser, W. (2003). *Warning: Psychiatry can be hazardous to your mental health.* New York, NY: HarperCollins.

Glasser, W. (2005). *Treating mental health as a public health problem*: A new leadership role for the helping professions. Chatsworth, CA: William Glasser Inc.

Glasser, W., & Breggin, P. R. (2001). *Counseling with choice theory.* New York, NY: HarperCollins.

Glasser, W., & Zunin, L. M. (1973). Reality therapy. In R. Corsini (Ed.), *Current psychotherapies.* Itasca, IL: Peacock.

Gloria, A. M. (1999). Apoyando estudiantes Chicanas: Therapeutic factors in Chicana college student support groups. *Journal for Specialists in Group Work, 24,* 246–259.

Glosser, G., & Wexler, D. (1985). Participants' evaluation of educational/support groups for families of patients with Alzheimer's disease and other dementias. *The Gerontologist, 25,* 232–236.

Golden, L. B. (1987). Prosocial learning groups with young children. *Elementary School Guidance & Counseling, 22,* 31–36.

Goldman, E. E., & Morrison, D. S. (1984). *Psychodrama: Experience and process.* Dubuque, IA: Kendall/Hunt.

Golkaramnay, V., Bauer, S., Haug, S., Wolf, M., & Kordy, H. (2007). The exploration of the effectiveness of group therapy through an Internet chat as aftercare: A controlled naturalistic study. *Psychotherapy and Psychosomatics, 76,* 219–225.

Gonzalez-Lopez, G., & Taylor, B. A. (1997, April). Contributing to the empowerment of inner city immigrant families: Group therapy in a Latino barrio school. *Family Therapy News, 28,* 20–21.

Goodnough, G. E., & Ripley, V. (1996). Structured groups for high school seniors making the transition to college and to military service. *School Counselor, 44,* 230–234.

Goodrich, K. M. (2008). Dual relationships in group training. *Journal for Specialists in Group Work, 33,* 221–235.

Goodrich, K. M., & Luke, M. (2010). The experience of school counselors-in-training in group work with LGBTQ adolescents. *Journal for Specialists in Group Work, 35,* 143–159.

Goodrich, K. M., & Luke, M. (2011). The LGBTQ responsive model for supervision of group work. *Journal for Specialists in Group Work, 36,* 22–40.

Goodrich, K. M., & Luke, M. (2012). Problematic student in the experiential group: Professional and ethical challenges for counselor educators. *Journal for Specialists in Group Work, 37,* 326–346.

Goodyear, R. K. (1981). Termination as a loss experience for the counselor. *Personnel and Guidance Journal, 59,* 347–350.

Gordon, T. (1970). *Parent effectiveness training.* New York, NY: Wyden.

Gordon, W. (1961). *Synectics: The development of creative capacity.* New York, NY: Harper & Row.

Gore-Felton, C., & Spiegel, D. (1999). Enhancing women's lives: The role of support groups among breast cancer patients. *Journal for Specialists in Group Work, 24,* 274–287.

Gossett, T. F. (1998). *Race: The history of an idea in America* (2nd ed.). New York, NY: Oxford University Press.

Gough, P. B. (1987). The key to improving schools: An interview with William Glasser. *Phi Delta Kappa, 68,* 656–662.

Goulding, M., & Goulding, R. (1979). *Changing lives through redecision therapy.* New York, NY: Brunner/Mazel.

Goulding, R. (1975). The formation and beginning process of transactional analysis groups. In G. Gazda (Ed.), *Basic approaches to group psychotherapy and group counseling* (2nd ed.). Springfield, IL: Thomas.

Goulding, R. (1987). Group therapy: Mainline or sideline? In J. K. Zeig (Ed.), *The evolution of psychotherapy* (pp. 300–311). New York, NY: Brunner/Mazel.

Graber, J. A., & Brooks-Gunn, J. (1996). *Transitions through adolescence.* Hillsdale, NJ: Erlbaum.

Greason, D. P. B. (2011). The transition stage in group work. In B. T. Erford (Eds.), *Group work: Processes and applications* (pp. 103–120). Upper Saddle River, NJ: Pearson.

Greeley, A. T., Garcia, V. L., Kessler, B. L., & Gilchrest, G. (1992). Training effective multicultural group counselors: Issues for a group training course. *Journal for Specialists in Group Work, 17,* 196–209.

Greenberg, I. A. (1974). Moreno: Psychodrama and the group process. In I. A. Greenberg (Ed.), *Psychodrama: Theory and therapy* (pp. 11–28). New York, NY: Behavioral Publications.

Greenburg, S. L., Lewis, G. J., & Johnson, J. (1985). Peer consultation groups for private practitioners. *Professional Psychology: Research and Practice, 16,* 437–447.

Greene, R. R. (1986). *Social work with the aged and their families.* New York, NY: Aldine de Gruyter.

Greenstein, M. (2000). The house that's on fire: Meaning-centered psychotherapy pilot group for cancer patients. *American Journal of Psychotherapy, 54,* 501–511.

Greenstein, M., & Breitbart, W. (2000). Cancer and the experience of meaning: A group psychotherapy for people with cancer. *American Journal of Psychotherapy, 54,* 486–500.

Grimes, J. (1988). Transactional analysis in group work. In S. Long (Ed.), *Six group therapies* (pp. 49–113). New York, NY: Plenum.

Gross, A. D., & Shakespeare-Finch, J. (2013). Positive experiences for participants in suicide bereavement groups: A grounded theory model. *Death Studies, 37,* 1–24.

Grossmark, R. (2007). The edge of chaos: Enactment, disruption, and emergence in group psychotherapy. *Psychoanalytic Dialogues, 17,* 479–499.

Guarnaschelli, J. S. (1994). Men's support groups and the men's movement: Their role for men and for women. *Group, 18,* 197–211.

Guerney, B. G., Jr. (1977). *Relationship enhancement: Skill-training programs for therapy problem prevention and enrichment.* San Francisco, CA: Jossey-Bass.

Guez, G., & Gill-Lev, I. (2009). A psychoeducational group for adolescent girls to facilitate egalitarian, non-abusive relationships. *International Journal of Group Psychotherapy, 59,* 385–405.

Gumaer, J. (1986). Working in groups with middle graders. *School Counselor, 33,* 230–238.

Gumaer, J., & Scott, L. (1986). Group workers' perceptions of ethical and unethical behavior of group leaders. *Journal for Specialists in Group Work, 11,* 139–150.

Guy, J. (1987). *The personal life of the psychotherapist.* New York, NY: Wiley.

Haberstroh, S., & Moyer, M. (2012). Exploring an online self-injury support group: Perspectives from group members. *Journal for Specialists in Group Work, 37,* 113–132.

Hackney, H., & Cormier, L. S. (2012). *The professional counselor: A process guide to helping* (7th ed.). Upper Saddle River, NJ: Pearson.

Hage, S. M., Mason, M., & Kim, J. (2010). A social justice approach to group counseling. In R. K. Conyne (Ed.), *The handbook of group counseling* (pp. 102–117). New York, NY: Oxford University Press.

Hage, S. M., & Nosanow, M. (2000). Becoming stronger at broken places: A model for group work with young adults from divorced families. *Journal for Specialists in Group Work, 25,* 50–66.

Hagedorn, W. B., & Hirshhorn, M. A. (2009). When talking won't work: Implementing experiential group activities with addicted clients. *Journal for Specialists in Group Work, 34,* 43–67.

Haight, B., & Gibson, F. (Eds.). (2005). *Burnside's working with older adults; Group process and technique* (4th ed.). Sudbury, MA: Jones & Bartlett.

Haight, B., & Haight, B. (2007). *The handbook of structured life review.* Baltimore, MD: Health Professions Press.

Hall, E., Hall, C., Harris, B., Hay, D., Biddulph, M., & Duffy, T. (1999). An evaluation of the long-term outcomes of small-group work for counsellor development. *British Journal of Guidance and Counselling, 27,* 99–112.

Hall, G. S. (1904). *Adolescence.* New York, NY: Appleton.

Hall, J., & Hawley, L. (2004). Interactive process notes: An innovative tool in counseling groups. *Journal for Specialists in Group Work, 29,* 193–205.

Hall, K. R., Rushing, J. L., & Khurshid, A. (2011). Using the Solving Problem Together psychoeducational group counseling model as an intervention for negative peer pressure. *Journal of Specialists in Group Work, 36*, 97–110.

Hamburg, D. A., & Takanishi, R. (1989). Preparing for life: The critical transition of adolescence. *American Psychologist, 44*, 825–827.

Haney, H., & Leibsohn, J. (2001). *Basic counseling responses in groups*. Belmont, CA: Wadsworth.

Hansen, J. C., Warner, R. W., & Smith, E. J. (1980). *Group counseling: Theory and process* (2nd ed.). Chicago: Rand McNally.

Hare, A. P., Blumberg, H. H., Davies, M. F., & Kent, M. V. (1994). *Small Group Research: A Handbook*. New York, NY: Ablex.

Harel, Y., Shechtman, Z., & Cutrona, C. (2012). Exploration of support behavior in counseling groups the counseling trainees. *Journal for Specialists in Group Work, 37*, 202–217.

Hargaden, H., & Sills, C. (2002). *Transactional analysis: A relational perspective*. East Sussex: Brunner-Routledge.

Harman, M. J. (1991). The use of group psychotherapy with cancer patients: A review of recent literature. *Journal for Specialists in Group Work, 16*, 56–61.

Harman, M. J., & Withers, I. (1992). University students from homes with alcoholic parents: Considerations for therapy groups. *Journal for Specialists in Group Work, 17*, 37–41.

Harman, R. L. (1988). Gestalt group therapy. In S. Long (Ed.), *Six group therapies* (pp. 217–255). New York, NY: Plenum.

Harper, F. D. (1984). Group strategies with black alcoholics. *Journal for Specialists in Group Work, 9*, 38–43.

Harper, R. L., & Ellis, A. (1975). *A new guide to rational living*. Upper Saddle River, NJ: Prentice Hall.

Harris, H. L., Altekruse, M. K., & Engels, D. W. (2003). Helping freshmen student athletes adjust to college life using psychoeducational groups. *Journal for Specialists in Group Work, 28*, 64–81.

Harris, S. A. (1996). Childhood roles and the interpersonal circle: A model for ACOA groups. *Journal for Specialists in Group Work, 21*, 39–48.

Harris, S. A., & MacQuiddy, S. (1991). Childhood roles in group therapy: The lost child and the mascot. *Journal for Specialists in Group Work, 16*, 223–229.

Harris, T. A. (1967). *I'm OK—You're OK*. New York, NY: Harper & Row.

Hartsell, T. L., Jr., & Bernstein, B. E. (2013). *The portable lawyer for mental health professionals: An A-Z guide to protecting your clients, your practice, and yourself* (3rd ed.). New York, NY: Wiley.

Harvill, R., Masson, R. L., & Jacobs, E. (1983). Systematic group leader training: A skills development approach. *Journal for Specialists in Group Work, 8*, 226–232.

Harvill, R., West, J., Jacobs, E. E., & Masson, R. L. (1985). Systematic group leader training: Evaluating the effectiveness of the approach. *Journal for Specialists in Group Work, 10*, 2–13.

Hatch, K. D., & McCarthy, C. J. (2003). Challenge course participation as a component of experiential groups for counselors in training. *Journal for Specialists in Group Work, 28*, 199–214.

Havighurst, R. J. (1972). *Developmental tasks and education* (3rd ed.). New York, NY: D. McKay.

Hawkins, B. L. (1983). Group counseling as a treatment modality for the elderly: A group snapshot. *Journal for Specialists in Group Work, 8*, 186–193.

Hayashi, M. (1990). On the significance of co-facilitator relationship in their encounter group. *Japanese Journal of Psychology, 61*, 184–187.

Hayes, R. L. (1990). Developmental group supervision. *Journal for Specialists in Group Work, 15*, 225–238.

Hayes, R. L. (1991). Group work and the teaching of ethics. *Journal for Specialists in Group Work, 16*, 24–31.

Hays, D. G., Arredondo, P., Gladding, S. T., & Toporek, R. L. (2010). Integrating social justice in group work: The next decade. *Journal for Specialists in Group Work, 35*, 177–206.

Hays, D. G., & Grimmett, M. A. (2014). Racism and White privilege. In D. G. Hays & B. T. Erford (Eds.), *Developing multicultural counseling competence: A systems approach* (2nd ed., pp. 82–104).

Helm, K. M., & James, L., Jr. (2010). Individuals and families of African descent. In D. G. Hays & B. T. Erford (Eds.), *Developing multicultural counseling competence* (pp. 193–215). Upper Saddle River, NJ: Pearson.

Henderson, D. A., & Gladding, S. T. (2004). Group counseling with older adults. In J. L. DeLucia-Waack, D. A. Gerrity, C. R. Kalodner, & M. T. Riva (Eds.), *Handbook of group counseling and psychotherapy* (pp. 469–478). Thousand Oaks, CA: Sage.

Henderson, D. A., & Thompson, C. L. (2011). *Counseling children* (8th ed.). Belmont, CA: Brooks/Cole.

Hendrix, F. G., & Sedgwick, C. (1989). Group counseling with the elderly. In G. M. Gazda (Ed.), *Group counseling: A developmental approach* (pp. 195–211). Boston: Allyn & Bacon.

Hendrix, H. (1988). *Getting the love you want*. New York, NY: Holt, Rinehart & Winston.

Hensley, L. G. (2002). Teaching group process and leadership: The two-way fishbowl model. *Journal for Specialists in Group Work, 27*, 273–286.

Heppner, P. P. (1981). Counseling men in groups. *Personnel and Guidance Journal, 60*, 249–252.

Herlihy, B., & Corey, G. (2014). *ACA ethical standards casebook* (6th ed.). Alexandria, VA: American Counseling Association.

Herlihy, B., & Remley, T. P., Jr. (1995). Unified ethical standards: A challenge for professionalism. *Journal of Counseling and Development, 74*, 130–133.

Herlihy, B., & Remley, T. (2001). Legal and ethical challenges in counseling. In D. C. Locke, J. E. Myers, & E. L. Herr (Eds.), *The handbook of counseling* (pp. 69–90). Thousand Oaks, CA: Sage.

Hern, B. G., & Weis, D. M. (1991). A group counseling experience with the very old. *Journal for Specialists in Group Work, 16,* 143–151.

Hersey, P., & Blanchard, K. H. (1969). Life-cycle theory of leadership. *Training and Development Journal, 23,* 26–34.

Hershenson, D. B., Power, P. W., & Waldo, M. (2003). *Community counseling: Contemporary theory and practice.* Long Grove, IL: Waveland.

Higgs, J. A. (1992). Dealing with resistance: Strategies for effective group. *Journal for Specialists in Group Work, 17,* 67–73.

Hill, M., Glaser, K., & Harden, J. (1995). A feminist model for ethical decision making. In E. J. Rave & C. C. Larsen (Eds.), *Ethical decision making in therapy: Feminist perspectives* (pp. 18–37). New York, NY: Guilford.

Hillman, B. W., & Reunion, K. B. (1978). Activity group guidance: Process and results. *Elementary School Guidance & Counseling, 13,* 104–111.

Himes, C. L., Hogan, D. P., & Eggebeen, D. J. (1996). Living arrangements of minority elders. *Journal of Gerontology, 51A,* 542–548.

Hines, M. (1988). Similarities and differences in group and family therapy. *Journal for Specialists in Group Work, 13,* 173–179.

Hines, P. L., & Fields, T. H. (2002). Preschool screening issues for school counselors. *Journal for Specialists in Group Work, 27,* 358–376.

Hinkle, J. S. (1991). Support group counseling for caregivers of Alzheimer's disease patients. *Journal for Specialists in Group Work, 16,* 185–190.

Hitchings, P. (1994). Psychotherapy and sexual orientation. In P. Clarkston & M. Pokorny (Eds.), *The handbook of psychotherapy* (pp. 119–132). London, England: Routledge.

Hoffmann, L. L., Gleave, R. L., Burlingame, G. M., & Jackson, A. P. (2009). Exploring interactions of improvers and deteriorators in the process of group therapy: A qualitative analysis. *International Journal of Group Psychotherapy, 59,* 179–198.

Holmes, P., & Karp, M. (Eds.). (1991). *Psychodrama: Inspiration and technique.* New York, NY: Routledge.

Homrich, A. M., & Horne, A. M. (1997). Multiple family group therapy (MFGT). In S. T. Gladding (Ed.), *New developments in group counseling* (pp. 51–53). Greensboro, NC: ERIC.

Hopson, B., & Hough, P. (1976). The need for personal and social education in secondary schools and further education. *British Journal of Guidance and Counseling, 4,* 16–27.

Horne, A. M. (1999, January). *Working with men in groups.* Paper presented at the Association for Specialists in Group Work Group-A-Rama, Albuquerque, NM.

Horne, A. M. (2001). *Family counseling and therapy* (3rd ed.). Itasca, IL: Peacock.

Horne, A. M., Levitt, H. M., Reeves, T., & Wheeler, E. E. (2014). Group work with gay, lesbian, bisexual, transgender, queer, and questioning clients. In J. L. DeLucia, C. R. Kalodner, & M. T. Riva (Eds.), *Handbook of group counseling and psychotherapy* (2nd ed., pp. 253–263). Thousand Oaks, CA: Sage.

Horne, S. (1999). From coping to creating change: The evolution of women's groups. *Journal for Specialists in Group Work, 24,* 231–245.

Horswill, R. K. (1993). Are typical senior center group activities better suited for women than for men? *Journal for Specialists in Group Work, 18,* 45–48.

Horvatin, T., & Schreiber, E. (Eds.). (2006). *The quintessential Zerka: Writings by Zerka Toeman Moreno on psychodrama, sociometry and group psychotherapy.* New York, NY: Routledge.

Hoskins, M. (1984, April). *Guidelines for writing therapeutic fairy tales.* Paper presented at the Fourth Annual Conference of the National Association for Poetry Therapy, Hempstead, NY.

Howlin, P., & Yates, P. (1999). The potential effectiveness of social skills groups for adults with autism. *Autism, 3,* 299–307.

Hudson, P. E., Doyle, R. E., & Venezia, J. F. (1991). A comparison of two group methods of teaching communication skills to high school students. *Journal for Specialists in Group Work, 16,* 255–263.

Huffman, D. D., & Fernando, D. M. (2012). Adapting the interpersonal process model of intimacy to enhance the co-leader relationship during training. *Journal for Specialists in Group Work, 37,* 152–167.

Hulse-Killacky, D. (1993). Personal and professional endings. *Journal of Humanistic Education and Development, 32,* 92–94.

Hulse-Killacky, D., Killacky, J., & Donigian, J. (2001). *Making task groups work in your world.* Upper Saddle River, NJ: Prentice Hall.

Hulse-Killacky, D., Schumacher, B., & Kraus, K. (1994, April). *Effective group leadership.* Presentation at the annual convention of the American Counseling Association, Minneapolis, MN.

Hulse-Killacky, D., Schumacher, B., & Kraus, K. (1999). Visual conceptualizations of meetings: A group work design. *Journal for Specialists in Group Work, 24,* 113–124.

Hummel, D. L., Talbutt, L. C., & Alexander, M. D. (1985). *Law and ethics in counseling.* New York, NY: Van Nostrand Reinhold.

Hurst, J. B., & Vanderveen, N. (1994). Effective management of polarities: Educating men to manage unsolvable problems. *Journal for Specialists in Group Work, 19,* 211–216.

Huss, S. N., & Ritchie, M. (1999). Effectiveness of a group for parentally bereaved children. *Journal for Specialists in Group Work, 24,* 186–196.

In, J. K., & Hwang, M. G. (1997). The effect on internal control and achievement motivation based on R. T. group activity—Making the world I want. *Korean Journal of Counseling and Psychotherapy, 9,* 81–99.

Ivers, N. N., & Newsome, D. W. (2011). Forming and orienting groups. In B. T. Erford (Ed.), *Group work: Processes and applications* (pp. 88–102). Upper Saddle River, NJ: Pearson.

Ivey, A. E. (1971). *Microcounseling: Innovations in interviewing training.* Springfield, IL: Thomas.

Ivey, A. (1973). Microcounseling: The counselor as trainer. *Personnel and Guidance Journal, 51,* 311–316.

Ivey, A. E., Ivey, M. B., & Zalaquett, C. (2014). *Intentional interviewing and counseling: Facilitating client development in a multicultural society* (8th ed.). Belmont, CA: Brooks/Cole.

Ivey, A. E., Pedersen, P. B., & Ivey, M. B. (2001). *Intentional group counseling: A microskills approach.* Pacific Grove, CA: Brooks/Cole.

Jacobs, E. (1992). *Creative counseling techniques: An illustrated guide.* Odessa, FL: Psychological Assessment Resources.

Jacobs, E. E., Masson, R. L., Harvill, R. L., & Schimmel, C. L. (2012). *Group counseling: Strategies and skills* (7th ed.). Belmont, CA: Brooks/Cole.

Jacobs, E. E., Schimmel, C. L., Masson, R. L., & Harvill, R. L. (2016). *Group counseling: Strategies and skills* (8th ed.). Belmont, CA: Cengage.

James, L., & Martin, D. (2002). Sand tray and group therapy: Helping parents cope. *Journal for Specialists in Group Work, 27,* 390–405.

James, M. (2002). *It's never too late to be happy: Reparenting yourself for happiness.* Sanger, CA: Quill Driver Books.

James, M., & Jongeward, D. (1971). *Born to win: Transactional analysis with Gestalt experiments.* Reading, MA: Addison-Wesley.

James, N. (1994). Cultural frame of reference and intergroup encounters: A TA approach. *Transactional Analysis Journal, 24,* 206–210.

Janis, I. L. (1972). *Victims of groupthink.* Boston: Houghton Mifflin.

Janis, I. L. (1982). *Groupthink: Psychological studies of policy decisions and fiascos* (2nd ed.). Boston: Houghton Mifflin.

Johnson, D. W. (2013). *Reaching out: Interpersonal effectiveness and self-actualization* (11th ed.). Upper Saddle River, NJ: Pearson.

Johnson, D. W., & Johnson, F. P. (2013). *Joining together* (11th ed.). Upper Saddle River, NJ: Pearson.

Johnson, I. H., Torres, J. S., Coleman, V. D., & Smith, M. C. (1995). Issues and strategies in leading culturally diverse counseling group. *Journal for Specialists in Group Work, 20,* 143–150.

Johnson, W. Y., & Wilborn, B. (1991). Group counseling as an intervention in anger expression and depression in older adults. *Journal for Specialists in Group Work, 16,* 133–142.

Jones, K. D. (2002). Group play therapy with sexually abused preschool children: Group behaviors and interventions. *Journal for Specialists in Group Work, 27,* 377–389.

Jones, K. D., & Robinson, E. H. (2000). Psychoeducational groups: A model for choosing topics and exercises appropriate to group stages. *Journal for Specialists in Group Work, 25,* 356–365.

Jourard, S. M. (1971). *The transparent self* (2nd ed.). New York, NY: Van Nostrand.

Juhnke, G. A., & Osborne, W. L. (1997). The solution-focused debriefing group: An integrated postviolence group intervention for adults. *Journal for Specialists in Group Work, 22,* 66–76.

Juntunen, C. L., Cohen, B. B., & Wolszon, L. R. (1997). Women and anger: A structured group. *Journal for Specialists in Group Work, 22,* 97–110.

Kaczkowski, H. (1979). Group work with children. *Elementary School Guidance & Counseling, 14,* 44–51.

Kalodner, C. R., Coughlin, J. W., & Seide, M. (2014). Psychoeducational and counseling groups to prevent and treat eating disorders and disturbances. In J. L. DeLucia-Waack, C. R. Kalodner, & M. T. Riva (Eds.), *Handbook of group counseling and psychotherapy* (2nd ed., pp. 484–494). Thousand Oaks, CA: Sage.

Kane, C. M. (1995). Fishbowl training in group process. *Journal for Specialists in Group Work, 20,* 183–188.

Kapur, R., & Miller, K. (1987). A comparison between therapeutic factors in TA and psychodynamic therapy groups. *Transactional Analysis Journal, 17,* 294–300.

Karpman, S. (1968). Fairy tales and script drama analysis. *Transactional Analysis Bulletin, 7,* 39–43.

Katzenbach, J., & Smith, D. (1993). *The wisdom of teams.* Cambridge, MA: Harvard Business School Press.

Kauffman, E., Dore, M. M., & Nelson-Zlupko, L. (1995). The role of women's therapy groups in the treatment of chemical dependence. *American Journal of Ortho-psychiatry, 65,* 355–363.

Keat, D. B. (1974). *Fundamentals of child counseling.* Boston: Houghton Mifflin.

Keat, D. B. (1979). *Multimodal therapy with children.* New York, NY: Pergamon.

Keat, D. B., Metzgar, K. L., Raykovitz, D., & McDonald, J. (1985). Multimodal counseling: Motivating children to attend school through friendship groups. *Journal of Humanistic Education and Development, 23,* 166–175.

Keats, P. A. (2009). Time-limited service alternatives: reply to commentators. *Journal for Specialists in Group Work, 34,* 202–208.

Keel, L. P. (1998). A task group practitioner's response to Waldo and Bauman's article on regrouping the categorization of group work. *Journal for Specialists in Group Work, 23,* 192–195.

Keene, M., & Erford, B. T. (2007). *Group activities: Firing up for performance.* Upper Saddle River, NJ: Prentice Hall.

Kees, N. L. (1999). Women together again: A phenomenological study of leaderless women's groups. *Journal for Specialists in Group Work, 24,* 288–305.

Kees, N. L., & Jacobs, E. (1990). Conducting more effective groups: How to select and process group exercises. *Journal for Specialists in Group Work, 15,* 21–29.

Kees, N. L., & Leech, N. (2014). Women's groups: Research and practice trends. In J. L. DeLucia-Waack, C. R. Kalonder, & M. T. Riva (Eds.), *Handbook of group counseling and psychotherapy* (pp. 506–520). Thousand Oaks, CA: Sage.

Kellerman, H. (1979). *Group psychotherapy and personality: Intersecting structures*. New York, NY: Grune & Stratton.

Kelly, J. F., Myers, M. G., & Rodolico, J. (2008). What do adolescents exposed to Alcoholics Anonymous think of 12–step groups? *Substance Abuse, 29*, 53–62.

Kelly, V. A. (2006). Women of courage: A personal account of a wilderness-based experiential group for survivors of abuse. *Journal for Specialists in Group Work, 31*, 99–111.

Kennedy, G. J., & Tanenbaum, S. (2000). Psychotherapy with older adults. *American Journal of Psychotherapy, 54*, 386–407.

Kenny, M. C. (2009). Child sexual abuse prevention: Psychoeducational groups for preschoolers and their parents. *Journal for Specialists in Group Work, 34*, 24–42.

Kepner, E. (1980). Gestalt group process. In B. Feder & R. Ronall (Eds.), *Beyond the hot seat: Gestalt approaches to group* (pp. 5–24). New York, NY: Brunner/Mazel.

Kerr, M. E., & Bowen, M. (1988). *Family evaluation: An approach based on Bowen theory*. New York, NY: Norton.

Keyton, J. (1993). Group termination: Completing the study of group development. *Small Group Research, 24*, 84–100.

Khattab, N., & Jones, C. P. (2007). Growing up girl: Preparing for change through group work. *Journal for Specialists in Group Work, 32*, 41–50.

Khng, R. H. H. (2001). Tiptoe out of the closet: The before and after of the increasingly visible gay community. *Journal of Homosexuality, 40*, 81–97.

Kilmartin, C. (2014). Using humor and storytelling in men's work. In A. B. Rochlen & F. E. Rabinowitz (Eds.), *Breaking barriers in counseling men* (pp. 20–29). New York, NY: Routledge.

Kim, B. S. K., Atkinson, D. R., & Umemoto, D. (2001). Asian cultural value and the counseling process: Current knowledge and directions for future research. *Counseling Psychologist, 29*, 570–603.

Kim, B. S. K., Omizo, M. M., & D'Andrea, M. J. (1998). The effects of culturally consonant group counseling on the self-esteem and internal locus of control orientation among Native American adolescents. *Journal for Specialists in Group Work, 23*, 145–163.

Kimmel, M. S., & Messner, M. A. (2013). *Men's lives* (9th ed.). Upper Saddle River, NJ: Pearson.

Kincade, E. A., & Kalodner, C. R. (2004). The use of groups in college and university counseling centers. In J. L. DeLucia-Waack, D. A. Gerrity, C. R. Kalonder, & M. T. Riva (Eds.), *Handbook of group counseling and psychotherapy* (pp. 366–377). Thousand Oaks, CA: Sage.

Kirk, G., & Okazawa-Rey, M. (2009). *Women's lives: Multiple perspectives* (3rd ed.). New York, NY: McGraw Hill.

Kiselica, A. M., & Kiselica, M. S. (2014). Gender-sensitive group counseling and psychotherapy with men. In J. L. DeLucia, C. R. Kalodner, & M. T. Riva (Eds.), *Handbook of group counseling & psychotherapy* (2nd ed., pp. 521–530). Thousand Oaks, CA: Sage.

Kiselica, M. S., & Robinson, M. (2001). Bringing advocacy counseling to life: The history, issues, and human dramas of social justice work in counseling. *Journal of Counseling and Development, 79*, 387–397.

Kissane, D. W., Bloch, S., Miach, P., Smith, G. C., Seddon, A., & Keks, N. (1997). Cognitive-existential group therapy for patients with primary breast cancer—Techniques and themes. *Psycho-Oncology, 6*, 25–33.

Kit, P. L., & Teo, L. (2012). Quit now! A psychoeducational expressive therapy group work approach for at-risk and delinquent adolescent smokers in Singapore. *Journal for Specialists in Group Work, 37*, 2–28.

Kitchener, K. S. (1984a). Ethics and counseling psychology: Distinctions and directions. *The Counseling Psychologist, 12*, 15–18.

Kitchener, K. S. (1984b). Intuition, critical evaluation, and ethical principles: The foundation for ethical decisions in counseling psychology. *The Counseling Psychologist, 12*, 43–55.

Kitchener, K. S. (1986). Teaching applied ethics in counselor education: An integration of psychological processes and philosophical analysis. *Journal of Counseling and Development, 64*, 306–310.

Kivlighan, D. M., Jr., & Luiza, J. W. (2005). Examining the credibility gap and the mum effect: Rex Stockton's contributions to research on feedback in groups. *Journal for Specialists in Group Work, 30*, 253–269.

Kizner, L. R. (1999). Small group counseling with adopted children. *Professional School Counseling, 2*(3), 226–231.

Klaw, E., & Humphreys, K. (2004). The role of peer-led mutual help groups in promoting health and well-being. In J. L. DeLucia-Waack, D. A. Gerrity, C. R. Kalodner, & M. T. Riva (Eds.), *Handbook of group counseling and psychotherapy* (pp. 630–640). Thousand Oaks, CA: Sage.

Klein, C., DiazGranados, D., Salas, E., Le, H., Burke, C. S., Lyons, R., & Goodwin, G. F. (2009). Does team building work? *Small Group Research, 40*, 181–222.

Kline, T. J. B. (1999). The Team Player Inventory: Reliability and validity of a measure of predisposition toward organizational team-working environments. *Journal for Specialists in Group Work, 24*, 102–112.

Kline, T. J. B. (2001). Predicting team performance: Testing a model in a field setting. *Journal for Specialists in Group Work, 26*, 185–197.

Kline, W. B. (1990). Responding to "problem" members. *Journal for Specialists in Group Work, 15*, 195–200.

Kline, W. B. (1997). Groups as a whole dynamics and the "problem" member: Conceptualization and intervention. In S. T. Gladding (Ed.), *New developments in group counseling* (pp. 93–95). Greensboro, NC: ERIC.

Knight, B. G. (2004). *Psychotherapy with older adults* (3rd ed.). Newbury Park, CA: Sage.

Kondo, C. T. (2009). Benefits of job clubs for executive job seekers: A tale of hares and tortoises. *Journal of Employment Counseling, 46*, 27–37.

Konstam, V. (1995). Anger: A neglected group treatment issue with cardiac transplantation recipients and their families. *Journal for Specialists in Group Work, 20,* 189–194.

Korchin, S. J. (1976). *Clinical psychology.* New York, NY: Basic Books.

Korda, L. J., & Pancrazio, J. J. (1989). Limiting negative outcome in group practice. *Journal for Specialists in Group Work, 14,* 112–120.

Kormanski, C. (1982). Leadership strategies for managing conflict. *Journal for Specialists in Group Work, 7,* 112–118.

Kormanski, C. (1999). *The team: Explorations in group process.* Denver, CO: Love.

Kormanski, C., & Eschbach, L. (1997). From group leader to process consultant. In H. Forester-Miller & J. A. Kottler (Eds.), *Issues and challenges for group practitioners* (pp. 133–164). Denver, CO: Love.

Kormanski, C. L., & Mozenter, A. (1987). A new model of team building: A technology for today and tomorrow. In J. W. Pfeiffer (Ed.), *The 1987 annual: Developing human resources* (pp. 255–268). San Diego, CA: University Associates.

Kottler, J. A. (1983). *Pragmatic group leadership.* Pacific Grove, CA: Brooks/Cole.

Kottler, J. A. (1994). *Advanced group leadership.* Pacific Grove, CA: Brooks/Cole.

Kottler, J. A. (2010). *On being a therapist* (4th ed.). San Francisco, CA: Jossey-Bass.

Kottler, J. A., & Englar-Carlson, M. (2014). *Learning group leadership: An experiential approach* (3rd ed.). Thousand Oaks, CA: Sage.

Kranz, P. L., & Lund, N. (1993). A reflective analysis through the vision and voices of an undergraduate psychodrama class. *Journal of Group Psychotherapy, Psychodrama, and Sociometry, 46,* 32–39.

Kraus, K. L., DeEsch, J. B., & Geroski, A. M. (2001). Stop avoiding challenging situations in group counseling. *Journal for Specialists in Group Work, 26,* 31–47.

Kraus, K. L., & Hulse-Killacky, D. (1996). Balancing process and content in groups: A metaphor. *Journal for Specialists in Group Work, 21,* 90–93.

Krieg, F. J. (1988). *Group leadership training and supervision manual for adolescent group counseling in schools* (3rd ed.). Muncie, IN: Accelerated Development.

Krieger, K. M., & Stockton, R. (2004). Technology and group leadership training: Teaching group counseling in an online environment. *Journal for Specialists in Group Work, 29,* 343–359.

Krivatsy-O'Hara, S., Reed, P., & Davenport, J. (1978) Group counseling with potential high school dropouts. *Personnel and Guidance Journal, 56,* 510–512.

Kübler-Ross, E. (1973). *On death and dying.* London, England: Tavistock.

Kulic, K. L., Horne, A. M., & Dagley, J. C. (2004). A comprehensive review of prevention groups for children and adolescents. *Group Dynamics: Theory, Research, and Practice, 8,* 139–151.

Kymissis, P. (1993). Group psychotherapy with adolescents. In H. Kaplan & B. J. Sadock (Eds.), *Comprehensive group psychotherapy* (3rd ed.). Baltimore: Williams & Wilkins.

Lacoursiere, R. (1974). A group method to facilitate learning during the stages of a psychiatric affiliation. *International Journal of Group Psychotherapy, 24,* 114–119.

Lacoursiere, R. B. (1980). *The life cycle of groups: Group development stage theory.* New York, NY: Human Sciences Press.

LaGaipa, J. (1977). The effects of humour on the flow of social conversation. In A. J. Chapman & H. C. Foot (Eds.), *It's a funny thing, humour* (pp. 421–427). New York, NY.

Lake, R. G. (1987). *The sweat lodge: An ancient medicine for modern sickness.* Mesa, AZ: Self Discovery Magazine.

Lancaster, C., Lenz, A. S., Meadows, E., & Brown, K. C. (2013). Evaluation of a conflict resolution program for urban African American adolescent girls. *Journal for Specialists in Group Work, 38,* 225–240.

Landreth, G. L. (1984). Encountering Carl Rogers: His views on facilitating groups. *Personnel and Guidance Journal, 62,* 323–326.

Lanier, E., & Robertiello, R. C. (1977). A small group of patients discuss their experiences and feelings about working with therapists of different races. *Journal of Contemporary Psychotherapy, 9,* 42–44.

Lanning, W. (1986). Development of the supervisor emphasis rating form. *Counselor Education and Supervision, 27,* 331–342.

Lanza, M. L., & Schmidt, S. I. (2008). Group work with aggressive men: Group within a group within a group. *Journal of Contemporary Psychology, 38,* 197–203.

Lapworth, P., & Sills, C. (2011). *An introduction to Transactional Analysis: Helping people change.* Thousand Oaks, CA: Sage.

Larrabee, M. (1982). Working with reluctant clients through affirmation techniques. *Personnel and Guidance Journal, 60,* 105–109.

Larson, C. E., & LaFasto, F. M. J. (1989). *TeamWork.* Newbury Park, CA: Sage.

Latner, J. (1973). *The Gestalt therapy book.* New York, NY: Julian.

Laughlin, P. R. (1988). Collective induction: Group performance, social combination processes, and mutual majority and minority influence. *Journal of Personality and Social Psychology, 54,* 254–267.

Lazarus, A. A. (1976). *Multimodal behavior therapy.* New York, NY: Springer.

Lazarus, A. A. (1981). *The practice of multimodal therapy.* New York, NY: McGraw-Hill.

Lazarus, A. A. (1989). *The practice of multimodal therapy: Systematic, comprehensive, and effective psychotherapy.* Baltimore: Johns Hopkins University Press.

Leach, M. M., & Aten, J. D. (2010). *Culture and therapeutic process: A guide for mental health professionals.* New York, NY: Routledge.

Lefley, H. P. (2009). A psychoeducational support group for seriously mental illness. *Journal for Specialists in Group Work, 34,* 369–381.

Leavitt, H. J. (1951). Some effects of certain communication problems on group performance. *Journal of Abnormal and Social Psychology, 46,* 38–50.

LeCroy, C. W. (1986). An analysis of the effects of gender on outcome in group treatment with young adolescents. *Journal of Youth and Adolescence, 15,* 497–508.

Lee, C. C. (1995, Fall). Group work for a new millennium. *Together, 24*(1), 4.

Lee, C. C. (1997). Cultural dynamics: Their importance in culturally responsive counseling. In C. C. Lee (Ed.), *Multicultural issues in counseling* (2nd ed., pp. 15–30). Alexandria, VA: American Counseling Association.

Lee, R. S. (1993). Effects of classroom guidance on student achievement. *Elementary School Guidance & Counseling, 27,* 163–171.

Leech, N. L., & Kees, N. L. (2005). Researching women's groups: Findings, limitations, and recommendations. *Journal of Counseling & Development, 83,* 367–373.

LeMasters, E. E., & DeFrain, J. (1989). *Parents in contemporary America* (5th ed.). Belmont, CA: Wadsworth.

LeShan, E. (1990). *It's better to be over the hill than under it: Thoughts on life over 60.* New York, NY: Newmarket.

Lessner, J. W. (1974). The poem as a catalyst in group work. *Personnel and Guidance Journal, 53,* 33–38.

Letendre, J., Gaillard, B. V., & Spath, R. (2008). Getting the job done: Use of a work group for agency change. *Groupwork, 18,* 52–68.

Leung, G. S. M., Leung, T. Y. K., & Ng, M. L. T. (2013). An outcome study of Gestalt oriented workshops. *International Journal of Group Psychotherapy, 63,* 117–125.

Leveton, E. (2001). *A clinician's guide to psychodrama* (3rd ed.). New York, NY: Springer.

Levi, D. (2014). *Group dynamics for teams* (4th ed.). Thousand Oaks, CA: Sage.

Levin, J. S., Taylor, R. J., & Chatters, L. M. (1994). Race and gender differences in religiosity among older adults: Findings from four national surveys. *Journal of Gerontology, 49,* S137–S145.

Levin, L. S., & Shepherd, I. L. (1974). The role of the therapist in Gestalt therapy. *The Counseling Psychologist, 4,* 27–30.

Lev-Wiesel, R. (2003). The group stories fabric technique (GSFT): A clinical tool for understanding transference issues in group psychotherapy. *Journal for Specialists in Group Work, 28,* 227–243.

Lewin, K. (1944). The dynamics of group action. *Educational Leadership, 1,* 195–200.

Lewin, K. (1948). *Resolving social conflicts: Selected papers on group dynamics.* New York, NY: Harper.

Lewin, K. (1951). *Field theory in social science.* New York, NY: Harper.

Li, M-H. (2009). A model parent group for enhancing aggressive children's social competence in Taiwan. *International Journal of Group Psychotherapy, 59,* 407–420.

Lieberman, M. (2007). The role of insightful disclosure in outcomes for women in peer-directed breast cancer groups: A replication study. *Psycho-Oncology, 16,* 961–964.

Lieberman, M. A., Yalom, I. D., & Miles, M. (1973). *Encounter groups: First facts.* New York, NY: Basic Books.

Light, R. (1994, March). *Effective teaching.* Presentation at Faculty Development Seminar, Wake Forest University, Winston-Salem, NC.

Linton, J. M. (2003). A preliminary qualitative investigation of group processes in group supervision. *Journal for Specialists in Group Work, 28,* 215–226.

Locke, D. C., & Kiselica, M. S. (1999). Pedagogy of possibilities: Teaching about racism in multicultural counseling courses. *Journal of Counseling and Development, 77,* 80–86.

Lowe, R. N. (1982). Adlerian/Dreikursian family counseling. In A. M. Horne & M. M. Ohlsen (Eds.), *Family counseling and therapy* (pp. 329–359). Itasca, IL: Peacock.

Lowenstein, L. F. (1993). Humanism-existentialism as a basis of psychotherapy. *International Journal of Mental Health, 22,* 93–102.

Luft, J. (1984). *Group processes: An introduction to group dynamics* (3rd ed.). Palo Alto, CA: Mayfield.

Luke, H. (2010). *Old age.* Great Barrington, MA: Lindisfarne Books.

Luke, M. (2014). Effective group leadership skills. In J. L. DeLucia-Waack, C. R. Kalodner, & M. T. Riva (Eds.), *Handbook of Group Counseling & Psychotherapy* (2nd ed., pp. 107–119). Thousand Oaks, CA: Sage.

Maass, V. S. (2006). *Women's group therapy: Creative challenges and options.* New York, NY: Springer.

MacDevitt, J. W. (1987). Conceptualizing therapeutic components of group counseling. *Journal for Specialists in Group Work, 12,* 76–84.

MacKenzie, K., & Livesley, W. (1983). Developmental model for brief groups. In R. E. Dies & K. R. MacKenzie (Eds.), *Advances in group psychotherapy: Integrating research and practice* (pp. 101–116). New York, NY: International Universities Press.

MacNair-Semands, R. R. (1997, August). Using new instruments to enhance group therapy. In J. Corazzini (Chair), *Integral features of group psychotherapy.* Symposium conducted at the annual meeting of the American Psychological Association, Chicago.

MacNair-Semands, R. R. (1998). Encompassing the complexity of group work. *Journal for Specialists in Group Work, 23,* 208–214.

Mahler, C. A. (1969). *Group counseling in the schools.* Boston: Houghton Mifflin.

Mahler, C. A. (1971). Group counseling. *Personnel and Guidance Journal, 49,* 601–610.

Malekoff, A. (1997). *Group work with adolescents.* New York, NY: Guilford.

Maliver, B. L. (1973). *The encounter game.* New York, NY: Stein & Day.

Manaster, G. G., & Corsini, R. J. (1982). *Individual psychology: Theory and practice.* Itasca, IL: Peacock.

Mangione, L., Forti, R., & Iacuzzi, C. M. (2007). Ethics and endings in group psychotherapy: Saying good-bye and saying it well. *International Journal of Group Psychotherapy, 57,* 25–40.

Maniacci, M., Sackett-Maniacci, L., & Mosak, H. H. (2014). Adlerian psychotherapy. In D. Wedding & Corsini, R. J. (Eds.), *Current psychotherapies* (10th ed., pp. 55–94). Belmont, CA: Brooks/Cole.

Mann, L. (1967). The effects of emotional role playing on smoking attitudes and behavior. *Journal of Experimental Social Psychology, 3,* 334–348.

Maples, M. F. (1988). Group development: Extending Tuckman's theory. *Journal for Specialists in Group Work, 13,* 17–23.

Maples, M. F. (1992). Steamwork: An effective approach to team building. *Journal for Specialists in Group Work, 17,* 144–150.

Marbley, A. F. (2004). His eye is on the sparrow: A counselor of color's perception of facilitating groups with predominantly White members. *Journal for Specialists in Group Work, 29,* 247–258.

Mardoyan, J. L., & Weis, D. M. (1981). The efficacy of group counseling with older adults. *Personnel and Guidance Journal, 60,* 161–163.

Marmarosh, C., & Van Horn, S. M. (2010). Cohesion in counseling and psychotherapy groups. In R. Conyne (Ed.), *The Oxford handbook of group counseling* (pp. 137–163). New York, NY: Oxford University Press.

Marmarosh, C. L., Dunton, E. C., & Amendola, C. (2014). *Groups: Fostering a culture of change.* Thousand Oaks, CA: Sage.

Marrotta, S. A., Peters, B. J., & Paliokas, K. L. (2000). Teaching group dynamics: An interdisciplinary model. *Journal for Specialists in Group Work, 25,* 16–28.

Martin, V., & Thomas, M. C. (2000). A model psychoeducation group for shy college students. *Journal for Specialists in Group Work, 25,* 79–88.

Mash, E. J., & Wolfe, D. A. (2013). *Abnormal child psychology* (5th ed.). Belmont, CA: Brooks/Cole.

Maslow, A. H. (1962). *Toward a psychology of being.* Princeton, NJ: Van Nostrand.

Mathis, R. D., & Tanner, Z. (2000). Structured group activities with family-of-origin themes. *Journal for Specialists in Group Work, 25,* 89–103.

Matthews, C. O. (1992). An application of general system theory (GST) to group therapy. *Journal for Specialists in Group Work, 17,* 161–169.

Maultsby, M. C., Jr. (1984). *Rational behavior therapy.* Upper Saddle River, NJ: Prentice Hall.

May, R. (1983). *The discovery of being: Writings in existential psychology.* New York, NY: Norton.

Maynard, P. E. (1980). Group counseling with the elderly. *Counseling and Values, 24,* 227–235.

Mayo, E. (1945). *The social problems of an industrial civilization.* Cambridge, MA: Harvard University Press.

Mazza, N., & Vinton, L. (1999). A nationwide study of group work in nursing homes. *Activities, Adaptation & Aging, 24,* 61–73.

McArthur, M. J. (1990). Reality therapy with rape victims. *Archives of Psychiatric Nursing, 4,* 360–365.

McCarthy, C., Mejia, O. L., & Liu, H. T. (2000). Cognitive appraisal theory: A psychoeducational approach for understanding connections between cognition and emotion in group work. *Journal for Specialists in Group Work, 25,* 104–121.

McClure, B. A. (1990). The group mind: Generative and regressive groups. *Journal for Specialists in Group Work, 15,* 159–170.

McClure, B. A. (1994). The shadow side of regressive groups. *Counseling and Values, 38,* 77–89.

McCormick, P. (1995). Redecisions required for mental health. *Transactional Analysis Journal, 25,* 321–326.

McCullough, P. G., & Rutenberg, S. K. (1988). Launching children and moving on. In B. Carter & M. McGoldrick (Eds.), *The changing family life cycle* (2nd ed., pp. 285–309). New York, NY: Gardner.

McGaw, W. H., Farson, R. E., & Rogers, C. R. (Producers). (1968). *Journey into self* [Film]. Berkeley: University of California Extension Media Center.

McGovern, T. E., & Silverman, M. (1986). A review of outcome studies of rational-emotive therapy from 1977 to 1982. In A. Ellis & R. Grieger (Eds.), *Handbook of rational-emotive therapy* (Vol. 2). New York, NY: Springer.

McGregor, D. (1960). *The human side of enterprise.* New York, NY: McGraw-Hill.

McKelley, R. A. (2014). Pushing haystacks and cracking steel balls. In A. B. Rochlen & F. E. Rabinowitz (Eds.), *Breaking barriers in counseling men* (pp. 9–19). New York, NY: Routledge.

McMahon, H. G., Paisley, P., & Molina, B. (2010). Individuals and families of European descent. In D. G. Hays & B. T. Erford (Eds.), *Developing multicultural counseling competence: A systems approach* (pp. 333–366). Upper Saddle River, NJ: Merrill/Pearson.

McManus, P. W., Redford, J. L., & Hughes, R. B. (1997). Connecting to self and others: A structured group for women. *Journal for Specialists in Group Work, 22,* 22–30.

McMurray, D. (1992). When it doesn't work: Small-group work in adolescent sexuality education. *School Counselor, 39,* 385–389.

McRoy, C. R., & Brown, B. M. (1996). Effect of conceptual level on group conflict interaction. *Journal for Specialists in Group Work, 21,* 11–17.

McWhirter, B. T., McWhirter, E. H., & McWhirter, J. J. (1988). Groups in Latin America: Comunidades eclesial de base as mutual support groups. *Journal for Specialists in Group Work, 13,* 70–76.

McWhirter, J. J. (1995). Emotional education for university students. *Journal of College Student Psychotherapy, 10,* 27–38.

McWhirter, J. J., Nichols, E., & Banks, N. M. (1984). Career awareness and self-exploration (CASE) groups: A self-assessment model for career decision making. *Personnel and Guidance Journal, 62,* 580–582.

McWhirter, P. T., & McWhirter, J. J. (1996). Transition-to-work group: University students with learning disabilities. *Journal for Specialists in Group Work, 21,* 144–148.

McWhirter, P., & Robbins, R. (2014). Group therapy with native people. In J. L. DeLucia-Waack, C. R. Kalodner, & M. T. Riva (Eds.), *Handbook of group counseling & psychotherapy* (2nd ed., pp. 209–219). Thousand Oaks, CA: Sage.

Mead, M. (1972). *Blackberry winter.* New York, NY: Morrow.

Meara, N. M., Schmidt, L. D., & Day, J. D. (1996). Principles and virtues: A foundation for ethical decision, policies, and character. *The Counseling Psychologist, 24,* 4–77.

Melnick, J., & Wood, M. (1976). Analysis of group composition research and theory for psychotherapeutic and growth-oriented groups. *Journal of Applied Behavioral Science, 12,* 493–512.

Meneses, R., Ortega, R., & Navarro, J. (2008). Criteria for assessing the level of group development (LGD) of work groups: Groupness, entitativity, and groupality as theoretical perspectives. *Small Group Research, 39,* 492–514.

Merchant, N. (2009). Types of diversity-related groups. In C. F. Salazar (Ed.), *Group work experts share their favorite multicultural activities: A guide to diversity-competent choosing, planning, conducting, and processing* (pp. 13–24). Alexandria, VA: Association for Specialists in Group Work.

Merchant, N. M., & Yozamp, C. J. (2014). *Groups in community and agency settings.* Thousand Oaks, CA: Sage.

Merriam-Webster's Collegiate Dictionary (11th ed.). (2003). Springfield, MA: Merriam-Webster.

Merta, R. J. (1995). Group work: Multicultural perspectives. In J. G. Ponterotto, J. M. Casas, L. A. Suzuki, & C. M. Alexander (Eds.), *Handbook of multicultural counseling* (pp. 567–585). Thousand Oaks, CA: Sage.

Michaels, M. L. (2006). Stepfamily enrichment program: A preventive intervention for remarried couples. *Journal for Specialists in Group Work, 31,* 135–152.

Miles, J. R., & Kivlighan, D. M., Jr. (2010). Co-leader similarity and group climate in group interventions: Testing the co-leadership, team cognition-team diversity model. *Group Dynamics: Theory, Research, and Practice, 14,* 114–122.

Miles, R. (1993). I've got a song to sing. *Elementary School Guidance & Counseling, 28,* 71–75.

Miller, M. J. (1986). On the perfectionistic thoughts of beginning group leaders. *Journal for Specialists in Group Work, 11,* 53–56.

Miller, S. P., & Hudson, P. (1994). Using structured parent groups to provide parental support. *Intervention in School and Clinic, 29,* 151–155.

Milsom, A. (2011). Leading groups. In B. T. Erford (Ed.), *Group work: Process and applications.* Upper Saddle River, NJ: Pearson.

Milsom, A., Akos, P., & Thompson, M. (2004). A psychoeducational group approach to postsecondary transition planning for students with learning disabilities. *Journal for Specialists in Group Work, 29,* 395–411.

Mitchell, C. L. (1993). The relationship of clinicians' values to therapy outcome ratings. *Counseling and Values, 37,* 156–164.

Mitchell, J. T., & Everly, G. S. (1993). *Critical incident stress debriefing: An operations manual for the prevention of traumatic stress among emergency services and disaster workers.* Ellicott City, MD: Chevron.

Mitchell, R. (2007). *Documentation in counseling records: An overview of ethical, legal, and clinical issues* (3rd ed.). Alexandria, VA: American Counseling Association.

Mitchell, R. C., & Mitchell, R. R. (1984). Constructive management of conflict in groups. *Journal for Specialists in Group Work, 9,* 137–144.

Moleski, S. M., & Kiselica, M. S. (2005). Dual relationships: A continuum ranging from destructive to the therapeutic. *Journal of Counseling & Development, 83,* 3–11.

Moller, A. T., & Botha, H. C. (1996). Effects of a group rational-emotive behavior therapy program on the type A behavior pattern. *Psychological Reports, 78,* 947–961.

Monterio-Leitner, J. (2001, March). *Psychodrama: When and why to use doubling.* Presentation at the annual convention of the American Counseling Association, San Antonio, TX.

Moore, J., & Herlihy, B. (1993). Grief groups for students who have had a parent die. *School Counselor, 41,* 54–59.

Moore, M. M., & Freeman, S. J. (1995). Counseling survivors of suicide: Implications for group postvention. *Journal for Specialists in Group Work, 20,* 40–47.

Moreno, J. L. (1914). *Einladung zu einer Begegnung.* Vienna: Anzuengruber.

Moreno, J. L. (1940). The mental catharsis and the psychodrama. *Sociometry, 3,* 209–244.

Moreno, J. L. (1945). *Psychodrama.* New York, NY: Beacon House.

Moreno, J. L. (1953). *Who shall survive?* New York, NY: Beacon House.

Moreno, J. L. (1964). *Psychodrama: Volume 1* (rev. ed.). New York, NY: Beacon House.

Moreno, J. L. (1984). Reflections on my method of group psychotherapy and psychodrama. In H. Greenwald (Ed.), *Active psychotherapy* (pp. 130–143). New York, NY: Aronson.

Moreno, J. L., & Moreno, Z. T. (1959). *Psychodrama: Foundations of psychotherapy.* New York, NY: Beacon House.

Moreno, Z. T. (1949). History of the sociometric movement in headlines. *Sociometry, 12,* 255–259.

Moreno, Z. T. (1983). Psychodrama. In H. I. Kaplan & B. J. Sadock (Eds.), *Comprehensive group* (2nd ed.). Baltimore: Williams & Wilkins.

Moreno, Z. T. (1987). Psychodrama, role theory, and the concept of the social atom. In J. K. Zeig (Ed.), *The evolution of psychotherapy* (pp. 341–366). New York, NY: Brunner/Mazel.

Morgan, R. (2004). Groups with offenders and mandated clients. In J. L. DeLucia-Waack, D. A. Gerrity, C.R. Kalodner, & M. T. Riva (Eds.), *Handbook of group counseling and psychotherapy* (pp. 388–400). Thousand Oaks, CA: Sage.

Morgan, B., & Hensley, L. (1998). Supporting working mothers through group work: A multimodal psychoeducational approach. *Journal for Specialists in Group Work, 23,* 298–311.

Morgan, R., Romani, C.J., & Gross, N. R. (2014). Groups with offenders and mandated clients. In J. L. DeLucia-Waack, C. R. Kalodner, & M. T. Riva (Eds.), *Handbook of group counseling and psychotherapy* (2nd ed., pp. 441–449). Thousand Oaks, CA: Sage.

Morran, D. K. (1982). Leader and member self-disclosing behavior in counseling groups. *Journal for Specialists in Group Work, 7,* 218–223.

Morran, D. K., Robison, F. F., & Stockton, R. (1985). Feedback exchange in counseling groups: An analysis of message content and receiver acceptance as a function of leader versus member delivery, session, and valence. *Journal of Counseling Psychology, 32*(5), 7–67.

Morran, D. K., Stockton, R., Cline, R. J., & Teed, C. (1998). Facilitating feedback exchange in groups: Leader interventions. *Journal for Specialists in Group Work, 23,* 257–268.

Morran, D. K., Stockton, R., & Whittingham, M. H. (2004). Effective leader interventions for counseling and psychotherapy groups. In J. L. DeLucia-Waack, D. A. Gerrity, C. R. Kalodner, & M. T. Riva (Eds.), *Handbook of group counseling and psychotherapy* (pp. 91–103). Thousand Oaks, CA: Sage.

Mullan, H. (1992). Existential therapists and their group therapy practices. *International Journal of Group Psychotherapy, 42,* 453–468.

Muller, L. E. (2002). Group counseling for African American males: When all you have are European American counselors. *Journal for Specialists in Group Work, 27,* 299–313.

Muller, L. E., & Hartman, J. (1998). Group counseling for sexual minority youth. *Professional School Counseling, 1,* 38–42.

Munich, R. L., & Astrachan, B. (1983). Group dynamics. In H. I. Kaplan & B. J. Sadock (Eds.), *Comprehensive group psychotherapy* (2nd ed., pp. 15–23). Baltimore: Williams & Wilkins.

Murstein, B. I., & Brust, R. G. (1985). Humor and interpersonal attraction. *Journal of Personality Assessment, 49,* 637–640.

Myers, J. E. (1989). *Infusing gerontological counseling into counselor preparation.* Alexandria, VA: American Counseling Association.

Myers, J. E. (1990). Aging: An overview for mental health counselors. *Journal of Mental Health Counseling, 12,* 245–259.

Myers, J. E., Poidevant, J. M., & Dean, L. A. (1991). Groups for older persons and their caregivers: A review of the literature. *Journal for Specialists in Group Work, 16,* 197–205.

Myrick, R. D. (2003). *Developmental guidance and counseling: A practical approach* (4th ed.). Minneapolis, MN: Educational Media Corps.

Myrick, R. D. (2011). *Developmental guidance and counseling: A practical approach* (5th ed.). Minneapolis: Educational Media Corporation.

Napier, R. W., & Gershenfeld, M. K. (2004). *Groups: Theory and experience* (7th ed.). Boston: Houghton Mifflin.

Nasser-McMillan, S. C., & Hakim-Larson, J. (2003). Counseling considerations among Arab Americans. *Journal of Counseling and Development, 81,* 150–159.

Nasser-McMillan, S. C., Gonzales, L. M., & Mohamed, R. H. (2014). Individuals and families of Arab descent. In D. G. Hays & B. T. Erford (Eds.), *Developing multicultural counseling competencies* (2nd ed., pp. 245–277). Upper Saddle River, NJ: Pearson.

Nelson, J. R., Dykeman, C., Powell, S., & Petty, D. (1996). The effects of a group counseling intervention on students with behavioral adjustment problems.

Elementary School Guidance & Counseling, 31, 21–33.

Neukrug, E., Milliken, T., & Walden, S. (2001). Ethical complaints made against credential counselors: An updated survey of state licensing boards. *Counselor Education and Supervision, 41,* 57–70.

Newell, S. (2002). *Behavioural management in the classroom: A transactional analysis approach.* London, England: David Fulton.

Newsome, S., Waldo, M., & Gruszka, C. (2012). Mindfulness group work: Preventing stress and increasing self-compassion among helping professionals in training. *Journal for Specialists in Group Work, 37,* 297–311.

Niccols, A. (2008). "Right from the Start": randomized trial comparing an attachment group intervention to supportive home visiting. *Journal of Child Psychology and Psychiatry, 49,* 754–764.

Nichols, M. (1986). *Turning forty in the '80s.* New York, NY: Norton.

Nims, D. R. (1998). Search for self: A theoretical model for applying family systems to adolescent group work. *Journal for Specialists in Group Work, 23,* 133–144.

Niles, S. G., & Harris-Bowlsbey, J. (2005). *Career development interventions in the 21st century.* Upper Saddle River, NJ: Pearson.

Nims, D. R. (2002). A collaborative psychoeducational group work training program for residential workers in the juvenile justice system. *Journal for Specialists in Group Work, 27,* 287–298.

Nitza, A. G. (2005). Mechanisms of change: The contributions of Rex Stockton to group development and outcome in research and practice. *Journal for Specialists in Group Work, 30,* 271–281.

Nitza, A. (2014). Selecting and using activities in groups. In J. L. DeLucia-Waack, C. R. Kalodner, & M. T. Riva (Eds.), *Handbook of group counseling & psychotherapy* (2nd ed., pp. 95–106). Thousand Oaks, CA: Sage.

Nolan, E. J. (1978). Leadership interventions for promoting personal mastery. *Journal for Specialists in Group Work, 3,* 132–138.

Nykodym, N., Ruud, W., & Liverpool, P. (1986). Quality circles: Will transaction analysis improve their effectiveness? *Transactional Analysis Journal, 16,* 182–187.

O'Brien, C. R., Johnson, J. L., & Miller, B. (1979). Counseling the aging: Some practical considerations. *Personnel and Guidance Journal, 57,* 288–291.

O'Connor, G. G. (1980). Small groups: A general systems model. *Small Group Behavior, 11,* 145–173.

Ohlsen, M. M. (1977). *Group counseling* (2nd ed.). New York, NY: Holt, Rinehart & Winston.

Ohlsen, M. M. (1979). *Marriage counseling in groups.* Champaign, IL: Research Press.

Ohlsen, M. M., Horne, A. M., & Lawe, C. F. (1988). *Group counseling* (3rd ed.). New York, NY: Holt, Rinehart & Winston.

Okech, J. E. A. (2008). Reflective practice in group co-leadership. *Journal for Specialists in Group Work, 33,* 236–252.

Okech, J. E. A., & Kline, W. B. (2005). A qualitative exploration of group co-leader relationships. *Journal for Specialists in Group Work, 30,* 173–190.

Okech, J. E. A., & Kline, W. B. (2006). Competency concerns in group co-lead relationships. *Journal for Specialists in Group Work, 31,* 165–180.

Okech, J. E. A., & Rubel, D. (2007). Diversity competent group work supervision: An application of the Supervision of Group Work Model (SGW). *Journal for Specialists in Group Work, 32,* 245–266.

Okun, B. F. (1984). *Working with adults.* Pacific Grove, CA: Brooks/Cole.

O'Leary, E. O., Sheedy, G., O'Sullivan, K., and Thoresen, C. (2001). Cork older adult intervention project: Outcomes of a Gestalt therapy group with older adults. *Counseling Psychology Quarterly, 16,* 131–143.

Olson, M. J., & McEwen, M. A. (2004). Grief counseling groups in a medium-security prison. *Journal for Specialists in Group Work, 29,* 225–236.

Olson, S. K., & Brown, S. L. (1986). A relocation support group for women in transition. *Journal of Counseling and Development, 64,* 454–455.

O'Malley, F., & Allen, J. G. (1993). Adolescent group therapy. *Bulletin of the Menninger Clinic, 57,* 265–267.

Omizo, M. M., Cubberly, W. E., & Longano, D. M. (1984). The effects of group counseling on self-concept and locus of control among learning disabled children. *Humanistic Education and Development, 23,* 69–79.

Omizo, M. M., & Omizo, S. A. (1988). Group counseling's effects on self-concept and social behavior among children with learning disabilities. *Journal of Humanistic Education and Development, 26,* 109–117.

O'Neil, J. M., & Egan, J. (1992). Men's gender role transitions over the life span: Transformations and fears of femininity. *Journal of Mental Health Counseling, 14,* 305–324.

Ormont, L. R. (1984). The leader's role in dealing with aggression in groups. *International Journal of Group Psychotherapy, 34,* 553–572.

Ormont, L. R. (1988). The leader's role in resolving resistances to intimacy in the group setting. *International Journal of Group Psychotherapy, 38,* 29–45.

Osborn, A. F. (1957). *Applied imagination.* New York, NY: Scribner.

Ouchi, W. (1981). *Theory Z.* Reading, MA: Addison-Wesley.

Pack-Brown, S. P., & Fleming, A. (2004). An Afrocentric approach to counseling groups with African Americans. In J. L. DeLucia-Waack, D. A. Gerrity, C. R. Kalodner, & M. T. Riva (Eds.), *Handbook of group counseling and psychotherapy* (pp. 183–197). Thousand Oaks, CA: Sage.

Pack-Brown, S. P., & Whittington-Clark, L. E. (2002). I am because we are! Afrocentric approaches to group work. Framingham, MA: Microtraining Associates (www.emicrotraining.com).

Pack-Brown, S. P., Whittington-Clark, L. E., & Parker, W. M. (1998). *Images of me: A guide to group work with African*

American women. Boston: Allyn & Bacon.

Page, B. J. (2004). Online group counseling. In J. L. DeLucia-Waack, D. A. Gerrity, C. R. Kalodner, & M. T. Riva (Eds.), *Handbook of group counseling and psychotherapy* (pp. 609–620). Thousand Oaks, CA: Sage.

Page, B. J. (2010). Online groups. In R. K. Conyne (Ed.), *The Oxford handbook of group counseling* (pp. 520–533). New York, NY: Oxford University Press.

Page, B. J., Delmonico, D. L., Walsh, J., L'Amoreaux, N. A., Danninhirsh, C., Thompson, R. S., Ingram, A. I., & Evans, A. D. (2000). Setting up on-line support groups using The Palace software. *Journal for Specialists in Group Work, 25,* 133–145.

Page, B. J., Jencius, M. J., Rehfuss, M. C., Foss, L. L., Dean, E. P., Petruzzi, M. L., Olson, S. D., & Sager, D. E. (2003). PalTalk online groups: Process and reflections on students' experience. *Journal for Specialists in Group Work, 28,* 35–41.

Page, B. J., Mitchell, C., Olson, S., & Vernon, D. (2000, October). *Ethical issues in group work: What decisions will you make?* Paper presented at the Southern Association for Counselor Education and Supervision, Greensboro, NC.

Page, B. J., Pietrzak, D. R., & Lewis, T. F. (2001). Development of the Group Leader Self-Efficacy Instrument. *Journal for Specialists in Group Work, 26,* 168–194.

Page, R. C., & Berkow, D. N. (1998). Group work as facilitation of spiritual development for drug and alcohol abusers. *Journal for Specialists in Group Work, 23,* 285–297.

Paisley, P., Swanson, L., Borders, S., Cassidy, N., & Danforth, C. (1994, March). *Counseling children using play media and the expressive arts.* Presentation at the North Carolina Counseling Association Conference, Charlotte.

Pan, P. J. D. (2000). The effectiveness of structured and semistructured Satir model groups in family relationships with college students in Taiwan. *Journal for Specialists in Group Work, 25,* 305–318.

Paradise, L. V., & Kirby, P. C. (1990). Some perspectives on the legal liability of group counseling in private practice. *Journal for Specialists in Group Work, 15,* 114–118.

Paradise, L. V., & Siegelwaks, B. J. (1982). Ethical training for group leaders. *Journal for Specialists in Group Work, 7,* 162–166.

Parker, W. M., Freytes, M., Kaufman, C. J., Woodruff, R., & Hord, R. (2004). The mentoring lab: A small group approach for managing emotions from multicultural counseling training. *Journal for Specialists in Group Work, 29,* 361–375.

Parkinson, C. N. (1957). *Parkinson's law and other studies in administration.* Boston: Houghton Mifflin.

Parr, G., Haberstroh, S., & Kottler, J. (2000). Interactive journal writing as an adjunct in group work. *Journal for Specialists in Group Work, 25,* 229–241.

Parsons, T., & Shils, E. A. (1951). *Toward a general theory of action.* Cambridge, MA: Harvard University Press.

Passons, W. R. (1975). *Gestalt approaches in counseling.* New York, NY: Holt, Rinehart & Winston.

Patterson, C. H. (1958). The place of values in counseling and psychotherapy. *Journal of Counseling Psychology, 5,* 216–223.

Patterson, C. H. (1985). New light for counseling theory. *Journal of Counseling and Development, 63,* 349–350.

Patterson, C. H. (1986, April). *Gimmicks in groups.* Paper presented at the annual convention of the American Association for Counseling and Development, Los Angeles.

Paulus, P. B., & Nijstad, B. A. (Eds.). (2003). *Group creativity.* New York, NY: Oxford.

Pearson, J. E. (1988). A support group for women with relationship dependency. *Journal of Counseling and Development, 66,* 394–396.

Pearson, M. J., & Burlingame, G. M. (2013). Cognitive approaches to group therapy: Prevention of relapse in major depressive and bipolar disorders. *International Journal of Group Psychotherapy, 62,* 303–309.

Pearson, R. E. (1985). A group-based training format for basic skills of small-group leadership. *Journal for Specialists in Group Work, 10,* 150–156.

Peck, M. S. (1983). *People of the lie.* New York, NY: Simon & Schuster.

Pedersen, P. (1997a). *Culture-centered counseling interventions.* Thousand Oaks, CA: Sage.

Pedersen, P. (1997b, July). The positive consequences of a culture-centered perspective. *Counseling Today, 40,* 20.

Pedersen, P. (2000). *A handbook for developing multicultural awareness* (3rd ed.). Alexandria, VA: American Counseling Association.

Pender, D. A., & Prichard, K. K. (2009). ASGW Best Practice Guidelines as a research tool: A comprehensive examination of the critical incident stress debriefing. *Journal for Specialists in Group Work, 34,* 175–192.

Perls, F. (1969). *Gestalt therapy verbatim.* New York, NY: Bantam.

Perls, F. (1970). Four lectures. In J. Fagan & I. L. Shepherd (Eds.), *Gestalt therapy now.* New York, NY: Harper & Row.

Perrone, K. M., & Sedlacek, W. E. (2000). A comparison of group cohesiveness and client satisfaction in homogeneous and heterogeneous groups. *Journal for Specialists in Group Work, 25,* 243–251.

Persky, M. (n.d.). *Overlooked and underserved: Elderly in need of mental health care.* Retrieved from http://www.mhaging.org/info/olus.html.

Perusse, R., Goodnough, G. E., & Lee, V. V. (2009). Group counseling in the schools. *Psychology in the Schools, 46,* 225–231.

Peterson, A. V., Chang, C., & Collins, P. L. (1998). The effects of reality therapy and choice theory training on self concept among Taiwanese university students. *International Journal for the Advancement of Counseling, 20,* 79–83.

Peterson, C. H. (2012). The individual regulation component of group emotional intelligence: Measure development and validation. *Journal for Specialists in Group Work, 37,* pp. 232–251.

Pfeiffer, J. W., & Jones, J. E. (Eds.). (1969–1975). *A handbook of structured experiences for human relations training* (Vols. 1–5). La Jolla, CA: University Associates.

Pfeiffer, J. W., & Jones, J. E. (Eds.). (1972–1980). *A handbook of structured exercises for human relations training* (Vols. 1–8). San Diego, CA: University Associates.

Phelps, R. E., & Luke, E. (1995). A structured group for dealing with self-criticism. *Journal for Specialists in Group Work, 20,* 48–58.

Phillips, T. H., & Phillips, P. (1992). Structured groups for high school students: A case study of one district's program. *School Counselor, 39,* 390–393.

Piercy, F., Sprenkle, D., & Wetchler, J. L. (1996). *Family therapy sourcebook* (2nd ed.). New York, NY: Guilford.

Pistole, M. C. (1991). Termination: Analytic reflections on client contact after counselor relocation. *Journal of Counseling and Development, 69,* 337–340.

Pistole, M. C. (1997). Attachment theory: Contributions to group work. *Journal for Specialists in Group Work, 22,* 7–21.

Plotkin, R. (1978, March). Confidentiality in group counseling. *APA Monitor,* p. 14.

Polcin, D. L. (1991). Prescriptive group leadership. *Journal for Specialists in Group Work, 16,* 8–15.

Polster, I., & Polster, M. (1973). *Gestalt therapy integrated: Contours of theory and practice.* New York, NY: Brunner/Mazel.

Ponzo, Z. (1991). Critical factors in group work: Clients' perceptions. *Journal for Specialists in Group Work, 16,* 16–23.

Popkin, M. (2006). *Active parenting Now in 3: Your Three Part Guide to a Great Family.* Atlanta, GA: Active Parenting.

Posthuma, B. W. (2002). *Small groups in therapy settings* (4th ed.). Boston: Allyn & Bacon.

Price, G. E., Dinas, P., Dunn, C., & Winterowd, C. (1995). Group work with clients experiencing grieving: Moving from theory to practice. *Journal for Specialists in Group Work, 20,* 159–167.

Prinz, J., & Arkin, S. (1994). Adlerian group therapy with substance abusers. *Journal of Individual Psychology, 50,* 349–358.

Provost, J. A. (1999). A dream focus for short/term growth groups. *Journal for Specialists in Group Work, 24,* 74–87.

Rabinowitz, F. E. (2005). Group therapy for men. In G. E. Good and G. R. Brooks (Eds.), *The new handbooks of counseling and psychotherapy with men: A comprehensive guide to settings, problems, and treatment approaches* (pp. 264–277). San Francisco, CA: Jossey-Bass.

Rainwater, J. (1979). *You're in charge! A guide to becoming your own therapist.* Los Angeles: Guild of Tutors Press.

Rambo, T. (1997). The use of creative arts in adolescent group therapy. In S. T. Gladding (Ed.), *New developments in group counseling* (pp. 31–33). Greensboro, NC: ERIC.

Randall, D. A., Jr. (1995). Curative factor rankings for female incest survivor groups: A summary of three studies. *Journal for Specialists in Group Work, 20,* 232–239.

Rapin, L. S. (2010). Ethics, best practices, and law in group counseling. In R. K. Conyne (Ed.)., *The Oxford handbook of group counseling* (pp. 61–82). New York, NY: Oxford University Press.

Rapin, L. S. (2014). Guidelines for ethical and legal practice in counseling and psychotherapy groups. In J. L. DeLucia-Waack, C. R. Kalodner, & M. T. Riva (Eds.), *Handbook of group counseling and psychotherapy* (2nd ed., pp. 71–83). Thousand Oaks, CA: Sage.

Rapin, L. S., & Crowell, J. L. (2014). *How to form a group.* Alexandria, VA: Association for Specialists in Group Work.

Raskin, N. J., Rogers, C. R., & Witty, M. C. (2014). Client-centered therapy. In D. Wedding & R. J. Corsini (Eds.), *Current psychotherapies* (10th ed., pp. 95–150). Belmont, CA: Brooks/Cole.

Rath, J. F., Bertisch, H., & Elliott, T. R. (2014). Groups in behavioral health settings. In DeLucia, J. L., Kalodner, C. R., & Riva, M. T. (Eds.), *Group counseling & psychotherapy* (2nd ed., pp. 340–350). Thousand Oaks, CA: Sage.

Ratts, M. J., Anthony, L., & Santos, K. N. T. (2010). The dimensions of social justice model: Transforming traditional group work into a socially just framework. *Journal for Specialists in Group Work, 35,* 160–168.

Rayle, A. D., Sand, J. K., Brucato, T., & Ortega, J. (2006). The "Comadre" group approach: A wellness-based group model for monolingual Mexican women. *Journal for Specialists in Group Work, 31,* 5–24.

Redfoot, D., Feinberg, L., & Houser, A. (2013). The aging of the Baby Boon and I and the growing care gap. *Insight of the Issues, 85,* Washington, DC: AARP Public Policy Institute. www.aarp.org.ppi

Remley, T. P., Jr. (1996). The relationship between law and ethics. In B. Herlihy & G. Corey (Eds.), *ACA ethical standards casebook* (5th ed., pp. 285–292). Alexandria, VA: American Counseling Association.

Remley, T. P., Jr., & Herlihy, B. (2014). *Ethical, legal, and professional issues in counseling* (4th ed.). Upper Saddle River, NJ: Pearson.

Remley, T. P., Jr., & Reeves, T. G. (1989, March). *Beyond the formal classroom: Faculty/graduate student relationships.* Paper presented at the annual meeting of the American Association for Counseling and Development, Boston.

Resnick, J. L. (1981). Parent education and the female parent. *The Counseling Psychologist, 9,* 55–62.

Resnikoff, R. (1988, October). *Gestalt couples therapy.* Paper presented at the 46th Annual Conference of the American Association for Marriage and Family Therapy, New Orleans, LA.

Reuer, B., Crowe, B., & Bernstein, B. (2007). Group rhythm and drumming with older adults.

Riddle, J., Bergin, J. J., & Douzenis, C. (1997). Effects of group counseling on the self-concept of children of alcoholics. *Elementary School Guidance & Counseling, 31,* 192–203.

Rieckert, J., & Moller, A. T. (2000). Rational-emotive behavior therapy in the treatment of adult victims of childhood sexual abuse. *Journal of Rational Emotive and Cognitive Behavior Therapy, 18,* 87–101.

Riordan, R. J., & Beggs, M. S. (1988). Some critical differences between self-help and therapy groups. *Journal for Specialists in Group Work, 13,* 24–29.

Riordan, R. J., & Kahnweiler, W. (1996). Job support groups: Three configurations. *Journal of Counseling and Development, 74,* 517–520.

Riordan, R. J., & Matheny, K. B. (1972). Dear diary: Logs in group counseling. *Personnel and Guidance Journal, 50,* 379–382.

Riordan, R. J., & White, J. (1996). Logs as therapeutic adjuncts in group. *Journal for Specialists in Group Work, 21,* 94–100.

Ritchie, M. H., & Huss, S. N. (2000). Recruiting and screening of minors for group counseling. *Journal for Specialists in Group Work, 25,* 146–156.

Rittenhouse, J. (1997). Feminist principles in survivor's groups: Out-of-group contact. *Journal for Specialists in Group Work, 22,* 111–119.

Riva, M. T. (2004). Best practices in groups. In J. L. DeLucia-Waack, D. A. Gerrity, C. R. Kalodner, & M. T. Riva (Eds.), *Handbook of group counseling and psychotherapy* (pp. 63–64). Thousand Oaks, CA: Sage.

Riva, M. T. (2014). Supervision of group leaders. In J. L. DeLucia-Waack, C. R. Kalodner, & M. T. Riva (Eds.), *Handbook of group counseling and psychotherapy* (2nd ed., pp. 146–158). Thousand Oaks, CA: Sage.

Riva, M. T., & Korinek, L. (2004). Teaching group work: Modeling group leader and member behaviors in the classroom to demonstrate group theory. *Journal for Specialists in Group Work, 29,* 55–63.

Riva, M. T., & Lange, R. E. (2014). *How leaders can assess group counseling.* Thousand Oaks, CA: Sage.

Riva, M. T., Lippert, L., & Tackett, M. J. (2000). Selection practices of group leaders: A national survey. *Journal for Specialists in Group Work, 25,* 157–169.

Riva, M. T., Wachtel, M., & Lasky, G. B. (2004). Effective leadership in counseling and psychotherapy. In J. L. DeLucia-Waack, D. A. Gerrity, C. R. Kalodner, & M. T. Riva (Eds.), *Handbook of group counseling and psychotherapy* (pp. 37–48). Thousand Oaks, CA: Sage.

Rivera, E., Wilbur, M., Roberts-Wilbur, J., Phan, L. T., Garrett, M. T., & Betz, R. L. (2004). Supervising and training psychoeducational group leaders. *Journal for Specialists in Group Work, 29,* 377–394.

Rivera, E. T., Fernandez, I. T., & Hendricks, W. A. (2014). Psychoeducational and counseling groups with Latinos/as. In J. L. DeLucia-Waack, C. R. Kalodner, & M. T. Riva (Eds.) *Handbook of group counseling and psychotherapy* (2nd ed., pp. 253–263). Thousand Oaks, CA: Sage.

Robinson, R. (2001). *Survivors of suicide.* Franklin Lakes, NJ: Career Press.

Rogers, C. R. (1967). The process of the basic encounter group. In J. F. T. Bugenthal (Ed.), *Challenges of humanistic psychology.* New York, NY: McGraw-Hill.

Rogers, C. R. (1970). *Carl Rogers on encounter groups.* New York, NY: Harper & Row.

Rogers, C. R. (1980). *A way of being.* Boston: Houghton Mifflin.

Rokeach, M. (2001). *Understanding human values.* New York, NY: Free Press.

Rokeach, M., Smith, P. W., & Evans, R. I. (1960). Two kinds of prejudice or one? In M. Rokeach (Ed.), *The open and closed mind* (pp. 132–168). New York, NY: Basic Books.

Rolland, C. B., & Neitzschman, L. (1996). Groups in schools: A model for training middle school teachers. *Journal for Specialists in Group Work, 21,* 18–25.

Romano, J. L., & Cikanek, K. L. (2003). Group work and computer applications: Instructional components for graduate students. *Journal for Specialists in Group Work, 28,* 23–34.

Romero, E., & Pescosolido, A. (2008). Humor and group effectiveness. *Human Relations, 61,* 395–418.

Rose, S. D. (1982). Group counseling with children: A behavioral and cognitive approach. In G. M. Gazda (Ed.), *Basic approaches to group psychotherapy and group counseling* (3rd ed.). Springfield, IL: Thomas.

Rose, S. R. (1987). Social skill training in middle childhood: A structured group research. *Journal for Specialists in Group Work, 12,* 144–149.

Rose, S. R. (2001). Group work to promote the occupational functioning of Ethiopian minority men with disabilities who have immigrated to Israel. *Journal for Specialists in Group Work, 26,* 144–155.

Roseman, I., Antonion, A. A., & Jose, P. (1996). Appraisal determinants of emotions: Constructing a more accurate and comprehensive theory. *Cognition and Emotion, 10,* 241–277.

Rosen, K. H., & Bezold, A. (1996). Dating violence prevention: A didactic support group for young women. *Journal of Counseling and Development, 74,* 521–525.

Rothke, S. (1986). The role of interpersonal feedback in group psychotherapy. *International Journal of Group Psychotherapy, 36,* 225–240.

Rothwell, E., Siharath, K., Bell, S., Nguyen, K., & Baker, C. (2011). Joking culture: The role of repeated humorous interactions on group processes during challenge course experiences. *Journal of Experiential Education, 33,* 338–353.

Rubel, D. J., & Kline, W. B. (2008). An exploratory study of expert group leadership. *Journal for Specialists in Group Work, 33,* 138–160.

Rubel, D. J., & Okech, J. E. A. (2006). The supervision of group model: Adapting the discrimination model for the supervision of group workers. *Journal for Specialists in Group Work, 31,* 113–134.

Rudestam, K. E. (1982). *Experiential groups in theory and practice.* Pacific Grove, CA: Brooks/Cole.

Rugel, R. P. (1991). Closed and open systems: The Tavistock group from a general system perspective. *Journal for Specialists in Group Work, 16,* 74–84.

Rush, C. M., & Akos, P. (2007). Supporting children and adolescents with deployed caregivers: A structured group approach for school counselors. *Journal for Specialists in Group Work, 32,* 113–125.

Rybak, C. J., & Brown, B. M. (1997). Group conflict: Communication patterns and group development. *Journal for Specialists in Group Work, 22,* 31–42.

Sack, R. T. (1985). On giving advice. *AMHCA Journal, 7,* 127–132.

Saidla, D. D. (1990). Cognitive development and group stages. *Journal for Specialists in Group Work, 15,* 15–20.

Salgado de Synder, V. N. (1987). Factors associated with acculturative stress and depressive symptomatology among married Mexican immigrant women. *Psychology of Women Quarterly, 11,* 475–488.

Saltmarsh, R. E., Jenkins, S. J., & Fisher, G. L. (1986). The TRAC model: A practical map for group process and management. *Journal for Specialists in Group Work, 11,* 30–36.

Sampson, E. E., & Marthas, M. (1981). *Group process for the health profession* (2nd ed.). New York, NY: Wiley.

Sandhu, D. S. (Ed.). (1999). *Asian and Pacific Islander Americans: Issues and concerns for counseling and psychotherapy.* Commack, NY: Nova Science Publishers.

Salazar, C. F. (Ed.). (2009). *Group work experts share their favorite multicultural activities.* Alexandria, VA: Association for Specialists in Group Work.

Santrock, J. W. (2013). *Life-span development* (14th ed.). Columbus, OH: McGraw-Hill.

Saroyan, J. S. (1990). The use of music therapy in an adolescent psychiatric unit. *Journal of Group Psychotherapy, 43,* 139–142.

Saunders, D. G. (2008). Group interventions for men who batter: A summary of program descriptions and research. *Violence and Victims, 23,* 156–172.

Sayger, T. V. (1996). Creating resilient children and empowering families using a multifamily group process. *Journal for Specialists in Group Work, 21,* 81–89.

Schafer, M., & Crichlow, S. (1996). Antecedents of groupthink. *Journal of Conflict Resolution, 40,* 415–435.

Schimmel, C. J., & Jacobs, E. E. (2011). When leaders are challenged: Dealing with involuntary members in groups. *Journal for Specialists in Group Work, 36,* 144–158.

Schimmel, C., & Jacobs, E. (2014). *How to select and apply change strategies in groups.* Thousand Oaks, CA: Sage.

Schlossberg, N. K. (1981). A model for analyzing human adaptation to transition. *The Counseling Psychologist, 9,* 2–18.

Schultz, B. (1982). *Legal liabilities in psychotherapy.* San Francisco, CA: Jossey-Bass.

Schuster, E. (1998). A community bound by words: Reflections on a nursing home writing group. *Journal of Aging Studies, 12,* 137–147.

Schutz, W. (1958). *FIRO: A three dimensional theory of interpersonal behavior.* New York, NY: Holt, Rinehart & Winston.

Schutz, W. (1966). *FIRO-B: Interpersonal underworld.* Palo Alto, CA: Science & Behavior Books.

Schutz, W. (1967). *Joy: Expanding human awareness.* New York, NY: Grove.

Schutz, W. C. (1971). *Here comes everybody.* New York, NY: Harper & Row.

Schwartz, J. P., & Waldo, M. (1999). Therapeutic factors in spouse-abuse group treatment. *Journal for Specialists in Group Work, 24,* 197–207.

Schwartz, J. P., & Waldo, M. (2003). Reducing gender role conflict among men attending partner abuse prevention groups. *Journal for Specialists in Group Work, 28,* 355–369.

Scogin, F., & Pollio, H. (1980). Targeting and the humorous episode in group process. *Human Relations, 33,* 831–852.

Seligman, M. (1993). Group work with parents of children with disabilities. *Journal for Specialists in Group Work, 18,* 115–126.

Semmelhack, D. J., Hazell, C., & Hoffman, W. (2008). The impact of group-as-a-whole work on anxiety and depression in a severely mentally ill population. *Journal for Specialists in Group Work, 33,* 43–60.

Shaffer, J., & Galinsky, M. D. (1989). *Models of group therapy* (2nd ed.). Upper Saddle River, NJ: Prentice Hall.

Shaffer, W. (1997). Psychodrama technique in the middle school, or meanwhile back at Elsinore Castle. In S. T. Gladding (Ed.), *New developments in group counseling* (pp. 33–36). Greensboro, NC: ERIC/CASS.

Shapiro, J. L., & Bernadett-Shapiro, S. (1985). Group work to 2001: Hal or haven (from isolation)? *Journal for Specialists in Group Work, 10,* 83–87.

Sharma, A., & Cheatham, H. E. (1986). A women's center support group for sexual assault victims. *Journal of Counseling and Development, 64,* 525–527.

Shechtman, Z. (2007). *Group counseling and psychotherapy with children and adolescents: Theory, research, and practice.* Hillsdale, NJ: Lawrence Erlbaum.

Shechtman, Z. (2009). *Treating child and adolescent aggression through bibliotherapy.* New York, NY: Springer.

Shechtman, Z. (2014). Group counseling and psychotherapy with children and adolescents. In J. L. DeLucia-Waack, C. R. Kalodner, & M. T. Riva (Eds.), *Handbook of group counseling and psychotherapy* (2nd ed., pp. 585–596). Thousand Oaks, CA: Sage.

Shechtman, Z., & Perl-Dekel, O. (2000). A comparison of therapeutic factors in two group treatment modalities: Verbal and art therapy. *Journal for Specialists in Group Work, 25,* 288–304.

Shechtman, Z., Vurembrand, N., & Hertz-Lazarowitz, R. (1994). A dyadic and gender-specific analysis of close friendships of preadolescents receiving group psychotherapy. *Journal of Social and Personal Relationships, 11,* 443–448.

Shen, Y-J. (2007). Developmental model using Gestalt-play versus cognitive-verbal group with Chinese adolescents: Effects on strength and adjustment enhancement. *Journal for Specialists in Group Work, 32,* 285–305.

Shepherd, C. R. (1964). *Small groups.* Scranton, PA: Chandler.

Sherif, M. (1937). An experimental approach to the study of attitudes. *Sociometry, 1,* 90–98.

Shulman, L. (2011). *Dynamics and skills of group counseling.* Belmont, CA: Brooks/Cole.

Shulman, L. (2012). *The skills of helping individuals, families, groups and communities* (7th ed.). Belmont, CA: Cengage.

Shulman, L. (2014). Unleashing the healing power of the group. In J. L. DeLucia-Waack, C. R. Kalodner, & M. T. Riva (Eds.), *Handbook of group counseling and psychotherapy* (2nd ed., pp. 120–132). Thousand Oaks, CA: Sage.

Sichel, J., & Ellis, A. (1984). *RET self-help form.* New York, NY: Institute for Rational-Emotive Behavior Therapy.

Sidley, N. T. (Ed.). (1985). *Law and ethics: A guide for the health professional.* New York, NY: Human Sciences Press.

Sigmund, E. (1995). A five-step model for problem resolution in difficult relationships. *Transactional Analysis Journal, 25,* 211–214.

Sileo, F. J., & Kopala, M. (1993). An A-B-C-D-E worksheet for promoting beneficence when considering ethical issues. *Counseling and Values, 37,* 89–95.

Silverman, P. R. (1986). The perils of borrowing: Role of the professional in mutual help groups. *Journal for Specialists in Group Work, 11,* 68–73.

Simkin, J. S. (1975). Gestalt therapy in groups. In G. M. Gazda (Ed.), *Basic approaches to group psychotherapy and group counseling* (2nd ed., pp. 265–286). Springfield, IL: Thomas.

Simpson, D. (1977). Handling group and organizational conflict. In J. Jones & J. W. Pfeiffer (Eds.), *1977 annual handbook for group facilitators* (pp. 120–122). La Jolla, CA: University Associates.

Simpson, L. R., & Diambra, J. F. (2011). Person-centered and existential approaches to counseling and psychotherapy groups. In B. Erford (Ed.), *Group work: Process and applications* (pp. 202–212). Upper Saddle River, NJ: Pearson.

Simpson, L. R., Vernon, A., & Erford, B. T. (2011). Adlerian and Transactional Analysis approaches to counseling and psychotherapy groups. In B. T. Erford (Ed.), *Group work: Processes and applications* (pp. 237–248). Upper Saddle River, NJ: Pearson.

Singer, V. I., Tracz, S. M., & Dworkin, S. H. (1991). Reminiscence group therapy: A treatment modality for older adults. *Journal for Specialists in Group Work, 16,* 167–171.

Singh, A. A. (2013). The use of popular opinion leader (POI) groups and the reduction of "gay bullying" in middle school: A case study inquiry of group leader experience. *Journal for Specialists in Group Work, 38,* 184–206.

Singh, A. A., & Hays, D. G. (2008). Feminist group counseling with South Asian women who have survived intimate partner violence. *Journal for Specialists in Group Work, 33,* 84–102.

Singh, A. A., & Hofsess, C. (2011). Reclaiming the Maiden: Use of archetypes in a 6-week women's empowerment group. *Journal for Specialists in Group Work, 36,* 41–61.

Singh, A. A., Merchant, N., Skudrzyk, B., & Ingene, D. (2012). Association for Specialists in Group Work: Multicultural and social justice competence principles for group work. *Journal for Specialists in Group, 37,* 312–325.

Singh, A. A., & Salazar, C. F. (2010). The roots of social justice in group work. *Journal for Specialists in Group Work, 35,* 97–104.

Skibbe, A. (1986). Assessing campus needs with nominal groups. *Journal of Counseling and Development, 64,* 532–533.

Skinner, B. F., & Vaughan, M. E. (1997). *Enjoy old age: A practical guide.* New York, NY: Norton.

Sklare, G., Keener, R., & Mas, C. (1990). Preparing members for "here-and-now" group counseling. *Journal for Specialists in Group Work, 15,* 141–148.

Sklare, G., Thomas, D. V., Williams, E. C., & Powers, K. A. (1996). Ethics and an experiential "here and now group"; A blend that works. *Journal for Specialists in Group Work, 21,* 263–273.

Slavson, S. R. (1945). Different methods of group therapy in relation to age levels. *Nervous Child, 4,* 196–210.

Slavson, S. R. (1948). Group therapy in child care and child guidance. *Jewish Social Service Quarterly, 25,* 203–213.

Slavson, S. R. (1962). Personality qualifications of a group psychotherapist. *International Journal of Group Psychotherapy, 12,* 411–420.

Smaby, M. H., Maddux, C. D., Torres-Rivera, E., & Zimmick, R. (1999). A study of the effects of a skills-based versus a conventional group counseling training program. *Journal for Specialists in Group Work, 24,* 152–163.

Smaby, M. H., Peterson, T. L., & Hovland, J. (1994). Total quality groups in business: Opportunities and challenges for specialists in group work. *Journal for Specialists in Group Work, 19,* 217–226.

Smead, R. S. (1994). *Skills for living: Group counseling activities for elementary students.* Champaign, IL: Research Press.

Smead, R. S. (1996). *Skills and techniques for group work with children and adolescents.* Champaign, IL: Research Press.

Smiley, K. A. (2004). Structured groups for gay men newly diagnosed with HIV/AIDS. *Journal for Specialists in Group Work, 29,* 207–224.

Smith, D. C., & Maher, M. F. (1991). Group interventions with caregivers of the dying: The "Phoenix" alternative. *Journal for Specialists in Group Work, 16,* 191–196.

Smokowski, P. R., & Bacallao, M. (2009). Entre Dos Mundos/Between Two Worlds youth violence prevention: Comparing psychodramatic and support group delivery formats. *Small Group Research, 40,* 3–27.

Solomon, A., & Haaga, D. A. F. (1995). Rational emotive behavior therapy research: What we know and what we need to know. *Journal of Rational Emotive and Cognitive Behavior Therapy, 13,* 179–191.

Sommers-Flanagan, R., Barrett-Hakanson, T., Clarke, C., & Sommers-Flanagan, J. (2000). A psychoeducational school-based coping and social skills group for depressed students. *Journal for Specialists in Group Work, 25,* 170–190.

Somov, P. G. (2007). Meaning of life group: Group application of logotherapy for substance use treatment. *Journal for Specialists in Group Work, 32,* 316–345.

Sonnenblick, M. D. (1997). The GALSS club: Promoting belonging among at-risk adolescent girls. *School Counselor, 44,* 243–245.

Sonstegard, M. A., & Bitter, J. A. (1998a). Adlerian group counseling: Step by step. *Journal of Individual Psychology, 54,* 176–216.

Sonstegard, M. A., & Bitter, J. A. (1998b). Counseling children in groups. *Journal of Individual Psychology, 54,* 251–267.

Sonstegard, M., Bitter, J. A., & Pelonis, P. (2004). *Adlerian group counseling and therapy: Step-by-step.* New York, NY: Routledge.

Spira, J. L. (1997). Existential group therapy for advanced breast cancer and other life-threatening illnesses. In J. L. Spira (Ed.), *Group therapy for medically ill patients* (pp. 165–222). New York, NY: Guilford.

Sprei, J., & Goodwin, R. A. (1983). Group treatment of sexual assault survivors. *Journal for Specialists in Group Work, 8,* 39–46.

Stanley, P. H. (2006). Using the 5 P relay in task groups. *Journal for Specialists in Group Work, 31,* 25–35.

Starak, Y. (1988). Confessions of a group leader. *Small Group Behavior, 19,* 103–108.

Stark-Rose, R. M., Livingston-Sacin, T. M., Merchant, N., & Finley, A. C. (2012). Group counseling with United States racial minority groups: A 25-year content analysis. *Journal for Specialists in Group Work, 37,* 277–296.

Steen, S. (2009). Group counseling for African American elementary students: An exploratory study. *Journal for Specialists in Group Work, 34,* 101–117.

Steen, S. (2011). Academic and personal development through group work: An exploratory study. *Journal for Specialists in Group Work, 36,* 129–143.

Steen, S., Bauman, S., & Smith, J. (2008). The preparation of professional school counselors for group work. *Journal for Specialists in Group Work, 33,* 253–269.

Steen, S., Shi, Q., & Hockersmith, W. (2014). Group counseling for African Americans. In J. L. DeLucia-Waack, C. R. Kalodner, & M. T. Riva (Eds.), *Handbook of group counseling & psychotherapy* (2nd ed., pp. 220–230). Thousand Oaks, CA: Sage.

Stein, H. (1993). Organizational psychohistory. *Journal of Psychohistory, 21,* 97–114.

Steiner, C. (1974). *Scripts people live: Transactional analysis of life scripts.* New York, NY: Grove.

Steinglass, P., Bennett, L. A., Wolin, S. J., & Reiss, D. (1993). *Alcoholic family.* New York, NY: Basic Books.

Sternberg, R. J. (2004). Culture and intelligence. *American Psychologist, 59,* 325–338.

Stewart, I. (2014). *Transactional analysis counseling in action* (4th ed.). London, England: Sage.

Stewart, I., & Joines, V. (2012). *TA Today: A new introduction to Transactional Analysis* (2nd ed., rev.). Chapel Hill, NC: Lifespace Publishing.

Stockton, R., McDonnell, K. A., & Aldarondo, F. (1997). Application of a model for group leader instruction. In S. T. Gladding (Ed.), *New developments in group counseling* (pp. 129–131). Greensboro, NC: ERIC.

Stockton, R., & Morran, D. K. (1980). The use of verbal feedback in counseling groups: Toward an effective system. *Journal for Specialists in Group Work, 5,* 10–14.

Stockton, R., & Morran, D. K. (1982). Review and perspective of critical dimensions in therapeutic small group research. In G. M. Gazda (Ed.), *Basic approaches to group psychotherapy and group counseling* (3rd ed., pp. 37–83). Springfield, IL: Thomas.

Stockton, R., Morran, D. K., & Harris, M. (1991). Factors influencing group member acceptance of corrective feedback. *Journal for Specialists in Group Work, 16,* 245–254.

Stockton, R., Morran, D. K., & Krieger, K. K. (2004). An overview of current research and best practices for training beginning. In J. L. DeLucia-Waack, D. A. Gerrity, C. R. Kalodner, & M. T. Riva (Eds.), *Handbook of group counseling and psychotherapy* (pp. 65–75). Thousand Oaks, CA: Sage.

Stockton, R., Morran, D. K., & Nitza, A. G. (2000). Processing group events: A conceptual map for leaders. *Journal for Specialists in Group Work, 25,* 343–355.

Stockton, R., Morran, D., & Velkoff, P. (1987). Leadership of therapeutic small groups. *Journal of Group Psychotherapy, Psychodrama & Sociometry, 39,* 157–165.

Stockton, R., & Toth, P. L. (1996). Teaching group counselors: Recommendations for maximizing preservice instruction. *Journal for Specialists in Group Work, 21,* 274–282.

Stogdill, R. M. (1969). Personal factors associated with leadership: A survey of the literature. In C. A. Gibb (Ed.), *Leadership* (pp. 91–133). Harmondsworth, UK: Penguin.

Stogdill, R. M. (1974). *Handbook of leadership.* New York, NY: Free Press.

Stone, M. L., & Waters, E. (1991). Accentuate the positive: A peer group counseling program for older adults. *Journal for Specialists in Group Work, 16,* 159–166.

Storandt, M. (1983). *Counseling and therapy with older adults.* Boston: Little, Brown.

Stotts, M. L., & Dyer, J. A. (Eds.). (2005). *Handbook of remotivational therapy.* New York, NY: Haworth.

Streib, G., & Beck, R. (1981). Older families: A decade review. *Journal of Marriage and the Family, 42,* 937–956.

Strother, J., & Harvill, R. (1986). Support groups for relocated adolescent students: A model for school counselors. *Journal for Specialists in Group Work, 11,* 114–120.

Strupp, H. H., Hadley, S. W., & Gomes-Schwartz, B. (1977). *Psychotherapy for better or worse: The problem of negative effects.* New York, NY: Aronson.

Stuart, B. K., & Schlosser, D. A. (2009). Multifamily group treatment for schizophrenia. *International Journal of Group Psychotherapy, 59,* 435–441.

Sue, D. W., Arredondo, P., & McDavis, R. J. (1992). Multicultural counseling competencies and standards: A call to the profession. *Journal of Counseling and Development, 70,* 477–486.

Sullivan, E. M., Coffey, J. F., & Greenstein, R. A. (1987). Treatment outcome in a group geropsychiatry program for veterans. *The Gerontologist, 27,* 434–435.

Sullivan, M. (1983a). Introduction to women emerging: Group approaches. *Journal for Specialists in Group Work, 8,* 3–8.

Sullivan, M. (1983b). Women and career development: Group activities to overcome internal barriers. *Journal for Specialists in Group Work, 8,* 47–55.

Summerton, O. (1993). Games in organizations. *Transactional Analysis Journal, 23,* 87–103.

Sweeney, T. J. (2009). *Adlerian counseling and psychotherapy: A practitioner's approach* (5th ed.). New York, NY: Routledge.

Swenson, L. C. (1997). *Psychology and law* (2nd ed.). Pacific Grove, CA: Brooks/Cole.

Szymanski, D. M., & Owen, G. P. (2009). Group-level coping as a moderator between heterosexism and sexism and psychological distress in sexual minority women. *Psychology of Women Quarterly, 33,* 197–205.

Tamm, M. E. (1993). Models of health and disease. *British Journal of Medical Psychology, 66,* 213–238.

Tate, K. A., Rivera, E. T., Conwill, W. L., Miller, M. D., & Puig, A. (2013). Conceptualizing group dynamics from our clients' perspective: Development of the conceptualization of group dynamics inventory. *Journal for Specialists in Group Work, 38,* 146–168.

Taub, D. J. (1998a). Building community on campus: Student affairs professionals as group workers. *Journal for Specialists in Group Work, 23,* 411–427.

Taub, D. J. (1998b). Promoting student development through psychoeducational groups: A perspective on the goals and process matrix. *Journal for Specialists in Group Work, 23,* 196–201.

Taulbee, L. R. (1978). Reality orientation: A therapeutic group activity for elderly persons. In I. M. Burnside (Ed.), *Working with the elderly: Group processes and techniques* (pp. 206–218). North Scituate, MA: Duxbury.

Tauriac, J. J., Kim, G. S., Sarinana, S. L., Tawa, J., & Kahn, V. D. (2013). Utilizing affinity groups to enhance intergroup dialogue workshops for racially and ethnically diverse students. *Journal for Specialists in Group Work, 38,* 241–260.

Tedder, S. L., Scherman, A., & Sheridan, K. M. (1984). Impact of group support on adjustment to divorce by single, custodial fathers. *AMHCA Journal, 6,* 180–189.

Tedder, S. L., Scherman, A., & Wantz, R. A. (1987). Effectiveness of a support group for children of divorce. *Elementary School Guidance & Counseling, 22,* 102–109.

Terry, D. (2010, April 11). Drill team helps provide structure and a refuge. *Chicago News Cooperative.* Retrieved from http://www.chicagonewscoop.org/drill-team-helps-provide-structure-and-a-refuge

Texas A&M AgriLife Extension Service. (2013, October 31). *Reminiscence: An Important Task for Older Adults.* Retrieved from http://fcs.tamu.edu/families/aging/reminiscence/reminiscence_important_task.php

Thomas, K. W., & Kilmann, R. H. (1974). *Thomas-Kilmann Conflict Mode Instrument.* Tuxedo, NY: XICOM.

Thomas, M. B. (1992). *An introduction to marital and family therapy.* New York, NY: Macmillan.

Thomas, M. C. (1991). Their past gives our present meaning—Their dreams are our future. *Journal for Specialists in Group Work, 16,* 132.

Thomas, M. C., & Martin, V. (1997). Helping older adults age with integrity, empowerment, and meaning through group counseling. In S. T. Gladding (Ed.), *New developments in group counseling* (pp. 43–45). Greensboro, NC: ERIC.

Thomas, M. C., & Martin, V. (2010). Group work: Elderly people and their caregivers. In D. Capuzzi, D. R. Gross, & M. D. Shauffer (Eds.), *Introduction to group work* (5th ed., pp. 505–536). Denver, CO: Love.

Thomas, M. C., Martin, V., Alexander, J. J., Cooley, F. R., & Loague, A. M. (2003). Using new attitudes and technology to change the developmental counseling focus for older populations. *Counseling and Human Development, 35*(8), 1–8.

Thomas, R. V., & Pender, D. A. (2008). Association for Specialists in Group Work: Best Practice Guidelines 2007 revisions. *Journal for Specialists in Group Work, 33,* 111–117.

Thompson, E. C., III. (1987). The "Yagottawanna" group: Improving student self-perceptions through motivational teaching of study skills. *School Counselor, 35,* 134–142.

Thorne, B. (1992). *Carl Rogers.* Newbury Park, CA: Sage.

Tillich, P. (1952). *The courage to be.* New Haven, CT: Yale University Press.

Tollerud, T. R., Holling, D. W., & Dustin, D. (1992). A model for teaching in group leadership: The pre-group interview application. *Journal for Specialists in Group Work, 17,* 96–104.

Toseland, R. W., Naccarto, T., & Wray, L. O. (2007). Telephone groups for older persons and family caregivers: Key implementation and process issues. *Clinical Gerontologist: The Journal of Aging and Mental Health, 31,* 59–76.

Toth, P. L., & Erwin, W. J. (1998). Applying skilled-based curriculum to teach feedback groups: An evaluation study.

Journal of Counseling & Development, 76, 294–301.

Toth, P. L., & Stockton, R. (1996). A skill-based approach to teaching group counseling interventions. *Journal for Specialists in Group Work, 21,* 101–109.

Townsend, L., Gearing, R. E., & Polyanskaya, O. (2012). Influence of health beliefs and stigma on choosing internet support groups over formal mental health services. *Psychiatry Services, 63,* 370–376.

Treadwell, T. W., Kumar, V. K., Stein, S. A., & Prosnick, K. (1997). Sociometry: Tools for research and practice. *Journal for Specialists in Group Work, 22,* 52–65.

Trotzer, J. P. (1988). Family theory as a group resource. *Journal for Specialists in Group Work, 13,* 180–185.

Trotzer, J. P. (2004). Conducting a group: Guidelines for choosing and using activities. In J. L. DeLucia-Waack, D. A. Gerrity, C. R. Kalodner, & M. T. Riva (Eds.), *Handbook of group counseling and psychotherapy* (pp. 76–90). Thousand Oaks, CA: Sage.

Trotzer, J. P. (2007). *The counselor and the group: Integrating theory, training, and practice* (4th ed.). Philadelphia, PA: Brunner-Routledge.

Tsui, A. M., & Sammons, M. T. (1988). Group intervention with adolescent Vietnamese refugees. *Journal for Specialists in Group Work, 13,* 90–95.

Tuckey, M. R., & Scott, J. E. (2014). Group critical incident stress debriefing with emergency services personnel: a randomized controlled trial. *Anxiety, Stress & Coping: An International Journal, 27,* 38–54.

Tuckman, B. (1965). Developmental sequence in small groups. *Psychological Bulletin, 63,* 384–399.

Tuckman, B. W., & Jensen, M. A. C. (1977). Stages of small-group development revisited. *Group and Organizational Studies, 2,* 419–427.

Tudor, K. (1995). What do you say about saying good-bye? Ending psychotherapy. *Transactional Analysis Journal, 25,* 228–233.

Tyler, N. (1995). PAIRS and redecision therapy. *Transactional Analysis Journal, 25,* 347–349.

Tyra, R. P. (1979). Group guidance and the SIPA model. *Elementary School Guidance and Counseling, 13,* 269–271.

U.S. Census Bureau. (2001, March 12). *Census 2000 shows America's diversity.* Retrieved from www.census.gov/PressRelease/www/releases

U.S. Census Bureau. (2014). *United States Population 2014.* Retrieved from http://worldpopulationreview.com/countries/united-states-population

Vacc, N. A., & Wittmer, J. P. (Eds.). (1980). *Let me be me: Special populations and the helping professions.* Muncie, IN: Accelerated Development.

Vacha-Haase, T. (2014). Group work with those in later life. In J. L. DeLucia-Waack, C. R. Kalodner, & M. Riva (Eds.). (2014). *Handbook of group counseling & psychotherapy* (2nd ed., pp. 276–287). Thousand Oaks, CA: Sage.

Vacha-Haase, T., Archibald, K. B., Brescian, N. E., Martin, K. L., & Fitzpatrick, K. (2009). Current events groups in long-term care: A guide to facilitating a successful group. *Journal for Specialists in Group Work, 34,* 382–403.

Vacha-Haase, T., Ness, C. M., Dannison, L., & Smith, A. (2000). Grandparents raising grandchildren: A psychoeducational group approach. *Journal for Specialists in Group Work, 25,* 67–78.

Valdes, T. M., & McPherson, R. H. (1987). "Leaving home": A family of origin group for college students. *Journal of College Student Personnel, 28,* 466–467.

van der Pompe, G., Duivenvoorden, H. J., Antoni, M. H., & Visser, A. (1997). Effectiveness of a short-term group psychotherapy program on endocrine and immune function in breast cancer patients: An exploratory study. *Journal of Psychosomatic Research, 42,* 453–466.

Van Hoose, W., & Kottler, J. (1977). *Ethical and legal issues in counseling and psychotherapy.* San Francisco, CA: Jossey-Bass.

Van Hoose, W., & Kottler, J. (1985). *Ethical and legal issues in counseling and psychotherapy* (2nd ed.). San Francisco, CA: Jossey-Bass.

Van Hoose, W. H., & Paradise, L. V. (1979). *Ethics in counseling and psychotherapy: Perspectives in issues and decision-making.* Cranston, RI: Carroll.

Van Velsor, P. (2009). Task groups in the school setting: Promoting children's social and emotional learning. *Journal for Specialists in Group Work, 34,* 276–292.

Vander Kolk, C. J. (1985). *Introduction to group counseling and psychotherapy.* Upper Saddle River, NJ: Prentice Hall.

Vassilopoulos, S. P., Brouzos, A., Damer, D. E., Mellou, A., & Mitropoulou, A. (2013). A psychoeducational school-based group intervention for socially anxious children. *Journal for Specialists in Group Work, 38,* 307–329.

Verhofstadt, D., & Leni, M. F. (2000). The "magic shop" technique in psychodrama: An existential-dialectical view. *International Journal of Action Methods: Psychodrama, Skill Training, and Role Playing, 53,* 3–15.

Vernon, A. (2006). *Thinking, feeling, behaving: An emotional education curriculum for children grades 1–6* (rev. ed.). Champaign, IL: Research Press.

Vernon, A. (2011a). The Rational-Emotive Behavior Therapy approaches to group counseling and psychotherapy: Theory, techniques, and applications. In B. Erford (Ed.), *Group work: Processes and applications* (pp. 213–226). Upper Saddle River, NJ: Pearson.

Vernon, A. (2011b). Reality therapy and behavioral approaches to counseling and psychotherapy groups. B. T. Erford (Ed.), *Group work: Processes and applications.* (pp. 227–236). Upper Saddle River, NJ: Pearson.

Villalba, J. A. (2003). A psychoeducational group for limited-English proficient Latino/Latina children. *Journal for Specialists in Group Work, 28,* 261–276.

Villalba, J. A. (2007). Incorporating wellness into group work in elementary schools. *Journal for Specialists in Group Work, 32,* 31–40.

Villalba, J. A. (2010). Individuals and families of Latin descent. In D. G. Hays & B. T. Erford (Eds.), *Developing multicultural counseling competence* (pp. 277–300). Upper Saddle River, NJ: Pearson.

Villalba, J. A., Ivers, N. N., & Ohlms, A. B. (2010). Cuento group work in emerging rural Latino communities: Promoting personal-social development of Latina/o middle school students of Mexican heritage. *Journal for Specialists in Group Work, 35,* 23–43.

Vinson, M. L. (1995). Employing family therapy in group counseling with college students: Similarities and a technique employed by both. *Journal for Specialists in Group Work, 20,* 240–252.

Viorst, J. (1971). *The tenth good thing about Barney.* New York, NY: Aladdin.

Viorst, J. (1986). *Necessary losses.* New York, NY: Simon & Schuster.

Vontress, C. E. (1996). A personal retrospective on cross-cultural counseling. *Journal of Multicultural Counseling and Development, 24,* 156–166.

Vriend, J. (1985). We've come a long way, group. *Journal for Specialists in Group Work, 10,* 63–67.

Vriend, J., & Dyer, W. W. (1973). Counseling the reluctant client. *Journal of Counseling Psychology, 20,* 240–246.

Wagenheim, G., & Gemmill, G. (1994). Feedback exchange: Managing group closure. *Journal of Management Education, 18,* 265–269.

Wah, L. M. (2008). Asian men and violence. In R. Carrillo & J. Tello (Eds.), *Family violence and men of color: Healing the wounded male spirit* (2nd ed., pp. 195–214). New York, NY: Springer.

Walden, S. L. (1997). The counselor/client partnership in ethical practice. In B. Herlihy & G. Corey (Eds.), *Boundary issues in counseling: Multiple roles and responsibilities* (pp. 40–47). Alexandria, VA: American Counseling Association.

Waldo, M. (1985). A curative factor framework for conceptualizing group counseling. *Journal of Counseling and Development, 64,* 52–58.

Waldo, M., & Bauman, S. (1998). Regrouping the categorization of group work: A goals and process (GAP) matrix for groups. *Journal for Specialists in Group Work, 23*, 164–176.

Waldo, M., & Harman, M. J. (1999). Relationship enhancement groups with state hospital patients and staff. *Journal for Specialists in Group Work, 24*, 27–36.

Waldo, M., Kerne, P. A. IV, & Kerne, V. V. H. (2007). Therapeutic factors in guidance versus counseling sessions of domestic violence groups. *Journal for Specialists in Group Work, 32*, 346–361.

Waldo, M., Schwartz, J., Horne, A., & Cote, L. (2010). Prevention groups. In R. Conyne (Ed.). *The Oxford handbook of group counseling.* New York, NY: Oxford University Press.

Walen, S. R., DiGiuseppe, R., & Wessler, R. L. (1980). *A practitioner's guide to RET.* New York, NY: Oxford University Press.

Waliski, A. D., & Carlson, L. A. (2008). Group work with preschool children: Effect on emotional awareness and behavior. *Journal for Specialists in Group Work, 33*, 3–21.

Walsh, F. (1988). The family in later life. In B. Carter & M. McGoldrick (Eds.), *The changing family life cycle* (2nd ed., pp. 311–332). New York, NY: Gardner.

Walsh, R. (1989). Asian psychotherapies. In R. J. Corsini & D. Wedding (Eds.), *Current psychotherapies* (4th ed., pp. 546–559). Itasca, IL: Peacock.

Walter, C. A. (2005). Support groups for widows and widowers. In G. L. Greif & P. H. Ephross (Eds.), *Group work with populations at risk* (2nd ed., pp. 109–125). New York, NY: Oxford.

Walters, R. (1989). Nonverbal communication in group counseling. In G. M. Gazda (Ed.), *Group counseling: A developmental approach* (4th ed.). Boston: Allyn & Bacon.

Walton, M. (1991). *Deming management at work.* New York, NY: Putnam.

Wanlass, J., Moreno, J. K., & Thomson, H. M. (2005). Group therapy for eating disorders: A retrospective case study. *Journal for Specialists in Group Work, 30*, 47–66.

Ward, D. E. (1982). A model for the more effective use of theory in group work. *Journal for Specialists in Group Work, 7*, 224–230.

Ward, D. E. (1985). Levels of group activity: A model for improving the effectiveness of group work. *Journal of Counseling and Development, 64*, 59–64.

Ward, D. E. (1997). Factors influencing the development and quality of cooperative teamwork in groups. In S. T. Gladding (Ed.), *New developments in group counseling* (pp. 115–117). Greensboro, NC: ERIC/CASS.

Ward, D. E. (2006). Classification of groups. *Journal for Specialists in Group Work, 31*, 93–97.

Ward, D. E. (2010). Definition of group counseling. In R. K. Conyne (Ed.), *The Oxford handbook of group counseling* (pp. 36–51). New York, NY: Oxford University Press.

Ward, D. E. (2014). Effective processing in groups. In J. L. DeLucia-Waack, C. R. Kalodner, & M. T. Riva (Eds.), *Handbook of group counseling and psychotherapy* (2nd ed., pp. 84–94). Thousand Oaks, CA: Sage.

Ward, D. E., & Ward, C. A. (2014). *How to help leaders and members learn from their group experience.* Thousand Oaks, CA: Sage.

Ware, J. N., Ohrt, J. H., & Swank, J. M. (2012). A phenomenological exploration of children's experiences in a social skills group. *Journal for Specialists in Group Work, 37*, 133–151.

Waring, E. (1988). *Enhancing marital intimacy through cognitive self-disclosure.* New York, NY: Brunner/Mazel.

Wasielewski, R. A., Scruggs, M. Y., & Scott, C. W. (1997). Student groups conducted by teachers: The teachers As Counselors (TAC) program. *Journal for Specialists in Group Work, 22*, 43–51.

Waters, E., McCarroll, J., & Penman, N. (1987). *Training mental health workers for the elderly: An instructor's guide.* Rochester, MI: Continuum Center.

Watkins, C. E. (1985). Countertransference: Its impact on the counseling situation. *Journal of Counseling and Development, 63*, 356–359.

Watson, D. L., & Tharp, R. G. (1981). *Self-directed behavior: Self-modification for personal adjustment* (3rd ed.). Pacific Grove, CA: Brooks/Cole.

Watzlawick, P. (1983). *The situation is hopeless, but not serious.* New York, NY: Norton.

Weed, R. O., & Berens, D. E. (Eds.) (2010). *Life care planning and case management handbook* (3rd ed.). Boca Raton, FL: CRC Press.

Wegscheider, S. (1981). *Another chance: Hope and health for the alcoholic family.* Palo Alto, CA: Science & Behavior Books.

Weiner, M. F. (1984). *Techniques of group psychotherapy.* Washington, DC: American Psychiatric Press.

Weinrach, S. G. (1980). Unconventional therapist: Albert Ellis. *Personnel and Guidance Journal, 59*, 152–160.

Weinrach, S. G. (1996). Nine experts describe the essence of rational-emotive therapy while standing on one foot. *Journal of Counseling & Development, 74*, 326–331.

Weisman, C., & Schwartz, P. (1989). Worker expectations in group work with the frail elderly: Modifying the model for a better fit. *Social Work with Groups, 12*, 47–55.

Welfel, E. R. (2013). *Ethics in counseling and psychotherapy* (5th ed.). Belmont, CA: Brooks/Cole.

Wenz, K., & McWhirter, J. J. (1990). Enhancing the group experience: Creative writing exercises. *Journal for Specialists in Group Work, 15*, 37–42.

Werstlein, P. O., & Borders, L. D. (1997). Group process variables in group supervision. *Journal for Specialists in Group Work, 22*, 120–136.

Wessler, R. L., & Hankin, S. (1988). Rational-emotive therapy and related cognitively oriented psychotherapies. In S. Long (Ed.), *Six group therapies* (pp. 159–215). New York, NY: Plenum.

Westheimer, J. M., Capello, J., McCarthy, C., & Denny, N. (2009). Employing a group medical intervention for hypertensive male veterans: An exploratory analysis. *Journal for Specialists in Group Work, 34*, 151–174.

Westwood, M. J., & Ewasiw, J. F. (2011). Integrating narrative and action processes in group counseling practicum: A multimodal approach for helping clients. *Journal for Specialists in Group Work, 36*, 78–93.

Westwood, M. J., Keats, P. A., & Wilensky, P. (2003). Therapeutic enactment: Integrating individual and group counseling models for change. *Journal for Specialists in Group Work, 28*, 122–138.

Westwood, M. J., McLean, H., Cave, D., Borgen, W., & Slakov, P. (2010). Coming home: A group-based approach for assisting military veterans in transition. *Journal for Specialists in Group Work, 35*, 44–68.

Wheelan, S. A. (2009). Group size, group development, and group productivity. *Small Group Research, 40*, 247–262.

Wheeler, A. M., & Bertrum, B. (2012). *The counselor and the law* (6th ed.). Alexandria, VA: American Counseling Association.

Wheeler, A. M., & Bertrum, B. (2015). *The counselor and the law* (7th ed.). Alexandria, VA: American Counseling Association.

Whitaker, D. S., & Lieberman, M. (1964). *Psychotherapy through the group process.* New York, NY: Atherton.

White, J., & Mullis, F. (1997). Parent education groups. In S. T. Gladding (Ed.), *New developments in group counseling* (pp. 47–49). Greensboro, NC: ERIC.

White, J., & Riordan, R. (1990). Some key concerns in leading parent education groups. *Journal for Specialists in Group Work, 15*, 201–205.

Whitfield, C. L. (1987). *Healing the child within: Discovery and recovery for adult children of dysfunctional families.* Pompano Beach, FL: Health Communications.

Whittingham, M. (2014). Group work in colleges and university counseling centers. In J. L. DeLucia, C. R. Kalodner, & M. Riva (Eds.), *Handbook of group counseling and psychotherapy* (2nd ed., pp. 329–339). Thousand Oaks, CA: Sage.

Widdowson, M. (2010). *Transactional analysis: 100 key points and techniques.* New York, NY: Routledge.

Wilcoxon, A., Remley, T. R., & Gladding, S. T. (2012). *Ethical, legal and professional issues in the practice of marriage and family therapy* (5th ed.). Upper Saddle River, NJ: Prentice Hall.

Wilcoxon, A., Remley, T. P., Jr., & Gladding, S. T. (2013). *Ethical, legal and professional issues in the practice of marriage and family therapy* (updated 5th ed.). Upper Saddle River, NJ: Pearson.

Wilkins, P. (1995). A creative therapies model for the group supervision of counselors. *British Journal of Guidance and Counselling, 23*, 245–257.

Williams, B. (2000). The treatment of adolescent populations: An institutional vs. a wilderness setting. *Journal of Child and Adolescent Group Therapy, 10*, 47–56.

Williams, C. B., Frame, M. W., & Green, E. (1999). Counseling groups for African American women: A focus on spirituality. *Journal for Specialists in Group Work, 24*, 260–273.

Williams, C. U., McMahon, H. G., McLeod, A. L., & Rice, R. (2013). An exploration of secondary school counselors' experiences engaging in group work. *Journal for Specialists in Group Work, 38*, 96–120.

Williams, R. C., & Myer, R. A. (1992). The men's movement: An adjunct to traditional counseling approaches. *Journal of Mental Health Counseling, 14*, 393–404.

Williamson, E. (1958). Value orientation in counseling. *Personnel and Guidance Journal, 36*, 520–528.

Williamson, R. S. (1992). Using group reality therapy to raise self-esteem in adolescent girls. *Journal of Reality Therapy, 11*, 3–11.

Wilson, G. L., & Hanna, M. S. (1986). *Groups in context.* New York, NY: Random House.

Wisner, B. L., & Norton, C. L. (2013). Capitalizing on behavioral and emotional strengths of alternative high school students through group counseling to promote mindfulness. *Journal for Specialists in Group Work, 38*, 207–233.

Wolf, T. J. (1987). Group counseling for bisexual men. *Journal for Specialists in Group Work, 12*, 162–165.

Wolfe, J. L. (1995). Rational emotive behavior therapy women's groups: A twenty year retrospective. *Journal of Rational Emotive and Cognitive Behavior Therapy, 13*, 153–170.

Wood, J. K. (1982). Person-centered group therapy. In G. Gazda (Ed.), *Basic approaches to group psychotherapy and group counseling* (3rd ed.). Springfield, IL: Thomas.

Woody, R. H. (1988). *Protecting your mental health practice.* San Francisco, CA: Jossey-Bass.

Woody, R. H., Hansen, J. C., & Rossberg, R. H. (1989). *Counseling psychology: Strategies and services.* Pacific Grove, CA: Brooks/Cole.

Woody, R. H., & Mitchell, R. E. (1984). Understanding the legal system and legal research. In R. H. Woody & Associates (Eds.), *The law and the practice of human services.* San Francisco, CA: Jossey-Bass.

Woollams, S., & Brown, M. (1978). *Transactional analysis.* Dexter, MI: Huron Valley Institute.

Woollams, S., Brown, M., & Huige, K. (1977). What transactional analysts want their clients to know. In G. Barnes (Ed.), *Transactional analysis after Eric Berne* (pp. 487–525). New York, NY: Harper & Row.

Worden, J. (1991). *Grief counseling and grief therapy* (2nd ed.). New York, NY: Springer.

Wrenn, C. G. (1979). Proposed changes in counselor attitudes: Toward your job. *School Counselor, 27*, 81–90.

Wrenn, C. G. (1985). Afterward: The encapsulated counselor revisited. In P. Pedersen (Ed.), *Handbook of cross-cultural counseling and therapy* (pp. 323–329). Westport, CT: Greenwood.

Wrenn, C. G. (1989). Preface. In J. E. Myers (Ed.), *Infusing gerontological counseling into counselor preparation* (pp. 9–15). Alexandria, VA: American Counseling Association.

Wubbolding, R. E. (1987). A model for group activities related to teaching reality therapy. *Journal of Reality Therapy, 6*, 23–28.

Wubbolding, R. E. (1988). *Using reality therapy.* New York, NY: Harper & Row.

Wubbolding, R. E. (1991). *Understanding reality therapy.* New York, NY: Harper.

Wubbolding, R. E. (1992). *Cycle of counseling and supervision and coaching using reality therapy* (chart). Cincinnati, OH: Center for Reality Therapy.

Wubbolding, R. E. (1999, April). *Reality therapy in groups.* Presentation at the World Conference of the American Counseling Association, San Diego, CA.

Wubbolding, R. E. (2001). *Reality therapy for the 21st century.* New York, NY: Brunner/Mazel.

Wubbolding, R. E. (2011). *Reality therapy.* Washington, DC: American Psychological Association.

Yablonsky, L. (1976). *Psychodrama: Resolving emotional problems through role playing.* New York, NY: Basic Books.

Yalom, I. D. (1985). *The theory and practice of group psychotherapy* (2nd ed.). New York, NY: Basic Books.

Yalom, I. (1995). *The theory and practice of group psychotherapy* (4th ed.). New York, NY: Basic Books.

Yalom, I., & Josselson, R. (2011). Existential psychotherapy. In R. J. Corsini & D. Wedding (Eds.), *Current psychotherapies* (9th ed., pp. 310–341). Belmont, CA: Brooks/Cole.

Yalom, I. D., & Leszcz, M. (2005). *The theory and practice of group psychotherapy* (5th ed.). New York, NY: Basic Books.

Yalom, I. D., & Lieberman, M. (1971). A study of encounter group casualties. *Archives of General Psychology, 25,* 16–30.

Yamamoto, G. (1995). The problems and effects of structured encounter groups as assessed by a follow-up survey. *Japanese Journal of Counseling Science, 28,* 1–20.

Yeaworth, R. C., McNamee, M. J., & Pozehl, B. (1992). The adolescent life change event scale: Its development and use. *Adolescence, 27,* 783–802.

Yontef, G. (1990). Gestalt therapy in groups. In I. Kutash & A. Wolf (Eds.), *Group psychotherapist's handbook.* New York, NY: Columbia University Press.

Yontef, G., & Jacobs, L. (2014). Gestalt therapy. In D. Wedding & R. J. Corsini (Eds.), *Current psychotherapies* (10th ed., pp. 299–338). Belmont, CA: Cengage.

Yoon, S. G., & Johnson, S. D. (2008). Phases and patterns of group development in virtual learning teams. *Educational Technology Research and Development, 56,* 595–618.

Young, M. E. (2013). *Learning the art & helping: Building blocks and techniques* (5th ed.). Upper Saddle River, NJ: Pearson.

Young, T. L. (2013). Using motivational interviewing within the early stages of group development. *Journal for Specialists in Group Work, 38,* 169–181.

Zajonc, R. B. (1965). Social facilitation. *Science, 149,* 269–274.

Zimpfer, D. G. (1984). Patterns and trends in group work. *Journal for Specialists in Group Work, 9,* 204–208.

Zimpfer, D. G. (1986). Planning for groups based on their developmental phases. *Journal for Specialists in Group Work, 11,* 180–187.

Zimpfer, D. G. (1987). Groups for the aging: Do they work? *Journal for Specialists in Group Work, 12,* 85–92.

Zimpfer, D. G. (1991). Pretraining for group work: A review. *Journal for Specialists in Group Work, 16,* 264–269.

Zimpfer, D. G. (1992a). Group work with juvenile delinquents. *Journal for Specialists in Group Work, 17,* 116–126.

Zimpfer, D. G. (1992b). Group work with adult offenders: An overview. *Journal for Specialists in Group Work, 17,* 54–61.

Zimpfer, D. G., & Carr, J. J. (1989). Groups for midlife career change: A review. *Journal for Specialists in Group Work, 14*(2), 243–250.

Zinck, K., & Littrell, J. M. (2000). Action research shows group counseling effective with at-risk adolescent girls. *Professional School Counseling, 4*(1), 50–60.

Zinker, J. (1977). *Creative process in group therapy.* New York, NY: Vintage Books.

NAME INDEX

SUBJECT INDEX